FIRESIDE

KIDS
Day In and Day Out

EDITOR
ELISABETH L. SCHARLATT

PROJECT DIRECTOR
CHRISTOPHER CERF

◆

*A compendium of ideas, recommendations,
insights, inspirations, facts and suggestions, problems
and solutions for living with kids every single day*

◆

Research Director: Ronnie Shushan

Designer: Beri Greenwald

A FIRESIDE BOOK
Published by Simon and Schuster

Incidental drawings by Christine Swirnoff

Manufactured in the United States of America

PERMISSIONS

We have made every effort to trace the ownership of all copyrighted material and to secure permission from copyright holders. In the event of any question arising as to the use of any material, we will be pleased to make the necessary corrections in future printings. Thanks are due to the following authors, publishers, publications, and agents for permission to use the material indicated.

American Kennel Club: Excerpts from *The Complete Dog Book* by permission of The American Kennel Club, New York, N.Y.

American Toy Institute, Inc.: "Choosing Toys: A Grandparent's Guide," © American Toy Institute, Inc., 200 Fifth Avenue, New York, N.Y. 10010. Reprinted with permission.

Atheneum Publishers, Inc.: From *Down the Rabbit Hole* by Selma G. Lanes. Copyright © 1971 by Selma G. Lanes. Reprinted by permission of Atheneum Publishers.

Avon Books: From *Nutrition Scoreboard: Your Guide to Better Eating* by Michael Jacobson and Wendy Wilson. Copyright © 1975 by Michael Jacobson. Reprinted by permission of the authors.

James Baldwin: From the introduction to *The Chasm* by Robert Campbell. Published by Houghton Mifflin. Reprinted by permission of James Baldwin.

Ballantine Books: From *Diet for a Small Planet* by Frances Moore Lappé. Reprinted by permission of the author and her agents, Raines & Raines. Copyright © 1971,1975 by Frances Moore Lappé.

Bantam Books: From *Puzzles, Quizzes and Games* by Phyllis Fraser and Edith Young. Copyright © 1947 by Mrs. Bennett A. Cerf and Mrs. Lewis Young, renewed © 1975 by Mrs. Bennett Cerf and Mrs. Lewis Young. Reprinted by permission of Bantam Books.

From *Other Worlds* by Carl Sagan, produced by Jerome Agel. Copyright © 1975 by Carl Sagan and Jerome Agel. Published by Bantam Books. Reprinted with permission.

"Worm Grunting" and "Jig Saw Puzzles" from *The Great Escape,* edited by Min S. Yee and David K. Wright. Copyright © 1974 by Min S. Yee and David K. Wright. Reprinted with permission of Min S. Yee.

Guy Billout: Cartoon © 1978 by Guy Billout from *Games Magazine.* Reprinted by permission of Guy Billout.

The Boston Children's Museum: From *Bubbles* by Bernard Zubrowski. Copyright © 1973 by Bernard Zubrowski and the Boston Children's Museum. Reprinted with permission.

Chicago Review: "A Late Wanderer in Oz" by Jordan Brotman. First appeared in *Chicago Review,* Vol. 18, No. 2, 1965. Copyright © 1965 by *Chicago Review.* Reprinted with permission.

The Children's Book Council, Inc.: Excerpt from the article "Good Night, Hillary" by Caroline Feller Bauer written for *The Calendar,* Vol. xxxii, No. 3, Sept.-Dec. 1973, published by The Children's Book Council, Inc., 67 Irving Place, New York, N.Y. 10003. Reprinted with permission.

Closer Look: From *Facts You Should Know About Tax Deductions* by Closer Look; The National Information Center for the Handicapped, 1976. Reprinted with permission.

(Continued on page 527)

ACKNOWLEDGMENTS

HOW DO YOU SINGLE OUT anyone for special thanks on a project for which hundreds of people wrote or were interviewed, took photographs, offered advice, edited, proofread, typed manuscripts, sorted releases, obtained permissions, or tracked down addresses and prices?

We're deeply grateful, of course, to everyone who contributed, but there are a few whose efforts we'd especially like to acknowledge here:

First and foremost, Bea Hurwitz, whose dauntlessness was nothing short of astounding; Theresa Curtin, Janet Gari, Dee Ratterree, Michele Salcedo, Dolores Tangen, and Judy Maysles, who helped mightily with logistics; Diane Cleaver, our editor; Beri Greenwald, our talented and patient designer; Jonathan Dolger, Amy Ephron, and Bob Springer, whose suggestions and encouragement were vital at the early stage of the project; and, finally, Jennifer Rogers, Dabney Finch, Rusty Unger, Flavia Potenza, and Joni Evans, one of whom always seemed to be there when disaster loomed.

CHRISTOPHER CERF

CONTENTS

All grown-ups were once children—
although few of them remember it.

Antoine de Saint-Exupéry,
in *The Little Prince*

INTRODUCTION

WHY ARE AMERICAN CHILDREN CALLED "KIDS"? The young goat is a precise analogy—spirited, rambunctious, winning, uncontrollable, pretty, cunning, and all-consuming.

Until we had kids, most of us believed that raising children is fulfilling and "natural." It wasn't long before we discovered that this business of being a parent is not at all what we'd been told; nor, for the most part, does it come naturally. The myth of parenthood has harmed many good people, parents and kids alike. "If it's so hard, there must be something wrong with me" is the parent's secret lament, and then guilt and self-doubt abound. But it is hard—bewilderingly, painfully hard. The universal response I got when I mentioned this simple truth to the parents I talked to in the course of working on *Kids: Day In and Day Out* was: "Thank God! I thought I was all alone in feeling that way." You are not alone. You're merely the victim of the myth of parenthood.

It is this myth that has led parents to believe there must be a "system" of child-rearing that will make it easier. But in talking to hundreds of women and men and children, and in examining my own day-to-day efforts as a mother, I learned one truth: All systems of child-raising—strict, permissive, psychologically "correct"—are nonsense. Raising children is completely individual; it depends entirely on the child and the parent—and even on the incident and the time of day. The notion that children can be brought up by one formula or another may be the product of our technological age. If cattle can be bred and eggs laid and wheat produced by scientific methods, claim those who believe order can be imposed on anything, then why can't children be raised by this system or that system or another system?

The answer is: They can't because the kids and the parents and the issues they face, separately and together, can't be fitted or, more often, forced into a formula. Every family's problems and conflicts are in every way special, and the only way for parents to confront the daily challenge is eclectically. We watch and listen and share with other parents, and we choose what seems appropriate to us.

This book offers an eclectic look at living with kids. What you'll find in these pages are the voices of hundreds of parents (and some others who were children once themselves) saying, in effect: I tried this and here's how it worked (or didn't work) for me.

I've always felt that the parents know better than anybody else what to do with their own kids. Still there is that sense of isolation we all feel; we worry about doing things wrong; we feel guilty for wondering if we're cut out for it at all. In much earlier times, every mother lived in fear of her child's getting scarlet fever, polio, diphtheria, smallpox, or some other crippling or fatal ailment. Now that we're less worried about those problems, a whole new set of concerns about our children's *development* has taken their place:

What toys, books, and games should we get for our kids? how should they eat? what should they play? what shoes should they wear or sports should they learn? do they need pets? must they have fluoride? can they shower with us? do they need an allowance? when should they read? which schools are best?

If we raise our kids without sexism, without additives, and without TV, will they turn out all right?

The real question, of course, is: What is it to "turn out all right"? We wonder if we ourselves turned out all right. We listen closely to our friends' tales of childhood and wonder if, despite their aberrant youths, they turned out all right. We squint at them. We examine our own values. We think we've got it and then it eludes us. We think we should look at the larger picture: education, morality, good health. But all we want, really, is to get through each day. Our kids are there, day in and day out, and we are responsible for them.

ELISABETH L. SCHARLATT

CHILD-REARING
Some Thoughts About Living with Kids Rather More Calmly

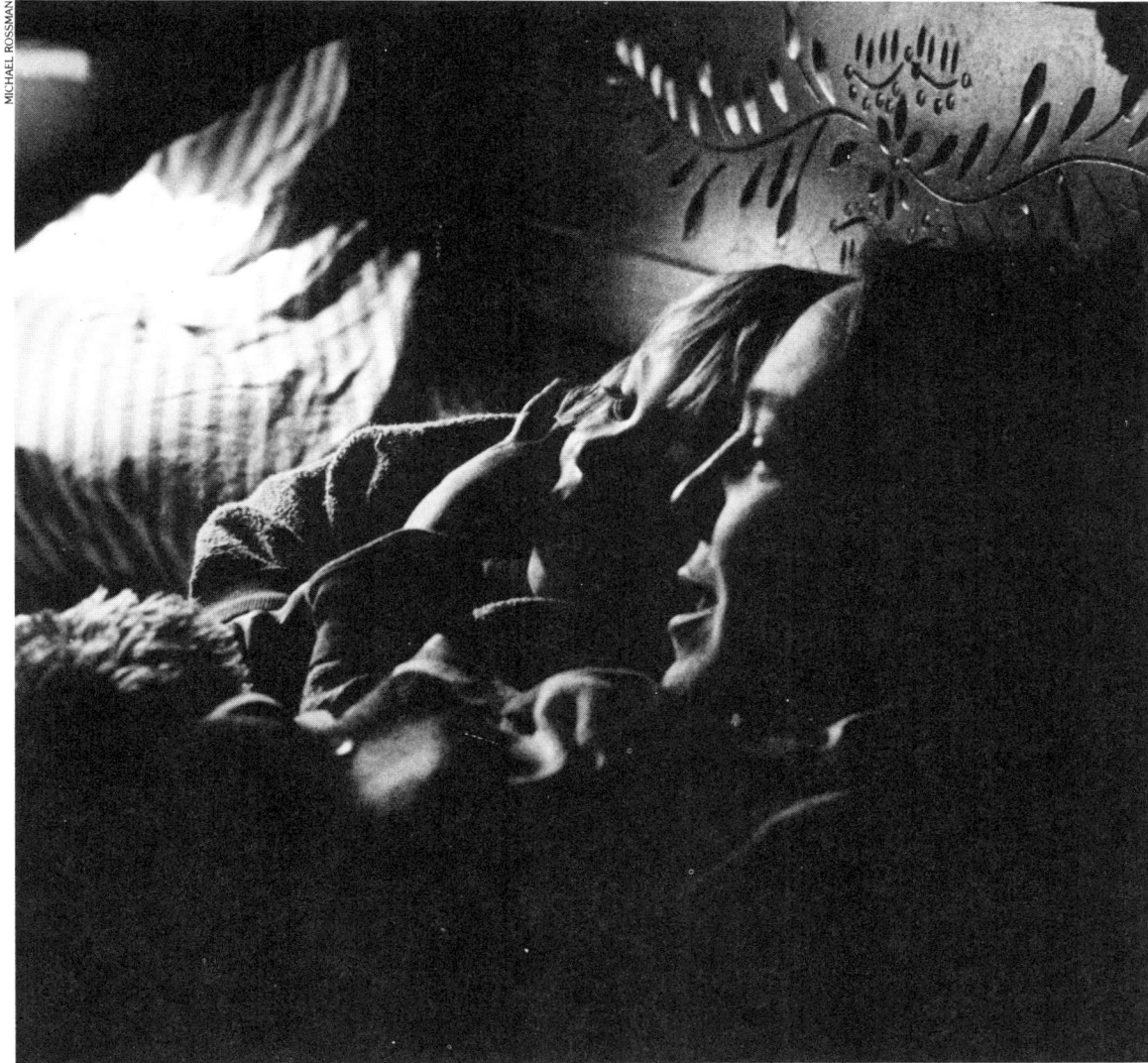

The irritating thing about ungoverned children is that they often make as orderly and valuable men and women as do the other kind.

MARK TWAIN

*I'm not going to say, of course, that I have become what I am
only as a result of your influence. That would be very much exaggerated
(and I am indeed inclined to this exaggeration). It is indeed quite
possible that even if I had grown up entirely free from your influence
I still could not have become a person after your own heart.*

FRANZ KAFKA
Letter to His Father

THE WAY THINGS ARE

The Greatest Eleven Minutes in the World

Being a parent is like a baseball game or sex: you're always interested; you wind up enjoying the whole game; you feel like you've enjoyed a whole sixty minutes or longer—but really there are only something like eleven minutes of action.

It's exactly the same with having a kid: after twenty-five years you've probably gotten eleven minutes worth of pleasures. The rest of the time you preoccupy yourself by watching and really believing you're enjoying it. You spend an awful lot of time watching your kids. An awful lot looking at them and listening to them and concentrating on them and spying on them and asking teachers how they are doing in school and asking friends what they're doing outside of school and putting them into situations that are stimulating to them and making sure they're okay. In fact, most of the time is spent anticipating the action.

The momentary pleasures notwithstanding, 99 percent of parenting is a tremendous burden. Having to buy your kid shoes is a burden. Having to buy your kid clothes and toys and books is an annoyance. Having to buy or make baby food is a chore. Having to make sure you have a supply of diapers is a pain in the neck. Even getting rid of a kid—like boarding him off to school or sending him off to camp—is a terrible burden, because you have to do it and you have to live with it and if you've done it with any ulterior motive your subconscious seems to seize you.

But it must be worth it somehow because people do it all the time. And those eleven minutes must be the greatest eleven minutes in the whole world. And like the baseball game—or

like sex—the momentary pleasure, the pure, raw, quick pleasure is what we're looking for and waiting for. And it comes only when the child's world and your world collide.

ALAN SAPERSTEIN

Father Knows Best

Fathers are really excluded from child-rearing. The kind of prejudice that women run into when they're trying to make their way in the business world I run into when I'm with my son Danny. Women, especially older women, see me out with him and say, "I'll take care of him" or "I'll do this or that." They've never seen him before, and I've been with him for his whole life, but they automatically jump to the conclusion that since they're women, they can take care of him better than I can.

CLAUDIO MARZOLLO

Hope Is One Year Old, and I Am Forty-nine . . .

I spent more time with Hope in her first year than with my four other children in all their first years combined. There is something sad in that, even though we are very close and they hardly feel deprived or forsaken. Those years in the 20s and early 30s, when most people launch their families, are usually hectic, uncertain, groping years. A father is mostly away in pursuit of whatever it is, and he catches only fleeting moments with his very young. But there is something very different, satisfyingly so, about the baby who comes in middle age. It is mainly the difference in her parents, who have developed the assurance and serenity and inner resolve that make coping a pleasure rather than a nervous burden. . . .

I have plunged in and done it all: changed her diapers while she twists and wriggles, splashed on Johnson's baby powder, struggled clumsily with undershirts and snaps and safety pins, fed her all the bland baby stuff that she disdains when she can cadge a mouthful of grownup food, nestled her in my arms for her bottle, bundled her in snowsuit and blanket against the biting winds of Lake Michigan,

rolled with her on the floor until she is laughing uncontrollably from way down deep in the delightfully round belly she will be dieting to flatten 15 years from now.

I have done all that and more, not just every so often on a let-Daddy-do-it-just-this-once basis, but at least some of the time on most of the days of Hope's first year on earth. That will always be with me. No one can take it away or wipe it out or foreclose on it.

WILLIAM H. RENTSCHLER
Harper's Weekly

FRANK DERBAS

. . . it never occurred to me that children, left alone, might find other areas of interest entirely; ones that did not fit at all within my value system.

MARGOT HENTOFF
Saturday Review

DISCIPLINE
A FEW CAUTIONARY WORDS

Telling Your Kid the Truth

Walking home from the park I saw a guy I know who recently split up with his wife and has custody of their child. It was a beautiful day and it was really quite late, and I heard the little boy, who was about four, say, "Daddy, I want to go on the ring-a-round." "No," the father said, and the kid kept on, "I wanna go, I wanna go." Then the father said, "Okay, you go and I'll go home, and you can come home by yourself."

I said to the father, "That's not fair. You don't really mean that." He said, "Well, I'm tired. I want to get home." I said, "So why don't you say that? Tell the kid you're tired and you want to get home. He can understand that." (Instead he'd said, "Later . . . maybe if we come earlier next time.") So he told the boy that he was tired, and that was the end of it.

These are common situations that everyone gets into. So often you can't imagine being straight with your kid. Somehow you think you're not a good parent if you're tired. You think you should never be tired.

We want to teach our kids to be considerate of others, but we never give them an opportunity. We're not real with our kids, we're not honest.

ZELDA WIRTSCHAFTER

How We Confuse Them

What I remember most about growing up was that my parents were so inconsistent. When I was upset and went to my room to cry, I never knew if they were going to come in and scream at me or come in and comfort me (or not come in at all). And I knew it depended totally on their mood, not on anything I had done or how I felt.

PAT HARDING STRACHAN

The Double Standard

Since as a child I was with you chiefly during meals, your teaching was to a large extent the teaching of proper behavior at table. What was brought to the table had to be eaten, the quality of the food was not to be discussed—but you yourself often found the food inedible, called it "this swill," said "that beast" (the cook) had ruined it. Because in accordance with your strong appetite and your particular predilection you ate everything fast, hot, and in big mouthfuls, the child had to hurry; there was a somber silence at table, interrupted by admonitions: "Eat first, talk afterwards," or "faster, faster, faster," or "there you are, you see, I finished ages ago." Bones mustn't be cracked with the teeth, but you could. Vinegar must not be sipped noisily, but you could. The main thing was that the bread should be cut straight. But it didn't matter that you did it with a knife dripping with gravy. Care had to be taken that no scraps fell on the floor. In the end it was under your chair that there were most scraps. At table one wasn't allowed to do anything but eat, but you cleaned and cut your fingernails, sharpened pencils, cleaned your ears with a toothpick. Please, Father, understand me correctly: in themselves these would have been utterly insignificant details, they only became depressing for me because you, so tremendously the authoritative man, did not keep the commandments you imposed on me. Hence the world was for me divided into three parts: one in which I, the slave, lived under laws that had been invented only for me and which I could, I did not know why, never completely comply with; then a second world, which was infinitely remote from mine, in which you lived, concerned with government, with the issuing of orders and with the annoyance about their not being obeyed; and finally a third world where everybody else lived happily and free from orders and from having to obey.

FRANZ KAFKA
Letter to His Father

Letting Them Do It Their Own Way

. . . even if in the end children do come to *our* way of doing things, we should let them do so in *their* way. Some might say, "Why waste time? If we know that a given way of doing things is best, why not just tell the children to do it that way?" But our way may not be the best way, but only the way we're used to. Also, the best way for us, or for some children, may not be the best way for all. Finally, it is *always* better, if he can do so at not too great cost or risk, for a child to find out something for himself than to be told. Only from making choices and judgments can he learn to make them better, or learn to trust his own judgment.

JOHN HOLT
What Do I Do Monday?

The Child in Search of a Kind Word

I was a timid child. For all that, I am sure I was also obstinate, as children are. I am sure that Mother spoilt me too, but I cannot believe I was particularly difficult to manage; I cannot believe that a kindly word, a quiet taking by the hand, a friendly look, could not have got me to do anything that was wanted of me. Now you are, after all, at bottom a kindly and softhearted person . . . but not *every* child has the endurance and fearlessness to go on searching until it comes to the kindliness that lies beneath the surface.

FRANZ KAFKA
Letter to His Father

You, Too, Can Teach Your Kids to Be Troubled

Children learn about behavior by imitating it. They will imitate behavior they find puzzling or frightening, as well as behavior they've learned gets rewarded. They try on behavior to see what it feels like. Children often "understudy" (the term is [Denah] Harris's) the parent whose behavior puzzles, frightens, or worries them, more than they do the parent they are less fearful of. They often grow up unconsciously understudying their parents' dysfunctional, troubling behavior, attempting to understand it without knowing they are asking questions. It's not the sins of the fathers and mothers that are passed on to the children, but rather all our unsolved problems.

STEPHEN M. JOSEPH
Children in Fear

GETTING DOWN TO SPECIFICS

Try a Little Craziness

I've found that when a kid is acting in a really irrational way, it's pointless to be rational. You have to do something just as crazy. Once my friend's child was having a terrible temper tantrum and was kicking and screaming and totally uncontrollable. Finally I took her in my arms, wrapped her in a towel like a straitjacket, and carried her into the bathroom and sprinkled water on her. She was so startled and looked at me and said, "Why did you do that?" And I said, "Because I didn't know what else to do." Then I asked her what she would have done if I had been kicking and screaming like that. She thought for a minute—and had no answer. We laughed about it, and a few minutes later she asked, "Would you do that again?"

She still says to me (two years later), "Remember that time you wrapped me in a towel . . ." and we laugh.

Another time when she was having a tantrum, I walked out of the room and screamed, "Hot dogs and ice cream!" She stopped screaming, followed me out, and said, "What do you mean, hot dogs and ice cream?" I said, "Well, we're going to get hot dogs and ice cream and I wanted to know if you wanted to come. And if you don't shut up you can't come."

Maybe I don't know what I'm doing, because I'm not a parent, but it worked, both times.

MARIA ROBBINS

A Lesson in Being Civilized

When my kid throws a tantrum I offer these choices:

1. If your anger can be expressed only through hitting and screaming, you can go to your room to scream and rage and also to think about what has happened.

2. If you're feeling bad or wronged and want to talk and to be held, we can do that.

3. If you will behave sociably, you may join us whenever *you* decide you're ready. Just tell me when you're ready and we will welcome your company.

ELS

The Subconscious at Work. Who? Me?

"I'll take you to the toy store and let you pick out anything you want," a mother promised her son, "if you do not bite your nails for a month." She knew bribing was a bad idea, but she'd tried everything else to no avail and she was desperate.

For thirty days the boy did not bite a fingernail. He broke the habit and collected his reward.

"I want a toy too. Mommy," his little sister announced. The mother was stumped. Already caught in a *quid pro quo* arrangement with her kids, she asked her daughter what she would promise in return. "I'll stop wetting my bed at night."

So it was agreed. If the child did not wet her bed for a month, she too could pick out any toy she wanted at the store.

For thirty nights the little girl did not wet her bed. Not once. The mother was delighted. The system worked, as shocking as it would seem to most parents of the Anti-Reward-and-Punishment-as-Motivation School of Discipline. The little girl got her toy.

But something went wrong. On the thirty-first day, this child did not wake up dry. "What happened?" the mother asked. "I thought you had stopped wetting your bed."

"I thought I had to stop for a month," the daughter replied, "and I did stop for a month."

ELS

The Mother Strike

One of my most strategic mother-moves is to go on strike. A strike is better than "I'm going to have a nervous breakdown," 'cause *they* know you ain't about to have a breakdown without a sitter. . . .

About my strikes. First, I make sure that there is enough food in the refrigerator and all the clothes are clean. And you can't strike when one of the children has a cold. It is best to strike on a school day in the afternoon near dinner time. What with homework and dinner, they stay busy. While on strike, it is a good idea to wear something flashy. The opposite of your usual presentation. I have a red mini dress I wear each time 'cause it dazzles them! Stay on strike 'til you get a definite commitment on things like sweeping the floor, making beds without being told, watering the plants, etc.

VERTAMAE SMART-GROSVENOR
Essence

A Positive Approach: Teaching Delayed Gratification

I've managed to avoid, for a time, the difficulties that always follow my saying no to my child. This I've done by saying yes—and qualifying it. "May I have a cookie?" "Yes—after lunch." "May I watch TV?" "Yes—after your nap." "May I have a look at your camera?" "Certainly—when I'm sure that you know how to take care of it."

By the age of three and a half, my son hadn't quite caught on that yes sometimes means no. [Update: By the age of four, he caught on.]

ELS

Logical Consequences: A New Approach to Discipline

This book, by Rudolf Dreikurs and Loren Grey (Hawthorn, 1969), $6.95 paperback), outlines an approach to child-rearing and discipline in which a child learns by not being protected from the consequences of his or her actions. For example, if a child comes home late for supper, the parent does not scold, but simply eats without the child. Assuming the child knew when to come home, can tell time, etc., the parent suggests the child find something to eat in the kitchen. That is described in the book as a "natural consequence." If this annoys the child, he or she will probably be on time in the future.

"Logical consequences" are slightly different in that they do not happen as a matter of course, but are arranged by the parent. Unlike punishment, the consequences are integrally related to behavior in some way that the child can understand, without the parent's making a moral judgment upon the child's behavior or getting angry. One example given in the book concerns a child who refuses to sit properly in his chair, and constantly tips it back. The teacher (this can happen at home, too) asked him whether he would prefer to go on leaning back in his chair or to sit like the rest of the children. When the child said he wanted to lean back, the teacher placed a book under each of the chair's front legs, which left the boy in an uncomfortable position. He soon gave up his leaning back, after using it for a time as an attention-getting device, and sought a way to get attention that would be more acceptable to his teacher. The authors warn that the adult must not place a child in danger in order to teach desired behavior through a logical or a natural consequence.

JOANNE BERNSTEIN

Commanding Respect: Be Yourself

I always turned to my father when I was in doubt about how to be a good example for my children. When he was alive he would show me. He would remind me of his stick. It was in the corner, and when he would be tired of putting up with our foolishness and mistakes, he'd walk over and grab the stick. He never used it. He never even came near us with it. We knew what he wanted. We became different. We stopped our noise and tears and went about our business. Now, I have to admit: I could never use a stick like that. I tried, but I found myself shaking. I had nothing to say, but my throat would catch. . . . I talked with my father, and . . . he said that his father never used a stick; he would stamp his feet hard on the floor. That was all he had to do. I asked my father why he did not do the same. He said he tried, but his feet just wouldn't oblige. All of a sudden they became heavy and he found them more disobedient than us! So, one day he took my mother's broom instead. Afterward, he decided he would find a stick for himself. . . .

So, you see, we each have to be ourselves. My father had helped me. I came home and thought to myself: why not be like my grandfather? The next day I stamped my feet when two of the boys needed to be told to stop fighting. But it was no good; they missed my point. I pounded on the table; and they heard. From that day on it was my way of being their father.

ROBERT COLES
From an interview in *The Old Ones of New Mexico*

SETTING LIMITS

The Metaphor

Too many adults seem to believe that if they are too strict, their children will not like them. The fact is that children find limits comforting and necessary. A metaphor which I have frequently used to convey this idea to parents and teachers involves their picturing how they feel driving over a high bridge, and then picturing that bridge without guard rails. The point is that children feel safer and more comfortable with firm, consistent, and objective limits.

ALLAN SHEDLIN, JR.

Not Exactly Summerhill . . .

In my totally naive and unrealistic world of early motherhood I thought if I allowed my children to "blossom naturally" and grow without structure, they would create their own structure and values without my imposing all of mine. There was no emphasis at all on daily living, simple problem-solving, task completion. No attention to adjustment. None of us had any responsibility, and the children were to make all decisions themselves. Of course it wasn't Summerhill around here at all, just angry, frustrated chaos and massive insecurity. Later, I did discover that power to the parent is freedom for the child.

BOBBIE MALONE

Making Deals

I sometimes let my son make deals with me to his own advantage—and it cuts down on the actual "discipline" arguments. For example, I tell him his hair needs washing. He says he doesn't want to do it tonight. I say his hair is disgusting and must be washed. He says he'll do it tomorrow. I ask him if he will *really* do it tomorrow. He promises. I say okay and make him write it down on his calendar so that the next day I can show him the note in his own hand.

It works.

Another example: I say it's time to leave the park or the party or the friend's house. He says he doesn't want to go. I ask him how much time he needs. He says, say, half an hour. We compromise at, say, ten more minutes (or two more turns at his game) and announce the time we will be going. To say "We'll stay until five o'clock" makes it easier to leave when five o'clock comes around. Even announcing a little in advance—"We have to leave in five more minutes"—helps. And is much preferable to interrupting something important to them by saying, "Okay, kids, let's go now." ELS

"I Won't Pick Him Up If You Won't"

The one thing I was really dreading was having to spend sleepless nights walking back and forth. But we just got into Danny's head right from the beginning that if he cried at night, he'd just get his diapers changed or he'd get fed, but that was it. We didn't play with him. It only happened a couple of nights that he cried and cried, and we just stood there and held on to each other and said I won't pick him up if you won't. And before long he was sleeping through the night. CLAUDIO MARZOLLO

"The Deeper Lessons About Limits Develop Slowly"

The first matter I had to set deliberate limits on with my son Lorca was hair-pulling. Gentle explanation proved useless. For a while I tried to evade or remove his hand, with no result. He might have learned from it eventually, but I lacked the patience. And the pain made me angry. He was so young that he had no clear idea of what another person *felt* when treated this way, let alone of how he should act to be acceptable.

In the end I resorted to a classic teaching situation: if you pull my hair hard enough to hurt, I'll pull yours. Since he was not barred from hair-pulling so long as he did it gently, he was also learning to evaluate and control his strength. In retaliating, I took care to pull his hair without spite, firmly and cleanly. Though I had confidence in how I was handling it, I also felt embarrassed by my primitive method and its brutality. For there was no escaping it: I was teaching my child a lesson through violence. No matter that the violence was minor, the motive lofty, the lesson necessary. Lorca is learning what is provocative under what circumstance, and when something is too much, in a world that refuses to be grasped as completely rational. I am learning, too. When I don't express my feelings at the time of the testing, at the time of my anger, and don't deal with them well later, they seep out fermented, in ways indirect and mystifying. I would rather the root fear be of direct reprisal than of the long withdrawal of love.

There's no escaping the fact that in the end we use superior physical power—even putting something out of reach is this—to resolve conflicts we cannot deal with otherwise. And I see as somewhat blurry the line between slapping a child and picking him up against his will, and also the line between these acts and taking away something he feels at the moment is a part of him: all seem to me to be acts of physical violence, whether they are done for his protection or for others', in anger or in calm. I guess I have accepted it. All that seems clearly wrong in practice now is excess and vindictiveness. We try to resolve conflict without force whenever we can, often by redirection. But we've been careful to avoid the strategy of buying him off with rewards: that teaches too crooked a lesson about the consequences of pushing our limits, and force against force seems more honest and freeing.

We had a hard time with Lorca and the ashtrays from the beginning. (Maybe it was because of our guilt about smoking in front of him.) Cigarettes were fascinating but a definite *no;* of course, he was into the butts and the ashes. It got so whenever we saw him coming we'd grab all the ashtrays and put them up high, or else he'd dump them quick as a whistle. After months of this I got a notion, and one day said, "Here, man, why don't you take this and *empty it in the garbage* and *bring it back* here. *Both hands,* now." He was seventeen months old. I wasn't sure he'd bring the ashtrays back. But he did, the very first time, and soon our ashtrays were safe and clean—sometimes puff by puff. The solution lay in finding a way to move with the flow of his energy rather than against it, and making, or letting, his needs and ours fill each other.

Likewise with the dog's food. Lorca would spill it whenever we were incautious enough to leave it on the floor after meals, and we'd walk to the bathroom barefoot over broken kibble in the dark. Now he leaves it mostly alone, since I got him into the ritual of taking the dish from me after I fix Bull's food and setting it down before him.

So the old lessons present themselves brutally anew, as parenting goes on. Whenever we've made a big emotional deal out of something, it has become a minor battleground: a certain kind of negative force breeding a certain provocative resistance.

"But surely there must be limits!" Of course. No pencils stuck in my eye, no messing with the stove since one pilot doesn't light, don't go into the streets. And beyond safety, limits are necessary for character to be defined against in growth.

Perhaps all the no's may remain no's, but their implications change. No stick in my eye, but you may touch it with your finger, very gently, as I touch yours, exploring the sensations. Don't mess with the key when I'm driving; but carry it for me and present it to be put in the ignition, and play with the switch on your electric dog, understanding the equivalence. Not simply "don't go into the street" but from the first days of carrying him abroad, his involvement in the slow process of Entrance into the Street: chanting "Red light don't walk/ Green light walk walk" at every corner; beginning to define and emphasize the white lines; exploring country roads where no cars come.

The deeper lessons about limits develop

slowly. Already Lorca studies how they are formed, as in daily experience we explain: "Because this happened, that limit (or law) is necessary." In unselfconscious ways, he begins to involve himself in making them—"I don't *like* to be kissed any more, just hugs!"—and in changing them, as he assures us, sometimes successfully, "If you let me, I will be very careful."

This is participatory democracy. We have learned how even our most intimate conscious- ness depends on the gross operations of social power. Right now Lorca learns wonderfully, in the spontaneous invention of play. Yet I think that if he is to grow up as a fully free man, in his learning and other pursuits, he must have a society in which he learns to see himself as empowered, as actively sharing in making and changing the rules and other decisions that govern collective reality.

MICHAEL ROSSMAN

"If compulsion is damaging and unwise, its antithesis—a vacuum of free choice— is unreal."

My own demands were . . . an important part of José's experience. They were not simply the demands of a teacher, nor of an adult, but belonged to my own way of caring about José. And he sensed this. . . . And when he learned that he *could* refuse—could refuse altogether, could terminate the lesson, could change its direction, could insist on something else—our mutual interest in his development was taken quite for granted. We became collaborators in the business of life.

. . . All of the children could refuse. They needed a good reason to do it, and they had to stand up to the adults. But they discovered that good reasons were respected. Boredom, for instance, is a good reason. The beautiful days of spring are good reasons. An ardent desire for something else is a good reason. Anxiety is a good reason. So is a headache or a toothache. And there are many things which if they arise during the course of a lesson deserve and must be given full precedence, such things as considerations of justice, self-respect, friendship. We and the children, in short, were in an on-going experience of attraction and repulsion, of cooperation and conflict. Out of this flexible and many-faceted encounter, the actual structure of our time together evolved. The essential thing was the absence of compulsion. . . .

. . . Often at First Street the children knew fairly well what they wanted to do instead of sit in class: a trip, a picnic, a project of some sort. But usually they did not quite know what it was, though a lesson was clearly not it. . . . It is part of a teacher's job, then, to help his students find out what to do instead of sitting in class.

GEORGE DENNISON
The Lives of Children

EDWARD KOREN

"A rigid attempt to be relaxed and spontaneous can be far worse than rigid conformity to rigid rules."

Margaret Mead drew this conclusion after observing American mothers who, after three generations of dependence on schedules and formulas and recipes for child care, were as rigid about a relaxed or self-demand schedule as they had learned to be about a rigid schedule.

Permissiveness is the principle of treating children as if they were adults;
and the tactic of making sure they never reach that stage.

THOMAS SZASZ

PUNISHMENT

When my kids dismantled the TV one day, I knew I was supposed to say: "I am very, very angry with you. I love you, but I must tell you that you must never do that again—it was a destructive thing to do." And it comes out: "GO TO YOUR ROOM!"

And to my other son, my nice sweet little boy, I hear myself saying: "ATTEN-SHUN!"

DOM DE LUISE

Not Bad

Your children will get plenty of reinforcement for the idea that they're bad, from society, without your help. But I think we need to redefine these concepts of good and bad. Children and adults often act destructively, but are they "bad" for doing it? What are we actually seeing in this behavior we've learned to call bad? Isn't problematic behavior the result of thinking, and "badness" a learned idea about behavior?

Because I don't think people are good and bad, I don't punish but I also don't praise children, because I don't want to condition behaviorism. We shouldn't train children, we should educate them; training is for dogs and horses. I'll tell a child, "That was very helpful," or "That was very thoughtful," instead of "That was nice" or "That was good." I'll say, if I see her act destructively, "That wasn't thoughtful" or "That was destructive," or "That hurt! Get off my toe!"

I try not to use "destructive" too often, because it might be closely associated with "bad" in her mind. I know it's awkward, and I have to search for words, but I don't want to maleducate the child to the idea that she's good if she's done this, and bad if she's done that.

The critical difference between this approach and the moral one is that I don't punish the children or withdraw my affection if they act destructively, and I don't base my empathy for them on their constructive behavior, or their conformity to my ideas. Or at least, I try hard not to.

STEPHEN M. JOSEPH
Children in Fear

Slam! Bam! "Don't Hit!"

A child learns to hit from seeing other people do it, and it's his way of asking why people hit. I try to answer the question I perceive in hitting. Of course, hitting him back or punishing him would be an answer, too, but not a helpful one. . . . I gently hold him away if he's still hitting, and then I answer those questions which I perceive in his behavior, rather than punishing him for punishing me. Human beings have been doing that for thousands of years, and it doesn't solve the problem.

STEPHEN M. JOSEPH
Children in Fear

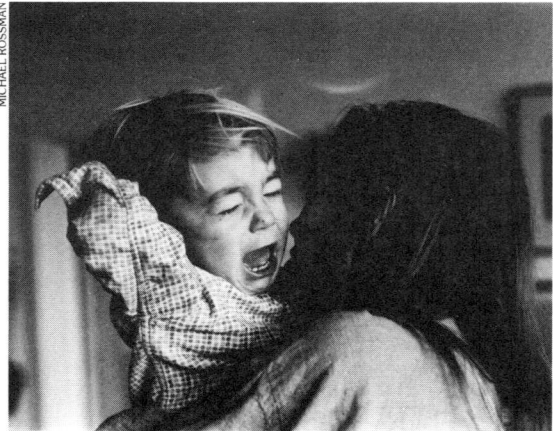

I always had a guilty conscience and was aware of both actual and potential faults. For that reason I was particularly sensitive to reproofs, since all of them more or less struck home. Although I had not in reality done what I was accused of, I felt that I might have done it. I would even draw up a list of alibis in case I should be accused of something. I felt positively relieved when I had actually done something wrong. Then at least I knew what my guilty conscience was for.

C. G. JUNG
Memories, Dreams, Reflections

The Klobber System:
A Letter from Moss Hart to Bennett Cerf

Dear Bennett:

Do you remember, one lovely starlit evening on the desert a few weeks ago, our discussing, at some length and with a good deal of parental acrimony, the proper method of bringing up children? That usually discerning and extremely wise lady, your wife, disagreed violently and somewhat haughtily, I thought, at the method we use in our house, but I thought you showed unusual interest in our experiment and silently longed to apply it yourself, so I pass it on to you and to any other frantic and harassed parents who, like ourselves, were damn near ready for the booby hatch until the Klobber System came into our home.

The Klobber Method was discovered, or rather invented, by Ernest J. Klobber, a Viennese psychiatrist who, at the time of the discovery of the method which was to bear his name, was a staunch believer in the modern and accepted formula for rearing children. Give them a reason for everything—watch out for traumas—plenty of love and security—and never a harsh word. So great an exponent of this formula was Professor Klobber that, at the time of his discovery, the Professor, who has six children of his own, was about to be carted off to a sanitarium in a state of complete nervous collapse, a condition any modern parent will understand at once. As the stretcher was being carried out of the house one of the children aimed a kick at it which, with unerring childlike aim, landed exactly where it was meant to land. The Professor, though thoroughly used to being kicked by his children, was under mild sedation at the time, and it may have been this that caused a curious reflex action on the Professor's part. Bringing his arm up from the stretcher, he brought his hand down with a good sharp crack on the child's head. There was an anguished howl from the child—first time in its life no reason had been given for an action—but the effect on the Professor was startling. He leaped up from the stretcher and gave each of the other five kiddies in turn a good smart crack over the head—a Klobber, as he afterward termed it—and never went near the sanitarium. Instead, in suddenly excellent spirits and health, he began to develop the Klobber Method. No reason was given for anything. "No" meant "no" and "yes" meant "yes," and trauma or no trauma, at the first hint of an argument the children got a Klobber, and life, for the Professor and his good wife, was livable for the first time since the patter of little feet had thundered through the house.

Like all great discoveries, however, the Klobber Method met with furious opposition on the part of educators and progressive parent organizations, and it was not until a refinement of the Method was suggested by an assistant of the Professor's that it began to meet with popular, if secretive, approval. The Professor's assistant, one Heinrich Klonk, suggested that—since a good Klobber usually left a telltale lump—a short side swipe, or a Klonk, in other words, would do the trick just as well, and to hell with PTA's and such. Heinrich Klonk is one of the unsung heroes of our time for, though he gets small credit for the Klobber Method, his little refinement worked like a charm, and the word "Klonk" echoes through thousands of peaceful homes like a balm.

The charm of this method, my dear Bennett, is its utter simplicity. In place of long hours of dreary explanation that Daddy cannot work if Junior bangs on the radiator and if Daddy cannot work and make money, how will we go to the circus; in place of that tortured quiet between husband and wife in the long night hours as to which one warped the childish id by refusing to allow the hot foot to be applied to Uncle Robert; in place of all that—just "Klonk!" and serenity reigns. It is the greatest invention since the wheel, my dear fellow, and as your wife seems to object to it, try it on her first instead of the children and let me know the results.

Ever yours,

Moss

How Should You Spank?

I want to make it clear that there is a "right" kind of spanking and a "wrong" kind. By the wrong kind I mean a cruel and sadistic beating. This fills a child with hatred, and a deep desire for revenge. This is the kind that is administered with a strap or stick or some other type of parental "weapon." Or it could also mean a humiliating slap in the face.

The right kind of spanking needs no special paraphernalia. Just the hand of the parent administered a few times on the kid's bottom. The right kind of spanking is a positive thing. It clears the air, and is vastly preferable to moralistic and guilt-inducing parental lectures.

Some of you may have heard the old saying "Never strike a child in anger." I think that that is psychologically very poor advice, and I suggest the opposite: "Never strike a child except in anger."

A child can understand very well when you strike him in anger. He knows you are mad at him and he understands why. What a child cannot understand is when he disobeys mother at 10 a.m. and . . . then when Dad arrives home he is expected to administer a spanking that will "really teach the boy a lesson." That's the kind of cold-blooded spanking a child cannot understand or forgive. . . .

What you should do is tell your child once or perhaps twice what you want him to do or to stop doing. Then, if he refuses to obey your reasonable request, and you have become frustrated and angry, let him have it right then and there!

FITZHUGH DODSON
How to Parent

DOUGLAS HOPKINS

One of the problems with long-term punishments is that while the punishment is still going on, the crime has been long forgotten.

ELS

Q: How did you discipline your children?
Rose Kennedy: *I spanked them with rulers—and then, as they got older, I spanked them with coat hangers, since there was always a closet nearby and always a hanger in the closet.*

*Having spent a lot of time with children, I've observed two very
striking things about the relationship between parents and their children.
Firstly, that kids don't listen to their parents. Secondly,
that parents don't listen to their kids.*

BEATRICE LA MOTTE D'INCAMPS

COMMUNICATING WITH YOUR KID:
"IT'S GOING TO BE ALL RIGHT . . ."

What Some Kids Think About Their Parents

A group of kids, aged ten to seventeen, aired their grievances about their parents on the "Not For Women Only" TV program. Their gripes, not surprisingly, ran something like this:

1. Adults worry about us too much.
2. They tell me what to do too much. When I'm baking, for instance, my mother tells me how to do it, or that I'm doing it wrong.
3. They always interrupt you in the middle of something to do something else.
4. They tell you they'll take you somewhere and then they never do.
5. They ask too many questions. Like when I come home from a friend's house: How was this, how was that. I just want to go to sleep.
6. They set bad examples. They tell you not to smoke, and then they smoke.
7. Parents are too set in their ways, too closed-minded.
8. Parents press subjects in an attempt to "communicate." They're too aware of being aware. Maybe a kid doesn't want to discuss sexual problems with a parent.
9. Parents stereotype kids; they think we're all alike.

RS

◆

Getting Rid of the Accusation

It took me some time to learn not to ask a child, "What's the matter?" When I did, or varied it with "What's wrong?" children withdrew. They reacted as if I'd said, "What's wrong with *you?* What's the matter with *you?* . . . A better question and a better way of learning about the problem is, "Why are you crying?" or "What happened?" or "Would you tell me what you're thinking now? You seem sad or worried." Such questions elicit answers. Children like to hear specific and personal questions which don't imply that the problem is anyone's fault, particularly when there has been an argument between them. Children learn that if something painful or unfortunate happens, it must be *somebody's* fault.

STEPHEN M. JOSEPH
Children in Fear

Dog
Room
Homework
Love,
E.J

The modern mother's note. Estelle Jacobs says, "By the time your kid is ten years old, you've dispensed with the long harangues on how to fill his after-school leisure time. You've dispensed with the niceties. The notes are stripped down to the bare essentials."

Why Kids Lie (or, Worse, Withdraw)

The heroine—the perfectly normal, virtuous, and slightly deceitful heroine—has become the happy wife of a perfectly normal, virtuous, and slightly deceitful husband. She will shortly become a mother of a perfectly normal, virtuous, slightly deceitful son or daughter. A happy ending, that is what it works out at.

FORD MADOX FORD
The Good Soldier

Many parents seem to believe that it is not just necessary but that it is all right for them to lie to their children—in large ways and small. Given this belief, it is inevitable that children end up by trying to deceive their parents in turn, partly because in all the swirling froth of bewilderment and fantasy that is childhood there must be some knowledge of what is true, and partly because the only way a helpless child has of defending herself or himself against what she or he senses is deceit is by deceit. As a child, I remember, there was much duplicity on my parents' side and on my own. They thought, and often *knew,* what was right for me, but unfortunately for the three of us they thought that what was right for all children was right for me. They didn't seem to wonder who *I* was, for I was simply a child. In fact, it wasn't until I was ten or so that they saw I was different from my older brothers, and began treating me differently, though only in small ways. By then, it was too late, for my shield against them was the same as their shield against me—deception—and I couldn't cast it aside in their presence even many years later when I wanted to.

RICHARD HARRIS

◆

Grown-ups—Even Parents— Have Rights Too

I had always thought I had an obligation to my child to play with him when he wanted me to play, to have the energy when he required it, to talk about sequoia redwoods or nightmares or how turtles lay eggs whenever he felt like asking. But then I discovered that I had rights. When I realized this—for instance, that it's all right not to know the answer to a question (or just not *feel* like answering one), that I can say I don't want to play, that I can admit to being

tired or grumpy—our relationship soared. I found out that my kid came to accept my frailties and idiosyncrasies and, in fact, seemed to respect me more for letting him see me as I am. If I weren't free to act as I feel, I'm sure I'd be resentful, and make him feel that I was making great sacrifices for him. My own mother never made me feel that way, and I learned from her, as I hope my son will learn from me, that people—even parents—must be allowed to be who they are.

ELS

Keeping Promises

Children are probably the toughest and the most fragile human beings in the world, and, bar none, the most important. They are also the most exasperating, cunning, devious, self-centered, ruthless, unpredictable, and exhausting people in the world; a hard day's work in the mines can be less grueling than walking a child through the park. The reason, for me anyway, is that while it is virtually impossible to fool a child, it is very easy to betray him.

Children, for example, do not believe in Santa Claus for very long, and without our testimony, neither could nor would have believed in him at all. The belief in Santa Claus is nothing more than an opportunity for the child to exercise his imagination, an opportunity, in fact, to play games with us. The child lets go of Santa Claus without a qualm since, after all, *we* are Santa Claus, and he knew that all along. He is very smug and happy to have so shrewdly seen through his elders—one of the complex of reasons that he does not immediately make public his discovery. He waits, as it were, to see if *we* are as smart as *he* is. The point is, however, that *we* are there, and as long as we are there, who needs Santa Claus?

And if we are *not* there, who needs Santa Claus? For, on the other hand, if you promise a child that you will see him at a certain hour, on a certain day, everything in the child concentrates and hurls itself forward into that day and hour: if you do not keep your promise, the child begins to get lost. If you tell a child that he need only pray to God for something he deeply desires and that God will answer his prayer, the child will believe you; he will take you at your word. And if the child prays and his prayer is not answered, it is not God whom he will reproach, for it is not God who has betrayed him. He can live without God, as he can live without Santa Claus; a child can live on astoundingly little, but he cannot live without love.

JAMES BALDWIN

You're a Grown-up, Remember?

You often have to watch very closely to spot changes in your kid, to recognize a different stage. A friend confided that she was so angry with her child for so long that she hardly noticed when he changed from a fairly difficult bully to a very nice and well-adjusted, considerate, intelligent, mature adolescent. It's good if you can see the change—and respond to it—before your child moves out of the house.

What a child can nicely do is tap the child in you. If you are not in control of your childish impulses, you will find yourself in a continuing conflict to work out who's in charge here. Your kid knows your soft spots better than you know them yourself. She knows your unconscious, your moods, and how to hurt your feelings. Certain kinds of conflicts can take you back to when you were ten yourself, and it's all you can do to keep your ego intact and respond like a grown-up.

When my three-year-old told me he won't be my friend any more, I said, "Okay, I'll be your friend anyway. But you still can't have the candy before dinner." When my twelve-year-old stepdaughter threatened never to speak to me again, I told her, "You can be mad at me, but you still have to be home by nine thirty." My son told me I make him sad; I told him I was sorry. My stepdaughter, at seven, told me she hated my cooking. My feelings were hurt

then, but I should've told her that I was sorry, that I hoped she'd change her mind.

The hardest thing to do is to keep in mind always that the child must test herself against the world, and you're it, for a while anyway. And she must also test you. To find out the ways in which you are vulnerable. To find out if you will love her even when she is "bad." To learn how best to get your attention. Some kids crave any kind of attention and learn that they will be noticed more by misbehaving (and in many cases they are right). You must keep your own ego out of it—and stop taking the insults personally. It is difficult to pass those tests. What is more difficult is getting over them. Or knowing when it's time to forget they happened.

One of the things I always felt uncertain about was the length of time one should stay mad at one's kid. As a sometime-grudge-holder, I would've been quite comfortable staying mad all day, or even into the next day. I consulted with friends, other parents. "How long does it take for the lesson to be learned?" Only one friend had an answer. "Either right away or not at all," she concluded. "Say what you have to say and be done with it. The one who will suffer most from stored-up anger is you."

So I seek better, more constructive, more grown-up ways of suffering.

ELS

A Storehouse of Information

. . . The earlier you start giving [children] accurate information about themselves and the world around them, the better they'll be able to cope with the maleducation they're sure to get when they go out in the world. . . .

Psychologist Denah Harris once told me about a four-month-old baby who used to cry each time her mother left the room, but stopped when her mother came back in. Her mother constantly checked to see if the baby was hungry, if a diaper pin was sticking her, if she was wet, had defecated, or if she was lying in an uncomfortable position. The baby cried when she picked her up, and cried when she put her down. Her mother finally figured out that the baby cried when the mother went out of the room and turned the light off, but not when she went out and left the light on.

Mrs. Harris suggested she carry the baby over to the light switch, place her hand gently on the switch, and help her to move the switch up and down, turning the light on and off, while explaining that this is called light, which comes from electricity, which is energy, and that the thing they're moving together is called a switch, which makes the light go on and off. When the mother did this a few times, two things happened: participating in the experience comforted and soothed the baby, even though she didn't completely "understand" what was happening. Also, the experience and the procedure were recorded for future recall. There was no threat of punishment associated with it, it satisfied the baby's innate need to know, and the information was recorded by the cortex. If parents follow this procedure consistently, a baby will have a storehouse of non-moral, non-punitive information to call upon when she gets old enough to use language, and this will be the type and quality of information with which she'll start her conscious, conversational life.

STEPHEN M. JOSEPH
Children in Fear

Feiffer

I HATED THE WAY I TURNED OUT...

SO EVERYTHING MY MOTHER DID WITH ME I HAVE TRIED TO DO THE OPPOSITE WITH MY JENNIFER.

MOTHER WAS POSSESSIVE. I ENCOURAGED INDEPENDENCE.

MOTHER WAS MANIPULATIVE. I HAVE BEEN DIRECT.

MOTHER WAS SECRETIVE. I HAVE BEEN OPEN.

MOTHER WAS EVASIVE. I HAVE BEEN DECISIVE.

NOW MY WORK IS DONE. JENNIFER IS GROWN.

THE EXACT IMAGE OF MOTHER.

9-22 ©1974 JULES FEIFFER

I guess women's lib helped me to stop trying to be what I wasn't anyway—

supermom. As soon as I stopped worrying about how wonderful I

was or wasn't, the mothering went easier.

JILL SCHICKEL

THE BOOKS

I don't know any new parent who hasn't consulted at least one of the child-rearing manuals (watching your kid sputter and break out in rashes can be quite bewildering). But I also don't know too many people who've found the books really essential after, say, the first year of the first child. By then you've got the hang of it; you finally believe that you're as good a judge as anyone.

ELS

One Kid Talked Too Late and Walked Too Early

I used to be heavy into Dr. Spock and the Gesell Institute. But both gave me a problem. Dr. Spock assumed that women have a sixth sense about newborn babies. His book was like those cookbooks that tell you to sauté the blah-blah and add the roux. It assumes you know about roux and sauté. Those books made me feel like that. . . .

[T]hat damned Gesell Institute book . . . gave me a fit. From the git, my children didn't act like the book said they was spozed to. One talked too late and walked too early. The other one talked early but didn't have no teeth. I tried not to worry, but things didn't get no better. The equilibrium and disequilibrium never hooked up so I put the book away.

One evening, when Kali was eight and Chandra was six, [after one of our "caucuses," a note was slipped to me under the door and] I picked up the paper and read "You better let us have our way or you will be sorry when we have tremas and we have to go to the doctors and you can't get no babysitter cause we are going to have them at different times. In that Gesell book on children's behavior it say on page 211 and page 209 under mother-daughter relationships our behavior is normal for our ages." The note was unsigned.

I didn't do anything that night, but the next day, I searched their room and found the book under Chandra's pillow. . . . I took the book, and put it on a big brown bag—the supermarket kind. Then I called the children and asked both of them to accompany me to the incinerator.

VERTAMAE SMART-GROSVENOR
Essence

The ABC's of Child-rearing: *G* Is for Guilt

What we often do—and why shouldn't we?—is seek out the theory that agrees with our own child-rearing philosophy, and make that our authority.

If a book says toilet-train at age one, and we want to toilet-train at age one, we can point to that book and say, "Look here, this is right." But if that same authority, whom we've taken to heart for agreeing with us on so many things, says "Don't let your child suck after age two," we look at our four-year-old's pacifier with panic and humiliation. If that same authority, whom we trusted on Cradle Cap Disorders, is now telling us that Mother should be home with baby for the first five years, we suddenly feel shame and remorse and can hardly look the babysitter in the eye ("*She* knows I'm not doing my job").

If there were a sure way to avoid the guilt most of the child-rearing manuals too often impose, we could use the kind of reassurance that some of the books offer. Spock is so thorough, for example, that his index all but lists "Penny" if your kid swallows a penny and "Nickel" if he swallows a nickel. Surely, an authority's acknowledging that a problem exists is reassuring. Spock's telling us that there really is no way to judge how much milk a nursing baby is getting helps us feel less anxious. His mentioning a thousand symptoms we may someday see in our children makes us feel better—ours is not the first and only child ever to have a red navel, thank God—even though 80 percent of the time he finishes a paragraph by telling us to call our pediatrician, which is what we'd have done anyway if we'd never seen his book.

But I'm not sure how far I'd go with him on the more general issues. "The main source of good discipline is growing up in a loving family—being loved and learning to love in return." Okay, great. I know people who've had different reactions to statements like that. The first is: So what else is new? The second, a little more complex, is where the guilt comes in: suppose you don't have a particularly loving household? Does that mean your kids are doomed—and you along with them? Ginott has said mothers of infants shouldn't go out to work. But suppose you have to work; or, worse, what if you really want to? Won't Baby adjust? Lee Salk says talk to your child about death so that she'll understand should someone die. But what if you read his book after the fact? What will be the consequences of your not having handled it his way?

"The books are a comfort just to have in the house," one mother told me. "Though I seldom consult them, you never know when you'll want an opinion." On what, I wondered, would this woman seek an opinion from the child-rearing books? Her six-year-old will not go to sleep without a bottle. Her twelve-year-old is still wetting his bed. One peek in a book by a doctor would reveal where she'd gone "wrong" with her kids on every count: she works, is permissive, gave them solid foods early, once put thumb-sucking deterrent on her boy's thumb, used a playpen for both, let them watch too much television and eat too many cookies after school. The kids, as infants, had prickly heat, diaper rashes, and indigestion.

There is, it would seem, no hope for this woman. Were she to consult these books now, chances are she'd fix on the page that tells how the years from one through six are the most important in a child's development. If not, then she would find the chapter that offers the most reassurance about how everything will be all right anyway even if your twelve-year-old does wet his bed, and she will glean from it whatever she feels is most comforting.

ELS

Trying to Decode the Manuals

A group of mothers met to consider the available child-care manuals. They were in high good humor, and settled around a table with a tower of guides in the center, plus a plate of cookies. The idea was to chart how the books differed as to wisdom on toilet training, routines, sex awareness, sanctions, etc.

Toilet training was first. Everybody silently read a different book and made notes. There was quiet.

The first book said that the way in which a child's posture develops will influence whether or not he is able to use the potty successfully. Also whether or not he will be prone to relapses at any given time. That book said to wait until around the age of two before introducing toilet training to the child. The second book said that if parents train their children much before the age of two, it is really themselves they are training. The third book suggested "making friends with the potty" around two. And so it went. One book listed manufacturers who could supply specialized sheets that would shock the child

awake should he—in the years after two—wet his bed.

The mothers moved on to oral gratification—bottles, pacifiers, thumb-sucking, and so on. All the books said that it was important that an infant be able to suck. One of the mothers remarked that her child liked sucking so much he had used a bottle at night well into his third year. Another mother, upset, commented that her child would have liked this too, but that she had read somewhere that protruding teeth could result, so she had taken it away. "If only I'd known what *you* were doing," she said.

The mothers went back to the books.

After a time one blurted out, "This project turns out to be very boring."

"These books all say essentially the same thing," agreed another.

"How are we going to show the differences?" worried a third. "Maybe by emphasis," she mused. "Some books talk mainly about development. Others have a psychological orientation."

"Go on to another topic," suggested the leader.

Now everyone turned to the subject of routines—bedtime, dinnertime, etc. The books agreed that punishment should never be a part of these activities. (They also assumed that these activities would in fact occur, implying that every American child faced daily a table with dinner on it.)

"I wish I had known about your child's bottle," said the mother who had removed her own child's, still thinking about the earlier conversation. "It just makes me so mad. The only reason I ever read these books is for reassurance. But I'm so obedient I do exactly what they say. It never occurred to me that other people went their own ways. I wish I could just talk to parents more, share experiences more."

Agreeing, a mother whose children were of elementary school age said she thought the books could even be dangerous. Suppose parents reading them felt they didn't measure up as parents, or, worse, that their boys and girls didn't measure up as children? Wouldn't there be resentment and bad feeling?

"I can't *tell* you the weeks I made everyone miserable, while I tried to talk like Dr. Ginott," another parent joined in. "I can't remember much about what those sentences were like any longer. But what I do remember is how guilty I felt all the time, trying to get the phrasing just right, and positive that I never was. Finally I concluded that the way I talk to my children is the way I talk, and that we would all be a lot more relaxed if I just went about it."

"Why did you get so hung up by it?" she was asked.

"I think because I felt a little lonely. I wanted very much to do a good job with my children, but I wasn't really confident. No one was around to help me. So I listened to any expert I could read. I guess I sort of turned the books into authorities. Then I submitted to them."

"I'm sure that wasn't what the authors had in mind," someone remarked.

"No, of course not. But there it is. I suppose way down deep, scared as I was, it was some sort of evasion of the parent role. This is really weird, but what I think was happening was that I was trying to get Spock—or whatever book it was at the time—to take some responsibility off me. But I finally figured out that my husband and I were the parents around here, and that we had just better grow into that."

"I wonder, if you think about the books as a phenomenon, how they came to be published in such numbers," someone said.

"Well, it's probably because people don't have their own parents around so much anymore helping out and advising. It used to be that support was available through the extended family. Now we turn to books. Also, the books reflect the child-rearing styles—and the style keeps changing. Parents are currently accepting their instincts more than ever before—no one is conforming to the perfectionist image. The books are just catching up with this notion."

"That's not wholly true, though," one mother said nervously. "We're all a bit insecure. We want to make sure we're right. We want someone to say: 'You're doing fine.' The interesting thing is that you can find a book to agree with you no matter what you think."

"I just wish they all said in big bold type, though, that *everyone* can make mistakes—kids, parents, books," said the mother who had never mastered Childrenese. "That child-care manuals are just to give you help if you can use it. Obviously, they don't know your particular child, they don't mean to dictate."

"But you're supposed to know that already," said the leader.

JENNIFER CARDEN

◆

I've read a lot, and my reaction to most of what I've read is reflected in my reaction to Ginott. I've read his books and know the script of just what I'm supposed to say in a given situation. The trouble is that my five-year-old has not read the script.

MARJORIE SMITH

Child-Care Manuals: A List from *Our Bodies, Ourselves*

Ainsworth, Mary D., et al. *Deprivation of Maternal Care.* New York: Schocken Books, 1966.

Anthony, E. James, and Theresa Benedek, eds. *Parenthood: Its Psychology and Psychopathology.* Boston: Little, Brown & Co., 1970.
   Heavy psychoanalytic and pathological bias.

Bettelheim, Bruno. *Love Is Not Enough.* New York: Avon Books, 1971 (paper).
   Although the book is not about "normal" children, it has some important things to say about all kids. Good sections on food, in-between times, and space.

Bowlby, John. *Maternal Care and Mental Health.* New York: Schocken Books, 1966.
   A report prepared on behalf of the World Health Organization as a contribution to the U.N. program for the welfare of homeless children.

Brazelton, T. Berry. *Infants and Mothers: Differences in Development.* New York: Delacorte Press, 1969. (Also available in Dell paperback.)
   Follows three "typical" infants from birth through the first year, with emphasis on the effects the infant can have on his/her environment, and the mother-infant interaction.

Fraiberg, Selma. *The Magic Years.* New York: Charles Scribner's Sons, 1959 (paper). $2.45

Ilg, Francis L., and Louise Bates Ames. *Gesell Institute's Child Behavior.* New York: Dell, 1955. (Get the revised edition.)

Montagu, Ashley. *Touching: The Human Significance of the Skin.* New York: Columbia University Press, 1971.
   Fascinating account of human needs and emotions relating to physical contact at all ages, includes some animal studies, etc. Especially shows artificiality of society in the United States.

Nelson, Waldo E., et al. *Textbook of Pediatrics.* 9th ed. Philadelphia: W. B. Saunders Co., 1969.

Prenatal Care, Infant and Child Care, Your Child from 6 to 17. U.S. Department of Health, Education and Welfare. Children's Bureau pamphlets.

Salk, Lee, and Rita Kramer. *How to Raise a Human Being.* New York: Random House, 1969.
   Interesting, readable, and very clear approach to various developmental stages, without rigid norms. Better than Gesell.

Spock, Benjamin. *Baby and Child Care.* New York: Pocket Books, rev. ed., 1968.
   Still a classic, and if you haven't read it, do. (Much misquoted.) Not good on breast-feeding or socialization, but good for basic everyday troubles.

N.B.: Also worthwhile, really helpful reading: books by psychiatrists such as R. D. Laing, Fritz Perls, David Cooper, Arthur Janov, and other modern "existential" psychiatrists; and books by educators John Holt, A. S. Neill, Sylvia Ashton-Warner, George Denison, Jonathan Kozol, and Herbert Kohl.

BOSTON WOMEN'S HEALTH COLLECTIVE

GETTING THE KID ON THE POT

Allowing My Child Out of His Diapers: An Interview with Nikki Giovanni

Interviewer: How did you toilet-train your child?

Nikki Giovanni: My system is based on the theory that no grown man or grown woman wets on himself or herself.

Thomas was in diapers until he was ten months old and we were going to London. After carrying Pampers all over the world, I said I am not going to carry Pampers to London. It was just a decision that I made. So I stopped the diaper service and bought him training pants and we left for London. Now he did not like to have his urine run down his leg—it would annoy him and he'd point and say, "*Uh.*" And I would say, "If you don't go in the potty, that's going to happen." I realized that he would be more disturbed by the urine running down his leg than I would be. That he would tire of it sooner than I would.

So every time he would toddle over to the potty I would reward him—with everything from kisses to candy to "Thank you" to "What a big boy you are." I was very patient. So he did it, I didn't.

Interviewer: There's something else you're not telling me.

N.G.: I never screamed at him. Whenever he wet on himself or had a bowel movement on himself, I would change him. There was never any punishment. (Now my mother's a very gentle lady, but I'm sure she probably hit me about potty training. She doesn't admit to it, but I'll bet she did.) While changing him I would say, "Now you got a little dirty, didn't you?" I don't think I pushed him, but I do think I did *allow* him out of his diapers. It finally got through to him—if you're out in the park and you're all wet, you have to go home to change.

It's No Big Thing

When Sarah, my first child, was about two, I realized that I would have to face toilet training. I asked around about how it should be done.

"It's just like with a dog," an older woman who had been through it told me.

"You put paper down?"

"Well, no, but you reward success and discourage failure."

"I should swat her nose?"

"Well, no."

I decided what she meant was to *ignore* failure—certainly a courtesy I appreciate when it is extended to me. Failure, I learned, could be called an "accident." I consulted a pamphlet in my pediatrician's office.

"Buy a potty," it said. "Let your child make friends with it. Don't press the issue."

I bought a potty and told Sarah she could have it.

I consulted my mother. "You're lucky it's summer," she said. "You don't have to deal with snowsuits and a lot of clothes. Just let her run around in her pants. She'll manage." I bought six pairs of training pants, double thickness.

Still not knowing what I was doing, and still thinking of toilet training as a Big Thing, I finally made one smart move of my own. I consulted Sarah.

"Lookit," I said. "You probably don't want to wear diapers any longer."

"I know, you never can find the pins," she answered, lying on the changing table.

"So I got the potty for you. When you feel like you'd like to let go, just sit on it, and then we'll dump whatever you make into the toilet."

"Okay," she said.

"Oh, there's one other thing," I told her, opening her dresser drawer. "These are called training pants. You can just wear them instead of diapers."

"Okay," she said. "I want to wear them now."

Certain things then began to happen. Later in the week Sarah was talking on the telephone to her father at the office. "You know, I have big-girl pants," she confided to him.

"I know," he said. "That's great. I am proud of you."

A package arrived in the mail. It was from her grandmother; lace pants with pink rosebuds. A confection.

We considered showing extravagant approval for all this—should we be yelling bravo in the bathroom? It seemed a little silly, so beyond a few initial shouts, her father and I decided no.

The end.

That's about all I remember. The potty stayed in the bathroom for several years because of brothers and sisters, but somewhere along the line, Sarah must have given it up. When she was three we talked about not wearing diapers at night, and she thought she could manage that. The strange part about this is that I literally can't recall it with any of the other three younger children. Did Sarah do it for me? Or do children really do it for themselves when they're ready and able and have the proper supplies? That must be it.

JENNIFER CARDEN

Nothing Ventured . . .

I'd promised my son that whenever he used the toilet I would push him on the swing. And I remember many a cold night when I'd have to put on my hat and coat and put on his hat and coat and out we'd go into the yard for a swing.

CHARLOTTE SAGOFF

When kids are ready to be toilet trained they'll be toilet trained—if you let them into the bathroom with you. Anything a kid sees you do, he wants to imitate. But if you're uptight about letting the kid in the bathroom when you're in there, he has nothing to imitate.

CAROLYN AND ORSON BEAN

Toilet training in the summer, in the country: if your child can spend the better part of the day outdoors (at least at the beginning of this effort), try letting her or him run around bare-bottomed, pee in the bushes, go in the house and sit on the potty at any time. This half-naked method seems to give kids a heightened awareness of that moment of elimination. For relaxed parents only.

ELS

I never put my child on a toilet until she was two and a half, when, seeing me in the bathroom, she came around and just looked. "Do you want to use the toilet?" I asked her.

"Yah."

"Do you know what to do?"

She looked at me assuredly and said, "Yah."

That was it. She's used the toilet ever since.

LYNNE CLEAVER

The Bribe: A Psychologically Sound Method?

No one was more surprised than I, who'd read more child-rearing books than anyone would need, by the toilet-training method I finally ended up using and which worked. I call it the French-Fry-and-Gum Reward and Punishment Method. Whereby the child is advised that if he doesn't deposit his bowel movement into the nearest toilet he will have no French-fried potatoes or chewing gum until the next bowel movement. And when he does use the toilet for a bowel movement, he will then have all the French fries and gum that he wants.

(*Note:* This seemed to work because at this particular time my child was obsessed with the two items being denied him. Also, he knew very well how to use the toilet—and I knew he knew.)

To me this seemed as psychologically sound as any method I'd read or heard about—there was no hitting or screaming, no coaxing or expressions of disappointment. I was utterly calm but firm about the decision. And surprised to learn how many others had used a similar system with equally successful results. When it comes down to the wire, you burn the books.

ELS

[Readers will note that this is definitely not in accordance with our general theories on bribing versus non-bribing.]

◆

The Need to Toilet Train

Toilet training is a subject of concern to many, though not knowing too many adults who make in their pants led me to believe it was an overrated problem. We felt that our child would get the idea himself, eventually, and we let him do it that way. It seemed rather basic to take that approach. If one can divide humanity into segments, it can be said there are those who feel reality comes from them and others who believe it is thrust at them. Forcing toilet habits on a child conveys a vision of hostile reality. However, since we didn't toilet-train our child, and since we wanted the pleasure of toilet-training something in a toilet-training society, we trained our toilet.

HARVEY JACOBS

Last Resorts

A few things to try when you begin to worry about your kid's not being toilet trained and you've already tried everything and read every book.

1. Say nothing and do nothing. Drop the subject. It is likely, if your kid is two anyway, that she knows exactly what she is expected to do. The only thing keeping her from actually doing it is that she won't. Leave her alone for a while and see what happens. And for goodness sake, stop worrying that you've ruined her for life by urging her to pee in the pot in the first place.
2. Without mentioning the "failure," you can, from time to time, say something like "Gee, won't it be nice when you stop wetting your pants—you'll be able to sleep over at Grandma's house."
3. Become less involved in the cleanup, if you can stand to. Let her wear training pants and tell her it's okay if she wets them (and convince yourself that it *is* okay). "Oh, don't worry about it," you can say if she comes to you saying she's wet. Then hand her a clean dry pair and let her change herself. This reassigning the responsibility for changing can work miracles: the child will soon find cleanup as much of an annoyance as you do, and she'll think more about how she can get out of doing it. Of course, this works only with the training pants, not diapers. (I've always thought it unfortunate that kids can't be taught to change their own diapers.)

ELS

SIBLINGS

I once owned two white mice, but . . . one ate the other and then died of loneliness.
GRAHAM GREENE

Getting Rid of Sibling Rivalry: Re-Creating the Extended Family

A pat phrase of our time is "sibling rivalry." We take as healthy and right what is only "normal" in the sense that it is all too common—that the children in a family should actively dislike each other and compete frantically and ruthlessly for the too scarce attention and "love" of their parents. Why should the competition be so frantic? Because the wanted and needed attention, concern, advice, companionship, and protection are so scarce. Why so scarce? Because there is no one but the parents to give it.

Children need many more adult friends, people with whom they may have more easy relationships that they can easily move out of or away from whenever they need to or feel like it . . .

What we need is to re-create the extended family. Or rather, we need to allow, encourage, and help young people create extended families of their own. There is no reason why the adult friends of a child should be friends of his parents.

JOHN HOLT
Escape from Childhood

RONNIE SHUSHAN/THE PHOTO WORKS

A Little Reassurance: You Were a Baby Once Yourself

Shortly before our second child was born, I spent some time with John (then three) going over his old baby pictures, digging out footprints, remembering certain gifts that he particularly loved (or continually spit up on), looking at pictures of grandparents doting over their first grandchild, reliving the first tooth, the first birthday, the first word. It seemed to be a tremendous help, and we both enjoyed it.

If ever there was a good reason to keep baby memorabilia (in the fashion of old baby books with satin covers), it is to help a young child know what to expect from this new baby about to join the family, and then, once the baby has arrived, to provide reassurance that the older child received all the same attention.

SUSAN LAWRENCE

Letting the Kids in on the Truth

I discovered, unwittingly, a way to get the kids, against all odds, to enjoy the presence of the new baby. As the due date grew nearer and my belly larger, I knew it was time for a heart-to-heart with my son, two and a half, and my stepdaughter, twelve and a half, both of whom (for their own reasons) I thought were apprehensive about the pending arrival of this mysterious being who already, even before she was born, was taking up space in our house and taking up much of our conversation.

Inspired by the notions of Dr. Lamaze, who thought that a lot of knowledge and understanding makes an experience a lot easier, I began talking to the kids about exactly what would happen—starting with labor (which, for these purposes, needn't be *too* detailed) and the days I would have to be in the hospital (and what would go on there and what a terrible rule they have there about brothers and sisters not being able to visit and why they have that rule), through the first days (including how left out everyone, everyone in the family, will feel when the neighbors and friends come to the house to kitchey-coo, and what an annoyance it will be when many of them bring presents for the baby and not for us), to all the days afterward (how some things will be delightful—especially when any of us get to be alone with the baby and watch it slowly learn and change—and other things will be unpleasant like dirty diapers and night crying). They should know that it's natural to feel left out (because so much attention seems to be paid to the new baby) and that when they do feel left out, it's okay to say something about it. (The new-brother-new-sister type of books generally don't acknowledge the negative aspects enough.)

There are two tricks to this whole thing: the first is to be wholly honest—your child will be much less suspicious if you are absolutely truthful about the good things for everyone that will come from this child's being born as well as those that will be a drag, even (hah!) for you. The second thing is to make certain they know

more about birth and labor and babies than any of their classmates. They should know that a baby gets hungry after about four hours and needs to eat and cries in order to make that known—even when it's the middle of the night. In short, they should be made to feel a part of the whole event, and the best time to work on that is before the baby is born, though you can start late and still get results.

A final tactic is to squelch those giddy relatives who breeze in and tell the older kid how lucky he is to have a new sister. "What's so lucky?" I said to auntie. "Right now it's mostly a pain in the neck." My son loved hearing that said out loud, in front of him, and with a kind of bold irreverence. It relieved him of a lot of the anxieties and resentment he would be afraid to express himself. And the baby, well, her feelings weren't hurt.

ELS

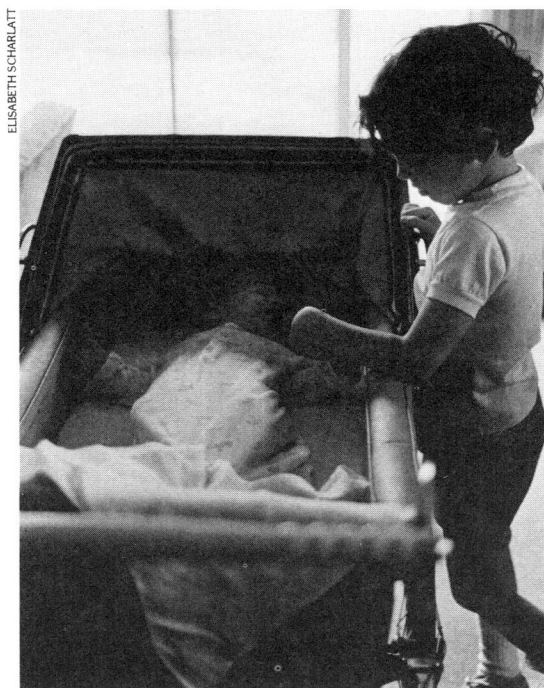

ELISABETH SCHARLATT

A Newborn Baby Is No Great Playmate

Before Dick was born, my parents made the common mistake of promising me a playmate in the new baby. As a result I found his newborn ineptitude very exasperating. I have been told that I once got him, as a toddler, behind a door and furiously demanded, "Can't you say anything but 'da da da' all the time?"

MARGARET MEAD
Blackberry Winter

Notes of a Newborn Father, or How the Second Child Has the Advantage

When we had our first child we felt a terrible impatience with his development. No stage arrived and departed quickly enough. As soon as we heard "goo" we listened for "good morning." As soon as Matthew crawled we shopped for sneakers.

But then when number two came along we automatically gave baby Stephen all the time in the world. We didn't decide to, it just happened. It just seemed natural and right, the way being call Daddy or Mommy one day seemed natural and right.

Conventional wisdom points out that a second child is often more relaxed. But the truth is, it's the parent who's more relaxed. My wife was first to notice. She gave Stephen a thorough examination the second he was brought to her hospital bed. But she had been so afraid of mishandling Matthew, she remembered, that she wouldn't even put all ten fingers on him at once lest some of them unconsciously pull a bottom brick out of nine months and five days of delicate construction. I first noticed the change the day we brought Stephen home. It was rainy, windy, and raw, but all that meant to us was the futility of taking moving pictures of mother and son's grand exit. Five years ago we would have waited for a break in the weather even if it meant camping in a hospital corridor from December to May.

Once home, both parents immediately enjoyed Stephen's infancy—the crying, the gurgling, the uncontrolled motor explorations, the gassy smiles, the sleepy eyes, the fleshing out of his face and limbs—everything. Previously all these developments were either startling or frightening or regarded as necessary steps toward some more fathomable, enjoyable plateau. With Stephen, each thing he did or tried to do was cherished for itself. The pressure was off. When he smiled he didn't have to be reacting to a bit of cleverness or foolishness we were offering. When he accidentally punched himself in the nose, we didn't rush to straitjacket him in that innocent-looking baby wrap you can fold shut at the sleeve ends.

We realized that with a week-old baby you can do almost anything common sense suggests. You can try to ram cereal down his throat, you can take him outdoors even if you don't live in Tahiti, you can let him cry a little longer, let him sleep a little longer, let him wear his own mess a little longer. It also struck us that drafts are not whistled in by the Devil's own breath, that the ghost of Baron Lister does not screen every visitor, and that a little rash or a touch of colic isn't always cause to rouse your pediatrician at three in the morning.

More important, we recognized the probable effect on Stephen of our new found relaxation and patience. Of all the thousands upon thousands of words we read concerning child-rearing, the ones most frequently repeated and most profound, I think, explain that a child has a special ability to sense adult attitudes. If you are overly protective and quickly panicky, a child soon develops an unreasonable fearfulness about his life. If you are impatient with your child's development because you just can't wait for him to "say the darndest thing," this pressure can place disproportionate emphasis on achievement and, consequently, give rise to feelings of inferiority in the child.

These thoughts were a little unsettling to someone who had been overprotective and impatient with his first child for four and a half years. But a curious thing happened. The change that took place had a retroactive side effect on Matthew. Months and years of parental mismanagement were wiped away. Matthew sensed the change in us and took immediate delight in it. He was noticeably freer, noticeably more confident and relaxed. When the nervousness and impatience disappeared in us, they disappeared for Matthew too.

In some people parenthood grows inside them along with the baby and then blossoms brilliantly at birth, never to wilt or strangle. Others are built differently. After nine speculative months they are shocked and thrust into an uncomfortable role which worries and intimidates them. For these less blessed souls, I hope the lesson my wife and I learned will be helpful: use your heart as well as your head, and all ten fingers.

ALAN SAPERSTEIN

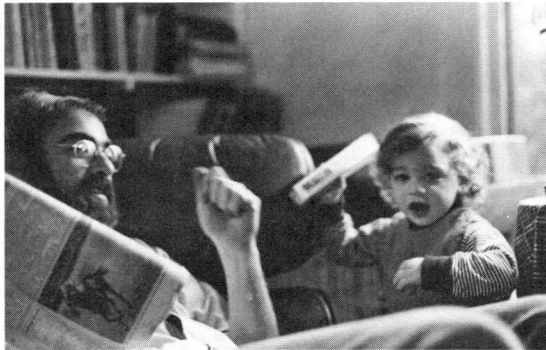
ELISABETH SCHARLATT

Your Parent or Your Sibling?

With Ann and me, our mother was not often blithe, nor were we with her. It's odd. We were thought in our circles to be amusing, and so was she in hers, but regrettably seldom did we laugh together. We never developed enough rapport. Sometimes mothers and daughters do have strong rapport; I have seen it. But in those cases, the daughters seem less close to each other or to their brothers. Can this be some new maxim of human nature, or is it somewhere written that you can have real, ready access to your parents or else to your siblings, but not to both?

JANE HOWARD
A Different Woman

When to Separate the Boys from the Girls

The parents of a seven-year-old girl and a five-year-old boy had kept the two together since the younger one was born. They shared a bedroom, bathed together, played together. The parents kept wondering how they would know when the time had come to separate them. One afternoon the two were splashing about in the bathtub, and the mother decided the time had come when she heard her little boy say to his sister, "Oh, wash out your own vagina!"

WALTER JERROLD

Dividing the Pie

Here's how my two kids piecefully solve as easy as, well, pie the problem of dividing the last piece of pie, cake, or anything: One cuts the piece into two. The other makes the choice of which "half" he or she wants. Without fail, the original piece is cut 50-50.

What I'm working on figuring out now is how to use a similar technique for three pieces.

JEROME B. AGEL

Siblings As Only Children

With four kids, we find that each one needs to have time with us alone, without the other three kids. Even if it's only once every two months that we take one of them out alone with us, it's important. We do whatever the kid wants to do, whether it's going bowling, or roller skating, or to the pizza parlor. One of them likes to go to very grown-up restaurants. To another, where we take him is far less important than making sure that none of the other kids finds out our destination.

CAROLYN BEAN

"Siblings" for an Only Child

Only children should be brought up close to other only children, so they will not someday have to reminisce alone.

JANE HOWARD
A Different Woman

PARENTS AT WORK:
How Many Kids Know What Their Parents Do?

Instead of always asking your kids questions about their day and what they did in school, tell them about yours. Describe it in detail; help them understand just what it is you do all day long. ELS

The question is not whether women should work. Of course we work. The real question for many is whether men will take equal responsibility in raising children so that we are not the only partner holding two jobs.

ABIGAIL HEYMAN
Growing Up Female

Taking Your Kids to the Office

Dad was a landscape architect. He used to take me with him to the office and I'd poke around and look at his drafting materials and other stuff. I had my own little place in the office, and my own projects. Dad's clients would come in, and the students that Dad was teaching would come in, and Dad's boss would come in. And everything that they talked about together I'd hear. Nothing was private or personal or that kind of thing. When Dad was criticizing a student's work and giving him a grade, I could sit there in his lap and watch the whole process, look over his shoulder. And I spent time there with him even when I was older. I knew exactly what my father did for a living, where he belonged in space and time.

How many parents take their kids to the office anymore, how many kids know what their parents do?

ELIOT WIGGINTON

I work in a creative teaching center—a small group in a big old house. My three-month-old baby is always with me at work. There's no problem. And my two-year-old child joins us at lunch and sometimes naps at the center. She's gained an amazing amount of poise from always having been a part of a social ritual with several caring adults.

SUSAN RUSSELL

I find with my son and with my daughter, five and four, that they seem to enjoy more than anything else going to my office with me. They do this a lot on weekends, usually for only a couple of hours at a time, and then their favorite toys become typewriters, Scotch tape, scissors, copy paper, Pentels, staplers, and all the other tools of my business. The fact that I have a television set in my office doesn't hurt, either. I find that when they play—and "work"—in my office, they are much neater and behave much better than they do at home. They seem to give the office some kind of respect. My son, particularly, seems to take great pride in knowing where the light switches are, and which button to press in the elevator, and, all in all, it seems like a good time. They also get a big kick out of going to the barber with me; they force him to spend as much time making them go up and down in the electrically operated chair as he spends cutting my hair.

What I'm saying, I guess, is that these fringe things, office tools and barber shop frills, appear to be more fun than the standard toys, most of which I find totally appalling. The best comment from my son on all of this was: "Daddy, when I grow up, I'm going to work for you so that you'll be able to see a lot of me." (A rather sad comment on the amount of hours I spend working.) "But, at night, I've got to go home, of course, to see my own children."

DICK SCHAAP

KIDS' RIGHTS

The Right to Get Away from It All

Parents can usually get away from their kids when they feel like it, but kids can't get away from their parents when *they* feel like it. In the South Sea Islands, kids can wander about and anyone will take them in as they come by. The kids all know how to swim and aren't going to fall in the water. In a city, kids have to be so dependent on the parents that it's terrifying.

If our kids want to visit their grandparents without us, we would have to drive seven hours to take them, drive back seven hours, and then go pick them up, so we end up all going together.

I'm not sure what you can do about kids' independence, but it's terribly important to try to do something.

CAROLYN BEAN

Letting a kid venture out into the world on her own without a list of instructions and without a send-off and a ten-piece band offers her a chance at becoming her own person. Allowing visits with friends and relatives you trust is a good place to start. Or encouraging a friendship with someone else's grandmother. Above all, it helps to remove some of the weight of the parent–child interdependence.

ELS

The Right to Be Destructive

It's very hard to know what to do. My kid says to me, "Is this toy mine?"

"Yes," I tell him, "it's yours."

"And can I do anything I want with it?"

"Well, yes, it's yours to do with what you want."

Before I know it, he's setting the toy on fire. Seventeen dollars worth of plastic melting away. What do you do?

DOM DE LUISE

The Right to Be Selfish

Respect for property is something all parents hope their kids will grow up with. You give them a book and you hope they take care of it. You don't want them to destroy your stuff, write on the walls, or mark up the piano. Respect for property grows out of ownership of property. But children are rarely allowed absolute ownership of property, they're always given *provisional* ownership. For instance, when a kid is given something, he is expected to take care of it. Can you imagine a friend giving you something and saying, "Now, I expect you to take care of this."? But we say this to our kids all the time. When you give a kid a tricycle and expect him to share it with his brothers and sisters or friends, he is aware that he doesn't own it. Until a kid is free to be selfish, he's not free to be generous.

It might help the kid to know that if ownership of property is absolute, it is yours to do with as you wish—to destroy, to waste, and above all to share with no one.

ORSON BEAN

The Right to Be Impulsive

One of the most mindblowing moments for a would-be free parent is to discover yourself in the act of authoritarian role-playing, especially in reaction to a child's act of healthy personal expression.

Holly, ten, was reading the ingredients on the label of a can of hoummous Mediterranean dip. Then the instructions. "Empty contents of tin into a bowl. Serve with cucumber slices, celery sticks, white bread or crackers . . ." She said in mock horror: "White bread!" And went for a pen to cross it out.

I told her, "That's not necessary," and became an instant candidate for kids' lib consciousness-raising. After all, if Ken Kesey had started to ink out the word "white" I would've thought it totally appropriate. Why shouldn't I give my own daughter at least as much respect?

PAUL KRASSNER
Soho Weekly News

The Right to Disagree with Dad

When asked what he would want for his children, besides privacy, Dustin Hoffman answered:

"The first thing I would want for them is freedom. The biggest thing I can give them is themselves, the chance to develop their own individuality. Let them form their own taste, different points of view. My older child comes home and starts asking: 'Daddy, is there a God?' And I say, 'Are you asking me what I think? Sometimes I think there is; sometimes I don't think there is.' 'What does Mommy think?' 'Mommy is more of an atheist.' 'What's an atheist?' and I explain that. And she says, 'Well, there's a God.' I ask, 'How do you know?' She says, 'I just know. We've been talking about it on the bus.' 'I see.' I like the fact that my opinion is questioned. That the answers are to be found everywhere."

DUSTIN HOFFMAN
Playboy interview

INGE MORATH MAGNUM PHOTOS. INC.

The Right to Be Aloof

What about the right of a small child not to be kissed? When you're twelve you can sulk in a corner and the relatives will shrug it off and call it an adolescent "phase"; when you're two you can blurt out a raspberry and run away and they'll call it the terrible twos, but there are so many times in between when kids have no defense. If you're five and shy, you get grabbed and smooched by every tanta who passes through. If you're an infant, you're at their mercy.

At the risk of antagonizing even my own grandmother (whom I love dearly), I will come to my own kid's defense, say something like, "He doesn't feel like kissing you right now, Grandma," if I see that, indeed, he doesn't. Grandma gets the point, stops asking, and gets her kiss voluntarily—and the kid feels better, too, I think.

ELS

I don't touch or approach children unless they touch me first. So far no one has, though I've just come from my grandchildren. The way things are going, they may never come to me at all. At least I can leave their fingers alone until they voluntarily touch me. Children are not common property just because they're small.

SYLVIA ASHTON-WARNER
Spearpoint

I'm dropping by in a hurry because I've got this incredible job. I'm leading an insane life...

...but I wanted to see how you're doing, Poor dear... he is adorable this one!

Me, I have to go to the airport to pick up the ambassador of Bajo and going to the airport is such a mess and then I have to stuff myself into a press conference

and then I have to lug the dumb wife of the ambassador to Yves Saint-Laurent. You know the type... It's all nonsense...

but I have to earn a living. Say, I'm going to Iran next week... if you need a rug just let me know... Oh he is more and more adorable this guy...

and what about you? It's decided you won't go back to work! Me, I'm for individual liberty. And Robert? Still a bureaucrat? No probleme? Good!

Once in a while I ask myself if I don't envy you... and then happily you have him! Well, ciao!

Happiness can be ruined by children, by financial anxieties, by so many secret things.

GRAHAM GREENE

THE BIG TABOO: KIDS ARE A DRAG

Breaking the Silence

An old friend with two children under three wrote in a recent letter: "The girls are, today, very nice. Each day is different. Some days I am so dreadful to them I shudder to think about it." I am moved by these words because they echo deep feelings I have about my own three-year-old daughter. But I was also moved by the woman's honesty. I wrote to my friend and thanked her for sharing her bared self with me.

Another woman I know once introduced me to a friend of hers as "my fairy godmother"—not so much because I had given her the maroon Perego baby carriage I was so fond of, but for telling her that parenting was sometimes very difficult for me.

The substance of both these stories—that parenting is sometimes painfully hard—is no news at all, I know, at least not to any parent. But it has been my experience, and that of many friends, that frank discussion of the nitty-gritty realities of this problem is all too rare.

Still another friend, a fellow alumna of a childbirth class (with whom I've shared some tentative parental confidences), speaks of a parental "conspiracy of silence." Somehow, there are feelings and experiences that are just damned hard to talk about. How do you say—and to whom—that at times you feel you're a lousy parent, or that you don't like being a parent, or (bite your tongue) that you don't know why you ever became one in the first place?

Yet the truth is that many of us have these feelings—including those of us who generally cope happily and successfully with our children, and at our best moments consider ourselves terrific parents and enjoy it all tremendously. I think most people will agree that sharing the problems helps. My point is that we have to work very hard at that communication, because confidences come rarely, hesitantly, awkwardly, with apologies, indirection, nervous laughter. The most revealing remark is dropped accidentally, or in a casual aside:

■ *Item.* Two of us pussyfoot around the topic of how maddening it can be to care for an infant, joking sophisticatedly that the aristocratic practice of having a governess present a clean, quiet child at the end of the day wasn't such a bad idea.

■ *Item.* I apologetically ask close friends with children of their own to think of counting me and my daughter in on their weekend fun, awkwardly admitting that long weekends alone with a toddler can be "difficult" (meaning tense and even lonesome).

■ *Item.* A mother, irony heavy in her voice, says that she can spend hours just looking at her son asleep in his crib at night. (She doesn't talk about the daylight hours that are not so easy.)

On occasion, happily, there are more direct moments of communication:

■ *Item.* An experienced mother drags a reluctant me and my six-month-old, breast-fed daughter on a spree around the city, assuring me that she never left the house for the first two years after childbirth unless her mother accompanied her.

■ *Item.* I tell a friend agonizing through the first weeks of breast-feeding that I was on the verge of quitting for Lord knows how long of my eventually successful ten-month experience at it.

■ *Item.* My sister, supermother of four, remembers that with her first, she never managed to get herself dressed until dinnertime.

■ *Item.* My daughter is at my office charming the pants off everyone, and I tell one admirer (a parent) that she's not always so terrific, but can also be embarrassingly shy, grouchy, and a genuine pain in the ass.

■ *Item.* I confess to a friend that I am impatient with my child when she is sick and out of sorts. I have spoken because this woman is trying to write an article on parental anger and I feel intellectually committed to honesty; but I am still rather horrified and ashamed.

People I know *are* trying to break down the old communication barriers on intimate topics. At thirty-four, I can remember when very few of us, even after marriage, discussed sex or contraception. I think the pill, in large part, has changed that. And only a few years ago, no one I knew talked frankly about marital problems. I can remember an evening about five years ago when four of us (two couples, old friends) realized that we hadn't understood there were going to be difficult moments in marriage because our proper parents had hidden *their* tensions from us as children. (We thereby made the great admission that we did have problems—without going so far as to talk about them directly.) I needed my supportive women's group before I ever began to open up that can of worms.

The conspiracies of silence about having children are something else. Before my time (thank goodness), there was a conspiracy about the physical act of childbirth. ("Why didn't you tell me what it was like?" my friend wailed from her hospital bed to a visitor. But that was nearly eight years ago.) The enormous issue of whether or not to bear children at all is just barely surfacing now.

The parental problems on my mind these days are those in the beginning—especially during that first difficult year, which at its worst can be frustrating, exhausting, and frightening. Nothing can be so maddening to the new mother as the traditionally condescending attitude toward postpartum depression. For be-yond any psychological reactions to hormonal changes lies the enormous challenge of coping with a whole new life, possibly the greatest single life-change that many of us ever undergo. There is responsibility for another life, and an inescapable commitment to the future. There are dirty diapers and cries in the night and multiplying expenses and no more truly free time.

Now some of us thrive on all this, but some of us have trouble coping. Perhaps my most telling "item" of proof of the silence conspiracy is that it is taking all my courage to write these thoughts down and all my self-restraint not to apologize for concentrating on the negative aspects of parenting. But that is my subject here—and if it is ever yours, I suggest you try sharing it with another parent.

My friend with the baby carriage, just emerging from her first year of motherhood, has an interesting insight. Knowing of her interest in the subject of the difficulties of parenting, I had asked if she wouldn't write down some of her thoughts. She answered that she and another friend had wanted to, countless times, but somehow hadn't been able to find—or make—the time. Maybe, she concluded sadly, that's why nothing satisfactory had been written. That first difficult year, when we were so well qualified to speak, was a time too harried—and disturbing—to be able to communicate what was happening to us.

Some years ago I cherished the friend who told me she had disliked the tedium and mess of feeding an infant. I believed her to be a good parent of a nice kid, and it gave me hope that I could nourish my own without always relishing the experience of shoveling mashed egg yolk and banana into that delicious little mouth.

NAME WITHHELD

A Matter of Time

Spock says Mother has to rest, which is very nice. But it's a lie. One gets used to not sleeping and being on twenty-four-hour demand. One also gets strung out!

FLAVIA POTENZA

Everyone says, Can't you get any work done while the kid is napping? Well, no, dammit, I can't get the kind of work done that I do when I'm alone. There's always the feeling that the kid is going to wake up any minute. In some cases he does, but even when he doesn't I find myself sitting and waiting for him to wake up, feeling the pressure of the limits of time.

ELS

After having been a parent for two months, one thing I realized is that parents don't have time to sit down for a while.

MARK GERZON

You're Not Alone

You become a parent and all of a sudden you think you know (or you're expected to know) how to do it—and when you discover that there's something tricky, you feel incompetent. It's a common feeling. It always seems that everyone else is raising terrific kids with such ease, coping beautifully. But they're not, not necessarily.

ZELDA WIRTSCHAFTER

Tired-Mother Syndrome

What hits a new mother the hardest is not so much the increased work load as the lack of sleep. . . . If you have never been awakened and required to function at one in the morning and again at three, then maybe at seven, or some such schedule, you can't imagine the agony of it. All of a woman's muscles ache and they respond with further pain when touched. She is generally cold and unable to get warm. Her reflexes are off. She startles easily, ducks moving shadows, and bumps into stationary objects. Her reading rate takes a precipitous drop. She stutters and stammers, groping for words to express her thoughts, sounding barely coherent—somewhat drunk. . . . In response to all the aforementioned symptoms she is always close to tears. . . .

This lack of sleep is rarely mentioned in the literature relating to the Tired Mother Syndrome. Doctors recommend to women with newborn children that they attempt to partially compensate for this loss of sleep by napping during the day. With one child that may be possible, with several small ones it's sort of a sick joke.

Quoted by BENJAMIN DE MOTT
Surviving the 70's

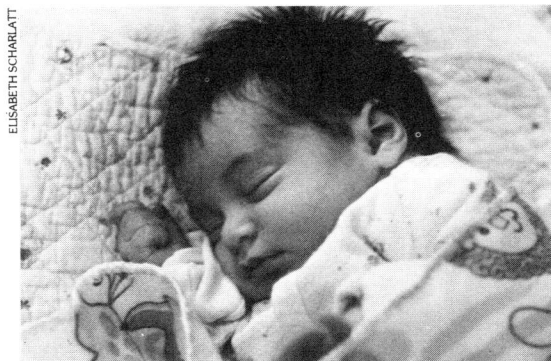

Privacy and Child-rearing

My son was out of school (his half day of insecurity and play) for two days and then there was the weekend, giving us four days in a row of full, concentrated togetherness and testing. After the third day in the house, out of desperation we went to the supermarket, sniffles and all. I stopped the cart in one of the aisles trying to think of what spice I'd told myself to remember to be sure to buy, when this usually charming three-year-old began asking questions and pointing out items of interest on the shelves until I finally had to shout at him to please keep quiet for one minute while I thought of something. "What are you thinking about?" he wanted to know. "Just a minute," I next said, slowly building up to that rage which, I finally figured out, comes from not having one minute for a private thought—even if you use the time to think about which lousy spice you used in the spaghetti sauce last time.

But I love this kid, I love this kid. But why is he talking to me all the time?

And in the bathroom, where there's no lock on the door so that this adventurous little person won't lock himself in, I have no privacy at all. "Please," I ask, "let me have some privacy. Don't I give you privacy when you want it?" It starts out in a calm, controlled tone. The next scene shows me holding the doorknob on the inside with all my might and a little boy pulling on the other side with all his might. Before long we are both screaming. He wants to "be with" me; I want to change my Tampax alone.

But I love this kid, I love this kid. But what is he doing here all the time? A life of being watched constantly, of not being able to open the refrigerator door without an audience, of not being able to sit down and read a book because of a three-year-old's presence, is outrageous. And frustrating.

Once recently he was at my sister's for a weekend and I went crazy with longing for him. Where's my son, I thought. Why isn't he here with me, his mother? But I never ever think about that when he's following me into the bathroom.

ELS

◆

Waiting Out the Worst Part

I figure I'm probably one of these mothers who enjoy their kid more after the age of five. Birth through four is so hard. I've spent so much time as a mother waiting for the time when my kid will pass through such-and-such a stage into the age when he enjoys doing with me the things that I do best.

FLAVIA POTENZA

There are some ages when people really like their kids, and others when they don't. Some people can't relate to two-year-olds because they can't talk to them. And as soon as the child hits seven or eight, suddenly the relationship blossoms. That usually applies to people who are verbal.

I hated it when my daughter was nine. There were physiological reasons for it as well as psychological: there was a little estrogen shooting into her system, and "bitchy" really is the appropriate word for what she became, as much as we hate to admit it. Also unreasonable, irrational, illogical, and stubborn. So when she was nine I took many long walks alone, and I kept telling myself not to collapse, that I knew I'd like the next age better. (It was a little bit easier for me to recognize it as a stage because I work with kids.)

With some kids, there's a stage, for example, at which they go berserk if some other child hasn't promised to be their friend that day. The stages vary with different kids at different ages. And there are some ages that are just very difficult, and you're not a hideous person because you feel like running from it. Parents of middle-aged kids don't talk as much about their kids. If they did, they would have a better perspective and recognize stages more easily.

JO BUTLER

THE BODY

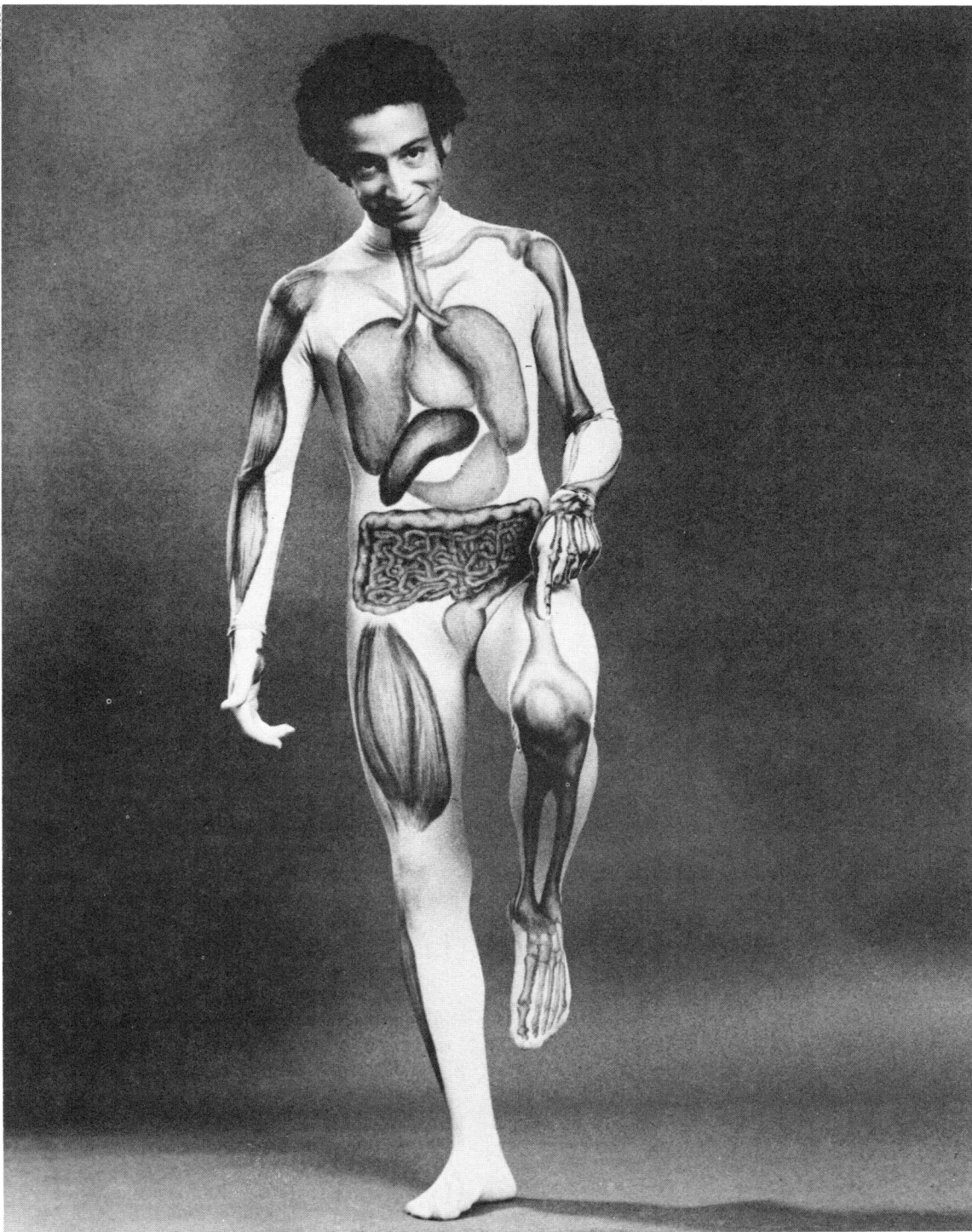

CHILDREN AND HEALTH
HOW TO TAKE CARE OF SICK KIDS AND HURT KIDS (AND ALSO YOURSELF)

How Do You Keep Them in Bed?

The big question is, How do you keep them in bed after they've seen *Sesame Street* and it's only 10 A.M.? The real question to answer first is, Do they have to stay in bed? Before you let yourself in for one of motherhood's worst sieges, make sure it's necessary. Check with your doctor. As it happens, I've been able to let my kids remain ambulatory and in clothes with fevers up to 105 degrees.

If you like keeping the child in bed, give a thought to the possibility that you're using its illness as a way to be super mother in an area where you're gifted. Especially if it seems to get sicker than most kids and really wants to stay in bed. It may have discovered sick as a great attention-getting device.

Assuming, however, that there's a reason or a medical order to keep them between sheets, there are a few small things you can do to make life more bearable for the kids and, more important, for you. (While it may be interesting to consider whether the superniceness that mothers deal out to sick kids is a kind of guilt reaction to the resentment they feel at having to take care of them, there are more interesting routes to martyrdom.)

Stock a bedside table with necessary paraphernalia—tissues, a pitcher and glass, and something to drink if the child is old enough to pour without spilling; a thermometer and vaseline, and whatever else your little invalid needs. The main idea is to keep from having to run relay races forty-seven times a day obeying the latest in royal fiats. You might stick a lazy susan on the table if you have one, so that the child can rotate it and not ask you for something that's three inches out of its reach.

A wastebasket by the side of the bed is far more esthetic than picking sneezed-into tissues off it one by one six times a day.

A table for eating or playing is handy. If you don't happen to still have the white wicker breakfast tray that came with your English breakfast china, you can use your ironing board, pushed down to a convenient height, with the narrow end over the bed.

If you have the fortitude, you can keep hidden a bunch of toys and produce them with a flourish. This does not mean a box of dolls with two arms missing, since most kids are even more demanding when they're sick than when they're well.

Little kids are frequently confused by being sick and scared way out of proportion—especially if they're going through a stage of being concerned about their bodies. They may think that something they did that was naughty just caught up with them and made them sick. (You can see how some fantasies get started.) They can even think they're going to die. So it's a kindly gesture to at least listen to their nutty questions and give an answer if you can.

An old grown-up shirt makes a great home hospital gown if there's a lot of throwing up or spilling of medicine, or if you just didn't get around to washing the pajamas.

If you desperately need a humidifier and yours is broken because you forgot to clean it for the last two years, you can use your electric coffee maker with the inside parts and top removed. Fill it with water and plug it in by the bed.

CAROL EISEN RINZLER

◆

The Famous Ice Cube Remedy

I find ice cubes are a great remedy for pain, rebukes, heat, fever, bitten tongues, loose teeth, and teethers. I honestly can't say why. All forms of hypochondria (to which children are subject) can be hastily dispatched with "Let's put an ice cube on that," or "How about a nice, soothing ice cube?" Don't laugh—it works!

JILL SCHICKEL

◆

Ice Cubes and Honesty

Before medicine-taking: put an ice cube on the child's tongue—it deadens the tastebuds until the medicine has gone down.

Another help in this area is called honesty. I find that if I tell my kids, "This one tastes really terrible," or "This isn't great, but not as bad as some," they'll really believe me and trust me and feel better about the whole ordeal.

CAROL EISEN RINZLER

Soaking: Try the Bathtub Instead of a Bowl

When three-year-old Gaby had a very sore thumb that needed constant soaking, I discovered that rather than keeping one little thumb in a bowl, sitting in a full bathtub required less effort (from us both).   PAULA GLATZER

Of Splinters, Bayonet Clamps, and Merthiolate

Go to a surgical supply house and buy a bayonet clamp, a kind of tweezers that makes removing splinters much easier. If you're having trouble locating the splinter, especially after the kid has pointed to six different places as the seat of its agony, wash the area (which is, nine times out of ten, filthy) carefully and paint around the suspected site with Merthiolate or iodine. The splinter should show up as a dark sliver.

CAROL EISEN RINZLER

What Should You Keep in the Family Medicine Cabinet?

The Medicine Show, put out by Consumers Union (*Pantheon, 1974, 272 pages, $8.50 hardcover; $3.95 paperback*), has a section on "everything really needed to meet the common medical problems of an ordinary family" and lists no more than half a dozen drugs needed in a medicine cabinet: aspirin; sodium bicarbonate or calcium carbonate ("as good as anything else for occasional treatment of heartburn or . . . indigestion"); calamine lotion for mild skin eruptions such as mosquito bites or mild poison ivy; phenylephrine hydrochloride solution ¼% U.S.P. (Neo-Synephrine) for head colds; a laxative; and rubbing alcohol.

They recommend that aspirins be thrown away when they crumble or smell of acetic acid (like vinegar), and suggest breaking up a regular five-grain plain aspirin to get the proper dosage for children (crushing it and mixing it with honey or jelly). They warn that candy-flavored aspirin, too tasty for children, may be responsible for the large incidence of fatalities in children from excessive ingestion of aspirin.

A sensible reminder: drugs packaged under a generic name are cheaper and conform to U.S.P. or N.P. standards; ask your doctor to prescribe them.

For first aid, they recommend the first aid textbook from the American National Red Cross as "the most comprehensive and authoritative of its genre."   ELS

The Dark-Colored Washcloth Method of Reducing Trauma

Another sneaky measure for common catastrophes is to keep a red or a black washcloth (preferably red, since you probably don't have a black one around and would have to go out and buy one) by the sink where you wash off bloody wounds. Not seeing all the gore on a light-colored washcloth somehow reduces the degree of trauma.

CAROL EISEN RINZLER

Stopping Tears

To stop tears in a little kid, take a bottle and enlist the child's cooperation in collecting some tears for you to save. This is one of those rather corny things that seem to work quite nicely.

CAROL EISEN RINZLER

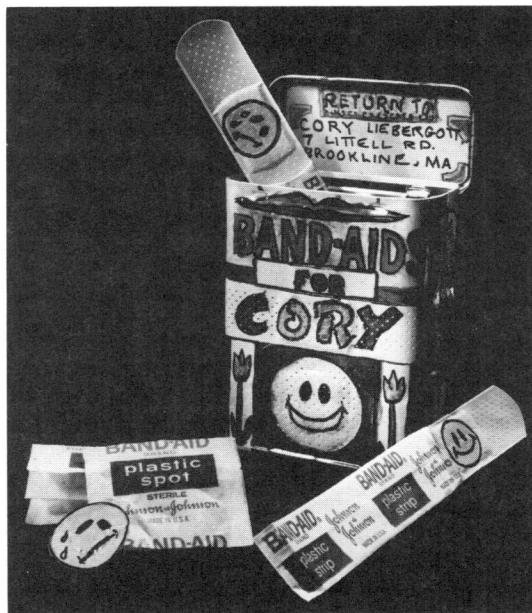

Band-Aid Kisses Can Make It Better

In order to persuade my twenty-month-old daughter, Allegra, not to remove Band-Aids as soon as I applied them, I would draw a red kiss on them and tell her that the kiss would make it better if she would let it remain on the sore for a few days. It worked, but ever since, she has insisted that all Band-Aids be decorated. All her day-care buddies wanted them, too, so I soon found myself in the Band-Aid decorating business and eventually began to paint the boxes as well.   JUDY SAMELSON

Sickbed Specials

1. Small tabletop building toys are perfect for sickbed trays. One of the best is Lego, a Danish import, small interlocking multicolor plastic building cubes. The main problem with Legos is that when they're new they're sometimes difficult to unlock, and can be frustrating for some younger children. And they are expensive. Still, one parent told us that Lego saved her sanity when her child was laid up in a body cast for two months. For the smaller child: beads to string, or macaroni (colored with Magic Markers) on a shoelace. Tinkertoys, plastic interlocking disks, or any kind of small building blocks are equally adaptable to bed trays. (You can often find a tin tray with fold-up legs in the dime store for under $2; or cut arches out of the open end of a cardboard box to fit over the legs.)

2. *Altair Designs* and *More Altair Designs* (Random House, $2.95 paperback) provide pages and pages of intricate geometric designs that make for hours of coloring. They're more sophisticated than regular coloring books; older kids seem to like that.

3. Being sick is a good time for just looking. Share some of your own picture books with your child—natural history books, "adult" artists like Hieronymus Bosch and M. C. Escher, catalogs with lots of pictures.

4. Hallmark makes jigsaw puzzles that can be solved in less than an hour by most kids over six. Called Springbok Miniature Art Puzzles, they're 7 by 7 inches and enable your child to make a Gauguin.

5. Play a record you're as happy to listen to as your child is. Play a card game, teach your child a new version of solitaire, read an unfamiliar story, or a favorite old one.

6. Art and architectural supply stores are full of wonderful writing and drawing pads, stencils, graph paper, and pencils and felt-tip pens in colors that will make your child's eyes widen.

RS and ELS

FIRST AID

A Trio of Basic Handbooks

The Emergency Family First Aid Guide (A Fireside Book, Simon and Schuster, $1.95 paperback) is a book that can literally be a life-saver. In clear, simple language, combined with numerous line drawings, it gives step-by-step first-aid directions for a bewildering array of alphabetically listed emergencies, from appendicitis, fainting, fever, frostbite, poisoning, shock, snake bite, stings and vomiting to wounds of various types. The book is carefully organized for quick reference and is set in extra-large type, presumably so you won't lose your place even if you panic.

In a similar format, though larger and much more expensive (8½ x 11 inches and $6.95, to be precise), is Martin I. Green's *A Sigh of Relief: The First Aid Handbook for Childhood Emergencies* (Bantam, 1977, paperback). It's thumb-indexed so you can find life-saving instructions in a hurry, and it also contains a helpful section on accident and disease prevention. There's even a drug identification chart with full-color drawings (including three particularly spiffy ones showing, respectively, four marijuana cigarettes, a hashish pipe and a quart of whiskey). Although certain key items seem to be missing (appendicitis, snake bite), *A Sigh of Relief* is an attractive and useful book.

Then, finally, there's the classic of the field, the American National Red Cross's *Standard First Aid and Personal Safety* (Doubleday, 1973, 268 pages, $1.95 paperback). It's the most authoritative of the three books reviewed in this article and, as such, deserves a place in the family library; however, its more traditional format makes it a bit harder to use in an emergency.

CBC

SAVE YOUR CHILD'S LIFE!

Save Your Child's Life! is certainly an over-dramatic title, but David Hendin's little paperback (Dolphin Books, $1.45) really is extraordinarily handy. In its 118 pages, Hendin has gathered such diverse information as "How to Accident-Proof Your Home," "How to Decrease the Chances of Your Child Being Poisoned in Your Home or in Your Garden," "How to Apply First Aid for Burns, Shocks, Cuts, Bruises and Bites," "How to Treat Your Child for Poison Ivy," and so forth. There's even a special checklist for buying safe toys, and a special form you can fill out to give to your baby-sitters, And finally—hallelujah—there's an index.

CBC

A First Aid Book Kids Can Use

Can a first aid book be exciting enough to interest a child? Harriet Margolis Gore's *What to Do When There's No One But You* (Prentice-Hall, 1974, 47 pages, $4.95 hardcover) is no thriller, but it does fill a need. A guide to what to do when an accident occurs, the book covers everything from a cure for hiccoughs to bleeding (nose, finger, tooth, and knee), burns (sun and flame), and bites (dog, bee, and snake). It can be used by a wide age range of kids who aren't ready for the adult first aid books. Each page or two presents a particular accident in story form: Anthony thought that if he ate a lot of vitamins he'd "grow up big and strong. . . . When Michelle found the empty bottle she gave him three glasses of water to drink. Then she called the Poison Control Center." For the more serious accidents, the reader is always advised to see a grown-up (one who's read the *Emergency Family First Aid Guide,* we hope).

ELS

DOCTORS AND NURSES

Tell Your Child the Truth

If your child is going to have an injection, tell him, "You are going to have an injection, and it is probably going to hurt; if you want to cry, that's all right, because when something hurts, it may make you cry." Following this preparation, if your child has his injection and cries, you can take an understanding attitude by saying, "Yes, I know it hurts—that's why you're crying." Then you can comfort your child. However, if your child has the injection and doesn't cry, you have put yourself in a position to say, "My, you were very brave—I know it hurt, and you didn't even cry."

When you prepare your child this way, that is, honestly, you cannot harm him. If your child handles the situation bravely, you can tell him so. Your praise will enhance his self-esteem and will help him deal with the next similar situation. If he cries, you will have predicted a response that did occur. At least he has faced an unpleasant situation, had an appropriate response, has received your support, and has not lost face. No matter which reaction your child has, you have given him the opportunity for mastering a situation, but most important, you were honest with him. He will remember your honesty and will continue to trust you. . .

DR. LEE SALK
*What Every Child Would
Like His Parents to Know*

Take a Crayon with You to the Doctor's Office

If there's usually a long wait in the examining room at your pediatrician's office: take along a crayon or marker for making pictures on the big piece of white paper that covers the examining table.

ELS

The Pediatric Nurse Practitioner: A Service to Help Your Child . . . *and* You

In the mid-1960s, a hospital in Denver started a program for the pediatric nurse practitioner, a health worker trained both in nursing and pediatrics who works in collaboration with a physician to provide well-child care and treat many childhood illnesses. People who've used the service—in out-patient clinics, group practice, and private physicians' offices—seem to feel that the care they get is as good as, if not better than, that which they would receive if they relied solely on pediatricians. Even many doctors estimate that over 70 percent of the out-of-hospital care now provided by pediatricians could be administered as well, or better, by PNPs.

KATHY MESSENGER

◆

We've had two nurse practitioners since we started the program. My husband and I were especially pleased that they helped us not only with medical problems but with developmental things and behavioral problems. When the child is sick, the nurse practitioners take into consideration that it's hard on parents as well as on children and they give advice to all of us. I found that most of what they've given to me starting with my oldest child, I've carried over to the second one, so I use their advice frequently.

JUDY BRISTOW

◆

For more about pediatric nurse practitioners or other new types of medical personnel, write to National League for Nursing, Inc., 10 Columbus Circle, New York, N.Y. 10019

DON'T FORGET TO IMMUNIZE YOUR CHILD

"Epidemics could erupt . . . in the United States because immunization against childhood disease has dropped to dangerously low levels," warns *Consumer Reports*.

One of the most convincing cases the article relates is that of 637 children affected by a measles epidemic in Texarkana, that Texas–Arkansas border town: ". . . 621 [children affected] lived on the Texas side of town. Only 16 of the measles cases—less than 3 per cent—lived on the Arkansas side, even though 35 per cent of the city's children live in Arkansas.

"The main reason: The county health department had an active measles immunization program on the Arkansas side of town. The health department in Texas had none."

While encouraging immunizations for children and adults, the article warns also that tetanus boosters "should *not* be routinely administered every year, as required by some schools and summer camps." Ask your own doctor.

The following chart is printed with the permission of *Consumer Reports*.

A FAMILY GUIDE TO IMMUNIZATION*

Here are the recommendations, as of January 1977, of CU's medical consultants. Included as a reminder is the tuberculin test. Consult a physician about your individual immunization. Immunization practices may vary according to local needs. Adverse reactions to vaccines occur in some people.

When	Immunization needed	Comments
2 months old	1st diphtheria-tetanus-pertussis (DTP) 1st trivalent oral polio vaccine (TOPV)	Can be given at same visit.
4 months old	2nd DTP 2nd TOPV	Can be given at same visit.
6 months old	3rd DTP 3rd TOPV	Can be given at same visit. The 3rd TOPV is optional, except in high-risk areas.
1 year old	Tuberculin test	
15 months old	Measles Mumps Rubella	Can be given together.
18 months old	4th DTP 4th TOPV	Can be given at same visit.
4–6 years old	5th DTP	On beginning school.
	5th TOPV	On beginning school; can be given at visit for 5th DTP.
Up to 15 years old	Measles	If not immune. (Little danger of getting measles after 15.)
14–16 years old	Tetanus-diphtheria (adult type)	And every 10 years thereafter.
All adults	Tetanus-diphtheria (adult type)	Repeat every 10 years following basic immunization.
All adults	Mumps	If not immune (by having had disease or vaccine).
All females before puberty	Rubella	
All females after puberty	Rubella	If a blood test determines you're not immune. Must not be pregnant and must not become pregnant sooner than 2 months after immunization.

*This table is designed for immunization on a regular basis, beginning a few months after birth. A physician will, of course, follow a different schedule for those who begin immunization at a later date.

SPECIAL NOTE TO TRAVELERS

For current recommendations as to immunization for foreign travel, consult CU's publication *Health Guide For Travelers*. It covers cholera, diphtheria, infectious hepatitis, measles, plague, poliomyelitis, smallpox, tetanus, typhoid, typhus and yellow fever. (Request an order form from Book Dept., Consumers Union, Orangeburg, N.Y. 10962.) Also check with your local health department, which is notified of any emergency health problems abroad.

CHILDREN AND HOSPITALS

Dress Rehearsal

Marsh has had two operations, both relatively minor—a front tooth extracted when he fell and broke it, and a hernia operation. I really looked Maine over for good, honest, real-life hospital books. I didn't find much. I personally think it's important that the book be about a real person, not a Curious George (H. A. Rey) or Nicky Bunny (Richard Scarry).

Lacking good books, what we did was this: We got a Hasbro doctor kit—stethoscope, syringe, thermometer, etc.—so Marsh could play with these things about a month before the operation. Then we found out from the surgeon the sequence of events, and told Marsh exactly what would happen when, and honestly what would hurt and for how long. Even at two, he could accept and understand this.

We took two trips to the hospital beforehand, and snooped around the ground floor (no patients) and got to meet some nurses, see rolling beds, wheelchairs, etc., to make it a less scary place. We arranged to meet one of the orderlies (in his white suit and mask) who would be with Marsh during the operation. He (and I) became much happier about the hospital in general. We did several hernia operations on "Teddy" at home, and treated him like a real person (which he is, of course). Our surgeon gave us the name of a little boy who had had the same operation a year before. This was great because here he was, all done, and still alive and beautiful. We saw his scar, and it was very reassuring.

Probably the most important thing, though, was to have one of us with Marsh all the time (except in the operating and recovery rooms; that wasn't allowed). I checked in with him at 2 P.M. and stayed till Rob came at 11 P.M. Rob stayed all night, and I went back at 8 A.M. The worst parts of the experience turned out to be things we hadn't prepared him for (blood test from finger, X-ray of chest where they strapped Marsh into a rack-like contraption—awful). Anyway, we all came through it with a positive feeling about doctors, operations, and hospitals, so I consider it a huge success.

I do think you can over-prepare a child, and it's hard to know how much is enough. If you go over it too much they start to sense how afraid the parent is, and it frightens them even more. My strongest suggestion to parents would be to try to get over their own fears, so that their confidence will be transmitted to the child.

ANNE GARDINER

You Have a *Legal Right* to Stay with Your Child in the Hospital

Our daughter was hospitalized—initially at ten months, then twice at two and a half years old. First, just for tests, then two eye operations. From that first awful experience grew an organization started by people who had all experienced the same attitude on the part of doctors and nurses—that kids are better off without parents when hospitalized. Our group—Children in Hospitals—is nationwide and includes many health-care professionals. Parents who want to stay with their children are grateful to learn that they are within their legal rights and that there is medical, psychiatric, and legal literature supporting them.

BARBARA POPPER

Children in Hospitals (31 Wilshire Park, Needham, Mass. 02192) advises:

■ You have the right to stay with your child whatever hours you wish to stay . . . whether you are a clinic patient or a private patient.

■ Children become fearful of even routine tests and exams without the reassuring presence of a parent. Often they withdraw and become silent and good. Hospital staff often interpret this as adjusting, but medical literature tells us this is a sign of emotional upset.

■ Be sure to tell [your child] there may be pain or discomfort for a short time but that each day he will feel better and be getting ready to come home.

■ Some children will ask no questions or will refuse to talk about a planned hospital stay, but mention the subject in the days before he is admitted.

■ Be honest about how much time you will spend with him. Always tell him when you are leaving. . . . It may seem easier to slip away when he is playing happily, but when he finds you gone he will feel more confused than if he had seen you go. Children often are afraid you won't come back or that they won't go home again.

■ After a hospitalization, parents often notice signs of upset that continue for days or weeks. Some children wake at night, cling more by days, fear doctor visits, and wet their beds. Some try hard to behave perfectly fearing a return to the hospital as a punishment.

You Can Help Hospital Personnel Get to Know Your Child

Some hospitals have a questionnaire for parents to fill out to acquaint hospital personnel with their child. If your hospital doesn't, you can easily provide the information for the nurses yourself. Certainly they should know the child's nickname, siblings' names, pets, eating preferences, fears, allergies, special interests, habits (play, reading), what terms are used for bowel movements and urination, attitude toward being in the hospital, and so on. You might tape up a sign in your child's hospital room telling all who cross the threshold what her favorite food is, her best subject, her dearest friend's name.

ELS

Here I am in the hospital playroom as Mark, eleven years old, rips open his snap-button pajama tops like Clark Kent and says to Matthew, nine years old, "Hey, wanna see my open-heart surgery?"

Without even looking up from the toy cow he's milking, Matthew matter-of-factly says, "No."

Just as matter-of-factly, Mark says, "Okay," and snaps up his pajamas.

Leave it to kids to express perfectly the drama, tension, fear, and paroxysmal emotions we are sure they are suffering.

ALAN SAPERSTEIN

Books That Can Help Kids Deal with a Hospital Experience

The problem with most books about hospital experiences is that they're boring, dishonest, condescending, or all three. Misleading preparation makes no sense. Recognizing that even a straightforward description of what the child should expect can be useful, both before and after hospitalization (also for kids whose siblings or friends are hospitalized), Anne Altshuler, instructor of pediatric nursing at the University of Wisconsin, offered the following annotated list of books from her booklet *Books That Help Children Deal with a Hospital Experience*. The booklet contains over fifty titles, and single copies are available free by ordering Publication No. (HSA) 77-5402 from the Department of Health, Education and Welfare, Bureau of Community Health Services, 5600 Fisher's Lane, Rockville, Md. 20857.

MADELINE, *by Ludwig Bemelmans (Viking, 1939, 27 pages, $6.95 hardcover; $1.75 paperback). Full-color illustrations by the author. Ages 3–9 years.*

A classic, much loved by children ever since it was written in 1939. This book uses rhymed verse to describe the adventures of a little girl at a French convent school. Madeline is pictured crying from a stomachache, going to the hospital by ambulance, showing her friends her scar after the appendectomy, staying in a bed which cranks up and down. . . . The book has little actual information about hospital experience.

DEE DEE'S HEART TEST, *Children's Hospital of Philadelphia, Public Relations Dept., 34th Street and Civic Center Boulevard, Philadelphia, Pa. 19104, 1976, 14 pages, 15 cents. Illustrated with black-and-white photos. Ages 3–12.*

A clearly presented, step-by-step account of a boy who is having a cardiac catheterization. Story follows procedures at Children's Hospital of Philadelphia, but can be easily adapted for children undergoing the procedure at other institutions.

DANNY'S HEART OPERATION, *Children's Hospital of Philadelphia, Public Relations Dept., 34th Street and Civic Center Boulevard, Philadelphia, Pa. 19104, 1976. 14 pages, 15 cents. Illustrated with black-and-white photos. Ages 3–12.*

A detailed and matter-of-fact account of Danny, who is having an operation on his heart. Discusses preoperative tests and preparation, intensive care unit, postoperative recovery period. Injections and postoperative pain are mentioned but not dwelled upon.

THE HOSPITAL BOOK, *by Barbara Schuyler-Haas Elder (John Street Press, 1975, 48 pages, $3 plus 30 cents postage and handling). Coloring book illustrated in black and white by Lun Harris. Ages 4–10.*

Presents a balanced view of possible pleasant and unpleasant aspects of hospitalization. Introduces admission procedures, hospital food, beds, call bell, injections (using leg in illustration), blood test, temperature, blood pressure, use of otoscope, x-ray, oxygen tent, intravenous fluid therapy, wheelchair, traction for broken bones, play-program. Diagrams of major organs and bones. Current edition is geared toward Johns Hopkins Hospital, but a general edition is under preparation.

A HOSPITAL STORY, *by Sara Bonnett Stein (Walker and Co., 1974, 47 pages, $5.95). Black-and-white and color photographs by Dick Frank and Doris Pinney. Ages 3–10.*

One of a series of Open Family Books for parents and children to read together. Suggestions for parents in helping a child cope with a hospital experience are included side by side with a large-print text for children. The story follows Jill through her hospitalization for a tonsillectomy. The parents' feelings are dealt with openly and honestly in the parents' text. An outstanding book.

I THINK I WILL GO TO THE HOSPITAL, *by Jean Tamburine (Abingdon Press, 1965, 48 pages, $4.50). Illustrated in four-color drawings by the author. Ages 3–10.*

A beautifully illustrated, honest presentation of both unpleasant and pleasant aspects of having a tonsillectomy. Susie does not feel ready to go to the hospital, so she visits first. Not wanting to go is accepted as a natural feeling. The book introduces such aspects as the hospital smell, casts, wheelchairs, temperatures, x-ray, blood tests, having a throat examination with a flashlight, going to the operating room on a cart, use of a call bell to summon a nurse, eating soft foods such as ice cream and soup, and having a few days of sore throat postoperatively.

ELIZABETH GETS WELL, *by Alfons Weber (Thomas Y. Crowell Co., 1970, 29 pages, $5.95). Full-color illustrations by Jacqueline Blass. Ages 5–9.*

A well-told, beautifully illustrated story, with much information about the hospital experience. Includes reference to siblings and their feelings about Elizabeth's illness as she goes to the hospital for an appendectomy. Describes Elizabeth getting sick at school, doctor's visit to home, going to the hospital, preoperative injection which causes a dry mouth, operating room, intravenous fluids, progression from inability to take fluids to a more normal diet, thirst as a problem, presence of stitches, scar, blood tests from finger (described as feeling like a "mos-

quito bite"), arm casts and their removal, taking of x-rays. Nurses are seen as helpful and caring persons. Much to look at and discuss in the outstanding illustrations.

MOM! I BROKE MY ARM, *by Angelika Wolff (Lion Press, 1969, 45 pages, $5.95). Three-color illustrations by Leo Glueckselig. Grades K–4.*

All about having a cast put on. Well told, realistic. Does not deal with hospital experience. Six-year-old Steven breaks his arm, goes to the doctor's office for x-rays, has a cast applied, wears it for six weeks, and has it removed. Discusses discomforts of casts in an honest, matter-of-fact manner.

CURIOUS GEORGE GOES TO THE HOSPITAL, *by Margaret Rey and H. A. Rey (Houghton Mifflin Co., 1966, 48 pages, $5.95; also available in paperback from Scholastic Book Services, $1.25). Illustrated in red, black, and white drawings. Ages 3–8.*

George is a mischievous monkey, already known to many children from his adventures in six previously written books. In this lively story he swallows a piece of a jig-saw puzzle and has to go to the hospital for an operation, taking his favorite rubber ball along for comfort. He has a barium test in the x-ray department. He cries when his visitor leaves and lets out a scream even before he gets his preoperative injection, only to find it was not as bad as he expected it to be. Illustrations show details of the clinic waiting area, operating room, children's ward and playroom. George recovers and is able to delight other child patients, including the frightened little girl in the next bed.

WHAT HAPPENS WHEN YOU GO TO THE HOSPITAL, *by Arthur Shay (Reilly and Lee, 1969, 27 pages, $5.95). Illustrated with black-and-white photos. Ages 3–10.*

Karen is a black child, about seven years old, who goes to the hospital to have her tonsils out. She brings her doll with her, is curious about the other children, makes friends with her nurse, cries over an x-ray examination until she finds it doesn't hurt. She is also upset when her parents leave for the night, and voices objection to the siderails on her bed. She is shown smiling and holding up a bottle with her tonsils in the recovery room, and also enjoying all the ice cream she can eat—both unrealistic situations—but otherwise the story portrays an honest picture of a one-night hospital stay, with overemphasis on neither the pleasant nor the unpleasant aspects.

So Your Child Can Play-Act His First Visit to the Hospital . . . An Animated Book

GOING TO THE HOSPITAL, *by Bettina Clark with technical guidance of Lester Coleman, M.D., illustrated by Walter Swartz (A Random House Pop-Up Book, $3.95).*

"Psychiatrists believe that it's the *unknown* that frightens children," Dr. Lester Coleman writes. "In recent years, more and more parents, surgeons and hospital personnel have become aware that when a child is properly prepared for his operation—*when he knows what to expect in the hospital*—he can take the whole experience in stride, with little or no fear or unhappy emotional after-effects."

In *Going to the Hospital,* Bettina Clark, and Dr. Coleman, her husband, have put together a pop-up book that can bring to life, in an exciting and amusing way, the realities of a first hospital experience. As a child turns the pages, he'll find, among other things, a doctor's mirror that really reflects; a model hospital with doors and windows that actually open and an elevator that goes up and down; even a gauze doctor's mask that he can take out of the book and put on.

The result (despite some remarkably prosaic artwork by Walter Swartz) is a book that should greatly ease your way if you're told your child must undergo surgery.　　　　CBC

POSTURE

The Alexander Technique

Back pain, fatigue, and general physical tension are not usually kid problems. But often they arise from poor posture and poor carriage, which are kid habits before they become problems at all. Through something called the Alexander Technique, kids can learn to use their bodies without strain, and with increased pleasure, for the rest of their lives.

The use of the body is what the Alexander Technique is a technique *for.* You practice it while you walk, stand, sit, bend, speak, type, sing, dance, or play. The technique is particularly helpful for kids who play musical instruments or do anything else that requires unusual body performance.

The late F. M. Alexander was an Australian actor who kept losing his voice on stage. After years of agonizing self-observation, he discovered, with the aid of mirrors, that the way he held his body while acting, although it "felt right" to him, put severe stress on his throat. This led to the discovery that most of us habitually use our bodies in a way that puts severe stress somewhere.

Since what's wrong with the body's alignment "feels right," it is impossible to correct by prescribed exercises alone. During a lesson you *think* a set of simple instructions to your body, as the teacher gently leads you through movements that correspond to the instructions. In time, you learn to give the instructions as you go through the routines of daily living, and your body knows what they mean. Because kids have not yet lost touch with their bodies, they take to the process easily and have fun with it.

Like peanut butter, the Alexander Technique is something kids like that is also good for them. But it is harder to describe than peanut butter is. To learn more about it, and where in the United States it is taught, you can write to the American Center for the Alexander Technique at 142 West End Avenue, New York, N.Y. 10023. (To learn more about peanut butter, write to the Peanut Butter Manufacturers & Nut Salters Association, 5101 Wisconsin Avenue, Suite 504, Washington, D.C., 20016.)

RALPH CAPLAN

The Rolfing Technique

Karen is eleven years old. She is tall for her age and beginning to develop breasts. Like many young girls who develop early, she was walking slumped over to minimize her height and to mask her self-consciousness over her maturing body. Several months ago she came to me at Esalen for rolfing. So far she has had four rolfings. Her shoulders have settled back and she now carries herself with poise and confidence.

Eric was shy and lacking in self-confidence when he started his rolfings. He was eleven years old then. Now at fourteen he is self-assured and has made the usually awkward transition from childhood to adolescence with relative ease.

Rolfing, a technique named after its developer, Ida P. Rolf, is a method of deep body manipulation, by hand, of the connective tissue (fascia, ligaments, tendons) that surrounds the different muscle groups and connects them to the skeletal system. The body is brought toward a more normal and efficient position. This brings about more balanced movement and usually a positive change in attitude.

When rolfers look at a body, they view it always in relation to the gravitational field. Once you consider that there is a constant force pressing down everything—including our bodies—you can appreciate the energy used to perform such simple acts as standing. For example, the more forward the head is held, the more energy is used to hold it up. If you draw an imaginary line from the top of your head through your ear, shoulder, elbow, hip, knee, and ankle joints, you will probably find a line that does not go straight. The rolfer's aim is to balance the different muscle groups in such a way that a straight line could be drawn between these points. As this reorganization occurs, gravity then becomes a supportive force rather than a destructive force. The energy formerly used to hold oneself erect is now available for other purposes.

While many adults are interested in rolfing to correct long-standing postural aberrations, the child's body is still forming and can be set on a more balanced growth path. To give some examples: Many young people have slight curva-tures of the spine, which, if corrected early, can allow the child to grow with a straight, healthy spine. Lower back pain, which plagues many adults, can be avoided once the body segments are "stacked" into horizontal planes by the rolfing process. And the pelvic basin, which is actually a basin to support and hold the viscera, can be made horizontal so that it functions in the way it was meant to, as a support system.

Since rolfing requires a cooperative effort between two people, a feeling of communication and trust is essential. The child should talk with the rolfer before deciding to start the process. It's important to feel right about the person with whom one is going to be involved.

Rolfing can be a painful experience, but when the child wants to be rolfed the pain becomes secondary and almost insignificant when compared to the positive results. But if there is resistance to the manipulation, the pain becomes the primary focus.

The rolfing process is designed as a series of ten hourly sessions spread out over a period of months. The cost is approximately $400. Further information, including names and addresses of qualified rolf practitioners through the country, can be obtained from the Rolf Institute, P.O. Box 1868, Boulder, Colo.

BEVERLY SILVERMAN

Father: "Brush your teeth."
Four-year-old Matthew: "Why, are these the cavity-prone years?"

TEETH, GUMS, AND TOOTH DECAY

No one should ever get tooth decay.
THOMAS MCGUIRE, D.D.S.
The Tooth Trip

More Than I Thought I Wanted to Know About Teeth

THE TOOTH TRIP *by Thomas McGuire, illustrated by Amit Pieter (Random House/Bookworks, 1972, $8.95 hardcover; $4.95 paperback).*

The conversational style and humorous illustrations made me read more than I ever thought I wanted to know about my dental system and its decay: how to examine gums and teeth for disease and decay, so you can catch it in the early stages and sometimes cure it at home, and how to brush, really brush. Dr. McGuire discusses flossing (essential) and Water Piks (good) and electric toothbrushes (not recommended), and even tells you how to make some of your own dental equipment. His information on diet is some of the best I've read anywhere, although it's secondary to his subject and not complete.

There's an excellent chapter on children. And the book is written simply enough for you to share it with your kids to make them understand what all the brushing and "no sugar" is about.

RS

The following is excerpted from *The Tooth Trip*.

In order for [tooth decay] to occur, three things are needed:
1) Germs (Bacteria). . . .
2) Food. . . .
3) Teeth. . . .
At least one of the three must be eliminated in order to prevent decay. . . .

When the germs have eaten and digested the food you've left them, their nature also demands that they eliminate the waste products of their bodies. This natural function occurs almost immediately after eating. The waste products which each of these millions of germs eliminates are very acidic, producing a substance that has the ability to dissolve certain materials it may come in contact with; sadly for us the enamel of our teeth is one of the substances this acid can dissolve.

JOAN BINGHAM

1) Raw fruits and vegetables are excellent natural cleansers of teeth and excellent massagers of gums. Man used this method successfully for nearly two hundred million years, during which time he had neither the dentist nor the Tooth Trip to aid him. The abrasiveness and fibrous nature of raw food is the reason that it cleans and massages. This, in essence, aids in the prevention of tooth disease. The fact that raw fruits and vegetables do not cause decay also adds to their preventive character. This value is lost if the fruits and vegetables are excessively cooked or canned; the sugar and preservatives that are usually added destroy the naturally cleansing effect and add the stuff that can cause decay. If a fruit or vegetable is excessively cooked, it loses its fibrous nature. Compare the difference between cooked and raw cauliflower, and thus their beneficial massaging action.

2) Even the natural raw sugars found in many fruits are not harmful to the teeth, as the size of the natural sugar molecule is still much too large for the decay-causing germs to eat. The fact is that natural raw sugars need to be left in the mouth for days before the enzymes of the mouth can break them down to a size small enough for the germs to digest. Honey is a natural sugar and its molecules are too large for the germ to eat without help from the mouth's enzymes. Of course, brushing your teeth, you never will leave anything in your mouth long enough to do damage.

3) Salad should be eaten at the *end* of the meal; or at least one-half of it at the end and one-half at the beginning. There are two reasons for this: the salad (a mixed vegetable salad, not the restaurant salad of just lettuce) acts as

a) a cleanser for the teeth and
b) as a source of bulk for the stomach and intestines. This is important, since the intestines rely on bulk to move the food along at a normal rate. Most refined and processed foods, or cooked vegetables and fruits, are either so broken down and/or dehydrated that they have no bulk. This means that under any form of pressure, this type of food loses its form and in essence, collapses. You can readily see this and test it by feeling and difference in bulk and texture between a raw carrot and cooked, canned or mashed ones.

Carbohydrates and Tooth Decay

The role of carbohydrates in producing cavities was dramatically illustrated in World War II. The English, Dutch, and Danes were the world's leading consumers of "sweets." During the war, the population barely subsisted on a starvation diet. Despite the lack of milk for children and proper diet, the decay rate fell to almost nothing. The lack of carbohydrates obviously led to the lack of cavities. After the war, the consumption of chocolate and refined sugars rose to their former levels, and the decay rate with it.

BURTON STEINBERG, D.D.S

Consumer Reports notes that toothpastes of documented efficacy decline in potency after packaging. Since the normal product life is about a year, the Federal Drug Administration should require fluoride pastes to be labeled with an expiration date.

Fluoridation

People do not seem willing or able to reduce their carbohydrate intake or to brush after each meal. So dental researchers turned away from fundamentals to search for a cure-all. It was observed that among the large groups of men being inducted into the armed services, many from Texas, Colorado, and Arizona were cavity-free. The decay-resistant enamel of this group was believed to be caused by the presence of fluoride salts occurring naturally in the drinking water of these areas. It was decided to test the thesis by artificially fluoridating the water in selected communities. A pilot project was set up in two neighboring New York towns of similar size. One community drank untreated water, and the other water to which one part per million of sodium fluoride had been added. In ten years the decay rate of the "treated water" town dropped an amazing 80 percent. The other town continued at its previous decay rate.

So why do we still suffer tooth decay twenty-five years later when a known preventive is available? This preventive is low in cost, easily added to a city's water, and has been endorsed for safety and efficacy by the American Medical Association, the American Dental Association, the National Institutes of Health, and the Surgeon General.

Some opposition comes from those who will not be benefited by drinking the fluoridated water. It is only effective in childhood while the teeth are forming. There are groups of laymen and scientists who feel that some toxic effects will be discovered (sodium fluoride is a deadly substance and is used in rat poisons).

Many feel that fluoridation is "mass medication" and that it violates their constitutional rights. Older people are afraid it causes brittle bones and damage to the organs.

More than three parts per million of fluoride can cause an unsightly brown "mottling" of the tooth enamel.

Many cities have gone ahead and treated their water, including New York City and Washington, D.C. But the controversy has delayed any nationwide effort.

For those who live in an unfluoridated area and wish their children to have the benefits of the chemical, it is available in several prescription forms. The daily dosage may be had in pill form, as a liquid, or in combination with vitamins.

If a mother-to-be takes fluoride during her pregnancy and the child continues to take it until about the age of twelve, the chances of decay are reduced to almost zero.

In addition to systemic action, it was found that fluoride applied by a dentist to newly cleaned teeth has a topical action. A twice-a-year topical application reduces decay by about 25 percent. It gives those who may have doubts about possible harmful systemic effects of sodium fluoride a chance to get some of its benefits without its possible risks. Fluoride is now commonly added in toothpastes. Several leading brands heavily advertise their fluoride content, and they do indeed reduce decay.

BURTON STEINBERG, D.D.S.

The Tooth Fairy Is a Shrewd Manipulator

A toothbrushing hint good for five- or six-year-olds who believe in the tooth fairy: inform them that the tooth fairy, a shrewd manipulator, pays dimes for damaged merchandise and a whole dollar for teeth without cavities or fillings.

CAROL EISEN RINZLER

TEACHING KIDS ABOUT THEIR BODIES

Help Is On The Way

Children are anxious to know how their bodies work, and how your body works, and why does it look that way, and what are those things hanging there, and what's inside? They ask questions like, "Will this cut on my finger make me bleed to death?" and "Why do mommies stuff paper up between their legs to make themselves bleed?"

Though you know the answers to these stoppers, can you explain them to your children? They *need* to know. Accurate answers to questions about body functions help to relieve anxiety and promote their confidence (and yours) in this magnificent organism, the human body. Help is on the way:

BODY BOOKS FOR PARENTS

Reading THE BODY, *by Anthony Smith (Avon, 1969, paperback),* is like listening to an old friend with a sense of humor tell you everything about sex, snoring, slimming (he's English); about hearts, brains, blood, reproduction, yawning, pregnancy—fascinating!

". . . most medical books," Smith writes, "concentrate on disease and on breakdown. This book does not totally disregard such failure, but regards a pumping heart as more interesting than a heart failing to pump. . . ."

Smith quotes Enrico Fermi: "Before I came here I was confused about this subject. Having listened to your lecture I am still confused. But on a higher level."

Smith will not confuse you, though; he will enlighten and entertain you. His book is out of print, but look for it in your library.

THE TEXTBOOK ON MEDICAL PHYSIOLOGY, *by Arthur C. Guyton, M.D. (Saunders, 1971),* has a forbidding title to most non-medical people, and a forbidding price ($25). But it's relatively easy to read, and Guyton's approach to the body, like Smith's, is non-pathological; he won't scare you into thinking that something is wrong with *every* organ in your body. You can get used, older editions for much less than the price of the new edition at medical school bookstores. Here's Guyton on the circulatory system:

The most important feature of the circulation that must always be kept in mind is that it is a continuous circuit. That is, if a given amount of blood is pumped by the heart, this same amount must also flow through each respective subdivision of the circulation. Furthermore, if blood is displaced from one segment of the circulation, some other segment of the circulation must expand unless the blood is lost from the circulation.

THE WISDOM OF THE BODY, *by Walter B. Cannon, M.D. (Allen Unwin, 1970, $10.95),* is an essential book. Subtitled "How the human body reacts to disturbance and danger and maintains the stability essential to life," this book, and the aforementioned two, will enable you to answer most "How does my body work" questions for yourself and your children. Cannon developed the concept of homeostasis: "the means employed by the more highly evolved animals for preserving uniform and stable their internal economy. . . . We shall see that the nervous system is divisible into two main parts, the one acting outwardly and affecting the world about us, and the other acting inwardly and helping to preserve a constant and steady condition in the organism itself."

THE HUMAN BODY, *by Paul Lewis and David Rubenstein (Bantam Knowledge Through Color Series, 1972, paperback),* has beautiful color illustrations by John Bavosi, and is a bargain at $2.25.

Breathing supplies the body with oxygen and removes carbon dioxide from it. Energy is produced in the cells through the oxidation of carbohydrates; carbon dioxide is a by-product of energy release, and if allowed to build up it will poison the cells.

The adult brain weighs about three pounds. It contains the cerebrum, its longest region; the brainstem, which joins up with the spinal cord; and the cerebellum, which lies behind the brainstem below the cerebrum and is concerned with the fine control of movement. [Lewis and Rubenstein, *The Human Body*]

BODY BOOKS FOR CHILDREN

When I taught at a nursery school and children were worried about scratches or stomachaches, or wanted to know how babies were born, they said, "Take out the body books," referring to the physiology and anatomy books I brought to

school just for them. Here is a short list of helpful books. You can find them, or books like them, in large bookstores or the book department of department stores. I've found librarians and bookstore managers most helpful in searching out books to meet children's special needs.

A note about age appropriateness: I don't think it's ever too early to begin to give children information about the world around them, and in this case, their own bodies. You know your child. Start at the level at which she or he can comprehend, then upgrade your estimate two to four years. Most children are much more advanced, potentially, than we think. In more advanced books, you can translate the words to the child's vocabulary level. You probably do that now.

YOUR WONDERFUL BODY, *by Robert J. Follett (Follett Publishing Co., 1971, $2.50 hardcover),* is nicely illustrated and integrated (blacks and whites, boys and girls). Most other physiology and anatomy books show only Caucasians when skin is shown at all. Inside the skin, all anatomy books are integrated:
"Bones give the body its shape," Follett writes. "They are the frame on which the body is built. Bones are hard. Some of them protect important parts of the body. The skull protects the brain. The ribs protect the heart and lungs."

USE YOUR BRAIN, *by Paul Showers, illustrated by Rosalind Fry (a Let's-Read-and-Find-Out Science Book, Crowell, 1971, $1.45 paperback),* is one of many books available on individual parts or systems of the body.
"A fire truck sounds its siren. The noise comes into your ear. The nerves of your ear send messages to your brain. You know a fire truck is passing outside." The illustrations are fine, but be advised that the telephone switchboard analogy, used in this book to describe how the brain sends and receives messages, is now in serious question. Most physiological laws are immutable, but as a Canadian poet whose name I can't remember said, "A fact is a compromise with time."

THE QUESTION AND ANSWER BOOK ABOUT THE HUMAN BODY, *by Ann McGovern (Random House, 1965, $3.50 hardcover),* answers questions like: What happens when you cry? Do boys have more muscles than girls? What are black-and-blue marks? Why do you sleep? How do you grow? What is fever? How do you taste? Why do you sniff to smell a flower?

MY BODY AND HOW IT WORKS, *by Jane Werner Watson (a Golden Read-Together Book in Cooperation with the Menninger Foundation, 1972, $2.50),* has nice drawings, and lots of white space to rest your child's eyes and yours. And the text isn't too dry: "When the food is all soft, I swallow it. The food goes down a long tube called the esophagus. It goes into my stomach and on into twisty tubes called intestines. Juice comes from the walls of my stomach and intestines to turn the food into liquid."

You'll find many more body books. The ones I've chosen here for children are inexpensive, non-sexist, and more or less integrated. If your child has questions about a specific part of the body, or a specific bodily function, search out a book that best answers that question. You don't need to be a doctor or a physiologist or a genius to begin to learn, with your child, about what goes on inside the body.

STEPHEN M. JOSEPH

It's *Gray's Anatomy!*

GRAY'S ANATOMY, *(Crown, 1977, $6.95 paperback)* is a vivid and detailed map of the meat you inhabit. If you missed out on this basic and intimate knowledge because the schools flashed it by so briefly, that's no reason to keep your kid from it. Where does the food go when I eat it? What are those blue lines on your hands? How does the baby grow? The pictures alone are worth the price. And thick with technical terminology though the text may be, it is well organized and clear, and bears deciphering by a literate layman, or a child growing up with the book, as far as his curiosity will take him.

I think it's a mistake to see this sort of learning as abstract. People's having control over their body's powers of healing seems to depend a lot upon their ability to visualize clearly what is happening inside their bodies, and what their healthy state is. I don't know of any more useful aid to this than a good anatomy text.

MICHAEL ROSSMAN

A Vote for Talking

While adults are educating themselves as health-care consumers—poring over everything from *Gray's Anatomy* to the new wave of oversized physical, mental, and spiritual health guides (some very good, some a sham)—the kids have been left with books which, as harmless as they are unimaginative, seem less effective than even a parent-initiated game of "doctor" to introduce the subject to young children. Since it certainly isn't necessary to introduce every new experience by way of a book, don't feel you should buy a book on a subject that can be covered by lots of talking.—Eds.

The Visible Woman

THE VISIBLE WOMAN, *manufactured by Revell, is available at good toy stores or can be ordered from Edmund Scientific Company, $8. 1776 Edscorp Building, Barrington, N.J. 08007.*

She is darling, just the gift for a child who delights in dolls. Beneath her transparent skin fit the bones, so cunningly articulated; her digestive organs and lungs; her segmented brain and clacking jaw; and either of two interchangeable wombs, one swollen to show her pregnant state. She comes as a kit, and *you* have to do the work of assembling her various parts and painting her organs. But once you do, you have a pretty good model of the real thing, which you can take apart and put together to puzzle out why your belly hurts *here* instead of *there.* An absorbing project for one child to tackle, the Visible Woman is also a fine classroom or playgroup accessory, especially in conjunction with a good anatomy text. They make a Visible Man, too, for the same price. Replacement parts are available.

MICHAEL ROSSMAN

[Revell, manufacturer of the Visible Woman, provides replacement parts free. Write to them at 4223 Glencoe Avenue, Venice, Calif. 90291.]

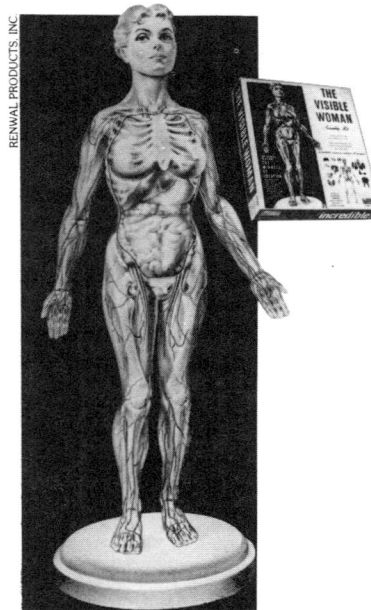

Anatomy Lesson

Would you believe a singing, dancing anatomy lesson? In his skin-tight body suit, John Burstein, calling himself Mr. Slim Goodbody, does his remarkable act in schools and community centers. He has produced a record with thirteen songs about bones and hair and muscles et al.

> One is connected to two is connected
> To 27 bones in your wrist and hand.
> One is connected to two is connected
> To 26 bones in your foot.
> Head in the sky, feet on the ground,
> Bones hold you up, and I have found
> For moving about,
> You can't do without—bones. . . .

Hard to argue with the man.

For more information about performances and the record, write to John Burstein, P.O. Box 773, Canal Street Station, New York, N.Y. 10013.

Why do we teach our children parts of the body as if they were objects? Why teach arm, finger, leg, long before we teach breathing, standing, running, jumping, talking, fighting? Why are namings of objects given precedence over namings of actions? Is this the child's demand? Who has defined the fundamental precepts of the children's questions?

WARREN BRODY
Earthchild

Brian and the Visible Woman

I experienced a child's intense fascination with physiology during the summer weekend when [my wife] Barbara and I assembled and painted the Visible Woman while staying with friends. Brian, their four-year-old son, watched us and listened carefully as I read the complicated assembling instructions to Barbara. We took turns fitting the bones together and putting the organs in place. Brian, usually very active, listened quietly.

His mother, Ellen, was in the kitchen making dinner. "Don't you know four-year-olds can't understand a lot of words?" she yelled, over the sound of the running water. "You have to show them, not tell them. My God, that sounds like a textbook for doctors!" . . .

Ellen couldn't hear our answer and we were almost finished, so we kept working, while Brian went on observing.

A few hours later, a friend of Ellen's arrived, along with her daughter, who was Brian's age. "Do you know how your esophagus works?" Brian greeted them. He showed them the completed Visible Woman, and began to explain the parts and their functions, almost verbatim. He remembered most of it, and he understood the relationships. We were all amazed, but my experience in the school had convinced me that most children share Brian's ability to retain physiological information.

STEPHEN M. JOSEPH
Children in Fear

◆

What Makes Blood Come Out?

Once a five-year-old asked me what made our blood come out if we cut ourselves. I began to talk about the heart. His face showed me right away that this was not in his experience. I asked if he knew where his heart was, or what it did. No, he didn't. I then asked him to jump up in the air, ten times, as high as he could. He did this, with great seriousness. Then I asked him to put his hand over the left side of his chest. His eyes grew wide. Something was *thumping*, right inside him. He had never felt that thing in there before, never knew it was there. Now that he had felt it, I was able to say something about that heart being like a fist, squeezing with each thump, and making the blood run round through little pipes, some of which we could see under the skin of our wrists. That, at least for the moment, was enough.

JOHN HOLT
Instead of Education

CHILDREN AND SEX

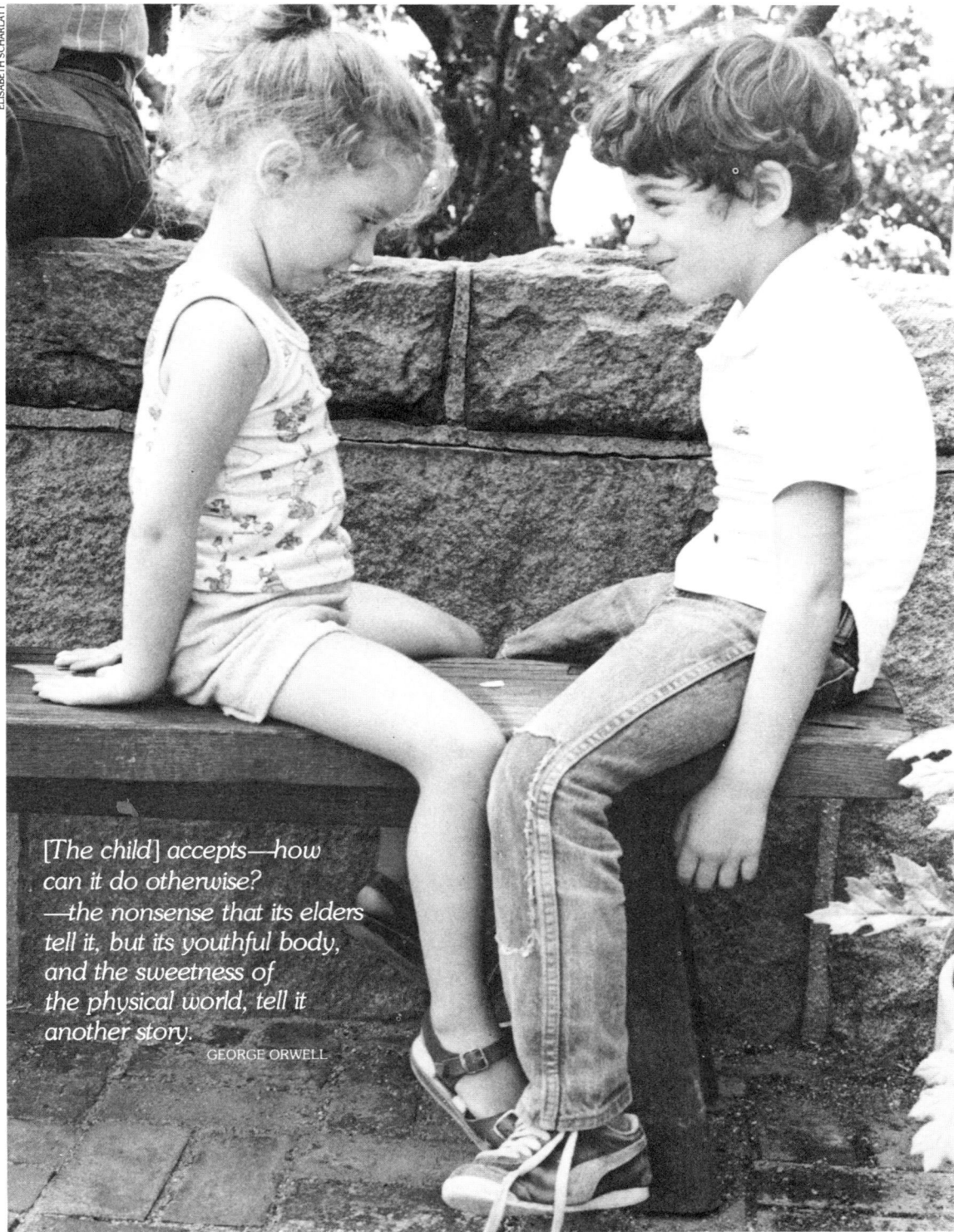

[The child] accepts—how
can it do otherwise?
—the nonsense that its elders
tell it, but its youthful body,
and the sweetness of
the physical world, tell it
another story.

GEORGE ORWELL

ACKNOWLEDGE YOUR CHILD'S SEXUALITY

The most striking phenomenon in the current conflict between generations is that each generation, in different ways, attempts to disallow the sexuality of the other. . . .

Parents are more reluctant to reveal sexual impulses to their children than any other characteristic, because their primary function is to control such impulses.

PHILIP SLATER
The Pursuit of Loneliness

The Mystery Remains

When you've just come up from magic and have learned not to believe without evidence, when you have discredited witches because you never *saw* one, sneered at fairies because you never *saw* one, the process of procreation as described by the adults in the child's world strains the child's new-found reality sense to its utmost. There is the sperm that can't be seen. The egg that can't be seen. The special opening in girls and women that can't be seen. And the mysterious process of sexual union that cannot, of course, be seen or even imagined well by the child. So we must not be surprised that the child who "knows everything," according to his parents, understands very little of it.

SELMA FRAIBERG
The Magic Years

Kids Are Teeming with Affection

When the kid ostrich's tail feathers caught on fire, mama and papa ostrich yelled, "Put your head in the hole, kid. Ain't nothin' happenin'!" Somehow the kid didn't believe them.

It's the same with us parents when it comes to sex. Kids are teeming with affection and tactile sensitivity (which is basically what sex is), but we try to deny that this is so.

First, it's healthy to acknowledge what sex is, for us and for our children. For someone who has cut through all the fears from his or her own childhood, sex is touching another person because the sensations are very nice and a feeling of friendship is expressed more easily than with words (which seem to elude both young and old).

Unlike adolescents', children's nervous systems haven't yet been supercharged by hormones, so the drive to orgasm is not nearly so imperative, though it can occur. And, unlike adults, children are present-oriented, readily willing to forget about sex play for a good game of tag, and not desperate to consign themselves to another for life. Actually, they're more realistic than we who pretend that sex is such a "heavy trip" with reverberations that extend forever, even though we know full well that when lovemaking is over we can read a book, go to work, or shop at a store as though it never occurred. Indeed, what is *less* significant than last week's or last month's orgasm?

Children also touch their own penises or vulvas, which discomfits lots of moms and dads. Why, I don't know, since almost every mom and dad did and does do this, too, with no bad consequences. But just because we can't give them a good reason to stop (or "1,000 good reasons not to" as my kids demand for every no-no) doesn't mean we won't discourage them nonetheless. We'll just be vague about why.

Fortunately, most children are not so perverted as to divorce themselves from their bodies just because Mom or Dad seems to prefer it. They'll just be a bit secretive—and apprehensive—about sexual feelings. When questions about sex arise, they'll just take them to their buddies, who know the subject inside out.

Come the teens, when all signals are GO, STOP, PROCEED WITHOUT CAUTION , WORRY, they'll be well prepared. They'll know a girl can only get pregnant when she's having her period. A boy with a penis less than eight inches long is a "morphodite." Pimples come from marathon masturbation. If boys (girls) don't fall in love with me, I must be homosexual. I'm the only one in the whole school who is a virgin. I'm the only one in the whole school who is not a virgin. You can't get VD (or pregnant) if you only do it once. You can't get pregnant if you take one of your mother's birth control pills after sex.

When they grow up, the guilt and ignorance will lead to all sorts of blossomings—impotence or premature ejaculation, mutual recriminations for unenjoyed sex relations, promiscuity as substitute for intimacy. In brief, the quiet and tumultuous desperation of marriage à la mode.

See how *unnecessary* good communication about sex is between parent and child? They'll learn it, *when they're ready!* And we don't need any school butting in, either! *This is strictly a matter between parent and child!* ("And what do you teach your child at home about sex?" "Well, er, ah . . . nothing.")

Perhaps you're beginning to think it is worthwhile to recognize your children's sexuality.

LEONARD GROSS

"Children live at the level of their parents' sexual organs.
That's where their heads are! They know what's going on."

Dr. David Reuben, of all people, came up
with this gem in an interview in *Family Health* magazine.

DISCUSSING SEX WITH YOUR CHILDREN

Sex Instruction Should Be Part of Natural Childhood

If the child's questions are answered truthfully and without inhibition on the part of the parents, sex instruction becomes part of natural childhood. The pseudoscientific method is bad. I know a youth who was taught sex in this way, and he claims that he blushes when someone uses the word *pollen*. The factual truth about sex is, of course, important, but what's more important is the emotional content. Doctors know all about the anatomy of sex, but they are not better lovers than the South Sea Islanders—most likely they are not nearly as good.

The child is not so much interested in daddy's statement that he puts his wee-wee into mother's wee-wee as he is in *why daddy does it.* The child who has been allowed his own sex play will not need to ask why.

Sex instruction should not be necessary for a self-regulated child, for the term *instruction* implies previous neglect of the subject. If the child's natural curiosity has been satisfied all the way by open and unemotional answers to all his questions, sex will not stand out as something that has to be specially taught. After all, we do not give a child lessons on his digestive apparatus or his excretory functions. The term *sex instruction* springs from the fact that sex activity is inhibited and made a mystery.

A. S. NEILL
Summerhill

By the time an American boy or girl reaches maturity he or she has so much symbolic baggage attached to the sexual impulse that the mere mutual stimulation of two human bodies seems almost meaningless. Through the mass media everything sexless has been sexualized: automobiles, cigarettes, detergents, clothing. (A recent TV commercial showed a lovesick man donning, with many caresses, and to the accompaniment of "I'm in the Mood for Love," a pair of shoes.) The setting and interpretation of a sexual act come to hold more excitement than the act itself.

PHILIP SLATER
The Pursuit of Loneliness

Doing Nothing as a Solution

I've always been great at theoretical discussions about children's sexuality. I could easily feel "safe" since my own child is a mere five-year-old naïf. Recently I discovered, however, that my sweet innocent baby is being corrupted by an eight-year-old hussy who sneaks off to the bathroom with him in school, where they take down their pants, show each other what they've got, and do God knows what.

I always thought that I would be open with my child about sex; treat it as the matter of course it is for most adults; free him from any future hangups; be comfortable in allowing him to experiment with his friends; let him play "Doctor" and "House" and see naked bodies so that there'd be no chance of sexual repression here. But I expected all that to happen when he was twenty-eight or something (or at least eleven)—certainly not at the age of *five!* Five years old is no time for a boy to be looking inside an eight-year-old's panties, I thought. But I was mistaken. Five years old is indeed the time—in fact, any time is the time, as long as there is someone whose panties are there for the looking and the kid is ready to look, I found out.

Anyway, my kid comes home with a batch of papers which I later discover are drawings of penises and vaginas and people fucking (this I know because they are captioned "Let's fuck" and "Why don't you fuck me") and have been written by this precocious girl to my innocent (and, I might add, pure—as far as I know) son.

Why have I kept these drawings for weeks? It is because I do not know what to do about this. I am not going to try to stop my son from exploring the subject—that would make him become even more involved. But neither am I going to *approve* of his carrying on in the bathroom with his young lady friend (that would likely confuse him and possibly make him lose interest in the exploration—which I also don't want to do). I think, finally, my doing nothing is a conscious decision: I cannot stop it and I will not approve of it. And maybe it'll all turn out fine.

ELS

The Question of What and How to Teach Your Child About Sex Is Up to You, but . . .

While there are a number of books which explain factual matters pertaining to sex and reproduction that are helpful, none can apply perfectly to your own life situation. Neither a child nor a parent–child relationship is an assembly-line product for which you can buy a care and maintenance manual. After all, the question of what and how to teach your child about sex is largely the question of how and what to teach your child about life. Some would presume to tell you, no doubt. Not I.

Some basic areas can be elucidated, however. Briefly, these are:

Homosexuality. Many little boys and girls kiss and explore the bodies of playmates of the same sex. These are usually isolated experiences and have no lasting significance. Behavior such as mutual masturbation also often occurs at the time of puberty, again reflecting experimentation and showing off new capabilities, rather than homosexual preferences.

A belief taking hold among some today is that homosexuality is as good as heterosexuality. Of course, homosexuals have been unjustly discriminated against. However, as I see it, a parent who wants his child to develop with a heterosexual preference should not consider himself or herself a bigot. Parenting means doing what you think is best for your child. Whether homosexuals can have as rewarding lives as heterosexuals, whether society will be better or worse off with increased homosexuality, whether *your child* will be happier as heterosexual, homosexual, or bisexual are all moot questions. To the extent you can influence these matters, it is your responsibility to exercise your judgments (including your biases) with respect for your child's predilections and convictions.

Sex and parent–child interactions. No harm will be done a child by seeing Mom or Dad nude or even in the act of love on rare occasions, so long as the parents make it clear their feelings toward each other are loving (sexual intercourse can appear violent to a child). Child psychiatrists believe it is wrong to frequently expose children to parental sex because it is overly stimulating and exacerbates the child's oedipal conflicts. If children are awed by Dad's penis or

Mom's pubic hair and breasts, assure them they'll be like that too someday.

Kids also like to snuggle in bed with Mom and Dad. Different doctors say different things about the wisdom of this, which gives me liberty as a parent to do what I feel comfortable and natural doing; that happens to be cuddling and hugging without eroticizing the affection.

Masturbation. Most experts say make the child aware that this is an okay activity that people do privately. Frequent masturbation may indicate anxieties, which the child tries to allay with the temporary calm that follows climax. Or, it may be caused by a more prosaic problem, such as a sore on the genitalia. Incidentally, all boys ask why their penis stands up sometimes. For your information, it does so in response to all sorts of internal states, not really sexual in the adult sense.

Dirty talk. Kids use taboo talk for dramatic effect because they have observed it gets attention. If you don't like it, cool the reaction and watch it diminish. Or give the child attention *before* the scatology erupts.

Sexy pictures. My children go wild over the pictures in *Playboy*. Obviously, clothes are intended to cover the body, and nudity is naughty. So how can they not be curious about these hidden delights? If such interest is sick, it's also universal.

How babies are made. Tell 'em. Clearly. At least to the extent they want to know. Don't be the father who went through the spiel of sperm, egg, womb, fallopian tubes, and the rest only to have his child say, "I mean *where* did I come from? Eddie says he's from Chicago, but where do I come from?"

Sexual development. Many girls menstruate at ages ten, eleven, or twelve. Prepare them for this event so they won't think they are injured or even pregnant, as has happened. Boys may develop before age twelve, too, on rare occasions. Let them know about the normalcy of the ejaculation of semen and noctural emissions.

LEONARD GROSS

——————◆——————

Sex and the Single Parent

For the first year and a half after the dissolution of my marriage I shared the custody of our two children (then three and eight), who spent four or five nights a week with me. This arrangement allowed me ample time for sexual liaisons while not with the children, and if any hanky-panky or the opportunity for such presented itself irresistibly during my nights "on" it was easy enough to arrange it so that the lady would arrive after the older child went to bed at nine, and not stay overnight.

When my wife and I signed a separation agreement, the situation changed. I was to have the children six nights a week. It also happened that a combined job/vacation offer opened for me in Maine which meant that I would have the children with me there for seven weeks straight. I wondered how I would be able to handle this; mused on it many nights.

The first problem was the seven weeks in Maine. One friend had offered to come visit for a long weekend. Not only did it seem silly for her to stay at a motel instead of with us, but certainly neither of us had the heart for such game playing as setting an early alarm.

A week before A's arrival I told Nat, the older boy, that A was coming up to visit. "Where will she sleep?" "You know where she'll sleep, honey!"

Naturally he was terrified at the prospect, and became more so as the week progressed. His younger brother seemed unconcerned. They both knew A, had spent a couple of delightful afternoons with her and me, and Lem looked forward simply to having someone else to play with. Nat was less sanguine, and I asked him to talk out his worries with me. He couldn't say very much, but I was as supportive as possible, saying that A was coming to visit because she liked us, and because she needed a little vacation too, and pointing out that he would be able to show her the island, since she had never been there.

On Friday, the day of her arrival, Nat asked if he could wait up with me to greet her. Since she was due in about ten or so, I said sure, and he did. Of coure he was nervous as a cat, and when she came he was stand-offish. After a few minutes of that I had him get ready for bed and tucked him in.

The next morning I came awake about 7:30, having set my mental alarm, and, knowing that the kids had been waking about then, made sure I was out of bed and partially dressed when they came in to see us. Lem jumped in bed with A, obviously delighted to see her, and they tussled and hugged a bit. Nat stood ramrod straight, observing. After breakfast he told me he wished she weren't there. I said, firmly, but without anger, that I was glad she was there, and that maybe he would have a good

time too, now that she was. That afternoon we spent several delightful hours exploring their favorite places and taking A to lunch at our most special eating place, and that night Nat took me aside to say that he was glad now that she'd come, that it was a lot of fun. I smiled and asked him if he'd noticed that I was easier to get along with too, now that I had a friend to play with.

A week or so after this I met another woman who ended up staying over. I had told Nat and Lem that she might, since she lived an hour's drive away, and that our date might end too late for her to drive home. This also went satisfactorily, but I realized that somehow I was going to have to work out a basic philosophy that Nat could accept without being bugged.

One day we started talking about love, and about friendship. Originally I thought to put the sleepovers in the love category, but I realized that (1) this would nail sex and love together in a way that I'd spent my life trying to disconnect, and (2) Nat had once told me that he knew people fuck and sleep together to find out if they like each other enough to live together. So I changed my tack to say that people often sleep together when they like each other a lot, and that sometimes love grows out of it, and sometimes it's just fun. He seemed to accept this, and is no longer quite so uptight if someone does appear in the morning. Of course, I try to warn him when someone will be here. Lem, as yet, has raised no problem, and my hope is that his Oedipal or whatever problems won't interfere any more than they would have with a mother-father scene, simply because he's already had some time to accept such situations.

Care must be taken, naturally, to keep one's child abreast of possible "friendships," so that he doesn't live in a world of constant shocks. Also, he must be reassured that every breakfast mate is not about to become his "mother." Like everything else, it takes patience and love. And there's no doubt in my mind that my particular situation is helped by the fact that the two boys have each other, and that they are boys. How it would be, for example, if I had one daughter is impossible for me to imagine.

The obvious thing is, of course, that we must avoid guilt trips. Children worry about losing us, about being presented with a new authority figure, about finding new children in the family, and all these threats must be discussed and dismissed. We are entitled to some love, or the simulation of it, and children are capable of realizing this if we present it correctly.

JOEL OPPENHEIMER

THE ANATOMY OF SEX

"Mommy, You Don't Have a Penis"

The other day I was taking a bath with my almost-three-year-old daughter. I was lying down and she was sitting between my legs, which were spread apart. She said, "Mommy, you don't have a penis." I said, "That's right, men have penises and women have clitorises." All calm and fine—then, "Mommy, where is your clitoris?" Okay, now what was I going to do? I took a deep breath (for courage or something), tried not to blush, spread my vagina apart, and showed her my clitoris. It didn't feel so bad. "Do you want to see yours?" I asked. "Yes." That was quite a trick to get her to look over her fat stomach and see hers, especially when she started laughing as I first put my finger and then hers on her clitoris.

At least, I feel that I can have some greater ease and openness about sexuality with my daughter than my mother had with me. It took us time to develop bad feelings about our sexuality, and we must allow ourselves more time to undo those feelings and develop new and healthier ones.

from *Our Bodies, Ourselves,*
by the Boston Women's Health Book Collective

[This story seemed so supportive, especially for anyone who's ever faced this issue. But while we're touting the clitoris as being comparable to the penis, it was a man who reminded us that the two cannot be compared. The penis is a multipurpose organ; the clitoris, single-purpose and part of a larger and more complex system, the vagina.—RS]

The Naked Truth?

We've had very little trouble explaining sex differences to our children, as we often wander about the house naked, or damn near. That and some good anatomy books with charts and the matter has been totally a non-issue with our three children, by age five.

NAME WITHHELD

I think it's shocking the way some people parade around without any clothes on in front of their children. Kids make dangerous comparisons between their genitals and their elders' and develop a concern for this earlier than is healthy. There is plenty of time to learn about adult bodies as an adult. And whatever erotic fantasies kids do develop about their parents don't need encouragement.

NAME WITHHELD

[Revell makes two $8 kits—the Visible Woman and the Visible Man—which might be the perfect tools for your discussions about the anatomy of sex. They can be built into transparent people, complete with skeletons and organs (including the sexual ones).

The Uterus, *Not* the "Tummy"

The seed does not grow in the mother's "tummy," or even in the mother's stomach. The seed grows in the mother's uterus. For some strange reason, people are hesitant about using the word *uterus* and use *stomach* instead. The substitution can confuse a child and cause problems. . . .

I would like to say flatly that there is no reason why your child cannot understand and learn that the uterus is *the* place in the body where the seed grows and that it is *near* the stomach.

DR. LEE SALK
What Every Child Would Like His Parents to Know

When my friend Susan was pregnant with her second child, her nearly-four-year-old daughter decided that she, too, wanted a "big belly," and she held in her bowel movements for days and days at a time. Her belly was big, all right, and so were her stomachaches.

ELS

The Beauties of Nakedness . . . Without Peeking

Often my little sister Anne and I, while Father shaved, bathed in the extra-big tub he had brought with untoward extravagance from Michigan. We loved these steamy sessions, and sang softly so that it would not disturb Mother: "Waltz Me Around Again, Willy" and "Camptown Racetrack" and "Onward, Christian Soldiers" . . . lifetime favorites of us all, even at five or six.

. . . Anne and I floated around in [the tub] like happy tadpoles, and Father hummed and occasionally scrubbed at us, and played tricks on the best mornings with his lather. All of us were of course stark rosy naked, and it was a special treat when he would casually put a dollop of the foam on his handsome and unbothered penis, and then dab us on our shoulders or noses or little pink breast-buttons. It was part of the satisfaction. We were nice well-made healthy children, and he was a manly fine man, and it was a good way to see the beauties of our bodies.

A few doors up from us lived two other little girls for a while, with an ailing mother who ate chalk. One time we must have been talking about how men are made, but I cannot remember why, and they said that they had peeked at their father, an action that had never occurred to us, and he had *two* things he could put lather on if he wanted to. We were sure Rex had only one main one, sufficient as it might be. We felt embarrassed to think anybody had more of anything at all than he had, and went at once to Mother to ask her about it.

She assured us that he was made as all men were made except perhaps better, and that she believed our little friends were mistaken about their father's attributes, owing to their hasty view. Then, it seems plain to me now, she and Father must have decided to give us a final demonstration and call a halt to further neighborly exchanges on the subject.

Rex stood up in the lovely steam one more time to shave himself while Anne and I bathed, and he dabbed a little foam here and there on all three of us, and after that he wore his BVD's in the bathroom when we were there. It is too bad. Perhaps it was another of the breaks between innocence and evil.

M. F. K. FISHER
Among Friends

Statues

When confronted with questions like what does a penis look like, we refer to pictures of statues in the encyclopedia for details.

NANCY MERLING

INTERCOURSE

Getting Right to the Point, or, They Know, They Know

Jenny (six or seven at the time): Did you and Daddy fuck to have me?

Me: Yes, of course, sweetie [*in a natural voice*]. That's how babies get made.

Jenny: I was just wondering—that's what V—— [*a school friend*] said.

Me: Do you know what fucking means?

Jenny: Well, sort of. The man puts his penis in the woman, but I don't really know how he does it.

Me: When a grown-up man and woman care about each other or want to feel close to each other, sex is one of the things they do, because it feels good to hold each other and touch. It's probably hard for you to imagine now, but when you're grown up, and you feel loving toward a man, like I do with—— [*friend*], you want to be as close together as you can be, and your vagina gets bigger and the man can slide his penis right in and it's a nice warm feeling. Usually people don't say "fuck" unless they're angry. They usually say "making love" or "having sex" or "sleeping together."

Another time, Jenny asked about sex and babies. I responded: When the man has his penis inside the woman he begins to feel as though waves were moving inside and then the sperm that he has inside him come out into the woman and go up into the womb. But sometimes when people make love they don't want to have a baby right then, so there are ways of keeping the sperm from going into the womb— the woman can take pills or put in a diaphragm, or sometimes the man wears a little thing over his penis.

Still another time, Jenny asked: Do you think I've ever fucked anyone?

Me: I don't know, have you?

Jenny: Yup, me and C——[*my friend's son*] fucked one night but you didn't know it.
Me: Did it feel good?
Jenny: Yeah, it was okay. Can I have a baby?
Me: Well, sweetie, I don't think you were probably having sex exactly like grown-ups do; and you can't have a baby until you start menstruating. But if it felt nice, it's okay. But sometimes, especially when you get a littler older, boys who don't really like you may want to play sex games that won't be fun.
Jenny: Yeah, I know. Like a lot of kids think it's dirty—but they're dumb.
Me: Right. But the thing that makes the difference is how you feel about the person and that you like each other.

ZELDA WIRTSCHAFTER

People Have Sex for Pleasure Too

Talking about sex with my daughters (I felt it was time—they were ten), I confessed that until I was twelve years old I thought that people only had sex to make babies. One night, I explained, I happened to see my parents, who slept in twin beds, under the covers together in my mother's bed. I understood what they must be doing and watched my mother's belly for the nine months that followed. When nothing happened, I confronted her: "Hey, how come you're not growing bigger?" I told her what I'd seen months before and wanted a reasonable explanation. My mother laughed and told me the shocking news. Only then did I understand, for the first time, that people have sex for pleasure, too.

My daughters started giggling. They thought it so funny that their mother, this wise old lady, was ignorant once. After that they were much more open, more comfortable asking what they might've thought were stupid questions.

"How long did you know Daddy before you had sex?" the girls later asked me.

"A week."

"A week?" they exclaimed. "*Before* you were married?"

"Yes . . . and I've told you that people don't have to be married to have sex. Why do you insist that they do?"

"Because it just seems to go together," they admitted, then thought about it some more before asking, perhaps, the most perplexing question: "But how did you decide to take off your clothes?"

LETTY COTTIN POGREBIN

Explaining Child-Free Lifestyles to Children

"Someday, you'll grow up and have a baby of your own," says a mother to her daughter who is playing with a doll. A casual remark. Yet children's memories have areas of startling permanence: remarks made by adults to youngsters can have profound impact on later attitudes and values. Thus statements such as the above can do much to create a strong predisposition toward a certain role (parenthood) which may be unsuitable or undesirable for the child when he or she becomes an adult. In the world of the future, sociologists predict, parenthood will be a specialized occupation, not a universal role. Both overcrowding and an increasingly specialized society make this inevitable. Integrating this future world view with a child's everyday scenes of play is really not so difficult. It's as easy, in fact, as saying "Someday, you know, you may want to have a baby of your own."

Just as important are unconscious attitudes which parents give children about parenthood, as when they view child-free adults skeptically or unfavorably.

Finally, when explaining sexuality to children, a purely reproductive frame of reference is to be avoided. "Babies are made when a man's body and a woman's body come together" should be, instead, "A man's body and a woman's are made to be united—sometimes that union makes a baby."

ELLEN PECK

Let's not perpetuate these Sexual Myths and/Misconceptions

—Masturbation stunts growth, causes acne, warts, blindness, impotence, etc.
—An intact hymen indicates virginity, and a broken or absent hymen indicates non-virginity.
—A baby grows in a woman's stomach.
—A young girl or woman should not swim, bathe, or exercise during menstruation.

—VD can be picked up from a toilet.
—Penis size is an indication of masculinity.
—Women ejaculate, as do men.
—"Wet dreams" or nocturnal emissions indicate sexual problems.

HOWARD KIRSCH and
CAROL GOLDBERG KIRSCH

DAVID KORR

Dirty Words

Empty Sewer Pipe Therapy, or, Dirty Word Class

A friend told me that when she was ten years old, she and a friend once crawled into a big, empty sewer pipe and for an hour and a half screamed every dirty word they could think of. It was so cathartic that she completely lost interest in obscenities.

For people who don't have access to empty sewer pipes: Aggie Aurbach recommends a "dirty word class" (her third-grader has one at school)—all dirty words spoken, defined, gotten out in the open.   RS

Cursing Well

The secret of good cursing lies in cadence, emphasis and antiphony. The basic themes are always the same. Conscious striving after variety is not to be encouraged, because it takes your mind off cursing.   A. J. LIEBLING

MENSTRUATION

Menstruating Is a Positive Experience

When I started explaining about menstruation to Valérie, I learned that she knew all about the physical aspects from a sex-education class in school. However, I told her something she hadn't learned, i.e., that menstruating is a positive experience for a girl, that it is a very happy event when it first happens, one she should look forward to, that it is a sign of growing up and she should feel proud when it happens. Children may have learned what to expect physically, but that doesn't mean that they feel good about it or really understand it. They may be terrified but not let on because they are ashamed. You have to intuit their fears without mentioning them, just trying to explain them away. Besides, they should be pleased with changes in their bodies as they grow up.

When talking about sex, we always insist that lovemaking is the culmination of a love relationship. In this way, we hope she will identify sex and strong feelings for another person, rather than thinking of it as something just physical and relating to herself alone.

ANNE BORCHARDT

Is It Fun?

The girls have always known and taken for granted menstruation because I've asked them to get me a Tampax when I found myself in the wrong place at the wrong time. They've watched kittens and a calf being born, and recently I told them (separately) the basics of sexual intercourse and reproduction. One wanted to know all about the technical aspects. The other wanted to know if it was fun.

RUTH PELMAS

BOOKS FOR ADULTS

Before laying down anywhere from $1.50 to $7 for a specialized book on sex education, try consulting any general child-rearing books you happen to own for whatever information they might provide. Look in the index (fie if there is none) under appropriate topics (sex, masturbation, homosexuality, dirty words—the labels themselves belie our alarm as a culture).

Looking through several books on our shelves, I found they all agree that:

—Too much information can confuse a child; take cues from the child's questions, and go, not too far, from there.

—Masturbation and sex play (i.e., sexual curiosity) are normal and healthy, and generally progress from public to private by around age eight.

—Communication is the key to healthy relationships.

RS

THE MAGIC YEARS, by Selma H. Fraiberg (Scribner's, 1959, 302 pages, $7.95 hardcover; $2.95 paperback).

A helpful book on the subject of sex education is Selma Fraiberg's *The Magic Years,* because she helps you to perceive what the kid understands about sex, or, more often, doesn't understand. Fraiberg's detailed examples from the children she has worked with provide a good and adaptable framework for the questions children are likely to ask. Below is an excerpt from *The Magic Years:*

"The daddy plants a seed . . ." At least two generations of parents have been grateful for this circumlocution introduced by books on sex education. In this way, it appears, we have introduced the agricultural fallacy into the large collection of fallacies which the child brings to sexual knowledge without any help from us. I recall a certain literal-minded fellow of six who was led into minor delinquency by the hopes engendered in him by this piece of information. He stole a package of cucumber seeds from the dime store and planted them (package and all) under a telephone pole "so's me and Polly can have a baby next summer."

Things are really not much better if the parents offer the additional piece of information that "the daddy plants a seed in the mommy." . . . One boy of six figured out that it flew into the mother, a perfectly sensible theory when you follow his thinking. He argued strongly and effectively for the air-borne theory, citing pollination as the analogy in the plant world. Other children attribute the feat of planting the seed to advancements in modern medical science. The doctor is frequently cited as the mediator in this process. Obviously, such a complicated and delicate process as getting the seed out of the father and planting it in the mother demands the highest medical skill and should not be left to amateurs.

YOUR CHILD AND SEX: A GUIDE FOR PARENTS, by Wardell B. Pomeroy (Dela-

corte, 1974, $6.95 hardcover; Dell, 1976, $1.50 paperback).

Much of what is in this book is obvious (the importance of communication and openness), some gratuitous ("the double bed is an aid to marital happiness"), and some open-minded without solving any immediate problems (an adequate discussion of homosexuality). But if you want a book on children and sex within the context of the traditional family, this was recommended by people who have used it and found it to be the best and most comprehensive book on the subject for parents. Dr. Pomeroy? He's co-author of *The Kinsey Reports* and president of the American Association of Marriage and Family Counselors. Here is an excerpt from Dr. Pomeroy's book:

Children ought to be taught the proper words for things, even though they may use slang. It is a kind of sentimental pandering, I think, to say "wee-wee" when penis is meant, or "grunt" for defecate. These useless euphemisms are in the same class with "bow-wow" for dog and "moo-moo" for cow. People seem to believe that a child is deprived of his childhood if he isn't permitted to use these "baby" words, and in any case, they think it's cute. Cute it may be to the self-indulgent parents, but unnecessarily crippling to the child's vocabulary. The idea of "baby talk" was not a child's idea of speech; it was conceived by parents.

Two recommended books for parents dealing specifically with adolescence are *The Sexual Adolescent: Communicating with Teenagers About Sex,* by Sol Gordon (Duxbury Press, 1973, $7.50 hardcover, $4.95 paperback) and *Sex and Your Teenager,* by Eda LeShan (Warner Paperback Library, 1973, $1.25).

HOWARD KIRSCH and
CAROL GOLDBERG KIRSCH

BOOKS FOR CHILDREN

Most of the books provide the facts in clear, elementary terms, but their differences in graphic design and depth of information make one suitable for your home and another just right for your neighbor's. Look through a few and see what feels best for you.

The guides to approximate age ranges should be interpreted imaginatively, as with all children's books. Even if your child can read the words by herself, it will mean more if you read it together.

The titles of many of the books sound confusingly similar, so it's a good idea to note the author and publisher of any that you want to seek out.

HOWARD KIRSCH and
CAROL GOLDBERG KIRSCH

FOR YOUNGER CHILDREN

WHERE DO BABIES COME FROM? A BOOK FOR CHILDREN AND THEIR PARENTS, *by Margaret Sheffield, illustrated by Sheila Bewley (Knopf, 1973, $5.95).*

One of the nicest books around for very young children. The descriptions of anatomy, conception, and birth are clear and simple. Intercourse is dealt with unemotionally, but the lovely pastel illustrations create a warm and gentle mood.

MAKING BABIES: AN OPEN FAMILY BOOK FOR PARENTS AND CHILDREN TOGETHER, *by Sara Bonnett Stein, photographs by Doris Pinney (Walker & Co., 1974, $5.95). Recommended for all ages.*

Making Babies is part of a series of "Open Family" books all of which include two texts on each page—one in large print for children, and one in smaller print for parents. In this particular volume, the text for children is very general, giving little detail, and the parents' text provides guidelines for ways to supplement discussions of the pictures. The ultimate success of the book, then, depends largely on the parents' ability to embellish the children's text. The book is illustrated with photographs, mostly of children and animals; two stark photographs of a fetus might be difficult for children to comprehend.

THE TRUE STORY OF HOW BABIES ARE MADE, *by Per Holm Knudsen (Children's Press, 1973, $3.95). Recommended for age 4 and up.*

This book, first published in Sweden, approaches the story of reproduction through a description of intercourse as an act of love between parents, sometimes resulting in conception. Unlike most other books for this age group, it clearly implies that love making is not solely for the purpose of making a baby. The text is straightforward, but occasionally oversimplified, as are the cartoon-like illustrations.

[This book may annoy feminists, says *The New York Times,* "because it makes the sex act sound like something that is initiated by the man's arousal."—Eds.]

HOW BABIES ARE MADE, *by Andrew C. Andry and Steven Schepp (Time-Life Books, 1968, $5.95). Recommended for ages 3–10.*

Another good book for very young children. The story of reproduction is described first in plants and animals (chickens and dogs), then in humans—a good approach, allowing children to think of reproduction in terms of other aspects of their environment. The illustrations—color photographs of paper sculptures—are unusual, but may strike some parents as being flat and uninspiring.

FOR OLDER CHILDREN

THE WONDERFUL STORY OF HOW YOU WERE BORN, *by Sidonie Matsner Gruenberg, illustrated by Symeon Shimin (a Doubleday Zephyr Book, 1970, rev. ed. $1.49). Recommended for ages 10–12.*

This book, originally published in 1952, has long been considered a classic. Speaking directly to children's conceptions of themselves, the story begins with a straightforward description of reproduction and unfolds into the emotional aspects of love and sex, preparing children for puberty. Highly recommended.

THE KIDS' OWN XYZ OF LOVE AND SEX, *by Siv Widerberg, illustrated by Michael Grimsdale (Stein & Day, 1972, $4.95 hardcover; $2.25 paperback). Recommended for ages 7–13.*

Originally published in Sweden, this book is probably the most candid and liberal of its kind.

In confronting questions on everything from the facts of reproduction to abortion, prostitution, and pornography, the author takes a stand for open attitudes about sex. This is an excellent book for parents who want to participate in teaching children what they might otherwise pick up outside the home (e.g., slang words for sex organs and intercourse), but it should be used with discretion.

[*The Kids' Own XYZ of Love and Sex* really goes into the things that kids wonder and worry about—i.e., masturbating, experimenting with peers, etc. Jenny really dug it (at age nine), and I felt it was "right on"—not condescending, or using technical language as so many of these books do, but warm, informative, reassuring, and straight.—Zelda Wirtschafter]

WHERE DID I COME FROM? *by Peter Mayle, illustrated by Arthur Robins (Lyle Stuart, 1973, $7.95 hardcover; $3.95 paperback).*

This is my favorite book on sex education. It appeals to my perverted sense of humor—I can't look at it without giggling. It's whimsical in an adult way, it doesn't talk down, and it's absolutely accurate. But I'm not at all sure it's for children.　　　　　　　　　　ELISABETH BING

THE HUMAN STORY: FACTS ON BIRTH, GROWTH, AND REPRODUCTION, *by Sadie Hofstein in consultation with W. W. Bauer, M.D., Lothrop, Lee & Shepard Co., 1969, $5.95). Recommended ages 10–14.*

An excellent book for helping young people deal with the onset of puberty. The author de-scribes the physical and psychological changes of puberty, including such common problems as acne and moodiness, in a frank and reassuring way. The second half of the book provides a "refresher course" on reproduction, and also contains information on heredity. A useful glossary is included.　　　HOWARD KIRSCH and
CAROL GOLDBERG KIRSCH

ALSO GOOD, BUT NOT ON THE CHILDREN'S SHELF

OUR BODIES, OURSELVES, *by the Boston Women's Health Book Collective (Simon and Schuster, 1976, $12.95; $4.95 paperback).* Don't underestimate a ten- or eleven-year-old's ability to comprehend this collection, in which women share information about their bodies with other women.

A SEASON TO BE BORN, *by Suzanne Arms, and John Arms (Harper & Row, 1973, $3.50 paperback),* might be useful for an older child who is embarrassed by or particularly interested in a mother's growing middle. It's a photojournal of one couple's preparation for and experience of childbirth, reassuring if somewhat romanticized.　　　　　　　　RS

When our son asked, "How do babies grow?" "What do they look like in Mommy's tummy?" we took out a copy of Lennart Nilsson's A CHILD IS BORN: THE DRAMA OF LIFE BEFORE BIRTH *(Dell, $4.95),* which is the best source I can think of for the answer.
　　　　　　　　　　GERALDINE O'DWYER

Further Resources For Sex Education

The following organizations, all of which are concerned with human sexuality, offer resources for sex education.

AMERICAN ASSOCIATION OF SEX EDUCATORS AND COUNSELORS (AASEC), 5010 Wisconsin Avenue N.W., Suite 304, Washington, D.C. 20016. Books, bibliographies, and pamphlets on sex education, primarily for professionals.

E.C. BROWN FOUNDATION, 710 S.W. Second Avenue, Portland, Ore. 97204.

JEWISH BOARD OF FAMILY AND CHILDREN'S SERVICES, Room 309, 120 W. 57 Street, New York, N.Y. 10019. Especially recommended: The annotated bibliography *Family Life and Child Development* ($2.50).

NATIONAL COUNCIL OF CHURCHES, Commission on Ministries and Human Sexuality, 475 Riverside Drive, New York, N.Y. 10027.

NATIONAL SEX FORUM, 1523 Franklin Street, San Francisco, Calif. 94109.

SIECUS, 137 N. Franklin Street, Hempstead, N.Y. 11550. In addition to materials on sex education in the schools, SIECUS offers bibliographies, books, articles, and other resources, many of which are also available in Spanish. Write for their most recent Publications Catalog.

SYNAGOGUE COUNCIL OF AMERICA, Committee on the Family, 432 Park Avenue S., New York, N.Y. 10016.

UNITED STATES CATHOLIC CONFERENCE, Family Life Bureau, 1312 Massachusetts Avenue N.W., Washington, D.C. 20005.

The following organizations operate anonymous telephone information services:

Community Sex Information, Inc., New York: (212) 677-3320

San Francisco Sex Information: (415) 665-7300

The single most useful list of resources we've seen to date is included in the book THE SEXUAL ADOLESCENT: COMMUNICATING WITH TEENAGERS ABOUT SEX, *by Sol Gordon (Duxbury Press, 1973, 208 pages, $4.95)*. The Selected List of Resources, which is thirty pages long, includes books, pamphlets, articles, journals, organizations, and audio-visual materials on human sexuality for teenagers and adults. This list, combined with the seven-page Glossary that follows it, is well worth the price of the book.—Eds.

GO AHEAD AND TOUCH

I believe that the need to touch and embrace should be encouraged. It is a natural human activity too long restricted and distorted in our culture.

DR. DANIEL CASRIEL

At the time that my child was growing up, it was true that girls could be fondled and cuddled from the moment of birth. They could be kissed, squeezed, hugged, pinched, nuzzled, and held. But boys presented a different problem for parents. In the early years you were entitled to pat a bare behind or kiss a bellybutton. At tuck-in time or bath time, you could cop a feel with aplomb. Up until the boy was about four. After that, for reasons linked to Oedipus and virility, it became harder, sometimes impossible, to make physical contact—to "make nice" we used to call it—except by clever and devious means. Sports are a terrific way to accomplish this. I once played a horse named Horo and got ridden around the apartment. A sudden show of temperament and Horo the horse reared and dumped my son the jockey, and I could slip a hand under his pajamas and tickle—typical horse behavior. I devised a "bee" game at bedtime. While murmuring, "There was a bee, a busy bee, a fuzzy buzzy bumble bee," I buried my face into my son's middle and gave him the zzz's at maximum vibration. He liked the game, and I liked the buzzing.

It's delicious to touch your kids, though the urge is not often spoken of. I remember once when a dance troupe from Bali, made up of six- to eleven-year-olds, came to New York, all the critics praised their skill and never mentioned the extraordinary sensuality of the dancers. Adults sat in the audience wondering if they were simply perverts or totally insane, reacting to the liquid loveliness of the young bodies doing their dance, enough to quiet the volcano and make rain on Times Square. Kids are sensual, warm to the touch, and touching them is an affirmation of all life. You can feel the warmth of life and the hopeful heat of the future. Physical contact with your children is nourishing. Sensual memory of my parents is stronger in me than all their spoken wisdom.

HARVEY JACOBS

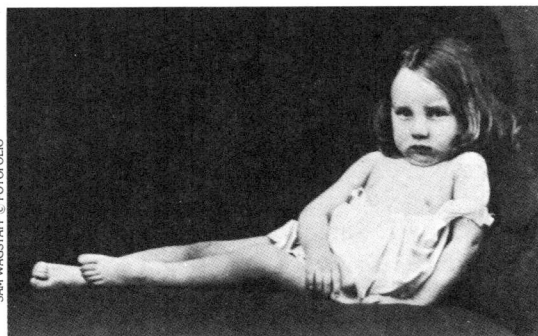

BY LEWIS CARROLL, C. 1859 FROM THE COLLECTION OF SAM WAGSTAFF © FOTOFOLIO

SEX EDUCATION IN THE SCHOOLS

If we were to teach sex the way we teach other things, it'd go out of style.

New York City teacher, quoted in *Herman Kahnsciousness* Produced by Jerome Agel

"Integrate the Spiritual and Romantic . . ."

Even in discussions of anatomy and physiology, I think it is important to integrate the spiritual and romantic aspects of sexuality. . . . This means that sex should be discussed in school, not so much by the school doctor or nurse, gym teacher or biology teacher, but by any and all teachers who are mature emotionally, who are respected by the students and who feel comfortable talking about sex.

DR. BENJAMIN SPOCK
Raising Children in a Difficult Time

Moralizing Can Be Hazardous To Your Health

Inclusion of sex instruction in the public school curriculum provides dangerous opportunities for encouraging sex repressions by moralizing. The mere term *sex instruction* suggests a formal, awkward lesson on anatomy and physiology by a timid teacher who fears that the subject may slip over the border into forbidden territory.

A.S. NEILL
Summerhill

Does Teaching Sex Destroy Sex?

To an adult who feels that he has had a good sex life for many years and was never "taught" anything about sex as a child, school courses in "sex education" sound like the best way to destroy sexual enjoyment once and for all. Since lovemaking between any two people is always different from lovemaking between any other two people—or even between one of the same people and someone else, or between the same two people at different times—it seems absurd to try to say anything general. What can diagrams of sexual organs and texts on physical responses tell a child—or an adult—about tenderness, or excitement, or passion, or lust?

It is far more likely that clinical explications of the sexual act will tend to destroy the personal and intensely private response that alone makes sex wonderful. What words can teach as much as the lessons learned through fumbling, covert

pleasures experienced during one's youth? Sexual needs, sexual delights, sexual adventures not only cannot be taught, they cannot be described, any more than all the poetry in the world can tell us what love is.. But sex education conceivably can destroy the pleasures of sex, because the attempt to make general what is so personal may compel children to conform—to do in bed what the books say to do in bed, not what she or he wants to do in bed—and finally to make the individual merely a person performing an act, not a man or a woman, a boy or a girl, expressing their needs and desires personally through the endless variations of their own bodies.

A. OLSON

But Do It Well!

I'm hesitant on the whole subject of sex education because if it's going to be done in school at all, I want it to be done really well. You could have a bad teacher for math and it might not be so terrible for the rest of your life, you could get over it, but when I think of some of the nuns who taught me . . . it makes me hesitant.

JO VINCENT

Don't Wait Until Your Child Goes to School

While I am in favor of schools offering instruction about sex, I do recommend that you do not wait until your child goes to school before you tell him the facts. Most children begin asking questions long before they go to school. The school can amplify sexual knowledge and keep your child from feeling that discussing reproduction and sex is taboo. But it is not the school's responsibility to inform your child.

DR. LEE SALK
*What Every Child Would Like His
Parents to Know*

FEARS KIDS HAVE

FEAR

"Fear Is Real and Reasonable and Okay to Feel . . ."

There are three things about fears in a child that I feel strongly about: (1) that whatever the fear is, it's real and reasonable and okay to feel; (2) that there are many things you should be afraid of; (3) that fears are a part of life because things aren't always happy and warm and safe. If there is still a need for God and policemen and whatever else makes grown-ups able to deal with airplanes and war and sudden diseases, then it is important for me to be there for a child, no matter how silly the fear is. I think a child should be dependent upon a parent or grown-up to feel safe and secure, so that eventually these feelings can be transferred to the world around him. After all, escalators and airplanes and monsters are what make life never dull and nearly always an adventure.

MARY-CLAIR VANDER WAL

In helping my kids to overcome fears, we act out the things that frighten them, pretending to *be* the scary thing, acting out the scary fantasy, exploring a safe resolution to the fantasy—e.g., monsters that are overcome by a little boy, airplanes that fly up over mountains and land safely.

SUSAN KIERR-BAIN

I told my son that if he ever feels really bad or sad or frightened he should ask to be held. "Please hold me," he is able to say, and I do for a moment of very quiet, very close connecting. And he's none the worse for it.

ELS

"I'm Not Going Anywhere . . ."

Whatever security I could offer my son had to be based on the feeling that I'm not going anywhere and that nobody is going to take his place in my life or my place in his. Our security is tied in to our feelings about each other—not to an apartment or a toy or whether or not I come home at six o'clock.

NIKKI GIOVANNI

At my child's school, parents are requested to stay with their children who are new at the school until both the child and the parent are ready for the separation. One of the children, when asked if she thought it was time, replied: "I want my mother to stay every day, but she can go now."

ELS

When I'm going off on a trip for overnight or longer, I prepare a little "book" with drawings or even magazine pictures telling the story of where I'm off to, how I'm getting there, what I'll be doing there, and most important, that I'll be coming back. Even for a very young child, this seems to be a comfort.

MARJORIE SMITH

You can also make a big calendar with words or drawings of what you'll be doing. The child can mark off the days.

CAROL EICHLER

If you are to be away from your child, have him or her keep a diary with drawings and details of each day to share upon your return.

ELIN EWALD

"What If . . .?" (A Game to Counter Fear)

One approach I have found helpful with my son when he feels fearful or upset or threatened by something is to play a game I call "What if?" Using his expressed feeling as a springboard, we play out the disturbing situation with a variety of imagined outcomes. Usually he discovers (sometimes to his own surprise) that he has a strategy or answer already in his head. When he lacks the information to work out a solution, or when he misses other options, I help him out.

For example, David once expressed concern about what would happen to him if he got lost in a crowded department store. I asked him what he thought he would feel if the situation occurred and what he thought he could do to cope with it. He first said, "I'd be upset, I'd cry, I'd feel scared and frightened, I'd be lonely," and then said, "I guess I could ask someone to help me find my mommy—like a salesperson." I added that usually when a child appears lost, someone who works in the store takes the child to the office. Then if the mother can't find the child (she too feels upset and concerned), she knows to go to the office. I told him that some stores announce on the loudspeaker the name of the lost child and that next time we went to a large store we could listen for such an announcement.

I have used this "What if?" approach with such serious concerns as: What if you or I were in an automobile accident, or injured, or hospitalized, or mugged; what if I died. David is reassured to feel he could cope with or manage a given situation, that he has options other than feeling overwhelmed and helpless. He is not reassured to hear "That would never happen," or "Don't worry about that—I'll take care of everything." Children are observant enough to know that these things do sometimes happen and that parents aren't always around to help them out.

SALLY LANGENDOEN

The Night . . .

One thing that may possibly have delivered my child from nighttime fear of shadows is my talking about shadows during the day. Whenever we went walking on a sunny day, we looked for shadows of *every* shape. In the afternoon we looked for shadows in his room and made some new shadows, now and then, with a flashlight in his crib. Then, when he saw them at night, they were like old friends.

ELS

To help a child be less fearful, try a radio playing music softly. Little transistors are good, and a child can turn them on and off easily. Zaps ghosts and other shadowy things in the night.
If a child is introduced at age two to the beauty of the night—walks viewing the sky, moon, etc.—in a positive, exciting way, he will not be afraid of the dark. Parents often instill their own fears in their children.

ANNA MAY NIES

. . . and Things That Go Bump in It

A ritual search for monsters—and a constant lack of them—sometimes helped in overcoming my daughter's fears. We went through a period of "filling the room with love," which was elaborate placing of love all around, especially on her bed. That helped for a while, too.

LESLIE HARRIS

One night, when a child for whom I was babysitting couldn't sleep because of these monsters in her room, I told her matter-of-factly that the monsters' mommies had just put *them* to bed, too, so they wouldn't have a chance to come into the room even if they wanted to. It worked.

AMANDA GARI

We've flushed all our monsters down the toilet.

SHEILA HUTMAN

To help my son feel in control of his life and his most feared intruders (imagined mice, dogs, cats, even buildings), I coached him to say, in a gruff voice: "Go home now. Go away, dog."

Of course this doesn't work when the dog is not imagined, but is barking up his sleeve and very real—but it does help against the imaginary animals and other beings, which is something anyway.

ELS

FRANK DERBAS

At two years old, Vaj had real night fears—mostly because the people upstairs clumped around in their wooden shoes. He was terrified. We asked the people to clump around one day after I got home from work, and then we listened with Vaj (still terrified), telling him who it was. Then we went upstairs and watched them clump around. He eventually made the connection, but still jumps when there's an unexpected clunk from upstairs. Now when he's going to sleep and there's noise, he'll say, "Go to sleep, noise," or "Good night, noise," or good night to the people upstairs, and he's okay.

FLAVIA POTENZA

Fear and Anger: "Beating Up on the Lion"

When my son was around three or four, he was terribly afraid of lions. It got to the point where we couldn't go to the zoo, it upset him so. There's nothing terrible about not going to the zoo, and I don't ordinarily spend twelve or fifteen dollars on stuffed animals, but I decided to get him a lion he could be comfortable around. So I bought him a very soft lion with sort of a funny face. At first he didn't pay any attention to it, but after a few months he was sleeping with it, beating it, acting out his anger on it. He named it the Cowardly Lion. Books say that kids are sometimes frightened by things that make them confront their own anger and hostility. Really though, to this day I don't know what went on in his head when he was so afraid, or what went on in his head when he knocked the shit out of the stuffed lion. I do know that now we go to the zoo and it's as if the fear never existed.

DONNA BARKMAN

Feiffer

I DON'T LIKE TO GO TO SCHOOL

I'M SCARED THAT WHEN I COME HOME, MY PARENTS WILL HAVE MOVED

I DON'T LIKE TO GO OUT TO PLAY

I'M SCARED THAT WHEN I TRY TO GET BACK IN, NO ONE WILL ANSWER THE DOOR.

I DON'T LIKE TO GO TO SLEEP.

I'M SCARED THAT WHEN I WAKE UP, MY PARENTS WON'T BE BREATHING.

I DON'T LIKE BEING A CHILD.

IT'S TWENTY-FOUR-HOUR-A-DAY GUARD DUTY.

"Jules Feiffer Strikes Again"

Some of us have a pipeline to our childhood; Jules Feiffer remembers his anxieties with accuracy and wit. A friend of mine, the artist Charley Stark, has a six-year-old son named Timmie who developed a series of fears after the death of his grandparents: he insisted that his mother, Margie Stark, not leave school after taking him there in the morning; he wouldn't go to sleep without someone in his room; and when his father left for work he'd follow him around the corner wanting to go along.

Timmie had always been a street kid, his territory as secure outdoors as in, but suddenly he would not go out to play; he refused to leave the house.

Charley and Margie were helpless in the face of this awful thing that was happening to Timmie; Margie felt that she had never really known her own child. At work, Charley confided Timmie's hang-ups to a sympathetic co-worker; she asked him whether he had seen the previous day's Feiffer cartoon in the *Village Voice*. Charley got the cartoon strip and gave it to Timmie to read. Timmie thought that Charley had drawn the cartoon himself: Who else could have understood his inmost fears so well? After Charley convinced Timmie that he had not drawn the cartoon, Timmie wanted to know whether Charley had told the artist about him. Charley assured his son that he had never met Jules Feiffer.

Once again, Timmie read the strip, at first solemnly, but then with a real sense of the humor: "This kid thinks and feels just like me . . . it's really funny." After reading it all day, Timmie colored the strip and put it up on his wall.

Soon after, Timmie began playing outside with his friends; went to school; was able to sleep alone in his room; he had regained his old aplomb. Jules Feiffer had struck again.

SHERMAN DREXLER

Exorcising Our Dracula

Our child, five, developed a fear of vampires. At night in bed, after lights out, he would ask his mother or me to stay with him. Vampires might be waiting in his closet or fluttering around the window in bat form. We found it best to deal with the fear on its own terms. It could not be allayed by saying things like, "That's ridiculous, there are no vampires," or, "How could a vampire get past the doorman?" We would look in the closet and out the window, while telling him that vampires were creatures of television, films, and stories.

Patience was the key word in exorcising our Dracula. And the most effective weapon was not a cross, mirror, or silver stake but stories by his parents of their own fears and how they went away or were conquered. One story he liked was about how my older brother used to torture me by rising from his bed at night and hopping madly around the room in the dark. He explained he had a devil-sickness and would hop himself to death. Then he would fall on the floor dead as a doornail. At this point I would tear-ass into our parents' bedroom, wake them, and tell them my brother had hopped himself to death. When our parents came to investigate, my brother would be peacefully sleeping in his bed and wake to deny the whole experience.

Stories like that, where the fear of the victim was obviously without real cause, helped. The vampire thing lasted a long while, and took much of the old patience. Finally, one day our son bought a Dracula poster and hung it over his bed. That signaled the end of the problem. It was our feeling, during this time of haunting, that the Dracula fear involved feelings about sex and death and power. Its immediate genesis was the media, i.e., television promos for Dracula films, kid tales in school, etc. When the fear took hold, it was used in many ways, to prolong stay-awake time, to manipulate parental sympathy, as a conduit for other fears and anxieties.

It is our hope that, with détente, our son may one day be ambassador to Transylvania, but then, all parents have dreams like that.

HARVEY JACOBS

Kids' Aggressiveness: Is It Related to Fear?

Why are some children bullies while others have the image of being cowards? Why are some children physically aggressive and brutal toward their playmates? Why do children taunt and tease one another to the point where the one subjected to taunts can be reduced to tears or blind physical retaliation?

Teacher Stephen M. Joseph spent months working with children in a New York nursery school in an attempt to find the answers to these basic questions about child behavior. . . .

The result of Joseph's research . . . is *Children in Fear,* (Holt, Rinehart and Winston), a small, disturbing book that contains valuable insights for any adult who has wondered about the cruelty of children to one another . . .

Joseph's basic premise was that there are no bad children, per se. There were reasons for their harmful behavior and that somehow this behavior was connected to their acting out of deep basic fears. Central to his premise was the theory of a psychiatric social worker he knew and respected, Denah Harris. . . .

"If a child hits me," Joseph explains, "I think he's asking if I'll punish him if he's bad and why other people punish him when he's bad, and why people hit each other. I gently hold him away if he's still hitting, and then I answer those questions, which I perceive in his behavior, rather than punishing him for punishing me. Human beings have been doing that for thousands of years and it doesn't solve the problem. . . ."

Solving problems was the theme Joseph stressed in all his encounters with the children. *Children in Fear* is filled with incident after incident of how he got children to think about why they were hitting someone or behaving badly.

The reader, of course, may reject his theories as impractical and hopelessly idealistic. There is still a strong urge to teach children that life is a constant challenge and retaliation or suspicion is more rewarding than understanding and dialogue as a basic system of human relations. But whether one rejects or accepts Joseph's premise that there are no bad children, only those with varying skills in "problem solving," the story of his exploration of young minds and ancient fears makes fascinating reading.

MARTIN BUSKIN
Women's American ORT Reporter

> Books for children on the subject of fear—and on anger, death, divorce, separation, etc.—even when they are not good books, are often better than nothing. At least they acknowledge the feelings, and a child should be helped to know that she or he is not the only one in the world going through that particular torment.—Eds.

DIVORCE

"Don't Try to Talk Them Out of It . . ."

One June my parents told me they were getting a divorce. It was a very sad moment. All of a sudden, I started bursting out into tears, and I said to them, "You're kidding." And my mother said, "No, we are going to get a divorce." I was very scared. But I didn't know what about.

About five months later, the agreement between my mother and father to get a legal separation was signed by both of them, and about a month after that, my father moved out. Right now, my father lives with a stockbroker named Vivian, and we are with our mother. I hope that my father will get married again, and so will my mother, but I know the legal separation does not allow it for one year yet. I'd like my mother to get married because I am the only boy in the house now, and it would be nice to have another man.

The only advice I can give is don't try to talk them out of it because when I tried that, it didn't do any good and it will just make you feel bad. At the beginning, it seems really awful, but then in three or four weeks, you realize that it's not all that bad. When my mother and father told me about the divorce they said it was for my good too, and I didn't believe them. They thought divorce was good, but I thought just the opposite. But now that my father has moved out, it isn't all that bad. So, your parents will think that the divorce is good for you, but I still think that divorce is dumb.

MICHAEL RINZLER
Age nine

P.S. If you are really sad, find a friend whose parents have been divorced, and talk to them about it.

Air Your True Feelings

By the end of my marriage, my husband had become so violent and verbally abusive that there was no question that divorce was the only solution. After we separated, however, I tried to speak of him only in kindly terms to the kids until one night. My son and daughter and I were sitting around the kitchen table, when she, out of the blue, gave a little sigh and said, "I love Dad and everything, but gee, it's a relief not to have him around!" My son looked as if he expected the skies to fall on him when he dared to agree, and I suddenly realized that expressing my own anger was far more honest than the whitewashing I had been attempting. We all aired our feelings more frequently, and the healing process began. Today we're all friends, and the kids see their father frequently and voluntarily, which they simply weren't able to do when they were filled with bottled-up emotion.

JANET HANSEN

Some Really Good Books About Divorce and Single Parents

A MONTH OF SUNDAYS, by Rose Blue (Watts, 1972, $4.90 hardcover). Ages 8–12.

A ten-year-old boy wishes his father would return home and then learns he must reconcile himself to his parents' divorce. Guilt is only one of the emotions he feels.

IT'S NOT WHAT YOU EXPECT, by Norma Klein, (Pantheon, 1973, $5.99 hardcover; Avon, 1974, 95 cents paperback). Ages 12–16.

A story of parents separating because of middle-age wondering and wandering is told from the viewpoint of the adolescents who are in the middle of it. There is explicit sexuality and an abortion is part of the plot, but mature twelves could probably handle it.

WHERE IS DADDY?, by Beth Goff (Beacon Press, 1969, $5.95 hardcover). Ages 4–8.

This book hits hard at the emotions children feel during a divorce: guilt, anger, wishful thinking.

BOYS AND GIRLS BOOK ABOUT DIVORCE, by Richard Gardner (Aronson, 1971, $10 hardcover; Bantam, 1971, $1.25 paperback). Ages 9 and up.

This is a honey of a book. It gives practical hints about coping with relationships with mother and father after divorce, as well as dating, remarriage, etc. It is quite revolutionary—it offers advice on how to tell if your parents love you and what to do if they do not.

IT'S NOT THE END OF THE WORLD, *by Judy Blume (Bradbury, 1972, $6.95 hardcover; Bantam, 1977, $1.25 paperback). Ages 9–12.*

A young girl realizes that her parents' separation is final and that it is best that way. She meets another child of a broken home who recommends Richard Gardner's book (see page 68).

VERONICA GANZ, *by Marilyn Sachs, (Doubleday, 1968, $4.95 hardcover; Archway, 75 cents paperback). Ages 9–12.*

A family's adjustment to the fact that the father is not much interested in them is a subplot in this novel, but it's an important motivating factor for the rest of the action.

JOANNE BERNSTEIN

HEADS YOU WIN, TAILS I LOSE, *by Isabelle Holland, (Lippincott, 1973, $5.95 hardcover; Dell, 1977, $1.25 paperback). Ages 12–16.*

Melissa is fat, and the boy she likes doesn't care for her. She has to cope with her parents' sarcastic fights and hostile attitude toward her. When her father walks out, her mother becomes an alcoholic. Melissa tries to diet with pills, nearly winds up a zombie. It is done well, in spite of all this.

ME TOO, *by Vera and Bill Cleaver (Lippincott, 1973, $7.95 hardcover; NAL, 1975, $1.25 paperback). Ages 9–12.*

A child has to cope with a father's desertion and a sister's handicap.

I'LL GET THERE. IT BETTER BE WORTH THE TRIP, *by John Donovan (Harper & Row, 1969, $5.95 hardcover; Dell, 95 cents paperback). Ages 12–16.*

This book concerns death, divorce, loneliness, adolescent homosexuality.

MOM, THE WOLFMAN AND ME, *by Norma Klein (Pantheon, 1972, $5.99 hardcover; Avon, 1974, 95 cents paperback).*

People think they have to feel sorry for kids living with just their mother. But this is a good book because it lets them know what it is like, and that it can be good. KARREN BAIN

Fortunately I found a novel—*Mom, the Wolfman and Me*—that my pre-teenage daughter could read and love and share with me even though it is about being married and unmarried and loving again and living arrangements. It is a good book for children and parents who are "embarrassed" by single parenthood or divorce. SUSAN KIERR-BAIN

MOVING

"All the Other Houses Were Strange . . ."

We moved four times a year, because for the fall and spring we returned to the house in Hammonton.

All the other houses were strange—homes that had to be made our own as quickly as possible so that they no longer would be strange. This did not mean that they were frightening, but only that we had to learn about every nook and corner, for otherwise it was hard to play hide-and-go-seek. As soon as we arrived, I ran ahead to find a room for myself as far away as possible from everyone else, preferably at the top of the house where I would always be warned by footsteps that someone was coming. After that, until we were settled in, I was busy exploring, making my own the new domain. Later, when I was about fourteen, I was in charge of unpacking, getting beds made, food

in the icebox, and the lamps filled and lit before nightfall.

The next step was to explore the neighborhood. I had to find out what other children lived nearby and whether there were woods, wild flowers, tangles, or jungles—any hidden spot that could be turned into a miniature primeval forest where life could be quickly shaped to an imaginary world.

MARGARET MEAD
Blackberry Winter

Let Your Children Participate

I moved around a lot as a kid, and my parents always made my sister and me feel that we were participating in the decision of whether or not to move. Once it was decided, they created a wonderful sense of adventure about meeting new people and learning about a new environment. But they also were honest about the negative aspects of moving: the strangeness of a new place, leaving friends behind, and the overall inconvenience.

After the first decision to move was made, my sister and I helped pack the household items as well as our own things. I was given responsibilities, which seemed very important to me, such as making lists or inspecting rooms to see that everything was packed.

My parents explained the differences between our new home and the old one, and the similarities. All I'd known was Arizona, and growing up in the desert. I had read about snow, about cold weather, about cities, and I was very excited about moving to New York.

Our driving rather than flying to our new home allowed more time to prepare for the change and enabled us to see the country and to feel and understand the distance we were moving. We stopped at friends' and relatives' homes along the way, and this added to our feeling of continuity. And when we arrived at our destination we went sightseeing in the places we'd been told about long before.

After the first move, each succeeding one was easier for me, though my sister never grew to enjoy it. Still, moving was never traumatic for either of us because of the way we were prepared for it.

CHIP BLOCK

Have A Backyard Sale

My mom and two other ladies decided to have a backyard sale to get rid of some of our things before we moved. My brother and sister and I and the three sons of one of the other ladies decided to have our own sale at the same time. We sold iced tea and lemonade to the people who came to the yard sale and penny toys and nickel books to their kids. Aaron Melnick and my sister Steffi, who is only five, drank up most of the lemonade and gave away some of our penny toys, but we still made a profit of 49¢ for each of the six of us. My brother and sister and I are saving our money to spend in Canada, where we'll be living for about ten months.

FLIP POSTOL
Kids Magazine

When Your Child's Best Friend Moves Away

It's easy to find books for the child who gives up familiar windows and trees, the mailman, and friends all at once, but the only book we know of that considers the kid who is left be-

hind when her best friend moves is *Janey,* by Charlotte Zolotow, pictures by Ronald Himler (Harper & Row, 1973, $3.95), a slightly too sentimental book, but one that will comfort the loneliness of a child who feels abandoned by a close friend.

ELS

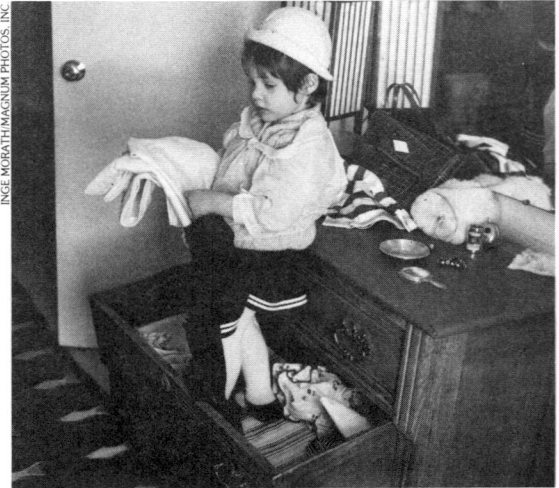

INGE MORATH/MAGNUM PHOTOS, INC.

Moving: A Bedtime Story That Helped

Once upon a time there was a little boy named ____ and he lived with his Mommy in a very nice house. One day his Mommy said, "You know, this house isn't so good for us any more; it's too far away from the place where I work. If we move to a new house that is closer to my office, then our life will be better." And the little boy thought about it and thought about it, but still he wasn't sure he wanted to move out of his house.

Soon they began to pack up all their stuff in boxes, big boxes, small boxes, square boxes, tall boxes. Boxes with tops, boxes from mops. And when they had everything all packed up, the big moving van came and three movers put everything on the truck: the couch, the lamps, the kitchen table, Mommy's bed, the little boy's bed, all the books, a big box full of all the dishes and pots, toys, the rocking horse, Grover, Teddy, Raggedy Andy and Raggedy Ann. Mr. Zebra, Ms. Elephant, all the sweaters and jeans and underwear in the house—everything. Then the truck was packed tight and the movers drove the truck along the big highway to the city and their new house. And that new house was wonderful. It had lots of stairs for climbing up and down, many, many windows for looking out of, and there were at least two fire hydrants on the block, and so on and so on.

And the little boy and his mommy were very, very happy to be in their new place. But they weren't very happy about the big mess of boxes that had to be unpacked. ELS

Mister Rogers to the Rescue

When we moved back from Latin America, my twins were four. One afternoon right after we moved I flipped on *Mister Rogers* and by complete chance he was doing his moving number. He says you can take the crib with you, and he moves the dollhouse crib with the little child, and talks about how it's all right to feel a little strange when you move. The children were so excited by it that they sat down and wrote to Mr. Rogers. A month later they got a typewritten card with his picture on it, saying Dear Charlie and Timmy. He mentioned their sister, and remarked how nice it was to live in a new country, and how lucky they were to have all those other experiences to tell their new friends. It's obviously a PR thing, but it's still marvelous.

GAY LORD

Note: Fred Rogers' Platt and Munk book, *Mister Rogers Talks About . . . ,* contains a simple and straightforward photo story on moving.—Eds.

DEATH

Those people who pretend that the death of a goldfish can teach little children about death are refusing to face reality. The death of a goldfish and the death of a father? Oh, no. That is no equation.

LYNN CAINE

Never Far From Their Minds

In talking to four- and five-year-olds, Stephen Joseph found that "the fear of death was never far from their minds." In his book *Children in Fear,* he states: "They thought that death was a continuation of life, that the dead person was buried 'alive,' and that they 'knew' what it felt like to be locked in a dark coffin with the cold rain dripping in, and the worms eating them."

ELS

I realize now that I have not always given replies to [my daughter's] questions and comments that were appropriate. When she tells me she wishes she were dead, I tell her she will be, sooner or later.

JOSEPH HELLER
Something Happened

What Will Happen to Me If You Die? . . . I'm Going Out to Play Now

Ours is a two-family home. In December 1970 Mark and Joan and their five-year-old daughter Sara lived downstairs, and Terry and I and our two-and-a-half-year-old son David lived upstairs. That December, Joan, thirty-one years old, was diagnosed as having terminal cancer. She died in the hospital in August 1971.

When faced with the situation of when to tell who, what, and how, our guiding principle as individuals and as parents was to be "straight" with the children and with each other. We expressed our feelings and concerns as openly as we could, and when we didn't have answers to questions (e.g., "Why did Joan die and not someone else?") we simply said so.

One day in June 1971, after wondering how to introduce the concept of death to David, I quite spontaneously told him a "cycle of life" story: "In order to grow flowers, seeds are planted in the ground. These become bigger and eventually turn into green plants which produce flowers. After the flowers have made everyone happy for a while, they produce more seeds and then the flowers die. Later the seeds fall on the ground, and with the help of warm sun and rain, they grow into plants and develop more flowers, which produce more seeds which produce more flowers, and on and on life goes.

"The same is true for animals. Kittens and puppies are born and they grow bigger until they become grown-up cats and dogs. Then they have their own kittens and puppies. The mommy and daddy cats and dogs get older and older while their babies get bigger and bigger. Eventually when the grown-up cats and dogs get very, very old, they die, while their kittens and puppies become cats and dogs and have more kittens and puppies. And so around and around life goes.

"The same is true for people. Little babies are born, they grow bigger and bigger and finally they are all grown up. After a while they have their own babies and become mommies and daddies. These babies grow up to be adults and have more babies while the older adults become grandparents. Finally, the very, very old adults die. And so life goes on and on and round and round—babies, children, mommies and daddies, grandparents, old age, death, birth, babies, and so on—like flowers and kittens and puppies.''

David responded enthusiastically to this story and asked to have it repeated for days and weeks on end: ''I like that story, Mommy. Tell it to me again!''

About this time David became involved with both indoor and outdoor gardening and in helping to set up and tend an aquarium. Both activities enabled him to observe the cycle of life firsthand in a way he could easily relate to.

A month later came the question, ''Do people come alive after they're dead?'' ''No,'' I answered, ''people's *bodies* do not come alive again—they can never walk and run and jump and hop again. But they do stay alive in our memories of them—what we did with them, how we loved them, and how they loved us. All these memories become part of us inside our heads, and as long as we're alive we can remember the people we love and care about who have died.''

On several occasions we visited Brooklyn's Greenwood Cemetery. Although I realize many people would hesitate to take a child to a cemetery on an outing, Greenwood is a beautiful environment—rolling hills, planned open spaces, magnificent vistas, all handsomely planted and well maintained. David enjoyed his visits there.

When David was almost three years old, I presented the concept of heaven (complete with angels) to him as a place where some people believe that persons go to stay after they die. Interestingly, he responded with, ''That's a silly idea, Mommy. There is no place out there in space where people go—you bury people in cemeteries and then grass and flowers grow on their graves and make that place more beautiful.'' I did not mention the concept of heaven again, nor did he.

In August, I was Joan's private duty nurse during the last few days of her life in the hospital and was with her when she died. David understood whom I was with and what I was doing, and he talked with Joan on the telephone. He asked her to get well soon and come home because he missed her.

When Mark and I returned home from the hospital after Joan's death, we found both children playing happily together outside. (My husband, Terry, was out of town.) We said we wanted to talk with each of them alone for a while, Mark with Sara and I with David. Since David and I were standing next to the very flowers that had often provoked my telling the ''cycle of life'' story in the past, I asked him if he'

remembered it. He nodded and proceeded to repeat his memory of the story to me. When he finished, I told him that Joan had just died, that he would not see her again, that he would now have to remember her in his head.

Mark, Sara, David, and I all spent the evening together walking around the neighborhood and talking about how sad we felt that Joan had died and how thankful we were that we still had each other to care about and love. For the next few months we lived as an extended family—sharing many meals, leisure activities, long talks, laughter and tears. It was a time of great closeness for all of us.

During this period David questioned incessantly: ''How old are people when they die?'' and ''When will [various grandparents/relatives/friends] die?'' ''Was Joan old?'' and ''If she wasn't old, why did she die?'' ''What is cancer?'' ''Did it hurt?'' ''Did the doctors [the nurses/you] kill her?'' ''I thought people went to hospitals to get well. Why did Joan die in one?''

I answered him as well as I could. I stressed that Joan's dying so young was very, very unusual. I said, ''People who are very sick go to hospitals because the doctors and nurses can take care of them better than at home. Most people do get better and go home. The doctors [the nurses/I] did not kill Joan. We tried to make her better, but her sickness was too strong for anyone or anything to cure. That's why Joan died.''

In January and February David was obviously depressed along with the rest of us in the house. He would lie on the living room rug curled up in the fetal position and suck on a bottle for long periods of time, day after day (only occasionally had he used a bottle as an infant, as he had breast-fed until weaned to a cup). He said he did not want to go to nursery school (though he did go); he did not seem to want to do much of anything.

One day I asked him outright, ''David, why do you suck on your bottle so much?'' to which he replied, ''I want to stay a baby, because if I stay a baby I won't grow up and grow old and die.'' I said I could understand why he thought that way and that none of us *wanted* to die, but that usually only old people die and that a lot of happy and good and fun things happen to people as they grow up.

On another winter day David cried on and off for hours. Finally I took him aside alone, put my arms around him, and asked, ''What is upsetting you so much today?''

''I'm worried about my friends,'' David replied. ''I haven't seen them for a while and I wonder if they're all right.''

Intuition prompted me to ask, "Are you worried about death again?"

Suddenly he turned to me with an expression I'll never forget and said sobbingly, "Yes, I worry about what will happen to me if you die."

I said I knew he would be very sad and upset if I died but that if it happened, his daddy would love him and take care of him and try to help him feel better just like Sara's daddy was taking care of her.

"What would happen to me if Daddy dies?"

"Then I would take care of you."

"What if you *and* Daddy die?"

"Sara's daddy would take care of you and Sara together."

"What if all three of you die together?"

"That's very unlikely—it is just about impossible. There will always be at least one of us, and most likely, all three of us will remain alive and together and able to care for you a long, long time. Joan's dying so young was unusual. It is extremely unlikely that would happen again to any one of us."

As spring came, David's spirits gradually lifted, though it seemed a large portion of his basic concerns were still tied to some aspect of death. Finally I spoke to the school psychologist, who quickly perceived that although death had not been a "hush-hush" subject in our home, it had become a "big deal." She suggested that I cut off lengthy periods of questioning about this subject as I spontaneously did with other topics.

From then on, when I had had enough, I simply began to say so: "We've talked long enough on this subject for now and I need a rest—we can continue talking later on." This new approach worked well. Questions relating to death came up less frequently and were more academic: "What dies first—the heart or the brain?" and "How can too much radiation cause cancer?" Occasionally he still comes out with, "I never want to die. I love life too much," to which I respond that everyone feels the same way.

The unveiling of Joan's gravestone took place in late May with both children present. They spent their time planting flowers and grass seed on the gravesite. It seemed to form a natural continuity for them with the "cycle of life" story.

About a year later, when David was four and a half, he asked me to explain cremation, an idea he had heard about in school. Then he wanted to know if bodies could be frozen, so that if I died, he could still see me. When I told him that this was an expensive and difficult process, he said, "Then I want you to be buried and I want you to have a gravestone with your name on it so I can come and look at it whenever I want to."

"Fine," I responded, "if that's what you want to happen to my body if I die, that's what will happen. I will write it in my will."

While lost in my tearful eyes and I in his, he said, "That's good." Suddenly he jumped off his chair, ran into my arms, and, embracing me tightly, he said, "I love you, Mommy," followed shortly by "I'm going out to play now."

I will never forget that exchange. It seemed to be a kind of resolution of the death crisis for both of us, a way of making peace within ourselves and between us.

SALLY LANGENDOEN

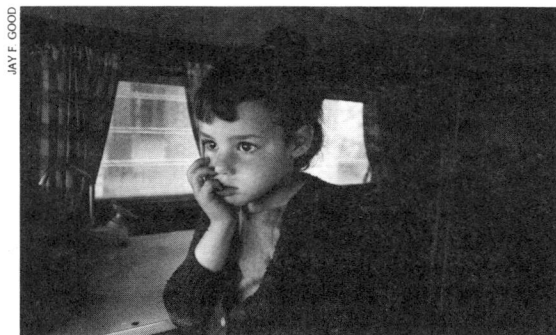

Time and Space to Think

When my child's father died unexpectedly, I decided to wait for a day I could be home with him all day before telling him (which happened to be the day following the funeral). He'd asked in the interim: Where's Daddy? I wasn't ready to tell him—it was so important that it be right. "He's not here," was my answer. And that was okay with him. Frequently Daddy was "not here." (But now I'd get busy after answering, change the subject, avoid telling him more.) It had, as I said, to be right. And it was, three days later. After a lapse that would probably shock the psychologists' books off their shelves, I was ready—and I have never felt more right about anything than about waiting those days. I told him. "Let's talk about what has happened to Daddy," I began.

"What happened? Where did he go?" asked this child barely knowing how to speak in complete sentences.

"Daddy died," I explained. I knew he didn't know what "died" meant. So I clarified: that means we're not going to see him anymore. Not really see him—we can look at his pictures and think about him in our imagination and remember all the happy times we had with him, but he is not coming home.

That served for a couple of days. We carried on the routine as much as possible. I didn't want him to feel that every aspect of his life would be disrupted, for that wasn't so—he would still eat, sleep, play, read with me. I didn't let my friends and family mill around the house. It was business as usual, and besides, I needed time and space to think about the answers to questions that were still to come up. And they did . . .

Concerning euphemisms: To equate death in any way with sleep would be to end all of the ease and pleasure and comfort of sleeping—for my child as well as for me—for all time. He would be afraid to let me sleep and afraid to sleep himself.

To say that death has anything at all to do with "going away" would mean that I would not be able to go away, not feel free to leave the house without causing my child great anxiety. And I would not have wanted to be stuck in my house from that day to this.

Heaven. Heaven becomes, well, more than a religious question. It's a way out. I needed to believe that my husband's spirit would live on somehow and, though I am not particularly religious, I must admit that heaven crossed my mind when I was faced with the question: "But where did Daddy go? I know he died, but where is he?"

A two-year-old kid—he didn't even remember last summer's garden—how can I explain the cycle of life to him so that it makes some sense? I didn't answer the question for ten minutes, needing time to grasp for an answer. Finally I said simply: "Daddy returned to the earth, as all living things eventually do. He's part of the earth now, allowing for new life." I could feel comfortable with that explanation and, for the moment and with a vague understanding, he seemed satisfied (though probably more with my tone than anything else). He didn't know what I meant, really, I am sure (nor did I, really); but his question had been taken seriously and answered and somehow that made it a little better.

A year later, when someone asked him about his father he answered, "My father is dead," and some people looked at this three-year-old kid and could see that he accepted this as a fact of his life. We talk about his father a lot, that is, whenever it comes up: "So-and-so was a good friend of your Daddy's"; "Daddy and I once took you to this restaurant when you were a baby and you spilled a glass of water all over the table and we got all wet."

ELS

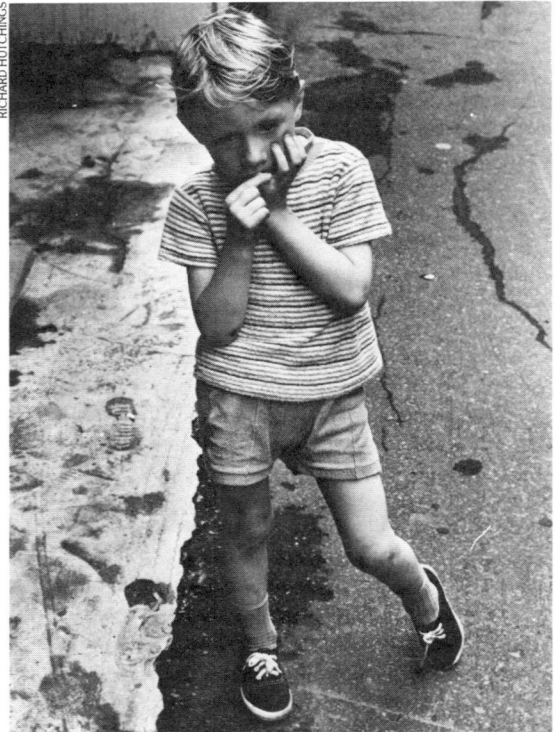

RICHARD HUTCHINGS

Wanting to Be Alone

My brother died in a plane accident when I was twelve. The main thing I remember was the steady stream of people coming to the house. Part of my obligation as a member of the family was to be there, in the living room, which meant I couldn't be alone, which is what I wanted. I can remember sitting at the big round table putting together a huge jigsaw puzzle. It was the only time I ever got involved in a big puzzle like that, I guess because it was the only way I could deal with what was happening around me.

CAROL PULITZER

Should Your Child Go to the Funeral?

Somehow I think it's worse for the children to be left home when everyone else in the family is off to the funeral. Their imaginings of what goes on are bound to be far more frightening than the actual events, and being left out is probably the worst part of it all. Seeing grown-ups crying? Relatives are usually horrified at the idea, but what could be more real and make a child feel more comfortable with his own sadness and confusion?

When his sister died, I asked my son if he

wanted to come say goodbye to her and say a prayer for her. You won't be able to see her, I told him, but we can try to *feel* close with her. No, he didn't want to go, he said. Okay, I said, but at least I'd made him feel that he had as much right as anyone else to be there. And I think he appreciated that.

ELS

Why Were You Smiling When You Came Home?

I didn't tell my children—aged four and six—about my father's death until after I got home from the funeral. They were hurt that I had been away and kept this from them. I could only explain that it would have been too sad to tell them about Grandpa's death without my being there with them. We were all crying together, and four-year-old Matthew asked why I had been smiling when I got off the plane, returning from the funeral. I told him that with all the sadness I felt, I was so glad to see the children, and he accepted this.

BOBBIE MALONE

A Difference in Timing

There is a distinct lack of synchrony between the generations in the rhythms of grief and the other processes of mourning. The latency child, who in the first week after his parent's death can freely bicycle, roller skate, and play ball at a time when his family is shrouded in the blackest grief, may nevertheless be bitterly loyal to the same deceased parent when years later the time comes for remarriage. Beneath the surface, completely out of step with the rest of his family, the child is still mourning. A respect for this difference in timing is the first step in preventing it from becoming an obstacle in family harmony.

GILBERT KLIMAN, M.D.
Psychological Emergencies of Childhood

Grandma Would Have Stayed with You If She Could

When my mother died it left a terrible gap in my children's lives. Wendy, who was eight, understood, but Dari, age three, thought her grandmother was angry at her and that was why she moved away. No one could persuade her to the contrary. After looking in all my child guidance books, I had just about given up. One day I walked in a room and heard Wendy asking her younger sister if she remembered the marionettes on *Mister Rogers*. Dari said she did. "Well," said Wendy, "the same way that the man yanked the puppets up when he was finished and the puppet had no control, that's what God did with Grandma, so Grandma had no choice and would have stayed with you if she could." This is the explanation that finally got through to Dari.

LYNNE BOOKSTEIN

THE BEREAVED CHILD AMONG HIS PEERS

The Burden of Sympathy

[My mother] died of cancer when I was ten, and I still can't talk about it easily. I was in fifth grade at the time, and having a dying mother was, aside from the sadness, an acute embarrassment to me. It sounds strange to say that, I know, but any kid who has been through it at such an age would know what I mean. Or would he? Some kids might enjoy the added attention, I suppose, but it killed me. I had the bad luck to be the only kid in my class, or that I had ever heard of, it seemed, who had had such a thing happen to him, and it was excruciating. I already felt conspicuous because of my deep voice and my shortness and the loathsome fact that I was considered a "brain," and

this added burden of sympathy was just too much.

For me it was doubly hard because, unlike most kids, I couldn't get through the dying part without everybody knowing about it. Because the teachers knew my parents, solicitous inquiries were everywhere, and I remember asking my father what I could possibly say when the junior high kids I met walking home from school asked how she was. The true answer was "She's dying," but this was out of the question. My father suggested "About the same." It usually got the reply "That's good."

DICK CAVETT
Cavett by Dick Cavett
and Christopher Porterfield

Don't Pretend It Didn't Happen

Among the major tragic events which have happened to families in The Cornerstone School was one which was especially unexpected: the death of a child's father six weeks after the beginning of school. The death occurred in a car accident over which the man had no control. Since the community at large was increasingly in possession of this information and it was not privileged, the matter was brought to the attention of each family member of the school. Each mother decided to tell her own child of the death, so that when the children arrived in school the next day they were all informed. The child whose father had died also came to school. There was a good deal of talk about the death between him and the other children with direct questioning as well as play-communication. It seemed that the experience of other children's being frank in their questions about the topic was of some help to the bereaved child.

GILBERT KLIMAN, M.D.
Psychological Emergencies of Childhood

INGE MORATH/MAGNUM PHOTOS, INC.

BOOKS ABOUT DEATH

Some Very Good Books in Which the Plot Involves Death

Picture books enlightening young children about death seem to fall into two categories: death of an animal and death of a grandparent. The animal (usually a pet) death stories are apparently written to prepare children for human deaths. Too often a description of funeral rites attempts to serve as an explanation and no more clarifies the painful reality of losing a loved one (animal or human) than the usual circuitous, evasive mumblings parents have been known to give their children for at least the last couple of generations.

The following books are good and, if possible, the one you choose should be read to your child before he or she has to face the subject in real life.

ELS

FOR YOUNG KIDS

NANA UPSTAIRS AND NANA DOWNSTAIRS, written and illustrated by Tomie de Paola (G. P. Putnam's, 1973, $4.99 hardcover)

This is a wonderful, wonderful picture book about Tommy, who is four, his grandmother, who looks to be in her sixties, and his great-grandmother, who is ninety-four. It is also about showing your love in the ways you are able, about families, about a life style which ignores the generation gap, and about the flow of life and death. Along the way we learn that people who are old are often weak in body, and so need caring for, much as the very young do. Nobody in this book is at an old people's home or golfing at Leisure World. Each generation enriches the other, and each character touches the others.

Tommy's grandparents and great-grandmother live together. He visits them every Sunday. His grandmother is involved in running the house, so she spends a lot of time bustling around the kitchen. Tommy calls her Nana Downstairs. Nana Upstairs, on the other hand, stays in her room, getting out of bed only to sit in her big Morris chair—to which she must be tied so that she won't fall out. Tommy asks to be tied in a chair too. He shares that with Nana Upstairs. There, side by side, they have marvelous chats in which they pretend there are little imaginary figures skittering about. Tommy loves the way Nana Upstairs' silvery hair looks when her daughter (his grandmother) brushes it for her, even though his big brother thinks with her hair down she looks like an old witch.

Nana Upstairs is very, very old, and so she dies. Tommy goes to the house when this happens. He is faced with her empty bed when he races up to the room where he has always found her. His mother says he can be with Nana Upstairs in memory, but he is still lonely for her. One night shortly after her death he sees a falling star from his window, and his mother tells him that that is Nana Upstairs sending him a kiss.

When we were reading this book (the children hearing it had been absolutely held by it) we thought that was where the story would end. How kind and wise it was of the author, though, to give us the fine last page:

A long time later, when Tommy had grown up, Nana Downstairs was old and in bed just like Nana Upstairs. Then she died too.

And one night when he looked out his bedroom window, Tommy saw another star fall gently through the sky.

Now you are both Nana Upstairs, he thought.

JENNIFER CARDEN

MY GRANDSON LEW, by Charlotte Zolotow, illustrated by William Pène du Bois (Harper & Row, 1974, 32 pages, $4.95).

In this sweet story a mother underestimates the memory of her six-year-old son, who, it turns out, recalls very clearly moments he spent with his grandfather, who died when the boy was two. An intimate and moving exchange takes place between mother and son. She sits at the edge of Lew's bed and listens to his recollections: a trip to the museum, his grandfather's smell of powder and tobacco, his "eye-hugs nights like this when I woke up and called." William Pène du Bois's illustrations work perfectly with this simple story about sorrow and the best of warm memories. "I want him to come back . . . and I miss him especially tonight," Lew says. "I do too," says Lew's mother. "But you made him come back for me tonight by telling me what you remember."

ELS

© 1974 BY WILLIAM PÈNE DU BOIS

THE TINY SEED, by Eric Carle (Crowell, 1970, unpaged, $5.95).

This is a beautifully illustrated and poetic story of the changing seasons and the life cycle of a flowering plant.

SALLY LANGENDOEN

THE DEAD BIRD, by Margaret Wise Brown, illustrated by Remy Charlip (Young Scott Books, 1958, unpaged, $3.95).

The simplest of all the picture books concerning to death, *The Dead Bird* could be considered a folk tale. There is no characterization. There are no feelings at all between the children and the bird—who is not a pet, simply a bird they discovered already dead in the woods. But I came back to this book because I thought it a good way to show my child what happens—burial in this case—to a dead thing.

It's everyone's favorite, on every book list. It is, however, a difficult book to read to a child because the illustrations and the passages relating to them appear on different pages. Most pre-readers like to have a picture to look at while the text is being read (and most parents like to have something to read while the child is looking at the pictures).

ELS

THE STORY OF BABAR, *by Jean de Brunhoff (Random House, 1933, 48 pages, $1.95 paperback).*

I used this book as a way to talk with a five-year-old girl whose mother was dying of cancer. The child reacted strongly to the scene where Babar's mother is killed. "What's going to happen to him?" she asked. "Who's going to take care of him now?" Later in the book an elephant dies of mushroom poisoning, with illustrations in green tones. "Do people turn green when they die?" I answered her questions simply and directly and stressed that although Babar obviously felt very sad and lonely when his mother died, he was able to find someone else (the Old Lady in the story) to love him and help him grow up and live a happy life.

SALLY LANGENDOEN

FOR OLDER KIDS

TUCK EVERLASTING, *by Natalie Babbitt (Farrar, Straus & Giroux, 1975, $5.95).*

While other contemporary writers offer ten- to twelve-year-olds super-realistic stories contrived to make a point about death (or some other "harsh reality"), Natalie Babbitt writes of an adventure with eternal life.

Journeying westward in the late eighteenth century, the Tuck family unwittingly drinks from a spring of immortality. Some eighty years later, still unchanged in age and appearance but isolated by their immortality from other human beings, they are discovered by young Winnie Foster. Their brief adventure together—the mortal and the immortal—is not easily forgotten.

RS

ON BEING ADOPTED

Starting at the Beginning

A friend told me that it's a good idea to keep saying the word "adopted" from the very beginning: "When we adopted you . . ." or "Before you were adopted . . ." The word then will not have the weight and mystique it used to bear when an older child would "find out" he was adopted.

ELS

Discussing Origins

I'd always imagined that when it came time to talk to my daughter about her being adopted,

ELISABETH SCHARLATT

we'd sit down at a table, composed, loving, the whole family together, having hot chocolate with fresh whipped cream, a fire blazing in the fireplace, snow on the windowpane. But when she asks questions about her "real" mother, it's always when she's on the john, or I am, or when she's late to bed and I am tired. "I'm your mother!" I end up shouting. "Now go to bed!"

MARY ANN SHORE

And Now We Are a Family: Old-fashioned . . . but Loving

"A man and a woman love each other, and decide they want to live together always—to be married—and they decide they want to share their love with some children . . . Children may be born to them. . . . Do you remember that lady with the big fat belly who smiled at you in the park? . . . I bet she was wishing her baby would grow up to look like you. Other times, a man and woman do not grow their children. They adopt them. . . . Adopting a baby means doing the mothering and fathering for a baby who was born to someone else." So explains Judith C. Meredith in her slim book AND NOW WE ARE A FAMILY *(Beacon Press, $4.95).*

Her attitudes are very traditional, even old-fashioned (she implies that people make babies only when they love each other), but of course the point is to make an adopted child feel good, and Ms. Meredith's descriptions are so loving. "Your first mother and father . . . must have been nice, because you are," she assures the child. She then goes on to give a couple of hypothetical born-out-of-wedlock explanations ("Perhaps [the mother] was very young and

had not even finished school yet. Or perhaps she could not earn the money she would need to take care of her baby . . .").

The book can be very helpful for a parent to read to an adopted child, but you should note that it cannot be applied to single-parent adoptions.

ELS

OTHER WORRIES

Getting Lost

If your kids have a propensity for getting lost: put a whistle around their necks and tell them to blow.

In a crowded place, invest in a helium-filled balloon and tie it to a button.

DOROTHY LOHMAN

◆

My kids were emphatically warned that if they ever got lost, they were to stand absolutely still and I would find them. This really worked one day when my daughter and I were separated on a subway platform. For five of the longest minutes of my life I was afraid she might have gotten on a train hoping to find me, but she remembered not to move, and I found her hidden in a crowd at the end of the platform, crying her eyes out. We grabbed each other and hugged and kissed, and when she saw that I was crying, too, she got so busy comforting me that her own fear was forgotten.

JANET GARI

Negative Energy from Adults: "What Have I Done This Time?"

I've found that the world of most of my kids is filled with so much negative energy imposed from outside sources that they have no choice but to withdraw into themselves and their circle of friends for sanity, safety, and some sense of belonging. Examples come to mind immediately: the shopkeeper who automatically suspects the kids are going to steal; the waitress who automatically assumes the kids are going to make a mess and be a pain in the neck; the dormitory, home, or classroom where, whenever the kid hears an adult call his name, he

recoils, wondering, "What am I going to have to do now?" or "What have I done this time?"

ELIOT WIGGINTON
The Foxfire Book

Hard Questions: There Are No Easy Answers

Parents worry about what to say to a kid when he asks "What does dead mean?" or "What is sex?" or "What does it mean to be free?" The reason parents don't have easy answers to those questions is that they are not easy questions. We don't start suddenly being adults; we work with all those questions all our lives. In a way I think it's dishonest for a parent not to say: "Those are hard questions and people think a long time about them. And what I think right now is this . . . But I'm not always sure." Sometimes kids need absolute answers, and they'll say "But you know, it's really true that . . . Isn't it?" And you can say, "Well, I mostly think that that's true now."

BECKY CORWIN

"She Didn't Want to Go Steady at Ten . . ."

When Renee was ten she had an "intense love affair" with a little boy who kept calling her up and writing her letters and mailing her valentines. What I did was be there if she wanted me and let her handle it. I didn't pry; if she was ready to share something she would. I would call her to the phone and was very careful not to tease her about it, though it was sort of funny. It was hard not to treat it as cute. It was two little human beings trying another kind of relationship, both of them very scared, pretty much like all the singles in the singles bars but without the verbal sophistication to cover their fear a little. Renee decided she wasn't ready and ended up backing off, which upset the young man. She began asking me to say she wasn't home: "Would you please do that for me, Mommy? I really don't want to explain, and I'm really not sure why but . . ." And I did.

Later on she began to articulate that she was frightened, that she didn't know what to do and it was frightening. She really didn't want to go steady at age ten. A child has a right to private emotions, but as a parent you're still there, ready to intervene if that's really needed. And it helps if you're sensitive to what isn't verbalized.

JO BUTLER

HANDICAPPED KIDS

If a language does not have a reasonable word for a situation, it may not be surprising if the society which uses that language has no reasonable place within it for the situation which the word would describe.

The Handicapped Child in America

Some people have trouble communicating with me. They look at me more as the wheelchair, not as the person.

A boy interviewed on an ABC News report.

Kids Are Better Than Adults at Accepting the Disabled

It need not be traumatic for a "normal" child to walk down the street, go to school, to the supermarket, to the movies and see a person in a wheelchair, on crutches, with an artificial limb, a muscular dysfunction, a harelip. When my kid was two he saw, possibly for the first time, a man in a wheelchair being pushed along by a friend. "Look, Mom," my son called out, "a big man in a stroller."

The man laughed and so did I. "No, that's called a wheelchair—it's for people who have something wrong with their legs and can't walk," I told him. "This man's friend is taking him out to see the sights, just the way you and I go out."

"Oh," said my kid, and went on playing.

The man smiled at me.

Some time later when his grandmother broke her hip and was in a wheelchair for a time, my son was totally sympathetic—fetched things for her, helped her align her leg supports, talked about the things she was unable to do but which he hoped she would be able to do when she got better. He assumed that a physical abnormality didn't mean that its victim was abnormal; it was just someone in a wheelchair.

Perhaps if our environment were more suited to the needs of disabled people—if elevator buttons were set low and doors widened to accommodate people in wheelchairs (Columbia University, I've read, has done this in one of its buildings, along with installing Braille numerals on the elevator buttons and flashing light alarm systems for the deaf), if ramps were installed in public buildings and at street crossings, if our culture would face the fact that there are lots of people with physical handicaps—our children might have a better perspective of the real world. If able-bodied children went to camp and school with disabled kids, perhaps they would learn a little better how to consider the needs of others. (Of course, many, indeed very many, disabled children need special equipment and trained personnel, but some can manage very well with ordinary facilities.)

If you're the parent of a handicapped child, you would do everyone a service to include your child in the activities that "normal" kids participate in. A friend of mine sent both his kids, children with normal hearing, to a nursery school for the deaf "because it was in the neighborhood" and there was a better teacher–student ratio than at other nearby schools. He felt that everyone benefited from that choice.

Except for those people who still believe that everyone should look and think alike, most of us could learn to accept a hooked hand as readily as we do braces on the teeth or eyeglasses. Kids are better able to do this than adults—at least until we teach them otherwise. One recent summer at the beach, there was a boy with a brace from his foot up to his hip. My nephew was playing with him, and told me, "Patrick can't run as fast as we can, so we'll just hang around here and play with our trucks."

ELS

Does Anyone Have the Right to Suggest That My Child Be Quarantined?

Knowing that I have a child who had been diagnosed as "mildly autistic," the editor of this book asked me if I would ever send him to a camp for autistic children.

What she was really asking was if I believed in isolating abnormality for its own benefit and for the benefit of the rest of society. I had answered that question the day of the diagnosis, when the psychologist said that although she was optimistic, if the problem degenerated I might have to consider institutionalizing my four-year-old son.

That night I swore to myself I would never pluck my boy out of the real world and put him where he could only conclude that he himself was unreal. I foresaw myself in a poor room, cooking on a hot plate for a sad but still defiant old man and his dear, defective, fully grown son. Everyone else had abandoned us. It seemed that some undefinable "they" were waiting for one of us to die so the survivor could be put away for his own good. One thing was certain: together we had the strength and will to resist the world.

There are circumstances under which I don't think I would have reacted with such a terrible vision. If my son were radically autistic, if he rocked and stared and walled out all but the eerie objects of his obsessions, then I would have wanted him to be where he had the best if not the only chance to laugh and learn and re-develop more normally. Or if his problem were physical, if he could not stand or eat or sleep, if his limbs were so crippled or his brain so inhu-man, then, yes, please, put him where it will be easiest to find a little peace.

But what if the symptoms are not so extreme? What if there are signs both good and bad in the child's development? What if one minute he's babbling baby talk, but the next minute he's reading three grades above his level? What if he can't put together a simple jig-saw puzzle, but he can tie his own shoelaces?

Does anyone have the right to suggest that my child be quarantined? Do the parents of his playmates and the teachers at his school and the other children in his life and even his own parents have the right to be annoyed or af-fronted or embarrassed or intolerant? Is that why there are special camps and special classes and special counselors and special medicines and special institutions—to preserve everyone else's sanity? To assure some imaginary synco-pation by which everyone crawls together and walks together and talks and prints and adds and works and marries and bears more children who do exactly the same?

When I think of my son going to school I think of my own school days: the classmates who were smarter than me and dumber than me; those who could mix easily and those who were tragically shy; kids who stuttered or limped or sometimes wet their pants; others whose mother's or father's premature death left them confused or whose deprived environment left them stigmatized. Two of the best and brightest grew up to have breakdowns which wasted their lives. So many of the ones the best and brightest had to wait for grew up to inherit the world.

I don't want my son in a special place where he will learn to live with his problem. I want him to detest his problem. To spite it like a wild ge-nius. Beethoven was deaf. Milton was blind. Einstein had a maturational lag. Alexander the Great was epileptic.

My answer ends as it began—with another diagnosis. They decided to test my son because sometimes he was disruptive in public kinder-garten. The implication was that maybe every-one would be better off if he attended a special school. But the results of all the testing—the IQ tests, the learning tests, the neurological tests, the psychiatric tests, the psychological tests—in-dicated that he should stay. That perhaps he may need special help, but that he should go on to regular first grade. And a sad but defiant old man rejoiced.

ALAN SAPERSTEIN

Introducing Eighth-Graders to "People Who Are Different"

Emily Perl Kingsley and Ellen Genauer, two Westchester County, New York, women whose young sons were both born with Down's syn-drome, have made it a practice to visit junior high school classes with their sons, Jason and Jared, to contribute to twelve- and thirteen-year-olds' understanding of retardation. Fol-lowing is Emily Kingsley's account of Ms. Genauer's and her procedure:

When we arrive, Ellen and I sit in front of a large room in which the students sit around on chairs or on the floor. We put the two babies on the floor and let them roam around. Jason starts by toddling around the room waving hello to everybody. Jared does not walk yet, but he waves and smiles and is held and cuddled and played with by the students on the floor as we talk.

We begin by explaining some of the technical terms—we define retardation and Down's syndrome and explain how it happens and what the implica-tions are in terms of physical and mental develop-ment. Before long we are talking about our feelings—the feelings we had at the time the babies were born, the shock, the disappointment, and then the process of adjustment. Then we talk about the commitment to work with our kids, the classes, the exercises, the homework, the stimulation programs, and parents' groups. And we talk about the enor-mous joys and rewards we've had.

The students are penetrating in their questions. How do siblings react? What about having more chil-dren? What about the future? Will they work? Will they marry? We talk about amniocentesis. We talk about financial burdens. We talk about expectations and about the fact that we really don't know what to expect.

I am so gratified to think that the young people we have talked to may go into their adulthood with a more accurate, more open, and more compassionate understanding of what mental retardation is all about; that the archaic stereotypes still present in our society may not take hold in these boys and girls just starting out; and that they may go on to influence other peo-ple whom they come in contact with.

YOU AND YOUR SPECIAL CHILD: THINGS YOU SHOULD KNOW

A Parent's Checklist on the Diagnosis of Learning Disabilities

Do begin by discussing your concerns with your child's physician and determine what you hope to accomplish by the diagnosis.

Do insist on a complete multi-disciplinary diagnosis. This could include, in addition to a pediatric examination, a neurological examination, a battery of psychological tests, a psychiatric examination, a language evaluation, and an educational diagnosis. (One or more of these tests might be omitted upon the discretion of the coordinating specialist with the agreement of the parent.)

Do insist that someone be responsible for coordinating the diagnosis because this will save you considerable time and effort. This can be done by any one of the specialists involved, but it is always best . . . to work with that individual with whom you have the best relationship.

Do be aware of the fact that no one person or no one discipline alone can make a complete diagnosis of learning disabilities since there are too many factors which must be taken into consideration.

Do have the final results of the diagnosis sent to your child's physician or clinic as well as to your child's teacher. Discuss the findings with them, because the more you know about your child, the more he can be helped.

Do be prepared to spend several months before you are through. Assess your budget before you start and try to get the best and the most for your money. Contact your Association for Children with Learning Disabilities and ask for information about diagnostic programs.

Don't stop in mid-diagnosis if one of the specialists tells you he has discovered your child's problem . . . only a complete diagnosis will tell the whole story.

Don't be afraid to disagree. The best specialists occasionally make mistakes, and even diagnostic teams sometimes show their bias. A professional opinion is just that—an opinion. You can always ask for a second opinion if you have doubts.

Don't be afraid to ask questions if there are things you don't understand. That is part of the service you are paying for, whether out of pocket or as a taxpayer.

Don't get discouraged. Your child can be helped, but you must first determine the problem before the remedy can be prescribed.

Association for Children with Learning Disabilities
Northern Virginia Newsletter

Learn Your Legal Rights

Learn your legal rights so that you don't get pushed around. You have options—still not enough of them, but there are facilities and services which are required by law to help you, which will be improved only as you use them and make demands of them. Item: a new education law mandates a free and appropriate education for all handicapped children (and legally empowers the parent to be involved in deciding what is appropriate). Item: a law in Massachusetts extends special parking privileges to handicapped persons whose cars have an HP license plate. (The parent or guardian may be entitled to the special plate if the car is registered in the name of the child.) Item: a law in Connecticut specifies that the local board of education must provide special education for preschool-age handicapped children, identified as those whose educational potential would be diminished without special education; but the Connecticut law does not require local school systems to search out such children. Parents must bring the children to the school's attention.

Legal Resources for Handicapped Children

The National Center for Law and the Handicapped, organized to promote the legal rights of handicapped persons, publishes a free bimonthly newsletter, AMICUS. Write to them at 1235 North Eddy Street, South Bend, Ind. 46617.

LEGAL CHANGES FOR THE HANDICAPPED THROUGH LITIGATION, edited by Alan Abeson is a useful booklet that identifies steps and defines terms in the litigation process. It's $3.75 from the Council for Exceptional Children's State-Federal Information Clearinghouse, 1920 Association Drive, Reston, Va. 22091.

ALLAN SHEDLIN, JR.

INFORMATION BY COMPUTER

Parents suspecting their child may suffer from learning disabilities can receive immediate assistance from the New Jersey Association for Children with Learning Disabilities. In less than an hour information will be gathered by a computer-based retrieval system developed at the Massachusetts Institute of Technology. Information will include where to locate evaluation centers, professionals specializing in the treatment of the handicap, and so on. The retrieval system is currently in operation for states from Maine to Virginia. Does it sound like a good idea for your state? Write to the New Jersey Association for Children with Learning Disabilities, Box 249, Convent Station, New Jersey 07961

Based on information in
Teaching Exceptional Children

Facts You Should Know About Tax Deductions for Your Handicapped Child

FEDERAL INCOME TAX DEDUCTIONS

There are two major types of deductions that apply to families of the handicapped: (1) medical expenses; (2) dependent care.

MEDICAL DEDUCTIONS

Medical expenses may be claimed for the taxpayer, spouse (on a joint return) and dependents to the extent that these expenses exceed 3% of the taxpayer's adjusted gross income. Expenses that have been compensated by insurance *may not* be deducted. Besides hospital costs, doctors' bills and prescription drugs, many other items qualify as "medical expenses." *Almost anything that helps a handicapped person to function better may be deducted, such as:*

Eyeglasses
Elastic stockings
Cost of maintaining a seeing-eye dog
Hearing aid
Special foods prescribed by a doctor for treatment of disease
Capital expenditures made for medical reasons
Oxygen equipment
Mechanical lifts, ramps or elevators
Special plumbing fixtures
School guide for a blind child

Other items that qualify as medical deductions include:

Medicine and drugs. Actual costs of medicine and drugs may be deducted, whether or not a prescription is required, to the extent that they exceed 1% of the taxpayer's adjusted gross income.

Food and lodging. Food and lodging costs included in a hospital bill are deductible. Food and beverages prescribed by a doctor as a supplement to a normal diet, and extra charges by restaurants to prepare required special diets, are deductible.

Insurance. One-half of all medical insurance premiums may be deducted, subject to the 3% rule. This includes premiums for hospitalization, accidents, disability, physicians' care and general health insurance, and supplementary health insurance premiums under Medicare. If a taxpayer contributes to an employee group medical plan, the amount paid for this insurance is also deductible. (The company bookkeeper keeps records on the amount each employee contributes for medical insurance.) The remaining one-half of those premiums paid specifically for medical *care* insurance may be added to other medical expenses and deducted, subject to the 3% rule.

Special aids. Special aids are deductible if they assist in the education of a handicapped person, such as: tape recorders, special typewriters, projection lamps to enlarge reading material, etc. Almost anything will qualify, provided the item helps to alleviate a physical or mental handicap. (For example, elevators for heart patients, air conditioning for asthma cases, etc.)

Transportation. Transportation "primarily for and essential to medical care" is deductible.

Commuting costs, even for a disabled person, are *not* deductible. Taxpayers may itemize transportation expenses or estimate costs using a standard mileage rate determined by IRS. Parking fees and tolls are deductible as separate items. Some examples of allowable expenses are:

> Travel expenses of a parent who accompanies a minor child to medical care.
> Taxi fares incurred in traveling to and from a doctor's or dentist's office, or a hospital or clinic.
> Visits of parents to their handicapped child in an institution or residential care facility, if the visits are considered by a doctor as part of the child's therapy.

Moving expenses. Moving expenses may be deductible if the move is made to a different climate to alleviate an illness.

Special schools. Although ordinary education is not medical care, the costs of attending a special school for the mentally or physically handicapped may be deductible. The taxpayer must show that the student is enrolled at the school *primarily* to help the student's handicap.

Costs of care and supervision, treatment or training of a handicapped person at an institution or sheltered workshop are also deductible.

A recent Revenue Ruling (75-303) allowed parents of a handicapped child to deduct advance payments made to a private institution for future care of their child. The parents entered into a contract with an institution specializing in the care and custody of the handicapped to insure that their handicapped child will receive proper care after their death, or at such time as they are unable to care for her. The institution required advance payments, no portion of which is refundable. The Internal Revenue Service allowed deduction of the payments as medical expenses.*

Medical expense checklist. The following items may qualify as medical expenses:

> Automobile hand controls
> Ambulance hire
> Artificial teeth
> Artificial limbs
> Braces
> Crutches
> Cost of operations
> Dental fees
> Dentures
> Diagnostic fees
> Drugs and medical supplies (which exceed 1% of adjusted gross income)

* "Federal Agency Rulings," *The United States Law Week,* Washington, D.C., August 5, 1975, p. 44, LW 2060.

> Eyeglasses (including examination fee)
> Hearing devices
> Hospital bills
> Lab fees
> Medical insurance
> Membership fees in associations furnishing medical services, hospitalization, clinical care
> Nurses' fees (including nurses' room, board and Social Security taxes)
> Obstetrical expenses
> Physician fees
> Psychiatrist fees
> Seeing-eye dog and its maintenance
> Special instruction or training
> Surgical fees
> Therapy treatments
> Transportation to obtain medical service
> Wheelchair
> X-rays

DEPENDENT CARE

The cost of hiring a person to care for a dependent may be deductible. The following criteria must be met:

- The person must be hired primarily to enable the taxpayer to work outside the home.
- The dependent must be either under 15 years of age or physically or mentally disabled.
- If the dependent is the taxpayer's spouse, he or she must be physically or mentally incapable of caring for himself or herself.
- The person hired *may not be* a relative of the taxpayer or his or her spouse.
- The deduction must be taken as an "itemized deduction" on Schedule A.
- *The deduction is not available if the taxpayer takes the standard deduction.*
- The deduction is available both to single and married persons.

Married persons taking this deduction must file a joint return or both must be gainfully employed or actively seeking fulltime employment, unless one spouse is disabled.

Child-care deductions may be claimed for services outside the home (i.e., at a day care center or preschool). Check with IRS for amount of deduction allowed.

FEDERAL INCOME TAX EXCLUSIONS

Certain amounts of money received by the taxpayer may be excluded from gross income.

Typical exclusions included:

- Damages received for personal injuries or sickness. It doesn't matter whether the amounts were paid as a result of a lawsuit or by agreement.
- Amounts received through accident or health insurance policies or a life insurance policy which paid disability payments. (Note: If an employer paid part of the policy's cost, the exclusion is reduced by the same percentage paid by the employer.)
- Amounts paid through accident or health insurance to reimburse the taxpayer for medical care expenses. It does not matter whether or not an employer paid for part of the plan. These expenses can be for the employee, his or her spouse, or dependents. (Note: These expenses paid by a health or accident plan *cannot* also be claimed as a medical expense deduction, since the taxpayer suffered no loss in meeting these expenses.)
- Amounts received under an employee's accident or health plan, if they are in payment for:
  Permanent loss of a part of the body
  Permanent loss of use of a bodily function
  Permanent disfigurement

Payments can be for injuries to the employee, his or her spouse, or dependents. But they must be paid because of the *nature* of this injury and not because of how long the employee is absent from work.

FILLING OUT FORMS

Where to get forms. Federal tax forms are available at local Internal Revenue Service (IRS) offices, post offices and at many banks and savings and loan offices. Additionally, some tax guide books contain copies of more commonly used forms. Taxpayers may use facsimiles if forms are not readily available.

Taxpayer assistance. The IRS will answer questions regarding individual tax situations. The IRS Department of Taxpayer Assistance and Information provides:

- *Telephone service.* The IRS will answer simple questions over the phone. It may be necessary, where figures or other specific information is involved, to use the Walk-In Service. Questions requiring study or research are usually referred to an agent, who will then relay the information back to the taxpayer.
- *Walk-in service.* The IRS will help taxpayers fill out federal income tax forms. Visit the local IRS office and *be sure to take all necessary papers, receipts, cancelled checks, forms, etc.*
- *Retroactive claims.* Persons who are eligible for any of the deductions in this section and who have not filed for them in previous years may file an amended return, retroactive for the past three years. The return must be filed before April 15 of each year, to allow for previous 3 years deductions.
- *Private tax firms.* For complex tax situations, taxpayers may obtain the assistance of any number of accounting or specialized tax firms. Be sure to check out the firm's reputation and *ask in advance* about the fees they charge.

[This guide was based on a section of *Rights Handbook for Ohio's Physically Handicapped,* Ohio Easter Seal Society for Crippled Children and Adults, Inc., 5 North Broadleigh Road, Columbus, Ohio 43209, October 1975. It is reprinted here by permission of *Closer Look,* a project of the U.S. Department of Health, Education and Welfare, Office of Education, Bureau of Education for the Handicapped.]

A TV EXPERIMENT: *SESAME STREET* FOR EXCEPTIONAL CHILDREN

Greg and Laura are partners for Bert and Ernie in a game of balloon volleyball on *Sesame Street*—as part of an experimental program created to reach mentally retarded kids. The special segments are broadcast during the first twenty minutes of each Wednesday *Sesame Street* program (in a few areas, this schedule may be different). Many of the activities in the special programming are modeled after the "Families Play to Grow" activities of the Joseph P. Kennedy, Jr. Foundation.

© CHILDREN'S TELEVISION WORKSHOP
© MUPPETS, INC.

KIDS WHO ARE BLIND

You'd Never Believe Joe Is Legally Blind

The remarkable thing about Joe is that he is legally blind. He is a tiny little pale thing with a shock of black hair which sticks out every which way, but because he is the son of working-class country folk he has never been treated as disabled. He's just gone on to regular school, makes good grades, is a testy fighter and aggressive as hell. He'll have a corneal transplant this summer (they had to wait until he was twelve to do it), and that will make it possible for him to see more than the gray shadows he sees now. But he does have the ability and desire to be a writer and the aggression to be a hard-news man. You would howl if you could see him at school. He plays baseball—bats, catches, runs—does everything the others do.

He told the coach that he can't play ball next year because of the operation in the summer but would sure try out for the team the following year.

When I write on the blackboard, he comes right up, cups his hand around his eye, squints the other shut, and reads what is written on the board. To read a book, he cups his hand over the eye and puts the book practically on his nose, then reads fast as a whip. He told me last week he was into his fourth library book for the week.

The doctor says that Joe sees only a small tunnel of light with no peripheral vision at all but that the corneal transplant, if it works, will improve his vision at least to the point that he can wear glasses or contacts and lead a normal life. Frankly, he leads the most normal life I've ever seen for a kid with a serious disability.

LINDA WEST ECKHARDT

Braille Playing Cards and Watches with Raised Dots . . .

You'll find Braille playing cards ($2.60), wood chess sets with raised and lowered squares ($16.95), watches with raised dots, and more in the *Aids and Appliances* catalogue for the blind and visually impaired. It's available from the American Foundation for the Blind, 15 West 16th Street, New York, N.Y. 10011.

Talking Books

I wonder what percentage of eligible people know that the Division for the Blind and Physically Handicapped of the Library of Congress (1291 Taylor Street, N.W., Washington, D.C. 20542) offers a free library service (including delivery and return delivery) of talking books and magazines, talking-book machines (specially designed phonographs), and attachments for the machines such as remote control and speed control devices and headphones. Eligible persons include anyone (child or adult) who cannot see (or see well enough to read a book), who cannot hold a book (loss of hand or use of hand, or physical weakness), or who has a visual or perceptual disorder that prevents the reading of print. Write to the above address for a list of regional libraries in your state and for application information. Other sources:

NATIONAL ASSOCIATION FOR THE BLIND, 200 Ivy Street, Brookline, Mass. 02146.

RECORDING FOR THE BLIND, 216 East 58th Street, New York, N.Y. 10022.

ALLAN SHEDLIN, JR.

Expectations

EXPECTATIONS, *an annual anthology of stories, poems, and prose in Braille, edited by Betty Kalagian (Braille Institute of America, 741 North Vermont Avenue, Los Angeles, Calif. 90029.) Available free to legally blind children. Funded by private donations.*

Many blind children in the eight-to-twelve age group look forward each year to this anthology of children's literature from the Braille Institute of America. . . . [Recent editions of the book contain] a variety of quality stories and poems along with embossed pictures and even scratch-and-sniff stickers that produce odors of ginger-snaps, peach, paint, sage and chocolate.

The editors have understood the supreme importance of providing blind children with the opportunity to make direct contact with the literature available to their sighted companions. Although willing readers are a great and necessary help, sightless children need the experience, early in life, of private and direct access to the stories, poems and games children enjoy. This lessens the sense of dependence on others that can be one of the crippling effects of blindness.

JOHN HOWARD GRIFFIN
New York Times Book Review

Large Print Editions

A number of publishers offer large-print editions. To check the availability of any title, ask your librarian for *Large Type Books in Print* (available for $12.50 from R. R. Bowker, 1180 Avenue of the Americas, New York, N.Y. 10036).

RS

Seeing What the Blind "See"

HOW CAN I MAKE WHAT I CANNOT SEE, *by Shiro Fukurai, (Van Nostrand Rein-* hold, 1974, $5.95 hardcover), is a little book that can help you "see" the art of blind children. It is an amazing documentary of a Japanese teacher who really wants to understand what blind children can create.

Instead of training the children to make things that a sighted person can easily identify, Mr. Fukurai trains his children to record the world as they perceive it. The result is a completely different kind of art, created from the perspective of touch and sound.

The book contains photographs, drawings, personal accounts. If a member of your family is blind, it will provide you with another way of seeing what that person experiences. If you are interested in creativity, the book will point you to another direction to explore.

BERNIE DE KOVEN

THE HEARING-IMPAIRED

The Word "Deaf": Be Careful How You Use It

Very few people of any age who have major hearing losses are totally deaf. All but a very small percentage have the ability to hear some sound, if it is sufficiently loud to begin with or is properly amplified by a hearing aid. Many are able to comprehend speech when they hear the sound and simultaneously watch the speaker's lips, facial expressions, and gestures. For practical purposes, they need not be called deaf.

In addition, labeling someone as deaf may actually make him functionally deaf, even if his hearing loss is only moderate. This is particularly true for a child. If people do not speak to him, do not expose him continuously to language and ideas, do not secure auditory training, a hearing aid, and special educational opportunities, and do not expect him to succeed socially, intellectually, and eventually vocationally, he may in fact become deaf for practical purposes.

SAMUEL MOFFAT
Helping the Child Who Cannot Hear

Teaching Kids Who Can't Hear: Don't Let Them Fool You

About ten years ago I was teaching science to deaf children. For the first month, I told them the important things that I had been taught in school: "Light travels in a straight line," "Ontogeny recapitulates phylogeny," and other such gems. They smiled and nodded, smiled and nodded. I had been informed by the head of the School for the Deaf that my students could read lips; all I had to do was speak slowly: "ontogeny recapitulates phylogeny." I spent that month telling the kids all about science, and telling my wife how easy it was to teach deaf children.

And then I gave my first and last exam. It was a disaster. They had learned nothing. In the years they'd been going to school the kids had discovered how to make it appear that they understood. They knew no science. What they knew was how to make me feel good, how not to hurt my feelings. Even at the expense of their own feelings about themselves, they were working together with me to play out the charade of "school."

The solution for my class of deaf children—as in every class of any kind I've taught since then—was a workshop-classroom. Ten kids and I filled up a tiny room with raw materials of all kinds: hammers, nails, scissors, glue, wood, paper, gels, animals. The important thing was that all the materials could be *handled* by the kids. Once the environment started to get concrete, once there were tools like a binocular dissecting microscope, the kids reached out to one another or to me for help and instruction. And the responsibility of learning moved from me to them to a cooperative relationship.

Probably the most important lesson I learned that year was supplied by our mother guinea pig. The kids adored her. She was absolutely the best teacher in the school as far as some of the kids were concerned. One afternoon she gave a lesson on childbearing, which held the kids entranced from three o'clock to six at night. Then the pups were born, eyes open, quickly nursing. Some time later the mother got ill, a tumor on her neck, and I didn't know what to do. It was a $2 guinea pig. I wasn't really prepared in my head to take her to the vet. The kids put my coat on, handed me the guinea pig, pulled me out the door. There was no hesitation there, their instincts were much better than mine. The vet operated, removed the tumor,

and two days later gave us back the pig; and two days after she returned, as per the vet's instructions, the kids removed the sutures. She went on to produce many more litters, and I think her great-grandchildren are still at the Lexington School for the Deaf.

The kids' involvement with the creatures in our room led to their writing books on fish and crystal growing and other things. Reflecting on how terribly important reading and writing are in most schools today, I think deaf children only highlight something about the nature of learning in human beings (and particularly children, deaf or hearing): that if they're allowed to get involved in physical and natural reality, then they will reach for books, then they will create the written material.

ALLAN LEITMAN

© CHILDREN'S TELEVISION WORKSHOP

Signing: For the Hearing as Well as the Deaf

HANDTALK is a dictionary of finger spelling and sign language by Remy Charlip, Mary Beth, and George Ancona (Parents' Magazine Press, 42 pages, $5.95 hardcover). It's an activity book that was conceived as much for hearing people as for deaf people, and kids seem to love it, intrigued as they are by secret codes. Black-and-white close-up photographs demonstrate finger spelling (in which each word is spelled out letter by letter using the fingers of one hand); color photographs dramatize signing (creating a picture with one or two hands to convey an entire word or idea).

Before you go out and buy this book for a child whose hearing is impaired, you should consider that the child's education might be de-emphasizing signing and finger spelling in an attempt to encourage "total communication," that is, speech as well as "handtalk." But for the hearing child, this book may be the beginning of communication with people who are different from themselves.

RS

Two Helpful Organizations

THE ALEXANDER GRAHAM BELL ASSOCIATION FOR THE DEAF, INC. (3417 Volta Place N.W., Washington, D.C. 20007), operates a parents' information service and a book lending library.

THE JOHN TRACY CLINIC (806 West Adams Boulevard, Los Angeles, Calif. 90007) is an education center for pre-school hearing-handicapped children and their parents. Its free *Correspondence Course for Parents of Preschool Deaf Children* is a valuable aid.

The data on the Bell Association and the Tracy Clinic was garnered from *Helping the Child Who Cannot Hear,* by Samuel Moffat (Public Affairs Pamphlet No. 479, 381 Park Avenue South, New York, N.Y. 10016, 50 cents). Very informative and concise, Mr. Moffat's pamphlet includes a lucid outline of the total communications (oral vs. hand language) controversy.

RS

[You'll find more information on organizations that may prove helpful to the hearing-impaired, as well as data on educational facilities and materials for the learning-disabled, in the Directory which follows.]

FREE HEARING AIDS

Kids who need but cannot afford hearing aids can get them free. For information, write to the National Hearing Aid Society, 20361 Middlebelt Road, Livonia, Mich. 48152.

SPECIAL CHILDREN: A DIRECTORY

Organizations

Possibly the most practical advice for parents of handicapped children is available, free, from CLOSER LOOK, the National Information Center for the Handicapped, Box 1492, Washington, D.C. 20013. If you need help for a child or youth with a mental, physical, or emotional handicap, write CLOSER LOOK (including such information as the child's age and disability—if it's been diagnosed). They'll respond with information on your legal rights, about how to arrange for appropriate services, and about groups you can work with "to eliminate barriers and open new opportunities." And you'll also receive a free subscription to their newsletter.

Most of the organizations listed below have local chapters. There you can often find other parents with whom to share information and your frustration (also anger and guilt).

GENERAL

ASSOCIATION FOR CHILDREN WITH LEARNING DISABILITIES (ACLD), 4156 Library Road, Pittsburgh, Pa. 15236. Primarily for parents, "a non-profit organization whose purpose is to advance the education and general well-being of children with normal or potentially normal or above average intelligence who have learning disabilities arising from perceptual, conceptual, or subtle coordinative problems, sometimes accompanied by behavior difficulties." Activities vary from state to state, but active chapters have monthly meetings and worthwhile newsletters, as well as occasional workshops.

BUREAU OF EDUCATION FOR THE HANDICAPPED, 400 Sixth Street S.W., Room 4030, Washington, D.C. 20202. ·

THE COUNCIL FOR EXCEPTIONAL CHILDREN (CEC), 1920 Association Drive, Reston, Va. 22091. A professional organization, but as a clearinghouse of educational materials of great interest to parents as well. Local chapter meetings are usually of value. Several publications are available free to CEC members.

THE FOUNDATION FOR EXCEPTIONAL CHILDREN, 1920 Association Drive, Reston, Va. 22091. Formed to advance the education of handicapped and gifted children. Federal law requires that one-third of the foundation's funds each fiscal year must come from the public.

NATIONAL ASSOCIATION FOR MENTAL HEALTH, INC., 1800 North Kent Street, Arlington, Va. 22209.

NATIONAL ASSOCIATION FOR RETARDED CITIZENS, P.O. Box 6109, Arlington, Texas 76011.

NATIONAL ASSOCIATION OF STATE DIRECTORS OF SPECIAL EDUCATION, INC., 1201 Sixteenth Street N.W., Suite 610 E, Washington, D.C. 20036. A nonprofit organization whose goal is to provide an appropriate educational program for every handicapped child.

THE NATIONAL EASTER SEAL SOCIETY FOR CRIPPLED CHILDREN AND ADULTS, 2023 West Ogden Avenue, Chicago, Ill. 60612.

NATIONAL FOUNDATION—MARCH OF DIMES, 622 Third Avenue, New York, N.Y. 10017.

STATE DEPARTMENTS OF SPECIAL EDUCATION.

AUTISM

INSTITUTE FOR CHILD BEHAVIOR, 4758 Edgeware Road, San Diego, Calif. 92116. Concerned mainly with autism.

NATIONAL SOCIETY FOR AUTISTIC CHILDREN, 169 Tampa Avenue, Albany, N.Y. 12208. An organization of parents, professionals, and other interested citizens working together to effect programs

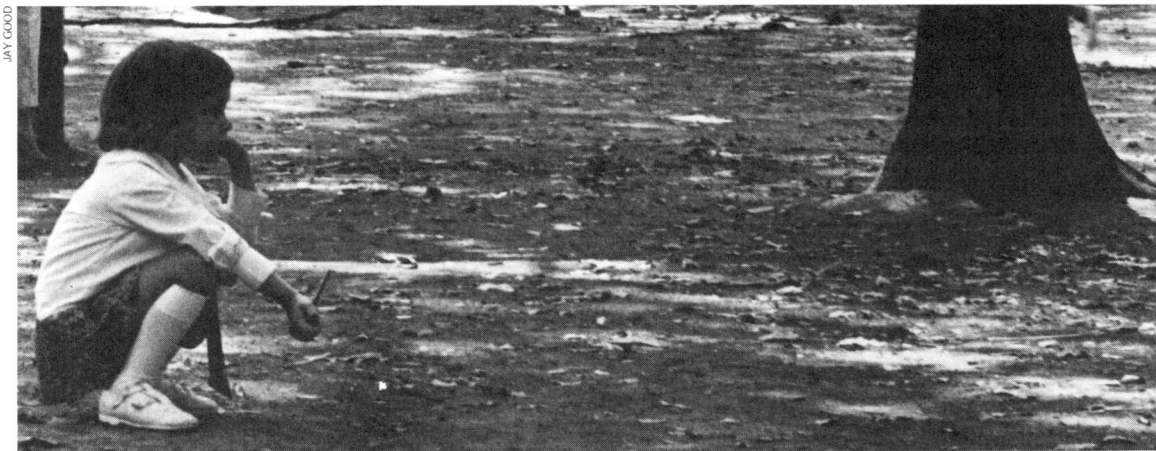

JAY GOOD

of legislation, education, and research for the benefit of all mentally ill children.

CEREBRAL PALSY

UNITED CEREBRAL PALSY ASSOCIATIONS, INC., 66 E. 34th Street, New York, N.Y. 10016. Local affiliates' services provided to children and adults with cerebral palsy and their families include medical diagnosis, evaluation and treatment, special education, and parent counseling.

DEAFNESS, SPEECH DEFECTS

THE ALEXANDER GRAHAM BELL ASSOCIATION FOR THE DEAF, 3417 Volta Place N.W., Washington, D.C. 20007.

AMERICAN SPEECH AND HEARING ASSOCIATION, 10801 Rockville Pike, Rockville, Md. 20852.

NATIONAL ASSOCIATION OF THE DEAF, 814 Thayer Avenue, Silver Spring, Md. 20910.

NATIONAL ASSOCIATION FOR HEARING AND SPEECH ACTION, 814 Thayer Avenue, Silver Spring, Md. 20910.

DIABETES

AMERICAN DIABETES ASSOCIATION, 600 Fifth Avenue, New York, N.Y. 10020

EPILEPSY

EPILEPSY FOUNDATION OF AMERICA, 1828 L Street, N.W., Suite 406, Washington, D.C. 20036. Nonprofit agency founded in 1967, with over 150 local chapters and affiliates.

MUSCULAR DYSTROPHY

MUSCULAR DYSTROPHY ASSOCIATION, INC. 810 Seventh Avenue, New York, N.Y. 10019

ALLAN SHEDLIN, JR.

[The local chapters of many of the organizations listed above should also help you seek out information on nearby special education facilities. —Eds.]

Source Books

The following directories should prove useful in researching both public and private special education facilities. The contents tend to be information supplied by the facilities listed, so you'll have to do your own evaluating.

ANNUAL DIRECTORY OF FACILITIES FOR THE LEARNING DISABLED AND CATALOGUE OF TESTS, published annually by Academic Therapy Publications, Inc., 1539 Fourth Street, San Rafael, Calif. 94901, free. Names and addresses of facilities (schools, clinics, camps—pre-school through adult), listed by state.

DIRECTORY FOR EXCEPTIONAL CHILDREN, (1,300 pages, $25 plus $1 postage and handling), from Porter Sargent Publisher, 11 Beacon Street, Boston, Mass. 02108. Descriptions of over four thousand treatment facilities and schools (public and private, residential and day) classified according to the special problems with which they deal. Updated every four years.

DIRECTORY OF THE NATIONAL ASSOCIATION OF PRIVATE SCHOOLS FOR EXCEPTIONAL CHILDREN (NAPSEC), free, updated annually. Published by NAPSEC, 130 East Orange Avenue, Lake Wales, Fla. 33853. This is a listing of members of this nonprofit organization "dedicated to establishing guidelines and maintaining standards for providing quality services for exceptional children."

DIRECTORY OF U.S. FACILITIES AND PROGRAMS FOR CHILDREN WITH SEVERE MENTAL ILLNESSES. Send $5 check or money order to Supt. of Documents, U.S. Gov't. Printing Office, Public Documents Department, Washington, D.C. 20402. Request number DHEW (ADM 77-47) 017-024-00689-1.

ALLAN SHEDLIN, JR.

[Also most helpful is Appendix II of Louise Clarke's *Can't Read, Can't Write, Can't Talk Too Good Either* (Penguin Books, 1975, $2.75). It provides detailed data, on a state-by-state basis, concerning "schools, public and private; clinicians, referral centers and sources of information."—CBC]

◆

Summer Camps and Recreational Programs for the Handicapped

The following directories of summer camps and programs are descriptive, not evaluative. The information included in them is supplied by the camps themselves.

CAMP PROGRAMS FOR AUTISTIC CHILDREN, available from the National Information and Referral Service for the National Society for Autistic Children, 306 Thirty-first Street, Huntington, W.Va. 25702. Revised annually.

A DIRECTORY OF SUMMER CAMPS FOR CHILDREN WITH LEARNING DISABILITIES, $1.25 plus 30¢ postage from the Association for Children with Learning Disabilities, 4156 Library Road, Pittsburgh, Pa. 15234. Lists summer programs, not only camps, by state (averaging two or three per state) with a brief description of each program.

THE EASTER SEAL DIRECTORY OF RESIDENT CAMPS FOR PERSONS WITH SPECIAL HEALTH NEEDS ($2 plus $1 postage and handling), from the National Easter Seal Society for Crippled Children and Adults, 2023 W. Ogden Avenue, Chicago, Ill. 60612. Camps are listed by state, by disability group served, and alphabetically.

SCOUT PROGRAMS FOR THE HANDICAPPED, Educational Relationships Service, Boy Scouts of America, North Brunswick, N.J. 08902. Some of the Scout literature (including *Boy's Life* magazine) is available in Braille; some of it on cassettes, tape, and large print as well.   ALLAN SHEDLIN, JR.

"ON HORSEBACK, EVERYBODY'S EQUAL"

You may be interested in the program sponsored by North American Riding for the Handicapped Association, Inc., Mrs. Lida McCowan, President, Cheff Center for the Handicapped, Box 171, Augusta, Mich. 49012. There are over thirty local programs registered with the NARHA working to encourage handicapped people to ride horses.

Several deaf and cerebral palsied kids enrolled in a riding program at Borderland Farms, Warwick, N.Y., exclaimed, "On horseback, everybody's equal," and "You don't trip and stumble." As one of the adult instructors said, it gives them "a certain amount of independence otherwise missing in their lives."   RS

Catalogues Offering Special Educational Materials

CHILDREN'S BOOK AND MUSIC CENTER CATALOGUE, 5373 W. Pico Boulevard, Los Angeles, Calif. 90019. The table of contents is good in that it differentiates between records "made especially for exceptional children," and those which are made for the general public but are also suited to the exceptional child. The catalogue also includes books, instruments, phonographs, etc., $1.

CHILDCRAFT EDUCATION CORP., 20 Kilmer Road, Edison, N.J. 08817. This general catalogue offers a large section of items with special educational uses. Some materials are cheaper elsewhere.

CONSTRUCTIVE PLAYTHINGS, 1040 E. 85th Street, Kansas City, Mo. 64131. In addition to being a comprehensive general catalogue of useful educational materials, it also features an interesting special education section.

CREATIVE PUBLICATIONS, P.O. Box 10328, Palo Alto, Calif. 94303. An interesting catalogue of manipulative math materials, books, and puzzles.

CUISENAIRE COMPANY OF AMERICA, INC., 12 Church Street, New Rochelle, N.Y. 10805. This catalogue lists some excellent manipulative aids and enrichment materials for effective mathematics teaching. It also includes a variety of math games and puzzles, reference books and texts, and other interesting materials. They are not cheap.

DEVELOPMENTAL LEARNING MATERIALS (DLM), 7440 Natchez Avenue, Niles, Ill. 60648. Offers well-made and professionally designed materials, often accompanied by manuals of suggested uses. Many of the items are produced by other companies also, but it's nice to have so many of them together. There is a section of materials for Spanish-speaking children, though it is less creative than the rest. Delivery of items is sometimes delayed.

IDEAL SPECIAL EDUCATION CATALOGUE, Ideal School Supply Co., Oaklawn, Ill. 60453. Not as comprehensive as the DLM catalogue, but a broader distributorship.

NOVO EDUCATIONAL TOY AND EQUIPMENT CORP., 11 Park Place, New York, N.Y. 10007. An extremely comprehensive catalogue but tough to sort through in terms of finding items specifically intended for special educational use. [Novo's prices are good; a spot check with Childcraft showed Novo selling items in the $4 to $15 range for a dollar less. Novo's isn't a fancy catalogue: you do some work, you save some money. —Eds.]

J. A. PRESTON CORPORATION SPECIAL EDUCATION CATALOGUE, 71 Fifth Avenue, New York, N.Y. 10003. A comprehensive selection of materials, well laid out according to primary use.

RECREATION EQUIPMENT FOR THE DISABLED, from North American Recreation Convertibles, Inc., P.O. Box 758, Bridgeport, Conn. 06601.
                                    ALLAN SHEDLIN, JR.

A Self-fulfilling Prophecy?

Kids don't feel weird or different or even deprived until we tell them they are. Grown-ups and other kids are probably responsible for the shame that handicapped kids develop about a "problem" they would otherwise likely take for granted and learn to live with. ELS

SCHOOLS AND LEARNING, OR, HOW TO EDUCATE YOUR KIDS

School is not a preparation for life; it is life. —JOHN DEWEY

I never let my schooling interfere with my education.

MARK TWAIN

The Given, the Questions

Given:
—That kids do need to learn A-B-C, 1-2-3.
—That kids don't need to rush into learning A-B-C, 1-2-3.
—That *most* kids, when left alone, will learn to read and write and count eventually if they need to, and if people around them are doing those things.
—That we all want our kids to be happy, fulfilled (and, maybe, go to college).
—That alternate education is, really, a class issue.
—That freedom for the children is not a bad thing, as long as they're learning. Nor are structure and discipline bad for the children.
—That the parent is the ultimate teacher.
—That the parent is not necessarily the best teacher.

So how do you educate your kid? There is so much written on every aspect of education and on every possible solution to every problem that it is near impossible to sort it all out. No responsible educator will tell you what's good or right, and few will even tell you the real differences between open and free and structured and nontraditional schools. It's all rather a mystery, especially since so many of the books seem to be saying the same things in different ways, or else they're making opposite points with strikingly similar explanations.

How many of the books do you want to plow through? Dennison's *The Lives of Children* is wonderful, moving. Kohl's *36 Children* is a learning experience, exciting. Holt's *Escape from Childhood* will raise your consciousness. *Summerhill* might open your eyes. Herndon will stir you. Ashton-Warner is exhilarating, revelatory. Ivan Illich will inspire you.

But how do you focus on the "problem," assuming there is one? The books do not always address your particular concern or the problems in your community. Must you change the school? Or is it enough simply to teach your child that the school is not the only place to learn?

ELS

CONSIDER THE ALTERNATIVES

A Dictionary of Terms

The School Book (Delacorte, 1973, $7.95 hardcover, Dell, 1975, $3.25 paperback) is packed with information that we think would be useful to parents. The authors, Neil Postman and Charles Weingartner, finally set us straight on school issues, although not without bias (as the title of their earlier book, *Teaching As a Subversive Activity* would imply). The information is general; there aren't any real live children in actual schools confronting real live teachers. But there is a useful dictionary of the terms thrown about, often incorrectly, in contemporary school talk, a clarification of who's who in education, and a valuable resource list—books, films, magazines, and games—"for people interested in improving what happens to kids (and teachers) in school."

We see no reason to redo what they've done so well. The following is a sample:

ALTERNATIVE SCHOOL

This widely used term has several distinct meanings. . . . In general, an alternative school is one whose conventions are entirely different from those we associate with most public schools. An alternative school may be private or public. It may be Summerhillian or not. It may be good or bad. What makes it an "alternative" is that it offers an arrangement for learning that is in sharp contrast to what is offered in the "regular" school. Harlem Prep is one of the best known, and best, alternative schools in the country. Summerhill, in Leiston, England, is probably the best known alternative school in the world.

CHILD-CENTERED CURRICULUM

The phrase is intended to communicate the simple

and irreproachable idea that what you do in school ought to grow mostly out of the needs and interests of children. The problem is that some people have difficulty locating the line that separates responding to the needs of children from being destructively indulgent toward them. . . . More than a few promising progressive schools have been ruined by the assumption that children can thrive in an environment in which they are treated exactly as adults. The effect of this is to deprive them of their childhood, which is the reverse of responding to their needs. . . . Curiously, the worst traditional schools and the worst progressive schools exhibit the same fatal tendency: dealing with children not as they are, but as someone wishes them to be.

COMMUNITY CONTROL

When segregationist southerners want to keep black children out of white schools, they holler, "Community control!"

When stylish northern liberals want to keep black children out of white schools, they holler, "Community control!"

When despairing militant blacks want to keep white teachers and administrators out of *their* schools, they also holler, "Community control!"

Obviously, community control is one of the most flexible terms we have in the language of school politics. What it means depends on how you feel. . . . Most people favor the idea that whenever possible (assuming, for example, there is no conflict with state and federal laws), school policy should be formulated by the people who are directly served by the school. But that's just the beginning of the problem. Who *is* "the community"? . . . The truth is that every community is dozens of communities, and the only way to resolve who should control what is through the ballot.

COOPERATIVE SCHOOL

In the best populist tradition, parents who disapprove of available public schools, and particularly of elementary schools, are increasingly starting their own schools. Such schools are called cooperatives. Parents rent space for the school, administer it, finance it, clean it, and even teach in it. In this way, they believe they can get exactly the kind of school they want. But the price is high—in time, energy, and money. As a consequence, the life span of most cooperatives is short.

DIDACTIC TEACHING

This is a technical-sounding term for a situation that is perfectly familiar to almost everybody: a classroom in which the teacher is at the front of the room telling students, straight out, what he thinks they ought to know. The teacher may ask few questions or many, but they are usually of the "What Am I Thinking?" variety; that is, the student is expected to give an an-

swer that the teacher has previously determined is "right."

FREE SCHOOLS

The "free" refers to the atmosphere, not the tuition. In fact, free schools are essentially private schools, but with this difference: the people who start and run them generally reject the entire gamut of traditional school conventions. This includes the grades, the lectures, the tests, the competition, the courses, and especially the authoritarianism. As a consequence, in many free schools, the children have as much to say about what happens as the adults, which has the effect, sometimes, of helping the children to grow up— and sometimes of making the adults more childlike.

MONTESSORI METHOD

The Montessori Method refers to a series of techniques developed by Maria Montessori. The aim of the method is to help children develop what she called their mental, spiritual, and physical personalities. Originally designed to be used with what we currently call "disadvantaged children" (Montessori called them "deficient children"), the techniques require careful teacher observation of the child and carefully kept records of his or her physical growth, motor skills, and cognitive development.

The physical environment in which learning takes place is an integral part of the Montessori Method, and the setting is supposed to include an open-air playground with enough space for gardening, as well as for active play. The classroom itself should contain movable furniture and equipment especially chosen to stimulate sensory experience. Through such arrangements, children are encouraged to learn self-discipline in their movements, and to observe the things in nature that surround them.

. . . On the one hand, the Montessori Method stresses what she called "the prepared environment." That is, the teacher controls the learning experience by carefully designing what the environment will contain. The teacher also has a well-formulated idea of how sensory experience helps to build intelligence, and of what the stages of cognitive growth are. In this sense, then, the Montessori Method *is* well organized with clear objectives. On the other hand, Montessori also insisted that teachers not correct a child unless asked to, and, in general, be "invisible" as much as possible. She even urged teachers (if you can believe it) to animate the classroom by their *silence*. In short, she wanted her method to represent "freedom in a prepared environment." In this sense, the Montessori Method is informal, and not dominated by a lot of teacher talk and direction.

OPEN CLASSROOM

This implies that the activities of students will, to a large extent, be determined by *their* interests and needs, not the convenience or predisposition of the teacher. Since one obvious need of young children is for mobility, the open classroom tries to provide ample freedom of movement. But the "openness" of the open classroom is not mainly physical. Children also need to communicate with each other, to ask their own questions, to seek answers in their own ways, and to pursue individual interests. All of this, the open classroom tries to do. If this sounds to you like warmed-up progressive education, you're right.

SCHOOL WITHIN A SCHOOL (MINI-SCHOOL)

Another form of alternative school produced largely by the search for relevance that characterized the schools in the 1960s is the "school within a school." What distinguishes SWAS from most other forms of alternative school is the fact that it has occurred mostly within the public school system. . . .

IVAN ILLICH

. . . Illich believes that a good educational system should provide anyone who wants to learn anything with an opportunity to do so, by making resources and people easily available. Such a system would not exclude anyone, for example, by demanding diplomas, certificates, records, or anything else. Nor would it force anyone to submit to an obligatory curriculum. Naturally, Illich believes that a school system such as we have in the United States, and which most countries in the world have copied, does not qualify as a decent educational system. . . . As an alternative, Illich proposes a network of resources that would bring together things, people with special skills, other learners, and even educators. Some critics of Illich have remarked that his network sounds an awful lot like a "school." But Illich denies this and promises something close to paradise if his ideas were seriously and carefully implemented. Many of these ideas are expressed in detail in his book *De-Schooling Society* (1970).

A. S. NEILL

If there were an All-Star team of great and influential school critics, A. S. Neill would certainly be on it. He is, of course, the founder of Summerhill, probably the best-known foreign free school in the world. Summerhill was started in 1921 in the small, wool-producing village of Leiston, England. From the outset, Neill tried to make Summerhill a noncoercive, nonrepressive educational experience for children from ages five through fifteen.

Neill believes that children are basically both good and wise, and that a school, therefore, should fit the child, rather than bend him to fit the school. As a consequence, at Summerhill, courses are optional, tests and grades are not given, university preparation is disdained, teachers and students transact freely and equally, and the entire school—teachers and students alike—participate in self-government.

JEAN PIAGET

. . . [Piaget's] main interest has been in the cognitive development of children—that is, how they develop powers of perceiving, remembering, recognizing, generalizing—in a word, thinking. He insists that all children go through certain stages of intellectual development *in the same order,* the difference between a bright child and a dull one being that the former passes through these states more quickly than the latter. . . . He is both skeptical about and amused at educators' attempts, especially in America, to speed up cognitive development. (He calls that problem "the American question.") He has been sending out warnings for years that parents and teachers should not trifle with nature by trying to force children to learn things they are not ready to learn. For example, Piaget believes that reading instruction should probably not begin until the age of eight or nine for most children.

Another Alternative: Jail

If kids in America do not go to school, they can be put in jail . . . If their parents do not see that they go to school, the parents may be judged unfit and the kids go to jail.

You go to jail. All of the talk about *motivation* or *inspiring* kids to learn or *innovative* courses which are *relevant* is horseshit. It is horseshit because there is no way to know if students really are interested or not. No matter how bad the school is, it is better than jail. Everyone knows that, and the school knows it especially. A teacher comes into the teachers' room and says happily, I had the greatest lesson today! and goes on to tell the other envious teachers what it was that they hadn't thought of themselves and says, The kids were all so excited! It

is horseshit. The teacher has forgotten (as I forget) that the kids have to be there or they will go to jail.

JAMES HERNDON
How to Survive in Your Native Land

◆

Taking Your Kid Out of School

Phyllis and I, both one-time teachers, became so disillusioned with public schools that we just *had* to withdraw our two boys at the end of their fourth and sixth grade years and oversee their education ourselves. . . . I'd like to [report] how we're doing.

First, who does the teaching? Frankly, we don't have much teaching. We believe that children learn best what they want to learn when they want to learn it. Too often adults actually get in the way of learning. Taken to its infinite end, one could wonder whether schools with all those instructional hours don't sometimes hinder learning.

So we sit back and let our older son Kevin read. For six months he read almost nothing but books and articles about astronomy. For awhile he got hooked on the American Revolution after seeing the play *1776*; then he got back into the A's again with astrology, architecture, and archaeology. They're not subjects ordinarily offered in grade school, but who are we to dictate a child's interests? Our youngest child, Clifford, who is no reader, is always taking engines apart or building something or fixing a leaking radiator in my car. Is this learning? Why not? Since he has more "personality" than almost anyone you'll meet, we recently were gratified to learn from the Christopher Jencks study that personality (along with luck and graded performance) had much to do with success in life.

Our own children seem to learn without that omnipresent teacher. Probably Professor Louis Agassiz demonstrated this in the way he taught his student Nathaniel Shaler; he had poor Shaler spend over a hundred hours examining a fish without telling him anything about the fish. He wanted Shaler to learn *for himself*. In the same way, we feel the most important thing is for a child to learn *how to learn*. The trouble with school is that too much is "taught." Too often a teacher is positioned between a child and the material, blocking natural access to that material.

Curriculum: The word is anathema to us. If we laid out a course of study for our sons, they'd surely feel they were back in school again with those narrow subject areas of history, English, geography, and math. Sometimes I get the idea that the mere defining of a subject is the first step toward robbing it of its mystique. When Kevin is reading about some archaeological discovery in Mexico, he isn't consciously thinking, "Now this is archaeology." In the truest sense, subjects all fuse with one another. Once Kevin became absorbed in Transcendental Meditation (and took a college credit course in it at Queens University in Kingston, Ontario), he began to delve into psychology, religions other than Christianity, the culture of India, mysticism, even elementary Sanskrit—all sorts of things, almost none of them offered in school. Who are we to fence in his learning with narrow subject areas of math, history, English, and civics? All right, so far as American history goes, he knows nothing whatever about corrup-

tion in the Harding administration, probably doesn't even know a man named Harding was ever President. But I'll bet he knows more about the American Revolution than anyone on our block. Is this bad?

And if you tell me he isn't becoming well-rounded, I will show you most of his school contemporaries . . . who know *nothing* of architecture, archaeology, astronomy . . . to say nothing of zen, penology, psychology—well-rounded *indeed!*

Social Life: It's the same as before: Kevin, our introspective reader, is still a loner without friends as he was throughout the first six grades. Clifford, our gregarious one, has dozens of friends *of all ages* just as *he* always did. We don't try to change either one and admire Kevin's self-sufficiency. In general we feel American schools are too obsessed with "interpersonal relationships" and thus give the "loner" a complex. By the way, either boy may return to school anytime he wants. So far, no takers.

Physical Education: They exercise as they used to—i.e., one boy is very athletic, the other somewhat sedentary. Both have ten-speed bicycles and do a lot of cycling. Our so-called non-athletic one has lately been entering 18-mile bicycle races and spends time "training." Both take swimming lessons to perfect their crawl strokes. Clifford is an ardent bowler. Both ski. By the way, not *one* of these sports was offered in school where the concentration was on sports requiring large groups.

Compromises: Kevin does take a course in guitar and an adult education course in touch typing.

Classrooms: Who needs a room with thirty desks facing north and one desk facing south? Take away all that glass and brick and learning is likely to take place anywhere. Since our boys left school, we spent six months in Mexico. I'm not going to make big claims our children learned sociology and geography out in the field, but I do hereby solemnly attest that Clifford picked up elementary but fluent Spanish, and nobody set out to teach him a single word of the language. Incidentally, he was the only one among us who could understand rapid Spanish spoken to us, and often translated before the rest of us could say *despacio, por favor.*

Diplomas, Certificates, Regent Exams, Report Cards, College Boards: We have successfully weaned our children away from all these tons of paper. When we feel they've "finished high school," we'll get our friend Kari, an artist, to make them up diplomas with more scrolls, ribbons, and fancy printing than anything the high school offers. A college admission director has already told us (at a cocktail party, not in his office) that a home-educated applicant would be most appealing—what a challenge to track him along all those traditional high schoolers with their grade-point averages! This admissions director told us Kevin's application would undoubtedly stand out among many others as rather intriguing—it would be hard to turn down flat.

Legally: Although we both feel that our state's compulsory school laws are unconstitutional and were once prepared to stand on these grounds as long as the money held out, we reached an accommodation four years ago with the city school system. Our attorney found a provision of the state's education laws pertaining to the education of a child at home. Granted the provision was undoubtedly drafted for the infirm who couldn't make it daily to a classroom, but still this section of the law happened to be marvelously applicable to our situation, for it allowed at-home education provided that the instruction offered was substantially parallel and equivalent to that provided in the schools.

Once we'd dug this provision out and shown it to the school authorities, they began to be more reasonable. Also I spent a weekend writing for them in term-paper length our philosophy of education and how we'd expect to proceed once our children were weaned from those brick school buildings. In good term-paper fashion, we listed the writers who had influenced us—Holt, Kozol, Leonard, et al. Finally the school "authorities" mellowed and eventually agreed to let us try to provide this "alternate and equivalent education" ourselves rather than continue with their legal harassment which had already caused them to give us an enroll-or-else-go-to-court ultimatum.

At first, regarding our venture as a sort of experiment, they appointed a go-between, a school system staffer with a doctorate in education. He was charged with getting us off to a good start. Fortunately he seemed surprisingly sympathetic to our ideas and immediately understood when he handed over to us a bunch of dull textbooks that we really weren't going to use them; he seemed to sense that we felt schools emphasized the printed word too much and that traditional textbook-learning was something we wanted to get away from. In the four years since we had this first meeting with our "go-between," we have left each other alone. Once he hinted that we really ought to keep some kind of record or documentation of what we were doing—"just in case," but nei-

ther he nor the system has bothered us. In turn, we have borrowed through him such things as a microscope, but have had no long dialogues. In a word, I guess he has confidence in us and feels we are making it all right.

ARTHUR S. HARRIS, JR.
Will It Grow in a Classroom?

If Kids Learn What They Want to When They Want to and How They Want to, When and How Are They Going to Learn What They May Not Want to But Will Need Later On in Life?

Most progressive or innovative schools strive to encourage the child's imagination to flourish. Since imagination is essentially undisciplined, educators who favor such schools seem to have concluded that whatever might stifle imagination is wrong. In other words, all formality—required courses, tests, compositions, grades, attendance—is destructive. But the problem, if my premise is correct, is that imagination is finally meaningless, even to the imaginer, if it is not given some form. And the more faithfully the imagination is translated into form, the more it expresses. Whether that expression is for the sake of the person who imagines something or for the benefit of others who might see or hear or touch or sense it, that expression is the end, the fulfillment of what is imagined.

Even if one assumes the extreme—that children possess total understanding and feeling, and that growing up limits or destroys their profundity—one must concede that children also lack the physical and mental dexterity to give objective form to their ideas that will have meaning for others. (Spontaneity may be wonderful, but often it doesn't do anyone any good except the person who expresses spontaneously.) After all, the child is not alone but usually wants desperately to communicate the feeling that overtakes her or him to others—both other children and adults. And, above all, the growing human wants to develop, to express herself or himself more and more fully. To do that, one must refine one's thoughts and feelings by getting rid of the extraneous and adding what has been left out. I see no way of doing this—whether the imagination takes the form of art, of science, of physical construction, of language—without the most intense kind of discipline.

One cannot write a coherent collection of

good sentences to express a thought unless one has a pretty good grasp of grammar (which is not simply the logical construction of a sentence but an attempt to translate speech into an understandable form), unless one appreciates the generally imprecise meaning of words and learns by endless trial and error to find the combinations of words that will finally convey the right meaning, and unless one develops the feeling for rhythm and balance that transmit the songs that are in all of us and that make language most compelling. And one cannot paint a picture, make a piece of sculpture, design a building, teach a class, or run a business until one has understood, studied, and experimented with the endless possibilities that are inherent in it. There are no shortcuts—even for geniuses, who work harder at what they do than anyone.

Apart from the question of imagination, most undisciplined schools are designed to let children determine for themselves what they are interested in and want to know more about. This approach seems to me to ignore the fact that most kids are prone to cling to what is familiar. They fear the unknown, and are often seized by unwarranted fear of something they do not understand at once. While they may be put off a given subject for life if they are *forced* to learn about it—as in a regular kind of school—that is usually the fault of the way it is taught rather than the subject being taught. I went to a college where the entire curriculum was the same and mandatory for all students—no electives at all, and about 60 percent of the four years was devoted to science. To my surprise, I found that some of the subjects I had been worst at and feared most—geometry, for instance—were subjects that I became best at. In the end, those four years proved to be the most interesting of my life.

If the purpose of education is, among other things, to give everyone a chance in life—to develop, to express, to go on learning, to earn a living—how can any education fulfill that purpose if those who go through it are not exposed to *all* kinds of studies? How can children be exposed to the breadth of the possible and demanding world that lies before them if they are not made to experiment? I wonder whether the system that supposedly frees children doesn't actually imprison them.   RICHARD HARRIS

◆

"But There Will Still Be Winter"

What does the school hate so much about this word "authority"? I don't mind authority myself when I know it is informed and fair. I miss very much a headmaster at school to go to for directions, someone accomplished in the mechanics and nuances of running a school, knowing the techniques in a classroom also, the interplay among teachers. I look for all this every day. As it happens, Life is authority, the headmaster of a global school. I found that out as early as my teens . . . if not earlier. Life says, "Obey my laws or perish." He says, "Take what you want from me but pay for it." He pronounces, "Now there will be winter."

No, no, I don't want winter!

But there will still be winter. The seasons are part of my rhythm.

Who are you to impose your seasons on me!

Save your breath, mortal, and I'll save mine. It's below zero today so put on warm clothes.

No, no, I dowanna!

Then perish, wretch.

SYLVIA ASHTON-WARNER
Spearpoint: Teacher in America

CHOOSING A SCHOOL

I think the only hope a parent has in making a valid judgment about a school is to observe in as many classrooms as possible in each school, making a body-count of good teachers versus bad; then send the child to a school where the percentages are in his favor, no matter what the educational philosophy.   ANNE NAVASKY

Picking The Right School: A Checklist

Don't concentrate all of your observations on the teacher. Look at the youngsters while the teacher is performing and also look at the environment, the walls and the floors. Here is a checklist:

(1) Do the kids look happy or oppressed or bored?

(2) Is there a physical restlessness present? What is the movement in the room like? Does the teacher always have to give permission for the slightest variation in routine?

(3) Do the kids ever talk to each other casually and not only when instructed to do so?

(4) Do the kids care about the classroom, or do they throw their trash on the floor?

(5) Are the bulletin boards barren? Are they a wreck with stuff torn down and scribbled on? Are they neat but completely managed by the teacher and filled with commercially produced material? Or is there a sense that the students have participated in dressing the room and that they care about it? Is the room a static environment? When do you feel it was last decorated or the bulletin boards changed?

(6) Does the teacher seem tired? Or excited about the subject being taught? Does the teacher seem to know the kids as individuals, or does he or she treat them as objects to be moved around and controlled with the least effort? Is there a sense that the teacher and the kids are comfortable with each other?

(7) Do you hear any laughter? Teacher or kids? Cynical or mocking or joyous?

(8) Does anyone stop to talk to you? Do the kids have an opportunity to express curiosity?

(9) Would you like to spend several hours a day in that environment? Would you like to see that teacher every day for a year? Would you be interested in hearing what that person has to say about your child?

(10) Are the materials and books available to the kids? Or are they under lock and key and carefully doled out? Does the environment seem stingy? Do the materials seem used? Abused? Cared for?

(11) Do the kids have to ask for permission to leave the room, and is the only permissible reason to leave the need to go to the toilet? Are there kids constantly trying to escape?

(12) What does the teacher's desk look like? Is it a private and sacred place for the teacher? Is it neat, or messy, or barren, or cluttered with kids' work?

(13) Do the kids have access to the teacher in a private way? Can they get up and go to the desk and ask a question? Do they shout out questions? Or do they keep their mouths shut?

(14) What is the nature of competition in the room? Do the kids try to help each other, or are they driven to be competitive and selfish with their work and their knowledge? What is the nature of praise and blame in the classroom? What behavior is rewarded and what punished?

(15) How does the teacher punish? Does he or she shout, scream, hit, sulk, insult, cajole, or use grades punitively, or threaten to send for parents or administrators? Does the teacher seem at ease with the kids so that discipline is not a problem, or are the reins held tight so that threats and admonitions are always in the background?

After a few visits one can get a reasonably accurate impression of the quality of life in a classroom, can tell whether it is interesting and attractive to young people, or whether it is stifling, boring, or oppressive. It is always good to explore a few classrooms in the same school to see whether there is a general tone in the school or whether there is a wide variation of style. This will tell a great deal about the administrators in the school and their relationship to the teachers. It is important to figure out whether the principal, for example, tries to impose his style on the school or whether he lets things happen; whether he supports all of his teachers, or whether he likes only the docile ones.

It is useful to know these things about a school before your child attends, and picking the right teacher can avoid a considerable amount of anguish during your child's school career. Further, if you ever have to battle the school, the information provided by the checklist can be used to create a document describing what you find good or impossible about the teacher you are supporting or trying to eliminate.   HERBERT KOHL

How Do You Spot a Good Teacher?

Private schools with fancy philosophies can have lousy teachers. And public schools can have good teachers. Before you decide to send your child to a particular school, you should spend as much time in as many classrooms as possible. That is your right.

So how do you find or spot a good teacher? I visited two first-grade classrooms in the same school, and the difference became clear.

At the front of one room stands Mrs. G., reading from a book. The children's desks are arranged in modular units, not in the old formal row after row. At each unit there are four or five children, seated looking at the same book as Mrs. G. I wonder why some of the children are sitting with their backs to the front of the room and not all seated sideways so that everyone can see the teacher easily.

"Now, children, on this page we must find all the objects which are grouped in threes. Does everyone see them? Circle them with your pencil."

I notice that one little boy has not even bothered to pick up his pencil. I also see that the girl sitting in front of me has not circled the right number of objects.

Mrs. G. does not seem to have noticed these things. She goes on. "Now on the next page we have to circle all the objects in fours. Does everyone see that?"

As the lesson ends Mrs. G. says, "Now, children, I want you to hand in your homework from last night. Amanda, will you collect all the homework. Silently. I want you to do this silently. Steven, put your hands on your desk. And do not talk."

"My homework is in my desk."

"Quiet. You can get it out when Amanda comes to your place. Now who does not have the homework? Carol, you will pass out the cookies to all those who have done their homework."

After spending some time in this room I realize that there does not seem to be excitement or smiles or interest on the faces of the children. Instead their faces show sullenness and fear, and when I look at Mrs. G., she too looks sullen. And a little bored.

I moved to Mrs. S.'s room. The desks again are arranged in modular form. But the children are sitting sideways to the front of the room. They all can see Mrs. S. simply by moving their heads slightly. She is reading the same lesson as Mrs. G.

"Children, we must circle the figures which are grouped by threes. Billy, what animal are they in the first column?"

"Ahhh, elephants."

"Right. Did everyone else get that?" Mrs. S. begins to walk slowly around the room, looking over the shoulder of each student as she passes. "Now which fruit is it for the next column? Colette?"

"The oranges?"

"Correct." She continues her stroll around the room. She bends over a young boy to point something out. She touches his back gently while she is talking to him.

"Now we must go on to the fours."

When she is finished with the lesson she says, "Will everyone take out the homework from last night. I'll be around to collect it." She goes over to one little boy who clearly does not have his homework. "Eddie, is there any reason why you haven't brought in your homework?"

"I didn't do it, Mrs. S."

"Eddie, you know if you do not bring in any tomorrow I will have to send a note home to your mother."

"Yes, Mrs. S."

"All right. Mary, will you go up to my desk and get the cookies. And pass them out to everyone. Only two to each person today. You may talk but stay at your desks while Mary passes out the cookies."

ALLAN LENZNER

[*You-Can't-Win Department:* The only problem with all this is that you audit Mr. Jones's class and it's wonderful, and your child ends up in the school with Ms. Smith for a teacher and she stinks.—ELS]

What I Look For

What I first look for in a school . . . are two things. To begin with, a head or a principal who sees teachers as well as children as quite disparate individuals, and who therefore does not try to lock both groups into a predetermined catechism of what "education" ought to be. I would not and do not send my children to schools where memorization and the acquiring of test-taking skills are confused with learning how to learn. But on the other hand, my wife and I have removed our children from a school that has become a shrine to John Dewey (misunderstood by the head). It is a fascinating museum piece of early "progressive" education, but since everyone is expected to follow the house line, the natural heterogeneity of the children is continually being constricted to fit the school's righteous model of how *the* child should "naturally" develop. . . .

Secondly, I look for teachers who are chronic learners . . .

NAT HENTOFF
Saturday Review

A Parent in Search of a School

Benjamin, who's seven, has a verbal capacity that's several years above his hand–eye capacity, and it's difficult to deal with a kid who's that bright and that uncoordinated and can't read. The psychologist who tested Benjy last spring told me that he needed a special school, but there aren't any decent ones in this city. On the other hand, Benjy's teachers and his analyst thought that a special school would be the worst thing in the world for him, that it would give him the stigma of having some kind of a learning disability, which isn't the case.

One day when I was talking about this and crying—I thought I was going to have to move to another city to get Benjy the help I believed he needed, and I was really going crazy—my doctor suggested that I at least look at an open-classroom school. I went down to the school and talked about Benjy with the principal, and she said, "It really is such a responsibility to educate a gifted child. You know, that's really my specialty." It was the first time anyone I'd ever talked to had treated my child as other than a piece of pathology.

Benjy's father and I took Benjy down to look around the school. Afterward, the principal asked Benjy what he thought of the place. "I don't see enough science projects or Montessori equipment," he answered. "And no rock collections."

She said, "Well, we do what the children here are interested in. Obviously when there's a scientist like you around, we'd like you to write a book on rocks."

"I can't write. I can't even read," he said.

"That won't stop you," she told him. "You can tell your teacher what you want to say, and she'll write the words down, and of course you'll be able to read your own words because they're yours."

It was all so positive that Benjy got confused and decided to tell her some bad things, like the way he fought with his friend Marcel.

She said, "You're concerned about being strong?"

"Yeah."

"Is Marcel stronger than you are?"

"Well, he's got stronger muscles, but I've got stronger feelings," Benjy answered.

"Well, how's your brain then?"

"Oh, I've got a really strong brain," Benjy said, all dimples and a big grin.

"Then you'll have to learn to use your strong brain to teach your strong feelings."

A little later, she asked, "What would you do if you brought some good rocks to school and someone took them?"

"I wouldn't care."

"Yes, you would," she said, and then asked, "What would you do if an older kid came up and said, 'Give me your lunch money'?"

"I'd say he couldn't have it, because I need it for my lunch," he answered.

She nodded. "That's good, because all new children get asked for their lunch money by some of the older ones," she told him. "That's the answer you should give, because the children who give up their lunch money keep on getting asked for it until they stop giving it."

Afterward, when we walked out the front door, Benjy said, "Did I get in?"

"That's where you're going to school, Benjy," I said.

"Good! I like it. And I really like that lady."

Benjy really likes physical beauty, the principal was very pretty, so I asked him, "Because she's so pretty?"

"Yeah, and 'cause she told the truth."

BOBBIE MALONE

Don't Waste Your Time

In selecting a private school, consider whether or not your child will be "selected" by the school. I once solicited four recommendations, had three interviews, paid a $15 application fee, and subjected my daughter to a three-hour exam at a school that did not accept her. When pressed, the admissions director admitted that there had been only *one* opening for a female in her grade (seventh) and over a hundred applications. Had we known that, we wouldn't have bothered, of course. So try to feel out the admissions practices and possibilities of the schools that interest you.

ANNA JANE HAYS

To Find Out What the Schools Say About Themselves . . .

A *Publishers' Weekly* review of *Private Independent Schools: The Bunting and Lyon Blue Book* (published by Bunting and Lyon, $30) says that the directory reflects "the tremendous changes in admissions, curriculum, student body, physical plant, costs, faculty, that are taking place in some 1,200 American private and elementary schools of all kinds in the U.S. and 31 other countries. . . . The information on each school was obtained from detailed questionnaires filled out by the schools themselves, from numerous on-the-spot inspections, from catalogues and yearbooks."

There are also two directories of public alternative schools. One is published by the National Alternative Schools Program, School of Education, University of Massachusetts, Amherst, Mass. 01003; the other by the New Schools Exchange, Pettigrew, Ark. 72752.—Eds.

Who's in Charge Here? A Vcte for Private Education

I . . . had never seriously considered the public schools, less because they might not be "good" than from a fundamental aversion to committing my children to the hands of the state. If they are to be miseducated, I prefer that it be my mistake rather than the state's.

MARGOT HENTOFF
Saturday Review

FRANK DeRBAS

Why Public Schooling Is Better Than Private Schooling

When I used to commute to college, on certain days I would ride home on the bus with young girls from a local parochial school. They would chatter about boys mostly, but one afternoon the subject of their conversation centered on the original Latin text of *The Aeneid,* a book I was then studying in what was reputed to be one of the best translations.

At first I was stunned and then depressed that these giggling little high school girls were being so much better educated than I was. Imagine, reading the *Aeneid* in the original. But today I look back on that experience with an entirely different philosophy. Because today I wonder what they failed to learn during the time it took them to learn Latin and concentrate on Virgil. Whatever it was that they sacrificed, I can be sure I got at least a healthy smattering of it somewhere along the line in my traditional public school upbringing.

And, to my mind, that's why public schools are better than private ones.

While it's the privilege and often the rule for private students to delve more deeply into this or that, it's the grand advantage of mass education that a public student is at least introduced to everything mankind currently judges to be important. And although some things are worth profound study, nothing is really irrelevant. Even small bits of information which by themselves do not enable you to make an incision or philosophize or challenge Einstein, even these insufficient bits have their proper places in reminding us that our lives are constantly affected not only by what we do, but by what others do as well.

Surely public schooling is far from perfect. But the very nature of mass education assures us that a student will not get an education that is oriented toward the prejudices of his parents. And that gives me great comfort when seemingly unaccountably I know the source of a line of English poetry or I can put my finger right on Madagascar or I can countersink as though it were instinctive.

When you pay for something outright you have the right and the inclination to exercise a good measure of control over your purchase. So when you buy an education privately you're bound to look for those selling features that as an adult you favor—a shiny science lab rather than a modern gymnasium, an impressive art staff rather than brilliant mathematicians and so on. But the "less fortunate" public students must have a taste of every dish, like it or not, for the state has calculated how to accomplish the most for the mass even though the geniuses and the poor learners may have to mark time. I, for one, would not trade my looser lock on Latin for my truly general education. If eventually I did drink deep from a Pierian Spring I have mainly my public schooling to thank for those shallow, intoxicating draughts of physics, penmanship, economics, driver's ed., typing, music, dodge ball, et al., which somehow whet a mightier thirst, and for that too maligned roll of public sheepskin, which has proven itself so sturdy a straw.

ALAN SAPERSTEIN

Living with Someone Else's Values

Our local school resembles too closely the school I attended. I'm looking for more openness in dealing with children and in working with parents. But the qualities fostered at school are not necessarily the same as we stress at home. Rather than change schools or teachers, we work within this context, pointing out to our child our values and views and explaining how they may differ from those heard at school.

BARBARA POPPER

HOW SOME CHILDREN FARE IN SOME SCHOOLS SOME OF THE TIME

Our daughter has attended kindergarten in a "conventional" public school and in an open classroom. Although she misses (as she often remarks) the "peace and quiet" of the closed classroom, she is sociable and outgoing and enjoys the freedom to move around and associate with different people that the open classroom provides. She has been encouraged to progress more rapidly (we feel) in the open situation, without a great deal of pressure. It seems to us that the advantages of the open classroom could be coupled with a little more discipline to produce even better results. But surely this must vary from one specific situation to the next.

MRS. DAVID ASHTON

My children's elementary school invites specialists in a number of fields (dance, sculpture, weaving, music, etc.) to come and be in residence for one or more weeks. The children are given a great deal of access to these people. It has been extremely valuable to both the children and the artists.

MARY ANN SHORE

The Montessori nursery schools in Rochester and New York City both gave my children the kind of academic curiosity and skills and ability to concentrate which is partially responsible for their present relaxed confidence in school. Montessori schools I've known range from insanely rigid to relaxed but still highly structured. To me, the ideal is liberal Montessori, or what I call the swinging West Side version. Best of all worlds.

ELEANOR DIENSTAG

My older child felt self-conscious in an open classroom set-up, wanted to bring more work home. In a traditional classroom, she felt more secure, worked better.

FRANCES LATERMAN

People ask if the kids at the Fifteenth Street School, because it's a Summerhill school, might be so far behind that they will have to do makeup work when they go on to a regular school. When my wife and I were involved with the school on a day-to-day basis, our teachers were in touch with parents and were aware of which kids would be leaving after what year. And if there was a student who hadn't done any work, we'd get together with the kid and teachers and say, "Look, next year you're going to ———, and you don't know a damn thing about math. You're pretty good in reading, even if you're no scholar in that either, and you're going to a traditional school where the rules are going to be entirely different, and you're going to be in bad trouble. Now what do you want to do?"

The kid would have two choices: he could be the dummy of the class, or he could catch up with what the other kids would be doing—not because he wanted to, but because he knew that if he did, his life would be more pleasant the next year. For him and a lot of other kids in the same spot it was a case of "I don't want to be the only kid who can't count past 100."

He had been in a reasonable environment where it was reasonable for him not to learn math because he didn't want to. But the reasonable thing for him to do now is to learn math—simply because that's life.

ORSON BEAN

My child attended a cooperative school in which parents were asked to participate in the daily activities. It was a marvelous educational experience for me, during which I learned more about children than at any other time in my life. The active participation of parents was beneficial to all.

SARAH KLEE

Yes, I'm dissatisfied with my child's school: (1) no physical education program; (2) no art; (3) no music; (4) no playground, but blacktop; (5) no lunch program; (6) vending machines with candy and potato chips. One or two of these things would be bad, but all together they distress me. I'm sorry to say I've taken no action at all except to try to feel out the opinions of other parents, and I keep getting the same answer: "It's always been this way, ever since I went to school here." (It is a local parochial school.) We have considered public school, but the one in our neighborhood has had two rapes and a murder and several teachers attacked in the halls in the last year. I feel really trapped on this one. We would switch to a private school except for the huge tuition.

JOY KLOTZ

David had been at a private school with the same kids and the same teacher for two years. Now in a totally new and alien environment with new kids and new teachers and bars on the windows, he kept saying he didn't like it and didn't want to go there. Finally, after three weeks, he could admit that he was scared. It was the new environment, but it was also that he was afraid of failing.

It was a twenty-four-hour one-to-one counseling: I listened and listened and listened and held him and held him and held him and played with him and played with him. I was exhausted. But the other day he came home and said he liked school. "I tell my brain now to hold my feelings calm," he said.

SALLY LANGENDOEN

Kate had an open kindergarten (which she loved) and a rigid first grade. The transition was murderous. She literally had to stay home one day every week and a half in the beginning of first grade. But I would like to keep my children home one day a week to fill in the gaps left by the school the other four days.

The obstacles? Others' opinions (particularly the school's) and my being a bit too disorganized.

MARY ANN BUCKLEY

School doesn't bother me, really, but you have to work so hard to stay in. When I work at it, I get an A+, but I just don't like to work that hard. Usually I get Cs and Ds.

I'd want to change schools, except we have the best basketball team and I like the kids in my class.

KEITH MILLER

Why I'm Not Changing My Kid's School This Year, Even Though I Hate a Lot of Things About It

With all the reservations I have about my son's school, it is essentially a decent place where no harm will come to him and he might learn something anyway. I looked around at other schools and decided against a move for my son for the following reasons:

He knows the school—the kids, the teachers, the geography of the building (there is something to be said for the comfort and security one gets from knowing where the bathroom is and where the pencils are kept)—and he is comfortable there.

He is doing fine at the school. It is I who am uneasy there: I don't like the noise, the clutter, the dirt. My son doesn't mind any of that.

He will not necessarily like the new school to which I would move him. In fact, it could turn out to be much worse (and then what would I do? Change again?).

In this case, I have decided, it is definitely easier to leave things as they are rather than go into an unknown situation which might have even more drawbacks than the first.

ELS

"Christopher has never been treated unkindly by adults. He trusts us implicitly. I hope, Miss Forbes, you won't in any way betray that trust."

. . . using energy to express anger and discontent is a diversion from the business of building something that will satisfy.

HAL BENNETT
No More Public School

WE *CAN* IMPROVE OUR SCHOOLS

SOME IDEAS THAT SEEM TO WORK

"To Begin With: Why Not Have a Garden?"

As a public school parent, I can think of at least one way the school could become a more enlightening, less rigid experience without adding one cent to the school budget. To begin with: why not have a garden come spring—turn over a piece of unused ground for kids to work with their hands, to plant, water, and care for living things. Each grade or individual child would have a section, later to reap the rewards by eating the fruits and vegetables in school. They can enjoy the flowers as well, learn about mulching, etc.

CAROL EICHLER

One thing I've learned is not to delay what you want to do because it's not exactly the right moment. I've always wanted to have an outdoor garden at the school where I am the principal. Last January when our resident craftsperson suggested we plant some trees and I hesitated because I really wanted more of a real park, which we weren't yet in a position to do, he said, "Listen, it's January, tree planting time, Mother Nature won't wait," and we did it, and it's nice.

LUCI ANN CARMICHAEL

◆

Cambridge Central School— Parents and Kids Together

About forty-five children, a racial and socioeconomic mix of three-to-five-and-a-half-year-olds, attend the Central School in Cambridge, Massachusetts, from nine to noon every day. This cooperative nursery-kindergarten is unusual—perhaps unique—in that it is combined with an adult learning center.

"We consider our work with parents as Central School's most important contribution to education," says Lisa Dittrich, who started the

school in 1967. "Many parents confess to us after a year in the school that they intended at first to just drop their children here and run, until some facet of our program intrigued them and they stuck around.

"Many of these parents in the community are concentrating so hard on daily survival that the idea of actually affecting the 'system' they are caught in is unknown to them. Hostility and a certain fatalism exist in the community toward social agencies, universities, and between people of different racial and social backgrounds. As a consequence, people tend not to use the resources available to them. Our parents leave this school with the knowledge of many resources that will help them at times of family stress. They have developed communication skills to use with people they might not ordinarily feel comfortable talking to—a school principal, for instance. And they've gained confidence necessary for a positive contribution to their children's public school education."

The school's homey family room, a bubbling coffee pot, cribs and babysitter for toddlers, do much to encourage parents to get involved. And a special staff member, the parent coordinator, is on hand to chat with them. Some may want to return to school after dropping out; others may face divorce and be confused and frightened; others need help in managing jobs and raising children at the same time; and others can help and be helped by sharing their experiences as parents.

An in-service teacher-training program has enabled a number of parents—mostly on low-income levels who have not finished high school—to take courses leading toward a degree in education and to take salaried jobs in the school, which may start them on their way to a career in education.

Central School also offers support to local public school teachers who come to observe and to try out some of their own ideas as well.

MAURICE SAGOFF

School Within a School,
Or, What You Can Do When the Principal Says No

The prime job of a school principal involves public relations and the avoidance of trouble. For this reason he is usually reluctant to support any change within his school that might possibly lead to controversy. However, it also means that if enough pressure is brought to bear on him, he will usually yield a bit, if he feels that there is no way of wiping out the opposition. A good example of the kind of pressure that can be mobilized happened in Berkeley several years ago. Two teachers in one of the junior high schools wanted to have 100 students, three classrooms, and their own books and supplies within the context of the junior high. They did not want to start a private junior high, but rather have a semi-autonomous public junior high that would be open and involve student and parent governance, and yet share the facilities and resources with the existing junior high.

The first time the teachers approached the principal with this idea he looked at them as if they were mad. The idea was unheard of, what would the parents say, and how would the rest of his staff respond? He gave the teachers a thousand reasons why they couldn't have their minischool, though none of the reasons questioned the educational soundness of the idea. The teachers were discouraged, but decided that they probably could get their school eventually if they started more modestly. The next day they proposed to the principal that instead of having the school, they be allowed to develop an elective class, called contemporary education theory, for the next semester. The teachers wrote up a class outline and created a reading list using some of the contemporary educational literature. On paper the teachers seemed to be proposing to read about and study educational change without actually implementing it, and that was less of a threat to the principal. In actuality the teachers intended to use the class as a planning time for the school they were determined to have the next year.

At first the principal had many objections to the class. He claimed that the students weren't interested. The teachers went out and signed up the students to prove that they were interested. Then he objected that it would involve too much juggling of schedules, so the teachers got the schedules and developed a feasible plan for having the elective the last period of the school day.

The teachers were not demanding or pushing or threatening the principal, and he finally yielded to the pressure and the teachers had their elective course.

The course met five times a week from February to June. The students read the books and visited free schools and community schools. Parents were invited to join the class, and several potluck dinners were given for teachers, parents, and students. Halfway through the course, the idea of a mini–junior high based on open principles was broached to the parents, many of whom were definitely interested. By the end of the school year a plan was developed, a proposal written, and community support mobilized. In June the teachers once again—along with the students and parents—approached the principal with their plans for a new school. He still opposed their plan, but this time he was more cautious since he was dealing with parents as well as the teachers. He didn't exactly turn them down. He claimed that he didn't have the power to grant their request and sent them to the assistant superintendent, who also claimed he had no power to act and sent them to the superintendent, who told them he would study the matter. In a slick professional maneuver, the issue was almost filed away. But the parents were not willing to quit. The step-by-step battle up the hierarchy was a form of political education which had made them more committed to the minischool than before. At this point the school was given a name, and the teachers and parents and students talked about it as if it already existed.

The parents went to the school board and requested action. They did not want to be put off by a feasibility study that would last a year, so they did not ask for any extra money. After the whole history of the planning and development of the school was presented, as well as the fact that the principal had allowed the elective course, the board voted that the superintendent should find a way to make the school exist. By the next September the school came into existence, and it is still going on.

If the school board had said no, the teachers would have had several options: try to close down the junior high and gain strength through confrontation; run a candidate in the next school board election or work on the school board members in private; have their own school without public money and continue to confront the public school system with its own failure to respond to the needs and demands of the community; go back into the school and subvert it; or finally quit and return to business as usual.

I have known many people who have won school battles by having the patience to exhaust all the channels and document their struggle and at the same time indicate to members of the bureaucracy that they were willing to do anything, from cajolery to battle, to get what was necessary for their children.

HERBERT KOHL

The Challenge:
To Make a Subject Come Alive in the Classroom
One Solution: MATCH Boxes

If you put on an Eskimo's goggles and find them way too big, what can you deduce about the Eskimo? That his head is broad. That the glare of the snow is so bright it requires protective eye shields. It is this kind of experience that makes the MATCH Box learning method one to consider.

MATCH Boxes are portable kits, each the size of a large suitcase, containing a selection of materials and activities for two or three weeks' intensive work in social studies. MATCH stands for *Materials and Activities for Teachers and Children*, and the subjects covered include: Animal Camouflage, Grouping Birds, Houses, Medieval People, Musical Shapes and Sounds, Netsilik Eskimos, Rocks, Waterplay, and Paddle-to-the-Sea. Each of these units combines books, films, records, models, and a large number of real objects in a learning system that allows children to work in small groups and as a class, to handle, study, experiment, record, conjecture, communicate, and learn.

In one kit called "The City," the students construct and analyze a city and try to solve some of our actual urban problems. In another, "A House of Ancient Greece," six teams excavate an ancient Greek villa and use their archaeological "finds" to reconstruct the life and structure of that community. A creative teacher might initiate the discussion of this MATCH Box by kicking over her wastebasket and having the class deduce the activities of the morning from the contents (which might contain a half-eaten apple, a broken pencil, a secret note). After this preliminary activity, the class will study the MATCH Box contents as members of an archaeological expedition.

The Boston Children's Museum rents out these kits at fees ranging from $20 to $40 for a two-week or three-week period. Six of the kits have been duplicated for wider commercial distribution by American Science and Engineering, Inc., 20 Overland Street, Boston, Mass. 02215. These are priced for sale, from $495 to $525, with some units available at a lower price if ordered without the 16-mm. film that is part of the kit. Each kit comes with a Teacher's Guide.

MAURICE SAGOFF

COURTESY OF THE BOSTON CHILDREN'S MUSEUM

The Zephyros Education Exchange

The Zephyros Education Exchange (1201 Stanyan Street, San Francisco, Calif. 94117) has put together a series of tabloids, called "deschool primers," which sell from $1.50 to $5. There's one called "Your City Has Been Kidnapped," which sensitizes kids about their environment. In Primer #9 there's a section on how to program an inchworm. In #12 you learn how to use comic books as a source for things like figures of speech and onomatopoeia (*kwam! arrgh! ahhh!*).

For $10 a year, anyone can subscribe and get whatever happens to be published by Zephyros during the year, plus two boxes full of bizarre fun.

BERNIE DE KOVEN

SETTING UP A SCHOOL CO-OP

Transportation: Comradeship for the Kids, Extra Time for the Parents

The school we chose for our son is half an hour from our home and out of our school district. Last summer I talked to some parents of other kids who went to my son's school and also lived in our part of the city. Most of them worked, and had to drive their children to school each morning, often in the opposite direction from their jobs, and then drive on, come back to pick up the kids in the afternoon, and return to work—an arduous and time-consuming task all around. I suggested that we hire a bus, and took it upon myself to place an ad in the local paper, inquiring about other parents who might be interested in the scheme and requesting any interested bus driver to contact me. Eight parents called me. So did a man who owned a small van and drove kids out on field trips every day from a day-care center; he wanted to know how much we would pay. I had no idea, so I called a local community-center director to ask what the going rate was: $28 per child a month, he said. The potential driver needed twelve children to make any profit, so I persuaded the principal of our school to let me look through the roster to find another four families that also lived in our area. We made the arrangements with the driver, who took care of the special insurance requirements. To make sure this had been done properly, I checked out what he had done with the local motor vehicle department, and found it was all in order.

Then, finally, one Monday morning up drove the van, and out ran my son to join six other kids who were already aboard. He enjoyed the comradeship, and the parents had all those extra hours away from the frantic rush-hour traffic.

Everything was going smoothly so far as I knew, until the driver quit on one week's notice. The job had been consuming more time than he'd anticipated, he told us, and he couldn't take the kids' bad language and fighting. Knowing my son was one of the worst offenders, I asked the driver if he'd set limits: No Throwing Things Out of Windows, No Fighting, etc. No, he hadn't; he'd not wanted to take the responsibility of setting up a manageable situation, then had lost his temper when the kids got the best of him in 4 p.m. traffic.

We found our replacement by calling limousine and transportation companies listed in the yellow pages. (Many such companies use camper-type buses to drive groups of business people in from the suburbs, and it seemed logical to extend this sort of service to school children.) Our approach was: "Here's a way for you to make $336 regularly (twelve kids at $28 per month) for two forty-five-minute stretches daily at times when you wouldn't be carrying your regular loads."

Our new driver is more professional than the previous one, *and* he's willing to deal directly with each parent, rather than insisting on going through me.

BOBBIE MALONE

Food: A Produce Market in the Basement

I was talking with some of the parents from our school, and everyone was complaining about food prices. I suggested the idea of a food cooperative at the school. The parents were very skeptical, but interested. Finally, two of them said they would work on it, and we started.

I wanted kids involved too, so our project could be educational as well as a service to the community. We got a group of interested kids and parents together and we dragged a handcart down to the market (luckily, it's just two blocks away). We came back with several cases of produce and sold it, with great success, in the school basement. The next step was to send notes home to all the parents. Less than a year later, our co-op was well established both in terms of the people who worked on it and those who bought from it. Now we're planning to begin taking food stamps—any group that's incorporated (our parents' group is) can accept food stamps as long as it's willing to go through the red tape.

LUCI ANN CARMICHAEL

KIDS
TEACHING KIDS

"Our Classroom Is the City We Live In"

I teach a class at Berkeley High School, which is euphemistically titled Children's Theater. There are twenty young people in the class and we do improvisations, events in supermarkets, buses, anywhere in the community at large. The class meets formally in the costume room of the Berkeley Community Theater, though our classroom is the city we live in. I have found myself increasingly unable to accept the four walls of a schoolroom as the boundaries in which learning is supposed to take place. . . .

The classroom not only segregates young people from society. It segregates them from each other. We have elementary schools, junior high schools, high schools—six-year-olds never meet ten- or fifteen- or seventeen-year-olds in school. It is absurd. Not only do we not let children of the same age teach each other by insisting upon silence in the classroom, we make it impossible in the context of school for older children* to teach younger ones. Our "Children's Theater" class has moved away from this, and once a week we visit a kindergarten.

The first time ten high school students came to the kindergarten we were all anxious about the visit. No one knew what would happen. A few improvisations were tried and they were fun but something unexpected and perfectly natural happened. The kindergarten children wanted to know who the high school students were, what they did and cared about. They wanted a chance to find people they liked, or whose interests fascinated them. The high school students felt the same way. The teacher and I, adults and the presumed experts in the room, stepped aside and let things happen.

Groups formed and dissolved, a few people went outside to take a walk, one high school student started to explain drawing to the young children and attracted a crowd, another began to use a typewriter, and got another crowd. I don't know everything that happened that morning, because so much was going on at the same time.

HERBERT KOHL
The Open Classroom

*I feel uneasy about this word. It makes some sense when applied to kindergarten or first grade people but none whatever when applied to high school students.

Youth Tutoring Youth Programs

We often observe an older child teaching a younger child—how to play a game, to put on skates, to take a first cigarette.

Since 1967 the National Commission on Resources for Youth has helped to initiate Youth Tutoring Youth programs all around the country. The emphasis is not so much on teaching basic school skills of reading, arithmetic, etc., but on developing a relationship between two young people where they can explore learning through their personal interests.

The NCRY distributes materials for tutors (and supervisors) and occasionally holds workshops to set up new programs. (They also publish a free quarterly newsletter about other student-run programs.)

For information and materials, write to the National Commission on Resources for Youth, 36 West 44th Street, Room 1314, New York, N.Y. 10036.

RS

The Perils of Primogeniture

[My] older sister Randy . . . taught me to shoot craps when I was seven (and she was twelve) but she used to change the rules around from minute to minute depending on what she rolled. After a ten-minute session with her, I would be divested of the entire contents of my carefully hoarded piggybank, while she (who started out broke) wound up as flush as Sky Masterson. No matter how Lady Luck had smiled on me, I always ended up a loser.

"Snake eyes— I win!" my sister would yelp.

"You do?" (I used to hoard my dollar allowance like the ant while she spent hers like the grasshopper—but she always wound up flush and I wound up bankrupt.) The perils of primogeniture. And I the perennially second-born.

ERICA JONG
Fear of Flying

"Somebody Looking Up To Me"

For two years now, I've participated in a special program at my school. The class has twenty-five people, split up in groups of five each. One day a week each group goes down to a room called room 2 (the ages of the kids range from three to five years old). We help the kids do art projects, read them books, play sports, and help them build and make things.

Once before, we taught seven-, eight- and nine-year olds. Me and my best friend Pete, we took two of those kids and taught them to use butane burners. We took glass rods, cut them in half with a file. We made bubbles, dripped glass, and bent it in shapes. Those kids had a real good time, and so did we. I'd rather teach the older kids, they're more sensible and easier to handle.

This project made me feel there was somebody looking up to me instead of my always looking up to somebody. I felt like a grown-up instead of a child.

DAVID ALMOND
Age ten

Learning Sympathy

"Most parents think the younger kids have the advantage in our mixed-grade classroom," said Laura Schwartzberg, a teacher in New York City. But it works both ways. "As a result of mixing with first- and second-graders, many of the kindergarteners have learned to read, add and subtract, sew, and much more. What the big kids are learning, though, is sympathy. They have a concern for their classmates' difficulties. And they remember their own struggling when they watch the younger kids trying to learn their lessons." And besides, to teach a five-year-old a math lesson, a seven-year-old would have to have the answers.

ELS

INSIDE THE WALLS

Found Space: Hallways

Most American secondary schools are . . . a series of . . . cells (i.e., classrooms) strung along hallways. The hallways themselves are the students' only common room, but their function is to keep people moving and minimize interaction. Access to the hallways is further limited to five minutes at a time and otherwise requires a permit.

MICHAEL SHAMBERG
Guerrilla Television

IDEAS FOR HALLWAYS

—Sand and water tables. Limit the number of children allowed at one time if noise becomes a problem.
—An intra-school post office. Kids take turns tending the office and delivering the mail. (In the school where I saw such a post office operating, mail was delivered in the middle of classes without any disruption.)
—Tables for individual and small-group reading, writing, and discussion.
—Shuffleboard and hopscotch halls.
—If the hall is deep enough or has a dead end, it could be used for slide shows and films.

RS

Thoughts to Accompany Your Next Building Fund Contribution

I have recently seen a large city school system plan and build more than one hundred kindergarten rooms under severe time pressure, using one design and calling in its teachers and consultants after there was no time to change that plan; they managed only to add a light slit in an otherwise totally windowless room. Building one such room would be no crime, but building all of them alike . . . denied that school system and [others] an opportunity to learn from the variety of plans which might have been used for classrooms two, three, four. . . .

When we started to rebuild the Hilltop Head Start storefront kindergarten, the teachers and children tried to tell the architects what they wanted. But a few weeks later, even with the plans in front of them, the teachers still had no idea of what the structure would look like, if built.

We then built a model of the architect's plan and presented this "doll house" to the staff. . . . They saw problems in the architect's plan [and worked with it.] Finally, when they knew what they wanted and where they wanted it, we drew in the details and handed the finished plan to a local contractor.

ALLAN LEITMAN
*Educational Arts Association
Conference, 1974*

STARTING WITH A CLEAN SLATE
(AND OTHER SMALL IMPROVEMENTS)

A small example of the difference between freedom and license that A. S. Neill always talked about is language. So-called bad language goes on in all schools, mostly *sub rosa*—you furtively say shit. In the Fifteenth Street School you can openly say shit, as long as there isn't someone around who does not want to hear it. A word is not in and of itself offensive. It becomes offensive if it is said to the ears of someone who is offended by it and the person saying it knows that. For instance, there was a rule at the school that you couldn't say shit on Thursday afternoons between 1:30 and 3 p.m. when visitors were there. The kids in time came to understand the difference between being against language *per se* and being against the intent of what language is used for.

ORSON BEAN

[Music in the Schools: For a good, reasonably priced way of getting music and dance into the school, see "Young People's Concerts," page 294.]

I would like to buy some empty, unlined notebooks and place them in the library at the kids' disposal, so that when they're in the library and don't feel like reading, or do feel like writing, they can have these notebooks. Just to see what they do with them.

RON PADGETT
*Teachers and Writers
Collaborative Newsletter*

Someone has finally realized that school pictures don't have to show vacant faces smiling into the camera. My son was photographed at school doing the activities he does there, with his classroom in the background. At least if you're going to pay something like $13.50 for the pictures, they might as well be interesting.

FLAVIA POTENZA

THE IDEAL SCHOOL

"I Want to Establish an Institution of Learning . . ."

I want to establish an institution of learning. I form no programme which is based on my theoretical conceptions, and on the basis of this programme look about for teachers, but I propose to all people who feel that they are called to furnish information to lecture or teach such subjects as they know best. Of course, my former experience will guide me in the selection of these lessons, that is, we shall not try to offer subjects such as nobody wants to listen to—in a Russian village we will not teach Spanish, or astrology, or geography, just as a merchant will not open shops of surgical instruments or of crinolines in this village. . . .

It is quite possible that there will turn up one teacher of zoology, one teacher of medieval history, one of religion, and one of the art of printing. If these teachers will know how to make their lessons interesting, these lessons will be useful, in spite of their seeming incompatibility and accidentalness.

LEO TOLSTOY
On Education

The Ideal School: "Open to the Group Imagination of Its Inhabitants . . ."

Soon my son will be in school. I hope it will offer him a full chance to follow his own rhythms and focuses of learning. I hope it will operate, beyond this private freedom, in a way which leads the children slowly but clearly toward determining collectively what they do together, setting their own limits as a key part of their curriculum. Many teachers and schools, even in the public school system, are now trying to encourage children's self-directed learning. But it is rare to find educators concerned with their growth in self-governance, and willing to lead them toward shared control of their education. This process can and should exist from kindergarten on. If it did, we would find it easier to imagine what schools would be like were they genuinely open to the group imagination of their inhabitants.

MICHAEL ROSSMAN

A Classroom on Wheels (Perhaps Not "Ideal," But a Possibility . . .)

The important features of the mobile classroom are:
- mobility, which provides access to a wide variety of experiences
- stability of work spaces, which keeps personal belongings, materials, and tools within easy reach for everyone.

The mobile classroom is thus quite similar to the general operation of the storefront school, with mobility added. The following will help clarify this:
- Here's what you will need to do:
  a. get a large school bus: a new 50 passenger model costs about $15 thousand; a decent used one can be found through the truck ads in your newspaper for as little as $15 hundred, which is about what you'd pay for a year's rent on a storefront.
  b. remove all but five or ten double seats, depending on the number of students you want to carry: limit to no more than 15 kids.
  c. convert the open space in the back of the bus for work spaces . . . Keep everything compact.
- You'll need a teacher-driver, and one assistant.
- Bus will travel . . . but will also provide familiar work spaces inside.
- Establish an itinerary, but keep it flexible. Start with trips which relate directly to subject matter being taught, then loosen up with trips which don't seem immediately relevant:
  a. Subject-related trips include: a bank (Arithmetic), or a farm (Biology, Ecology, Geography), or a newspaper office (Reading and Writing).
  b. Non-subject-related trips include: seashore, camping, fishing, watching a house being built.

Auto clubs often have maps showing points of historical interest. Once you get started many other possibilities will open up to you; mobility will lead to discovery. Note: Always phone anyone you're going to visit at least a week in advance, to ensure their co-operation.
- Travel itinerary would include:
  a. day trips
  b. weekend trips using bus as living space
  c. extended trips to other cities, states, countries
- Would require expensive insurance:
  a. Liability: $250 annually
  b. Medical: $5 per year per child
  c. Fire, theft, vandalism: $75 to $100 annually
- Potentially high maintenance costs
  a. Toll roads about four times that of auto
  b. Gasoline: five miles per gallon
  c. Tires: $45 and up per tire
  d. Tools for maintenance and repair: $85
  e. Valve job on engine: $400 and up
  f. Major overhaul of transmission: $250 and up
  g. New battery: $45 and up
  h. High license costs: $40 if registered as a "motor home" in California, to $1,000 per year if registered as a "commercial carrier." (Check with your Department of Motor Vehicles.)
- Would expose children to a large variety of experiences . . .
- Would not be hassled by inspectors from the Health Department, Zoning Board, etc.
- Would be practical only in the better climates.
- Over a period of years, the costs of maintaining the bus would probably be comparable to the costs of maintaining a building.

HAL BENNETT
No More Public School

"I Dream of What I Haven't Got . . ."

I dream of what I haven't got, of what I wish I had, and wonder how to go about getting it.

In mind only, I see a place on the fringe of the town with trees and a hill nearby, and a building there attuned to the scape, broad with a rearing roof. At one end of the length is a glassed-in wall backing a hooded veranda, from which a ramp slopes down gradually to the place where children play. Out there on the grass is a generous heap of not too heavy timber, close to a shed with a lock on the door housing real tools: real saws, hammers and thousands of nails and spades to dig in the bank.

Why the ramp? Much of the equipment is wheeled outside and back in for the night: water tank on wheels, sand tank on wheels and the mud container. The easel can be wheeled outside too when the day is fine; the paint, water and brushes table and the construction set to build with.

There are steps to the veranda, of course. Across the veranda the glassed-in wall, folded back in summer, closed in winter, yet permitting the light and the needed sight of the wide white outside. Inside is a large and spacious room, tall-ceilinged and abounding in air. Wide windows open up the other walls, low for the use of young children, and the floor is bare so they can hear the sound of their own steps; a living sound like children's voices with meaning and rhythm in it.

From the walls jut several mobile screens forming open alcoves: one for reading, another for writing and two for science and math. One is a place to play house in or assemble a playshop in and another a corner for pets. There's a piano in one, a good guitar and other musical instruments.

Three doors open off the three walls: one for a porch for their clothes and lockers and a toilet compound, a room at the back with a concrete floor for cooking and kiln work, and the third is a room where teachers go to regroup their faculties; to review the last hour, conceive the next and to think in privacy.

Only well-trained teachers work here, both men and women, and in the style of the future. Dead grades give way to interflowing movements from the reception class up. Each teacher knows each technique of each of the four movements, though responsible for his own, so that any child has access to any teacher in family fluidity.

Not only teachers are here but the whole range of life, from a baby to age, maybe a teacher's baby. Maybe an old man snoozing here to be considered and passed his paper and, like the baby, not to be waked. It's a dream . . .

SYLVIA ASHTON-WARNER
Spearpoint

The School that Ought to Be

The school that ought to be has teachers that know how to handle their classes (keep them interested) and know *what they are teaching.*

Subjects:

Pleasurable* Human Behavior
   *for the people you behave to and yourself
Historydrama
Naturemath
Creative Cookery (on a Budget)
The Long-Neglected Art of Observation
The Long-Neglected Art of Walking
The Long Neglected Art of Thinking Clearly
   (Meditation)
Mastery of the Elegant Insult (optional)
Examination of Fantasy

These classes require small classes in large rooms with easy access to everywhere.

HERBERT KOHL
The Open Classroom

"Special" Education for All

An estimated 10 to 15 percent of the school-age population, grouped together because they are "different" from the "normal" population, receive an education that is labeled "special." To qualify, you have to be cerebral palsied, retarded, learning disabled, deaf, visually impaired, emotionally disturbed, or perhaps gifted. This special education is usually characterized by more varied educational approaches than the normal school programs, and by a smaller teacher–student ratio to allow for a greater concentration on individual needs. I have mixed feelings when a kid in my special ed program progresses to the point of being able to enter the regular school. I know that child is being moved out of a learning environment suited to his needs and into one where he is expected to conform.

One hundred percent of the school-age population ought to have an opportunity to benefit from an education which is special and responsive to individual needs, strengths, weaknesses, and interests. By maintaining the present staff size as the elementary school population now decreases, it would be possible to move in the direction of all education as special, and special education programs as currently conceived would be eliminated for all but the most severely handicapped.

ALLAN SHEDLIN, JR.

◆

"We Want Our School to Be . . ."

We want our school to be a community endeavor in the sense that we the teachers cannot create a school by ourselves; the school system can't simply plunk down a school and say: Now, that's a school. There must be a meeting of the expediters, who might be the school system; the actual implementers, who are the teachers; and then the great supporting group, the parents in the community. And without all three working closely together, we can't get closer to the ideal school.

I think the parents need to understand that we view anyone entering this building as part of the entire teaching staff, whether it's a custodian or secretary or a parent or a delivery man: any person a child is going to interact with is a person he is going to learn something from. Parents join that group, and we need them for several reasons. We need them because the children need to see that they're interested and involved and supportive and connected to the school.

Secondly, the teachers need it. We talk about all kinds of marvelous things for children—developing their greatest potential, giving them freedom, allowing for divergent thinking and creative expression—but we rarely mention such things with regard to teachers, the support that teachers need, the opportunity for creative development that teachers need, the kind of atmosphere that teachers need to live in. (I think traditionally teachers have been treated in a very authoritarian way, and if this is what we do to the teachers we can expect that this is what they do to the children in the classroom.) Parents need to know that teachers need them as human beings, need them to come in and say can I help you, need them to say I think you're doing a good job, to say let me give you some advice about my child, or can I help make something for the classroom.

LUCI ANN CARMICHAEL

There will be Latin and rhetoric, and they will exist another hundred years, simply because the medicine is bought, so we must drink it (as a patient said).

LEO TOLSTOY

THE ROLE OF THE SCHOOL

Beauty Versus Truth

While student-teaching in a middle-class school, Herb Kohl writes in his book *36 Children,* he once spent a morning discussing the building of a cathedral and showing the class slides and pictures of it:

They had been studying technology so superficially that I wanted them to understand how problems arose and were solved—and for a change I wanted to show them something beautiful in school.

The morning had seemed to go well, only I was surprised to see a little committee waiting for me after class. There were five children looking nervous and distressed, their faces grave and serious. The spokesman stepped forward and cleared his throat.

"Mr. Kohl, there is something that distresses us. We spent the morning looking at that cathedral. It was very beautiful but, Mr. Kohl, will it help us? . . . How will it get us into college?"

The Cow on Main Street

People used to go to school to get information. They came off the farms and away from the cows and sat in rows because school was the only place they could get information. But today, homes are full of information—books and magazines and television provide an overload. And so kids go to school to learn how to plant and how to milk a cow.

JEAN MARZOLLO

"Primitive Education"

I once lectured to a group of women—all of them college graduates—alert enough to be taking a fairly advanced adult-education course on "Primitive Education" . . . I described in detail the lagoon village of the Manus tribe, the ways in which the parents taught the children to master their environment, to swim, to climb, to handle fire, to paddle a canoe, to judge distances and calculate the strength of materials. I described the tiny canoes which were given to the three-year-olds, the miniature fish spears with which they learned to spear minnows, the way in which small boys learned to caulk their canoes with gum, and how small girls learned to thread shell money into aprons. Interwoven with a discussion of the more fundamental issues, such as the relationship between younger children and older children, I gave a fairly complete account of the type of adaptive craft behavior which was characteristic of the Manus and the way in which this was learned by each generation of children. At the end of the lecture one woman stood up and asked the first question: "Didn't they have any vocational training?"

MARGARET MEAD
American Journal of Sociology

Parents' Rights: Not for the School to Decide

In some schools—mostly, though, in the very contemporary, hip schools concerned with kids' rights and with the "emotional well-being of the children"—the *parents* are put on the defensive: sneered at for not participating enough, scorned for not giving enough money, generally demeaned for ever putting their own interests or needs before the child's.

Parents, do not despair. The teacher, or even the headmaster, of a swanky school does not necessarily know better what's better for our children. We're doing the best we can do. There is enough guilt coming from other places so that we need not get it from the school, too. It's *not* the role of the school to control the parents.

You have the right to be who you are and not to conform to the school's notion of the kind of parent you should be. One way to make this clear is to brace yourself and talk back to the school's administrators. Another is to be grumpy and quickly establish a reputation as an eccentric. These things being difficult, you may prefer simply to sneak out at night and throw tomatoes at the school's windows.   ELS

How Much Is Learned at School Anyway?

I am not sure that we don't expect too much from school. I am very casual about it: I assume children learn most at home and that school is where they learn to get along with kids and teachers whether or not they like them.

REP. PATRICIA SCHROEDER

GETTING INTO THE ACT AT YOUR KID'S SCHOOL

Sneaking a Look

The usual way to pay a visit to your local school is through the principal's office. In the school everything has to be controlled, even the visits of parents, and so a school secretary will usually ask you what you want, and if your visit seems harmless, you will be issued a pass just like the kids. Harmless visits are generally those that occur during lunchtime or before nine o'clock in the morning or after three in the afternoon and deal with problems you as a parent might have with your child. It is important to notice that visits to the classroom are considered bad form during the school day when the youngsters are in class. However, that is the only time that you will be able to find out what actually happens in the school.

If your school is open to the community and there is no problem with visiting, get a pass and wander around the halls and drop into a number of classrooms and see what is happening. If you are denied permission to wander around, come back another day and don't ask for permission. Enter by a side door, and if anyone questions you, say that you are delivering a message or finding out about classrooms for your child or some other nonsense. If they send you to the office, as they would a disobedient child, leave and come back another day or wander down the hall in the direction of the office and then go about your business. If you pretend to be a dumb parent, ignorant of the rules of the school and unable to learn quickly, you can get away with hanging around and observing. Also there are a few teachers in almost all schools who welcome parents and community people and, once identified, they can help you get around the tightness of the institution.

HERBERT KOHL

How to Make the PTA Work

1. Get into the school, hang around, and know where all the information is stored—e.g., the confidential records, the financial information, the supplies and equipment inventories, the principal's bulletins to his teachers, the minutes of the union meetings, etc.

2. Identify potential allies within the school, including teachers, administrators, teacher aides and other paraprofessionals, janitors, secretaries.

3. Use PTA meetings to share information—books, films, ideas.

4. Develop alliances with parents of children in other schools in your district. (The head of the PTA should attend meetings of the district PTA.)

5. Become active in the PTA and take it upon yourself to invite teachers, and especially teacher aides, to meetings. Have potluck dinners (serve some wine) and get to know the people you will need as allies outside of the context of the school.

6. Do not ask the principal's permission for your actions. Establish your independence, not necessarily in a hostile manner. You do not work for the principal; remember that it is your school and he or she only works there.

7. Convince the teachers that the PTA will support them in whatever innovative programs they want to try. Some teachers will be more willing to take risks if they know that there is a group of parents that will fight for them and publicly support them. When a PTA endorses change within a school, it carries some public weight and puts the administration in the awkward position of opposing a respectable and official parent organization.

8. Let a few of the school board members know something of what you are doing. Bring them to your school a few times and let the principal and teachers see you with them.

9. Enlist volunteers to work on changing the school environment—painting the school, remaking the playground.

10. Ask the principal to help you plan ways of changing the school, and if he or she refuses, get specific reasons why.

11. Get to know as many of the students as possible and find out how they feel about different teachers and about the school as a whole. Invite them to meetings. Ask them what they would like to happen at school. Be careful, though, not to spring a question on a kid you do not know. He won't know what you expect and will probably tell you what he thinks you want to hear.

12. Move slowly and specifically. Do your homework, get your case together, and know how much support you have.

HERBERT KOHL

Be Brave: They Might Even Listen to You

Like most parents, I'm hopelessly afraid of the schools. I suppose this comes from being a little kid in continual fear that they're going to get me on something. So, in the honest tradition of middle-class parents, I made every effort to stay far away from my children's schools. I went near them only when I was called for a conference. Then I would go for the appropriate thirty or forty minutes, muttering to Miss So-and-So until it was time to go and we would each sigh our relief. I never was inside a school during regular classroom hours; I never went to a PTA meeting if I could help it unless there was a concert and my kids were singing. And it never occurred to me that there was any other way it ought to be.

Then the school began an effort to attract parents of children from six of the classrooms where they were trying out a new program. A meeting was scheduled and I went. The principal spoke about the administration's dissatisfaction with report cards, and said they were working toward a different kind of reporting. We were asked how we felt about that. I'd always felt that to speak in a large group like that you had to have some kind of status that means everybody else has to listen to you. But a few parents volunteered their feelings, which made me brave enough to talk.

So I said, Would it be possible to have narrative reporting now for anybody who wanted it? (I had seen my kids looking smug, thinking they were a lot snazzier than anybody else because they got As, when it was clear, at their age, that they weren't doing anything special; they just happened to learn to read before they went to school.) I suggested that parents be given a choice of straight narrative reporting or grades.

The principal said, "I never thought about that. Sure, we could try it." And it really made me feel terrific that anybody had accepted an idea that had just come off the top of my head. After the meeting, he came up to talk to me, and asked if I had any more ideas about how that could be done. I think it was from that point that I felt, Okay, they'll listen to me.

JUDY ALBAUM

Pulling Your Kids Out of School for a Day

There are times when it is absolutely valid to pull your kids out of school for a day, and you stay home from work for a day, and the two of you go off and have fun. The simplest thing can be special when not everyone else is doing it at the same time—the park or the supermarket at off-hours can be a wholly new experience. Pack a lunch (something unusual) and a sketchbook, and sit some place and draw (there's no such thing as not knowing how). Drive out of the city. Watch a building go up. Cook together, leisurely. Everything is different when it's done differently.

JO BUTLER

Everyone Has a Private Life

I'm really grateful to my daughter's preschool teacher for telling me that I didn't need to know what Holly did at school and who her friends are. That if she didn't want to tell me about her school life, it was okay. Finally, I stopped asking.

JACKIE SHAPIRO

TEACHERS (AND OTHERS) TEACHING

> There was an old lady of France
> Who taught little Ducklings to Dance;
> When she said, "tick-a-tack!"
> They only said, "Quack!"
> Which grieved that old Lady of France.
>
> EDWARD LEAR
> *Nonsense Poems*

What to Do When Boredom Sets In

It is part of a teacher's job . . . to help his students find out what to do instead of sitting in class. Here is an example. The five older boys had passed through a period of strife (largely racial) and had suddenly become united, almost as a gang. The warm weather had arrived. They were restless, hated the idea of lessons, ran out of the school, ran back, milled around in the hall, went out again and sat on the front steps, moping ferociously. They didn't know what to do. We suggested that they go out on bikes. That wasn't quite right. And they didn't want dodge ball or games in the park. They didn't want a supervised trip either. It became apparent that something real was lurking in their minds, something they vaguely agreed upon or vaguely sensed was important. What was it? Mabel intuited what it was: they wanted to do something *together,* some shared and purposeful activity that would confirm their new relationships. She suggested they make a pool table—and that was it! They trooped off to the lumberyard and bought a big piece of plywood, and strips for the sides, and some foam rubber, and green felt, and glue, and a coping saw to make the holes, and a file to smooth them. They worked at their table almost a week and it came out surprisingly well, and they used it when it was finished. And it was evident all along that this table was an embryonic clubhouse—exactly what they needed.

GEORGE DENNISON
The Lives of Children

Watch the Kids (and *Keep* Watching)

I am convinced that the teacher must be an observer of his class as well as a member of it. He must look at the children, discover how they relate to each other and the room around them. There must be enough free time and activity for the teacher to discover the children's human preferences. Observing children at play and mischief is an invaluable source of knowledge about them—about leaders and groups, fear, courage, warmth, isolation. Teachers consider the children's gym or free play time their free time, too, and usually turn their backs on the children when they have most to learn from them.

HERBERT KOHL
36 Children

Teachers, Do It Yourself!

I had no right as a teacher and a person to demand of the children what I couldn't demand of myself. Before each writing lesson I vowed to do the assignment myself. Often I spent evenings devising complex means of avoiding or "forgetting" my vow. At other times I wrote bad fables and bland poetry though I surprised myself with several parables that still please me. I drew a total blank when I tried to put a simple joke down in writing. These experiences sobered me: the children's struggle with language was my own and therefore it was easy not to force them to write things that embarrassed them, or that might lead them to reject writing altogether because they couldn't use one particular form of written expression. Teachers ought to attempt to do the writing assignments they give before deciding upon criteria to judge children's efforts. What would happen to the grading of children's poetry if teachers used examples of their own work instead of Robert Frost or Walt Whitman as models for grading?

HERBERT KOHL
36 Children

What's a Teaching Tool?

The term "teaching tool" has come into wide use among educators in the last few years. Many films are used as teaching tools; some games serve well as teaching tools; there are kits and packages and models and laboratory materials and "enrichment publications" and source lists and even people called curriculum consultants—all promoting the use of new teaching tools, which are supposed to help our children learn, grow, and become better citizens.

Actually many of these tools were in use when our grandparents went to school, such as blocks and boxes and beads and graph paper and compasses and rulers. The only difference is that modern marketing methods have won over teachers who might not otherwise have had the modest ingenuity to make use of these things in the classroom. Most of the "curriculum materials" aren't bad, mind you, and many of the magazines that advertise or promote them—*Learning, Teacher,* and *Instructor,* for example—are very good and helpful to teachers, but the popularity of these products is another example of how the public is fooled into believing that a product is necessary if their children are to learn.

As is the case with toys, if the package says "educational," many parents begin to think, Well, my kid should have it. The danger lies in the overemphasis on the need for these packaged forms of what can be found at the corner stationery store. And, more unfortunate, people lose sight of the fact that anything can be a "teaching tool." Herb Kohl said it best when he was asked if he'd come across some new teaching tools that he thought were terrific. "Yeah," he replied, "paper and a pencil."

ELS

How to Destroy Enthusiasm

The worst teacher I ever had was the one who taught me drawing in high school. I didn't know anything about drawing. But on the first day of school, I instinctively turned my paper upside down to check the composition. She made it clear that "artists don't do that." That's when I decided I would never draw again.

DR. SEUSS
as quoted in *Early Years* magazine

LEARNING: SOME THINGS TO THINK ABOUT

Whenever [children] ask their parents
Embarrassingly important
Cosmological questions . . .
Perversely, the parents
Tell them to forget the Universe
And to concentrate
With A,B,C,
1, 2 and 3—
Only with parts,
Which process the parents
Call "Elementary Education,"
And reflexively misconceive
As the essential beginning
Of all learning processes.

R. BUCKMINSTER FULLER
Intuition

Learning By Doing: It Still Works

American youth is still expected to spend 16 consecutive years on its collective butt learning how to pass an infinite series of computer-corrected exams devised in a cave located somewhere under Princeton, N.J. . . .

Luckily for us, organized education hasn't been able to secure a monopoly on the teaching of every useful task. Apprenticeships, or on-the-job training, continue to flourish. If you can no longer learn to be a lawyer by clerking that's still the way you learn to be a high-steel iron worker.

NICHOLAS VON HOFFMAN
New York Post

Learning
Is Where You Find It

Mother thought about every place we lived not only in terms of its schools, but also as a more or less promising source of "lessons." Whatever form such lessons took—drawing, painting, carving, modeling, or basketry—she thought of them as a supplement to formal education within the context of the most advanced educational theories. In Hammonton I had music lessons and also lessons in carving, because the only artist the town boasted was a skillful woodcarver. In Swarthmore we were taught by an all-round manual training teacher under whose tutelage I even built a small loom. In Bucks County I had painting lessons from a local artist and later from an artist in New Hope. And one year Mother had a local carpenter teach Dick and me woodworking. She was completely eclectic about what we were taught in these lessons, provided the person who was teaching us was highly skilled.

MARGARET MEAD
Blackberry Winter

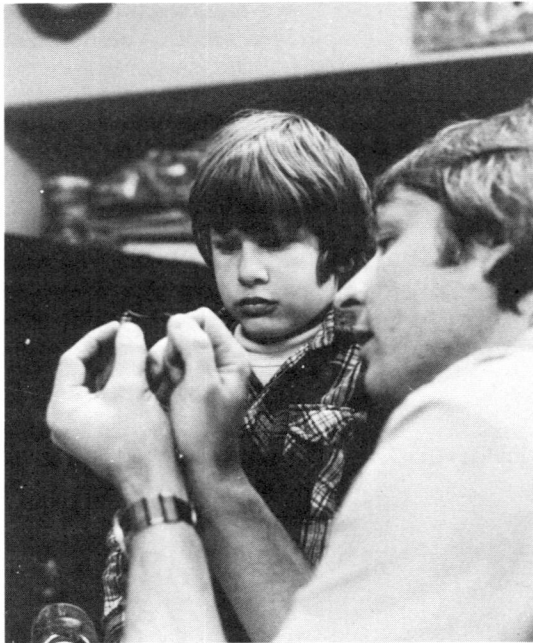

FRANK DERBAS

Making Connections

. . . one day we were looking at a picturebook of the Pilgrims. José understood that they had crossed the Atlantic, but something in the way he said it made me doubt his understanding. I asked him where the Atlantic was. I thought he might point out the window, since it lay not very far away. But his face took on an abject look, and he asked me weakly, "Where?" I asked him if he had ever gone swimming at Coney Island. He said, "Sure, man!" I told him that he had been swimming in the Atlantic, the same ocean the Pilgrims had crossed. His face lit up with pleasure and he threw back his head and laughed. There was a note of release in his laughter. It was clear that he had gained something more than information. He had discovered something. He and the Atlantic belonged to the same world! The Pilgrims were a fact of life.

GEORGE DENNISON
Lives of Children

◆

Left Behind at Howard Johnson's

I told the math class that to let something go by in class without knowing what it means, and without saying anything, is like leaving something in Howard Johnson's on a long car trip. You are going to have to go back for it eventually, so the sooner the better. This foolish metaphor has helped the kids, or so they say. . . . They have learned to recognize, if only a little, the feeling of panicky confusion that slowly gets hold of them. To be able to say "I'm getting left at Howard Johnson's" helps them to control this feeling, and if it gets too much for them they can always tell me that they have been left behind; then I can do something about picking them up.

JOHN HOLT
How Children Fail

◆

Out of the Fire Into the Frying Pan

. . . our children today live in a world in which the environment itself is a teaching machine made of electronic information. . . . The youngster today, stepping out of his nursery or TV environment, goes to school and enters a world where the information is scarce but is ordered and structured by fragmented, classified patterns, subjects, schedules. He is utterly bewildered because he comes out of this intricate and complex integral world of electric information and goes into this 19th Century world of classified data much like any factory set up with its inventories and assembly lines. The young today are baffled because of this extraordinary gap between two worlds.

MARSHALL McLUHAN
Perspecta: The Yale Architectural Journal, 1967

On "Wrong" Answers

It's important for parents and teachers to understand that when children answer a question incorrectly, they're often not "wrong"—rather, they're answering a question they haven't been asked. I don't think there's any confusion in a kid's mind when he says "the moon" in answer to the question "Which is nearer—the moon or New York?" When pressed for an explanation, he's likely to say he can *see the moon,* but he can't see New York. What's happened is that he has misunderstood the question: what he means by the word "near" is quite different from what the adult had in mind.

If we want our children to *learn* from our questions, therefore, we really must listen to their answers to make sure that they're answering the same question that we meant to ask them.

CHRISTOPHER SARSON

Competition Can Be Detrimental to Performance

. . . if you place children in competitive situations too early, before skills are proficient, they will generally perform more poorly. . . . When a child is still struggling to learn skills, the additional burden of being placed in front of an audience and being pitted against a rival is bound to have a negative effect [which] may be magnified if the child is highly anxious as a result of being placed in a competitive situation that "really counts."

TERRY ORLICK and CAL BOTTERILL
Every Kid Can Win

To Learn Is to Take Chances

It's very difficult to convince young children that it's O.K. to make mistakes, that mistakes can help them to learn. They don't believe me, because their experiences have taught them that it's not at all O.K. to make mistakes, and if they do, they'll be punished or ridiculed. They've learned to be frightened to make mistakes; that there is only one correct way to do everything. The most fearful children are would-be perfectionists who won't attempt any task unless they can do it perfectly, the first time, without an error. They are afraid to risk being "wrong"; being called "stupid"; and so their learning process is crippled, because to learn is to take chances.

STEPHEN M. JOSEPH
Children in Fear

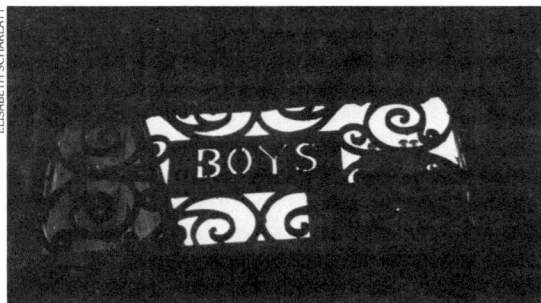

Learning to Skate in the Summer and Swim in the Winter

I used to know an old lady who'd been a teacher all of her life and lived in the state of Maine. She used to say: Kids learn to skate in the summer and swim in the winter—meaning, you do a lot of learning in some odd part of your mind which is not conscious. You get the feeling of things. Things consolidate—I don't know what the process is, but things come together so that there could be a long inactive period and then *whoom!* you're flying because you feel like it.

Learning is not an orderly process—it cannot be scheduled and run like railroad trains.

JOHN HOLT

Adjusting Our Priorities

By the time a child is four years old he is using 50 per cent of his I.Q. By age 13, he is using 92 per cent. Educational funds should be applied during the formative years, rather than as they are now.

R. BUCKMINSTER FULLER
I Seem to Be a Verb

Learn or Else

I think the big mistake in schools is . . . using fear as the basic motivation. Fear of getting failing grades, fear of not staying with your class, etc. Interest can produce learning on a scale compared to fear as a nuclear explosion to a firecracker.

STANLEY KUBRICK
The Making of Kubrick's 2001

———————◆———————

[Do you have reason to suspect your child has a learning disability? If so, you may want to consult "A Parent's Checklist on the Diagnosis of Learning Disabilities," on page 84.]

LEARNING: A FEW SPECIFICS

"Now I've Learned My A-B-C's, Tell Me What You Think of Me"

You don't need to know the letters of the alphabet in order until you start learning dictionary skills. There's just no purpose in a three-year-old's learning to recite the alphabet except one: it is rewarded by teachers (also uncles and aunts).
SHARON LERNER

"How Can You Use a Word Like 'Represents' with a Three-Year-Old?"

I was trying to explain a calendar to my son: Each square represents one day, I told him. "How can you use a word like 'represents' with a three-year-old?" my friend asked me. What other word should I have used, I wanted to know. "I don't know," he said. "How about 'stands for'?"

What makes anyone think that "stands for" makes any more sense to a three-year-old than a word like "represents"? He will learn the meaning of the word by hearing it in its context, as kids learn most of their vocabulary from the very start.
ELS

Say What You Mean

An elementary school teacher of our acquaintance uses a little game to impress upon her fifth graders the necessity for precise description, for saying exactly what you mean.

She asks the youngsters to write down directions for making a peanut butter sandwich.

She collects the papers and the next day takes a loaf of bread and a jar of peanut butter to class. Then she asks the children to make sandwiches following their own step-by-step instructions. The results, she reports, are hilarious.

Some forget to include the need for a knife. So, they must spread the peanut butter with their fingers. Others omit mention of two slices of bread. They wind up with a one-sided sandwich that is no sandwich at all.

The kids have a great time. They giggle a lot. But the illustration is not lost on them—say what you mean.
BOB WIEDRICH
The Chicago Tribune

[To find out about some ideas and methods that have helped—or failed to help—children learn to read, turn to pages 247–254, in the BOOKS section.]

Teaching Kids Not to Hate Mathematics

The basic attitude toward mathematics in this country is, to put it bluntly, *intense hatred*. Math is just about the only subject taught in school that people are proud of failing. "I was never *very good at math in school*"; you hear that a lot. Why, then, doesn't anyone ever say, with a great big smile on his face, "I was never very good at *reading* in school"? It's very much an attitudinal thing.

I think this "mathephobia," as a colleague of mine calls it, starts at a very early age. It comes as a result of the way children are first exposed to mathematics. The concentration always seems to be on the numbers themselves, and ways of manipulating them, rather than on what the numbers mean in everyday life. By way of illustration, I heard about a child the other day who was trying to figure out how long a metal strip had to be to go around a circular table he was making. He had absolutely no idea how to

go about it, even though, as his teacher complained to him terribly unhappily, they had studied "radii" and "diameters" in class just the week before. The teacher began to go through it all again, and halfway through her explanation he suddenly said, "But that's math—what I want to know is how much metal I need to go around the table!"

It's important to try to change this attitude. Children have to realize that they use math—in a real sense—every hour of every day. They have to learn to feel comfortable with numbers, so that they're not scared of them; once they do, they can learn any math they're exposed to, whether it's the new math or the old math or the good math or the bad math.

From an interview with
CHRISTOPHER SARSON

Math and Mother Goose

When it's time to listen to Mother Goose rhymes, Rachel (age five) picks a title from the table of contents—when we first started she always picked the longest title—and I read whatever she picks. Over time, I've been able to teach Rachel how to find in the text the page number indicated in the contents. Here's how I did it. Suppose, for example, that the verse she selected was on page 28. I'd suggest that she open the book anyplace—let's say it turned out to be page 52. "Now, Rachel," I'd ask her, "is twenty-eight less or more than fifty-two? It's *less,* so you flip a little toward the front of the book . . ." And so on. The nice thing is that Rachel really started the game herself.

STEPHEN OLDERMAN

Designing a Mural: A Subtle Way to Teach Math

Not only is designing a mural a great art project for a group of children, it also can get across some difficult mathematical concepts in a subtle and non-frightening way. First the kids draw a miniature version of the mural on an 8½-by-11-inch piece of paper, then they put a grid over it and transfer the artwork on each section of the grid to pieces of paper two feet square, which are then hung up on the wall in the proper sequence. The kids can color in the outlines they've traced on the big pieces of paper, and before you know it they've completed a removable mural. Or, if you're lucky enough to have a space where a permanent children's mural might be appropriate, they can transfer their tracings from the large sheets of paper directly to the wall, before they proceed with their coloring.

Of course, all this can be a bit messy, so you should be careful to use washable paints, or take other precautions against permanent damage.

From an interview with
CHRISTOPHER SARSON

Theater Games: Not Just for Acting Students

Theater games are not usually thought of as activities for "ordinary" children, yet they can be tremendous fun and can help kids learn things about themselves, about each other, and about the adult playing with them that they might never discover in any other way.

Teaching theater workshops, I found that sometimes one exercise would hold the interest of the group for weeks at a time, and we would explore it from many different viewpoints. Other times we worked on one particular game for one session only, and went on to something else the following week.

Outlined below are sixteen of my favorite exercises, many of which were inspired by Viola Spolin, whose book *Improvisation for the Theater,* (Northwestern University Press, 1963) will inspire *you.* Some are appropriate for kids of all ages, and some are best with younger children. Some require a group; others work well with only a few children, or even a single child. In any case, kids should be told that they'll be most successful with these specific exercises if they *act* rather than *react;* if they plunge in without prior thought or preparation.

1. Walk around the room. Find a movement or an action that you can repeat, that expresses how you feel *today.*

2. Sit around in a circle. Each person tells a very brief *short story,* just using his or her face and hands—no words.

Go around again. Tell the same story, just using words, no movement at all.

Go around again. Tell the same story, using just three words and just one hand. Variations on this exercise are infinite.

3. Walk all around the room in many directions. Stop, enact a section of a recent *dream,* then go back to walking. Then try to remember the sound or voice from that part of the dream, then walk, then enact it again.

4. Stand around in a circle. One person makes a *mask-like face* and directs it (with eyes, tongue, lips and/or nose) to another, and that one to another, and so on. Try to keep your body still—just the head is active in this one.

5. Someone starts a story, the next person *continues the story* and leaves off at an exciting part, the next person takes it from there. This can also be done between mother and child, or just two children.

6. Set up a *small house* using whatever furniture and props are around. By your movements and voice, try to make the others guess what kind of environment you are in.

7. Think of a *character* you'd like to be today (folk, story, novel, movie, totally ima-

ginary, someone from your past) and act it out quietly with your eyes closed. Find one action for that character and a voice. If in a group, show each other your characters after you've worked on them by yourself, or put them together in a scene.

8. Here's one related to No. 7: Lie down, let your mind go, and imagine yourself doing *fantastic things*—like jumping over a building, flying through the air to the sea, constructing a village. Get one image and repeat it to yourself. Then get up and try to act it out, no matter how fantastic the fantasy.

9. For two children or a group separated into partners: One kid becomes an *object;* the other uses that object. Take turns being the object. (One could be an old writing desk; the other would write on him or her, pull out a "drawer"—an arm or a leg—and so forth.)

10. Another *story* idea—either for a mother and child or two children: One person is the voice, the other the body. One is the teller, the other the enacter. Switch roles often until the story is being batted back and forth rapidly.

11. For a group: Split into threes or fours. Have each group make up a simple scene to enact, but have the *entrance* take up most of the scene. Whatever happens in the middle should be very short and low-key. The exit should be fast and loud.
The entrance is what counts here—very exaggerated, drawn out, and colorful.

12. For one child: Make up an *argument* between two people. You must act out both people using different voices and different faces.

13. Yet another *story* idea—for a group sitting in a circle: Each person writes a very short story on a piece of paper, without an ending, folds it and throws it in the middle of the circle. Each picks one up and reads it to himself or herself. Then, going around the circle, each child acts out the story, adding an ending of his or her own. A variation: Each child acts out whatever story he or she got, but in silence, pantomime. Only the new ending is said in words, aloud.

14. Act out a whole *day in the life* of a person, compressed into a few minutes. Try to be as detailed as possible—different feelings, moods, physical aspects, facial expressions. For older children: Keep repeating this "day in the life," each time compressing the entire thing more and more until it's like shorthand; each action is abbreviated, the transitions get smaller and smaller, till the last time you come out with one or two actions.

15. Go to a place by yourself where you can concentrate. Pretend you have on a *costume* or a completely different set of clothes. Try to express that costume by acting out each part of the clothing in detail. (Pretend to be buttoning large buttons, adjusting a feather in a huge hat, putting on galoshes or a flowing cape.) Try to give us a picture of what kind of outfit you are wearing.

16. Good for a small group: Set up an *obstacle course* of chairs, tables, pillows, books, toys, etc. Decide where it begins and ends. Select four or five places where you have to make certain sounds (like going under the chair is a yell, climbing over pillows is a short song, going around toy soldiers is a soft moan). The first kid to go through becomes part of the obstacle course at the end, until all are through. Each one must make the sounds at the designated places.

LANNY HARRISON

BABYSITTING AND DAY CARE

I saw to it that [my daughter] was never left in a strange place with a strange person. First a familiar person introduced her to the new place, or the stranger who was to care for her was introduced to her in a familiar place. She went easily and happily to strangers and showed discomfort only in the presence of visitors who, like her grandfather, were themselves a little too anxious.

MARGARET MEAD
Blackberry Winter

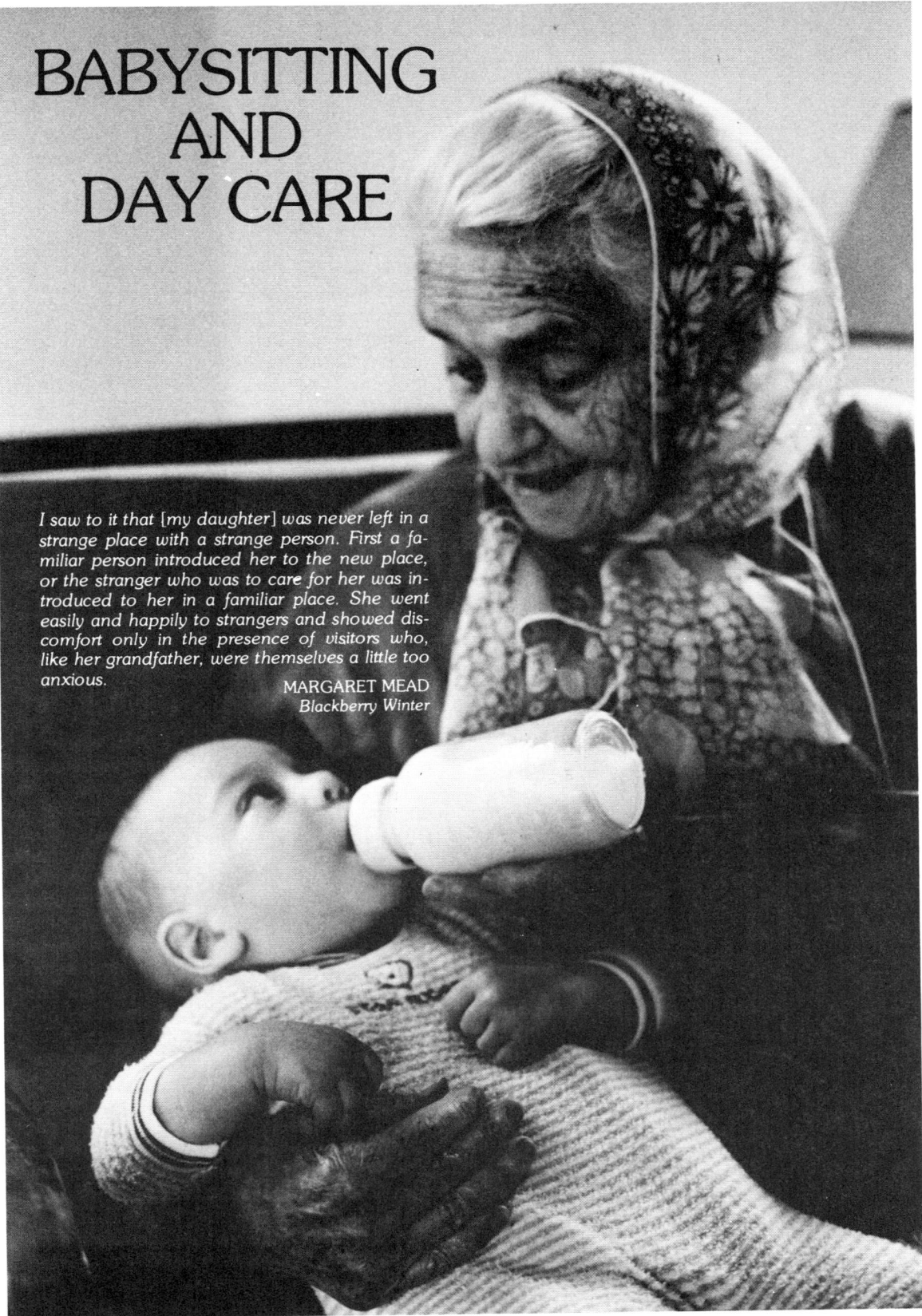

BABYSITTING

CHOOSING A BABYSITTER

Babysitters: The Possibilities

Probably no other job profile is superimposed upon so many different faces as the babysitter's. She or he is old or young, willing or not to put toys back on the shelf, able or not to stay out after midnight, available on a full-time basis or practically never. And your reasons for needing the sitter are just as varied. You have a job, you need to run an errand, you are going to the movies, you want some time off.

How do you choose the sitter best for you? Ask yourself whether you would be comfortable with this sitter if you were your child. Decide whether it is important to this particular occasion that the sitter wash the dishes, or whether all that matters is that he is pleased to give piggyback rides. (If the sitter is hired for the hours you are at the office, the tidying-up factor is probably important. If you are just out to dinner, it may not be.)

Here are some prototypical babysitters and the advantages and disadvantages they might present. (The full-time housekeeper who may also clean, launder, and cook is not discussed here. Nor are organized day-care programs, which are presented elsewhere in these pages.)

The teen-ager: She can be just marvelous or just awful. She can be very sensitive to children, having lately been a child herself. She can be interested in taking the time to play with your child. Or she can be using your home as a place to hang out, at the best doing her homework, and at the worst committing heaven-knows-what with a friend or friends, which is, of course, her business, but not when it involves the food in your refrigerator or neglect of your child. As a general rule, with exceptions naturally, steer away from teen-agers as sitters for infants, and use them as much as possible with grade-school-age children. Try boys as well as girls.

Because teen-agers tend to be busy with their own commitments, you might want to hire your sitter for one particular evening each week, or on some other regular basis. It is also wise to amass a list of teen-agers who babysit before you actually need one, so that you don't have to scramble for help. Sources? Word of mouth, a sign hung in the apartment elevator, at the store, etc. Also orphanages and high school guidance counselors.

With high school split sessions, many teen-agers end the school day quite early and are looking for steady afternoon jobs. For around $15 to $20 a week, you may be able to find a youngster who will pick up your children at school and act as a sitter or mother's helper in the afternoons. If you can't find one who is willing to give up every afternoon for the job, think about hiring two to split the week.

The person who takes children into her home: This is really an informal day-care arrangement, generally unlicensed. It can be convenient, as it is usually on a regular basis and always available so long as you deliver your child to the sitter. Go there a time or two just to observe (and be suspicious if this is an unwelcome idea). Is the person in charge involving the children in activities, or just parking them in front of the television set with a supply of potato chips? Are there too many children in the space? Do they go outdoors? Are they fed well? Does everyone seem healthy? Are there toys and equipment, however simple? Will your child feel displaced if he is sent here, away from his own territory and things, or is this a spot that provides the fun of other children and the stimulation of new surroundings? The rates should be cheap because other parents are paying in, too, but be cautious!

The person who answered your ad: Interview her. Ask for references and check them out. If you are advertising in the first place it is probably because you needed someone yesterday to look after your children on some sort of regular basis. No matter how swept away you are by her charm and willingness to work, however, put things on a trial basis for the first two weeks or so. Listen to what your children say about her. If her personality clashes with yours or your child's, it is just not going to do to have her playing an important role in your household. As to specifics, does she live nearby so that she can get to your home on time? Will she clean, too, if that is what you want? (Conversely, is there a danger that *all* she will do is clean—to the point of ignoring your child?) Do her long-range plans dovetail with yours? Would *you* like to have to stay home with her?

The older person: A retired person who has energy is a choice babysitter. It's a wonderful source of additional income for the older person, who often has that special grandparent instinct.

The babysitting agency: The woman sent by an agency is often elderly, and very expensive. Needless to say, she is not the one for a full-time job, not the one to secure if you are going back to work or otherwise planning days out on a long-term basis. On the other hand, if you need someone on very short notice, this may be the place to look. Most city telephone directories list babysitting agencies that are licensed and have been in business a number of years. You will have to rely on their judgment, as there is no way to screen the sitter—or often even learn her name—before she shows up at the door. But if the agency is one that your friends have used, you can sometimes request by name a sitter who has worked well for others. At the least, be frank with the dispatcher about the requirements: tell if your children are noisy and active, or whether you wish to have them taken outdoors.

You will have to pay for the sitter's transportation. To add to the expense, the meter will start running the minute she arrives, whether or not you actually leave at that point. And more. There is usually a four-hour minimum. In New York City, for example, to have one of these people from 7 p.m. to midnight for two children (more is extra) will run between $18 and $25.

Babysitting pools: (see page 130). A coalition of parents who pay in hours rather than money.

Friends: There is no need to be shy in asking for help from true friends. You, of course, must address yourself to the delicate question of reciprocating, but most people are really rather nice and like to help out. Try single people especially. As more and more adults have chosen a single life, they may welcome the chance to spend time with someone else's children. Offer, in exchange, dinner. Or use of your washing machine. Or a cake you've baked.

Relatives: No need to quote statistics here on the demise of the extended family, any more than on the disappearance of governesses and nurses. But if your children's grandparents or aunts and uncles live nearby and they like to help out, consider yourself very lucky. Chances are they love your child. And even if they are crazy or ill-tempered, you still know what you are getting, which in the babysitting game is half the battle.

Finally, some common sense. Tell all sitters, no matter how demure they may appear, that they are not allowed to hit your child, spank him, or use any kind of physical punishment. When you've hired a long-term sitter, try to spend at least a day at home together so that he or she will see how you do things. Always leave a number where you can be reached (if you plan an evening at the Coliseum in a crowd of thousands, plan to call in). Leave numbers of friends who will help in an emergency, and your doctor's number. None of this is hysterical, and it must be done. Discuss bedtime, meals, and the general plan you have for the children while you are away. (Make sure the children understand this as well.) Let the sitter know what is in the kitchen that she can eat, and what she can't. Be very specific. Don't expect the sitter to read your mind. Every parent wants something different.

JENNIFER CARDEN

What to Ask a Prospective Babysitter in an Interview

1. Do you have brothers and sisters? (A friend has found that the ideal babysitters are oldest siblings from large families who had to look after younger brothers and sisters while growing up and generally have a greater sense of responsibility. On the other hand, such a person may have resented always being given this responsibility and might now take it out on your child. Also, the youngest girl in a large family may have wanted this duty and responsibility and wants to prove to her mother—now transferred to you—how responsible she is.)

2. Did you have to look after your brothers and sisters as a kid? How did you feel then?

3. (For adult babysitters) Do you have a family of your own? What arrangements have you made to care for your family while you work?

4. How do you feel about the winter? Do you mind going out in cold weather?

5. Do you have specific ideas about babysitting—any general rules or guidelines that have helped you in this work? (Her answer will suggest how she feels about kids in general, and will give you a chance to learn whether her ideas work for you.)

6. How did you feel about the children you looked after in previous jobs? (Be suspicious if she gives an entirely glowing report. Ask if the children ever misbehaved and how she dealt with them.)

Remember, the point of asking any questions at all in an interview is that it helps you get a sense of the person you're interviewing. Make sure your child is around at least part of the time so that you can see how the prospective babysitter reacts to the child. This is your big chance to watch her in action.

ELS

Give the Kids a Voice

There is such a thing as the right babysitter. It is important, I think, to let the kids take part in the decision as to who sits. Ask them if they have a preference and discuss it with them. My children will voice their disapproval of one who is too rigid or too strict, or who spends too much time on the telephone or raiding the refrigerator.

The children have an important opinion as to whether or not the sitter is "good." And although you can't leave it up to the kids alone to determine whether the sitter is responsible or wholly trustworthy, their comments will give you important insights. If they were *too* comfortable with one sitter, I'd get suspicious.

CAROL EICHLER

◆

The Grandparent Solution

In order to be asked less frequently to babysit for her grandchildren, Shirley Bosin wrote in *Harper's Weekly,* she began charging for her services. She put the money into a savings account for the grandchildren's schooling, and that way everyone benefited.

ELS

◆

The Babysitting Pool

If your faithful and familiar babysitter demands a raise in pay and the thought of enlisting a lower-waged, thus lower-aged, sitter causes you anxiety, a babysitting pool may be the answer. It can be formed with a minimum amount of effort (better yet, with a lot of initial effort from one or two enthusiastic organizers) and, once formed, runs itself fairly simply without a lot of upkeep.

The model described below works well for our pool of seventy families, but you can start a pool with as few as five families who agree on two basic sets of rules: one governing the mechanics of the operation and one governing regulations of the babysitting itself.

One person acts as president and treasurer and one acts as a clearing house for information about the pool and about individual needs to sit or be sat for. These positions are filled by new volunteers each year. In order to join, a family needs three references and pays dues of 50 cents a year. When you join, you are given fifty free tickets, each ticket representing a half hour of sitting time. This first free twenty-five hours of sitting time is used as an incentive for people to

join and as a way for them to meet people in the group by asking them to sit. (For smaller collectives, fewer free tickets.) You also receive a current membership list (updated quarterly by postcards to all members). The membership list contains the following information for each family: father's and mother's names; names and birthdates of each child; a list of times and days when a family member is *not* available to sit. You then call people on the list and arrange for your needs, and once this begins to happen, you meet other families quickly and trade tickets back and forth.

Any difficulties in either finding a sitter or in replenishing your supply of tickets get reported to the clearing house member, who keeps a current list of people who especially need tickets and are eager to sit. When you leave the pool, you are expected to return fifty tickets, and those who need tickets in order to exit amicably are listed with the clearing house. In this regard the honor system (rather than an initial deposit) seems to have worked fairly well. Occasionally a voting questionnaire is sent out to determine special policy matters, and the only other demand on members is to attend a yearly meeting.

Rules governing the sitting evolve out of the nature of the parents and the group itself. Here are some samples from our pool:

- Kids needing care in the daytime are usually taken to the sitter's house, but in the evening kids are sat for in their own houses.

- Time is counted to the nearest half-hour, and time and a half is paid after midnight.

- Pediatrician's name and number—as well as other emergency numbers—must be left.

- The rate of payment is the same for any number of children in a family, but children from other families who are there must be paid for with tickets from their parents as well.

Most of the rules governing sitting are rules that each family has for itself, and the pool works very informally among people who have become friends. It is a great way to meet people, to leave your children with a parent rather than a teen-ager, and to combat poverty, guilt, and anxiety.

MARY-CLAIRE VANDER WAL

I stopped at a friend's house one night and said, let's go to a movie. She sat down at the phone with a list of numbers of parents in her babysitting pool and when she found a sitter on five minutes' notice I was convinced of the virtues and the possibilities of the babysitting pool. However, it can be an inconvenience: you might have to drag your kid out to the sitter's house at night in your evening gown, or if you've made an earlier commitment to sit, you might have to leave your mate behind with your own kids on a Saturday night when you feel like being together; and it's very hard to be a babysitter in a pool if you're a single parent. Still, it may work for you.

ELS

SO YOU'VE GOT YOURSELF A BABYSITTER. *NOW WHAT?*

I asked a friend recently how her kid got on with babysitters. "Quite well," she said; "she's discovered that most of them are there to entertain her." —RS

Adding That Magical Dimension

If your child is still clinging, it helps to give the babysitter, in the child's eyes, that special magical dimension. Recently, when my son was giving me a hard time for leaving him with the sitter, I told him that she was going to bake oatmeal cookies with him (something I'd never done). He fell for it and nearly pushed me out the door. (If you try this, don't forget to leave the ingredients.)

With teen-aged babysitters, you might prefer something that can be made without a stove, like a smoothie: orange juice and a banana mixed up in a blender (a little honey and an ice cube optional).

ELS

Be Specific

It helps to be very specific about how you want your household and child run. Babysitters will not do things your way unless you specifically describe the way you want things done. I once discovered how a babysitter achieved great popularity with my son by unearthing every hidden sweet in the house (many of which I'd tucked away for my own surreptitious nighttime consumption) and sharing these secret treasures with him unstintingly. I should've warned her. It's easiest to write out your instructions and leave them for all babysitters.

Even suggestions for disciplining or getting the kids to bed would help. Or a list of permissible bribes (and forbidden ones). A sitter once thanked me for making her job easier when I suggested that with my son she not give orders as orders. "Better get this traffic jam cleared up before the fire engine comes through" is one way of getting the toys picked up. Or: "Right after these crayons are picked up we can have a story (or a second dessert)."

ELS

Learn Your Babysitter's Needs

Nobody babysits for you because of money. Take that as a word of advice. You may pay someone very well—but really she is there because she loves you and she loves your child. I could pay someone twice as much and not get a person better than the woman who takes care of Thomas. I learn her needs and I pay attention to who she is and she responds to that.

NIKKI GIOVANNI

(If None of This Works) How to Fire a Babysitter

Think of a nice way of saying "You're fired!" ("I'm very sorry, but this doesn't seem to be working out for me," or "We've decided we need someone to work full time [part time/weekends], and we won't be needing you any longer"), but say it and get it over with. It's a mistake to keep on a babysitter who makes you uneasy just because it is so hard to let her go. If you think she may be vindictive, don't give two weeks' notice—it's worth the severance pay to preserve your child (and, perhaps, your Ming dynasty vase).

ELS

Leave a Number: The Babysitter's Checklist

Child's name/nickname _____   Police Emergency_____

Parents' names_____   Fire Department_____

   address_____   Poison Control Center_____

   phone_____   Doctor's name_____

Father's business phone_____   address_____

Mother's business phone_____   phone_____

Nearest friendly neighbor_____   Drugstore_____

Nearest friendly relative_____   Nearest hospital_____

Child's allergies_____

Child's blood type_____

Any medications, vitamins_____

Special house rules_____

Prohibitions_____

Eating habits_____

Don't forget to leave a number where you can be reached.

BABYSITTERS, FRIEND AND FOE

A Stabilizing Influence

One of the most stable influences in my kids' lives has been their babysitter. When they were very little, a cousin put us on to Gussie, who's in her fifties, married, and has no children of her own. She finished her shift in the pants factory in time to pick the children up from school. Over five or six years, she's come to look at my kids as hers. She has a grandmotherly instinct, spoils the hell out of the children in some ways, but is able to discipline them. Sometimes she'll come and have dinner with them even when she's not engaged to sit. Sometimes they spend the night at her house.

Since my wife and I have separated, it's been especially good to have Gussie sit for both of us.

STEPHEN SONTHEIMER

Siphoning Off the Hostility

Fraulein, to me, had the strong specific meaning of nursegirl. . . . Frauleins were my immemorial enemies, interposed between my parents and me, like wicked bailiffs between kind barons and their serfs. They were the bad doorkeepers of a benign sultan. Without their officious intervention, I was sure, I could have been with my parents twenty-four hours a day, and they would have been charmed to have me. . . .

The Fraulein, I have thought often since, was a remarkably effective device for siphoning off from the parents the hostility that analysts assure us is the parents' due. Careful bootleggers in Harlem during Prohibition used to pass suspect alcohol through an old felt hat, on the theory that the poison would remain there. The Fraulein had the function of the felt hat. As full of the discharged hostility as the hat was of fusel oil, she shifted to another job when the child outgrew her. She left it as harmless to its parents as a baby rattlesnake milked of venom. To the child who began conscious life under the rule of a Fraulein, even the least bearable mother appeared an angel.

The device seems to me, looking back, more sensible than that of the kind nanny described in English novels. The nannies siphon off not the hostility, but the affection, leaving the protagonists incapable of liking anybody else for the rest of their lives . . .

It never occurred to me to wonder why my parents paid the Fraulein who deprived them of the pleasure of my constant company. I was sure the witches, like those in the fairy tales with which they tried to terrify me, had imposed themselves on the kind king and queen by some cunning swindle.

A.J. LIEBLING
Between Meals

Taking the Pressure Off

As a single mother I have seen to it that my son has men in his life—men who are not necessarily in my life. His nursery school was run by a man; he's had male babysitters whenever it has been possible; he goes on outings with his godfather or uncle or the father of a friend. Such associations take the pressure off me (though I lose out on the opportunity to whine and wail at him: "I've been both a mother and father to you!").

ELS

Sometimes it's so hard to find a babysitter that you can't go out.

DAY CARE

DAY CARE: PROS AND CONS

Are Day-Care Centers an Acceptable Alternative for Families with Two Working Parents? Here Are Margaret Mead's Comments

I would first like to distinguish day-care centers—all day, twelve-hour care, for infants and older children—from nursery schools, for children from two to five. They are becoming confused today and this is unfortunate. I think that well-run day-care centers are preferable to poor and irresponsible care for the infants and young children of working mothers who have no other way to care for their children. But I consider them a very poor alternative to any kind of good care, where the infant and child up to two is cared for by at least one person who is continuously present in its life—a grandmother, a father, an aunt, a neighbor who is caring for two or three children. All that we know about child care suggests that continuity of care is a crucial ingredient in the development of children. For children over two, a nursery school, a few hours a day with other children—whether this is a neighborhood cooperative or a more professionally run school—is an addition, and a valuable one, to the home environment, and a corrective for any of its limitations: no siblings, contentious siblings, no other adults except parents, etc.

But the ideal situation is to have groups of people of different ages live close enough together so that young children can be cared for within the extended neighborhood, rather than in institutions.

I would also like to stress the great value of child-care centers where children can be taken when their parents are ill, or in other emergencies, or even while the mother is shopping. These supplements to isolated homes are most desirable.

In the modern world, with its surplus of population and its need for better-reared children, I see no excuse for two people who want to work full time having a child at all, unless they can provide for one or more individual caretakers to give their child continuity.

MARGARET MEAD

Best Company for Kids: Other Kids or Adults?

An article once suggested that to elicit potential genius from a child a parent should surround him with adults rather than peers and stimulate and encourage his fantasies—these conditions had prevailed in the childhoods of fifty or so reputed geniuses throughout history. On the other hand, psychologists and common sense never underestimate the importance of peer relations in normal development. The question of whether either emphasis is more desirable— peer or adult—is interesting only because thinking about it is so interesting. Both aspects are important in whatever sort of natural balance parent, child, and peers comfortably strike. But isn't it fascinating just to note the differences and implications between these two kinds of unconsciously powerful relationships.

You would think a child could learn a great deal from an adult, the way a beginner learns from an expert. But maybe a child isn't prepared to learn a great deal. Or maybe the inscrutable blitherings and extrasensory communication between peers is an invaluable learning, socializing, and psychologizing process. Still, one two-year-old doesn't teach another two-year-old the alphabet.

ALAN SAPERSTEIN

Most of What You Need to Know About Choosing a Day-Care Center

Comparing educational philosophies at a pre-school level can be a futile pastime, since the most important dimension of the school is the warmth and the patience of the teacher. What you might want to know, in the end, is: Does the teacher ever hug a student?

ELS

HOW TO START YOUR OWN DAY-CARE CENTER

Anyone can start a day-care center. It is a return to that old world of barn-raisings, quilting bees, and shoot-outs at the O.K. Corral. But before you read any further, let me warn you: once you get a taste of involvement in a day-care center, you're hooked. You start out wanting a good experience for your child and some free time for yourself, and you end up with a new and consuming identity: that of the day-care-center parent.

We began several years ago in a church basement in Brooklyn. Out of an original group of fifteen seemingly rational and loving parents came battles over political, social, educational, and philosophical questions so intricate, so paralyzing, and so bloody at times that the mere survival of the center seemed in jeopardy. But despite the intricacies and sensibilities of their parents, our kids have loved the center from the very first day it opened. They loved it just enough; we, on the other hand, have probably loved it too much.

This leads into my first basic advice to anyone wishing to begin a day-care center: Remember that the center is primarily for the children, not for the adults. Start out with a small group of like-minded people gathered from among friends and acquaintances or lured by signs in supermarkets or word of mouth around the sandbox, and try to involve people who have similar visions and needs. We had wanted to create an ideal, free, diversified world for our children in the center, but our resources were limited, and after five months of arguments and discussions someone said: Forget our differences; we're opening the doors on Wednesday; who's going to be there?

Advising that you avoid abstract arguments is tricky, because it is crucial to have an educational and philosophical policy in mind before you find a site, choose equipment, and appoint a staff; on the other hand, it is so easy and yet so devastating to lose sight of everything *but* your differences. It may perhaps help if at the first few meetings you try to make five basic decisions which should make divisions in the group fairly clear at the beginning if compromises are to be made:

How many children do you want in the center?

What age range will they cover?

What kind of program do you want for them?

How many hours a day/days a week will the parents need day care?

Can the parents staff the center, or will a paid staff be hired?

If your feelings on these questions—or those concerning what the children will be doing and growing into at the center—are not within reasonable agreement, it is better to split into separate groups.

We started out with seventeen children from six months to three years—the pre-nursery-school ages, the hardest ones to find day care for. We wanted a program that was centered on activities which our children could choose rather than be scheduled into. Ideally, there would be cutting and pasting going on in one corner of the room, story reading in another, a dollhouse or garage or make-believe supermarket set up in a third, and others depending upon the number of adults available to supervise each activity and area. The only scheduled events in the day would be snacks, lunch, naps, and diaper changes or trips to the bathroom. Whenever any activity lost interest for most of the children, it would be replaced by another, providing the adult had survived and was still able to function (which, on many days, was a big provision).

It was also important to us that children in all stages of development be allowed to play together and to learn from each other. We wanted no part of grouping arbitrarily by age, but instead encouraged exposure to as many different kinds of children and adults as possible. Most of the parents needed only part-time day care, and at least one parent of each child was free once a week to work a session at the center—the men as well as the women. Our basis then from the beginning was activity-oriented, age-integrated, parent-staffed day care, and we have spent the last three years trying to figure out what exactly these terms mean.

SITE

Theoretically, once you know what you want and what you need for your center, you can begin to work out the particulars, the first of which is finding a site.

Low-rent storefronts or basements can be found, but rent-free space is usually available somewhere. We found that churches, syn-agogues and civic groups seemed to be the most sympathetic to the day-care needs of the community. But usually free space has some strings attached, and while they may seem minor at the beginning, make sure you can live with them. You might have to make concessions such as observing special holidays or rituals, religious or political, or sharing the site with another group and clearing it nightly of all your things.

The temptation is to take the first available space offered, but don't. The limitations and potentials of the site will influence the day-to-day operations of the center more than you realize at first. We purposefully chose a large open basement in a church because we did not want walls and partitions to separate our children into groups and we wanted them to feel free to move about at will. After a year or two we realized that our kids were indeed moving about at will. In fact, we had managed to produce a robust don't-fence-me-in group of kids, so adept at Batman and Robin antics that the noise level (not to mention traffic mishaps) in the place had reached an unbearable level. After two years of parents warring over the partition question, we finally voted to divide and conquer. It took one weekend and forty-five old doors and a parents' emergency construction crew working around the clock to produce three partitioned areas; however, we are still trying to convince the highly skilled Batmen and Robins that they cannot scale insurmountable heights and leap from tall buildings. Probably the most important thing about a site is that it have the potential for changing as the needs and wishes of the parents and children change.

Finding a Site: Considerations

1. Is it safe and healthy for children? (What type of floors, walls, ventilation, fire exits, security from theft, things to trip over or bump into, etc.? Are there loose wires or lead-based paints that could pose a potential hazard?) If there are safety problems, how much will it cost to correct them?

2. Does it meet local fire and Board of Health regulations for occupancy by kids under five?

3. Is there an outdoor play area available with the site or close by?

4. Can it be fixed up to be bright, cheery, and comfortable?

5. Are there adequate bathroom facilities with easy, quick access and hot water? Fixtures low enough for children to reach?

6. Can the room or rooms contain the unimaginable noise level a group of children tends to produce?

7. Are there distractions built into the site, like people having to walk through on a regular basis or a boiler room next door?
8. Will the space be exclusively for your use, or does it have to be cleared nightly of toys, etc.?
9. And most important: does the layout of space provide the potential for developing the type of program you want? Is it large enough? (A minimum of 50 square feet of classroom space per child has been suggested, exclusive of kitchen and special-function rooms.) Is it partitioned so as to provide separate activity areas, or can it be if you wish?

EQUIPMENT AND SUPPLIES

If your experience is like ours, the initial joy of actually finding a site for the center will be overwhelming, and two days later the thought of what-to-do-with-it-now will be equally overwhelming. Most of the equipment you need to start operations can be donated or built, and it is better to think in those terms from the beginning and hoard any money you have for the extra things that kids love which can't be readily gotten for free: like playground equipment, indoor rocking boats, sand and water tables—all the things in the catalogues which are too big and too expensive to fit into your living room but which you'd still like your children to enjoy.

Work on donations first: toys, cribs, refrigerators, books—anything anybody from anywhere no longer needs for their kids or their house. You can advertise or put up signs for the equipment you need, and gather things not only from those directly involved but from as much of the community as possible. We wrote toy manufacturers for samples, offering to test and endorse their products; we suggested the use of the center for advertising photos if the equipment could stay once the lights and action were over. We visited hard-nosed New York City shop owners and painted lovely pictures of sweet children playing happily on the rugs we were sure they'd be eager to donate. There is often a doting grandmother or grandfather who's a soft touch, and many donations were extorted from local merchants by promises of future patronage (this was undoubtedly our best and most successful method).

Our tables and chairs for eating and for group activities were initially created out of metal milk crates (stealthily selected from neighborhood supermarkets sometime between dusk and dawn) or orange crates plus pieces of plywood for tops. Hooks were hung for clothing, gates installed, and shelves hammered together. And then we painted, washed, scrubbed, disinfected, de-bugged and, to announce our presence, we put a lovely sign outside our door (which was stolen within ten minutes, announcing other presences). With a lot of work and very little money, we finally reached the point one day when we looked around, breathed deeply, smiled proudly, and watched a flood of accomplishments fill the room like welcome sunshine. We were actually doing it!

So much for permanent equipment. The kinds of supplies you need for the center depend somewhat upon the ages of the children, but the sample list in the box should get you off to a good start.

We found one or two stores that would give us a discount for our standing orders on paper goods and cleaning supplies. We ordered everything in bulk: fresh fruit and vegetables (kids love to shell peas and clean beans) came from a neighborhood food cooperative, and we had milk delivered three times a week. Our crafts supplies were also ordered at a discount rate from a wholesale supplier. We were amazed once we began working with the children how many activities can be devised using free supplies like egg cartons, newspapers, old clothes, empty cereal boxes, and nearly anything else you can think of. In addition to conserving money, we got enormous satisfaction from the creative recycling of what resources we had.

Initial Equipment
1. Can be donated or bought:
   Refrigerator
   Stove or hot plate
   Mattresses, pillows, couches: for sitting, resting and jumping on
   Rugs
   Anything needed to decorate the room
   Wastebaskets
2. Can be built:
   Small tables for eating, crafts, games
   Small chairs and/or benches
   Easels for painting
   Cubbies or hooks for jackets
   Shelves and bookcases
3. Play equipment (donated used or bought):
   Blocks
   Toys
   Books
   Old clothes for dress-up

   The would-be-nice section:
   Sand and water table or box
   Indoor climbing apparatus and mats

Record player
Piano

4. For children two and a half and under (usually can be donated used):
Cribs for naps—and sheets
Changing tables
Gates
Potty seats

Supplies

1. Food (for snacks twice a day and emergency lunches for those who forgot or ate theirs on the way to the center):
Milk
Juice
Fruit
Cheese
Crackers
Peanut butter and jelly
Bread
Nuts

2. Paper goods, etc.:
Paper towels
Toilet paper
Soap
Cleaning supplies
Diaper-changing supplies
Trash bags
Pampers

3. Play supplies:
Clay
Glue
Paints, brushes, paper
Collage materials
String
Scissors
Books
Records
Crayons

"The Philadelphia Plan"

Those in the market for day-care supplies ought to obtain a copy of *Choosing and Using Materials in Child Care Settings*, by Ann Dintenfass and Bernie De Koven (available for $1.50 from The Training Office, 401 North Broad Street, Suite 895, Philadelphia, Pa. 19108).

Originally prepared for use in Philadelphia, this is a simple, fresh presentation of materials (commercial and homemade) and ideas that all early-childhood teachers will find useful. The many drawings will help you find what you're looking for, and charts in the back provide a checklist of materials and a list of catalogues which carry them (Childcraft, Edmund, See, Workshop for Learning, and others).
                                                                            RS

STAFFING

Staffing the center depends upon whether you have more time than money or more money than time, and upon how important you feel parent participation is in the center. We operated for the first nine months with parent staffing only. The center was open from 9 to 5 five days a week, and the day was divided into two sessions that ran from 9 to 1 and 1 to 5. This gave us ten sessions a week to staff. Each parent worked one session in exchange for three sessions a week for her or his child. (We have now upped that to five for part-time kids and ten for full-time kids.) We figured that for children under two we needed 1 adult per 3 children per session; for ages two and three, 1 adult per 4 children; and for ages four and five, 1 adult per 5 children. Later we decided to open the center at 8 a.m. and close at 6 p.m., giving an extra hour on each side only to those parents who worked full time and needed it; we then asked each parent to come early or leave later once a month, alternating among the four parents who worked a particular session.

We had wanted parent involvement in day care, and with this system we got exactly that. We also had people coming late, leaving early, not coming at all, or developing mysterious ailments once a week on the day they were scheduled to work. A lot of us had feelings about working in the center akin to the old Philadelphia joke: first prize, a week in Philadelphia; second prize, two weeks. Thus there came into being the system of paid substitutes. Either you worked your session or you hired an approved paid substitute (which generally took ten to fifteen phone calls to accomplish if you were lucky).

Having barely limped through the first summer, we decided to raise our fees and hire a director. We were ready to admit that although we were all terrific parents, sensitive and delightful, we somehow were lacking in knowing exactly what to do with that many kids for that many hours in that place. We needed leadership. More and more substitutes were appearing on the scene, and the children were having difficulty recognizing any adult on a regular basis. We felt that a director could not only provide consistency of activities and treatment of the children, but help in organizing as well, and then perhaps parents would be more eager to subject themselves to working four hours a week in the center. The director-led/parent-staffed center worked well at times; and not so well at others, but it was an improvement.

The following summer we accepted city funding, which meant we had enough money to increase our number of children to forty-five—fifteen full-time kids and thirty part-time—and to hire a staff of eight teachers plus a director, bookkeeper, and family counselor.

We have had staffing both ways: parent and paid, and it is still difficult to say which is better. We gave permanent positions to several of our substitutes whom the kids loved and the parents had for months appreciated. Many of them had no professional training or credentials, as many of the newer staff people do. Our feelings were that we wanted to avoid the kind of insensitivity to children that comes from either too much training or too little experience, and we have a good staff, well mixed in terms of age, sex, ethnic group, experience, training, and all the other good things. We have kept parent staffing to a degree by requiring that all parents who have at least four hours free a week work at the center on a regular basis every second or third week. It is much harder to make credible an every-third-week disability, and as the atmosphere in the center has changed, parent staffing has been easier to maintain, and paid staffing has worked well.

Staffing

1. Choices:
   Parent volunteers
   High school or college volunteers
   Neighborhood volunteers
   Partially paid/partially parent staff
   Paid staff
2. Considerations:
   If you have parent or volunteer staffing, your choices are somewhat limited, but you can hope for a few experts in exercises, dance, music, painting, storytelling, and survival.
   If you have a paid staff, you have to decide preferences of age, sex, training, experience, etc.
   The younger the children are, the higher the ratio of adults to children should be.

FINANCES

There are two parts to financing the center: initial funds to set things up, and money needed for ongoing expenses. Initially we did receive some money from neighborhood groups, but the response to our asking for funds from large foundations or corporations was negative. We found that unless we came up with a totally unusual or experimental program for day care, foundations were not interested. So, we began by paying in $25 initial expense money per

family, with the agreement that this would be refunded when we left the center.

To meet ongoing expenses we paid fees. At first it was a simple $5 a week for four sessions. Later one of the parents worked out an intricate sliding fee scale, which meant the more money earned by a family, the more they paid for day care, and the system worked well, probably because no one could comprehend it. With an income of $10,000, a family paid $11 a week for four sessions, but they were paid $6.80 for working a session, which ended up meaning about 25 cents an hour for day care. People who paid less than $6 basic fee did not get money back for working their session, and somehow things seemed to work out.

For us the determination of fees revolved around two basic questions: how much money we needed to pay our bills, and how much each of us could afford to pay. The first amount was fairly fixed, and when it moved, it was up. Initially we figured $3 per month per child for food and the same for supplies. In addition, there were utility bills, telephone bills, liability insurance coverage, and money to pay those substitutes who were not paid by the parents who hired them and who should have paid them (keeping track became difficult). The year we hired a director, our expenses were about $12,000 a year, with $7,500 going for her salary, but that year we had instituted the sliding fee scale and some parents were paying a considerable amount. It is important to agree from the very beginning whether or not you pay for all sessions your child is scheduled for, regardless of actual attendance.

A word about funding. Depending upon the area of the country you live in, city, state, or federal funding may be available. To find out, contact the local department of social services; in New York City, for example, funding is at times available through the Agency for Child Development. Individual requirements and policies regarding day care differ greatly from state to state, and at times from hour to hour, so it would not help to go into greater detail than this.

Our center collectively broke its heart over accepting and living with city funding, which we did two years after we began. Although it provided us large amounts of money for staff and equipment, and for accepting new members who needed day care desperately but could give neither time nor money to the center, the price we paid for these things was high.

The city, state, and federal governments introduced us to bureaucratic intricacies in great contrast to our usual muddling-through. Once we had accepted funding and expanded our responsibilities to many more families and to the staff, it was difficult to fight for our belief in universal day care and parent control when up against a threatened cutoff of funds.

Giving advice on the wisdom of seeking outside funding is difficult. It is necessarily true that with money come controls, and living with them can be galling. It is probably true, however, that our children have benefited greatly from the increase in funds.

Finances

1. Initial financing:
   Grant from a foundation
   Donation from church, civic, or block association
   Fund-raising
   Flat fee of $10 to $25 for initial membership
2. Ongoing financing:
   Flat fee per session
   Flat fee per week
   Fees paid on sliding scale according to income, number of children—either by the session or by the week.
   Decide: do you pay for the session your child is scheduled for whether he/she makes it there or not?
3. Ongoing expenses:
   Rent
   Salaries of staff
   Food
   Supplies
   Insurance payments
   Telephone bill
   Utilities
   Substitutes for absent staff

FISHER PRICE CO.

CONTINUING OPERATIONS

Once you have the children, the parents, the site, the equipment and supplies, the staff and adequate financing, all you have to worry about is keeping it all going.

We had initially agreed to be a collective—which meant that work was to be shared as equally as possible among members, but that we would try to avoid putting burdens, financial or otherwise, on anyone who couldn't handle them at any time. Members were required to be on a committee (rotating every six months), work in the center if they could or pay a substitute if they could not, come to general meetings twice a month, clean the center one weekend every five or 6 months, and pay fees. The collective works as well as anything dependent upon an average group of people: some people work all of the time, some work some of the time, and some do nothing at all and endure occasional but usually gentle abuse. (This is not to imply Utopia Revisited; we are quite accomplished at venting our anger in small groups or behind backs, but by the time it comes to an actual legal vote, our hearts are not in the kill and we retreat from you-must to it-would-be-nice-if-you-would.)

All parents and staff vote on important questions involving the center, and since everything seems important, we tend to vote a lot and lose track of many decisions. Our general meetings were for so long involved with mere survival that only now are we enforcing a rule to discuss the children for at least the first hour.

The hardest lesson for us to learn was that the safety and well-being of the children had to come first, before the needs or individual wishes of the parents. No one, for example, wants to tell a parent who is late for work that her child can't stay that day because his nose is running (and certainly not before spending hours at a meeting defining what constitutes an acceptable runny nose versus a nonacceptable runny nose. For the record, this is dependent upon such minute details as color and texture of mucus, which we have spelled out quite graphically). Yet the illness rate in the winter months is high and kids who are sick or on any kind of medication simply have to be kept out of the center.

Each parent should leave a sheet in the center giving emergency numbers, name and phone number of their child's pediatrician, a list of special health problems—allergies, etc. Children should be signed in and out of the center for each session—and the phone number of one parent put next to the name. This must be done faithfully.

We must be equally rigid in complying with fire regulations and holding drills (we have had one serious fire) and in determining how many children may be in the center in relation to the number of adults there to supervise. We have a policy of drop-ins, which means a parent may bring a child on a day not regularly scheduled if there is room, and the temptation is to say yes to be nice, when the answer should be no to be safe.

In the final analysis, starting a day-care center has to be based on the belief that it will be good for your children and good for you. It is much easier to hire a sitter, look for a nursery school, or start a playgroup. But none of us wanted that. We wanted a parent-controlled and -involved center which gave our children the opportunity to be with many different children and many different adults in one place. We have grown and changed as our children have grown and changed; and it has been good for all of us.

Operations

(Sample list of committees for ongoing problems and improvements)

1. Curriculum Committee:
   Responsible for getting and maintaining supplies relating to children's play, toys, books; responsible for activities in center: evaluating, instituting new ones, etc.

2. Finance Committee:
   Responsible for collecting fees; paying staff and all bills; giving reports and predicting rising costs and fees.

3. Maintenance Committee:
   Responsible for organizing four parents to clean center every weekend; seeing that laundry (mostly bed sheets) is done; making sure every child has a change of clothing at center; generally maintaining health and safety standards.

4. Construction Committee:
   Producing any new equipment needed in the center; painting; making sure gates work and shelves don't collapse.

5. Membership Committee:
   Handles all scheduling of children and changes in scheduling; schedules parents' sessions to work; maintains a waiting list of people who want to join; contacts and initiates new members.

6. Executive Committee:
   Generally oversees; enforces rules; prepares the agenda for general meetings; hears complaints; keeps track of things and tries to keep the peace.

7. Fund-raising Committee:
   This was abandoned after six months due to inactivity and lack of cooperation.

8. Personnel Committee:
   Formed only after we had a paid staff of eight; deals with parent/staff problems, city regulations, general employer/employee matters.

9. Standing Ad-hoc Committees:
   By-laws
   Personnel Manual
   Incorporation (Incorporating as a nonprofit corporation is a good idea but difficult. In New York you have to have a lease on a building proving you are a day-care center before you can be incorporated as nonprofit. Initially we had rent-free space and no lease; later we paid rent with city funding, but the building didn't meet city regulations so we had new problems.)

MARY-CLAIRE VANDER WAL

Books About Day Care

THE DAY CARE BOOK: THE HOW, WHAT, AND WHY OF RATIONAL DAY CARE, by Vickie Breitbart (Knopf, 1974, 209 pages, $5.95 paperback), is an inviting compendium of personal accounts, articles, analytical essays, wonderful graphics, and concrete suggestions on how to set up a day-care center. If you are at the stage of deciding what you think about day care, this book may be a comfort and a guide for you. It is a very political book—committed to community-run day care, to non-sexist roles, and to the struggle for "child care for all." Some readers may be offended by the polemical quality of the theoretical essays which argue these positions or by the articles denouncing the alternatives (that is, franchise day care or highly technologized pre-school "discovery centers"), but I frankly enjoyed these impassioned arguments because they were clear, cogent, and based on personal concerns. This is also a very human book: you can listen to the views of single mothers, of parents engineering a battle for a community-controlled child-care referendum, of parents coming to communes with high hopes and then discovering the pitfalls of communal child-rearing. And the book is practical: it has an appendix of "Resources," with charts on licensing, budgets, funding sources, equipment to make and buy, and a good bibliography.

For those at the stage of creating and designing their own day-care center, the richest source of information is a trio of books written by E. Belle Evans, each with different co-authors. I was tremendously excited by these books because they are direct, specific, and thorough. The broadest of the three is DAY CARE: HOW TO PLAN, DEVELOP, AND OPERATE A DAY CARE CENTER, by E. Belle Evans, Beth Shub, and Marlene Weinstein (Beacon, 1971, 337 pages, $3.95 paperback). It raises the issues and describes the factors involved in starting a center: deciding whom it will serve, finding and developing a site, hiring and training a staff, developing a curriculum, planning a budget, and raising funds.

DAY CARE FOR INFANTS: THE CASE FOR INFANT DAY CARE AND A PRACTICAL GUIDE, by E. Belle Evans and George E. Saia (Beacon, 1973, 216 pages, $3.45 paperback), has a similar format and range but is specifically concerned with the very different needs of children under three. Faced with the problem of finding good care for my five-month-old son while I work (infant day care is impossible to come by in most neighborhoods), I found this book useful in thinking about the issues involved in outside care for infants and in evaluating caretakers, even though I didn't end up using group day care.

The third book, DESIGNING A DAY CARE CENTER: HOW TO SELECT, DESIGN, AND DEVELOP A DAY CARE ENVIRONMENT, by E. Belle Evans, George Saia, and Elmer A. Evans (Beacon, 1975, 176 pages, $3.45 paperback), is a truly nuts-and-bolts manual; it would also be useful to any adult who wants to build storage equipment, children's furniture, room dividers, and lofts for the home. After examining the relationship between design and educational philosophy (without arguing for one particular philosophy), the book goes on to discuss site selection, renovation, and dividing and using indoor space. A neat little chapter which describes basic contruction tools is followed by the largest section: building instructions for everything from storage cubbies on through toilet seats to a complex but cozy library platform. The instructions tell which tool to use when, the diagrams are clear, and there are illustrations of the finished product in use. Insofar as you subscribe to the all-American do-it-yourself philosophy of day care for your child, you can't possibly wail "But I don't know how!" with these books at your disposal.

SHELLEY KESSLER

Community Day Care: A Book That Shows It Can Work

SHARING THE CHILDREN, *by Nora Harlow (Harper & Row, 1975, 154 pages, $7.95 hardcover; 1976, $2.95 paperback).*

It began as a small group of desperate mothers who took turns caring for each other's children in their respective apartments. It became a six-day-a-week community activity, in a rent-free Columbia University storefront, with mothers, fathers, and grandparents sharing the care of the children.

It wasn't easy for anyone. ("I was suffocating being all mother. I was scared to death not to be.") It certainly wasn't easy to get the university's help. ("We were an independent community group and letting us use some of their property would be setting up a possible hazard to their property rights. A very dangerous precedent for absentee ownership of property all over the world.") And it wasn't easy to involve the fathers. ("We had married nice . . . college professors, pipefitters, poets, park attendants, Ph.D candidates, numbers runners, security guards, small businessmen, taxi drivers, and a U.N. consultant. All with the assumption they couldn't work in a daycare center because they had jobs. . . . Only two men would jeopardize their jobs by spending half a day with the children." And: "Whitney cried because she was forced into the company of a grown man and she was afraid. . . . We had been dimly aware of the little girls' fear of men for some time but it hadn't been a problem since they rarely came into personal contact with men.")

The fact that one group, in its unique and imperfect way, was able to overcome such obstacles makes this book more than just another day-care book.

RS

(recommended by Jean Marzollo)

Nursery School, Home Style

If you don't want to (or can't) send your kids to a day-care center, but you do want to give them a taste of pre-school learning activities in your own home, try the Three Four Five Nursery Course (Macdonald Education Ltd., Holywell House, Worship Street, London EC2A. 2EN, England, approximately $30., plus postage—about $16. airmail or $9. surface mail.)

I saw an advertisement in *Nursery World* for this product, which is basically a nursery-school course for the home, and I found it an extremely imaginative and helpful aid for any mother with a pre-school child aged three to five. I have never sent my boys to nursery school, feeling that they would be in formal school for such a long time. But by the time you get to son number four, your ideas begin to run dry. My son and I looked forward each month to the arrival of his activity folder containing cutouts, rhymes, numbers, color work, a small record, and we subsequently dubbed the course Kitchen School.

KATHRYN CAHILL

Neighborhood Day-Care Centers—Another Way

One popular complaint today is that we have tried to solve too many of our personal problems by waiting for government—federal, state, or municipal—to take them out of our hands. If that doesn't happen, many of us try to pay someone else to solve them for us. Day care for small children is one of these problems. We either turn our kids over to an official day-care center (if one exists in our area) or pay a prince's ransom to a nursery school, where, we hope, they will be treated with the "care" we think they need and deserve. But this particular problem might be better solved if parents got together in a movement designed to persuade government to help them help their children.

In every sizable city, regulations could be put through to set up small day-care "dwellings." Under this system, apartment buildings with, say, more than twenty apartments would each have a two-room or three-room apartment set aside for use as a day-care center, under municipal order. The parents of small children in the building could send their kids to this center, take turns in staffing it, pay the cost of maintaining the place, provide equipment and food, and, if they hadn't the time to take their turn, pay extra for those who do. Twenty families who split the costs could expect to spend $10 to $20 a month each on the rent for the dwelling and perhaps twice that for other expenses—which in most large cities represents about one-quarter of what a decent nursery school charges for taking in a child for eighteen to twenty hours a week. Such a program would depend on the density of the child population in any given area. If there were not high-rise apartment houses, several buildings might share an apartment for day care in just one building in a neighborhood. And where there were only houses in a community, a small house could be taken over by the municipality, which could pay off the mortgage out of fees paid by parents.

Most important of all, though, parents would not only have control over these dwellings and their programs, but would have a far more essential advantage: the chance to participate with their own and others' kids in day-to-day teaching and learning.   RICHARD HARRIS

Tot Lots: Integrating Children into Everyday Life

I have three children, 8, 2½, and 1. They are beautiful children, and most times I delight in them. But there are times when I see them only as encumbrances, the objects of my frustration and anger. They are welded to me not only by birth, but by a society that sees them as totally my problem, my burden alone. Wherever I move, they move with me: to the drugstore, the newsstand, the fish market. Where once I moved on two legs, now I move on eight.

As parents, my husband and I are the sole providers, protectors, entertainers, and watchdogs for our young. We have no "extended family" to help care for them, no communal group to share the tasks. We are a total "nuclear family," the strain of which casts shadows of tension over what should be the joy of raising a family. When there are errands to be run or places we want to go—even for an hour—the scheduling and logistical arrangements that must be made would spin the most grizzled heads in the Pentagon. Society assumes not one iota of the burden for its future citizens. Business and industry make few provisions for people who are also parents.

Though free universal community-controlled child care is one goal, child-care service of another sort is equally important. Part-time child care. Hourly child care. Child care provided on the sites our dreary but necessary chores lead us to. Dragging the children along to places where adults don't even want to go doubles the frustration (in my case, triples it) and, more often than not, turns the children into the recipients of our frustrations.

In a Mother's Moment of Truth not too long ago, I realized how misdirected my anger was. After all, it's not the children's fault they have to be stuffed into shopping carts in the supermarket; not their fault that, out of sheer boredom, they whine and fidget while I puzzle over the unit prices of competing peanut butters. It isn't their fault that every time we assault the children's section of a department store, I shriek at them for not standing still while I try to find a pair of Toddler 3 training pants. It's not their fault that my blood pressure hits the red zone when we're on the outside of a "No Baby Carriages" sign at the stationery store. Do I dare leave two babies on a New York City sidewalk while I rush in to pick up a new magazine? Obviously not. I've learned to read less.

But I'm getting ahead of my Mother's Moment. It all happened a few weeks ago at our local supermarket. My supermarket survival syndrome consists of filling one cart with the two younger children, and letting my 8-year-old son take his own cart. This he fills with all the overstarched fantasies he's seen on television that week, and we don't have to have a scene until we remeet at the check-out counter. There I make him return half the Wing Dings, Pop-Tarts, and Cocoa Puffs he has happily collected.

Then I take another empty cart. Wheeling the children in front of me, and towing the empty cart, I convoy directly to the animal-cracker section. A box each occupies them for twenty minutes, exactly the amount of time I have to stock up for the week. In a blur of motion, I scoop the seven days worth of Beech-Nut baby food, King Vitaman (to offset the Cocoa Puffs), individually wrapped cheese slices, Baggies, the stuff our lives are made on, into the wheeled barge behind me.

It was while streaking toward the apple juice that it happened. Moving smartly past a tomato-juice display, a little hand snaked out from the cart and lassoed the bottom can on the pyramid, setting off 40 cans of tomato juice in a free fall. The crash brought screams of terror from the children. It also brought the manager at full run. In stony silence he watched as, on my hands and knees, I lunged after the rolling cans. Apologizing profusely for the disturbance, I snapped at the children over my shoulder to prove that I was certainly not one of those permissive parents, and that my children should certainly know how to behave in a supermarket.

On the way home, I alternated between seething martyrdom and screaming out loud. But then, looking at their three faces, the tear-stains melting rivulets through the slush of drooled animal crackers, I instantly and forever realized that the enemy was *not* the children, but the supermarket, its manager, and all the product manufacturers who spend fortunes on advertising and displays and fancy labels but have no idea what a shopping parent endures in the process of becoming one of their consumers. Why should I grovel at the manager's feet after I had just written a check for $69.82 for a week's groceries? Didn't the market owe *me* something? And didn't Beech-Nut baby food, Johnson & Johnson baby powder, St. Joseph baby aspirin, and the makers of Pop-Tarts owe my children something? We are their profit margin, their total market, their impulse buyers.

My course was set. Overnight I became a rev-

olutionary, demanding a place for parents and children to survive together in our society. The child-care situation is, as we all know, one of our major challenges. But asking for an hour's peace, a time when a parent can be an adult and a child can be a child, did not seem too outrageous a proposal. I was as tired of living my children's lives as I'm sure they are tired of living mine. . . .

Why has our society failed to provide for shared experiences—for parents and children together going about the business of life? It seems as if every five minutes, someone is building a new shopping center with parking for 5,000 cars, and the parking lots are landscaped and well designed. But a safe, attractive "tot lot"—a place to leave a child for 30 minutes while we fill a prescription—that seems to be unthinkable, unmanageable. But why? Aren't children as important as cars?

In fact, there are several notable experiments which inspire new ideas to prove it *can* be done.

A few years ago, New York's 14th Street Association subsidized a "check-a-child" facility in Union Square Park. The neighborhood merchants, primarily two large department stores, had raised $10,000 to renovate part of the park, and to equip it with toys, climbing cubes, and picnic tables. The supervision was provided by the City's Department of Parks for 25 cents for the first three hours, $1 an hour thereafter. Unfortunately, this example doesn't have a happy ending. With the slump in the city budget, the Parks Department canceled its supervision, and the merchants were unwilling to pick up the extra tab.

In [some] branches of Planned Parenthood . . . either a room or a corner of a room is provided for children. Filled with toys, blocks, and books for older children, and playpens for the younger ones, a supervisor looks after them for anywhere from fifteen minutes to two hours while their parents meet with the staff. . . .

Social Service Center 73 in the Brownsville section of Brooklyn is a notable example of inventiveness and self-help. The home economist there, Ms. Thelma Lovelace, watched the children "always crying and running all over the place, aggravating the mothers who were already depressed enough coming in here." She decided that, "if we could assist them at all with their problems, we would."

So Ms. Lovelace ran a cake sale. With the proceeds, she painted up a spare room at the welfare office and collected some used toys. She wrote to many children's equipment firms, and one came through with a baby tender, which means at least one baby at a time has a decent place to nap. Helped by four other employees, Thelma Lovelace managed for a while, but she has run out of money, and has had to ask for donations from the staff to buy juice and cookies for the 20 to 35 children they care for every day.

Beyond social conscience, it simply makes good business sense to take the distraction of children off the parent's back so that she or he can get on with whatever job has to be done. At Crocus, a small children's clothing shop in Brooklyn, the co-owners Val Gunning and Ginnie Hoyt, mothers with five children between them, set up a "children's corner"—stocked with toys and stuffed animals—which keeps the children occupied while parents shop unhindered.

"When adults feel unhassled," Ms. Gunning said, "they buy more things. In fact, the children feel so comfortable here, they drag their parents and babysitters in on their own. We have the most frequently used bathroom on Montague Street!"

In Atlanta, Georgia, Rich's Department Store, "the biggest store south of New York," has been providing free child care for 46 years in two of its seven branches. Supervised by a staff of five, the nurseries have toys, rocking horses, television sets and storytime. This service has been so successful that nearly 40,000 children had every reason to thank their parents for shopping at Rich's last year.

Child care isn't new to the Consumer's Co-op in Berkeley, California, either. For over 15 years, the Co-op has maintained "Kiddie Korrals" in some of their branches in the Bay Area. Any child old enough to walk can be checked into a Korral for as long as 90 minutes. There they are kept happily busy with a pre-school program of arts and crafts. . . .

The ultimate, of course, is in the "new city" concept, where social planners *start* with the idea of incorporating children into the lifestream instead of ignoring them and later dismissing children's facilities as an unworkable afterthought. In Columbia, Maryland, a "new city" being developed by the Rouse Corporation halfway between Baltimore and Washington, each neighborhood has a community center, which houses morning and afternoon cooperative nursery school programs and a Montessori program. There is also a by-the-hour day-care setup, where . . . children can be cared for on a part-time basis. . . .

Clearly, it *can* be done, and it isn't costly or unmanageable to those who keep priorities and public relations in mind. So I've got a plan. The manufacturers who make their money off our children's backs have just as great an obligation to us as do the stores that carry their goods. It seems to me they could split the cost of providing hourly child care for us, while we return the favor by becoming customers. I know I'd travel quite a distance to shop where my children could be cared for. Visions of Health-tex Activities Corners in department stores come to mind, or a section of the toy department where slightly damaged seconds on games, toys, and dolls would be available in a "Please Touch" area. One adult on duty for a transient group of kids couldn't tax a department store's operating budget any more than a community service ad would, and the public relations effect would be immeasurable. When the customer claimed his or her child, a small fee could be paid, or the customer could present a sales check showing a purchase of $5 or more.

And why can't Johnson & Johnson and Mennen set up space in drugstores in return for all the baby powder and Band-Aids we've bought over the decades? Supermarkets might divvy up the cost of children's corners with Beech-Nut and Gerber's or the cereal kings like General Mills and General Foods. Marx Toys, Mattel, Creative Playthings, and all the nameless toy manufacturers who barrage us with costly, irritating commercials might win more friends and customers by providing supervised programs in playgrounds or parks.

And why can't the children's book publishers kick a little back to the public libraries to expand children's reading-room facilities and staff so that parents can take the time to read and study, too? Mushrooming shopping centers around the country could be tithed to provide child care, and children's facilities should have at least the same priority as the parking lot. . . .

It's not enough to adore children at a distance, or to exalt our offspring as the hope of tomorrow. We must integrate children and parents into society. It's not enough to tuck the children away in school, or pack them off to the backyard, or hire a nanny every time we have to go to the laundromat. There must be creative alternatives—whether a blackboard in the butcher shop or a toy corner in the shopping center—that will allow parents and children to become companions again.

LINDA BIRD FRANCKE
Ms. Magazine

FOOD AND NUTRITION

ELISABETH SCHARLATT

The only emperor is the emperor of ice cream.
WALLACE STEVENS

You Don't Have to Be a Believer or a Non-believer

It's very important to keep in mind as you try to improve your diet that you don't have to do everything. You don't have to embrace any one authority; you don't have to read all the books at once; you don't have to be a believer or a non-believer—there are gradations of every shade. A good approach is to work on one element of your diet, such as convincing your family to switch from soda pop to apple juice. Or start reading the labels on a particular kind of food that you buy. Or find a place to get really fresh poultry. Or make the change from pro-

cessed to whole grains. Or grow your own vegetables one summer.

It just isn't necessary to alter your entire diet at once. MARY DUSTAN TURNER

Eat Well . . .

Good nutrition isn't just a matter of knowing what's good for us and then eating well. There are huge obstacles and problems. . . .

We feel it is important not to condemn ourselves for eating the way we do. Certain changes in our diets would clearly be more healthful, but it's not easy to make the switch.

From *Our Bodies, Ourselves,*
by the Boston Women's Health Book Collective

BEGINNINGS

Breast-feeding: Three Things the Books Don't Tell You

First, how much it can really hurt in the beginning. With all my reading about what a wonderful, rewarding, satisfying, virtuous experience it could be, I was not prepared for the initial pain and the disappointment that it didn't "come naturally" for me (nor for several of my friends, I discovered later)—you have to *learn* to hold the baby comfortably. Maybe the reason this news doesn't make the books is that you absolutely forget that pain very quickly. I can't even recall how long it lasted—and I only remember it at all from having discussed it at length with other nursing mothers at the time.

The books also don't tell you that you can work out your own routine in terms of schedules, weaning, relief bottles. When beginning to wean my son (who'd been getting a relief bottle at midday from the age of four weeks, when I was going to work), it came down to my nursing him once a day, in the morning, by the time he was nearly ten months old. This worked out quite well, as I got to nurse him and, finally, have my freedom too, and I began to realize that I might have gone on with that arrangement for quite a long time. The books don't tell you just how well your body adapts (I had milk

in the morning, but my breasts did not fill up all the rest of the day).

Lastly, the books don't tell you that, in fact, T-shirts are far better for inconspicuous nursing than are those button-down-the-front shirts everyone's always reminding you about. Nursing from underneath is far easier than opening up your shirt, and with the baby cradled in your arm, you can go unnoticed in the most public of places.

Now, knowing all this, consult the best book on the subject: The Complete Book of Breast-feeding, by Sally Wendkos Olds and Marvin S. Eiger, M.D. (Workman Publishing Company, $3.95 paperback). ELS

Bottle Weaning

Before I pass on this clever suggestion for helping a toddler give up the bottle, let me assure you that the whole experience was not as easy as it may sound. (My daughter was three before we went through with it.) But what finally worked was giving the bottles to Baby Ben, the lucky recipient of our used clothes and toys. Somehow Gaby found this more convincing and consoling than the doctor's admonitions about harming her teeth. PAULA GLATZER

Baby Food

What seems instructive about the history of commercial baby foods is that educated consumers *can* make a difference. Commercial baby foods are healthier and safer today than they were a decade ago, and consumer demand has played an important role in bringing about the changes.

Jim Turner briefly described that history up to 1970 in his book *The Chemical Feast*:

Twenty years ago a jar of baby food contained a given amount of fruit, vegetables, or meat. As the costs of these ingredients rose, baby-food companies began to replace part of them with starch and sugar—each of which is less expensive than the ingredient it was replacing. Naturally, foods thinned out with starch or sugar tasted blander or sweeter than the originals, so baby-food makers began adding salt and monosodium glutamate to please mothers who tasted their babies' food. Then it was discovered that the starches added to the food would break down and become watery if a mother fed her baby some of the bottle's contents and let the remainder sit, even in the refrigerator, overnight. The baby's saliva, which got into the food on the spoon the baby was fed with, was "digesting" it. The answer provided by the baby-food companies was to find a starch that saliva could not break down and add it to the bottle's contents. So now baby food contains . . . modified starch which baby saliva does not break down in the jar or the mouth and which some researchers fear may not be completely digested even by the rest of the baby's system. None of these additives in the food for purely economic reasons has been proven safe for consumption by babies.

Industry justifies the addition of sugar to baby foods by the assertion that it will make them tastier to infants. But, actually, most baby food is fed to infants early in their life, before they have developed the ability to discriminate by taste.

By 1977, Beech-Nut, Heinz, and Gerber's had all eliminated monosodium glutamate and salt from their baby foods. And all three manufacturers have cut back on the amount of sugar (although approximately one-third of each company's products still contain sugar). All three still add modified starch to many of their products, claiming it is necessary to prevent food separation; but perhaps someday this ingredient may also be eliminated.

Whether or not commercial baby foods are as healthy as homemade ones still will be endlessly debated. If you believe that foods prepared at home from fresh ingredients are more wholesome than commercially processed ones, the debate ends there. But if the kitchen is not your favorite place to be, you don't have to feel guilty. Homemade and processed baby foods are about equal in nutritional value. You may still want to check the labels and avoid the ones that include modified starch and added sugar.

The real difference between commercial and homemade baby foods, though, is one of cost and convenience. Any homemade food is cheaper; whether or not it's more convenient is largely a matter of opinion.

Some people actually do find it easier to make the foods at home than to buy and store and dispose of all those little jars. Easier, that is, if you avoid those baby food cookbooks that present ridiculously elaborate recipes for your eight-month-old. All you need to make baby food is a little food left over from your own meal (if it's not highly seasoned—no Szechuan or Indian curries) thrown in a blender or table grinder with enough liquid (water, milk, or juice) to make it the proper consistency for your child. It might be useful to invest in one book to provide tips on preparation, storage, and equipment.

Two books that keep homemade baby food simple are *Making Your Own Baby Food,* by Mary Dustan Turner and James S. Turner (Bantam, 1972, $1.75), and *The Natural Baby Food Cookbook,* by Margaret Elizabeth Kenda and Phyllis S. Williams (Avon, 1972, $1.50). Two sample suggestions follow. —RS

COTTAGE CHEESE FRUIT

Blend quickly: ½ cup cottage cheese, ½ cup fresh fruit (raw), 4–6 tablespoons orange or apple juice.

From Making Your Own Baby Food

QUICK-FREEZE BABY FOOD

. . . any cooked, puréed or strained meat, fish or vegetable may be frozen in meal-size amounts. One easy way to freeze quantities for your baby's meals is to quick-freeze the food you have prepared in ice cube trays. Store the frozen cubes in labeled containers. Plastic bags work well. Remove enough to heat for baby's meal, then reseal and replace in the freezer. Combination dinners, fruit juices, cooked and uncooked puréed fruits (except bananas) and most desserts can also be frozen successfully.

From The Natural Baby Food Cookbook

Baby Food: "The Pelmas Concoction"

When the girls were going through the "junior baby food" stage, I used to make up a concoction of cooked ground meat (lamb, beef, pork), mashed potatoes, and a cooked fresh vegetable (mashed up a bit) and mix it together. There would be enough for two or three dinners, and they loved it. So did I. It was tasty and easy, and since Roy and I always ate after they were in bed, I spent a minimum of time cooking for them and a maximum cooking for us.

RUTH PELMAS

You May Not Like the Food, but the Jars Are Fantastic

Let's face it, baby food jars are extraordinarily handy—for nails and screws, paper clips, thumb tacks, Baggie ties, paints—and are even the ideal containers for those homemade baby foods we're all advocating. However, you don't have to feed your child the food to get the jars—there are alternatives. If you have occasion to buy any of the following, save the jars: pimentoes, artichoke hearts, jam and jelly samplers, caviar, mushrooms, vitamins, spices, and shrimp (although the shrimp's not so hot).

ELS

A Safety Hint: Listen for the Pop

The indented circles found on the caps of baby food jars are really "safety buttons." The Glass Container Manufacturers Institute, Inc., Washington, D.C., warns: Check the buttons before you open the jar. If they are down (indented), the jar is vacuum sealed. When you open the jar, the button should jump with a "pop," indicating that the jar was properly sealed. If the button is up before you open it, you should not use the product.

Today's Health

"Eat! Says Fat Little Johnny's Mother"

It is nonsensical to say, "Eat your vegetables; they're good for you." To a preschool child, this is no reason at all to eat vegetables. . . .

The best solution to dawdling is to serve your child small portions—give him second helpings on request—and be patient. . . . It's much better to underestimate than overestimate his needs. . . .

Give your child a broad variety of foods when he's an infant. Don't force him to eat foods that he genuinely doesn't like, but have him try new foods frequently. Introduce a new food in a very small amount, along with another food that he particularly likes. Small portions really are the biggest secret in helping your child develop good eating habits.

DR. VIRGINIA M. VIVIAN
quoted by Clifford B. Hicks in *Today's Health*

PROBLEM FOODS

The Effect of Sugar on Behavior

We hear a great deal about the role of cane sugar in causing tooth decay, obesity, and heart disease; about how sugar-loaded foods spoil a child's appetite for good, nutritious foods and keep him literally "addicted" to sugar. But what has been overlooked in so many of the negative reports on refined sugar is the devastating effect which a sugar-loaded diet has on a child's *behavior*.

In the treatment of 1,000 children suffering from behavior disorders or learning disabilities, I have found that a significant percentage were dramatically improved by removing sugar and other junk foods from their diets. Those parents who were successful in enforcing the sugar-free diet achieved great success in helping their children to overcome the hyperactive behavior which was interfering with their learning and their peer relationships.

Most of the sweetened foods contain artificial colors and artificial flavors to which many children react with an allergy which is not manifested in the usual ways but by a sudden outburst of disturbed, disruptive behavior produced by a reaction in the brain. A high percentage of children have some disturbance of glucose metabolism, and in this group the eating of sugar-laden foods produces an initial rise in the blood sugar level, which is normal, but this rise is soon followed in an hour or two by a precipitous drop in blood sugar level to a point lower than the level at the time the sugar was eaten. This drop releases in the brain a large amount of a hormone which controls mood; the result is overactive and at times violent behavior.

When a child has been on a sugar-free diet for a period of time and his behavior has improved, members of his family can easily know when he has had some sweets by the return of his previous irritability and overactivity. I have seen a number of children who reacted to the withdrawal of sugar from their diet with the personality change and physical discomfort seen in the withdrawal of drugs.

ALLAN COTT, M.D.

[But let's face it, if you don't serve sweets at your child's birthday party, no one will come. —Eds.]

The All-American Sweet Tooth

The average [American] citizen is presently consuming two pounds of sugar a week.

JOAN GUSSOW
Consumer Action Now

SOME PARTICULARLY BIG OFFENDERS

Drink	Serving Size	Teaspoons of Sugar Per Serving
Hi-C Orange Drink	6 oz. (¾ cup)	5
Cola	12 oz.	9
Bird's Eye Orange Plus	4 oz.	2
Bird's Eye Awake	4 oz.	3
Tang	4 oz.	4
Kool-Aid	8 oz.	6

From *Nutrition Action*
Center for Science in the Public Interest

Avoiding Sugar: Advice for Label Readers

You should try to avoid foods that have sugar listed as the first ingredient—such a listing means that the product consists primarily of sugar. And, as you read the labels, remember that glucose, dextrose, fructose, maltose, lactose, and sucrose are just other names for sugar.

RS

"Do Not Offer a Lollipop to This Child Standing Next to Me, Please"

The first time my child ever saw a lollipop was in the doctor's office (I swear) when the nurse presented it to him for being a "good" patient. It was too late for me to stop her, but it would've been helpful if she'd bothered to find out that I'd been making a concentrated effort (and was successful at it) to keep my son from sweets for as long as possible. He didn't need to know about lollipops at the age of one (especially on a day when I was wearing a new dry-cleanable-only pair of slacks which weren't helped any by a sticky palm clinging to them). From that time on there was not a thing I could do short of wearing a sign on me that said DO NOT OFFER A LOLLIPOP TO THIS CHILD STANDING NEXT TO ME, PLEASE to forewarn the banker, the dry cleaner, and friendly vendors trying to drum up business. And any dentists who offer lollipops (and there are still a few who do) ought to have their tools taken away.

ELS

Killing for Cap'n Crunch

The whole problem of sugar and especially sugar-coated cereals is what we have the hardest time dealing with. It's a constant source of argument. Our kids are as socially self-regulated as you could hope for, but they would kill for Cap'n Crunch; they would eat it three times a day for life. People say, Let them have all the Cap'n Crunch they want, and after three weeks they will come to a balanced diet. It's not so.

I think that if the kids knew how we really feel about it—which they don't because even we are confused as a result of our own sugar-coated upbringing—we could come up with something we could all live with. That's the only thing that we're extremely inconsistent about. If you say, "Don't drink Coke, it's bad for you," and the kid sees you drinking Coke, he assumes it's all right, really.

ORSON and CAROLYN BEAN

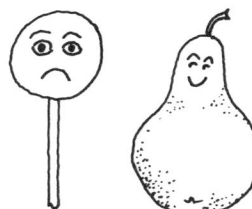

[To find out what happened to some young athletes who ate lots of sugar and others who had none, see page 384.]

What's Happened to the Glass of Water?

The heavy advertising of beer and soft drinks . . . delivers a message far more potent than the urging to buy any single product. In terms of this message it doesn't really matter whether someone going to the refrigerator gets out a Pepsi or a Coke, a 7-Up or a Budweiser. What matters is that a thirsty American . . . goes to the refrigerator to open up a container rather than to the sink to open up the tap. That behavior has been sold to us.

JOAN GUSSOW
Journal of Nutrition Education

"The Real Thing" Isn't

Soda pop: we drink $7 billion worth a year. Per capita consumption has doubled in the last twelve years! Coke costs more than milk or orange juice, and contains no vitamins, minerals, or protein. Soda pop contains only sugar (except for artificially sweetened ones) and these calories push better foods out of the diet. The ad budget for "the real thing" is about $70 million a year.

MICHAEL JACOBSON
Center for Science in the Public Interest

Additives Are Aptly Named, or Adding to the Corporate Coffers

Some food additives make foods safer, others make foods cheaper, others make foods more or less nutritious; all food additives help companies make money, and that, in a nutshell, is why additives are usually used.

MICHAEL JACOBSON
Eater's Digest

Additives to Avoid

The trouble with food additives is not that they're all dangerous; it's that we don't know for sure that they're all safe. Because many of them haven't been adequately tested, there are a few I consistently try to avoid:

Artificial colors and artificial flavors. To my mind, these are the most preposterous additives. Think about it: they're added to make a food look better so you'll buy it, or to make it taste like something it is not. There is no nutritional value in any artificial color or flavor, many of them have not been sufficiently tested, and they are now suspected as a possible cause of hyperactivity in children. (To learn more

about the possible connection between food additives and hyperactivity, read *Why Your Child Is Hyperactive,* by Dr. Ben F. Feingold [Random House, 1974, $7.95 hardcover].)

BHA and BHT. These chemicals, which prevent oils from going rancid, are among the most frequently used additives; food packagers use them to extend the shelf life of many cereals, packaged breads, potato chips, crackers, candy bars, and vegetable oils. BHT is known to accumulate in body fat, and it has not been determined whether this accumulation is harmful. BHA is suspected as a cause of hyperactivity in some children. Both BHA and BHT are classified by the Food and Drug Administration as "generally recognized as safe" by virtue of the fact that they were already being used in foods when the Food Additives Amendment was passed in 1958. If you don't require foods that stay "fresh" forever, and are willing to refrigerate your vegetable oils, you can always find brands that don't contain either of these additives.

Sodium nitrite and sodium nitrate. These are found in ham, bacon, hot dogs, and other cured meats and fish as a flavoring and a preservative; they are also found in many red meats as a totally unnecessary color preserver. They may be harmful because the nitrites combine with other chemicals in our food to form nitrosamines, substances suspected of causing cancer; they also add more sodium to our diets, which are already too high in salt.

Some butchers carry bacon cured without nitrites or nitrates. It is more expensive than the bacon with nitrites, keeps for only a week in the refrigerator, and is delicious. It's still unhealthily high in animal fat, however. As a replacement for bacon and eggs, try wheat berries and eggs. It sounds like an odd combination. But whole wheat berries are incredibly cheap (under 30 cents a pound) and, simmered like rice, mixed with a tamari (soy) sauce and olive oil (and cayenne pepper if your family likes spicy foods), they have a hearty, salty taste and are even the color of bacon.

RS

◆

MAGNETIC DETRACTION

Even nutritious additives have their drawbacks. Kellogg Co., for instance, recently reduced the iron content of its Frosted Rice cereal to 10% of the government's "recommended daily allowance" from 25% after consumers discovered they could move flakes of cereal around with magnets.

Nutrition Action, August 1977

About That Fortified Cake . . .

Hostess Snack Cakes seem to me to be a perfect example of what corrective advertising cannot do. Hostess Snack Cakes have been promoted as good nutrition because they have had what I call the three popular B's and one mineral added to them. Yet everything that is wrong with the American diet is rolled up in a Hostess Snack Cake or Pie. They are high in calories, high in sugar, high in fat. Encouraging a child—or his mother—to think of them as good nutrition in a country where the major nutritional problems are overweight, tooth decay, diabetes and heart disease is a little like teaching a four-year-old to smoke on the grounds that it will be good for his lungs.

JOAN GUSSOW
"Counter-Advertising—
The Handwriting on the Wall,"
Caveat Emptor

RICHARD HUTCHINGS

What's in a Fast-Order Burger?

Nutritionally, the fast-food chains offer questionable value. Dr. Jean Mayer, the Harvard nutritionist and author, has said that a McDonald's meal lacks Vitamin C and adds large amounts of fat, carbohydrates, calories, and sodium to the diet, especially if eaten too often, as it is by so many Americans. He further stated that it contains almost no roughage, and nothing served there "makes it necessary to have teeth." A nutritional analysis of meals from fast-food chains done by Assistant Professor Howard Appledorf at the University of Florida Institute of Food and Agricultural Sciences in Gainesville indicates other deficiencies. Testing samples of burgers, French fries, and vanilla shakes from McDonald's, Burger King, and Burger Chef provided some interesting conclusions. A seven- to ten-year-old child who eats a small hamburger, fries, and a shake from Burger King would get at least one-third his Recommended Dietary Allowances of calories, protein, calcium, phosphorus, magnesium, and zinc but would be low in iron. To get that iron, he would have to have the specialty Whopper, or Burger Chef's Super Chef. Burger King also came out best for eighteen-year-old males, who would get from a Whopper, fries, and a shake one-third R.D.A. of everything except iron and magnesium. While all three chains were remarkably alike in the quantities of food they sell at a given price, Burger King and Burger Chef were consistently superior to McDonald's, whose products were lower in every mineral tested, though close in protein and calories.

The Super Chef had more fat than the other specialty burgers, and both Burger King and Burger Chef weighed slightly more than McDonald's because of greater moisture. Less ash was considered an advantage for McDonald's, and all shakes were reported very high in phosphorus and, especially, in calcium—no surprise when one considers all the chalk they contain. In every case a shake would be necessary to make the meal nutritionally acceptable.

When I asked Professor Appledorf for some details about this survey, he said it is important to remember it was conducted only in Gainesville, which might not be typical of other franchise areas. He also admitted there was a great weakness in the analysis because it did not include vitamins. When I asked if the university had a grant from any of the fast-food chains, he admitted, as a matter of fact, one from Burger King, "but, of course, that wouldn't influence findings."

MIMI SHERATON
The New York Times

McDonald's on the Hoof

If all the cattle that have ever laid down their lives for McDonald's were to be resurrected for a reunion, they would stand flank-by-jowl over an area larger than Greater London.

Time, September, 1973

[Update: By now, those cattle would cover an area larger than London and Kent.—Ed.]

SOLUTIONS

Lacing with Protein

Frances Lappé says in her book *Diet for a Small Planet* that "children need one and a half to two times more protein per pound of body weight than adults, and babies from two to three times more." That's because adults need protein for maintenance, whereas kids obviously need protein for building and growing. Lappé suggests that the best way to ensure that kids get the protein they need is to lace their foods with high-protein ingredients such as wheat germ, brewer's yeast, sunflower and sesame seeds, dry milk, eggs, nuts.

The following are some pointers on how I add various high-protein ingredients to the dishes I like to cook. (I *still* haven't figured out what to do with brewer's yeast, which, as Frances Lappé points out, is high on the list of protein-rich foodstuffs.)

Most of the ingredients listed can be found in supermarkets, but some may require a trip to the health food store.

Seeds and nuts (unsalted, unroasted). Add these generously to cold cereals, vegetable and rice dishes, and salads. Peanuts and sunflower seeds eaten together have more usable protein than either one eaten separately. Cashews, black walnuts, pumpkin and squash kernels, and pistachio nuts are richer in protein per calorie than pecans, almonds, and English walnuts. (Note about buying unroasted seeds: heating foods to certain temperatures changes their molecular structure in a way that makes them more difficult for the body to assimilate. Buy unroasted nuts and seeds and toast them on a cookie sheet in a low oven, under 200 degrees.)

Yogurt (plain, unflavored, with "active cultures"). I use small amounts of yogurt in salad dressings, blended juices, sauces, and soups (a big spoonful in each bowl, instead of sour cream). Try a baked potato with yogurt and chives and you'll hardly miss the salt and butter. Toast a few spices—seeds like cumin, fennel, caraway, mustard—crush them and mix with yogurt, and you've a healthy condiment for grains and vegetables. A chicken marinated overnight in yogurt and spices makes a more succulent roast than you can imagine. If you want fruit yogurt, blend some plain yogurt with overripe fruit and a little honey or brown sugar (most store-bought fruit yogurts are full of sugar, artificial flavorings, and other additives); you'll end up with a delicious soupy snack or a dressing for fruit salads. (*Note*: The active acidophilus culture is a friendly bacteria found naturally in the lower intestines; when the bacterial balance in your stomach is upset, eating yogurt helps to restore it to normal.)

Tofu (soybean curd). Americans are beginning to discover this versatile food in Chinese and Japanese restaurants, and for home use the firm, custard-like squares are increasingly available in health food stores, Oriental food markets, and some supermarkets. Tofu is not only high in protein but remarkably low in calories and entirely free of cholesterol. It is also cheap. A half-pound serving of tofu costs about a quarter and has the same amount of usable protein as a 5½-ounce hamburger. For babies, just mash or purée the tofu with fruits, vegetables, cottage cheese, etc. For the family, cut the tofu cakes in small cubes and add them at the last minute to soups, salads, mixed vegetables. Tofu has such a mild flavor that it absorbs the flavor of whatever foods it is prepared with.

Wheat germ (unroasted). All the protein, vitamins (especially B and E), and minerals (especially iron) that are taken out of whole wheat to make it white are available to you in wheat germ. Keep it in the refrigerator (spoilage is the reason the germ was removed from the wheat to begin with), add it to meat or vegetable loaves and patties, to breads (wheat germ biscuits are delicious), cereals, soups, and mixed fruit drinks. You can also use wheat germ as a breadcrumb-like topping for vegetable dishes.

Cheese (unprocessed). Add to grains, vegetables, beans, and salads.

Non-fat dry milk. Add to breads and other baked foods, hot cereals, soups, peanut butter.

Mung bean sprouts. One of the highest protein per calorie foods around. Add them to salads, tuna fish, vegetables, soups, (just before you've finished cooking them), grains, eggs, cheese sandwiches. Use other sprouts—alfalfa, wheat, etc.—the same way. (Sprouts sautéed with tofu and vegetables in an olive oil, garlic, tamari [a naturally fermented soy sauce], and ginger base, garnished with yogurt and wheat germ, win my nutritious delicious award.)

RS

◆

[For more about Frances Moore Lappé's *Diet for a Small Planet,* see page 158.]

The Food Scoreboard: "How Many Points Do I Lose on Maple Syrup?"

We recently came across a useful approach to nutrition outlined in a booklet called the *Food Scorecard* (by Michael Jacobson and Wendy Wilson, 1974, 50 cents from the Center for Science in the Public Interest, 1755 S Street, N.W., Washington, D.C. 20009—a condensed version of Jacobson's complete 102-page book *Nutrition Scoreboard: Your Guide to Better Eating,* available for $1.75 from Avon publishers). Foods are scored according to their overall nutritional value—the better the food, the higher the score. A food gets points for the nutrients it contains (e.g., proteins, vitamins, minerals, starch, unsaturated fats) and loses points for saturated fat content and for additives such as sodium nitrite (negative points for sugar are figured separately). Useful in the system is the listing of commonly eaten foods, often by brand name (McDonald's small hamburger, Cap'n Crunch, Campbell's Chunky Beef soup), in average-size servings—both "good" foods and "junk" foods.

Presenting this scorecard approach to our six-year-old resulted in some significant changes in his eating habits and attitudes. After reading through several of the lists to check out the scores of various foods, he spontaneously elected to keep his own scorecard for several days. The following are some of his remarks overheard at random.

"I don't want all that chicken . . . How many points does chicken have? Sixty-two points! What is 2.7 ounces? Let's weigh the chicken. Oh, boy, I get sixty-two points for eating all that chicken . . . Look, Mom, I ate it all up!"

"I want some maple syrup on my pancake. Wait a minute. How many points do I lose on maple syrup? Look, just put a few drops on."

A friend went to the refrigerator to get something to drink and selected a can of Coca-Cola. Our son yelled out, "You lose ninety-two points if you drink that. I wouldn't drink it if I were you. Try milk, you'll gain thirty-nine points."

"Mom, can I have this lollipop?" "If you want it." "But how many points do I lose?" "About twenty-seven points." "I changed my mind. I don't think I want a lollipop."

Ham has been a favorite protein food for our son, but upon seeing the asterisk following its listing and learning that it meant that ham contained the additive sodium nitrite, which should be avoided—or at least not eaten very often—his request for ham has gone from once a day to once a week or less.

I don't know how long this will last, but food is no longer the horrendous argument it used to be.
                              SALLY LANGENDOEN

The following two charts are from Michael Jacobson's *Nutrition Scoreboard.*

Some All-Star Foods

FOOD	SERVING SIZE	NUTRITIONAL SCORE
Liver, beef	2 oz.	172
Broccoli	3⅓ oz.	116
Cantaloupe	¼ melon	99
Cod, broiled	3 oz.	40
Milk, whole	8 oz.	39
Tomato juice	4 oz.	37
Rye bread	2 slices	29
Peanuts	¼ cup	25

Some Junkyard Foods

FOOD	SERVING SIZE	NUTRITIONAL SCORE
Soda pop	12 oz.	−92
Morton coconut cream pie	¼ pie	−62
Kool-Aid	8 oz.	−55
Jell-O	½ cup	−45
Del Monte vanilla pudding	1	−43
Candy bar, average	1 bar	−34
Hot dog	1	6

Avoid fat, sugar, white flour

Snacks

FOOD	SERVING SIZE	NUTRITIONAL SCORE
Granola and milk	1 oz. plus ½ cup	45
Sunflower seeds	¼ cup	44
Almonds	¼ cup	31
Peach	1	29
Peanuts	¼ cup	25
Granola	1 oz.	25
Cashews	¼ cup	24
Walnuts	¼ cup	17
Raisins	1½ oz.	13
Apple	1	12
Triscuit crackers	4 (0.6 oz.)	9
Potato chips	¾ oz.	8
Popcorn (no butter)	2 cups	6
Oatmeal cookie	1	−4
Sandwich cookie	1	−7
Snickers candy	1 bar	−23
Mars Almond candy	1 bar	−27
Milk chocolate	1 oz.	−27
Brownie	1 (1⅓ oz.)	−30
Milky Way candy	1 bar	−33
M & M's candy	1 pack	−33
Cracker Jack	1 box	−39
Hostess Sno-Ball	1	−44
Popsicle	1 (3 oz.)	−45
3-Musketeers candy	1 bar	−55
Chuckles candy	1 package	−74

Some Nutrition Tips from the Boston Women's Health Book Collective

Whenever you can, make your own soups and whole-grain breads. They contain far more nutrients than canned soups and spongy, store-bought breads.

Use cast-iron skillets and pans when cooking. They are an important source of readily absorbed iron.

When cooking vegetables, use only a little water and keep the pot tightly covered. Also, try to save the water in which vegetables have been cooked for stews, soups and sauces, broths, and so on. Many vitamins are lost to the air (oxidized) or dissolved in water—save them when possible.

Make sure fresh fruit is really fresh. Old vegetables may have fewer vitamins than frozen or canned ones.   From *Our Bodies, Ourselves*

Improving the Family's Breakfast

After reading articles in everything from women's magazines to medical journals which all pointed out the empty calories which make up the bulk of the American diet, I decided to shore up our diet, beginning with breakfast. The first morning that I replaced corn flakes with unsweetened granola, my husband shrieked that it tasted like horsefeed. The children quickly joined in the chorus and I was left to finish the granola alone, munching along miserably, thinking it delicious but unable to sell it. From there we went to eggs every day, which soon bored everyone in the family. "Not again, Mother!"

Finally we arrived at a variety which seems nutritionally sound, is fairly quick to prepare, and ends up in the stomachs of the children instead of the dog. Our breakfast menus now include toasted cheddar cheese on whole wheat bread, scrambled eggs with sour cream, peanut butter (whole peanut butter, not the commercial

ELISABETH SCHARLATT

variety, which is 75 percent hydrogenated shortening and usually referred to on the label as "Old-Fashioned" or some such name) spread on whole wheat raisin bread, and farina or rolled oats in the winter when it's cold. The constants in our breakfast menu are fruit juices (and I don't mean Awake), whole milk, and whole wheat toast.

Our first meal of the day is not only nutritionally sound but interesting and stimulating. The kids don't even realize that it's "good for them." I gave up on granola.

LINDA WEST ECKHARDT

How to Choose a Cereal

The best way to judge the quality of a breakfast cereal is to read carefully the list of ingredients on the label. If sugar is listed first, avoid the product, regardless of how many nutrients have been added. Select cereals that contain whole grains and little or no sugar. Here are two labels:

WHEATENA INGREDIENTS	FRANKEN·BERRY INGREDIENTS
100% natural wheat. Contains no added salt or any other additives or preservatives.	Sugar, oat flour, degermed yellow corn meal, wheat and corn starch, corn syrup, dextrose, salt, gelatin, coconut and peanut oils, calcium carbonate, sodium phosphate, monoglycerides, artificial flavors, sodium ascorbate, artificial colors, niacin, iron, gum acacia, vitamin A palmitate, pyridoxine (vitamin B_6), riboflavin, thiamin, vitamin D and vitamin B_{12}. Freshness preserved by BHT.

What's wrong with Franken·Berry?
1) Sugar is listed first, which means that it is the major ingredient. The cereal also contains two other sweeteners, corn syrup and dextrose, which add calories without nutrients.
2) It contains starch, refined and degermed flour instead of whole-grain flour.
3) It contains artificial colors, artificial flavors, and the artificial preservative BHT.

What's right with Wheatena? It is made with whole wheat and does not contain added sugar or artificial coloring. It is also relatively inexpensive, 63¢ for 22 ounces (2.9¢ per ounce) compared to 65¢ for 8 ounces (8.1¢ per ounce) of Franken Berry.

MICHAEL JACOBSON
Nutrition Scoreboard

"Sugar in the Mornin', Sugar in the Evenin' . . ."

"When am I going to be able to eat sweet cereals?" my son inquired, as if it were an activity one grows into, like crossing the street alone.

"Never," I replied.

"Never? I can *never* eat a bowl of sweet cereal? For the rest of my life?" He was incredulous, as if I'd told him he'd never walk to school by himself, nor hit a ball.

We discussed my objection to sugar in what seemed our 480th such discussion in five and a half years. I told him this time that even though I had given in to cultural pressures and allowed him to eat sweets and junk food occasionally, I could not abide sugar in the morning. I admitted that I myself like Pepperidge Farm chocolate chip cookies and that, yes, I did have some hiding in the cupboard. But, I reminded him, I am all grown up: my bones are formed, my teeth are firmly rooted, my cells are all grown in; his body, on the other hand, is just now being made into what it will be for his whole life. I tried to explain about growth and change and how what we eat helps or harms us. I talked about proteins and vitamins and minerals and what they do and how we get them. It was a fairly long discussion. He heard only one thing.

"You mean I can *never* eat sweet cereal?" he said at the end of it all. "That's not fair."

We did finally reach a fair compromise, which I must say I don't find *completely* objectionable: I would agree to buy a sweet cereal if he would agree not to eat it in the morning. He could have it as dessert after a good dinner. Still not fair? He loved it. I think it was the aberration of having a bowl of Cocoa-Puffs when it's dark outside that appealed to him most.

And, fortunately, before the box was even empty, the thrill was gone.

ELS

Advice to Snack Eaters

It may be too late for the grown-up sweet freaks among us (though maybe not), but here are some snacks you can give your children which will not pour more sugar into them. (I proposed the following to the head teacher at The Studio on 11th Street School a few years ago when the students and the teachers were looking for ways of snacking more nutritiously. Before long, there were no sweets offered at the school, and the kids didn't miss them at all.)

TO DRINK

Apple juice. Red Cheek is the best commercial brand I know of; there are other pure brands but check the label to make sure they have no sugar or preservatives added.

Unsweetened grapefruit juice. Kids can get to love this. Mine did until someone said, Isn't that too sour for you?

Unsweetened orange juice. I'm not too confident about the fresh-squeezed that you get in a store, because they don't wash the outside of the oranges (which are undoubtedly covered with insecticides) before they put them in the squeezing machine. (You can't win.)

Mint tea, hot or cold. This is a real treat and tastes, you can tell the kids, like peppermint chewing gum. Combined with other herbal teas, the mint usually has a dominant taste. Experiment with them. Try adding a slice of lemon or orange or a cinnamon stick.

Any unsweetened fruit juice, even frozen. Beware of anything that says "punch" or "drink." Hi-C, Kool-Aid, and Hawaiian Punch are *not* fruit juices.

Banana milk (as dictated by Nicholas Scharlatt, at age 3—I think he had it in school. In any case, he told me how to make it). Take a glass of milk and a banana, put them in a blender, and you have banana milk. (The most important thing, we discovered later, is to add an ice cube. Nothing's worse than lukewarm banana milk.)

TO EAT

Nuts—any fresh unsalted, not roasted.

Raisins and other dried fruits. Some dried fruits, like apricots, though delicious and healthful, have more sugar in them than others. Check the label.

Fresh fruits. How many ways can you slice an apple? Fruits cut up differently each time are a little more welcome than the same old quarters.

Sliced carrots, celery, green pepper, cucumber, cauliflower, fresh string beans, peas in the pod.

Bread sticks with sesame seeds.

Pickles.

Cheese. American cheese and other processed cheeses contain preservatives and are disproportionately expensive compared with natural cheeses. Natural cheeses on whole wheat crackers or quartered slices of whole wheat bread are good snacks. (If you think that you have American cheese because the kids want it, consider which came first—their desire for it or their introduction to it by adults who think that's what kids want to eat.)

Granola. A handful can take the place of Cracker Jacks. (You can even put a prize at the bottom of the bowl.)

Jerky. A dried beef product which is pungent, chewy, and solid protein. (You can tell your child it's what the cowboys ate—and they did.)

Other good snack foods. Coconut, whole peanut butter on whole wheat bread, pumpkin or sunflower seeds.

If a kid doesn't like a healthful snack, then he doesn't have to have a snack. If he's really, really hungry, he'll eat cucumber slices, and if he's really thirsty, he'll drink grapefruit juice.

If he wants some ice cream, how about sprinkling some wheat germ on it—no choices, it should just come that way. And if a kid doesn't want it, he doesn't have to eat it.

Presentation matters. For some reason my child will eat a snack of meat or cheese when it's rolled up with a toothpick sticking through it. The same thing laid flat on a plate will not appeal to him at all.

ELS

It is as important for modern children to distinguish nourishing foods from junk foods in a store as it was for frontier children to distinguish between edible and poisonous berries in the wilderness.

MICHAEL JACOBSON

PHASING OUT THE JUNK

Halfway Home

We have trained our children to eat fewer junk foods by offering more dazzling junk foods as rewards for eating nutritious foods. It took tremendous discipline on their part, but they finally trained themselves not to want junk foods at all so they wouldn't have to eat anything nutritious. (We are working on the second half of this problem.)

ANNE NAVASKY

The Lesser Evils

It's better to buy a child a Hershey's chocolate bar than hard candy like sour balls and lollipops, which are basically sugar and water and caramel. Lollipops are devastating. They just create a film of sugar on the child's teeth. It's better still to buy a candy bar that has some nuts in it. Or one of those little peanut butter cups. There are health-food candy bars, and when we go to the health food store we usually buy some tiger's milk bars, which, although they are 30 percent sugar, at least contain some protein. Or we buy sesame bars, because in Christopher's mind these are candy bars, and yet they aren't as lethal as some of the candy bars you see.

JIM TURNER and MARY DUSTAN TURNER

Teas and Milk Shakes

Since we banned soft drinks in our house, our children have become real connoisseurs of teas. They've even gotten into the whole ceremony involved in brewing a pot of tea and enjoy showing off to their friends. They also keep the blender humming making milk shakes and fresh fruit drinks.

LINDA WEST ECKHARDT

The Eichler Snack Pack

We never go anywhere—movies, day trip, planetarium, beach, baseball game—without a little bag of food. I refuse to be robbed by vendors peddling 50-cent candy bars, and my snack pack, though not always nutritious, is always less junky than the commercial offerings.

CAROL EICHLER

The Peanut Butter Pop

I don't know how much longer I will be able to put this over on my son, but when he asks for a treat I offer him a "peanut butter pop"—a dollop of peanut butter scooped onto a small spoon and offered vertically for licking. Follow with a glass of milk and an "apple cookie"—a round, flat inside slice of the apple.

Candy Days

Polly Samuels, who at four and a half is a candy freak, asks for some every time she passes a store that sells it. "On Candy Day you can have whatever you like," her mother tells her. Thus, on that one day a week designated as Candy Day, Polly gets a quarter and can choose whatever she can afford. It works: you don't have to say no all the time, and she has a chance to talk all week long about what she's going to buy.

ELS

I have had some limited success with what we call the "Sunday Box" in our house. The idea is that all candy accumulated in the course of a week goes into this box, and on Sunday after lunch a veritable orgy of candy-gorging is permitted. There is, believe it or not, a limit to the amount of candy a child can consume in one sitting.

CAROL EISEN RINZLER

"An Unfortunate Solution"

When our family first began to make the shift from pure junk to more nutritious foods we had one son whose eyes clouded over as if he'd been condemned to a diet of bread and water. Once, while cleaning out his closet, I discovered a glass full of sugar and a spoon hidden under his sneakers and dirty underwear. For him, we've provided an artificial sweetener to make sweet drinks, an unfortunate solution, but the only one we've been able to come up with.

LINDA WEST ECKHARDT

Homemade Popsicles

My sister passed along to me a Tupperware popsicle tray—I've no idea of its proper name. Looking like an oversized ice tray, it has room for six homemade pops each with a plastic handle (half of which freezes inside the pop). I don't know that the Tupperware people designed this product for the purpose of helping us wean our children off junk-food snacks, but that's what's happened in our house. We've made yogurt pops (relished by a kid who never liked yogurt in any form), apple juice, cranberry, grape juice, and even grapefruit juice pops—plus the predictable ones made of orange juice and lemonade. When we're feeling really adventurous, we make combinations. (Add the flavors one at a time letting the first flavor freeze before you pour in the second one.)

For similar results, you can save your Good Humor sticks and make popsicles in small paper cups (Dixie makes a three-ounce size).

ELS

Winning Their Hearts with Red Cheek

While food shopping for a Sunday visit from our nieces, my husband and I considered buying some soft drinks for the kids. Going out of your way to buy Coke for a kid seems a rather perverted way to show affection; we resisted and won their hearts with Red Cheek apple juice.

RS

DRAWING BY KOREN. © 1974 THE NEW YORKER MAGAZINE, INC.

"No more carbohydrates until you finish your protein."
—Edward Koren

NUTRITION BOOKS FOR ADULTS

*If you read a dozen books on child care,
you're a conscientious parent;
if you read a half dozen on nutrition, you're a
fanatic. Something's wrong. —RS*

No one responsible will say, Here's the answer. But what they will say is that there are lots of contending ideas, and that what is good for one person to eat may not be good for somebody else. Everybody has a different need and a different way of supplying that need. I basically maintain that even though we may be eating the best way we know how, we're probably not doing it right. It's important to be skeptical about all these books. We can say you should know about Roger Williams' books, not because it's the answer but because it gives you some things to think about. You should have Adelle Davis, because hers is another way of thinking about it. Look at Beatrice Hunter, look at Jean Mayer, look at the AMA, and look at what they say. Sample them all, and then make the reasoned choices for your life. 　JIM TURNER

DIET FOR A SMALL PLANET, *by Frances Moore Lappé (Ballantine, rev. ed. 1975, 411 pages, $1.95 paperback).*

RECIPES FOR A SMALL PLANET, *by Ellen Buchman Ewald (Ballantine, 1975, 356 pages, $1.95 paperback).*

You don't have to be a vegetarian to be concerned about eating more meat than is good for you, more meat than you can afford, and more meat than our land can afford to produce. Through her best-selling book, Frances Lappé has given millions of people an understanding of the food chain, and she is *the* source of information on how to combine vegetables, grains, milk products, and other non-meat edibles to maximize their protein content (it seems tricky at first, but is easy to get the hang of).

The revised edition of *Diet* is half whys and hows (including some very useful general tips) and half recipes; *Recipes* is exactly that, by the woman who inspired Lappé to write her book. Both are good books; both are good cookbooks (though I inevitably spice up some of their dishes to suit my own taste). They've influenced my personal diet more than anything else I've read.
　　　　　　　　　　　　　　　　　　　RS

Pizza for a Small Planet

four 10-inch pizzas

half of one pizza=approx. 16 g usable protein
37 to 44% of daily protein allowance

Sauce:

3 tbsp olive oil	1 tbsp dried oregano
1 cup onions, finely chopped	1 tbsp fresh basil or 1 tsp dried basil
1 tbsp minced garlic	1 bay leaf
4 cups canned tomatoes, chopped	2 tsp honey
1 small can tomato paste	1 tbsp salt
	pepper to taste

In a 3- or 4-quart saucepan heat the oil and saute the onions until soft but not brown. Add garlic and cook 2 minutes more. Add the remaining ingredients, bring the sauce to a boil, then lower the heat and simmer uncovered for about 1 hour, stirring occasionally. Remove bay leaf and, if a smoother sauce is desired, you may puree or sieve it.

Dough:

2 tbsp dry baking yeast	1 tsp salt
1¼ cups warm water	2½ cups whole wheat flour
1 tsp honey	1 cup soy flour
¼ cup olive oil	garnishes

Dissolve the yeast in the water with the honey. Mix with oil, salt, and flours in a large bowl. Blend well and knead until smooth and elastic on a floured board. Let rise in the bowl in a warm place until doubled in volume (about 1½ hours). Punch down and knead again for a few minutes to make dough easy to handle.

To make four 10-inch pizzas, divide the dough into quarters, stretch each quarter to a 5-inch circle while you hold it in your hands, then roll it out to 10 inches and about ⅓ inch thick. Dust pans with cornmeal, place the pizzas on top, and pinch a small rim around the edge. For each pizza use ½ cup tomato sauce, ½ cup mozzarella cheese, and 2 tbsp Parmesan. In all, you need: 1 lb mozzarella cheese, grated; and ½ cup freshly grated Parmesan cheese.

Other garnishes may top your pizza: sliced garlic, sliced onion, mushrooms, sliced green pepper.

Bake 10 to 15 minutes at 500°F.

The pizza looks like work, but it makes a wonderful supper dish—high protein in content *and* quality.

　　　　　　　　　FRANCES MOORE LAPPE
　　　　　　　　　in Diet for a Small Planet

NUTRITION IN A NUTSHELL, *by Roger Williams (Doubleday Anchor, $1.95 paperback).*
A condensed guide to improved nutrition by an eminent biochemist who discovered certain B vitamins. In this concise volume he gives specific instructions about altering your diet and supplementing it with vitamins. A valuable book to have and use frequently.

LINDA WEST ECKHARDT

THE NATURAL FOODS PRIMER, *by Beatrice Trum Hunter (Simon and Schuster, 1973, 156 pages, $2.50 paperback).*

COMPOSITION OF FOODS, *by Bernice K. Watt and Annabel L. Merrill (Agriculture Handbook No. 8, Superintendent of Documents, U.S. Government Printing Office, Washington, D.C. 20402. Revised December 1973, 190 pages, $2.35 domestic postpaid, $3.60 GPO Bookstore).*
In the Hunter book I found helpful miscellaneous advice such as where different foods are best stored. (I never stopped to think that egg shells are porous and that the cardboard containers you buy them in allow for less passage of moisture, bacteria, and molds than do open egg slots in refrigerators. I wonder if the people who design refrigerators know this? I use my slots to hold lemons and limes, so at least the space isn't wasted.) RS

The Watt and Merrill book contains the most comprehensive tables available on the composition (water, calories proteins, fats, vitamins, minerals) of raw, processed, and prepared foods. No brand names are used.

NUTRITION SCOREBOARD: YOUR GUIDE TO BETTER EATING, *by Michael Jacobson (Avon, 1975, $1.75 paperback).*
A thoroughly refreshing approach to improving your children's diet—and your own. See Sally Langendoen's article about it on page 153.
Here's Jacobson writing on Adelle Davis:

The Adelle Davis approach to nutrition is a complicated variation of the detailed approach. In addition to details about how much of each nutrient is in each food, Ms. Davis discusses possible health benefits or hazards of the nutrients. This approach—making nutrition a study—has attracted hundreds of thousands of followers, perhaps as many as 2 percent of the population, and sparked much of today's widespread concern about food quality. But the other 98 percent does not want to preoccupy itself with foods and health and could well benefit from a simpler approach to nutrition.

[Adelle Davis has written the following books: *Let's Eat Right to Keep Fit, Let's Cook It Right; Let's Get Well,* and *Let's Have Healthy Children.*]

OBESITY

A Problem to Deal with Early

The number and size of fat cells in the body are established early in life. . . . When a too fat baby slims down into a skinny child, he will still have the same high number of cells capable of storing fat. When the child reaches adulthood . . . he has the built-in potential of becoming obese. It is only a potential . . . ; a thin adult may have a large number of fat cells but somehow avoids stoking them up to full capacity.

The New York Times

Two Helpful Children's Books

FAT ELLIOT AND THE GORILLA, *story and pictures by Manus Pinkwater (Four Winds Press, 1974, 48 pages, $4.95 hardcover).*
The author, who admits that a certain autobiographical element has crept into this book, ob-

viously understands how lonely it is to be fat, and how hard it is to lose weight. But he doesn't let the subject interfere with his storytelling, or his sense of humor. I mean, not every fat kid has a gorilla who chases him, takes his food away, and steals his candy money. RS

After supper, Elliot took the book and a plate of doughnuts to his room. He settled down on his bed and began to read:
"How to tell if you are fat: First, go to the zoo."
Elliot was about to reach for his shoes, when he read the next line:
"Study the hippopotamus."
Elliot had done that recently, so he read the next line:
"Now look in the mirror."
Elliot looked.
"If you see any resemblance other than the face, you are fat and need this book."
Elliot was aware of a vague similarity. He yawned wide, and made a few bubbling noises. Then he saw a big gray, sloppy, shiny fat hippo in the mir-

ror. Elliot rubbed his eyes, and there he was, Elliot again. He looked at the book:

"Why it is not good to be fat: If you are fat, you are probably miserable. Fat people have trouble moving around, get tired easily, feel hungry all the time, and are generally not every healthy."

Elliot nodded his head; he had a lot of colds every year.

"How you got to be fat: Most people get fat by eating too much and not moving around enough. Also by eating wrong things."

"I never knew that," said Elliot.

from Fat Elliot and the Gorilla

HUNGRY FRED, *by Paula Fox, illustrated by Rosemary Wells (Bradbury Press, 1969, $3.95).*

This is about a little boy who is always hungry—he eats his dinner, he eats his plate, he eats the table, he winds up eating the entire house. Then he goes off into the woods—still eating everything, even the trees—where he meets a rabbit. Hungry Fred says, "I'm hungry," and the rabbit says, "Yes, we've all heard about you." The rabbit suggests that they be friends, and Fred takes the rabbit back to the spot where his house used to be. When they get there, Fred's mother is crocheting a new rug and his father is building a new house and his sister is planting new trees. The point of the story: the reason Fred ate so much was that he felt nobody was paying any attention to him.

SHARON LERNER

KIDS IN THE KITCHEN

My son is a terrible terrible eater, but when I let him cook, he will eat whatever he cooks—even if it's something he ordinarily doesn't like.

CAROL EICHLER

The kitchen, reasonably enough, was the scene of my first gastronomic adventure. I was on all fours. I crawled into the vegetable bin, settled on a giant onion and ate it, skin and all. It must have marked me for life, for I have never ceased to love the hearty flavor of raw onions.

JAMES BEARD
Delights and Prejudices

Ordinary flour has provided my three-year-old with hours of fun and imaginary play. I put about 2 inches of flour in a deep roasting pan and he uses his Matchbox cars, trucks, and construction equipment, pretending the flour is snow, dirt, etc. This is especially effective when I am baking bread, as it allows him to use the same materials in a new way.

JEANNE DUN

My mommy puts the butter in the pan. And then I take it in one hand and tilt it this way and that and cover the whole pan with butter. I don't leave a spot without butter. Then I crack the egg and if it breaks I scramble it. And if it doesn't break my mommy fries it.

ANDY BERENSON
Age five

Whenever I can, I let my son cook and bake with me. I inevitably lose patience with him because something has to be done "right" (my way) or fast. It's helped to let him "help" me by putting his hand on mine while cutting or mixing, letting him hold the electric mixer, or, when I am making cookies, to give him his own corner of the table, his own tools, and his own dough (cookie dough can be handled as much as you like and still be edible). Then he's busy, but still close enough to me to watch, talk, and ask questions.

FLAVIA POTENZA

◆

Lunch (Without Cooking)

Many kids enjoy just being in the kitchen with all those wonderful pots, pans, and gadgets to play with. But the real fun for kids in the kitchen is helping to cook the food. No matter what age, there is always a cooking job a child can share with a parent or do alone. When kids help in the kitchen they have fun at the same time they learn to follow directions, to measure ingredients, to time the cooking process, to share their creations and, of course, to clean up.

Good cooking requires organization. Kids should wash their hands, read the chosen recipe, and gather all the ingredients and kitchen tools they will need. (If any ingredients are not on hand, a kid should make a note of what is missing and borrow it from a neighbor, or go along on the next trip to the food market. The food market can be fun for the young cook when he or she is doing the shopping.)

Only recipes that can be made quickly are fun for beginning chefs. Kids can become impatient or disinterested if the recipe takes a long time or cannot be eaten immediately. Each step of a recipe should be carefully followed until the "dish" is completed. But the next time the recipe is made a kid should experiment by adding a little of "this" and substituting a bit of "that."

A good cook always experiments a little to try to make the recipe taste better. Personal touches will make it the young chef's own recipe.

Here are three recipes to make a complete lunch—a main course, a beverage, a dessert—and a bonus recipe for a breakfast treat. None requires the use of the stove. There are no guarantees about nutritional value, only a chance to have fun, work with real kitchen tools, learn the rules of the kitchen, and make a lunch that really tastes good.

PICKLE DOGS

Serves one

2 slices American cheese
1 hot dog roll
1 long slice dill pickle
relish (your favorite kind, mustard or ketchup)

You will need a *knife* to cut the pickle, a *spoon* for the relish, and a *napkin*.

Cut each slice of cheese in two and put the cut slices on the inside halves of the hot dog roll. Put the pickle slice between the slices of cheese. Add relish, mustard, ketchup or whatever you like. Fold the roll together and serve with a napkin.

RASPBERRY FUZZ SHAKE

Makes one large or two small glasses

1 small jar raspberry cobbler baby food
(Other flavor shakes can be made from strained peaches, strained applesauce and apricots, or blueberry buckle baby foods)
1¼ cups cold water
1½ tablespoons honey
⅓ cup non-fat dry milk

You will need a *large jar* or *container with a tight lid* for mixing and shaking. A plastic container with a tight snap lid is safer for shaking than a glass jar. You will also need a *measuring cup*, a *tablespoon* and a *drinking glass*.

Put the raspberry cobbler, cold water, and honey together in the plastic container and fit the lid on tightly. Shake the container until all the ingredients are well mixed. Add the dry milk, put the lid back on tightly, and shake well for about a minute. Pour the shake into a drinking glass and serve.

A small variation is to add a tablespoon of baking soda with the dry milk to make a RASPBERRY FIZZ Shake.

SWEET CEREAL BALLS

Makes six to eight large cookies

½ cup chunky peanut butter
⅓ cup honey
½ cup flaked coconut
2 cups of your favorite cereal

You will need a *mixing bowl*, a *large spoon* for mixing, a *measuring cup*, a *large cereal bowl* and a *plate*.

Put the peanut butter, honey, and coconut into the mixing bowl and mix the ingredients well. Stir in ½ cup of the cereal and put the remaining cereal into the cereal bowl. Scoop out large spoonfuls of the peanut butter mixture and form it into balls with your fingers. Roll the balls around in the bowl of cereal so the cereal covers the balls completely. Serve on a plate.

NUT BUTTER (A Breakfast Treat)

Here's a bonus recipe that's a tasty breakfast spread for toast, crackers, pancakes or muffins. Unless you get up extra early, you had better prepare your NUT BUTTER the day before.

½ cup or more shelled walnuts or pecans
plastic sandwich bags

You will need a *rolling pin,* a *measuring cup* and a *spoon.*

Be sure all the shells are removed from the nuts. Put the nuts in a plastic sandwich bag and seal the opening. If the plastic bag seems thin, put a second or third plastic bag over the first for strength.

Place the bag of nuts on a hard surface, such as a kitchen counter or cutting board. Pound the nuts with the rolling pin until they break into small pieces. Then roll over the nuts with as much pressure as you can. A friend or anyone strong might help you press down very hard with the rolling pin. As you roll the nuts, the nut oil will ooze out and mix with the fine bits of rolled nuts to make the NUT BUTTER. Keep rolling until the NUT BUTTER is as smooth and creamy as you can make it.

For extra creaminess, you can mix a little regular butter with the NUT BUTTER. Spoon the NUT BUTTER out of the plastic bag and refrigerate it in a small covered container until ready to use.

STEVEN CANEY
Steven Caney's Play Book

Cookbooks for Children

Cookbooks for children, like dictionaries for children, can never impart their lessons with the richness that comes from another human being who savors the preparation of food or the nuances of words. Growing up in a kitchen that was regularly filled with the image of someone patiently tending a roux, and with the smell of that roux being transformed into gumbos and gravies—now that is not easily translated to the printed page.

Regrettably, the lesson taught by so many of the cookbooks written for children is just the opposite of the lessons we remember from our own childhood kitchens. With a few exceptions, the books range from mediocre and dull to downright insulting, not only to the palate but to the intelligence as well. You don't need a book to know how to make a peanut butter sandwich (a standard item in many of the children's cookbooks), or how to bake a cake using a cake mix (the directions on the cake mix boxes are just as good if not better than those in the books), or how to open a can to make soup (we've nothing against canned goods per se; but if you need ideas for what to do with them, the food companies will provide that literature free). Insulting also are the precious recipes for making a "Bunnysickle" or a "Yummy Delicious."

A good cookbook—for adult or child—must primarily tell you how to turn basic foods into interesting, appetizing dishes. It should explain how various procedures can transform foods from one state to another. One of the few cookbooks written and published for children that succeeds in these tasks is KIDS ARE NATURAL COOKS (*Houghton Mifflin, 1974, 129 pages, $3.95 paperback*). Developed by adults cooking with children at the Parents' Nursery School in Cambridge, Massachusetts, this book is outstanding both for its solid information and delightful style. The recipes are grouped seasonally, and there is an emphasis on using foods when they are available. Rather than shying away from a procedure that might be too complicated, the authors are masters at meeting problems head-on. To make pumpkin pie: One gets a pumpkin (not a can of orange goo), and so learns to distinguish between a "sugar pumpkin" grown specifically for eating and the variety grown for decoration only. Next, make a simple pie crust, and the pie filling. Then you find out how to turn that soggy mass of seeds into delicious roasted seeds. And with the leftover pumpkin, make pumpkin bread. Any child who learns to cook from this book can easily go on to use just about any "adult" cookbook.

There are recipes for pizza dough and pizza sauce, spaghetti alla carbonara, Norwegian oatmeal-raisin soup to be eaten with potato dumplings, chapatis, berry pudding, pretzels; for making cheese, yogurt, peanut butter, ice cream, grape jelly; and instructions for grinding flour, growing sprouts, baking cakes and cookies. The book is well designed, nicely illustrated, sensibly spiral-bound, and very reasonably priced.

Another book written for children that we recommend for cooks of all ages is COOKING WITH COLETTE, by Colette Rossant (*Scribner's, 1975, 198 pages, $7.95 hardback*). Colette Rossant used to have a television series for children called *Zee Cooking School,* and the kids who were on the show obviously enjoyed her simplified (but not bastardized) gourmet cooking course (though they did squeal, as many children will, when they first handled chicken giblets or beef marrow). The show has been discontinued, but the book serves well for any child who enjoys making classic dishes from fresh ingredients—coffee mousse, quiche lorraine, baba ganouj, pot-au-feu, poached striped bass. Colette begins with desserts (they are what children most love to eat, after all, and they are also where one learns the properties of those most basic of ingredients—flour, butter, milk, eggs, sugar), then appetizers, soups, vegetables, salads, and finally, poultry, meat, and fish.

Colette provides the kind of useful general information that will take readers beyond following recipes to an understanding of food. On how to choose vegetables: "To know if a string-bean is fresh, take one and break it in two. If it's crisp, and if the inside looks wet and bright, the string bean is fresh. The beans should be a nice light green color." On removing the brownish scum that forms on the surface of soup: ". . . every method requires a lot of time and takes away some of the flavor of the soup. If you

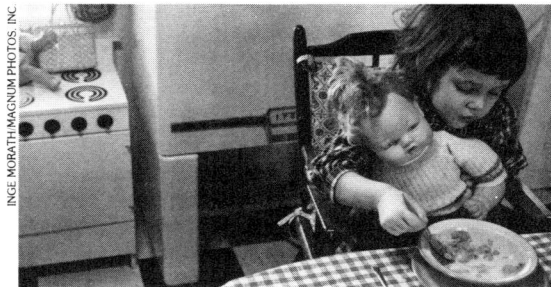

wash well all the ingredients, you will find that there's very little scum and you can remove it easily with a slotted spoon." The recipes themselves are clearly written and easy to follow.

But perhaps what stands out most in *Cooking with Colette* are the author's anecdotes revealing how or where she learned particular recipes, and her occasional dissertations on the importance of particular foods in different countries. Never pedantic, these discourses serve to remind us of the cultural importance traditionally attached to preparing and sharing food. If the traditions of cooking are indeed becoming extinct in our fast-paced contemporary lives, perhaps children can rediscover them through books such as Colette's.

MARIA ROBBINS and RS

ADVERTISING AND NUTRITION

5,000 Food Commercials a Year . . .

. . . that is the nutrition education of the moderate TV-watching child. That education is often supplemented by a school program whose materials are provided, usually free, by the same food manufacturers who advertise on television.
RS

One of the most important nutrition messages on children's television relates to what is *not* advertised. When we watched there was no milk (though . . . there were things to make milk "palatable"), and except for hot cocoa mixes there were no milk products—no cheese, not even ice cream. There were no eggs, no meat, no vegetables, and only one fruit. That nutrition message tells little children which kinds of foods we do not think it is important to excite them about. . . . Nothing on children's television is tart, fresh, crisp, spicy or meaty. Everything is fun, sparkly, gay, colorful, thick, chocolatey, magicky or crunchily delicious.
JOAN GUSSOW
Consumer Action Now

Edible Obsolescence

The most effective way that a manufacturer has of converting food additives to money is to use them to develop a new product. Food additives enable a chemist to translate an advertising man's wish into an actual product. . . .

One food industry man said:

The marketing of many standard food items—the bread-and-butter items that have been around for years—has by now degenerated into a profitless price squeeze. Therefore, food companies simply must make innovations to maintain sales growth.

New products mean money because they don't have any competition for a lengthy period of time. In this period they can become established as *the* brand to buy. The relative lack of competition enables a manufacturer to set as high a price as the public lets him get away with. . . .

MICHAEL JACOBSON
Eater's Digest

Premiums: Watch Out for Small Tricks

Watch out for small tricks. Apparently, since advertising the premiums inside cereal packages has been banned from children's TV by the Federal Communications Commission, some marketing genius at a cereal company has devised a new way of reaching the kiddies: boxes are placed *backward* on the lower shelves—all too enticing to kids whose parents might not *want* to buy junky sugar-coated cereals.

When your kid starts telling you what to buy, ask her if it's the cereal she wants or the prize (or premium). If you can get her to admit that it's the premium, talk about the foolishness of buying something you don't want simply to get something you do want. Suggest taking a trip to the dime store soon (*and do it*) to find a comparable item which she can have without the junky sugar-coated cereal (which, I'm afraid, usually does have the best prizes of all). ELS

Subliminal Advertising in Nursery Rhymes

Are you trying to cut down on the use of sugar in your household? You're blaming the television commercials for the pressures the kids put on you to buy sugar-coated cereals? Maybe it goes back further than that. Have you ever considered subliminal advertising in nursery rhymes? You bet. The subject is goodness, and the way to that goodness is sugar.

> Handy Spandy, Jack a Dandy.
> Loved plum cake, and sugar candy . . .

The next time you're reading nursery rhymes to your two-year-old, notice the number of rhymes in which sugar is mentioned, usually in terms of a reward for virtue or goodness. In our version of the venerated nursery rhymes there's about one verse to the page which extols the virtues of sugar.

One particularly annoying rhyme is the one which ends like this:

And when Jacky's a very good boy he shall have custard,
But when he's a bad boy he shall have mustard.

The kids would do better to be rewarded with mustard.

You can help your child develop values which will save him from the sugar monster by being a critical reader—even when he's a baby.

LINDA WEST ECKHARDT

FOOD IN SCHOOL

"Kitchen Science"

The Studio on Eleventh Street School in New York City has a course called kitchen science, an hour a day in which two kids at a time participate in lunch preparations. It incorporates lessons in math, science, food and nutrition. And what's more, the kids even seem happy to eat the healthful slop they concoct. ELS

Why School Breakfast?

There is little educational justification for feeding children lunch—indeed there is less educational justification for feeding children lunch than there is for feeding them breakfast . . . Most learning in school takes place before lunch, and while a meal might theoretically serve as a reinforcer for a hungry child, getting lunch is not—and probably should not be—made contingent upon a pupil's morning performance in the classroom. If we can feed hungry children only one meal, then let us not make them sit through a morning of classes on an empty stomach. Let us feed them breakfast, teach them something and send them home hungry. Maybe that way, they'll at least want to come back to school tomorrow.

JOAN GUSSOW
"Why School Breakfast"

Did You Eat All Your Lunch, Sweetheart? *Sure, Mom.*

At the Pleasant Valley School in Camarillo, California, the principal demonstrated to parents that the students were wasting enough food to feed an entire class each day. He dumped the contents of one trash bin onto a picnic table. The contents added up to: 41 sandwiches, 19 apples, 13 oranges, half a chocolate pudding, 14 cookies, 19 candies, 2 burritos, 2 cartons of milk, 2 pieces of chicken, 3 bags of potato chips, raisins, 4 carrot sticks, and a piece of Mexican bread. As a result of that demonstration there are now classes at that school on food-waste—*and* parents are packing smaller school lunches.

JO ANN YORK
with Jerome Agel and Eugene Boe
How I Feed My Family on $16 a Week

Lunchboxes: The Pros and Cons

I discovered the lunchbox as a great soother of anxiety. When Nick got his new super-hero lunchbox, he felt bold enough to face kindergarten. It was only when he was armed with the lunchbox that he agreed to have his lunch in school. No amount of cute drawings by Mom on the side of the brown paper bag could get those results.

ELS

I have often felt like mobilizing with other parents who've thrown away five dollars on their kids' lunchboxes, and picketing the manufacturers of those tin or plastic hunks of junk. The metal ones, of course, rust, often within weeks of purchase. If may be possible to give them a longer life if you stand outside the school with a dry cloth *every* day in order to clean and wipe dry the inside·of the box immediately. And it's a sure thing the inside of the box will need wiping up, since the thermos that comes with it usually leaks (until finally it breaks completely and the Styrofoam inside comes out—and you find yourself buying juice in those little cans).

Finally you give in and buy the plastic version, only to discover that this time the latches break or the plastic handle comes off. More than once, David's sandwich went tumbling onto the sidewalk. He had tape around his lunchbox for about three months and had to hold the thing in two hands. I know of one mother who was so frustrated that she bought a brass door handle and welded it onto her kid's lunchbox. It was a magnificent job. The final blow came, though, when, a week later, the rest of the box fell apart.

I'm definitely going back to the brown bag.

SUSAN WECHSLER

[Ironically, some of the worst food (aesthetically, nutritionally, and educationally) is served in institutions. Visit a hospital or school and what you'll probably find is white bread. They don't even give you a choice.—RS]

THE SUPERMARKET AS AN ECOLOGY CLASSROOM

If your kids accompany you when you shop at the supermarket, you can teach them a lot about ecology as they walk up and down the aisles with you. For example, you can show them a six-pack of orange juice cans—six cans, each containing six fluid ounces—and ask them ·to compare it to one large orange juice can, containing, say, forty-six ounces. Not only is there a difference in the price per ounce (which your children might want to figure out mathematically); you can also point out to them the extra amount of metal that's used in making six small cans as opposed to one large one (it's almost twice as much). You can point out the fact that the six-pack requires a cardboard package, while the large individual can does not. You can explain that the manufacture of the smaller cans and of the cardboard package requires the use of far more energy than the production of the individual can. You can tell them about the gasoline used in hauling the excess garbage produced by the extra metal and cardboard in the six-pack. And so on, all the way to the garbage dump.

A second lesson you might teach your kids in the supermarket is the wastefulness of display packaging: a plastic bubble, or blister-pack, over a product costs a lot more than a simple paper bag, and it's a lot harder to recycle. Did you know that about 40 percent of every purchase you make at the store is for packaging and not for the product itself? What's worse, when you get home, you have to throw that excess packaging away.

◆

Here's an exercise for your children while they're at the store with you: have them look for packages that are still useful once they're empty. A mustard jar designed to double as a drinking mug is a perfect example (Kosciusko

Mustard makes such a jar), and I'm sure your kids will be able to find others.

One day, on one of our shopping excursions, my daughter pointed out that an ice cream cone is really the ultimate package. Why? Because it can be totally eaten. Perhaps your children will help you find other examples of ''ultimate packaging.''
ILENE GOLDMAN

After the supermarket shopping is done and the bags are being emptied, remove all the wrappings and packaging from the food and put it in a large bag. Then look at the amount of trash. Try to figure out how many families there are in the city, and try to imagine how much trash there would be if you put yours together with the others. Okay? Now ask your children if individually wrapped cheese slices (for which you pay x cents extra per pound) really need that extra wrapping and if they want to add to the waste problem.
ELS

And Do Frogs Lay Legs? A Word About Kids' Vegetarian Instinct

My kid has acquired a taste for quarter-inch-thick gray hamburgers. When I served him a freshly ground sirloin burger that was pink and juicy, he said, ''Yuk, it's bloody!'' Even so, he tried it.

''Where do hamburgers come from anyway?'' he asked after a bite.

''From cows.'' I turned away so that he wouldn't see from my expression that there was more to be said on the matter. (He is a humane child.)

I trusted that if we left the subject there he would assume that cows lay hamburgers the way chickens lay eggs—after all, he knows that cows give milk without pain. But I'm not looking forward to his asking me where drumsticks come from. I'll say ''Chickens,'' and hope for the best.
ELS

KIDS' ROOMS
AND ENVIRONMENTS

RONNIE SHUSHAN/THE PHOTO WORKS

167

A Room to Grow In

Say "baby's room" and *shazam,* the image pictured is a pastel-hued, Lilliputian wonderland. Say "children's room" and the picture changes to a chaotic jumble of beat-up cast-offs from every imaginable source combined with an array of clutter that rivals the Collier brothers' collection. Here's a simple adapt-as-you-grow plan that should accommodate your darling from that first rosy-cheeked flush through the last bout with advanced acne.

Starting with a basic furniture plan is your first step. Childcraft (1 Park Avenue, New York, N.Y., [212] 868-0820), a furniture manufacturing company, has devised some ingenious pieces that are beautifully convertible. One is a changing table for a newborn that converts to a worktable and desk later on. Another piece is a crib with removable side rails that can become a youth bed or settee. Both are popularly priced.

We all know that young children respond to primary colors—red, yellow, blue—so instead of the traditional pastel nursery, start right off with colors that are bright and gay. Don't be afraid to paint a baby's room orange.

Walls should be planned to accommodate the needs of a growing child. One wall could be covered in cork or Foamcore for pinning up early masterpieces and later to exhibit posters, photos, and "I Hate Mother" signs. (Foamcore is a white surface, about a quarter-inch thick. It's inexpensive, sold by the yard in art supply stores, and washable.) Another wall could have a large piece of slate attached to it—a wonderful way to let the kids write on the walls. (Buy it at a local lumberyard.) Walls can also be painted with washable high-gloss paint or, much better, covered with scrubbable vinyl paper.

Flooring in a kid's room can present a tricky problem. Vinyl tile or linoleum is the most practical in terms of wash and wear, but it's cold to walk on and a bit hard to land on when a child is first learning to walk. Carpeting, though warmer and more of a cushion, represents a larger investment and may not last beyond the kid's first experiments with water, food coloring, and tropical fish food. One solution might be putting an inexpensive washable cotton rug over a vinyl floor, or using indoor-outdoor carpeting, a low-pile, synthetic covering designed for areas of heavy traffic. It requires minimum maintenance and is easily cleaned.

If you want your children to be orderly about their things, you need to provide plenty of storage space. Adequate shelving is vital; you'll get the most for your money if you build it yourself, or find an amateur carpenter to build it for you. And if you're tired of hanging up your kids' clothes, try setting closet poles at a height children can reach, and put some hooks inside the closet door.

NAOMI WARNER

A Kid's Bedroom Is a Place to Be Manipulated

My kids have a three-room cluster, two bedrooms and a playroom, and the main thing about it is that it's a space they can manipulate and change to create their own environments. The beds and dressers are just regular beds and dressers; that's all they need to be. Across the ceiling, there are beams for hanging things. Plastic milk crates are used to build steps up to the dresser, which becomes a look-out tower. I think my son sleeps in his bed about 10 percent of the time; usually he beds down wherever he made a sleep-place that day. Sometimes an indoor tent. And now a sleeping bag.

One of their favorite activities is weaving the room. They take out balls of string (which are always used over and over) and tie the string onto a doorknob and then tie it onto a dresser knob and then onto the bed and then onto a shoe and then onto the closet door. And once they weave the room they weave in everything in between, creating an enormous maze.

Now that my daughter is getting older—she's going to be eight soon—she's more concerned about her image, and she's becoming very orderly. She has gone from that random play decorating to functional changes to suit her needs. For instance, she doesn't have curtains in her room—you don't really need them in the woods—but she decided there was one place where the sun comes in in the morning, which she wanted to close off. Instead of "Buy me a curtain," she's figured out a way to weave that area.

STEVEN CANEY

CHILDREN'S FURNITURE

Bunk Beds

If you are considering bunk beds, be sure to get two single beds (or three) that can be used separately, as well as on top of one another. . . . Later, when your children are older and/or no longer thrilled about being in the top bunk (or when you want to separate them), you can use the bunks as useful single bunks anywhere. . . . Moving is easier with a less cumbersome unit, too, so try and remove the top bed from the bottom bed right in the store where you buy it.

If you can't move it there, you won't be able to do it any easier at home! Many bunk bed units can be purchased unassembled. They aren't that difficult to assemble, and it does save you money, especially in trucking bills. . . . Be sure you understand the instructions before you make your purchase, and when the beds are delivered count the parts you need to put them together, to be sure there are no parts missing. . . .

The Muurame bunk beds designed by Pirkko Stenros, a Finnish architect (purchased at Scandinavian Designs, Inc. [in New York City]), are cleanly designed, solidly built, and allow for maximum flexibility. There is a middle piece which separates the two beds, allowing adequate height between the two beds and creating a ladder. You can buy a bookcase that hangs on the side of the bed and also doubles as a night table or an extra surface for the one up top. You can buy drawers on rollers which slide easily underneath the bottom bunk. Buy one long drawer and you have a bed for a baby, a trundle bed, a box, or a storage drawer. Or, buy two square drawers to fit together under the bed unit. Make your own seat and add oars and you have a boat! . . .

Put a patterned sheet on the bottom of the upper mattress to cover the gray drab ticking.

ALEXANDRA STODDARD
A Child's Place

Reconsidering the Cradle

The story of the decline and fall of the cradle is a typical one of fads, fashions, fallacies, and of ill-informed and misguided authoritarianism. During the 1880's the view developed among physicians and nurses that there was danger in overindulging the child. It was thought that many of the complaints from which babies suffered were due to the well-meant interference of fond parents. It soon came to be "authoritatively" held that the clearest and first evidence of this spoiling of the baby was the cradle. . . .

And so the cradle was finally banished to the attic or lumber room and the baby consigned to a crib. . . .

[But] the baby assures itself that all is well largely through the messages it receives from the skin. The supports it receives in the enveloping environment of the cradle are very reassuring to it, for the cradle affords it something of a replication, a continuation, of the life it led so long in the womb, and this is good and comforting. When the baby feels uncomfortable or insecure it may whimper, and . . . rocking reassures [it], for in its mother's womb it was naturally rocked by the normal motions of her body. . . .

When the infant is too warm the rocking has a cooling effect, hastening evaporation from the skin. When the infant is too cold the rocking helps to warm him. The warming has a hypnotic effect on the infant, and it is soothing to his nervous system. Above all, the rocking motion produces a gentle stimulation of almost every area of his skin, with consequential beneficial physiological effects of every kind.

ASHLEY MONTAGU
Touching: The Human Significance of Skin

[If you're still wondering about spoiling, consider that cradle rocking is probably no more habit-forming than breast-feeding or bottle-feeding. And, as Ashley Montagu points out, "children are weaned from breast or bottle, unless it is done too suddenly, without any serious difficulty or after-effects."—Eds.]

Building a Plywood Bed Platform

(1) Cut the legs from a four-by-four. Each should be 13 inches in length.

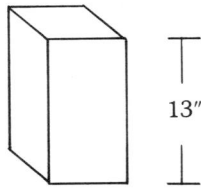

13"

(2) Buy a two-by-four and measure it exactly (you might find that its actual dimensions are 1¾ by 3½ inches). Now notch each leg to accommodate two two-by-fours as follows (we'll assume, for purposes of these instructions, that the 1¾- by 3½-inch measurement is the correct one):

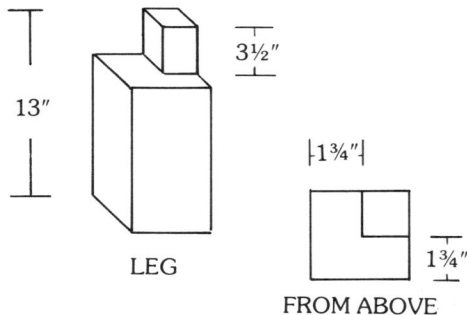

13"   3½"

                            |1¾"|

LEG   1¾"

FROM ABOVE

This can be done with a handsaw, but care must be taken to make the cuts perfectly straight or the legs on the bed will not stand vertically.

(3) Measure your mattress (there are at least three different "twin" sizes), and cut each of the two-by-fours 1¾ inches shorter than the corresponding side of the mattress. Glue (Elmer's is surprisingly good) and nail (or bolt for real stress-resistance) as follows:

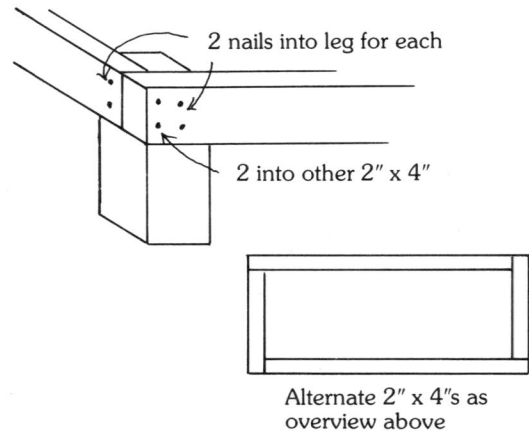

2 nails into leg for each

2 into other 2" x 4"

Alternate 2" x 4"s as
overview above

(4) Then nail on a ¾-inch piece of plywood the dimensions of the top of the frame. For finishing it off, cover with scraps of leather, fabric, Mylar, vinyl, etc., either by gluing or stapling.

PAUL DRYMALSKI

How to Turn a Bed into a Boat (or a Train or a Truck)

You don't have to buy a London-bus bed or have a double-decker storage-sleeping-climb-on built for $2,500. Once you get your kid to believe in the power of the imagination (by believing in it yourself, I suppose), you can turn a box spring and mattress into a boat, a train, a great big truck. It helps to have a few extra pillows to pile up for sides, a husky voice for motor sounds, and maybe a make-believe prop or two for atmosphere.

ELS

Pillows Are for Sleeping

We made great big pillows (four foot square) and it was this easy: sew fabric together like a pillow case, fill with shredded foam, then close up the fourth side. Keep the stuffing loose and floppy for cuddling and rough-housing. Whenever my friends sleep over, I offer them the single bed in my room but they always say, Oh, no! I want to sleep on the pillows.

KARREN BAIN
Age eleven

◆

The Wood-Box Bed: It's Inexpensive and It Doesn't Take Up Much Room

When my four-year-old son wanted a "real" bed, not a crib, I couldn't afford to buy one. Moreover, his room is tiny. So with money and space as limitations, I decided to build him a bed—which was simply a very strong open-topped wood box, constructed to fit around his crib mattress and mounted on casters (legs could easily be added). He's now six and has almost outgrown it, so it's about to become an under-bed storage box. I'm still broke, and his room is still tiny, so I guess I'll try a loft bed next.

DONNA BARKMAN

Do-It-Yourself Tube Chair

Education Development Center (39 Chapel Street, Newton, Mass. 02160) publishes a book called *Building with Tubes* ($1). In it they describe how to make these chairs from discarded industrial tubes or barrels.

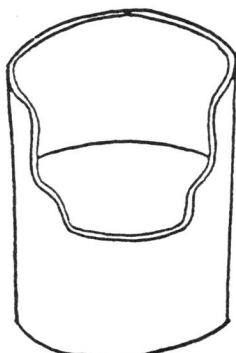

1.
CUT OUT
SHAPED TUBE

FRONT VIEW

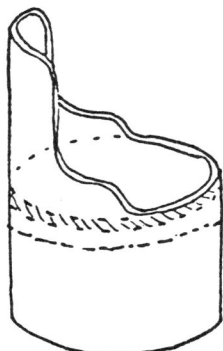

SIDE VIEW

2.
MAKE A SEAT BY
CUTTING A DISC OF
THE SAME DIAMETER
AS THE INSIDE OF
THE TUBE.

3.
CUT A RING OF TUB-
ING 2" OR MORE
WIDE. REMOVE A
PIECE OF THE RING
SO IT WILL FIT IN-
SIDE THE TUBE.
GLUE IN PLACE TO
SUPPORT THE SEAT.

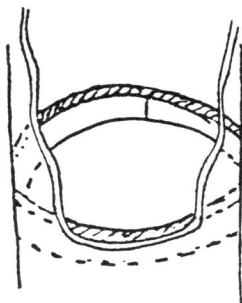

4.
GLUE THE SEAT IN PLACE.

Bean-bag Chairs

Child-size bean-bag chairs are more than for sitting, though they're fine for that too. Rolling,

throwing, practicing your first-base slide, tumbling off, building, if you have more than one: kids will concoct an amazing variety of functions. With all this action, two things are essential when purchasing a bean-bag chair: a double lining, and a stuffing of pinhead-size foam (squishier). Vinyl makes for easy cleaning. Added bonus: they slip easily under tables, desks, etc., when you want them out of the way.

RS

Milk Crates: For Storage and for Standing On

Milk crates, which you can only get at around three or five o'clock in the morning, can be stacked or hung from the ceiling and from one another by wire. The metal or wooden ones are better for standing on than the newer plastic ones, but the latter are better for storing books, toys, jeans, and sweaters.

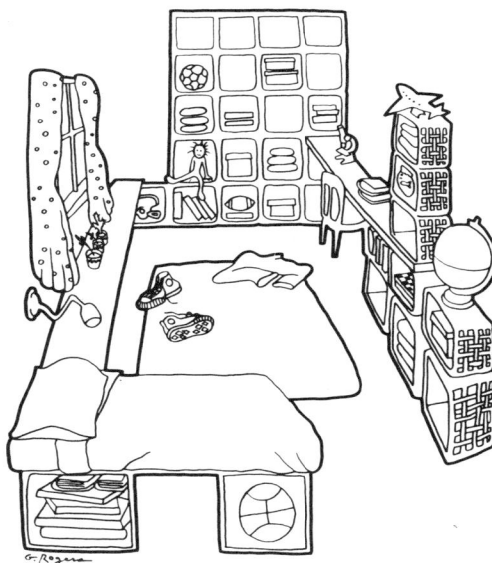

Instant Blackboards

Want to turn ordinary boxes and chairs and walls into chalkboard boxes and chairs and walls? You can do it by slapping on a coat of Chalk Board Paint, a lead-free latex-base paint that might be available at your local hardware store. (If it's not, you can order it, at $5.60 a quart, in colors of fuchsia, green, and Dutch blue, from the Workshop for Learning Things, 5 Bridge Street, Watertown, Mass. 02172.)

RS

How to Build a Child's Worktable

The idea grew out of a picnic table in the park—the kind with the benches attached. For aesthetic reasons, I chose to make straight legs on my table, instead of the traditional slanted ones (also because I thought it would be easier, which was true). Now I know better: the slanted legs give stability, while my straight-legged table tended to tip over if an adult sat on one side. My solution: I used metal angles to attach all four legs to the floor. Now it's like a rock.

I think a larger or squarer table wouldn't tend to tip over. However, the directions and dimensions I've given here are based on the table I built because it's the only one I know, and, finally, attached to the floor, it is strong, steady, and aesthetically pleasing.

I encourage you to take my experience and make whatever modifications you want to adapt the table to your particular situation.

STEPHEN OLDERMAN

MATERIALS

One sheet of ¾″ plywood
¾″ pine shelving, 10″ wide (amount of wood to be determined by the size of your table)
2″ x 3″ boards
1″ x 3″ boards

4 bolts with screws
Drill
Hammer
Nails
Saw

INSTRUCTIONS

1. Cut four 30″ legs from your 2″ × 3″s.
2. Cut four 46″ lengths from your 1″ × 3″s.
3. Cut two 18″ lengths from your 1″ × 3″s.
4. Nail one 30″ leg to each end of one of the 46″ 1″ × 3″s (see illustration).
5. Repeat with other legs.
6. Take the two remaining 46″ 1″ × 3″s and nail them to the legs about 9″ up from the bottom (see illustration).
7. Now take your 18″ 1″ × 3″s and nail the two sets of legs together. You should now have the legs and frame of your table standing up (see illustration).
8. Cut two 46″ lengths from your 2″ × 3″s.
9. Cut two 54″ lengths from your ¾″ shelving.
10. Place one of your 2″ × 3″s on the inside of the table legs along the short axis. The top of the 2″ × 3″ should be 20″ above the floor (see illustration).
11. Carefully mark its position on the legs and remove the 2″ × 3″.
12 Drill a hole in each leg for the bolt.
13. Carefully return the 2″ × 3″ to position. Mark it through the holes you've just drilled in the legs. Remove the 2″ × 3″ and drill matching holes.
14. Now replace the 2″ × 3″, put bolts through the holes, and secure with screws.
15. Repeat steps 10 to 14 on the other legs.
16. Center shelving over two supports, allowing about ½″ overhang, and nail down. Now you have your benches (see illustration).
17. Cut a 30″ × 54″ piece of ¾″ plywood.
18. Center over legs and nail plywood into all four legs.
19. That's it (see illustration).

STEPHEN OLDERMAN

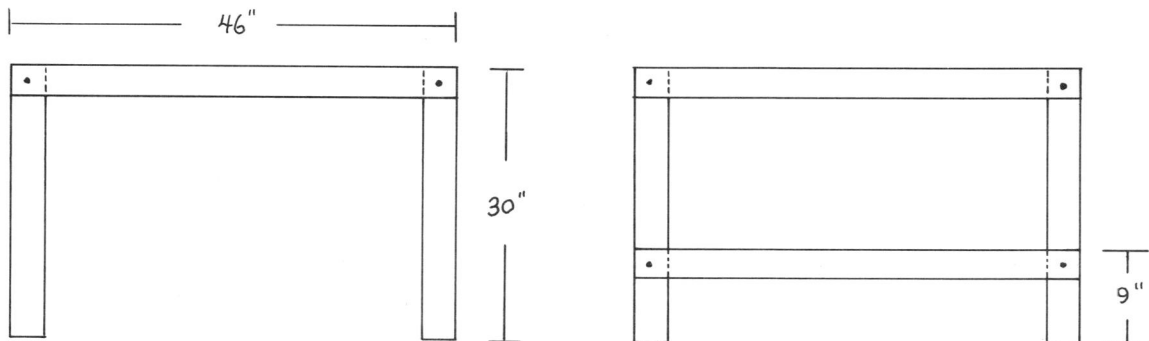

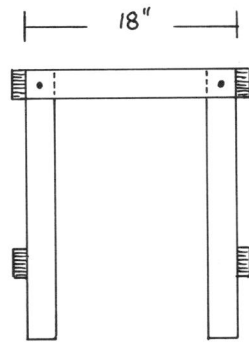

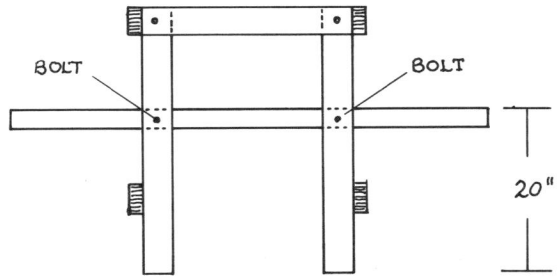

BOLT

BOLT

18"

20"

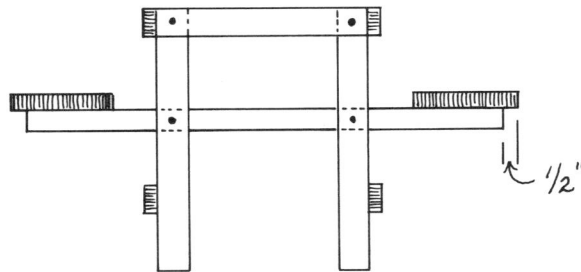

½"

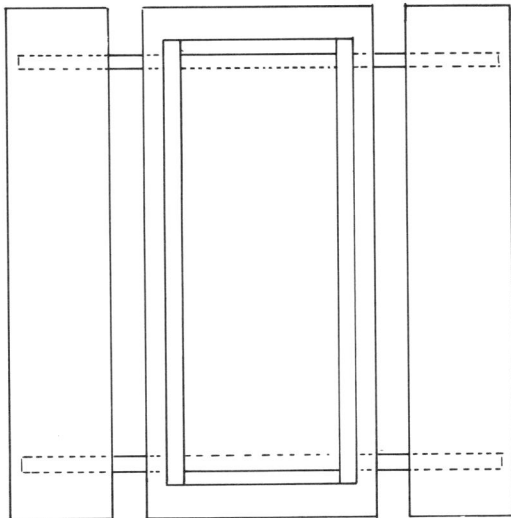

OVERHEAD VIEW

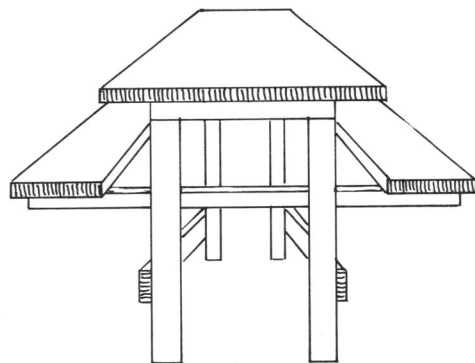

PERSPECTIVE VIEW

Murphy Play Table

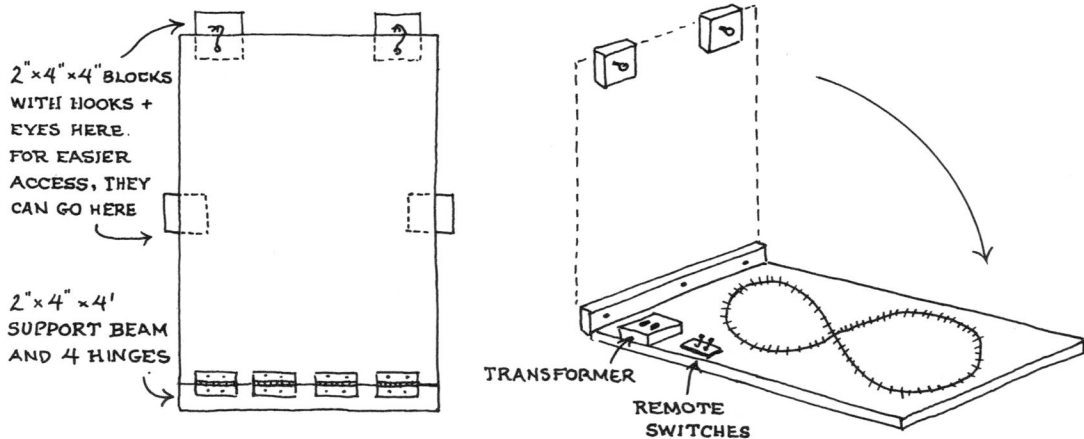

2"×4"×4" BLOCKS WITH HOOKS + EYES HERE. FOR EASIER ACCESS, THEY CAN GO HERE

2"×4"×4' SUPPORT BEAM AND 4 HINGES

TRANSFORMER

REMOTE SWITCHES

In a small city apartment that has trouble enough accommodating two adults and a child and their accouterments, accommodating the toys of a four-year-old presents a real problem. So when our son began badgering us for electric trains, we began looking for a larger apartment. But the solution came in the form of a murphy table.

We bought (for a total cost of about $20):
One 4' × 6' piece of ½" plywood
One 2" × 4" × 4' support beam
Four hinges
Two hooks and eyes
Two 2" × 4" × 4" blocks
Plastic anchors for ¼" screws for attaching beam and blocks to the wall.

We rigged it so the table would be kid height, about 20 inches, and used his small toy box (with wheels) and an oversized dictionary to support the end. (A more desirable support, however, would be legs—maybe two two-by-fours cut to the desired height, attached with hinges so they'd fold against the board when it's raised—our next project, I suppose.)

This can be any kind of play table, but for a train table, the tracks are tacked on. The transformer has to be attached each time you use the trains (a slight inconvenience) and the wires show when the table is up (we covered the underside with posters of trains). If you anticipate landscaping and building bridges, the two-inch clearance between wall and tabletop (when the table is folded) won't be enough. That can be remedied by increasing the width of the support beam and blocks.

Ours was a quick improvisation. I'm sure someone with more skill and more planning can easily rig a more streamlined and sophisticated version.

FLAVIA POTENZA

Children and Boxes

It's true, I haven't had much to do with children—some friends have them, and I see them around on buses—but from what little I've seen, they need sturdy, colorful, movable furniture; things to knock over, climb under, and hide their belongings in. Box furniture, perhaps, really comes into its own with children. Boxes are built to their size, and very little work is needed in putting things together for them.

A child's table is a simple matter of two boxes and a piece of plywood. Storage is created the same way on top of the table, if you like.

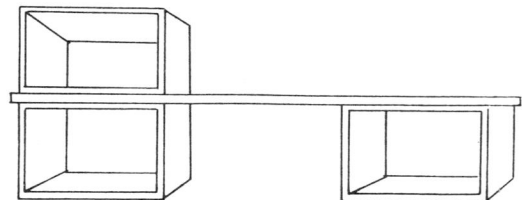

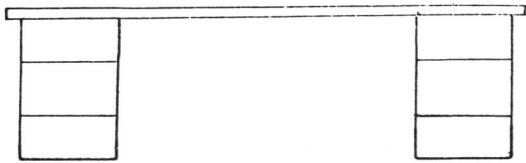

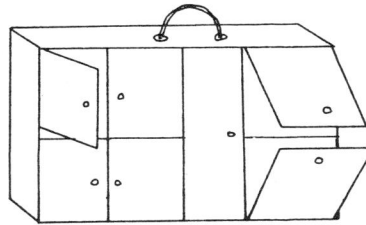

When the child grows taller, the boxes can be turned around and shelves added to them.

Another box, with a cushion, is an easy stool. . . .

From what I see of children they like places to look in, are fascinated by colors and doors, things they can move around all by themselves. A child's room is one place where boxes should be painted, rather than varnished to adult tastes.

Boxes make great toys. A tea chest can become a maze if you cut climbable-through holes in the sides, so that the children can chase each other through and around and over. Several tea chests must be heaven.

Small cardboard or wood boxes can be used as building blocks, either all the same size or ones that fit inside each other. The corners can be strengthened with masking or scotch tape and the whole box painted in bright colors.

Children like to carry bags and boxes around with them, to move their treasures along with them. A cigar box or something slightly larger is perfect. Put different compartments inside the box and little doors on the side of the box which open into the different compartments. A handle on top and the box makes it a magic suitcase.

Actually, there's no need to go to even this trouble. Put a child in a room full of boxes, leave him alone, and see what happens. Children know exactly what they need and what they want at any given time. They'll arrange it all themselves and be happy doing it.

DIANE CLEAVER
The Box Book

◆

Furniture That Folds, Knocks Down, Stacks, etc.

Nomadic Furniture, by James Hennessey and Victor Papanek (Pantheon Books, 1973, 150 pages, $3.95 paperback), has a section on children's environments and furniture that is very informative, along with directions on how to build the stuff cheaply and with your kids' help. Now that we know how important physical environment is to man and how important it can be to the development of mental and physical well-being in our offspring, there is no excuse for providing sterile, nonproductive environments for our kids in the name of good housekeeping.

LINDA SUGARMAN

WAYS TO ACCOMMODATE SWINGING, JUMPING, CLIMBING, AND EVEN PLAYING BALL INDOORS

The Swyngomatic

There are over a dozen Swyngomatic models. You can buy a fifteen-minute or a one-hour ride, in a nylon seat or a vinyl seat or a cradle bed, resting on a one- or two-piece tubular frame, with or without a music box, with or without a sunshade. A no-frills model will cost around $10 in discount stores, and as one parent reported, "You have to wind it up, and it's

very noisy, but when your baby doesn't want to be anywhere but in motion, it's a blessing." (Swyngomatics are also sold in many department stores and specialty shops, and the fancier models can run over $20.)

If you want to get a few more years' use from an outgrown Swyngomatic, remove the swing and cover the frame with a sheet, blanket, or fabric to make an impressive indoor play tent.

RS

The Jolly Jumper

I attribute Ian's general sturdiness, and particularly the strength in his legs, to his enthusiastic use of the Jolly Jumper from six to fourteen months of age. He enjoyed hell out of it, he soared and laughed. He'd futz around in there sometimes as long as half an hour. A valuable toy, if a toy is what it is.

IVAN GOLD

Unlike the Swyngomatic, the Jolly Jumper really isn't the place to leave a young child unattended, no matter what the manufacturer says. There's nothing inherently unsafe about the Jolly Jumper; in fact, we're quite enthusiastic about it. But it's good to watch for the occasional overzealous bounce that lands heads against doorways, or arms tangled in ropes.

You can buy a Jolly Jumper in many discount stores for under $10, and in many department stores for as much as $15.

RS

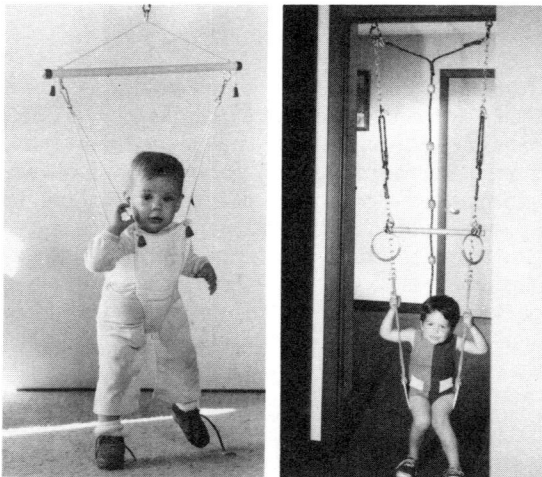

Now That You're Hanging, What Can You Hang?

Rope ladders, trapeze bars, indoor swings, and other active play items you can hang indoors are available, individually and sometimes as components of a set, from many of the toy catalogs. Galt, Creative Playthings, Childcraft, and Child Life all have some.

Lots of people make their own hanging contraptions. Says one friend, "A swing mounted on a beam in an open basement—a sturdy rope brought through the center of an octagonal seat (1-inch plywood) and knotted below—is great for circles, back and forth, and tricks. Wonderful physical activity on rainy days."

RS

A piece of indoor play equipment that many people said was one of the best investments they'd made is the Creative Playthings Indoor Gym House. It costs $43.95.

Hanging Play Equipment Inside

The problem: to find a beam in your ceiling from which to hang rope ladders, swings, ropes, and rings. The solution: It is not easy. And there's no shortcut. So-called beam finders that use a small magnet to locate nails definitely don't work. You must use the trial-and-error method of drilling through the ceiling until you hit a beam. In most instances, you will hit a wood lath (thin strips of wood to which the plaster is attached). However, the lath is only about ¼-inch thick and will not support a child of any size for any length of time. When you hit a beam, you'll know: your drill will continue to bite into the wood instead of popping out of the other side as it does with the lath.

Enlarge the hole so that you can see the whole beam, then screw into the middle of it the longest, biggest screw hook you can buy (a clothesline hook is best). Hang the equipment and patch up the holes with patching plaster.

If you haven't found a beam after a couple feet of test holes, your beam is probably running the other way, and you must reverse your direction 90 degrees.

If this doesn't work for you, call a friend or hang it in the door jamb.

STEPHEN OLDERMAN

Great Balls of Foam

Parker Brothers' Nerf Ball (4-inch diameter, about $1.80 at discount stores) and Super Nerf Ball (7-inch diameter, about $4.00 at discount stores) are light, squishy foam balls which are terrific for throwing around the house because they don't knock over lamps and tables. But

Consumer Reports blasted them, as I recall, because they're flammable, and because very small children who succeed in biting off a small piece of the foam could theoretically get it caught in their throats.

Some Nerf Ball items are a little more expensive than need be, because Parker Brothers chooses to sell a hoop with them, and all you really want is the ball.

JEAN GREEN

Nerf Balls come in many incarnations. There are softball-sized Nerf Balls, Nerf Footballs, Nerf Basketballs; even Nerf Frisbees and Nerf vehicles like the Nerfmobile. If you've become resigned to your kid's playing ball in the house, try the small Nerf with a small paddle like a Ping-Pong Paddle.

ELS and CBC

We think Super Puff Basketball (RBC Industries, about $7 at discount stores) is a good game because you can play it inside. It can be put on a door without bolts.

TIMMIE and CHARLES LORD

Super Puff Basketball is a godsend for apartment life. But a word of warning: the clamp that goes over the door has a knife-sharp edge; never play with it until installed.

GAY LORD

Note: Regular Puff Basketball has a smaller ball and a smaller rim (plastic instead of metal), and is attached to the wall with suction cups. It sells for around $3 in discount stores.

◆

The Childcraft Climbing House

The Childcraft Climbing House is the quintessential plaything. It's four feet square, two sides are seven feet high, two sides are four feet high. There's a pole to slide down, and a rope ladder attached top and bottom for climbing or swinging, a crossbar at the seven-foot height, and three adjustable planks for climbing over and under. It's made of beautifully finished highly lacquered wood, not a single possibility for a splinter. It accommodates three or four children, up through about age eight.

Because of the cost, making the decision to purchase the Climbing House was like buying a car. We shopped around at other places, like Community Playthings, but the Childcraft house was the only one that was physically challenging enough to hold our son's interest for several years. It was the only present we bought for our two children (age twenty months and four and a half) that Christmas, and was possible thanks to a donation from the grandparents. But I'm sure it will be resalable when our children have outgrown it.

People marvel at my two-year-old's physical adaptability, and I'm convinced she got it from the Climbing House. We feel privileged to have it in our home. My children's school has one, too, and whenever a child gets hyperactive or out of control, she is sent to the Climbing House to work it out.

The Climbing House is in Childcraft's institutional catalogue, "The Growing Years," not their Christmas catalogue. They don't encourage individuals who want to buy from their institutional catalogue; you really have to persevere if you want it. The assembly instructions, by the way, are quite specific and simple.

CYNTHIA STEIN

[*The Childcraft Climbing House costs $419.95, plus tax and an 8½ percent delivery charge outside the metropolitan New York area.*]

DECORATING

"I Hung Mickey from the Ceiling"

Here are some of the ideas I had when I first decorated my son's room:
CEILING. Hang plastic blow-up toys (i.e., Mickey Mouse, Donald Duck, etc.) on nylon string from the ceiling. They're very light, and any movement in the room starts them gently swinging. Also, if they fall down, no one gets hurt. This works best with high ceilings. I got the idea remembering how Gerrity used to watch his mobile in his crib; why, I thought, shouldn't he have something to look at in his regular bed, too?

WALLS. From any gas station you can get (if you tip the attendant) some of those colorful triangular flags you see waving in the wind, all strung together. Tack them up on the walls where the ceiling and wall meet, going all around the room—they look very colorful and festive.

If you ever see something in a window display you really like, go into the store, ask for the display department, and find out if you can have the item (or buy it) when the store has finished using it. I got three beautiful five-foot-high British soldiers from a display that F. A. O. Schwarz had used. I tacked them on the walls, and they became the focal point for my son's room.

Put a huge blackboard on the wall. Gerrity and his friends spend hours doodling, erasing, washing, etc.

FLOORS. I used vinyl tile—indestructible, sanitary, and fun for kids, as their toys move over this kind of surface very easily. There isn't any maintenance, either.

SYDNEY LANSING

◆

Posters—from $2 to $16

If you have any spare wall space—between your young artists' own masterpieces and the bulletin boards, chalkboards, and storage shelves—there's a wonderful array of inexpensive posters from which to choose.

Opening the pages of the Green Tiger Press catalog is like discovering a treasure-trove. This firm is in the business of producing posters and prints based on artwork from old children's books. Whether you are well versed in children's literature or not doesn't matter a bit. These posters are irresistible, priced from $3 to $6.

If your taste is for contemporary children's book artists, the Children's Book Council produces a Book Week poster and mobile each year, as well as bookmarks, friezes, and stream-

COURTESY OF GREEN TIGER PRESS

ers. The selection includes works by Richard Scarry, Maurice Sendak, Byron Barton, and Gerald McDermott, and the prices are reasonable.

Franklin Watts, Inc., has Brian Wildsmith posters that are delightful in their detail and design

and are printed in full color on a durable grade of paper that won't tear with handling. The Wildsmith "Circus of Color Posters," far and away the best of the series, is a set of eight designed to introduce children to color—they are 2 by 3 feet and cost $15.95; "Months" is a set of twelve posters, 2 by 3 feet, $15.95. (Posters are not available individually, but if you order a set you'll have a supply of birthday presents on hand.)

COPYRIGHT © 1972 BY EZRA JACK KEATS/MACMILLAN CO.

COPYRIGHT © PENGUIN BOOKS, LTD. 1972

Macmillan Publishing Company offers a set of three posters by Ezra Jack Keats ("In the Community," "In School," "At Home") for $4.95. These seem more school-oriented, but could open the way for a nice home discussion about pre-schoolers' experiences. Macmillan also offers the C. S. Lewis "Narnia" maps for $1.95 each. The colors are muted compared to the usual fare of bold primary colors, and will probably have the most appeal to children who have read the books. The posters in both sets measure 20 by 30 inches.

Gallery Five, a London-based company, prints some elegant full-color fairy tale posters which cost $2.50 apiece and come in varying sizes. These are all quite large.

Again, outside the realm of children's themes, the Sierra Club produces beautiful wilderness scenes, $2.50 each and approximately 25 by 35 inches, which are distributed through local bookstores or Sierra Club offices. They are full-color photographs printed on high-gloss paper and should be handled with care to avoid tearing.

Sports Illustrated offers 2 by 3–foot or 18 by 24–inch full-color posters of sports personalities in just about any sports category you can name. They are $3 each, or three for $8 plus $2 for each additional poster. Handle with care, as they tear and wrinkle easily.

FLAVIA POTENZA

TO ORDER POSTERS

The Green Tiger Press catalog: send 50 cents in stamps to the Green Tiger Press, 7458 La Jolla Boulevard, La Jolla, Calif. 92037.

Children's Book Council: write to them at 67 Irving Place, New York, N.Y. 10003; ask for their materials brochure.

Franklin Watts, Inc.: write to the Sales Department, 730 Fifth Avenue, New York, N.Y. 10019, to order their catalogue.

Macmillan Publishing Co.: write to Macmillan Order Department, 222 Brown Street, Riverside, N.J. 08075.

Gallery Five: for fairy tale posters, contact Marcel Schurman, Inc., 954 60th Street, Oakland, Calif. 94608.

The Sierra Club: 530 Bush Street, San Francisco, Calif. 94104.

Sports Illustrated posters: Marketcom, Lockbox 2257, Hampton Bank, 4301 Hampton Avenue, St. Louis, Mo. 63109

Wall Decorations: Two from *The Catalogue of Catalogues*

Maria Elena de La Iglesia, in her world-wide shopping guide, *The Catalogue of Catalogues* (Random House, $7.95 paperback), provides a wealth of information on art, graphics, and wall decorations. We found the following excerpts on posters and friezes for children's rooms particularly interesting:

John Paige, The Manor House, Kings Cliffe, Peterborough
PE8 6XB, England
Brochure, $1.

John Paige, a free-lance graphic designer, publishes and sells his own train friezes. The paper friezes are sophisticated, in restrained realistic colors, and can be joined together to stretch right across a wall. The British trains are just the thing for a train buff. Bought by the carriage, entire walls can be covered with them. John Paige suggests that until he publishes some (which he is planning to do), customers can add their own lineside features by making drawings or pasting up photographs of signal boxes, bridges, stations, smoke or anything else. The train friezes are 3" high, and engines cost 38 cents each, carriages 25 cents. Also two complete trains: the Silver Jubilee, which is 8'6" long, is hauled by a Silver Fox engine and costs $1.30, and the Coronation, 10'9" long, is hauled by a Dominion of Canada engine and costs $2.30.

Educational Graphics Ltd., 43 Camden Passage, London
N1 8EB, England, or P.O. Box 798, Oak Park, Illinois 60302
Leaflet, 25 cents; air mail 50 cents.

This English firm (formerly Posters by Post) had so many orders after its listing in the first edition of *The Catalogue of Catalogues* that it has now organized an American warehouse. The stock consists of a very good collection of posters and educational charts for children's rooms and schools. For decoration there are some beautiful animal photographs, and posters by Arthur Rackham, the famous illustrator of children's classics, and by Alfonse Mucha, an Art Nouveau painter. More educational, or at least practical, are posters to teach kids primary skills such as counting and time telling, kitchen nutrition and calorie charts, historical charts, and a collection of hobby charts illustrating subjects like postage stamps of the world, the history of steam engines, the history of sailing ships, and racing cars—these last make excellent presents for older children. All posters and charts are in color and cost around $2 each.

◆

"What is the point of making the beds, when in the evening we must unmake them?"
"Why should I sweep the floor when it will only get dirty again?"

From *Bubba and Baba,* by Maria Polushkin,
pictures by Diane de Groat

If cleanup time at your house sounds like this conversation between Maria Polushkin's lazy bears, this picture book may help you institute some reforms. Then again, maybe it won't. But the story is amusing, the illustrations are attractive and wonderfully detailed, and the book is nicely designed. What more could you ask for, except maybe a clean room?

RS

Postscript: Suggestions for Cleaning Up the Kid's Room

—Without judging, say what a mess the place is and offer to help with the job.

—Ask your kid to help you clean up your room and suggest that you'll then help her with hers.

—Threaten: Any toy that is still left out by bedtime will be given away or thrown out. (Variation: Anyone whose toys are not put away before dinner gets no dessert.)

—If all else fails, close the door.   ELS

CLOTHING

CLOTHES AND IDENTITY

Fauntleroy's Revenge

The worst thing I ever bought my son was a velvet suit with ruffled shirt. He drooled and spilled on it with the same disdain as he drooled and spilled on unstylish and cheaper outfits. And, most deserved blow of all, he outgrew it after wearing it twice.

ALAN SAPERSTEIN

"The Worst Is Yet to Come"

Recently I went into Lord & Taylor and bought two flannel robes with flowers and ruffles for my smaller girls—what on earth for? Do they pass hors d'oeuvres at dorm parties? Certainly not. Do they need robes for any purpose whatever? No! Have I prevented them from becoming brain surgeons by this unfortunate purchase? I have also bought them second-hand reindeer sweaters from a store on Macdougal Street. If I don't repair the holes perhaps they will become brain surgeons after all. Femininity and all the charged meaning of that word is not to be expressed in choice of clothes. One can be a mathematician and like silk shirts or a suburban housewife who never removes her jeans. Sexual roles and clothing choice do not have any connection any more.

Children's clothes theoretically go up to size 14, but there is a well known change after 11 years or so when the identity problem in the choice of clothes is not the parent's but the child's. In all the dressing rooms of the preteen departments can be heard the whining: "Mother, that's horrible," "I'll never wear it," "Ugh!" "Yuck!" "It makes me look fat. It's disgusting." Some mothers are reduced to tears, to hopelessness, feel rejected. The worst for them is yet to come. I am prepared to be tolerant. I have imposed no taste on my older children. They wear jeans and plaid work shirts, sweaters and sneakers with magic marker decorations. They wear thrift shop clothes, they wear cotton fabrics in December and Indian bedspreads and fake flowers. They wear green nail polish. They wear decals on their faces. Do I care? Yes, I care. Do I scream? Sometimes. Why do I care? The Dybbuk of my mother says, "You can't go out in a straw hat in November" and a memory of my teen-age self stalks out of the house furious at my old-fashioned hang-ups.

Clothes become almost too personal, too important, too close to the heart, at the center of the adolescent storm to be bought by even a well meaning adult. The very fact that a parent has chosen an item may make it undesirable to a restless soul filled with a sense of emotional turmoil beyond or beneath your understanding. Then, too, the fashions change so fast. My 13-year-old wanted long skirts and silver bracelets for her birthday—or so she told me a month ahead of time. As the date approached she let me know that long skirts were anathema and she really wanted overalls so she could spend the rest of her life on a farm like the heroine of a TV movie called "Sunshine," with music by a hero I had never heard of, John Denver. The only thing I know for sure is that Denver and the overalls will be replaced by something else. The new clothes abandoned on the floor of the closet are like mutations, evolutionary specimens that didn't work out on the way to an identity that will in an eon or so be hers. I sent back the long skirts to Bonwit Teller and went to an Army-Navy store and bought birthday overalls.

ANN ROIPHE
The New York Times Magazine

Clothes and Sex Roles

Too many clothing makers make light-color clothes for girl children and dark clothes for boy children, so a little girl goes out and plays in the mud and looks much worse for wear than a boy who goes out and plays in his navy blue togs. Parents get upset and encourage a little girl to sit passively by instead of being an active kid. One other thing: if a kid has overalls on, regardless of sex, nothing is going to show, but a little girl in a short skirt isn't going to turn over on a jungle gym or do cartwheels readily if she feels that her body's on display.

CARRIE CARMICHAEL

Imitations of Name Brands: A Target For Kids' Cruelty

If you buy for your child—particularly as he or she approaches adolescence—off-brands or discount specials or imitations of name brands, your child's classmates will tease him or her mercilessly. Hong Kong imitation Keds, called "Kreds" or "Kefs" or something, bring derisive laughter (usually from boys; girls don't go in for this sort of thing as much). If you find a pair of bargain sneakers called "High Leapers," your child will be called "High Leaper" for the rest of the school year.

"But they're just as good," you say, "and much cheaper."

You are probably correct, but your child's classmates won't applaud your thrift. It's a di-lemma. Do you go along for the sake of peace, or do you encourage your child to take a stand against the tyranny of peer pressure and name brands? Go gently, and remember, in the sixth grade, it's caveat conform.

STEPHEN M. JOSEPH

SHOPPING FOR KIDS' CLOTHING

It Matters a Lot

. . . many people appear to forget the atmosphere of their own childhood almost entirely. Think for instance of the unnecessary torments that people will inflict by sending a child back to school with clothes of the wrong pattern, and refusing to see that this matters!

GEORGE ORWELL
Such, Such Were the Joys

◆

Dressing A Younger Child: Comfort First

There are Plain Janes (and Johns) and Fancy Flossies (and Freddies), and the kind of clothes your child wears will probably depend on the way you dress. I'm a creature of comfort and easy care, often to the abandonment of fashion. My daughter, five, is now a creature of comfort as well. Here are some discoveries I've made in the name of convenience.

All clothing should be machine washable and dryable. You can definitely dress a child very well without ever hand-washing, ironing, or dry-cleaning. This dictum includes everything from party clothes to coats and snowsuits (all of which need frequent cleaning). If you insist on luxuries like real cotton party dresses that must be ironed and pure wool coats that must be dry-cleaned, be prepared to pay for them in time and money.

Most parents, especially new ones, will give in and buy a few irresistible but impractical items; you'll certainly receive them as baby gifts. My experience has been that these are more often than not disappointing—shrinkable, ill-fitting, or a hassle to put on. At the other extreme, bargain junk—cheapies that shrink or stretch out of shape, fade, lose their elastic in the first laundering—can also be a waste of money.

These things just don't seem to happen with a brand like Health-tex, whose clothing I've found to be good-looking, durable, and even fairly well sized (I was happy to discover this, having admired their "Easy Answers to Hard Questions" ad campaign ever since I was old enough to thumb through a Sunday newspaper supplement). I only wish someone made apparel for *my* age group that looked as good as my daughter's Health-tex outfits after several dozen machine washings and dryings.

Choose clothes that are easy to put on and take off. For infants, the most practical items are one-piece suits that open all the way down the front and on down at least one of the legs. Keep in mind two requirements:

1. Easy dressing: Suits that opened flat so that I could lay my baby on them and stick in her appropriate limbs (those over-the-head and fasten-in-the-back numbers were a pain in the neck) saved me endless frustrating tussles trying to turn my child into a double-jointed contortionist.

2. Easy diapering: You should be able to get at baby's bottom as easily as possible without a complete undressing. Properly placed closings will allow you to maneuver the baby's legs and bottom half without disturbing the head or arms. (Overalls with crotch snaps may be less chic than those without snaps, but what a great design concept!)

Warning: Infants grow quickly, so don't buy too much of anything in one size. You're better off having less and laundering more often.

Shirts and overalls make the most sense once the baby is sitting up or standing. In overalls, look for adjustable shoulder straps (for extra length when it's needed), some give at the waist (elastic or double sets of buttons—manufacturers, please note!), and snaps at the crotch. Shirts should be easy at the neck—many are made with snaps at one shoulder.

For three- and four-year-olds, there is a new requirement: clothes the kids can put on themselves. For coats, I swear by zipper fronts, which are fast and easy; also hoods, which always come in handy. Check the quality of the zipper for easy start and action (better still, have the child check it). To prevent losing the hood string in the washer or drier, tie it.

To encourage further self-sufficiency, elasticized-waist pants, long and short, are fabulous, particularly when girls start going to the bathroom themselves. Two pairs of Danskin stretch pants, though expensive, proved the best clothing buy we ever made. We got them loose-ish in the tummy and they lasted a few seasons (they have generous hems and they seem to be indestructible). There is one drawback, however: they have no pockets, and that's a problem for little collectors. Let Danskin add a pocket or two—a single patch pocket in the rear would do—and they'll receive my top award.

All too soon, little girls want grown-up zipper flies and snaps—even though they usually have to come to you to have them zipped and snapped. Stick with the semi-elasticized waists (at the back of the pants) for as long as possible. Non-elastic waists fit for too short a time at this stage.

Even for older kids, you should check the stretchability of all shirt necks, especially turtles. I've had to toss out several otherwise good shirts because of unstretchable necks. Again I recommend Danskin; their long-sleeve mock turtleneck shirts look good and are durable. I do not recommend Danskin for warmer weather, however. The deservedly famous leotard fabric is just too heavy for summer—except, perhaps, for bathing suits.

PAULA GLATZER

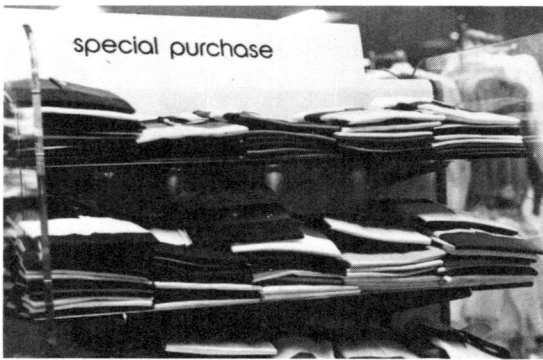

Sizing Will Madden You, But Here Are Some Clues

Sizes by age are almost always inaccurate—as a rule, much smaller than the tag says. Perhaps this is a problem throughout the clothing industry, but it's nigh on to criminal with kids, where you generally can't try on. It is confusing enough that your six-month-old is wearing size 18-month clothes but where a manufacturer actually lists poundage and the "20–25 pound"

size is too small even for your 15-pound baby, well, that calls for some consumer protest.

Even major companies are wildly inconsistent. Carter's, the underwear biggies, makes underpants to size or bigger (size 4 is large on my four-year-old), pajamas that run a year behind (four-year-old wears size 5), and undershirts that start small and shrink to minus 2 years (four-year-old needs at least a 6). The stuff itself is generally superior—we've tossed most of the fancy or cheap non-Carter's underpants as misfits—*if* you can find the size you need. Carter's outerwear, maddeningly, seems to run smaller than Health-tex.

The worst has got to be divining the right size cotton socks, which look larger than life on the rack, but then shrink drastically in the laundry. To make matters worse, the size number usually washes away, so you can't rectify the error in your next purchase. (Solution: Take an indelible marker and write the size and brand on the bottom of the sock before you wash it.)

Synthetic socks retain their sizing, but there ought to be a law against socks knit so tightly that a kid—even a parent—can barely put them on. I've thrown out the worst of these too (from Woolworth's).

PAULA GLATZER

Buying Unisex Clothes: You'll Get More for Your Money in the Boys' Department

Clothing manufacturers seem determined to believe that little boys play much harder than little girls. As a result, the jeans and overalls and tennis shoes sold in most boys' departments are almost always more ruggedly made than their similarly sized counterparts in the girls' department. So, over the years, when Alison has wanted an item of unisex clothing, I've bought her the boys' version.

ANNA JANE HAYS

Winning the Pajama Game

For pajamas to fit for more than one season, buy those that have a ribbed cuff around the ankles rather than the loose-bottomed ones. The latter, if they're a little large, will hang too long and trip your kid, while the cuffed kind can be bought with a little overhang that will lessen as your child grows.

Incidentally, pajamas with feet can be cut off at the ankle for another season's wear.

ELS

"The Pants Are Fine but These Buttons are Hideous"—One Mother's Solution

Sometimes I see a pair of, say, overalls, that have ugly buttons. If the overalls themselves are all right, I buy them and buy a couple of beautiful buttons as well to replace the ugly ones.

KAREN FELDGUS

Buster Brown 1, Corner Laundromat 0

By far my favorite plain kids' shirts are Buster Browns. They're all cotton, in decent primary colors, and they come in attractive T-shirt and long-sleeved turtleneck styles. And the price is right: about $5 for the long-sleeved shirt. Buster Browns look good even after a bout at the corner laundromat.

ELS

[Hooray, too, for Health-tex and Danskin. See Paula Glatzer's article, page 183.]

POLLY DESIGNS, 719 Greenwich Street, New York, N.Y. 10014, makes children's hand-decorated batik shirts with designs we think kids like—ice cream cone, clouds, teddy bear, truck, butterfly, airplane, dinosaur, Volkswagen, kite—in bright clear colors: red, blue, orange, purple, shocking pink. They're all cotton, pre-shrunk, and can be washed and dried by machine. Children's sizes (4 to 14) cost $6. Infants' sizes (6 months to 24 months) sell for a dollar less. And if you want infants' terry pants to match, you can buy a pair for $2 (New York residents add tax).

ELS

Up with Tubes

Tube socks can be the answer to all kinds of hosiery woes. First of all, they wear evenly, so your kids won't get holes in them quite so quickly. Second, they're easy to put on: children don't have to worry about getting the heel in the right place. And third, kids can grow with them.

SHARON LERNER

Three Cheers for Sears (But Buy Your Parkas from Montgomery Ward)

I recommend inexpensive "rough" clothes from Sears—the jeans, sporty turtlenecks, the western wear, the "toughskins," and all those pajamas that come with extra bottoms and cost half as much as the "designed" expensive clothes. They really do last, have reinforcements in the knees and, ironically, have more real style than the imitation Jonathan Logans.

I don't recommend Sears' more expensive dressy clothes. The catalog always makes the wools look richer and thicker than they are.

ELIN EWALD

You'll find excellent buys in underwear, T-shirts, and overalls to size 6x at Sears. For winter snorkel parkas, Montgomery Ward is your best bet.

ZELDA WIRTSCHAFTER

Sears is great for summer shirts and shorts sets. They last a long time.

RUTH PELMAS

A Word About Shoes

There is a soft-shoe-versus-hard-shoe controversy in this country, and it is not likely to be resolved in our lifetime. The arguments are strong by the proponents of both sides. You will have to decide for yourself whether you want your child's feet to have the support of a leather-soled shoe or the malleability of a soft moccasin or canvas sneaker. Both sides agree, however, that the shoe must be well made and properly fitted and that the material should be porous (leather and canvas are porous; vinyl and rubber are not) so that the feet can breathe. Some in each group feel that baby does not need shoes before she walks, and it is universally acknowledged that it is better for the feet to walk on soft country surfaces (or thickly piled carpet) than on the hard concrete surface of city pavement.

For a free brochure of good-quality soft leather moccasins that start at size 0, write to Quoddy Moccasins, 67 Monot Avenue, Auburn, ME 04210. Prices start at $4.50.

Stride-Rite and Buster Brown are proven, responsible hard shoes and tend to be sold where there are salespeople who know something about fitting children for shoes.

ELS

Mothercare: A Favorite for Mail Order Shopping

Mothercare is the name of a large chain of children's stores in England. They cater to children up to the age of four, and the clothes and toys are incredibly inexpensive and surprisingly durable. When the children were young I used to order from the catalogue. Pajamas purchased from Mothercare are known to have been worn by three or four children and still have seams intact. They also have a good selection of knit clothing and sweaters, not of terrific quality but comparable to American and less expensive. The sizes are given in inches.

I bought a great pair of red rubber boots when Polly was three, best quality boots ever. They came up to her knees, and she wore them for two years until her toes were curling in them, and then we passed them on to a friend. Mothercare also has bulky orlon cable-knit tights that are so warm for children. And lightweight shawls that are wonderful for baby covers—very hard to find in the United States and expensive when you do find them here. There are good buys on children's winter coats, too.

Have a look at Mothercare's catalogue and compare prices. The Mothercare catalogue is free: order it from Mothercare Ltd., P.O. Box 228, Parsippany, N.J. 07054.

JUDY THORN

---◆---

Absorba from France

The French Absorba outfits for infants and toddlers are expensive, but there's no American equivalent. You can roll the pants legs up and down and adjust the snaps to give twelve to sixteen months of growth and wear, and still pass the garment on to another child. Many Absorba items have nylon zippers which make them easy to get in and out of, and their bright colors and prints are a welcome relief after too many traditional pastels. Absorba outfits cost about $16, and are available in specialty shops and some department stores.

Recommended by JAYME STEWART

Three Good Cover-Ups

Instead of buying a smock for your kid, you can make one out of an old daddy-shirt. It's simple: cut down the sleeves, have your child put it on backward, and button it down the back.

SHARON LERNER

Terrycloth, used in the manufacture of most bibs, is terrific for soaking up wetness, but it retains stains as well. Cydney Kritzer and Andrea Winters-Weston make, by hand, three-ply bibs that are terry-cloth on the inside, cotton on the outside. Liquids pass through the cotton and are absorbed by the terry lining; stains wash out of the cotton, and if they remain on the surface of the terrycloth, well, they're hidden from view.

You can order a bib from them directly—or get more information—by writing them in care of the Mother-Maid Company, Garnet Street S.W., Atlanta, Ga. 30303. Bibs come in three styles: basic, bell-shaped (both with crumb-catchers), and heart-shaped. Several whimsical designs are available: a dinner jacket with bow tie, a "Stars and Stripes" motif, a girl's face complete with sewn-on braids, a four-star general's uniform (if you're feeling egalitarian, they'll make up an enlisted person's bib instead). Prices run from $3.50 to $4. That may sound like a lot for a bib, but it's extremely reasonable for a tuxedo.

CBC

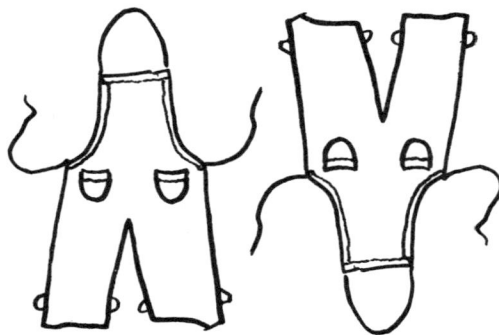

Here's the shape of my favorite unisex cover-up for kids who wear pants and overalls—from the crawling stage to the arts-and-crafts period. The apron stays put around the legs with an elastic "strap," and it ties around the waist. Try making one yourself, or send $6.50 and I'll make one for you with love. Mine are reversible: denim on one side and gingham or calico on the other. Send the child's age or size to 10 South Elberon Square, Elberon, N.J. 07740.

DOROTHY LOHMAN

MAKING CLOTHES FOR YOUR KID

Keep Your Creativity in Check

My mother used to make clothes for me, clothes which she'd design herself. She was a marvelous seamstress, and she put a lot of time and love into every last detail—making shoulder pads for each coat, lining each skirt. She even created little beanies to go with each outfit.

Today I feel very sentimental about those clothes my mother made for me. But at the time, I remember, I always felt a little funny wearing them, because they weren't quite what everybody else had on. My mother had her own ideas about style, and for a nine-year-old, that was just plain bad news.

ANNE HOFFMAN

Why I Buy My Kids' Clothes Even Though I'm a Good Seamstress

I once made a birthday dress for my daughter. It was beautiful, all pink and white and very festive indeed; she wore it to her party. Also for her birthday, she got a Big Wheels, on which she promptly went out for a ride. Half an hour later she came inside with two big holes in her pink-and-white dress, the dress whose tiny seams I'd carefully put together, whose tiny armholes I'd cut just right. I ended up having to put patches on the dress and it was a party dress no more.

Moral: Don't be a perfectionist about sewing clothing for your kids. The hems and seams and masterful details will not be appreciated.

MARY ANN SHORE

You've Read the Last Two Articles and You *Still* Want to Make a Dress for Your Kid? Then Try This Reversible One

I've never had girls, but I've given lots of gifts to people who have. A stunningly easy and very adorable little dress can be made by anyone, however inexperienced or clumsy. It is Simplicity Pattern No. 8165, and it comes in Toddler sizes 1–4.

The dress features ruffle and matching bloomers. I've never bothered to make the bloomers. I'm sure they're easy too, I just never thought they were necessary.

One little variation: The pattern calls it a "lined one-piece top." Instead of just lining the top, I choose two coordinating fabrics and the dress instantly becomes completely reversible. You get two dresses for the price of one. It is particularly charming with two different calicos or a calico with a gingham. I finish it off with a crisp white eyelet ruffle at the bottom.

The whole thing can be made in an hour, with or without a sewing machine.

EMILY PERL KINGSLEY

◆

What If Your Kid Isn't Toilet Trained Yet?

The manufacturers of clothing for little kids have decided that all children are guaranteed to be toilet trained before they are big enough to fit into a Toddler size 3.

Garments in infant sizes (6 months–24 months) are made with gripper snaps along the inseam of the pants to facilitate changing diapers. However, after a kid outgrows size 24 months, it is a real problem trying to find clothes that still have the snaps.

Health-tex (God bless them) do make a few overalls each year with snaps for Toddler size 4. This is a blessing for parents of children who just aren't ready yet and for parents of mentally retarded or handicapped kids whose training will be later than the norm.

If you can't find enough Health-tex overalls to get you through, you can, of course, sew your own overalls. But if you're not interested in sewing, at least try this. Many sewing stores have long rolls of gripper tape. (It's usually used by upholsterers for pillow closings or slipcovers.) Get the heavy-duty kind (the smaller size will never withstand the crawling around of an active youngster) and open up the inseam and sew the tape in. This way you can convert regular clothes into clothes which answer your special needs. Then changing diapers may still be messy, but it won't involve totally undressing and redressing the child top to bottom.

And there's another benefit: Somehow the kid always knows. Five minutes after you've finished sewing snaps into all the kid's pants, he'll announce that he's toilet trained and doesn't need diapers any more anyway.

EMILY PERL KINGSLEY

An Overall Strategy

If you're going to make overalls for a boy who's toilet trained, sew in an extra long zipper all the way down the front. My son won't wear overalls (which I love on him) because the fly (in the ones that have a fly) is never easy enough for a three-year-old. But his friend has overalls with a zipper from the top all the way down to the crotch.

ELS

◆

Clothkits

For very unusual knitted clothes which you can make from kits, write to Clothkits, 24 High Street, Lewes, Sussex, England, and ask them to send you their catalogue and their overseas-service leaflet. Their stock includes an intriguing selection of silk-screen-printed patterns for jumpers, blouses, skirts, trousers, baby suits (many with animal designs) and, my favorite—

for special occasions—a clown suit. That you cut these out and sew them together yourself, besides making you feel creative and ambitious, saves you money and allows for a proper fit.

ELS

[You—and your kids—can create your own personalized T-shirts. To find out how, see Steven Caney's article "Design-It-Yourself Iron-Ons" in the MAKING THINGS Section, page 333.]

HAND-ME-DOWNS

Hand-Me-Downs: A Second Look

Some people—me, for example—want everything new for the new baby. But I've changed with time. Between rapid growth requiring larger sizes and heavy use requiring frequent laundering, you'll need a shocking amount of clothing. And considering the expense, not to mention the time involved in shopping, *good* hand-me-downs are a blessing.

My daughter's treasured Danskins were hand-me-downs, and I'm bequeathing them to a dear friend with appropriate solemnity. If, like me, you've worn your own winter coat for four years, your little one can wear, for one year, the coat her cousin wore only one year—and still be able to pass it on. The practicality of accepting expensive and rarely used items that no single child will wear out—party clothes, spring coats, bathing suits, ice skates, cowboy/girl suits, Halloween costumes—is obvious.

I won't confess it to the shoe salesman, but I've even had a few real successes with hand-me-down footwear—rarely used Mary Janes in particular. An absolute necessity that not even an orthopedist could fault you for is hand-me-down rubber rain boots—the alternative is to buy a new pair for every new shoe size, which

can be every six months, with perhaps once-a-month use.

My personal favorites were toddler's two-piece pajamas, the uncomfortably tight elastic waists conveniently pre-stretched by the original owner. Our recipient appreciated them likewise.

There is a negative side—you'll get tons of stuff you don't want or need, so try (it can be difficult) to be firm about refusing such items, or you'll be drowning in them.

Line up donors *and* recipients; this is especially important early on, when the size changes are rapid. Keeping up with the backlog of outgrown items is almost as much of a problem as acquiring new ones.

If you plan to have more children, and you have the storage space, you'll probably want to keep things. You can, however, help a friend remember to *return* items if you lend them with your name tape sewn in (also useful for getting back things *you* prefer to pass on, or for sentimental keepsakes that you'd like to lend once again to a close friend).

To keep on top of it all, you should, ideally, constantly sort and discard—though it might be more helpful to you, finally, for me to confess that I've never managed to keep up with it all myself. (Ditto even for most of my more efficient friends.)

PAULA GLATZER

Old Scarves Make Wonderful Toys

I've found that old scarves of mine—especially richly colored ones—make wonderful toys for our six-year-old Jennifer. By wrapping them around herself in different ways, she makes halters out of them, or skirts, or shawls; she's even turned them into diapers when playing at being a baby. The kids use them to wrap their dolls in, too.
ANNE HOFFMAN

Save a baby-sized T-shirt or two. In a few years your kid can dress his dolls or stuffed bears in them.—ELS

Personalizing Hand-me-downs

Unless someone sings too highly the praises of spanking-new clothes, your child should be perfectly happy wearing hand-me-downs. But just to be on the safe side, make sure the clothes will become your child's very own by embroidering his or her name or sewing a special patch on the pocket.
ELS

CLOTHING SAFETY

The Great Fire-Retardancy Controversy: What Will They Think of Next?

It seems there's been, for years, a major debate over fire retardancy. Every article we read reaches a different conclusion about the need for flame-retardant materials, the Flammable Fabrics Act of 1953 keeps getting amended, and now they tell us that chemicals used to promote fire retardancy react toxically with urine. We cannot feel assured that the clothes our kids are wearing, if untreated, will not burst into flames at the slightest brush with Uncle Harry's cigar. But, if the garments are treated, then we must fear that the kiddies will be poisoned by noxious fumes should they wet their pants. What are we to do?

Of course, this is not a joking matter, but I cannot help being ironic about the flailing of the textile industry. My infant once received as a gift a kimono bearing a label reading "FLAMMABLE—(Does not meet U.S. Dept. of Commerce Standard DOC FF3-71.) Should not be worn near sources of fire." Feeling a bit alarmed, I wrote to the Good Housekeeping Institute, which had put their seal of approval on the ki-

mono. They reassured me that manufacturers using up their old stock of fabrics—fabrics purchased before the institution of today's stringent tests—must label "Flammable" all garments made from such textiles. "This does not mean that the textiles are necessarily *highly* flammable," the Good Housekeeping people explained, "but it does mean that they will burn faster than the standard presently requires."

While they are all busy deciding about fire retardancy, I will try to keep my kid in the cottons passed down from his cousin Todd, who was fortunate enough to have been small before the beginning of the Great Dynel-versus-Acrylic Debate of 1972.

I feel that it's best to employ safety measures like making sure there's nothing over the stove the kids will want to reach for.
CYNTHIA STEIN

Breathing Through Your Hat

A cap in which to sleep in very cold weather should be of knitted wool, so that if it slips over the baby's face he can breathe through it.
DR. BENJAMIN SPOCK
Baby and Child Care

DRESSING YOUR KIDS: THE LOGISTICS

Putting a Shirt On Your Little Egghead

When putting on sweaters and shirts with small openings, remember that a baby's head is more egg-shaped than ball-shaped. Gather the sweater into a loop, slip it first over the back of the baby's head, then forward, stretching it for-

ward as you bring it down past the forehead and nose. When taking it off, pull the baby's arms out of the sleeves first. Gather the sweater into a loop as it lies around his neck. Raise the front part of the loop up past his nose and forehead (while the back of the loop is still at the back of his neck), then slip it off toward the back of his head.
DR. BENJAMIN SPOCK
Baby and Child Care

The "Flip It Over Your Head" Method of Putting On Coats and Sweaters

Young kids often have difficulty putting on jackets and cardigan sweaters. They do fine until they have to put their second arm into its sleeve. Then everything falls apart: they're just not coordinated enough, and are apt to end up spinning around helplessly, their hand never quite catching up with that elusive armhole.

One way of getting around this problem is what I call the "flip it over your head" method. Here's how it works:

1. Lay the coat or sweater, open and front side up, on the floor.

2. The child stands or kneels at the top of the garment, with his toes facing the neck opening.

3. He bends over and sticks his arms into the sleeves.

4. Straightening up, he flips the coat or sweater over his head and pulls it on.

The good thing about the "flip it over your head" method: not only does it work, but it's lots of fun.

SHARON LERNER

The Bad Thing About the "Flip It Over Your Head" Method, Above

As the kid is flipping the jacket on, everything falls out of the pockets, including the house keys you entrusted to him. (One good thing about this bad thing is that the two dozen marbles he stole from the class's Chinese checkers game will also fall out.) Another problem: I don't like imagining the $75 Mighty Mac being swept across the schoolroom floor. But surely the kids don't mind the dust.

ELS

◆

The 1002nd Use for Baggies

Forcing a pair of galoshes over your child's leather shoes or sneakers is certainly one of life's unpleasant little chores (and it's one, as I'm sure you've noticed, that never seems to present itself unless your kid is already hopelessly late for school). But the folks at the Colgate-Palmolive Company (although they probably don't know it) have provided a solution: Baggies. Put one over each shoe or sneaker before galoshing—the slipperiness of the plastic will make your task so much easier.

ANNA JANE HAYS

A Cure for Stuck Zippers

If you've got a stuck zipper on your hands—especially one of the big, rugged ones like those featured on Mighty Mac outerwear—try lubricating it by whipping out a dry bar of soap and rubbing it up and down along the open tracks above the zipper pull. Then, if you can just succeed in forcing the zipper pull up a notch or two, your troubles should be over.

Incidentally, the little bars of soap they give you in motel rooms are just the right size for performing this operation, so make sure you steal one the next time you have a chance.

ANNA JANE HAYS

But Grandmother . . .

Babies and children who are reasonably plump need less covering than an adult. More babies are overdressed than underdressed. This isn't good for them. If a person is always too warmly dressed, his body loses its ability to adjust to changes. He is more likely to become chilled. So, in general, put on too little rather than too much and then watch the baby. Don't try to put on enough to keep his hands warm, because most babies' hands stay cool when they are comfortably dressed. Feel his legs or arms or neck. Best guide of all is the color of his face. If he is getting cold, he loses the color from his cheeks, and he may begin to fuss, too.

DR. BENJAMIN SPOCK
Baby and Child Care

New Life for That Old Down Jacket

A down jacket, though expensive for (usually) one winter's wear, is the warmest, most lightweight, most loved cold-weather covering for kids. Here's how to give it a second life: when the jacket is outgrown, cut off the sleeves and wear it a second season as a down vest over a sweater.

ELS

The Long and Short of It

We all know that when the knees wear out on our kids' pants we can cut them off above the knee to make great shorts, hemmed or ragged (kids seem to prefer them ragged), but you may not know to save the bottoms you cut off. When the next pair of knees wears through, and you've enough shorts already, those old bottom scraps will make perfect patches.

CAROL EICHLER

Portable Pin-on Pockets

Peter's Pockets, a book by Judi Barrett, illustrated by Julia Noonan (Atheneum, 1974, $4.95), may convince you to make portable pin-on pockets for everything your kid owns, especially if she or he is as much a collector as the three-and-three-quarters-year-old Peter of this tale. (In another year or three, let's hope Peter will be sewing his own pockets, eh?) Ms. Barrett has a good idea, and her nonstory (with counting and the names of lots of familiar objects) is one that kids will want to hear more than once.

RS

Priorities

If it has to be ironed, throw it out or give it away! Twenty years later the kid is going to remember that you had time to sit down and read a story, not that you spent fifteen minutes a day ironing his or her little shirts. Ironing is not nurturing.

CARRIE CARMICHAEL

◆

Extravagances-That-Are-Worth-It Department

Kids always seem to have knots in their sneakers (often made by teachers who tie a double knot so they won't be bothered with untied shoes the rest of the day). A friend who claims she's terrible at getting knots out keeps an enormous supply of shoelaces on hand ("They're very cheap if you buy them by the box"). To avoid the morning struggle with the knotted sneakers, she blithely cuts off the knot with a scissors and puts in a new lace.

ELS

Name Tags: Sew-ins, Yes! Iron-ons, No! (And a Stirring Debate on the Merits of the Indelible Laundry Marker)

As soon as your child goes to school, or even a playgroup, buy name tapes for all outerwear—a dollar should get you 100. A shortcut to sewing on all the tapes is an indelible laundry marker, invaluable in a multi-child family for identifying things like underwear without printed sizes. The indelible pen is also the best thing for marking boots and rainwear.

PAULA GLATZER

Iron-on name tags should be called wash-out name tags. I've yet to find any that will stay in place after the third or fourth laundering. And once they fall off, they're murder to sew back in—the fabric's too tough to pierce with a needle.

And what about indelible markers? They certainly work well—*too* well, in fact. If you want to hand an item of clothing on to someone else, that old name will always be there to remind the new owner that the garment is not really his.

There's no doubt about it: those old-fashioned sew-in name tags may drive you crazy, but they're still your best bet.

ANNA JANE HAYS

LETTING THEM DRESS THEMSELVES

What They Learn When You're Not Looking

As far as I can remember, I did not teach my kid anything about getting himself dressed, except to encourage him to try it. Eventually he just did it, as most kids do. He had dolls sporting buttons and zippers, and a book that had laces and snaps to do, but I never saw him "working" any of those devices. (It is, of course, possible that he practiced late at night and early in the morning until he had it mastered, then said to himself "I'll show them," and sure enough he did.)

What I was not prepared for was the independence of taste that accompanies dressing oneself. It had not occurred to me that my child would not select outfits as charming as those I'd always put on him as a toddler. Perhaps this is his way of getting back at me because I quit dressing him each morning. My dilemma, still unresolved, is whether I should put myself out of this misery by simply getting rid of the purple pants which my sister passed on to me with good intentions but which I can't abide. The alternative is to pretend I don't know him when he wears them, which I tried but which makes me uneasy.

ELS

Inside Out

Kids, usually after age six, seem to have some very strange fetishes about clothes. David's is that he loves to wear his clothes inside out—pants, shirts, pajamas. He doesn't do this every day, however. You see, when he takes the clothes off, they are right side out, and that is how he wears them the next day. There is nothing I can do to change this—it's like a religion to him—and there is one advantage: the clothes at least look clean on whatever side he's wearing. I thought my son was really peculiar. Then I met a woman whose kid does exactly the same thing!

SUSAN WECHSLER

Kids Know How They Want to Dress—And Maybe That's Okay

When it comes to dressing, kids have their own sense of what looks right and what doesn't, and if you challenge their judgment, you do so at your own peril. Our daughter Jennifer developed a taste at an early age for funny old hats. When she was four, her father bought her a wonderful flea-market straw bonnet: it was black, with an extraordinarily wide brim, and the crown was crushed flat, as if someone had been walking on it. Around the crushed part was a broad, off-white ribbon, tied in a big bow.

One really cold January morning, Jennifer was getting ready for her daily walk with her father to school. She had on her warm winter coat and her boots and mittens, and, of course, her big black summer bonnet. As she sailed out the door, I noticed that her coat was open at the top; she'd just gotten over a cold, so I asked her to put a muffler around her neck.

"No," she protested, but I was insistent.

"It's freezing and you'll get a sore throat," I told her, and off she went, bonnet and muffler and all, feeling very blue.

Moments later she was back, drenched with tears, dragging her very puzzled father behind her. "*Now* what's wrong?" I asked.

"I *can't* wear the scarf," she said flatly.

"Why not?"

"Because people might think I look funny on the street," Jennifer explained.

And then there's the case of my nephew, Donn. He used to have one outfit—a maroon jacket worn over a blue-striped T-shirt and a pair of jeans—that he felt made him look absolutely fine. No other ensemble would do: he even went so far as to hide the clothes under his pillow at night so his mother couldn't spirit them away to the laundry before he got the chance to wear them again just one more time.

As a parent, you have to evaluate incidents like this on a one-by-one basis. How terrible was it, really, that Donn wore a slightly gamy T-shirt to school once in a while, if it made him feel extra good to do so? Or how great were the odds that Jenna would actually catch cold on that six-block walk to school, when weighed against that special pride she felt walking down the street with her father, dressed just the way she wanted to be?

I must confess, though, that I made Dusty carry Jennifer's muffler to school that January morning, just in case.

ANNE HOFFMAN

What Do You Want to Be When You Grow Up? As Big As My Clothes.

We all remember getting new clothes when we were kids. They were scratchy and, for a while anyway, we were supposed to make a pretense of keeping them clean. All we really wanted was something comfortable that fit properly and looked like the kind of clothes that our parents wore. Of course, we settled for what we could get.

What we got was mostly things that never fit. At the times of our most rapid physical growth, anything that fit today would be too small tomorrow, so our mothers, naturally enough, bought everything at least a size or two too large. By the time we grew into the garment, it was worn to tatters and the whole process started over again.

KEN ROBBINS

MONEY

Are Pennies Money?

. . . walking along the inner edge of a sidewalk, I came upon a short projecting pipe that descended vertically into the cement. I lifted the iron cap on its hinge, and before I knew what I was doing, I dropped the pennies into the mouth of the pipe. They must have fallen a great distance, for I heard nothing for a few seconds, and then only a faint vibration of the pipe, not even a true sound.

Later my father asked me what I had done with the money he had given me. It is true that I had never thought of the pennies as money, to be exchanged in a store for toys or books, but I lied to him and said that they were in a box of marbles in my room. He saw the lie, like a sudden darkness that flows out through the eyes. I knew that he held it against me for not having spent the money as another child would have done.

ALFRED DUHRSSEN
Memoir of an Aged Child

ALLOWANCES

A Workable Approach to Allowances: A Fairy Tale

Once upon a time there was a family that tried to figure out who should get allowances (and why) and how allowances should be spent. The mother and father, like most parents, had gotten a dime when they were children.

First they thought their children's allowances should be Character Building. "My son," said the father, "you must cut the lawn, put out the garbage, walk the dog, do the dishes, or bring in and bale the harvest."

The son quickly chose garbage, and entertained himself with visions of the promised grant. For two days he took out the garbage zestily. Before long, however, he felt it important not to break from the episode of *I Love Lucy* he was watching. The garbage accumulated in a tower on the kitchen floor. Some spilled over. Not only that, the people next door complained about the cantaloupe rinds strewn about the neighborhood due to dogs getting into the pails because the lids had not been tightly replaced.

Now came the Character Building. The mother and father both yelled and nagged at the son. "We must Crack Down," said the mother. She thought that maybe she should just do the job herself, and rescind her son's allowance. "That will teach him a lesson," she remarked. It certainly did: that he was a worthless individual who could not perform a job well. The father, who was not entirely mean-spirited, decided his son's allowance should be reinstated even though he wasn't doing his job. That taught the son a lesson too: that he was a worthless individual who couldn't do a job well, but that it didn't matter because he would get paid anyway, so why bother trying?

It was the son himself who finally saved the day. He said, "If I am supposed to earn my allowance, I would like a job that is within the range of my capabilities so that I do not get frustrated trying to do it, and furthermore can take some pride in it." At that, the parents realized their son was developing feelings about work that were being reinforced by his getting an allowance. They taught him exactly how to put the garbage out.

There was another son too, a little brother. He was just learning some very complicated principles about money, and for that reason the family decided his allowance should be small so it would not overwhelm him. The things he was learning were: (1) Even though coins might look different, they are all money. So are certain wrinkled pieces of green paper, odd though that might be. (2) Money is used to trade for goods and services—certainly a merry notion, and probably magic. (All you had to do was present a round piece of metal to the storekeeper and he would give you back a candy bar.) (3) Dimes are worth more than pennies, despite the fact that any dope can see pennies are larger. (4) If you drop a dime behind the sofa, you can't buy anything with it at the store.

The younger brother, after months went by, began to think he should have a place to keep his money protected, but that is getting ahead of the story. (His parents supplied him with a strongbox and key from the stationery store. All agreed it was far superior to the Popeye the Sailor Man bank with the easily removable plastic plug, from which money was always disappearing.)

Now even younger was a toddler daughter. It seemed wise not to give her an allowance at all, as there was fear she might eat it. What the parents did with her was to take care of her needs as they arose. It took some time and energy to identify those needs, but they were able to do it. The older children could see that in this society at least, money and independence go together somehow. It made sense that a dependent baby would not get an allowance.

But there was also a much older daughter. She was ten or eleven, old enough to choose between saving her money for something special or spending it as soon as she got it each week. Once when her father saw her saving, he said, "You understand about delayed gratification." "It is because I am older, more mature, and have a better concept of time than my brothers and sister," she replied.

Her parents helped her open a bank savings account. She discovered interest, which made her happy (though not at the current rates); also accounting and budgets, because it turned out that she was expected to pay for some of her expenses herself, such as trips to the movies.

Indeed, the family had developed a workable approach to allowances: an allowance was always tailored to the individual and his current level of maturity. It was not used as a bribe, nor as a status symbol, nor to compete among the children's friends. The parents did not dole it out in place of other real things, like love, affection, or a hot meal. Nor did they constantly refer to the daring mother and father down the street who did not give allowances at all.

Some of the children's money paid for their continuing expenses; some paid for indulgences. And even though money and independence might be inextricably linked in this society, no one was allowed to squander his money on sweets. There was no need to be overawed by allowances. Besides, excessive sweets rot your teeth.

JENNIFER CARDEN

Beyond Allowances

For years many middle-class parents have given their children, even when quite young, an allowance. But this is usually a small sum, to be spent on trivia—though some thrifty children will save it for a long time to buy something more important. Some older children are given a larger allowance, from which to buy their clothes, entertainment, and the like. Even then the parents still buy for these children much of what they need and rarely ask them to account for what they spend themselves. We could go further than this. Parents could keep track for a year or two, perhaps with the help of the child, of all the money they spend on his needs. Then they could offer to put this much money into a special account under his control and let him buy these needs for himself. Many children might not care to do this, but those who did would learn important things about making priorities and choices—things better learned sooner than later. The point is always to offer the child the chance to take greater responsibility and to make more serious choices.

JOHN HOLT
Escape from Childhood

Is It Better Just to Give Kids Money When They Need It?

The great problem with living in the city is that kids are so huckstered to and it's so easy for them to spend their money. It's very difficult to convince them that they shouldn't just spend it on junk. Growing up as we did, with relatively little access to places we could spend money, we had perhaps a greater incentive to save up our money and use it for a particular thing. But now, in the city, kids can walk right out their front door and be in a candy store; and the money just disappears. We really tried to do the dollar-a-week thing, and expected the kids to be sensible about how they spent it. But it's almost impossible. Finally we cut back on allowances completely; now we give the kids money when they have what seems to be a sensible request.

MICHAEL FRITH

There's money scattered all over our house. Dimes, nickels, quarters, literally lying all over the place. It would be ludicrous of us to say to Evan, who's five, "Okay, here's your allowance, a dime." It wouldn't mean anything to her.

MATT HARRIS

Christopher shops pretty carefully. He gets 20 cents a week, a quarter for raking up the leaves and stuff like that, and he hoards all the money until he gets $4. When he's ready to spend it, he has a fairly clear notion of what it is that he wants.

I think his having the money to spend himself makes him, at seven, a little more alert, more aware of the fact that things cost money. He's more sensitive about being gypped than if someone had just given him the money.

JIM TURNER

A Tool for Preparing Kids for Life

I feel strongly that an allowance is one of the most underrated tools for preparing kids for life. As a pre-schooler, Renee got an allowance at the same time she started to count and discovered bubble gum machines and chocolate candy bars. She was given one nickel, and five pennies, an instant math lesson. It was only a short time before she was deciding whether to blow it on two candy bars, or something else. She then had to confront the crisis when the candy bars doubled in price. She has learned to negotiate for raises, save money, and, in general, manage. She also had the experience of being without that allowance, when Mommy was without work. JO BUTLER

An Allowance Is a Right, Not a Punishment or a Bribe

I really do think that kids deserve a certain amount of money a week, and to know that they're going to get it. I think that's their right as a member of the family. If they do something bad, withdrawing their allowance is not an appropriate punishment. JEAN GREEN

CHILDREN, MONEY, AND WORK

Explaining Money in Terms of Work

Don't try to explain money to your child without explaining work. After all, money is a relatively recent invention. In earlier times, kids needed very little explanation. They saw people bartering with what their work had produced. Now, however, they not only don't see barter; they don't see work. Daddy and/or Mommy leaves the house and returns several hours later—that's all a lot of kids, especially small ones, can understand.

Usually the subject of money will come up when a child wants something expensive. Don't tell him that he doesn't *need* the toy (or whatever) if the truth is that you can't *afford* the toy. Instead, explain that it takes six hours' work, say, to earn enough money to pay for what he wants, and that those earnings are needed to pay for essentials. Give examples: the electricity bill for running the toaster or the TV, gas for the car, baby sister's visit to the doctor when she had the flu, a winter coat, etc.

If pressed to explain why you don't have enough money to do everything, even though so-and-so down the street does, it's time for a little honest economics. Don't try to hide that your salary is only middle-sized. With a simple statement—"Son, teachers just don't get paid very much"—a lot of things can be clarified.

Sometimes it happens the other way around, too. A child in an affluent family may ask why his friend cannot afford to have a bike like his. It is not easy for parents who must explain their wealth, but they can explain that inequality demands a lot from children who are poor, and that it requires generosity of those who are not. MARK GERSON

Kids' Jobs Around the House: Which Ones Should You Pay Them For?

Giving money for jobs around the house can be a problem. It's hard to know what you should pay your kids for and what they should do as part of the family. You get into a thing where you say "Hang up your coat" and your kid says "Are you going to pay me?" Or, "Take out the garbage." "Pay job?" And so you have to say "No, that's your responsibility as a member of this family."

I paid my five-year-old a nickel to clean up the play yard. I felt it wasn't fair to ask him to put all the trucks away when he hadn't even been out there, so he was doing me a favor. When I'm really crazy and desperate, I get my nine-year-old to clean. And that is worth a fortune. He cleans the whole upstairs, and vacuums and everything; he does a perfect job, and he gets a dollar, which is cheaper than a maid. He knows how to arrange the toys so it looks like a toy store, and to arrange the books on the shelves neatly. What does he do with the money? He buys war toys. LIZA WERNER

Find Chores That Challenge Your Children

The jobs we tend to give children to do are terribly dull and inconsequential. They are the jobs we feel sure they can do; we never let them wash the dishes until we are sure they won't break every third one, so they feel no sense of challenge. They also tend to be the chores that *we* despise doing ourselves, so we end up teaching the exact opposite of what we want to teach: instead of demonstrating that work today can be a challenge to oneself, we are teaching that work is an unpleasant duty to others. One mother's attempt to solve this problem was by having every member of the family share the menial tasks equally, and at the same time every child got his chance to take on something more exciting, such as cooking a meal, planning a family picnic, or shopping at the supermarket. "We start when a child reaches his fifth birthday," this mother told me. "And you would be amazed at what a damned fine meal a five-year-old can prepare—if you're crazy about peanut butter and jelly, that is!"

EDA J. LE SHAN
Natural Parenthood

Money Is Hard Work

"Father," Almanzo said, "would you—would you give me—a nickel?"

He stood there while Father and Mr. Paddock looked at him, and he wished he could get away. Finally Father asked:

"What for?" . . .

"Frank had a nickel. He bought pink lemonade."

"Well," Father said, slowly, "if Frank treated you, it's only right you should treat him." Father put his hand in his pocket. Then he stopped and asked:

"Did Frank treat you to lemonade?"

Almanzo wanted so badly to get the nickel that he nodded. Then he squirmed and said:

"No, Father."

Father looked at him a long time. Then he took out his wallet and opened it, and slowly he took out a round, big silver half-dollar. He asked:

"Almanzo, do you know what this is?"

"Half a dollar," Almanzo answered.

"Yes. But do you know what half a dollar is?"

Almanzo didn't know it was anything but half a dollar.

"It's work, son," Father said. "That's what money is, it's hard work."

Mr. Paddock chuckled. "The boy's too young, Wilder," he said. "You can't make a youngster understand that."

"Almanzo's smarter than you think," said Father. . . .

"You know how to raise potatoes, Almanzo?" [asked Father].

"Yes," Almanzo said.

"Say you have a seed potato in the spring, what do you do with it?"

"You cut it up," Almanzo said.

"Go on, son."

"Then you harrow—first you manure the field, and plow it. Then you harrow, and mark the ground. And plant the potatoes, and plow them, and hoe them. You plow and hoe them twice."

"That's right, son. And then?"

"Then you dig them and put them down cellar."

"Yes. Then you pick them over all winter, you throw out all the little ones and the rotten ones. Come spring, you load them up and haul them [to town], and you sell them. And if you get a good price, son, how much do you get to show for all that work? How much do you get for half a bushel of potatoes?"

"Half a dollar," Almanzo said.

"Yes," said Father. "That's what's in this half-dollar, Almanzo. The work that raised half a bushel of potatoes is in it."

Almanzo looked at the round piece of money that Father held up. It looked small, compared with all that work.

"You can have it, Almanzo," Father said. Almanzo could hardly believe his ears. Father gave him the heavy half-dollar.

"It's yours," said Father. "You could buy a sucking pig with it, if you want to. You could raise it, and it would raise a litter of pigs, worth four, five dollars apiece. Or you can trade that half-dollar for lemonade, and drink it up. You do as you want, it's your money." . . .

Frank asked Almanzo:

"Where's the nickel?"

"He didn't give me a nickel," said Almanzo. . . . "He gave me half a dollar." . . .

"I'm going to look around," [Almanzo] said, "and buy me a good little sucking pig."

LAURA INGALLS WILDER
Farmer Boy

KIDS IN BUSINESS

My Son the Worm Salesman, Etc.

Last year I needed some money, so my father suggested that I sell worms for fishing. Since we live near two rivers, I thought it would be a good idea. So I went out to our compost pile . . . and dug some. Then I put up a sign and managed to stop a lot of passers-by. I sold the worms for 35¢ a dozen or three dozen for $1. Then I found a place where I could buy 1,000 worms for $6, and I was able to sell all of them. I made $25 altogether, and I have a big business going now. I plan to set up my business again next spring.

STEPHEN MEYERS
Kids

[If the fast turnover and high mark-ups of worm retailing intrigue your child (or you), you won't want to miss Charles Kuralt's article on worm grunting on page 385.]

When we moved to New York—I was nine or ten—I had my first business scheme. I started this company called Blocks 'n Bagels: Saturday night I'd go around our apartment building in Riverdale asking people for orders for lox and bagels. Then I'd take a cart to a delicatessen and pick up the food and mark it up nickels and dimes. And I did nicely, I made a few bucks. I spent some of the money on books and junk foods, but mostly I saved it.

CHIP BLOCK

Dad didn't give me an allowance. He gave me chickens. I'd get my money through them. I had a regular egg route. I'd get up early, clean the roosts and then sell the eggs door to door. It was called the George Company. When I went away to school, I sold the business to my sisters, Susan and Judy. It became the S & J Company.

GEORGE STEINBRENNER
Quoted by Ron Fimrite in *Sports Illustrated*

Benjamin is so shy and uncomfortable about performing that he hates even to be photographed. A friend called and told me that he needed a boy for a TV commercial and was Benjy interested. I thought Benjy would refuse—and he did, until he found out that he would be paid for the work and could keep the marbles they used in the commercial. Benjy forgot all hang-ups (he said he needed the money!) and was pleased with himself about having a *job*.

BOBBIE MALONE

American Seed Company [Lancaster, Pa. 17604] lets kids sell their vegetable and flower seeds for them and earn money or pick a prize. They send you 45 packages of seeds, which you sell at 45 cents each (you don't have to pay them until after you sell the seeds). From the $15 I earned I could keep $5 and send them $10 or send them the whole $15 and choose from about 50 prizes. I picked a stopwatch (Westclox), a terrific chrome one with a place for a chain. It came very quickly in the mail.

TODD EICHLER
Age six

I walk the dogs that belong to my neighbors. With the dog owners, I decide how often I should walk the dog (usually once a day) and how much I should be paid. My best customers are mothers who have to take care of their little children, and older people who find it tiring to walk dogs. I not only get money, but I have fun, too. I think this is a good job idea for anyone who loves dogs and animals, and wants to help people.

LINDA JACOBSON
Kids

I bought my first magic tricks with my birthday money when I was around eight years old. And then when Christmas came along I bought some more tricks. By the end of that year I had enough for an act, and people paid me $3 to go to their houses and do my show. Then I did a show for $5. And after about a year and a half I was charging $10. Gradually I started doing more and more shows, accumulating more money, and buying more tricks.

You really have to work at magic if you want to do shows. A lot of kids think they can just look at the instructions, which give you a really boring and predictable routine. I invented my own routines and my own stories. They were a little crude, but they were original.

MARK FRIEDBERG
Age eleven

[For more advice on magic tricks, see pages 436—40.]

Recently I discovered an ad in the newspaper from the American Can Company announcing that they would pay from $10 to $15 per ton of cans for recycling. I am in the seventh grade, and our class has hoped to do this collecting of cans two or three times a year, in Southborough (Massachusetts), until our high school graduation. The money will go toward a scholarship fund for one of the students in the graduating class who plans on attending a college with an ecological-conservational program.

I started the Can Crush Committee, and I was joined by several fellow students, who helped me pass out posters and spread the word. When enough washed and peeled cans were collected from the Southborough homes, we ordered several trucks, and we drove to Medham and dropped off 1,030 lbs. of mixed cans. We made approximately $5 on our first load. If the townspeople keep chipping in, we're sure to reach our goal.

STEVE BAKAL
Kids

One summer, I picked up Saturday movie money by renting my grandfather to my friends. For a dime, they could watch him whittle a chain and a whistle from one piece of birchwood and, as a bonus, he would sometimes talk as he whittled. During those lazy hot afternoons he told stories of Indians and blizzards and how barbed wire ruined the wilderness; he made us hear wolves howl and feel the ground shake as the buffalo stampeded. Week after week, Granddad gave my friends and me the gift of his past. He made the way our elders had lived intelligible and real. It was much more entertaining and exciting than the movies I saw with the money I collected.

SHARON CURTIN
New York Times Magazine

My brother and I made $2.95 on a rock sale. We sold our rocks for 5¢ and 10¢ apiece. We got two ink pens and some candy and bubble gum with the money we made. We had 10¢ left over.

VICTOR WRAY
Kids

"The Most Loathsome Job in the World"

Before I struck it rich with my magic shows I had to go out and earn my own pocket money in the usual ways—helping my father paint houses . . . returning pop bottles, and doing the most loathsome job in the world, caddying. Having caddied . . . I know what it must be like to be black. The goddam golfers would call you "you" and "boy" and treat you like a dog. The game bored me to idiocy, and no matter how hard I tried to concentrate, I was invariably looking somewhere else when my player took a drive, and I'd get hell for losing the ball. You had to attend the club's golf-course-etiquette courses if you wanted to work your way up from Class C caddy, which I never did. I think they invented a D category solely for me. So help me, we were told that when we came to the ball-washing machines on the fourth and eighth holes we had to say, "Can I wash your balls, sir?" I started dreading those words the night before, and by the time I had to deliver them my throat would constrict and make my voice crack, or else I would stammer on the b in balls.

I finally decided it was not worth the $1.25 a day I was getting paid, having to ask total strangers if I could wash their balls. On the way from the locker room to the caddy class I cut through the parking lot and went home, and never went back. Providence must have had a hand in my decision, because on the way home I found a five-dollar bill at the bus stop, which saw me through the rest of the summer. Five dollars went farther in those days. So did buses.

DICK CAVETT
Cavett by Dick Cavett and
Christopher Porterfield

"Every Kid's Guide to Making Money"

The best book I've seen on the subject of kids and work is *Good Cents* by The Amazing Life Games Company (and friends), published by Houghton Mifflin (1974, 128 pages, $7.95 hardcover, $3.95 paperback). Subtitled "Every kid's guide to making money," the book is just that: there are 128 pages of ideas for kids of all ages, and they are ideas that can actually be put into practice without too much difficulty. Many of the ideas are obvious ones, but they are presented so appealingly that if I were a kid I'd be inspired to try some. There are things to make and sell—fireplace logs out of old newspapers, doormats out of bottle caps, dog flea collars out of eucalyptus pods, paintings, potted plants, lemonade. There are things to collect and sell— records and books, fresh bait, recycled items, flea market treasures (which are found cleaning up basements and garages for money). Services to perform—window washing, yard cleaning, errand running, birthday party planning and organizing, laundromat sitting. There are suggestions for how to advertise, what to charge, how to *do* some of these chores you're being paid for, the best time to conduct business, the best customers and where to look for them. For the grand finale, they suggest a street fair and offer three pages of ideas that will make it a success: apple bobbing (losers get "a clean face"), guess your dog's weight (prize: a coupon for a free dog wash), quick portraits (for 25 cents a drawing), and a twenty-cent raffle (the winner gets two free hours of babysitting and you get "a lot of free advertisement for your service"). There's also a kind of appendix concerning taxes, banking, keeping track of one's money—assumedly for those to whom the book brought some success.

ELS

SAVINGS

Learning to Spend Is Important Too

Sometimes people who have money are the most inept at educating their children in ways of handling money gracefully. The method of denial for the purpose of not spoiling seems pointless, since the children notice their parents enjoying the pleasures and benefits of money. And it has been my experience that depriving kids of things that one can afford breeds greed, not prudence, in money matters.

Writer/composer Mary Rodgers insists that her kids learn how to *spend* their allowances; she does not like them to squirrel their money away. "I try to emphasize being generous; I buy them surprise treats and I love to see them buying surprise things for us or their friends. Some people spend so much time impressing their kids with how to save that the children never learn how to spend."

ALICE BACH

◆

The Case Against Piggy Banks

. . . it is wrong to teach children to save. The home savings bank asks too much from the child; it says to him, "Think of tomorrow," at a time when only today matters to him. To a child of seven, it means nothing that he has twenty-seven dollars in the bank, especially if he suspects that his parents will one day draw it out to buy him something he does not want.

A. S. NEILL
Summerhill

LEARNING ABOUT MONEY

"Do You Want To Be Careful, or Do You Want To Be Friends?"

In an examination of children's books for both their explicit and implicit approaches to consumer education, first prize goes to Russell and Lillian Hoban's *A Bargain For Frances* (Harper & Row, 1970, $3.95 hardcover). Frances' friend Thelma cons her into buying an ugly plastic tea set with red flowers, when she had her heart set on a real china set with pictures in blue of "trees and birds and a Chinese house and a fence and a boat and people walking on a bridge." Thelma tells her that that kind breaks, is very expensive, and besides, the stores no longer sell them. She kindly sells Frances her own ugly set for $2.17, all the money Frances has in the world.

Agreeing to a policy of "no backsies," Frances pays her money and trots home with her acquisition, only to discover that the set she wanted is readily available at $2.07. Using the same psychological trickery that was used on her, Frances eventually gets the tea set with the blue pictures, plus a dime left over. Along the way, the first- or second-grade reader for whom the book is intended receives several valuable lessons in consumerism. An analysis of Thelma's sales pitch shows that Frances was taken in by: (1) the immediate availability of the ugly tea set; (2) the misrepresentation of the saleslady (Thelma) about the availability of the competing product; and (3) the desire for a bargain without bothering to find out first if it indeed is a bargain.

Frances and Thelma agree to give up trying to trick each other because it's a big nuisance having to watch each other so closely when they play together. "Do you want to be careful, or do you want to be friends?" asks Frances, and the implication is clear that the buyer–seller relationship automatically precludes friendship.

KATHERINE M. HEYLMAN

Money: An Ecological Viewpoint

You ask what I want my kid to learn about money? I want her to learn that not everything costs money. That some items you might buy can be had for the time it takes to track them down from someone who might otherwise throw them away. That other things might be had in exchange for labor or services (one young friend had her eye on a camera at a store near her school; she worked a few hours in the afternoon as a delivery person for the store to pay off part of the cost of the camera). We used to make fun of people who reused aluminum foil and saved paper bags; now we realize that we save money—and the environment—that way.

SUSAN LAWRENCE

[A woman in Los Angeles tells us that her kid's school is teaching practical economics to kindergarteners. They buy, sell, earn, spend, save a little—and pay taxes. It sounds like an informal version of George Richmond's *Micro-Society School, A Real World in Miniature* (Harper and Row, 1975, $2.95 paperback). And Ilene Goldman, co-director of Consumer Action Now, uses her trips to the supermarket to help her kids learn how to be good consumers. For more about this, turn to Ilene's article, "The Supermarket as an Ecology Classroom," on page 165.—ELS]

Money and Discipline: Beware of the Double Standard

A mother will cry, half in jest, "I wouldn't sell my child for all the gold in the world," and five minutes later, she will spank her child for break-ing a 10-cent cup. It is the money that is at the root of so much discipline in the home. Don't touch *that—that* having cost money.

Too often children are balanced against money—but only children, not adults. My mother used to spank us if we broke a plate; but when Father broke a plate, it was just an accident.

A.S. NEILL
Summerhill

RICHARD HUTCHINGS

"Emotional Yardsticks": Money *Can* Buy Happiness . . . If You Use It Properly

In principle, money can buy happiness or anything else—if it doesn't, it is because people don't use it that way. The kind of commitment necessary to accumulate money often seduces people into responding to economic rather than emotional yardsticks—"It's overpriced," instead of, "I don't want it in my life." People abandon homes to which they have devoted decades of love and energy because they are "too expensive to keep up," and spend years in deep depression or even die in response to the loss of familiar and loved surroundings. The reasoning behind such an act is that money will thereby become available for many more reasonably priced goods and services which are not nourishing to the soul, however enjoyable or even necessary they may seem to be. This is called being "sensible" about money.

PHILIP SLATER
Earthwalk

SCIENCE:
EXPLORING THE
PHYSICAL WORLD

Science Is a Way of Looking at the World

Science is a way of looking at the world. You can look at anything scientifically. Anything is scientific material; everything is scientific material. The scientific method, which is only one of any number of ways of thinking about things—but a useful one—is "What happens if I do this and what happens if I do that and how come it does that and well maybe I can find out if I try this . . ." Even a baby is using the scientific method in his crib, although he doesn't think of himself as doing it.

JOHN HOLT

◆

Science Is Far More Exciting Than Science Fiction

I got turned onto stars and planets before I knew there was such a thing as science fiction. When I was maybe ten years old, I came upon Burroughs, Wells and Verne and thought them marvelous. At eleven I discovered *Astounding Science Fiction* at a newsstand and was exhilarated and delighted with its cosmic perspective. Since then, I have learned more science than I knew when I was eleven, and my literary tastes have perhaps improved. I am not the same person I was when science fiction carried me on soaring flights of the imagination. When I return to a science-fiction novel that I last read when I was a boy (and still remember with the greatest pleasure), it often seems to have deteriorated strangely over the years. What has really happened, I think, is my slow discovery that science is far more exciting than science fiction, far more intricate, far more subtle—and science has the additional virtue of being true.

CARL SAGAN
Other Worlds

◆

What Science Isn't

Answering a lot of questions isn't what science is about. It's about trying to reinforce what it is you and the kids see.

Let's suppose a kid asks you where the moon comes from. What you want from a reference book is not answers, but background to initiate a process of observations that will provide answers. How do I make observations about the moon's relative position in the sky each night, taken over a two-week or a six-month period? Are there things that I'm going to see that will tell me something about the moon, and about

how the moon acts, and why it acts the way it does?

Certain things are obvious: the moon has phases, and a different position in the sky each night. These sorts of observations are the major steppingstones to knowledge about the physical world. That the physical world is a beautiful place because things are consistent: water never runs uphill, the moon changes every night. Those constants are the basis from which we all derive our sense of the world as being a consistent livable place, where there is an underlying logic that works.

This is essentially what Piaget and all the other experientially oriented educational psychologists are saying: that it's terribly important for the child, especially the young child, to experience and observe directly the physical world. Adults have lost that sense, and try to answer all those questions with facts.

TONY SHARKEY

The "Flavor of Scientific Activity": It's More Important Than Memorizing Facts . . .

Children's vocabulary, toys, and television-watching are often cited as evidence of the generational growth in science-mindedness. Adults are impressed when children speak of rockets, orbits, moon shots, atoms, molecules, action–reaction, and other sophisticated things, but the ready use of these words can give a false impression. There is nothing scientific about mouthing words. It is much easier to talk of hovercraft or to manipulate a plastic working model than to disassemble a lock to see what makes the tumblers work, and it is less scientific. It may be *au courant* to watch space patrols on television, but it is less scientific than to sail a modest craft along the sidewalk after a heavy rain. In learning to watch what others have chosen to commend to their passive attention, children's senses have been dulled. When a child gives the name for something the adult feels rewarded by this evidence of his competence as a teacher. In the process the child's mind is dulled; he may well have responded with a word he does not even understand. . . .

There must be times when the adult, parent or teacher, says "I don't know." . . . It is salutary for children to learn that a parent, or even a teacher, than whom no wiser person has ever lived, does not know everything. This realization suggests to children the immensity of knowledge and the inevitable need to admit ignorance. . . .

Nevertheless the adult who assumes the responsibility for providing children with science experiences of good quality ought constantly to add to his fund of knowledge. It is certainly important to know—the more the better. But it is also indispensable to feel, to catch the flavor of scientific activity. American physicist Richard Feynman, the Nobel Laureate, once described how he first became interested in science. He did not speak of sophisticated equipment or of courses in physics, and certainly not of grades. Instead, he spoke very movingly about his father, a salesman, who used to spend his short vacations with his family in the mountains. Here the father took his son on walks and shared with the young, bright, impressionable boy the wonder he felt about natural events: how the birds succeed in coming back to precisely the same place each year, how the life cycle in the woods seemed to satisfy all the living things that depended upon it, and other remarkable puzzles. I do not know whether the father knew the names of the various birds, trees, rocks, and flowers. Richard Feynman did not mention it. Apparently it was not important. What was important was the spirit the father transmitted. Like good knowledge, the feeling endured. Richard Feynman did not forget it.

LAZER GOLDBERG
Children and Science

TOOLS OF THE TRADE
The Edmund Catalogue

The pleasures of the Edmund Catalog (from Edmund Scientific Company, 7782 Edscorp Building, Barrington, N.J. 08007) begin on the first page, with a picture of the president, Norman Edmund, and his son Robert, who is now old enough to be vice-president. They are pretending to inspect a new supply of low-priced microscopes, but really they are just looking proud, with good reason. "Small and inexpensive sets of chipped lenses, offered to experimenters, started this business thirty-one years ago," Dad says. "Ever since, our aim has been to discover and offer unique, bargain-priced, and hard-to-find items of a scientific nature. Today, you have your choice of 4,500 different products. We continually search for new and unusual items that will please you."

Twice a year they send me their catalog with its microscopic index, and I page through its latest wonders—starter kits in fiber optics and laser technology, cutaway Wankel engines, low-cost air-pollution testers, biofeedback machines. Someday I will succumb, but so far I've managed to keep our orders modest: a soil-testing kit for our garden, a prism to split the rays of the sun, a real rocket that soars on compressed water, a small supply of carnivorous plants, a pump for an indoor fountain, ten assorted lenses for $4.50 so the kid can explore optics and make his first telescope.

The Edmund Scientific Company may not be flawless—some of the commercial products they stock are overpriced, and I have heard some complaints about their telescopes. But their catalog is an incredible cornucopia, of generally high-quality items and many surplus and odd-lot bargains. In my own experience they have been prompt and efficient in their service, responsive to inquiry and criticism, honest, and constantly educational—not only through their catalog, with its hundreds of entertaining mini-lectures, but also through the information sheets and experiment booklets that they furnish with many items. They will send you the catalog free; for the idle gift (they also have gift certificates) or first serious exploration, it is unbeatable.

MICHAEL ROSSMAN

[NOTE: Since the above was written, Robert, "old enough to be vice-president," has become president. He still looks proud.—CBC]

MICROSCOPES

"Good Optics Are the Key, and You Get What You Pay For"

Using a good microscope is like getting glasses if you're nearsighted: a whole dimension of reality snaps into vivid focus. Everything bears looking at again: fabrics, the skin that peels from your sunburn, moldy bread, salt, a butterfly's wing. I keep a small bowl of water on the table beside my microscope. Seeded with a handful of mud and grass, it now hosts an intricate ecology of a hundred lives too small for the naked eye; and sometimes while we are still asleep, our five-year-old takes an eyedropper and goes exploring, tilting the mirror to catch the morning sun.

A good microscope isn't cheap, but with reasonable care it can last a century. Quality microscopes start at $120 and go to ten times that. They hold their resale value well, and you can often buy them secondhand in a college town. For those who don't want to make this initial investment, you can get a beginner microscope for as little as ten bucks at some toy stores. But beware: if it's too cheaply made, it can be so frustrating to the eye as to destroy all its pleasure. Good optics are the key, and you tend to get what you pay for: sharp images, color-corrected. For this reason, stay away from packaged kits with bottles, prepared slides, and exotic appliances, and put your money into the best unadorned basic instrument you can buy. Whether buying it new or used, check it out: the focusing should be smooth and without free play, and the images should be sharp through each objective (prick your finger to get blood cells to see). Even new instruments vary, and if you feel yours is flawed, take it back to the store.

Our local toy and hardware stores carry several brands—Skilcraft, Perfect, Tonka—ranging from $15 to $40. They look flashy: they have four-turret objectives and boast 600X to 900X magnification; but they are all pretty junky, cheap metal and minimal optics. The least you should ask for are optically ground achromatic objectives, coated if possible. Edmund Scientific Company has a three-turret microscope (50X, 150X, 300X) which sells for $40 with a carrying case (#70,008). The cheapest full-sized microscope costs double that, but sometimes you can find an old two-turret German one with superior optics for $50 or less.

MICHAEL ROSSMAN

An Opposing View: "It Doesn't Make Sense to Spend a Lot of Money"

A microscope is a learning tool. And the first thing you should learn about a microscope is how serious is your interest in owning one. It doesn't make sense to spend a lot of money on a microscope until you've learned whether or not you like using it.

Another mistake that people make is starting out with too great a magnification. When you're just beginning microscope work, you need to be able to relate some of the detail you can't see with your naked eye to what you can see with your naked eye. If you put a snowflake under the 25X lens, it's not very hard to find the snowflake, and it's easy to see what part of the snowflake you're focusing on because you can see enough of the whole. But as you begin to enlarge more and more, you see less and less; the area you're actually looking at is a tiny area and it's extremely hard to relate it to the whole snowflake.

We make a small, nearly indestructible, high-impact plastic microscope. It comes assembled but can be completely taken apart and easily put back together again. It serves young kids just starting, and it serves adults (in conjunction with other microscopes) doing field work.

GEORGE COPE

[When George Cope says "we," he means the Workshop for Learning Things, 5 Bridge Street, Watertown, Mass. 02172.

The microscope he mentions is 25X, and can be purchased by mail from the Workshop for $11.95 plus handling ($1 on all orders under $20) and postage.

Also available from the Workshop for Learning Things: an "illuminator": a small lamp (using a night-light bulb) to be used near a single microscope. The mail-order price is $5.95, plus handling (see above) and postage.—Eds.]

The Dissecting Microscope . . .

A binocularscope, which has two eyepieces, so that you get magnification and a sense of depth as well, is available from Bausch and Lomb. You can actually move things around while you're looking at what you're doing; that's why it's called a dissecting microscope. You can put big things under it, like an apple or an orange. It doesn't replace the microscope we make (see above), it's a whole different experience. I think parents are crazy to pay more than $10 for a microscope, but if they're willing to spend over $300, this is the one to buy. I think there's nothing worthwhile in between.

GEORGE COPE

[You can write for a free catalogue of Academic Stereozoom Microscopes, Bausch and Lomb, Dept. 6606, 1400 North Goodman Street, Rochester, N.Y. 14602.]

. . . and the Agfa Lupe

The Agfa Lupe, available in camera shops for under $4, is an 8-power magnifying glass that's so good that all the people who really know about magnifying glasses use it.

PHYLIS MORRISON

[A discussion of telescopes, and how to buy one, can be found on page 216.]

SCIENCE KITS

The Kafkaesque World of Do-It-Yourself Science Kits

After six weeks of researching, purchasing, and putting together a good-sized sample of science kits available for kids, I have come to the conclusion that a great many of these kits, while admirable in their intent, can be a veritable Franz Kafka nightmare for both parent and child unless caution in selection and assembly is exercised. (For Kafka's own views on child rearing, see pages 2, 4, and 5.)

I only hope that most readers will not be dismayed by my own misadventures and will give their children the opportunity to try some of the better kits on the market. I am convinced that both parent and child have much to gain from experimenting with these. In an age when technology is advancing at such a pace and affecting more and more of our lives, it seems to me crucial to have at least a rudimentary understanding of how things work.

There is really no great mystery about science. Like a foreign language, it can be mastered by anyone who is not prejudiced against it. I have learned enough about electricity, and electronics in particular, to fend off much unnecessary expense by doing simple electrical jobs around the house, as well as to avoid major rip-offs from television repairmen, electricians, and air-conditioning and heating installers. I am no longer reticent about fighting the computers which do almost all of my monthly billing and am quick to point out to potential offenders that computers, as I was taught in my programming classes, are designed for the service of people, not the other way around.

I think it's crucial for children to develop a positive attitude toward modern technology. Machines should not seem overwhelming, reducing us to seeming incompetents simply because we can't blink our lights as fast as they can. One sure way a child can learn that man has created the machines is by building one himself or herself. I also think that building a ham radio with a child is more fun for a parent than playing Crazy Eights or Old Maid. It's an opportunity for both to spend time and to solve problems together, as well as to learn something about the real world.

HEATHKIT
Heathkit (35-07 Broadway, Fairlawn, N.J. 07410) is one of the oldest electronic kit outfits. There are many Heathkit Electronic Centers throughout the country, all of which are listed in their catalogue (which is free and which you will receive every year once you are on their mailing list).

Heathkit kits are easy to build and have been rated by Consumer Reports as being among the most reliable in performance. Also, if you run into any difficulties you can go into your local center and receive advice or have the kit checked out free of charge by one of the experts-in-residence there.

In particular, I would like to recommend the Heathkit Jr. JK-18A Electronic Workshop "35." The "35" stands for the number of experiments that can be performed with this totally safe, preassembled breadboard on which the child makes the connections himself to spring-clip terminals. The experiments range from Morse code flashers and battery tester all the way up to a four-transistor radio. Also included are such really entertaining ones as an electronic organ and rain and burglar alarms.

The kit is priced in the catalogue at $39.95, which is a lot of money, but it is about the same as the other top electronic starter kits and it is far superior to the others in that Heathkit's instruction book is really a *book*, with some of the best instructions and explanations of how and why everything works. The circuit diagrams have little captions explaining what each element of the circuit does, and all through the book there are terrific cartoons depicting electrons with tiny sneakered feet rushing about over resistance "mountains," jumping capacitor "bridges," and spiraling around inductors in the most captivating fashion. I have to admit rather sheepishly that the transistor cartoon has done more for my understanding of that particularly mysterious cornerstone of modern electronics than a year and a half of graduate work in electrical engineering.

In addition, Heathkit has some of the best ham radio kits and courses for the beginner and an incredible selection of kits for everything ranging from home computers to guitar amplifiers and electronic organs for the budding rock star to such esoteric gadgets as electronic "Fish Spotter Sounders."

VANITY FAIR KITS

Suffice it to say about these kits that I purchased the 20-in-1 Electronic Project Kit for a sum which I choose not to remember, as it was a total waste. The kit came pre-wired by the factory for a two-transistor IC radio. All one had to do was connect the battery, which I did. Nothing happened but a lot of static. I checked the circuit. Still nothing. I grounded it, wired up an antenna and, you guessed it, again nothing but a few crackles and pops. But, unlike the Vanity Fair people, I *am* fair, so I rewired it for one of the more simple (though more ethically objectionable) circuits, No. 5, "Sound of Machine Gun." With growing smugness, I once again revelled in the sweet sound of silence.

Ditto for the Home Broadcaster Kit, which sounded as though it could have been a lot of fun, as it permits you to broadcast through your own home radio receiver. Don't even look at these kits if you see them anywhere. They're plain evil.

ACTION LABS KITS

These well-packaged and, to all outward appearances, well-conceived and designed experiments seem calculated to drive both child and parent to an instant dislike of science.

The kits come either singly for $2.50 or in a four-pack for $10. I purchased several four-packs and eagerly began building, thinking it only child's play (the Action Labs are recommended for "ages graded from six years," and I am many times that). After many increasingly frustrating hours of opening packages, sorting out parts, and following more or less lucid instruction booklets, I was forced to the shocking realization that my "Flapping Airplane" flapped like an expiring bat (the main crank kept getting stuck), that the "Turning Mirrors" wouldn't turn (the gears kept slipping), that "Fun with Magnets" was no fun at all because the compass wouldn't point north (the floating pointer would get stuck to the side of the case), and that my "Test Car" wouldn't start, though it looked terrific, because one of the metal parts was bent and created too much friction for the rubber band to turn.

My wrath as a consumer, a toy lover, and a science enthusiast was particularly aroused when I considered the fact that—with only a bit more care in design and production—these toys could have been marvelous. For one thing, whoever conceived them meant well. The instructions are chock-full of little "Caution" boxes such as "Do not play on the street" or for the Drawing Copier (which, by the way, actually does work), "Note: If you peep too long, you will get tired. So be sure to take a rest occasionally." There are also sets of questions accompanying the experiments which stimulate the child to think about what he or she is doing (unfortunately, however, Action Labs fails to provide the answers).

Secondly, it was a source of great excitement to my energy-crisis-buff husband to see that these toys could teach kids about wondrous unsung sources of energy, for some of which, such as "Rubber Band Power," he has been crusading more or less vigorously for years. Incidentally, a kit that did work and amused us considerably was the Waterspout Kit, with which you can make a water sprinkler (we made a wonderful drippy mess of the kitchen) and when you turn it over, it forms a little waterspout which can hold up and spin a small plastic ball.

LOGIX KITS

Logix or Logix-kosmos Kits are far and away the most elegant, brilliantly conceived, well distributed, and slickly packaged of all the science kits. However, of the three Logix kits that I purchased and tried to put together, none worked for one reason or another. The Electronic Computer (ages 12 and up, $30) is theoretically fascinating. But after hours of assembly time, I was still getting faulty contact with the slide bars and therefore was unable to get any of the programs to operate reliably. I just happened to notice on my way through the Bloomingdale's toy department last Christmas that the salesgirl who was demonstrating the computer was having an equal amount of difficulty. When I spoke to one of the engineers of the Logix Corporation in Montreal, he seemed surprised and said that they'd received hundreds of letters from kids around the world who had made it work and enjoyed it. Oh, well . . .

I then tried my hand at building the Motor Generator (ages 10 and up, $10). Again, after several hours of struggling with the super-thin copper wire with which you make the windings around the armature, I got to the next-to-last step: the installing of a bar magnet. Much to my dismay, the part which had been included in the kit was a piece of machined steel the same size as the magnet—but the wrong part. Again, the engineer at Logix expressed surprise and promised to send the bar magnet along with two long screws which were missing from the kit. By the time they came, I'd lost interest in the whole project.

As far as the Electronics Lab (ages 9 and up, $12.95) is concerned, I still think the Heathkit Lab provides far more value for the money, is far easier to put together, and contains a greatly superior instruction booklet. [Karen Mitnick, however, is an unabashed fan of the Logix Electronics Lab. See her review in the box below.]

Working with actual electronics elements sure beats theorizing any time. A mini-lab for beginners, the Logix Electronics Kit includes over one hundred precision components (clips, wires, seven resistors, two transistors, seven capacitors, a diode). The accompanying eighty-page guidebook is written with real compassion for a novice who needs to start from scratch. I've got forty experiments at my fingertips, culminating with a two-transistor radio I built by myself. I've already built a working console (I was thrilled when the circuit I built made a bulb light up), worked with transistors, and tested resistors. I've also got a card for free membership in the Electronics Club (entitling me to newsletters and club information).

The company also has kits for learning optics (build your own camera), computers (that's right—build your own), aeronautics, electricity. It's a great way to learn, because you're actually doing experiments (recalling the chemistry set I had in those ancient pre-transistor days). The box cover (which wisely shows both boys and girls) recommends the kit for ages nine to adult.

KAREN MITNICK

SCIENCE FAIR KITS

With unbounded admiration, I have to give the Science Fair kits (produced by the Radio Shack Division of the Tandy Corporation, Fort Worth, Texas 76107) four stars for the quality and fun they've provided all across the board. There are three thousand Radio Shack stores throughout the country, so availability is no problem. Their catalogue is free, and the stores even provide a free comic book, ''The Science Fair Story of Electronics,'' for kids.

My all-time favorite electronic kit is Science Fair's Two-Octave Electronic Organ Kit (Cat. No. 28-215, $13.95, ages 10–12 and up). I built it three years ago with a minimum of effort and when I pulled it out recently to check it, all I had to do was put in two fresh batteries and it worked perfectly. It comes in a nice wooden frame (boy, am I getting tired of cardboard, plastic, and styrofoam kits), and it contains all the parts your child will need, a very clear instruction booklet, two pages about how to read music, and ten wonderful tunes to play (among which are such immortal classics as ''The Marine Hymn,'' ''Dixie,'' and ''Adeste Fideles''). Worried about your eardrums? Relax. This modest little perfection is in better tune than a $10,000 Moog Synthesizer of my acquaintance.

ELECTRONIC LABS: I must start this section with a word of caution. Science Fair has an excellent series of Electronic Labs a noteworthy example: the 100-in-1 Electronic Project Kit, $24.95, which I recommend highly. Though their instruction booklets are not quite as good as the Heathkit Lab's, they have more experiments, such as Strobe Light and Computer Circuits. These are all excellent quality and you can recognize them because they come in wooden boxes.

SCIENCE FAIR P-BOX KITS: Once your child has expressed some interest and skill with one of the above starter kits, you might want to try some of these mini-kits, which, though a bit harder to put together, are low-priced and work (at least the two that I built did, a Visible Light Transmitter and a ''Goofy-Lite'' Kit). They start as low as $1.95 and none seems to be priced over $10.

MISCELLANEOUS: There are also some shortwave radio kits and terrific Fiber Optics Kits which you might want to consider. In addition, for the less handy youngsters, there are strobe lights and color organs in the catalogue which can be attached to your hi-fi system and could make nice gifts for the rock-'n-rollers in your family.

GENEVIÈVE CERF

A FEW SPECIFICS . . .

BUBBLES . . .

Blowing Bubbles

[*Bubbles,* by Bernard Zubrowski (Boston Children's Museum, Jamaica Way, Boston, Mass. 02130, 1973, $2.50) is, according to Becky Corwin, "the best book on bubbles yet. It provides the how-to-do 'ems (little or no equipment needed) for creating giant bubbles, tiny bubbles, oddly shaped bubbles—not to mention ordinary bubbles—to marvel at." The following is excerpted from Mr. Zubrowski's tome.]

In the beginning all you will need is some soap, a container of water, drinking straws, and a surface on which to blow bubbles.

Put some soap in warm water. You do not need a huge quantity of soap. Stir till soap mixes with the water. Experiment with different amounts and kinds of soap to see which gives the best results.

Make sure you try dishwashing soap such as Joy or Ajax. Add about three-quarters of a measuring cup to a gallon of warm water.

Put some soap solution in a tray and see what kinds of bubbles you can make by using a drinking straw.

BERNARD ZUBROWSKI
Bubbles

◆

The Definitive Bubble Book

SOAP BUBBLES, *by C. V. Boys, with black-and-white line drawings (Dover, 192 pages, $3),* is a classic (one preface dates back to 1911). The book will tell you about all kinds of interesting things—making wire frames to get different-shaped bubbles, putting bubbles in a jar (do it right and they'll keep for days and days), things you can do with a soap bubble that people just don't do much.

You'll have to glean from Boys' masterwork, though, because it contains a wealth of information that you really don't need and probably won't be interested in.

WILLIAM ACCORSI

Hemispheres

Here is one way of making a hemisphere:

Dip one end of straw in the solution.

Wet the surface you are going to blow on with the soap solution.

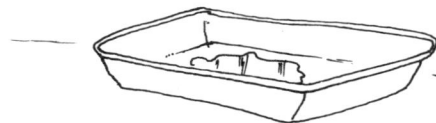

Hold the straw about two inches above the tray and blow gently.

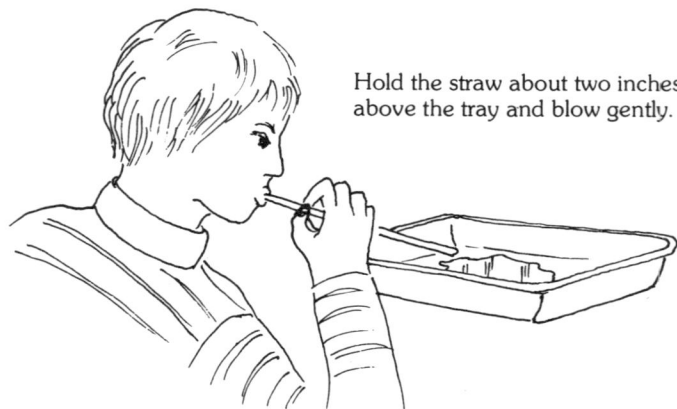

THE ENVIRONMENT . . .

You Can't Teach a Child Ecology (at Least Not in the Abstract)

"Ecology" should not just be a catchphrase for cleaning up your block. The young child can be introduced to larger concepts in nature—limits of resources, irreversibility, relationships in nature, the use of space.

The child will have as much a sense of the balance of nature as what he sees. If he sees his mother take six paper towels to wipe up a little spilled milk, that will not help him to understand that paper towels are made from trees that have to be cut down. If he rides in large cars he will not understand the need for energy efficiency. Your life style is the only ecology game that counts. The others just waste trees.

ELS

◆

Household Ecology

Life in the country on a two-acre mini-farm is considerably different from our former existence in the city (though much of what we've learned and become responsible for might well be incorporated in city life). There is a garden to tend, and that means seven days a week; there are chickens to feed and eggs to gather; there is garbage to be disposed of. Have you ever thought what you would do if the trusty garbageman didn't come around three times a week?

Everyone in our family has become more conscious of garbage since we became personally responsible for it. What do you do with it? First of all you eliminate as much garbage-producing matter as possible. No paper plates, paper napkins, processed foods in fancy boxes, no cardboard milk cartons, no throwaway pop bottles. You use returnable bottles for everything from milk to beer. Cans have both ends cut out, are washed and stuck in the garden to prevent those insidious cutworms from destroying the plants; recyclable paper is saved and turned over to the Girl Scouts the first Saturday of every month; recyclable bottles and aluminum cans are turned in at the collection center in town; wet garbage is never, repeat *never,* placed on top of throwaway refuse, it is placed in a container and thrown on the compost heap daily; and residual dry garbage is burned in an incinerator.

When the entire family must tend to the garbage, each becomes exquisitely aware of waste.

Recently we cleaned up the right of way between the highway and our fence. There was more trash there than we accumulate in a month. The kids were incensed. They kept shaking their fists at cars that drove by, calling their occupants jerks and other, less printable terms. It is unlikely that they will ever litter.

And how about water? You turn on the tap and there it is, right? Wrong. When you live in the country and have your own well, the pump sometimes fails. Then what? Then kids take five-gallon buckets and haul water from the river to wash in, we drink bottled water until the repair person comes, and when it's fixed we resolve to store some water for emergency use next time. Do we bathe, run the washing machine, water the grass, and use the dishwasher all at once? Not since the time we burned out the pump on the well. We are learning to conserve energy and water. We're even getting more parsimonious about the use of clothes. Nobody pitches a garment into the dirty-clothes basket anymore merely to get it out of sight. Now we examine it. If it can be worn again, we wear it. This saves water.

And do we use high-phosphate detergents? Not since they clogged up the septic tank and made a bubbling seething mess in the side yard. Now we know from personal experience what "biodegradable" is all about.

Are the children assigned busywork or enrolled in *every* lesson from ballet to judo to keep busy? Not now. They are a necessary part of the family. We honestly couldn't keep up with the work without their participation. And they're beginning to be something of experts on chickens and gardens and garbage and conservation.

LINDA WEST ECKHARDT

Schools: The Ideal Recycling Centers?

There must be hundreds of thousands of people like me who'd really want to recycle all their papers and bottles and cans, if only it were a little easier, a little more convenient to do so. If the neighborhood school ran an ongoing collection center, you could send the kids off to school once or twice a week with the family trash, often enough so that sorting and storing bottles and cans and newspapers and magazines and cardboard boxes wouldn't be much of a problem. Many people without school-age children would also find schools conveniently enough located for regular deposits of recycla-bles, especially if the center were open one Saturday a month.

The kids could pretty much run the operation on the school end. There's science and math in it, social studies too, as well as a chance to participate in some real and useful activity. The recycling center might even make some money for the school's equipment or library fund. —RS

On the Preservation of Places to Poke Around In

One thing my Dad and I used to have a good time doing was just truckin' through the woods—just walking and looking and picking up rocks. Sometimes Dad would get this crazy idea and we'd walk up the middle of the creek, for as long as we felt like walking. Sometimes a mile, two miles, just going right up the creek, with no shoes on. I'm convinced that's one of the reasons that now, as an adult, I feel a good deal of sensitivity toward the environment. I want to keep places like that where kids can have that experience of poking around without somebody coming around and telling them to get the hell off. If they want to walk all day and poke around inside rock houses and cliff houses, I want them to be able to do that. Because I'm convinced that that was a formative experience for me.

ELIOT WIGGINTON

RICHARD HUTCHINGS

An "Honest" Ecology Book

The faith of publishers in word magic has brought to stillborn existence many a small volume with the magic word "ecology" in its title. *Populations: Experiments in Ecology,* by A. Harris Stone and Stephen Collins, (illustrated by Peter P. Prasencia. Franklin Watts, Inc., $5.95), seems, among a dozen, the most honest and useful for young readers. It is organized around a number of tasks in the wide domain of population studies among humans and other living forms, each of them readable, pointed and practical for many children of school age. They are mostly counting, interviewing, weighing or modeling tasks. Only two (one with lima beans and the other with fruit flies, and both far from easy because of time span or technique) involve the use of living forms whose husbandry the experimenter must first master. These are real experiments just the same: weighing one's own meals (and finding their gross equivalents), counting human sex ratios at supermarkets, movies, and construction sites, totting up the floor space in one's own house, counting heads in a fine photograph from the stadium during the Rose Bowl game, sampling marble populations, and so on. The experiments are not dramatic on the surface, but they cut to the real problems of a science. Children—or any group of people who are serious about this weighty topic—will enjoy and profit for a long time from this book by an experienced author–artist team.

PHILIP AND PHYLIS MORRISON
Scientific American

Kids to the Rescue!

Here it is. A big environmental education in one small, nifty package. *Save the Earth!, An Ecology Handbook for Kids,* by Betty Miles, illustrated by Claire Nivola (Alfred A. Knopf, 91 pages, $2.50 paperback) is a book created for kids that is clearly a boon to parents and teachers. Author Betty Miles and artist Claire Nivola in separate chapters lovingly describe the land, air and water around us, and offer simple ways for all people to save these renewable resources. They suggest easy experiments for kids to carry out to dramatize abuses of resources. The last chapter is full of how-to-do-its—everything from how to write a professional newspaper story to ways of forming a block association.

The young critics I showed *Save the Earth!* to think it is a good book. My 9-year-old stepson Josh, for one, likes the words best. Me too. I like them because they are clear and simple. But I'm delighted by the whimsical drawings, including one of a kid glowering at cigarette-puffing grown-ups, and by such dramatic photographs as one showing gorgeous clouds of black industrial smoke billowing into the sky. There is no fuss here. The book is fresh and clean, a pleasure to read and look at.

Josh yelled with surprise at the story of Mt. Trashmore. Building a mountain of garbage was a peculiar idea to him. But why not? It all has to go somewhere—an elementary lesson that runs like a refrain throughout this book. Other lessons are surprisingly adult, such as ad-

vising kids how to acquire a healthy skepticism.

This handbook is full of simple but staggering facts: sounds of 180 decibels can kill you. Each chapter contains a story to show what people can do: the sloop *Clearwater* sails the Hudson River reminding us of better days and serving as a scientific classroom. The experiments are as simple as putting a white sock over the end of a car's exhaust pipe and running the engine to see how dirty the sock gets.

And last but not least is an important theme. *Save the Earth!* stresses over and over ways for kids to be aware of self and of personal responsibility.
BETTY MADISON KARLEN
The New York Times Book Review

MINERAL COLLECTING . . .

Tips for Rock-Hounds

Mineral collecting . . . can combine outdoor and indoor activity—outdoors for digging and hunting when weather permits, and indoors for sorting, polishing and cataloguing. And it can be as high-priced or as inexpensive a hobby as one wishes. Specimens can be acquired by digging in sites near home, or the hobbyist can travel miles to search for rare or exotic additions to his collection. (Some people spend entire vacations this way.) New materials can also be added by trading with other collectors, or by shopping at local auctions or regional "shows."

The tools needed for mineral collecting are comparatively inexpensive and easy to locate. The only "unusual" one would be a good mineral pick. I recommend the Estwing brand. It costs about $9 and comes in several weights or sizes . . . Most rock-hounds will also want a couple of cold chisels, plus a shovel and a small sledgehammer weighing from five to eight pounds.

WILLIAM B. SANBORN
The New York Times

The Fossil Places of the City

"Gravity pulling stones from walls and cliffs," says the sharp, simple text of *City Rocks, City Blocks, and the Moon,* by Edward Gallob (photographs by the author; Charles Scribner's Sons, $6.95). Equally sharp and even more vivid, the view the lens caught shows a brick wall in some waste lot, the bricks fallen away from a big patch. The magnified penny in another shot gives scale to the small curled shells there in the builder's limestone; still another picture shows the dark, fine-grained trap basalt, ballast among the railroad ties. So, through 40 photographs with their connecting text, this author-artist leads a young big-city reader into a sense of material and of change; into the continuity between a city and its mineral substances. Gallob is sensitive of eye and thought; he knows the fossil places of the city—muddy playgrounds, soft asphalt, wet pavements—and he has seen its history. He understands collectors, too, and he properly connects the moon rocks with the fun of real collecting open to a small child in the city. . . .

PHILIP AND PHYLIS MORRISON
Scientific American

CHEMISTRY . . .

Experiments in Applied Chemistry, or How to Make Your Own Non-slip Floor Wax

The young chemist is a well-known type, eager for new chemicals, generally seeking the excitement of bright color or unusual gas or even a good-sized bang. . . . The challenge is the ability

to create novelty in matter. *The Formula Book,* by Norman Stark (Sheed & Ward, Inc., $5.95), is entirely different in its aim, although it is closely related in activity. In a way the two styles mirror the relation of scientific research to technology. Here are collected what amount to some 200 "recipes" for an entire range of household preparations that can be realized in an ordinary kitchen, given a number of containers for the product. What you make is not particularly novel. Rather, it is useful. By your own understanding purchase of materials, by skill and careful work, you can produce what you might buy at the hardware store or the supermarket. (You will not understand it much better, however; this book has two excellent pages on alcohol and its denaturing, but almost no other background material beyond the how-to level. We would have welcomed even a few pages more.) Here are formulations for non-slip floor wax, contact lens fluid, anti-knock additive (benzene, a little doubtful), horse-hoof grease and tennis-net preservative. The tasks are often finicky and sometimes tedious, but they are first-class family activities, safe under supervision; they could pay for themselves, with the time spent charged to recreation. They might in some cases form a new way to make contact between parents and basement chemist.

PHILIP AND PHYLIS MORRISON
Scientific American

[The Formula Book is also available in paperback, from Avon, for $1.75. —Eds.]

Fire

Most young children learn one thing about fire—that it's a no-no. Instead, parents might create an opportunity for kids to learn all about fire—that it's a no-no under certain circumstances, enormously useful in others, and a very interesting phenomenon all the time. You can give kids some practice on what will catch fire and what won't, and under what circumstances. Experiments can be controlled so that there's no likelihood of anything serious happening. You can light a candle and predict whether something you hold in the candle flame will burn or not. You can try a stainless steel spoon, a toothpick, a piece of newspaper, maybe a tree branch from the backyard. Eventually the child will suggest trying something that is not a very good idea (a book of matches, for example), and you can open up the discussion to what should not be put in a flame, and how to put out a fire. A child who is taught cause and effect will be a lot safer than the child who is simply told to stay away from the stove and never to play with matches.

GEORGE COPE

ASTRONOMY . . .

Space is nice. And it's pretty empty. It's as empty as a building 20 miles long, 20 miles wide, and 20 miles high that contains only a single grain of sand.

CARL SAGAN

The Stars: A New Way to See Them

I suppose it's a bit melodramatic to say that *The Stars: A New Way to See Them* (Houghton Mifflin, 160 pages, $10.95 hardcover, $5.95 paperback) is a book that changed my life. But if you consider the fact that some of my greatest pleasure as a teen-ager came from star-gazing (including the construction of a telescope made from a gigantic mailing tube and a curved mirror purchased from an optical shop), that I've spent an inordinate amount of my adult life running around the countryside chasing eclipses, and that I married a woman whose attention I first attracted by showing her Jupiter in the night sky, then maybe I'm really not exaggerating.

For indeed, H. A. Rey's remarkable book, presented to me as a twelve-year-old, made astronomy as a hobby far more simple and enjoyable a prospect than anything else I've ever seen on the subject. (H. A. Rey, as you may recall, is the author-illustrator of the famous series of children's books about Curious George, the monkey.) It's Rey's theory that most of us—children or adults—don't know the stars because of the way astronomy books have always represented the constellations.

"Some books," he points out in his introduction, "show, arbitrarily drawn around the stars, elaborate allegorical figures which we cannot trace in the sky. Others . . . show the constellations as involved geometrical shapes which don't look like anything and have no relation to the names. Both ways are of little help if we want to find the constellations in the sky . . ."

So, what Rey has done—and God knows why no one did it before—is simply to redraw the lines connecting the stars so that Gemini, the Twins, really *looks* like a pair of twins, Leo, the Lion really *looks* like a lion, and so forth. The resulting shapes are much simpler to remember, and once you remember them, you really can retrace them in the sky.

Figure 1:
The Twins—A Group of Stars

Figure 2: The Twins—Allegorical

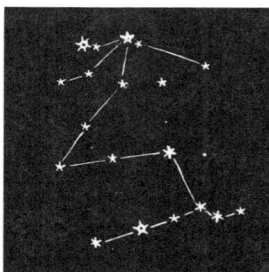

Figure 3: The Twins—Geometrical

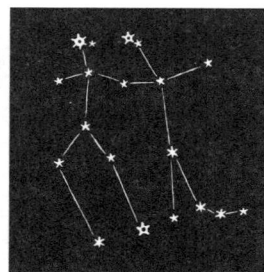

Figure 4: The Twins—Graphic

In addition, Rey fills his book with other radical departures: he uses English names for the constellations instead of the more common Latin ones; he divides the sky up into groups of constellations, which makes them far easier to find; he concentrates on the practical side of star-gazing, rather than on the complexities of astronomical mathematics; and he scatters amusing cartoons and whimsical observations through his pages.

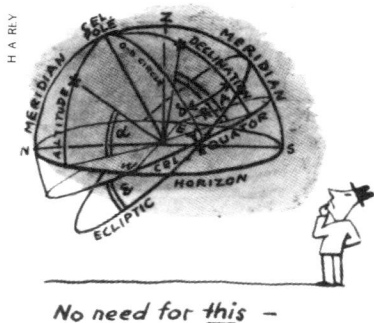

No need for *this* —

if all you want is **this** !

Since *The Stars: A New Way to See Them* was published in the early 1950s, H. A. Rey's drawings have gained wide acceptance even among serious astronomers (and many of them could use his help: one of my best friends is a leading expert on the solar corona but he hasn't a clue how to find even the brightest stars without the use of a computer-set telescope). And Rey himself saw fit to do a simplified version of his text for the pre-teen set, called *Find the Constellations* (Houghton Mifflin, 72 pages, 1954, $4.95). CBC

The Sky Show in Your Backyard

To me, the most exciting part of astronomy—and one that's as easy for the beginner as it is for the expert—is following the planets as they make their way around the sky. Venus and Jupiter, in particular, are almost always spectacularly bright, and therefore, when they're in the evening sky, they're remarkably easy to spot. And, as you watch them—and Mars, Saturn, and Mercury (when they're at their best)—change their place night after night, you get a sense of the wonderful order of the universe.

Particularly interesting are the moments—there are usually a few each year—when one planet passes another. Astronomers call this a conjunction, and a child with no astronomical knowledge at all can watch and enjoy this if he knows where and when to look. All he need do is go outside at approximately the same hour on a few successive nights around the date of the conjunction and watch as the two gleaming points of light draw inevitably closer together and then, after an evening of looking like a spectacular "double star," begin to draw apart again.

But how can you know when a conjunction is due? Well, the *World Almanac* and the *Information Please Almanac* have Astronomical Events sections that refer to them. But far more useful to the beginner is the Abrams Planetarium *Sky Calendar* by Robert C. Victor; it presents simple directions and charts for observing conjunctions and other events astronomy enthusiasts wait for. You can order the calendar, at a cost of $2 per year, from the Abrams Planetarium, Michigan State University, East Lansing, Mich. 48824. (See next page.)

SKY CALENDAR

ROBERT C. VICTOR/ABRAMS PLANETARIUM

SUNDAY	MONDAY	TUESDAY	WEDNESDAY	THURSDAY	FRIDAY
Diagrams labeled *Morning* or *Evening* show sky during mid-twilight about 3/4 hour before sunrise or 3/4 hour after sunset, respectively, from latitude 40° N. Diagrams for Jan 13,16,27,28 are for other times, as noted.	Look at Jupiter **1** with binoculars in late evening. Note cluster of stars 1° north (upper left) of Jupiter: the *Beehive!* The quadrilateral of 4th and 5th magnitude stars surrounding it provides a useful reference for plotting Jupiter.	January 2, morning: Face SE. ✳ Venus ✳ Antares ✳ Mercury	Quadrantid meteor **3** shower activity peaks sharply tonight. Maximum numbers of meteors may be seen in Canada and northernmost U.S. around midnight E.S.T. Shower continues until dawn tomorrow.	Have you ever seen moon within 24 hrs of New? If you see it Jan 27 or 28, please send report. Include date, time, instrument used, description of moon, and your location. See *SKY AND TELESCOPE*: 4/78 p 358; 6/77 p 440; 2/72 p 95; 8/71 p 78.	🌓 **5** First Quarter (evening half moon). Scale of diagrams on this calendar: See box before December 1 on last month's *Sky Calendar.*
In two weeks, **7** Pluto moves inside the orbit of Neptune and becomes the eighth planet until 1999. Regulus ✳ ○ Moon Tues morn — Morning: Face west Jan 14-16.	Evening: East **8** ♪ Pleiades ○ Moon ✳ Aldebaran	Evening: East **9** ♪ Pleiades ⋯ ⋯ ✳ Aldebaran Moon ○	January 10, morning: SE. ✳ Venus Look for β Scorpii 3° S (lower right) of Venus. Can you still see Mercury? ✳ Antares Mercury	One week from to- **11** day, Venus at greatest angular distance, 47° west or upper right of rising sun). At sunrise it will be nearly 30° up in SSE. Telescope will show its half-lit phase: ◖ Venus remains morning star until July.	Evening: **12** ENE • Castor ✳ Pollux Full ○ Moon tonight
○ Moon Monday morning Jupiter ✳ ○ Moon Sunday morning	Morning: ✳ **15** SE. Venus Watch Venus ✳ pass Antares Antares this week ✳ (closest Wednesday, 8° apart).	4½ hrs after **16** sunset: ✳ East. ✳ Regulus ✳ ○ Moon Saturn ✳	Morning: WSW **17** ✳ Saturn ○ Moon ✳ Regulus	Top view of solar **18** system today. Venus at greatest elongation west of sun. Angle at Earth = 47°. ✳ Sun • Venus •Earth	Sun enters **19** Capricornus. That constellation is hidden in the sun's glare, but Cancer is in opposition to the sun and visible all night. What bright "star" is visiting Cancer until it leaves evening sky in July?

Choosing a Telescope: You Don't Need Mount Palomar To See the Rings of Saturn

There are three basic kinds of telescopes: the *refractor,* which uses a lens to gather light and an *eyepiece* to magnify it; the *reflector,* in which a concave mirror is substituted for the light-gathering lens; and the *catadioptric,* or compound, telescope, in which a combination of mirrors and lenses is used to gather and focus light beams.

Which kind should you buy? Well, each has certain advantages. Refractors are simple and straightforward, and, at least in the size most suitable for beginners (most experts recommend one of 2.4 inches in aperture), are widely available at camera shops and department stores. Reflectors definitely offer the most light-gathering—and hence magnifying—power for the money, but they are a bit more cumbersome to operate than refractors, their open-tube design can lead to maintenance problems, and they tend to be available only by mail. Catadioptric scopes are amazingly compact, since their lens-plus-mirror design allows them to have far shorter tubes per inch of aperture than either refractors or reflectors. Their portability and general high standard of performance make them an ideal choice, except for one thing: they are very, very expensive.

The best guide to purchasing a telescope that I've seen is an article by Thomas Cave and James Mullaney that appeared in the October 1977 issue of *Astronomy* Magazine. It clearly details each of the three types of telescope and suggests various brands. To obtain a copy of the issue, send $2.50 to Rosemary L. Pickart, *Astronomy* Magazine, 411 East Mason, 6th Floor, Milwaukee, Wis. 53202.

As a child, I found it an unparalleled thrill to look through my telescope and see the craters of the moon, the satellites of Jupiter, and the rings of Saturn. If that's your goal—for you or your kids—the simplest three-inch reflector, as long as it's sturdily mounted, should prove more than satisfactory. (My first instrument—known as the Ross Stellarscope—was little more than a cardboard tube with a concave mirror at one end and a cheap flat mirror-cum-magnifying lens at the other.)

Now mind you, such a telescope may not give you perfect color images, and it won't be easy to locate faint objects, and you won't have much luck taking celestial photographs, and the tube may vibrate annoyingly every time you touch it. But you *will* be able to see those craters, moons, and rings—and that's plenty exciting enough for the beginning astronomer.

A better-than-minimally-acceptable reflecting telescope is the three-inch Space Conqueror, available for under $60 from Edmund Scientific Company, 150 Edscorp Building, Barrington, N.J. 08007. If I were you, I'd try one out before investing $1,000 or more in a Questar Catadioptric. (I sure do love my Questar, though . . .)

CBC

INFINITY

The Other Side of the Wall

When I was around three years old I asked my mother, How big is the world? When she said it is very very big I asked, Is there a wall around the world? She said no, and explained about outer space. I insisted on asking again, Isn't there a wall somewhere that's the end? And she again said no. If there was a wall there would have to be something on the other side.

Once I grasped this idea of infinity in space, it was an easy analogy to infinity in time.

CHIP BLOCK

Teaching a Three-Year-Old About Infinity

When Nick saw the small plastic flashlight he wanted it and I said Oh no, we need that for the house. But then I thought, why shouldn't he have it, he's never had a flashlight and I'm always saying what a wonderful plaything it is for a kid. So he spent the afternoon flashing it on everything and I forced myself to say nothing, for once, about using up the batteries. His favorite discovery was that shining it on the ceiling made a star shape. And we had our dinner with the flashlight sitting on the table shining a star onto the ceiling.

After dinner we had to go out, and Nick took his flashlight. It was starting to get dark, so it was a good time to be flashing it on the buildings and cars we passed. He then flashed it up into the sky hoping to create a star just like the one on our kitchen ceiling. "Hey, Mom," said Nick, "how come I can't make a star?" Because the sky never ends—it goes on and on and there's nowhere for the light to land as it does on our ceiling.

ELS

◆

The Universe in 40 Jumps

COSMIC VIEW: THE UNIVERSE IN 40 JUMPS, *by Kees Boeke (John Day, 1957, 48 pages, $6.95 hardcover),* is a great book, as valuable for parents who have a difficult time answering some of the cosmic questions their kids ask as it is for kids (from four up). Each of a sequence of photographs shows a child in relation to the school, to the street, to the earth, to the universe.

There's also a remarkable film based on the book—*Powers of Ten,* by Charles Eames—which is available to libraries and schools. You can see it at the Smithsonian Institution's Air and Space Museum in Washington, where it's on permanent display.—RS

SCIENCE BOOKS

Two Books That Make Science Fun

In the foreword to Joe Abruscato's and Jack Hassard's oversized paperback *The Whole Cosmos Catalog of Science Activities* (Goodyear, $9.95, Santa Monica, Ca. 90401, 134 pages), there is a quotation from Jerome Bruner: "There is something antic about creating, although the enterprise be serious." It is in that spirit that the authors have assembled the projects, games, experiments, puzzles, craft activities, biographies and articles to be found in this fascinating book.

In *The Whole Cosmos Catalog,* your kids and you will learn how to make a continental-drift flip book, how to plot earthquakes, how to make your own weather instruments, how to suspend a paperclip in mid-air (hint: there are

magnets involved), how to build a telescope similar to the one Galileo used, how to play that remarkable new urban-blight board game *Litterburg,* and much more. All the activities are arranged carefully by subject, and the book is well-indexed.

MAGIC WITH SCIENCE *by Walter B. Gibson (Grosset and Dunlap, 120 pages, $2.95 paperback)* is also based on the premise that kids will learn science if they approach it with a spirit of fun. Gibson has collected some 140 magic tricks, all performable with props available around the house or from neighborhood merchants, and all of which demonstrate a simple scientific principle. The book never becomes heavy, and, happily, the "magic" effects are stressed more than the technical explanations of why the tricks work. A clear—if uninspiring—illustration accompanies each trick.

CBC

Nature Guides: Two Excellent Series

There are several inexpensive nature guide series. You really do need to own these rather than borrow them from the library, so they'll be there when you need them. Two series of pocket-size books—both published by Golden Books—were specifically recommended to us:

THE GOLDEN NATURE SERIES (*Fossils, Trees, Insects, Stars, Seashells, Rocks and Minerals, etc.*) (*paperback, $1.95 each*).

They're cheap, they're good, they're beautiful, they're thoughtful," Phylis Morrison tells us. "When a paperback is tiny, it wears beautifully; and these are better illustrated, if somewhat less complete, than much grander field guides." Alan Leitman agrees: "I can't imagine that any elementary school or junior high classroom would be without them."

GOLDEN FIELD GUIDES (*Trees of North America, Birds of North America, Seashells of North America, paperback, $4.95 each*).

These guides fit easily into a pocket and have plastic-coated covers (anyone in the field on a wet day or working near water will appreciate their moisture-resistance). The author of each guide is an expert in his field (Tucker Abbott on shells, C. H. Robbins on birds). Pictures (color drawings) and text are conveniently placed on facing pages, and there are geographic range maps which help beginners know that the species they've "identified" couldn't possibly be within a thousand miles of their particular region at that time of year. The guides contain good background introductions and bibliographies.

JEFF SIMON

If You're Looking for Science Books for Children . . .

No one seeking science books for children should miss the December issue of *Scientific American,* in which Philip and Phylis Morrison present an annual review of the year's offerings. He is the magazine's book editor (and a physicist at MIT), she a wonderful teacher with an uncommon respect for kids. Together they select over forty books each year, including some that might not be labeled either children's books or science books. If you want to read reviews from previous years, you can find back issues of *Scientific American* in most libraries.

RS

PETS
AND OTHER ANIMALS

JAY GOOD

E. Barf '78

Any Animal Can Be a Pet

It is generally thought that you have to walk into a store and pay money and get papers to have a pet. Not so. Any tame animal for which you have space can be considered as a pet if you are going to love it, take care of it, clean up after it, and make it part of your life.

If you can't keep a rabbit (they chew everything), how about a dog (so responsive, but a responsibility, I know). If not a dog, a cat (the litter box in a small apartment—ick). If not a cat, a fish? If not a fish (you can't cuddle a fish, and they die easily), a hamster (lost behind the bookcase). Then how about a guinea pig (it will stay in the doll carriage). If not a guinea pig, then certainly a desert tortoise, much easier to sustain than those little ones with the awful plastic trees. Think of Galápagos.

But if you can't keep any, why not have a visitor? Aren't we borrowers, anyway? How about some earthworms, a cricket, or a toad for a little while before you return it to its habitat? One helpful book on care, feeding, and catching is *Odd Pets* by Lib Hess and Dorothy C. Hogner (Crowell, 1951, hardcover). [Unfortunately, the book is out of print now, but you might be able to find a copy in your local library.]

BETTY RADENS

[In some towns, if you don't want to *own* an animal, you can take one out of the library. See Toy and Pet Lending Library, page 454.]

DOGS

Putting Off the Dog

We live in a city apartment. We did not want a dog. Our son, half-past four, wanted a dog. In order to avoid getting a dog I became a horse. My name was Horo. I galloped around the house with our son as jockey. I reared up on my hind legs. I was tied to doorknobs and drank from a bowl on the floor on special occasions. I learned to jump the hurdle of our son's bed. I could count with my hoofs. I was quite a good horse and might have had a fair shot at the Triple Crown and early stud except that at five our son discovered my faulty breeding. When we could put off the dog no longer we got a dog. I was among those who scowled at dogs in the elevator and muttered when they defecated on the street. The other day a man howled at me because our dog was peeing on a patch of green around a tree on the sidewalk. I took the dog's side and said that city grass must learn to endure such indignities. Then I whinnied and stomped off snorting fire.

HARVEY JACOBS

Some Swell Pup

Written in collaboration with Matthew Margolis, director of the National Institute of Dog Training, [*Some Swell Pup, or Are You Sure You Want a Dog,* by Maurice Sendak (Farrar, Straus & Giroux, 1976) tells] . . . a cautionary tale of two kids and how they learn to train and love their rambunctious new puppy—which ironically takes on the role of the stereotypical unruly child—with the guidance of a caftanned canine saint. . . .

It's certainly the wittiest tale about how to get gently and humanely socialized that I've ever read.

JONATHAN COTT
Rolling Stone

Computer Mating

Our son wants the dog to mate. The dog wants to mate. He is in perpetual heat and has taken to watching Errol Flynn films on the late show. With babysitting money, our son sent five bucks to a computer dating service for dogs advertised in The New York Times. *They cashed his check but never sent the name of a single, eligible girl. Meanwhile, our son dressed Frisky for his wedding. You can see that the groom has honorable intentions. If you know of a likely lady, send her punch card.*

Some Hints on Buying a Dog— From the American Kennel Club

The following notes are excerpted from *The Complete Dog Book* (Howell Books, $7.95 hardcover), which contains, according to the American Kennel Club, "the photograph, history and official standard of *every* breed admitted to A.K.C. registration, and the selection, training, breeding, care and feeding of purebred dogs." It's a useful book indeed for the serious dog owner, and even if you're looking for the most unpretentious of pets, it contains many useful bits of information. Herewith some of the A.K.C.'s hints on buying a dog:

To begin with, the family's receptiveness to having a dog must be established. The attitudes, habits and dispositions of all who will have responsibility for the dog must be taken into account. A new puppy is a delight, but there will be need for housebreaking, training to the leash and the obeying of commands, and, of course, his daily care.

All puppies seem irresistible, but the full-grown animal must be visualized. Adult height, length, weight, appetite, disposition, amount of grooming required must all be carefully considered before brining home a cuddly ball of fur that can grow up to be a 100-pound terror. Consider, too, any limitations imposed by your environs; if it is to be a city dog, for example, the necessary excursions for exercise and elimination might prove a problem.

Do not buy a puppy under six weeks of age—eight weeks would probably be better. The important thing is to know that the puppy is fully weaned, and strong enough to be on its own away from the mother.

The puppy should be healthy, normal and alert. Never select from a litter in which disease seems to be present, and certainly never a puppy that seems ill with runny nose, watery eyes or fever. A cowed, trembling, shy puppy, or one that seems snappy and bad-tempered, should be avoided.

From the beginning, you should have a local veterinarian to whom you can turn. He can give you specific recommendations for the area in which you live, and can advise you on the vaccinations that are essential, from the outset, to provide immunity from the diseases that are fatal to so many puppies.

Because it has been subject to past misinterpretation, you should know that the designation "A.K.C., Reg." following the name of a kennel simply means that the kennel's name is . . . protected for the sole use of its owner in naming dogs to be registered or shown. It does not signify any special stamp of approval on the kennels—the American Kennel Club does not register or rate kennels as such. Nor does the A.K.C. buy or sell dogs.

Canine Tolerance: Dog Meets Child

Sensitive dogs are particularly gentle with the children of a beloved master; it is as though they understand how much they mean to him. And fear that the dog might harm the children is quite absurd; on the contrary, there is a danger that the dog, by being too tolerant of the children, may educate them to roughness and inconsideration. One must be on one's guard against this; particularly in the case of the large and very good-natured breeds, such as St. Bernards, Newfoundlands. In general, however, dogs know very well how to escape the attentions of children when they become tiresome— a fact of great educational value: since normal children derive much pleasure from the company of dogs and are correspondingly disappointed when they run away from them, they soon realize how they must behave in order to make themselves desirable companions from the dog's point of view. Children with a certain amount of natural tact thus learn at a very tender age the value of consideration for others.

KONRAD LORENZ
Man Meets Dog

CATS

Cats and Kids

Age and seniority are the important issues here. A kitten introduced into a child's life, even a baby's, should be a happy experience all around. The child benefits from early exposure to petdom and to the animal world, and the kitten adapts, fleeing or playing or ignoring the child's caprice as its view of the situation warrants. The young human is a part of the world the puss is given, and the puss adjusts.

But bringing an adult cat into the home of a babe or of a very young child is always unwise.

If the cat was there first, accustomed to its prerogatives and its share of affection, problems may ensue. Tales of smotherings in cribs are probably apocryphal (from the same paranoid drawer, very likely, as tales of the transmission of rare feline diseases from the stools of infected animals to pregnant women or the newborn; however, for the super-cautious, all the medical evidence is not yet in), but the suddenly neglected cat has other choices: it can flee; it can destroy property, however well behaved it was until then; it can become ill and pine away, even unto death. ·Thus, great care must be taken to see that the cat receives (at least) its customary ration of attention from new parents during the early going. If this is handled well, the presence of the babe will be accepted by

---

We like to put marbles in the bathtub for the cat to play with.
ELIZABETH EHRENFELD

I've thought about how I would like it if somebody picked me up by the neck and threw me around and held my legs. That's what I used to do to Kitty. Then I started to think how I would feel . . .
DAVID ALMOND
Age nine

the puss, his eventual manhandling of it toler-ated, and they may even, in time, become friends.

The wisest course, if both children and cats are contemplated, is to acquire both at the same time.
IVAN GOLD

PETER ALMOND

PET BIRDS AND FISH

Pet Birds: Make Sure the Store Will Guarantee Their Health

After buying three sick parakeets, arguing with the store for refunds, and comforting my thrice-disappointed son, we at last found a shop which would guarantee the health of its birds and so we bought Charlie. The children play with him every now and then—he is so tame he will walk around on the floor and play ball and let you kiss him and hold him very close. The kids like trying to teach him dirty words.
CAROL EICHLER

How do you know if a bird is healthy? I asked Virginia Belmont, a bird expert of forty-four years whose store in New York's Rockefeller Center has truly extraordinary caged creatures. "The eyes should be clear, the feathers should be smooth rather than ruffled, the nose should be absolutely clean and dry. But really," she continued, "there are so many signs to look for that the only advice I could give to parents is to buy from a reputable store."

That leaves two questions: (1) How can you tell if a store is a reputable store? and (2) Do you trust yourself to tell a clouded bird's eye from a clear one?
RS

An Aquarium Divided Against Itself

Those $1.98 plastic dividers that are professed to instantly convert one aquarium into two do not work very well. Our infant guppie popula-tion is slowly and mysteriously on the decline, from which we surmise that the older fish found their way into the "nursery."
CAROL EICHLER

[For information on how to construct your own backyard pond, turn to page 228.]

OF GERBILS AND SKINKS, FRUIT FLIES AND FROGS. . .
(AND OTHER EXOTIC PETS)

You can't always find exotic lizards, but when you do they should cost from $3 to $15. They eat mealworms, flies, crickets, and (are you ready for this?) cockroaches.

Gerbils, Chuckwallas, Iguanas, and Skinks

I would like never to see another gerbil. They're easy to keep, they don't stink up the cage, and that's why they're so popular. But they do so many really weirdo things. They release a big section of their tails when they're frightened, so when you pick one up, you may end up holding the tail while the gerbil is running around the cage with no tail. They eat their young, they bite, and for some kids growing up in the city, gerbils look a little too much like rats to make anyone very comfortable having them around.

Actually chuckwallas and iguanas probably make better pets than gerbils. They're little desert reptiles, and all they really need is to be hot. They'll go for hellishly long without being fed, and their defecation problem is just about zero. The only trouble is they lack charm, they don't lick your hand. In North Africa they have a quite pleasant lizard-type creature called a skink, about the size of a chameleon, which has more charm than the others and is still pretty easy to keep. And skinks don't do some of the bad things gerbils do.
GEORGE COPE

[In short, you won't be bothered by the piddle of the skinks.—CBC]

How to Catch Flies for Your Frog (or Chameleon)

If you need to catch flies for your pet frog or chameleon, you can spray them (on the wing) with water from a plant mister, which temporarily grounds them, and then proceed to pick them up and introduce them to the frog in question.
JUDY ALBAUM
New Ways

At Last: A Modular Rodent Housing System That Really Works

If you're determined to keep gerbils or hamsters, you should be interested in Habitrail, a "modular rodent housing system" (what self-respecting small mammal would want to be without one?) produced by Living World.

Habitrail is a series of houses, exercise wheels, climbing spaces, etc., all made of transparent plastic and all of which can be joined together by sections of tube tunnel (also of clear plastic). It makes for a pet habitat you can constantly modify or add to; you can get hours of pleasure watching your little darlings darting about the mazes you construct, and, what's more, Habitrail is a lot less messy than the standard wire cage. Habitrail is marketed through pet shops. The starter set sells for about $12.
CBC

All About Rabbits

The households which are the likeliest candidates for *Rabbits: All About Them,* by Alvin and Virginia Silverstein, photos by Roger Kerkham (Lothrop, Lee and Shepard Co., 1973, $5.95 hardcover), are, of course, the ones which keep rabbits. Right away there is a problem. Bunnies, according to the text and an accompanying photo, chew on practically anything, books included.

Be that as it may, this is the place to learn that rabbits aren't really rodents, and that there is a difference between rabbits and hares. Everything about how to care for, breed (the authors admit it isn't hard), and study rabbits is here, along with notes on rabbits' contributions to science and a bow to rabbits in literature (Flopsy, Mopsy, Cottontail, Peter, Br'er Rabbit, the March Hare, et al.).

Larger biological issues are approached from the rabbit's point of view: reproduction, ecology, genetics, disease, defensive actions, social habits, territorial behavior. A thorough and well-written book, and good reading either in the classroom or at home despite the several typographical errors which may confuse children developing their reading skills.

Hippity-hop.
JENNIFER CARDEN

On Owning (and Feeding) a Common Garden Snake

The common garden snake is a fine city pet for a child, and almost any parent can get used to it once they have seen all its virtues: it is noiseless, harmless, odorless, playful, interesting, and it doesn't need constant feeding. A pet snake is best bought at a reputable pet store, for around $5. They eat goldfish, which we were able to price variously at four for a dollar to ten for a dollar, so it pays to shop around. (Interestingly the store with the most expensive goldfish also suggested the snake eat more of them, three or four a week as opposed to one or two a week.)

Starting a Fruit Fly Colony (Don't Take the Top Off the Jar)

Every time my stepdaughter's friend, a geneticist, comes to visit he has to bring his fruit flies. My eleven-year-old daughter became fascinated, trapped some she found lurking on rotting grapefruit in our kitchen, and started her own colony. She soon had a burgeoning colony of hundreds of "wild" fruit flies. She'd learned from Mike all sorts of things like distinguishing eye color and sex, how to spot an adult or pregnant or sterile fly, etc. National Educational Television had some good things on genetics which she watched. (Kids don't turn to books nearly as much as the tube for information any-

more.) When she showed Mike her colony, he was impressed. She offered the flies to him. He couldn't use them because they didn't fit his research, but he took them to another geneticist who did research on wild fruit flies and now my kid is raising fruit flies for University of Texas experiments. She watches over them like a mother cat. I'm thrilled, except when the baby occasionally takes the top off the jar. Then we're inundated and it's like the African Queen until she catches the damn things.

LINDA WEST ECKHARDT

"So You Want to Import a Pet"

Harrods Ltd., Knightsbridge,
London S.W. 1, England

Harrods pet shop sends lion cubs, pumas, bush babies, otters, Siamese and Burmese cats, decorative waterfowl, aviary birds, etc., all over the world. In 1967 they sent an elephant called Gertie by air to Los Angeles. They will gladly give a quotation for any animal which doesn't have to undergo American quarantine, and say that British-bred dogs are in great demand in America.

A permit is needed to import an animal; for details write to the Commissioner of Customs [1301 Constitution Avenue N.W., Washington, D.C. 20229, and ask for the leaflet "So You Want to Import a Pet."

MARIA ELENA DE LA IGLESIA
The New Catalogue of Catalogues

POINTERS ON PET CARE

The World Pet Expo: An Animal Road Show

If your civic group can plan six months in advance, has roughly $5,000 to spend on a two-day animal show, can supply the space for it, and will agree to advertise it, the World Pet Expo may be for you. The people to talk to are R. W. Commerford and Son, Route 4, Goshen, Conn. 06756. (If your civic group can plan six months in advance and *doesn't* have $5,000, don't despair; Mr. Commerford is glad to discuss the renting of individual animals.)

Or maybe you are merely considering going to the show when it comes to your town. The World Pet Expo does not have much to do with pets as we know them—which is to say there are no dogs or cats. But it does feature elephant and camel rides (75 cents for once around the

ring), pony rides (50 cents), and a terrific thing called Jumping Jack which has nothing whatsoever to do with animals; for 50 cents you can go into a big plastic gazebo affair with an air-filled floor and jump, jump, jump for a nice trampoline effect.

Most of the animals are in unlabeled corrals and cages, a fact which leaves parents groping for the difference between llamas and emus. There are also "pets" in circus-wagon displays—beautiful birds, for example. Lots of goats, pigs, and sheep are on hand for petting, also smaller animals like rabbits, guinea pigs, and white mice.

Along with all this there are plastic inflatable animals you can buy for too much money, booths where you can spin-paint, and art on black velvet for sale. It costs $1.50 for adults and 99 cents for children just to get in, so if you are going to indulge yourself in any of the above-named treats, be forewarned. Our excursion—four kids and an adult—cost $13.90.

Commerford adds a new animal every year. We visited during the year of the zebra. He was penned up with two llamas, friends from a former life at the Clyde Beatty circus where they used to form a liberty act together with three stallions and a donkey. A liberty act is one in which the animals perform on spoken cue rather than in response to, say, a whip.

All the Commerford animals seem to be in pretty good physical shape. They travel up and down the East Coast from New England to Maryland. Not as good as the Bronx Zoo in New York, or even the Montgomery County Fair in Maryland, but pleasant enough for an afternoon when you've nothing better to do, are loaded with change, crave an outing to a combination amusement park, zoo, and farm, and want the kids to be able to get up close.

JENNIFER CARDEN

The American Humane Association

This is a rare case of getting a lot for a little. For 1 cent (when was the last time you got anything for a penny?) the American Humane Association (P.O. Box 1266, Denver, Colorado 80201) offers "Cats Need Good Care" (or dogs, horses, birds, fish, rabbits) bookmarks that have food and care instructions on the back. For 7 cents there's "The Care of . . . " pamphlets, which give more detailed instruction on the care and maintenance of a pet. For 12 cents there are two-color "Dogs Need Good Care" (or etc.) posters, and for 30 cents there are color cartoon posters featuring the pet of your choice with kindness slogans lettered on them. And if you think that's a bargain, for 75 cents a year you can get for your child, or he can get for his friends, a subscription to the *National Humane Junior Review,* a four-page monthly with photographs, animal stories, crosswords, brain teasers, and interesting tidbits of animal information. Here is an example of a bird-care bookmark.

FLAVIA POTENZA

FOOD: FOOD AND WATER ARE CRITICAL FOR A HEALTHY BIRD. SICKNESS OR DEATH CAN RESULT IF YOUR BIRD IS DEPRIVED OF FOOD OR WATER FOR EVEN ONE DAY.

Basic diet: a high quality, prepared parakeet seed mixture. Also, tidbits of vegetable greens, clover, carrots, celery and fresh fruits. Gravel, cuttlebone and fresh water at all times.

CARE: Cage should be out of drafts, in a lighted area but not in direct sunlight. Clean cage weekly; change paper and gravel daily.

To better care for your pet write for the free pamphlet, THE CARE OF BIRDS:

The American Humane Association
P.O. Box 1266
Denver, Colorado 80201

If you can't afford to make a donation to the ASPCA, you probably can't afford to properly provide for the animal they would give you.

"I Let an 8-Year-old Con Artist Talk Me into Buying Him a Dog"

DEAR ABBY: I am so mad at myself, I don't know what else to do, so I'm writing to Dear Abby!

I let an 8-year-old con artist (my son) talk me into buying him a dog! He cried and begged and promised to take care of it, so like a fool I gave in.

For exactly one week the kid "took care" of his dog. He even got up early to take the dog out. Well, the novelty soon wore off, and now guess who's taking care of the dog? The kid

does the dog a favor and plays with it (in the house) for maybe 10 minutes.

I guess I want to tell other parents that just because a kid begs for a dog doesn't mean he really wants it.

I wish there were a "rent-a-dog" outfit in business somewhere. I'd have rented this pooch first to find out if I really wanted to buy him.

—GROWLING MAD

DEAR GROWLING: Thanks for the tip. Put your kid in the doghouse and try to find a good home for the pooch.

from *Dear Abby* column
New York Post

WATCHING ANIMALS IN THE WILD

A Birdhouse an Eight-Year-Old Can Assemble

If you think a pet makes a nice visitor but not a permanent guest, consider an easy-to-assemble bird house. They come in kits. Assembling one is a nice project for a winter afternoon, and something to have ready for those spring bird visitors. Write to: Gallo Manufacturing Co., 1312 North Memorial Drive, Racine, Wisconsin 53404. Ask for Bird House (or feeder). [The house is just that; the feeder has a "roof" but no walls]. They cost $1.79 each, and an 8-year-old can put one together.

Consumer Action Now Newsletter
(also highly recommended by Gay Lord)

How I Make Bird Feeders

In the winter the birds do not have any food because it is hard to find. That is why I make bird feeders. Here's how I make them:

1. Ask the butcher for any kind of fat except bird fat.
2. Melt it down until it is liquid.
3. While it is cooling, take some cupcake papers and put them in a muffin pan.
4. Cut string into eight-inch lengths, one string for each cup.
5. Put birdseed into the fat and mix it up.
6. Pour the fat and birdseed mixture into the muffin cups, until each cupcake paper is between one-half and three-quarters full. As you do so, hold a piece of string in the middle of each cup.
7. Put cups in the refrigerator or freezer overnight.
8. In the morning remove the papers and tie the seed balls onto a tree.

(I learned this from Mrs. Sweeney and Mrs. Uman of Irvington, New York.)

DAVID GROSS, *age eight*

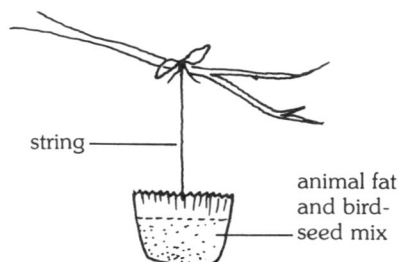

string ———

animal fat
and bird-
seed mix

The Bird Show in My Windowbox

When a bare windowbox stared me in the face this fall, I decided to fill it with birdseed. True, its generous size accommodates squirrels and raccoons as well as cardinals and juncos, sparrows and chickadees; and the bluejays peck away at the sides of the box. But the bird show in my yard is varied and amusing, and a real lift to the spirit on a cold winter day. In another corner of the yard, I've hung a piece of wood with suet-filled holes, and occasionally I stick mealy apples in the nook of an evergreen trunk, all of which makes for good traffic patterns. "Birds are all right," wrote E. B. White to his brother, "except you get practically nothing done, as they make everything else seem so unimportant."

RS

A Backyard Pond

Get an old washtub or bathtub—someone's got one lying around, or they can be bought for a few bucks at a salvage shop. Porcelain or concrete is best, but even a washtub of metal will do for a few years. Dig it into the ground, put some dirt in the bottom, cover with a few inches of water—shallow enough that a kid can't drown in it (or make a removable chicken-wire lid if you must)—and you've got a pond in your yard. I've lived with one most of my life; I think it's a form of worship. This year I put one in at my kid's school, and I go there one afternoon a week to sit beside it and talk to the kids about pond life.

We stock ours with whatever lives locally and fits the climate—half the fun is in going out collecting and in finding out what combinations will live together. Tangles of watercress, algae, and duckweed make it fertile with protozoans and shelter the fry of the fish whose droppings fertilize them. Goldfish are alien and gross; we use small schools of slim mosquitofish, supplied free by the county to put in ponds to eat mosquito larvae. Two newts and a crayfish prowl the clear waters, and a frog waits on an island for flies. (If you get a small turtle, be sure it's certified free from salmonella bacteria.) We have really too many carnivores for the ecology, but the kids drop in extra sow bugs and worms to supplement the lesser populations of water beetles, damselfly nymphs, and snails; and the big bullfrog tadpoles, which take two years to mature, browse on the algae that grows on the sides.

The deepest lesson of the pond is this: the more you watch, the more you see. It is hard to teach a youngster patience, but the pond is a pleasant place to try. In between handling the waterdog or fishing out a nymph to examine, we are still. The fish come out of hiding, darting in synchrony. A snail floats, foot turned up, mouth chewing the air and visible at last. The frog's imitation of a stone pays off, and, too quick to see, his long tongue lashes and a fly-wing dangles from his mouth. To watch the world of the pond is to worship.

MICHAEL ROSSMAN

◆

Books on Pond Life

If you frequent larger ponds that exist quite well without your assistance, Franklin Russell's *Watchers at the Pond* (Knopf, 1961, 241 pages, $8.95 hardcover) is a classic. Russell's writing is as poetic as it is scientific. I should think that an interested nine- or ten-year-old, experienced in pond-watching, could understand most of this re-creation of pond life from one winter through the next.

For straight identification and a description of the gross ecology of a pond, the little Golden Guide *Pond Life* (Golden Press, 1967, 160 pages, $1.95 paperback) is a useful and inexpensive aid.

If you fancy building something more elaborate than the washtub pond Michael Rossman describes above—say a concrete pond for ducks—*How to Build a Pond* (a Nuffield Mathematics Guide; John Wiley & Sons, $3.75 paperback) documents the building of one at an English junior school. The approach is as a math project, with lots of figuring of angles and areas and how many gallons of water the pond holds and how much the water weighs and how much it all costs. The Anglicisms may be confusing, and the size of the book (12 by 8½ inches) unnecessarily cumbersome; but it's a useful prototype from which teachers can work.

Even if you don't have a backyard, you can still have a pond, or at least an insect aquarium. *The Pond on My Windowsill,* written and illustrated by Christopher Reynolds (Pantheon, 1970, 192 pages, $5.99 library edition), is chock-full of information on collecting, maintaining, and studying plants and animals for the indoor pond, all clearly presented in a first-person narrative based on the author's apparently extensive experience.

RS

At every level of existence, constant competition for space and a share of sunlight, oxygen, and moisture made haphazard the lives of all creatures. The pond weeds pushed against each other for space in the shallows: the ones that reached the surface early would survive. The symmetrical lily pads stopped the sun from reaching into the water and so discouraged other plants from following them. The duckweeds were packing their leaves into place throughout the pond, and they prevented most other aquatic plants from getting a share of the surface of the water wherever they grew. Some plants, like cattails, strangled *all* competition. Tree leaves and needles spread in the air to catch as much of the sunlight as possible, making it difficult or impossible for new trees to sprout under them. Despite the pond's show of abundance, its resources were strictly limited. There was plenty of air but not an infinite supply of water in it. There was plenty of water in places, but not an endless supply of warmth and oxygen. There was plenty of sun, but never could it shine on all things equally. All the living things in the pond were racing to get a dominating share of the resources.

FRANKLIN-RUSSELL
Watchers at the Pond

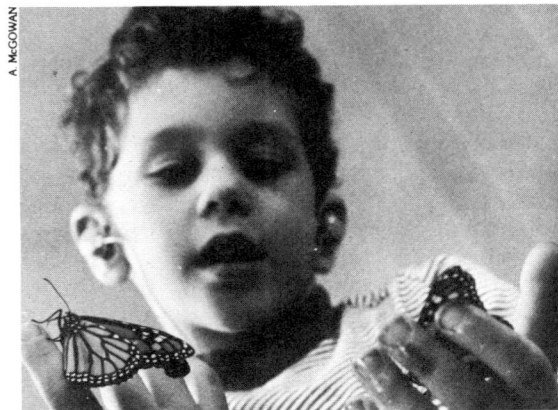

Monarching

We keep trying to give kids a greater sense of the world; what they get is secondhand. We seldom touch their need to experience natural processes, because that must be satisfied firsthand. The stuff that affords these experiences is sometimes so accessible that we overlook it: simple things like a sprouting potato, food changing on the stove, a bird eating at the window—or a Monarch butterfly. The distinction of the Monarch's life cycle is its consolidation of the maturing process into a short space of time and its very visible miracles. Once having been witness, you are led on to repeat the experience and cast about for comparable ones in things you may have been taking for granted.

Year after year in the fall, we watch the Monarch story unfold in our classroom. All you need for this is a willingness to patiently inspect milkweed.

We bring field flowers and Monarch butterflies into a big, walk-in cage in our classroom. When we are lucky, two butterflies mate. The female will then lay eggs on the milkweed. Each is about as big as a pinhead. We can watch through a magnifier, some ten days later, as the young caterpillars hatch—no bigger than snippets of thread. Every day they grow enormously. We measure them on graph paper and with cuisenaire rods. We count the days. In about another ten days, we will find one hanging upside down in the shape of a "J." Checking every few minutes to catch the moment of change, we observe the "J" suddenly begin to gyrate wildly. The caterpillar skin splits and is dropped. The gyrating slows and the chrysalis, or pupa, appears, waxy blue-green embellished with dots of what looks like gold leaf.

We watch as days pass, making observations. About twelve days later, we notice the chrysalis begin to blacken, as one child said, "like a bruised finger." You can see the wing now, someone notices a day or so later. It's perfect, and in miniature. The butterfly emerges finally, fat-bodied and with small wings. Gradually fluids from the body pump into the stretching wings as the butterfly swings gently, hanging from the now transparent chrysalis case.

Next day the children watch the new Monarch in netted cage. There the butterfly lights on the flowers and sips honey-water from the hands of the children.

When we release the Monarchs for their long migratory flight (from New York to perhaps Florida or even Mexico), the children run along under them on the ground until they disappear into the south.

Some experiences change our way of looking at things. One time in midwinter when the Monarchs were long gone, I watched a child arranging his triangular American cheese slices like a butterfly on his lunch plate. And five-year-old Lizzie wrote this poem:

A Monarch was turning into a Chrysalis.
He tried to wiggle, but he couldn't.
One day his chrysalis turned brown.
He was making his wings.
He felt like an orange ball in the sea.

BETTY RADENS

Experiencing the Monarch Butterfly at Home

Look for milkweed. On it look for the characteristic white, black, and yellow striped caterpillar. Then bring the caterpillar inside, along with a handful of milkweed. You can keep the caterpillar in a jar with holes in the lid or a screen top. Replenish the milkweed leaves as needed. When the caterpillar is very fat, it will start to wander about for a place to hang, and will probably choose the jar top. About twelve days after shedding the caterpillar skin, the chrysalis will begin to blacken and you can take the top off and suspend it so the butterfly will have space to spread its wings when it emerges. In a day you may start to handle the Monarch gently. It can be placed on a flower (it actually tastes with its feet) to sip nectar or on a paper towel to eat sugar-water. It needs fresh air, humidity, and light, but shouldn't be left where it can't find shade.

BETTY RADENS

ANIMALS AND HOW KIDS FEEL

Stubby Was a Mongrel

When I was about ten years old, I had a dog I loved named Stubby. One summer I went up to a playmate's cottage with his family for two weeks, and when I got back Stubby was gone. My mother told me that he had run away and that they had got another dog for me. Stubby had been a mongrel, and the new dog, MacGregor, was a thoroughbred—a wire-haired terrier. I hated it on sight, and I knew that Stubby hadn't run away but that my mother had wanted a more fashionable dog and had taken advantage of my absence to get one. I was broken-hearted, and would have nothing to do with Stubby's usurper. But, in time, I took to Mac—all quite secretly; in public I disdained him, but when we were alone we played together. Then, a few months later, my new playmate was killed by a car. No one could understand why I, who would have nothing to do with the dog, cried for three days.

WALTER JERROLD

Chickens I Have Known

We got a dozen chickens every spring, and I got to know them really well. We were really friendly with each other. First of all I went through the whole trip of trying to keep them happy. I'd get bored with the kind of food I was feeding them, so I'd take time to go pick bunches of chickweed and stuff and bring it in and give it to them—something green and fresh. And I'd watch how happy they were when they'd get that; they'd all just jump on it and I'd sit there feeling really good.

Sometimes I'd walk in the door and the chickens would squat down and kind of push their wings up to be scratched. They'd all come over and I'd scratch 'em and pet 'em. That kind of thing. There were times when it sounded so stupid that I thought I'd almost been dreaming, like that couldn't really have been, those chickens coming over to be petted. I must have made that up. But I went to a crafts festival in Addington, Virginia, recently and I was sitting on a porch talking to an old woman who makes baskets, and her daughter and granddaughter were sitting in the corner of the porch. So we're all sitting there and the old woman's making baskets and I'm taking pictures and all of a sudden across the porch comes this great big chicken and walks right straight to that little girl and she reaches out and puts her arm around it and pulls it into her lap and it sits there sort of picking at her ear. And I said sonofabitch.

Another thing about my experience with the chickens was that in the late fall Dad would take me along to my grandmother's to kill her chickens. Chickens that I had known. And he'd hold them by their feet and chop their heads off, and I had to slap the bushel basket over them, while they hopped around inside beating themselves to death. Then we'd hang them up and drip them and take them in to my grandmother so she could pluck them. It was all kind of grim in a way, but not a bad learning experience at all. It's one of the things that rural kids accept as a fact of life and that many urban kids don't ever experience.

ELIOT WIGGINTON

The Death of a Pet

Early one morning I received a telephone call from a friend—the mother of a five-year-old boy. "I'm calling from upstairs," she said in a low voice, "so Greg won't hear this." There was a pause. "Ernest died this morning! What shall I tell Greg?" "How terrible!" I said. "But who is Ernest?" "Ernest is Greg's hamster!" she said. "This will break his heart. I don't know how to tell him. Bill is going to stop off at the pet shop on his way home from work tonight and pick up a new hamster, but I just dread breaking the news to Greg. Please tell me what to say to him." "Why don't you tell him that his hamster died?" I said. "Died!" said my friend, shrinking at my crudity. "What I want to know is how I can break the news gently to him and spare him the pain of this whole experience! I thought I would tell him that Ernest went to heaven. Would it be all right to tell him that?" "Only if you're sure that Ernest went to heaven," I said in my best consulting-room voice. "Oh, stop!" my friend begged. "This is very serious. I don't mean the hamster. I mean this is Greg's first experience with death. I don't want him to be hurt."

"All right," I said. "Then what right do we have to deprive Greg of his feelings? Why isn't he entitled to his grief over the death of his pet?

Why can't he cry and why can't he feel the full measure of pain that comes with the discovery that death is an end and that Ernest is no more?'' ''But he's only a child!'' said my friend. ''How can he possibly know what death means?'' ''But isn't this how he will know what death means? Do we ever know more about death than this—the reaction to the loss of someone loved?''

. . . We need to respect a child's right to experience a loss fully and deeply. This means, too, that we do not bury the dead pet and rush to the pet store for a replacement. This is a devaluation of a child's love. It is like saying to him, ''Don't feel badly; your love is not important; all hamsters, all dogs, all cats are replaceable, and you can love one as well as another.'' But if all loved things are readily replaceable what does a child learn about love or loss? The time for replacing the lost pet is when mourning has done its work and the child himself is ready to attach himself to a new animal.

SELMA FRAIBERG
The Magic Years

◆

Our five-year-old son and four-year-old daughter had a black baby rabbit that died of exhaustion at the age of three weeks. My husband thought a full explanation and funeral were in order. Two hours later, while I was cooking supper, our son suggested digging up the rabbit and cooking it; and two years later, our daughter has taken to sadly announcing that she misses her little black rabbit. I now feel that dead baby rabbits should be ''sent to visit their mother'' while the children are out. My husband violently disagrees with me. I am afraid of dying. He is not.

ANNE NAVASKY

Ceremony: What We Don't Know About Kids

Bing Crosby is said to have told a story about one of his sons at the age of six or so who was inconsolable when his pet turtle died. To distract the boy, Bing suggested that they have a funeral, and his son, seeming only slightly consoled, agreed. The two took a cigar box, lined it carefully with silk, painted the outside black, and then dug a hole in the backyard. Bing carefully lowered the ''coffin'' into the grave, said a long, heartfelt prayer, and sang a hymn. At the end of the service, the boy's eyes were shining with sorrow and excitement. Then Bing asked if he would like to have one last look at his pet before they covered the coffin with earth. The boy said he would, and Bing raised the cigar-box lid. The two gazed down reverently, and suddenly the turtle moved. The boy stared at it for a long time, then looked up at his father and said, ''Let's kill it.''

WALTER JERROLD

[For more about helping kids learn to cope with death, see pages 71–78.]

A Fantasy

I go to sleep wishing desperately for a small animal to have near me, to share my loneliness and my wakedness, and my father's words answer me in the dark: ''An animal, my poor

child! Don't you think life is made difficult enough by people?'' I realize already how much of an intrusion I must be into my parents' separate lives, how much of a drag upon their pleasures. My obsession for something smaller than me to alternately love and torture grows to a crescendo and fixes upon the following fantasy: I am the owner of two small monkeys, which I imprison nightly in a small tight shoebox. They cry stridently until they are on the verge of suffocation, at which point I release them, rescue them from death, and bring them into my bed to pet them, feed them, and enjoy their gratitude. The cognizance of their suffering, my total power over them, the strident whining of their suffocating voices bring me a sensation of delight and power, which I rehearse, almost nightly, between my sixth and ninth year.

FRANCINE DU PLESSIX GRAY
Lovers and Tyrants

BOOKS ABOUT ANIMALS

This section contains reviews of books—fiction and nonfiction—relating to pets and other animals and how they actually live, on the farm or in the wild. More whimsical articles starring members of the animal kingdom are in the BOOK section, which starts on page 239.—Eds.

GREAT PETS, *by Sara B. Stein (Workman Publishing, 1976, 368 pages, $10.95 hardcover; $5.95 paperback).*

To introduce children and parents to "almost every pet a child could care for," Sara Stein has covered an amazing array of animals: from dogs, cats, canaries, and guinea pigs through such arcane companions as ants, boa constrictors, chameleons, flatworms, geckoes, goats, tortoises, and fruit flies.

"The animals included," says the author, "are those that could conceivably be kept, from overnight to permanently, by a child between 3 and 12. Where it's inevitable that parents will have to participate in care, warning is given, and animals that require a lot of care or quite technical equipment are mentioned only to point out the difficulties."

For every animal discussed there's a wealth of information provided; how to house it (including plans for building cages and shelters from such materials as baking pans and tuna fish cans), how to feed it, how to train it (if possible), how to shop for it or catch it in the wild, and so forth.

Perhaps the most appealing feature of the book is the wealth of full-color photographs it contains. (One series of pictures I found particularly instructive shows exactly how much to feed various kinds of animals per day.)
CBC

SYMBIOSIS: *A Book of Unusual Friendships, by Jose Aruego (Scribner's, $3.95).*

This is a delightful book about different kinds of animals that become close friends "in order to help each other." For example, learn why a bird called a plover plucks the food from the crocodile's teeth. (That way the plover gets his dinner and the crocodile gets his teeth cleaned.) Find out, too, why the ostrich and the zebra hang out together. ("The ostrich has very good eyesight, while the zebra has keen hearing. For safety, they often herd together so they can

warn each other when prowling lions are near.")

My son enjoyed the book when he was three, and a friend who is twelve found it fascinating as well.
ELS

GOBBLE, GROWL, GRUNT, *by Peter Spier (Doubleday, 1971, $5.95 hardcover).*

Some six hundred animals, all drawn with care, humor and visual clarity, fly, leap and graze in the pages of this book for preschool children and slightly older readers. The pictures are arranged with good zoological sense. One page takes you to the African veld, another to the deep sea, a third to the night woods, and so on; it is biogeography (or ecology, in the fashionable phrasing). . . .

The animals are noisy; next to each one is some apt phonetic rendering of the sounds it makes. These representations are conventional where that sounds right, as in the bullfrog's *jug o'rum more rum;* unexpected, as in the two-page chorus of seventy-one drab, gregarious starlings murmuring *fee-you* and *sweet, twee and weet,* or absolutely novel, as the *arrrf-arf* of the colorful toucan. . . . There is a hushed page too: the snail, the mute swan, the moth and the condor. . . . No other book this year combines as much observation, helpful pedagogy and sheer fun.
PHILIP AND PHYLIS MORRISON,
Scientific American

THE SHEEP BOOK, *by Carmen Goodyear.*

A farmer comes upon a newborn black lamb in her stable. When the lamb is grown, she shears its wool, cards it and spins it into yarn, then knits the yarn into a sweater.

On a cool spring night she puts on her

sweater and goes to the stable to discover her sheep has in turn given birth to a new lamb.

Children to whom I read this book seemed to find it very satisfying. Of course, I'm pleased with the female farmer, thinking we've all had enough of the farmer in the dell and "farmers' wives" in general.

You can order it from. (I'm really put off by the name) Lollipop Power (A Women's Liberation Collective), P.O. Box 1171, Chapel Hill, N.C. 27514. It costs $2.50 postpaid.

BETTY RADENS

[Some of the best shows on television are about animals. See pages 318, 319.]

PLANTS

Gardening is caught—not taught.
ALICE SKELSEY
and GLORIA HUCKABY
Growing Up Green

233

GARDENING WITH YOUR CHILD

Growing Up Green

"No other form of gardening can quite produce the remarkable satisfaction that comes from working with the land and bringing from it food for your own table," write Alice Skelsey and Gloria Huckaby in *Growing Up Green* (Workman, 1973, 204 pages, $4.95 paperback). Their book is full of good ideas about planting (everything—especially *every* kind of seed that you've been throwing away), collecting (little bits of our environment), and cooking with your child. The authors make it quite clear that you needn't be an old-time farmer to appreciate, and participate in nature, indoors and out. (Unfortunately, the book is hard to use because there is no index and the material is loosely organized; cross-referencing within the text helps, but not enough.)

There are lots of suggestions for projects parents and kids can do together and many that kids can do alone. For small garden plots, the authors recommend single-purpose gardens: a salad garden; or a Mediterranean garden with tomatoes, eggplant, green peppers, Italian squash, and onions. Or a Chinese garden with Chinese celery, cabbage, snowpeas, leeks, white radishes, cucumbers, bok choy, and coriander. Or even a circus garden with peanuts and corn (for popcorn). One of their best ideas: take a day off to celebrate a beautiful day—keep your child out of school and enjoy the things that grow and change.

ELS

◆

TWO IDEAS FROM *GROWING UP GREEN*

The Avocado

About the largest seed you'll come across in the kitchen is the avocado. . . . It surely must be the subject of more how-to instructions for impromptu gardening than any other seed. Here is all there is to it:

When the seed is removed from the avocado, it is covered with a rather thick brown skin. It doesn't matter whether you leave this on or take it off. Just insert three toothpicks at about equal distance around the "waist" of the avocado seed. Place it pointed-end up in a glass of water and suspend it from the rim by the toothpicks.

Keep the water level in the glass high enough so that the bottom of the seed is always covered, adding water as it evaporates. . . . (Adding a few pebbles of charcoal to the water discourages slimy happenings.)

As for how long it takes the seed to root, that's anybody's guess. Occasionally you will find an avocado with a seed almost at the sprouting stage. Other seeds will take a week or so to send down a root, and still others will sit in the glass week after week until the seed finally splits apart and the root emerges.

Next, a green shoot slowly emerges from the top of the seed, and after it reaches about 1 inch, things begin to move along at a faster pace. In a few days the shoot will be 3 or 4 inches tall, and the seed can be potted up.

Avocados can't take cold temperature, but they do quite nicely in the house with ordinary house-plant care. The avocado will head straight for the ceiling unless you or the children intervene. If you decide you would prefer a bushier plant, then pluck up your courage and when the avocado is a couple of feet high, whack off about one third of it. It will take a while, but new growth will appear along the sides of the stalk, and the plant will be off and growing again, and this time branching out instead of simply up.

Living Christmas Trees

Children—even from toddler stage—love having their "own" Christmas tree, one they can keep in their special place and decorate and undecorate as much as they wish, and any way they wish. So why not make their small tree a living one, and make it one that can grow up indoors right along with them? (Many families have already discovered the pleasure and advantages of making the *family* Christmas tree a living one and planting it outdoors after the holidays are over.)

Nothing will suit so well for an indoor Christmas tree as a Norfolk Island pine. These lovely, graceful plants can be purchased when they are only inches high, and can be found (not all the time, so keep an eye out for them) in discount, supermarket and dime stores as well as elegant nurseries. In fact, the small size is more likely to be found in the dime stores and such. They're inexpensive at that point and are a real bargain.

The pyramidal shape of the pine means that your youngster will have no trouble at all relating to this "house plant" as a Christmas tree, too. When he is old enough to manage them, a string of tiny sparkle lights as well as miniature ornaments he can collect or make himself will provide all the glitter he wants.

As the years go by, your investment in the tree grows, too. The toddler who starts out with a tiny tree costing under $1 will find himself as a teenager with a plant worth as much as $30 to $40. And priceless for you both as far as memories go.

ALICE SKELSEY and GLORIA HUCKABY
Growing Up Green

A Paper-Cup Grapefruit Orchard

The next time you and your family eat grapefruit, or oranges or lemons, why not plant some of the seeds and start an indoor "orchard." Simply punch a few holes in the bottom of a paper cup (for drainage), fill the cup almost to the top with soil (for best results, add a small proportion of sand and peat moss), pour on a few seeds, cover with a half-inch of soil, press down the dirt a bit, pour on some water (in continuous small doses, until some begins to trickle out the bottom of the cup), put the cup in the window and wait.

When the soil seems dry, water it a bit the same way you did the first time. Within two weeks (if you're lucky) you'll be rewarded by a sprout or two, perhaps more.

When (and if) the plants appear, they'll need lots of light. Keep them watered, too, but don't overdo it. Before long, you'll probably want to transplant your young sprouts to genuine pots. But, unless you live in a warm climate, don't expect to end up with fruit-producing trees.

CBC

Instant Flowers for Impatient Gardeners

If your kids are excited by the idea of watching things grow but too impatient to wait for results, then a variety of water lily known as colchicum (*kahl*-chi-kum) may solve their problem. All you have to do is wait till August, cover a colchicum bulb with three inches of soil, and, ten days or so later, a whole bouquet of huge flowers will pop out. (They will, that is, if Bebe Miles, writing in *Ranger Rick's Nature Magazine,* is to be believed.)

"These big bulbs are so eager to blossom," Bebe tells us, "that if you forget to plant them, they will flower right in the paper bag." Make sure you plant them right away, therefore. (Two more reasons to do so: the bulbs are poisonous and shouldn't be around for a kid to put in his mouth; also they will not survive if not given a chance to root.)

Colchicum bulbs—available in most garden supply shops—bloom perennially, so your family can enjoy them year after year. What are you waiting for?

[Answer: August!—ELS]

CBC

(This project, like the preceding one, comes from *Ranger Rick's Nature Magazine,* and is based on an article by Frances M. Miner of the Brooklyn Botanic Garden.)

CBC

[*Ranger Rick's Nature Magazine* is published by the National Wildlife Federation, 1412 Sixteenth Street, N.W., Washington, D.C. 20036.]

A Gardening Book That Allows for Failure

Although *How to Grow a Jelly Glass Farm,* by Kathy Mandry and Joe Toto (Pantheon, 1974, $4.50 hardcover), won an American Institute of Graphic Arts award for its illustrations, it is the text that is notable for its simple charm and humor. It suggests planting grass seeds in an old sneaker, "but don't let anybody walk in it." Instructions for planting sunflowers are given with the warning: "Be nice to this plant. In just a few months it could be bigger than you." But what is special about this book (and what is lacking in other, more serious plant books) is that it allows

for failure, and very matter-of-factly. From a pine cone, for example, "in less than a month you should have your own Christmas tree sprout. But if nothing happens, decorate the pot." Or: "You have to trick these [citrus] seeds into thinking they're home in the tropics [give them lots of sun and "a rainstorm when they feel dry"] or they won't grow at all. . . . Not every seed will believe you and sprout. But in two weeks you'll find out just how many fruits you can fool." Excerpts follow.

ELS

JELLY GLASS FARM

Stuff a yam half in and half out of a
jelly glass with a big mouth.
Make sure the fatter side is up.
Pour some water into the glass.
Make sure the water always touches the yam.
Yams can get very thirsty.
In about a week, roots will start to grow down
and shoots will grow up.
In about six weeks, the vine should be
about a foot long.
Put it next to something it can climb on.
If it climbs too high, trade it in for a cow.

FEATHER IN YOUR CAP

When your teeth crunch on a piece of carrot,
the carrot top can't be far away.
Find it.
Plant it with its round side up in a saucer full of
bird gravel or pebbles or potting sand.
But don't use sand from the beach.
The salt in it will make your plant sick.
Keep it moist.
In a few days, roots will grow down and
carrot leaves will start to feather out.
Carrot leaves don't taste too good.
But you can always invite a rabbit home for lunch.

KATHY MANDRY and JOE TOTO
How to Grow a Jelly Glass Farm

Room to Grow In

If you're interested in nurturing a garden but don't have any land, send for a copy of *Gardens for All* (P.O. Box 164, Charlotte, Vt. 05445), a free pamphlet describing ten community gardening projects in different parts of the country, some offering over 500 individual 15-by-30-foot plots. One even raises fish as well as greens. If you want to find out about a free community garden in your area, or perhaps start one through your parks commission, neighborhood, school, church, or place of employment, this nonprofit organization wants to help you.

RS

When a group decides it would like to lease a particular city lot for a garden, here is the procedure to be followed, according to community garden specialists:

Note the names of all streets that surround the lot, and the numbers of the adjoining houses.

Go to the Real Estate Registry . . . (listed in telephone directories) and consult the map that gives block, lot and index or parcel numbers. Then, from the Deed Index, find the name of the deedholder; or contact the owner through the lawyer listed on the deed.

If the lot is city-owned, a letter should be written to the Commissioner, Department of Real Estate . . . Describe the project planned; give block, lot and index or parcel numbers.

The lease for the lot should be in writing.

Before proceeding with any work, it is advisable that the group obtain "third person" liability insurance. *The New York Times*

OKAY, SO THE STUFF GREW.
NOW WHAT DO WE DO WITH IT?

Green Fun

Maryanne Gjersvik bills her photograph-filled book *Green Fun* (Chatham Press, 1974, 80 pages, paperback) as a collection of "instant toys, tricks and amusements anyone can make from common weeds, seeds, leaves and flowering things." And that's exactly what it is: for $1.95, Ms. Gjersvik tells you how to make finger puppets out of acorns, dolls out of cornhusks and hollyhocks, sailboats out of milkweed pods, a whistle from a blade of grass (this last takes skill, though: I never *could* master it*), and much more. Two samples of her wisdom follow.

                                                    CBC

   * ELS did, though.

A GRASS WHISTLE

You can make a very loud whistling squawk using only a wide blade of grass. Hold the grass with two hands between the tips and the base of both thumbs. With your lips against the space just below your thumb knuckles, blow very hard into your hands and onto the blade of grass. Be sure the grass is stretched tightly across the inside of the opening.

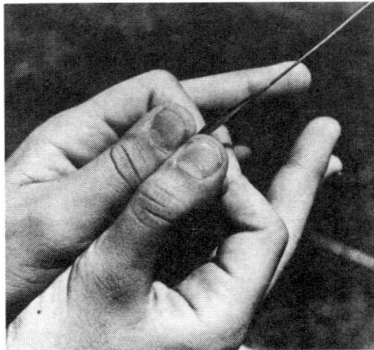

Though some people can never make a sound, I have a friend who tells me that her father is able to play the beginning of *"My Country 'tis of Thee"* on a blade of grass.

A MAPLE LEAF CROWN

A summer crown of green maple leaves is something special.

Break the stems off each leaf and save them to use as pins. Put the first two leaves down so that they overlap. Push a single stem pin through the center rib of both. Keep adding more leaves and pins in the same way until you

have a band long enough to reach around the head. When the size is right, connect the first leaf to the last with still another stem pin and your crown is ready to wear.

                                    MARYANNE GJERSVIK
                                              Green Fun

Making Your Own
Vegetable Dyes

Dyes don't have to be purchased at the store in little brown bottles. They come from plants. A class I visited last year had an assortment of colored yarns hung around their room, the subtleties of which were the game of nine-year-olds. They got some of their ideas from *Foxfire 2* (Anchor, 1974, $4.50 paperback), which told them how people used to boil down walnut hulls, hickory bark, pokeberries, and the like in iron pots, and used vinegar and salt as a mordant to fix the dye and keep it from fading. More straightforward in its how-to advice, and the best book on natural dyestuffs around, according to Phylis Morrison, is *Dye Plants and Dyeing* (Pamphlet number 46, $1.75 from Brooklyn Botanic Garden, 1000 Washington Avenue, Brooklyn, N.Y. 11225).

                                                    RS

LEARNING ABOUT THE PLANT WORLD

Pea Plants Make Perfect Teachers

Mature pea plants are priceless; for two-year-olds whose grasp of time is still weak they display every stage from tiny flower bud to heavy-bodied pod, simultaneously, in strict sequence along the climbing stems.   MICHAEL ROSSMAN
Saturday Review

Beyond Xylem and Phloem

The very same people who sell you plant food and insect poisons also put out some good gardening guides. *A Child's Garden: A Guide for Parents and Teachers,* from Chevron Chemical Company, Public Affairs Department, 575 Market Street, San Francisco, Calif. 94105, 50 cent paperback, is particularly interesting, since it provides clear explanations about the whole system of a plant, complete with do-it-yourself experiments. So many of the other child-oriented books never take you beyond using red food coloring to delineate xylem and phloem in carrots. But this one does. (Example: a way of observing the properties of auxin, the hormone concentrated at the growing tip, which causes the plant to branch when pinched back at the tip.)   RS

THE URGE TO IDENTIFY

It's lovely to have your own nature guides, so they will be around when you or your kids want to refer to them. Better than running to the library when you're stuck with the impulse to identify. Below are some good titles.

Identifying Trees and Shrubs

The Tree Identification Book, by George W. Symonds (Barrows, 1973, $16.95 hardcover; Morrow, $6.95 paperback) is wonderful. You can identify a tree by looking up virtually any one thing about it—its seeds, bark, leaves, flowers, twigs. And the book is thumb-indexed, making it easy to use. Also available is *The Shrub Identification Book,* by George W. Symonds (Barrows, 1963, $16.95 hardcover; Morrow, $6.95 paperback).
PHYLIS MORRISON

Do You Know What You're Eating? (This Book Will Tell You)

The Oxford Book of Food Plants, by G. B. Masefield, M. Wallis, S. G. Harrison, and B. E. Nicholson (Oxford University Press, 1969, 214 pages, $16.95 hardcover), would be a wonderful gift for a child who is interested in the world of cooking and planting. It is full of information (not how-to, but of origins and geographical distribution and nutritional value), with color illustrations. It lets you see, for example, the different varieties of cucumbers and gherkins, how they grow on the vine, and what their flowers look like. Coffee beans, watermelons, peas and lentils—the life cycle of every food you eat is here.
RS

And, for You City Dwellers With a Weakness for Weeds . . .

Plant books that are city-oriented are rare, but Anne Ophelia Dowden's *Wild Green Things in the City: A Book of Weeds* (Crowell, 1972, $8.50 hardcover) is one that you can take to the curbside where a plant is stubbornly growing in a crack, look at one of her drawings in the book, which shows the plants in their "natural" settings (amid bottle caps and matchbooks), and know the author really understands. The illustrations are clear enough to enable you to identify plants, in some cases through several seasons, and yet the drawings are not "clinical"; they leave the plants with their dignity.
JO BUTLER

[For a review of Golden Books' excellent field and nature guides, turn to page 218 in the SCIENCE section.]

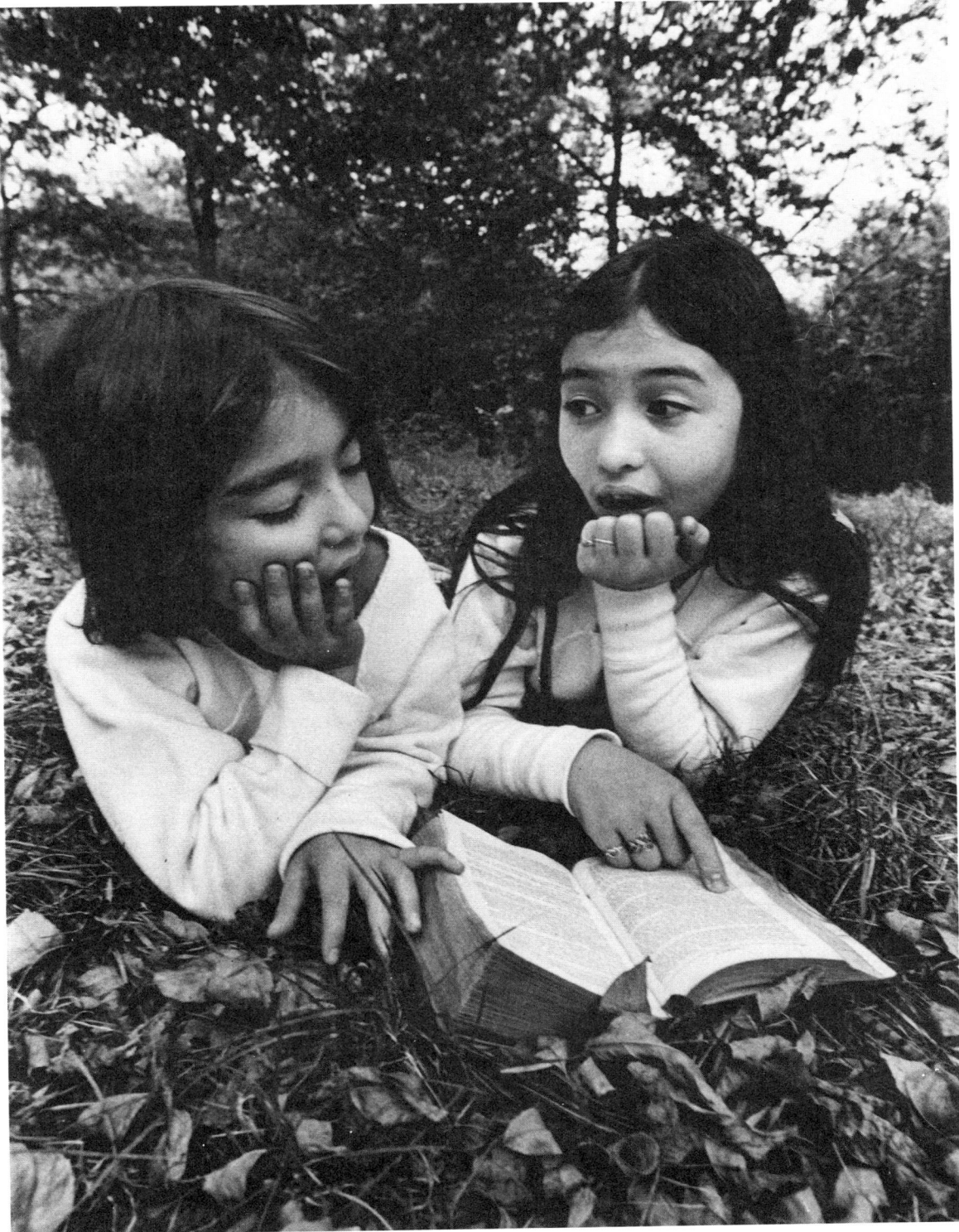

RICHARD HUTCHINGS

CHILDREN'S BOOKS:
HOW SHOULD THEY BE WRITTEN?
DO WE NEED THEM AT ALL?

I don't like what is known as children's literature; I don't recognize its validity. Children should be given only what is suitable for adults as well. Children enjoy reading Andersen, The Frigate Pallada, and Gogol, and so do adults. One shouldn't write for children; one should learn to choose works suitable for children from among those already written for adults—in other words, from genuine works of art. It is better and more to the point to learn to choose the correct medicine and to prescribe the correct dosage than to try to dream up some special medicine just because the patient is a child.

ANTON CHEKHOV
Letters of Anton Chekhov

◆

"A Good Book Cannot Be Written for a Particular Age"

I strongly believe that a new look needs to be taken at the whole idea of children's books; that the necessity for having them at all needs at least to be questioned. I am not referring to books for the illiterate under-fives, and have no criticism to make of them beyond the fact that publishers and authors seem to think that the smaller the child, the larger the book must be— for what reason, since their arms are short and their eyesight usually at its best, it is hard to imagine. But once these tasteful if unwieldy volumes have lost their charm, the child begins to be given novels which are intended to mirror what psychiatrists and school teachers call "the child's world." These are frequently sold with time limits stamped on them, like cream cheese or Kodak film—to be read between the ages of 10 and 13, with no suggestion that this is roughly speaking. These books are, of course, written by adults, usually selected by adults, paid for by adults, published and printed and reviewed by adults. . . .

The fact that seems to have been overlooked is simply that a good book cannot possibly be written for a particular age, sex, creed, or colour—if it is, the motive and the execution must be dishonest, and the result spurious. *Black Beauty* and *The Secret Garden* are more intelligent, even sophisticated, than the average women's magazine story; *Tom Sawyer* and *Huckleberry Finn* can be enjoyed by any fairly bright executive wanting a bit of escapism between ulcers. It is as foolish to confine these books to the nursery shelves as it is to assume that your ten-year-old is incapable of enjoying Colette or Kingsley Amis.

PENELOPE MORTIMER
"Thoughts Concerning Children's Books"
New Statesman

You Have to Write Up, Not Down

Anyone who writes *down* to children is simply wasting his time. You have to write up, not down. Children are demanding. They are the most attentive, curious, eager, observant, sensitive, quick, and generally congenial readers on earth. They accept, almost without question, anything you present them with, as long as it is presented honestly, fearlessly, and clearly. I handed them, against the advice of experts, a mouse-boy, and they accepted it without a quiver. In *Charlotte's Web,* I gave them a literate spider, and they took that.

Some writers for children deliberately avoid using words they think a child doesn't know. This emasculates the prose and, I suspect, bores the reader. Children are game for anything. I throw them hard words, and they backhand them over the net. They love words that give them a hard time, provided they are in a context that absorbs their attention. I'm lucky again: my own vocabulary is small, compared to most writers, and I tend to use the short words. So it's no problem for me to write for children. We have a lot in common.

E. B. WHITE
"The Art of the Essay"
Paris Review

A Freeman and an Equal

We must write for children out of those elements in our own imagination which we share with children: differing from our child readers not by any less, or less serious, interest in the things we handle, but by the fact that we have other interests which children would not share with us. . . .

Once in a hotel dining-room I said, rather too

loudly, "I loathe prunes." "So do I" came an unexpected six-year-old voice from another table. Sympathy was instantaneous. Neither of us thought it funny. We both knew that prunes are far too nasty to be funny. That is the proper meeting between man and child as independent personalities. Of the far higher and more difficult relations between child and parent or child and teacher, I say nothing. An author, as a mere author, is outside all that. He is not even an uncle. He is a freeman and an equal, like the postman, the butcher, and the dog next door.

C. S. LEWIS
"On Three Ways of Writing for Children"

◆

Dream Sources

I'm an artist who does books that are apparently more appropriate for children than for anyone else, for some odd reason. I never set *out* to do books for children—I *do* books for children, but I don't know why. And, to me, the greatest writers—like the greatest illustrators—for children are those who draw upon their child sources, their dream sources—they don't forget them. There's William Blake, George MacDonald, Dickens . . . that peculiar charm of being in a room in a Dickens novel, where the furniture is alive, the fire is alive, where sauce-pans are alive, where chairs move, where every inanimate object has a personality.

There's Henry James, whom I would call a children's book writer, why not? He would have dropped dead if you had said that to him, but his all-absorbing interest in children and their relationships to adults creates some of his greatest stories. Just the way he allows children to stay up and see what the grown-ups are really doing. In *What Maisie Knew,* children are constantly mixing in the most deranged adult society, and they're permitted to view and morally judge their elders. It's like a fantasy come true. It's like Mickey not wanting to go to sleep in order to see what goes on in the Night Kitchen. James' children stay up at night, too. Maisie hardly says anything, but we all know what she knows, and we see her know it.

Finally, there's Herman Melville. . . . It's the two levels of writing—one visible, one invisible—that fascinate me most about Melville. As far down as the whale goes in the water is as deep as Herman writes—even in his early works like *Redburn,* which is one of my favorite books. The young man coming to England for the first time . . . I swear, I'll never forget that walk he takes in the English countryside. There's a mystery there, a clue, a nut, a bolt, and if I put it together, I find me.

MAURICE SENDAK
quoted by Jonathan Cott
Rolling Stone

BOOKS FOR THE VERY YOUNG

I think there is nothing pleasanter or cozier than parents and children sitting down and reading a book together. It seems sad to suppose that there are a lot of parents who don't ever do that with their kids. I am most happy when I produce a work that appeals to both parents and children at the same time and for the same reasons.

ARNOLD LOBEL

◆

A Taste For Third-Class Mail

My son has two shelves full of books carefully selected to Enrich His Inner Landscape. I admit I wanted to control him, give him a "taste" for good literature before he was three, and that I used to be fairly rigid about reading to him; I tended to discourage him from choosing a book for bedtime that didn't appeal to me. What I discovered, however, by watching my own mother, who hates to say no to a request her grandson makes, is that you can read *anything* to a very young child and make it interesting. Example: anything that has pictures in it is a perfect conversation starter—magazines, mail-order catalogues, junk mail. If it doesn't have pictures, you can always talk about the letters—or even about the punctuation with a child who's up to that. The point is that if you're sitting with the kid, being loving and warm and relaxed, nearly anything you read will be suitable. As long as you're not trying to teach him how to punctuate a sentence properly, but simply showing what a question mark or an exclamation point is, the child will be quite content.

ELS

Where, When, and How You Read is Important

I think a lot of things have to be working together if a child is fully going to enjoy being read to—the right reader, the right book, the right time, the right circumstances. So many things have to go together to have a bit of perfection. Books are read at night sometimes, when a kind of tiredness has overcome us all, and something is lost. And don't take a children's book to Coney Island and expect you're going to have a successful reading session there on the beach on a golden Sunday afternoon. It just doesn't work that way.

From an interview with GEORGE WOODS

Read-Aloud Records Starring *You*

When *Sesame Street* writer David Korr was a child, his parents used to tape-record themselves reading David's favorite stories aloud; then whenever they had to go out for dinner, they'd leave a reel or two, along with the appropriate books, in the hands of David's baby-sitter.

David's mother and father didn't consider these recordings a substitute for reading aloud in person to their son, but the tapes were a thoughtful way of showing their child that they weren't abandoning him, just because they didn't take him with them *every* time they left the house. (And, to be honest, the recordings *did* come in handy when David asked them to read the same story for the seventh time in a row.)

If you have a cassette tape recorder, you may want to try out the Korr system yourself. You can make a separate cassette for each book and file it away for future use. Or mail one home if you're away on business or on vacation.

There's lots of room for creativity when you make your tapes. You can add sound effects or musical backgrounds. You can make a buzzing or beeping sound when it's time to turn the page, thus making it easier for your kid to read right along with you. Or you can include your child in the recording session, as a consultant, as an actor, or as a sound-effects specialist.

CBC

A Story Someone Made Up

A picture of the author on the book jacket of a children's book helps my child think of the story as one which someone made up and someone drew pictures for. Don't overlook the author's picture when there is one; if there isn't, just reading the author's and illustrator's names can help.

ELS

BEDTIME STORIES

"Good Night, Hilary"

There are many kinds of books to read at bedtime, but one kind is the book that deals specifically with bedtime. Although going to bed happens nightly no matter where you live, I became aware that "The right book for the right child at the right time" adage certainly applied in this seemingly universal area. The bedtime book needs to suit each household and each particular child. In our home we have found a few titles particularly appropriate.

Part of our "night-lite library" is a small book called *Good Night Little ABC* by Robert Kraus (Springfellow/Dutton). [*Good Night Little ABC* and *Good Night Richard Rabbit* are available back to back, upside down in paperback from Windmill/Dutton.] It's a rather playful tongue-twisting alphabet book whose theme is going to bed. The reason it is so popular in our house-hold is that for the letter "H," the rhyme uses our daughter's name:

> "Good Night Little H
> Hilary Haggerty Hedgehog
> Good Night Little H"

Hilary was just beginning to identify letters when this book came into our home. "H" was the first letter she recognized, but she was confused with the small letter "h." This little book prominently identifies the upper and lower case of each letter on the same page. Furthermore, everyone in the book is dressed in pajamas and it is obviously time to go to bed in *Good Night Little ABC*.

A participation night time book is *Hush Little Baby*, illustrated by Aliki (Prentice). Even though we can hardly carry a tune, we all join in singing this old lullaby. Lest we all get too excited in our bedtime singing, the last two illustrations in the book show a colonial household with a child being tucked in bed by mother.

Other portions of the book also fit our family life. The father in the book, as in our family, must often be away from home on business. The father appears as a bearer of gifts when he returns from these trips, and Hilary can identify her family experience with those in the book.

For those times when we don't need a quiet night time book, Pat Hutchins' *Good-Night Owl!* (Macmillan) brings a little laughter into the bedtime ritual. It is a rollicking, rhythmic, repetitive story with a burst-of-laughter type surprise ending. We imitate the singing birds; we identify the birds, which are illustrated clearly and simply; and we count the birds as they appear in the story. . . .

Luckily for Hilary, she has not experienced nightmares, and so her reaction to *There's a Nightmare in My Closet*, by Mercer Mayer (Dial) is that it is a "funny monster." She feels sorry for the nightmare when it begins to cry, as was Mercer Mayer's intent for us. We hope she will be less frightened when she has a bad dream.

Milton, The Early Riser, by Robert Kraus (Windmill/Dutton) sounds like a getting up book—and it is, for children who get up too early and wake the household. It's also a good night book because everyone is asleep in the book until the end when everyone wakes up and then Milton falls asleep. Even if Hilary insists on missing the point, it's still an amusing bedtime book.

The perfect night time book for our home, and no doubt many homes, is the classic *Goodnight Moon,* by Margaret Wise Brown (Harper). It's a quiet game saying good night to countless objects. It involves looking for the mouse in the pictures, identifying objects in the "great green room" of the book and in our own room. It is true the pictures are not lavish, but each object is identified in text and picture and the room in the book gets darker and darker as the good nights continue. At last Hilary announces of the bunny "She's sleeping"—and she is, while the mouse looks out at the moon and stars, and now Hilary is also going to sleep.

I can hardly wait to read *Bedtime for Frances* by Russell Hoban (Harper), *Hildilid's Night* by Cheli Durán Ryan (Macmillan), *Bunk Beds* by Elizabeth Winthrop (Harper) and share *A Sleepless Day* by John Hamberger (Four Winds) with a slightly older little girl. In the meantime,

Good Night, Hilary.
CAROLINE FELLER BAUER
The Children's Book Council *Calendar*

How to Turn *Any* Book into a Goodnight Book

Simple. When you get to the end of the story, say goodnight to everyone (and everything) pictured on that last page: goodnight owl, goodnight pussycat, goodnight palm tree, goodnight sea, sand, and moon, goodnight boat, goodnight conch shell. And you tuck your little cutie in with a kiss and wish him goodnight, too. (With thanks to Margaret Wise Brown, who made it okay to say goodnight to the moon and other inanimate objects.)

ELS

◆

Have a Few Dwarfs

I once told Jason a terrific bedtime story. It was called "Snow White and the Hundred Dwarfs." If your kid won't fall asleep and you think a story might help, try this one:

"Once upon a time a girl named Snow White knocked on the door of a little cottage in the woods. And who do you think lived inside? Some dwarfs! And their names were Doc . . . and Sneezy . . . and Sleepy . . . and Bashful . . . and Dopey . . . and Sleepy . . . and Happy . . . and Sleepy . . . and Florence . . . and Sleepy . . . and Philip . . . and Sleepy . . . and Standish . . . and Sleepy . . . and Henry . . . and Alfred . . . and Sleepy . . . and Elizabeth . . . and Sleepy . . ."

And so on. My husband fell asleep on about the thirteenth dwarf. Jason lasted until eighty-three.

EMILY PERL KINGSLEY

Four Books to Fall Asleep Over

HILDILID'S NIGHT, *by Cheli Durán Ryan, illustrated by Arnold Lobel (a Caldecott Honor Book, Collier Books, paperback, 1974, 95 cents).*

In *Hildilid's Night*, Cheli Durán Ryan and Arnold Lobel have collaborated to excellent purpose (their characterization of an old lady who spits at the night because she loves the sun is particularly marvelous).

There's nothing sentimental about *Hildilid's Night*. But it reads like a remembered classic, with a fine, galloping rhythm that leads us to a splendid good night at the end. A real bedtime story (and the price is right—95 cents).

SHERMAN DREXLER

THE SOMETHING, *by Natalie Babbitt (Farrar, Straus & Giroux, 1970, $2.95).*

Mylo is afraid of Something coming in his window at night. His mother explains away ghosts and robbers, but that's not what Mylo's afraid of. The fear is finally overcome when Mylo creates a statue of the Something out of modeling clay. That's not a bad idea for chasing away fears, especially when you have a Natalie Babbitt story and drawings to suggest it.

RS

DREAMS, *by Ezra Jack Keats (Macmillan, 1974, $5.95 hardcover).*

With *Dreams*, writer-illustrator Ezra Jack Keats returns to his familiar inner-city story of *Hi! Cat, The Snowy Day, Goggles,* etc. *Dreams* is a vibrantly illustrated book, which shares with us young Roberto's experiences one night when he knew or felt that everyone was dreaming but he. My three-year-old started talking about her dreams after we read this. And she also began to notice shadows. A young child can understand what a dream is, when it happens, and why it happens. With this book Keats once again has demonstrated his ability to relate poetically and graphically the everyday experiences of children.

MARIE BROWN

DR. SEUSS'S SLEEP BOOK *(Random House, 1962, $3.95 hardcover).*

From "a very small bug by the name of Van Vleck" (who "is yawning so wide you can look down his neck") to Snorter McPhail and his Snore-a-Snort Band (who "snore in a cave twenty miles out of town. If they snored closer in, they would snore the town down"), a myriad of improbable Seussian creatures nod, doze, and sleepwalk their way through the pages of this book. It's an energetic child indeed who isn't ready to turn out the light at the end of *Dr. Seuss's Sleep Book.* After all, "They're even asleep in the Zweiback Motel! And people don't usually sleep there too well."

CBC

NON-BOOKS AND GIMMICKS

Non-Books: Alan Saperstein Likes Them . . .

My child was going to have the head start I never had—an honest-to-goodness preface to life: Alice in Wonderland, Gulliver's Travels, Original Mother Goose with etchings by Gustav Doré, Lamb's Tales from Shakespeare, Oscar Wilde's Fables, all the literary primers I never saw till high school and college. I was going to spoon-read my son fantasy after proven fantasy on the supposition that a kid likes whatever he gets until he's old enough to compare. And while that supposition is undoubtedly true, comparisons are made much earlier than you'd guess. In fact, immediately.

The trick is that kids don't compare like things. So it's not a question of one book's being as good as another book. It's a question of one book's being as good as any other good thing in the child's experience.

As it turns out, when you're two or three, pudding is a very good thing. It looks good, it feels good, it smells good, and it tastes sublime.

Presumably, things that can live up to pudding are better than things that can live up to Edmund Wilson.

I know this because whatever I give my son he immediately turns into pudding. Not out of maliciousness or ignorance, but out of natural self-indulgence and impatience. Television has already made him feel a range of emotions it took his father twenty years to transliterate into a visceral alphabet of powerful feelings. And television has got him used to having his heart bounced around and his eyeballs popped by constant, disconnected information. These feelings of his are so easily grasped, so addictive, and so sensational that cerebral work has become just that—work.

Whatever your feelings about the death of literature and the so-called inanity of electronic media, it is easier to learn these days than it ever has been, and that's what I call progress. Happily or unhappily, no one has been able to obviate the real work—what you do with what you learn. But right now there's as much work involved in watching and listening and smelling and touching and tasting *Sesame Street* as there is in devouring pudding. The two phenomena are nearly identical. They're both protean, both spookily alive to the senses, both smoothly hypnotic, and both the ultimate in palatability. On the other hand, literature is rigid, hieroglyphic, non-seductive, and unappetizingly lumpy until translated into pictures or song.

It may sound as though I'm against books altogether or that I view them as obsolete or that I don't want them to say anything terribly inventive. The truth is my love for books causes me to root like hell for them to make a comeback, to do whatever they can to be as good as pudding and still maintain their traditional specialness as a ready source of imaginative stimulation. Consequently I was delighted to find that some publishers with an apparently keen appreciation for the importance of physically involving children in learning and of entertaining them (the greatest teaching method of them all) have put titles and bindings on pudding. And these "books," as I go on calling them, are far more valuable to pre-school-age children than Lewis Carroll's ageless prose.

Consider the pop-up book. Can a metaphor, a simile, can any great writer's greatest conceit in any way approach the dimension and impact of a picture that actually springs off the page, or moves as you move a lever, or gains color and life as you dial a cellophane tint over it? Can a word look so wonderful? Can it feel so good and real in the hand? Can it scare you or tickle you so quick? Ask your little Puddinhead.

Consider also the books with finger holes cut through them. On page one is an elephant with a hole where the trunk belongs. By sticking his finger through the hole the child has completed the information as no word could, as no picture could, as only his mind-wiggling little pinky could. Likewise his fingers become a puppy's legs, a clown's dancing feet, a gorilla's arms, and so on.

Then there are bathtub books. These float and absorb water and wring out dry again and behave like the seals and otters they depict. There are outsized books, touch-me books with sandpaper beards and string hair, books you can scratch a scent out of with your fingernail, pictures that reverse themselves like venetian blinds, eyes that follow you across the page, cows that moo, chicks that peep, jackets with real buttons, shoes with real laces. Some books even celebrate the classics, though many would think they debase them instead. But when Pinocchio's nose grows in fact as well as in print, that to me is cause to celebrate. Because that to

my son is pure pudding. And the object I think is not to prepare him for a literary life, but to prepare him for his life, whatever shape it takes.

So I like and I keep buying and I recommend these very unliterary books, these unorthodox pages of pudding. If the stories are profound or benignly traumatic, so much the better. If not, none the worse. If my child won't tolerate the slowness and illusoriness of verbal drama, it is not that he is dumb and it is not a warning that he will grow illiterate and non-expressive. It is only that he is very much alive and very much frustrated by a medium which is not quick enough, complete enough, powerful enough, and easy enough to satisfy his throbbing sense of reality.

ALAN SAPERSTEIN

While pop-ups may be to literature what Broadway musical comedy is to Ibsen, every child ought to experience at least one of these seductive productions. (*The Night Before Christmas* at [$3.95 from Random House] is probably the most magical of them all.)

SELMA G. LANES
Down the Rabbit Hole

◆

. . . and Fredelle Maynard Doesn't

The first thing to observe of many eye-catching newcomers is that they are not books at all. They are, in Jason Epstein's fine contemptuous phrase, "nursery fixtures made of paper." Consider, for example, *The Giant Comes to Town* by Michael Twinn, a Rand McNally Super-Giant book. Four feet high, weighing about five pounds (taller than most bookcases), it stands on the floor of juvenile book departments, a trap for indulgent uncles in search of a different gift. The child who crouches before this volume (no child could possibly *hold* it) can read all about the unkempt giant who's not allowed to play until he gets a haircut, takes a bath, dresses neatly and eats his dinner. "Now the giant looked so nice that he looked just like you." This mammoth novelty turns out, in short, to be a tame little lamb in wolf's clothing, an updated version of the moral tale in praise of cleanliness. . . .

Then there are the pop-ups, books designed to produce three-dimensional panoramas as a page is turned. Pop-ups are not new—they've been on the juvenile scene twenty years at least—though the most recent ones are perhaps unusually elaborate in what's called their "paper engineering." The case against pop-ups can be simply stated. They are expensive (all that cut-and-fold costs money); they tear easily, leaving the frustrated small owner with a tatter of cardboard bits; and, no doubt because so much thought goes into the book's mechanics, the text almost always seems an afterthought. . . .

Voguish adult interest in sensitivity training and sensory awareness probably accounts for another fairly recent innovation: the touch and smell book. Pictures in the Downy Books (Rand McNally) are upholstered with a fuzzy furry stuff, the tactile equivalent of chalk squeaking on a blackboard. Grosset and Dunlap's Touch and Smell Books have even poorer text, a more ambitious range of textures. *Fun in the Country,* for example, by Oscar Weigle, features rayon chenille grass and a patch of real plywood on its barn. (It's very much in the spirit of this contrived experience that the reader can smell the apples and violets—but not the horse or the barn.)

Is there anything, anything at all, to be said for these "toy" books? The usual argument in their favor goes pretty much like this. *One,* it's generally agreed that increased sensory awareness is A Good Thing. Well, here are some prearranged sensory experiences: the child scratches the chemically treated paper and gets the real smell of lemons or chocolate. *Two,* reluctant readers may be seduced by these novelties into the reading of other books.

Let's consider these arguments. *One,* a child doesn't need a book to smell lemons or chocolate; he can go to the kitchen. *Two:* the text of these books, almost without exception, is so abominable that no child would be inspired to read if that's what reading is.

FREDELLE MAYNARD
Guiding Your Child to a More Creative Life

Me-Books: Especially for Whomever

A well-meaning aunt sent my son one of the Me-Books. It may not be the *original* "Me-Book," but it's "a personalized story especially for you" just the same. The trouble is that these are not personalized stories at all, but standardized, badly written, badly designed fare—much like the letters you get soliciting magazine subscriptions and calling you by name—only this one includes your dog's name too. Whatever happened to the personalized story as one with which a child could identify emotionally? (If a kid in a story is feeling, say, sad in a way that will help the kid reading the story to come to terms with his own sadness—or confusion or insecurity or fear—that's a very important story.)

The particular book that came in our mail tells of an alligator who danced "when Nicky came to see him." Now my son Nicky might get a kick out of that for about five minutes, especially since this Nicky had the same last name and lived at the same address and had friends with the same names as his own friends. Pretty personal so far, eh? That the alligator landed on the front lawn of Nicky's house and the real Nicky doesn't have a front lawn outside his apartment gives the first clue to the story's being a phony, but on the next page this Nicky is chatting about the alligator with his father, and the real Nicky's father is dead. Okay, a lot of kids whose fathers are not dead read the book, but it's supposed to be a personalized story. Should we forgive the computer's presumptuousness if it doesn't ask the right questions at the outset?

Consumer note: The publisher of Me-Books was reported by *Time* magazine to have said: "A great thing about Me-Books is that one book can't be passed from child to child. Each kid must have his own!" There's a lot of money to be made from us dopey parents who'll usually grab up anything that has our kid's name on it.

ELS

MAKING BOOKS WITH YOUR KID

"Joey's Book of Letters, Colors, and a Little Bit of Learning"

My six-year-old daughter made a book for her younger brother called "Joey's Book of Letters, Colors, and a Little Bit of Learning." There are four pages in it. One is yellow, another page is "B," and another is something like "The sun will come up in the morning." Some of the stories she writes or draws we bind on the sewing machine.

JENNIFER CARDEN

Do-It-Yourself *Pat the Bunny*

Make your own *Pat the Bunny* type of "touch-and-feel book." Use heavy construction paper or pieces of cardboard (like flash cards). Some suggestions for textures: sandpaper, cotton, tin foil, velvet and other fabric scraps, zippers, a leaf, glued-on rice or macaroni, bristles from an old brush, ribbons, braids, bows, buttons, coins.

Watch out for swallowing.

ELS

Japanese Bookbinding

This is a very simple technique that can be used by very young children with little assistance (age five and up). It is especially useful for binding loose sheets of paper—stories, pictures, song or recipe collections, and so on.

1. Cut covers out of poster board, oak-tag, or even construction paper to size of paper to be bound.

2. Draw a straight line along edge to be bound, about ½" from edge. Put paper and covers together.

3. Make evenly spaced dots along line (½" to 1" apart); then punch holes at dots with an awl or other poking tool. Holes should go through covers and paper—it helps to use clothespins or clamps to hold it all together.

4. Thread yarn or embroidery thread and put it through first hole; wrap it over top edge and thread it back through same hole. Pull it from back through second hole, wrap around edge and return through same hole. Continue in this way until you reach the end of the line.

5. Wrap yarn/thread around end and do a simple running stitch (in one hole and out the next) back along line, so that all spaces are filled. Wrap around end and tie in a knot.

6. Crease cover at seam so pages will lie flat when book is open.

JIM BLAKE and BARBARA ERNST
The Great Perpetual Learning Machine

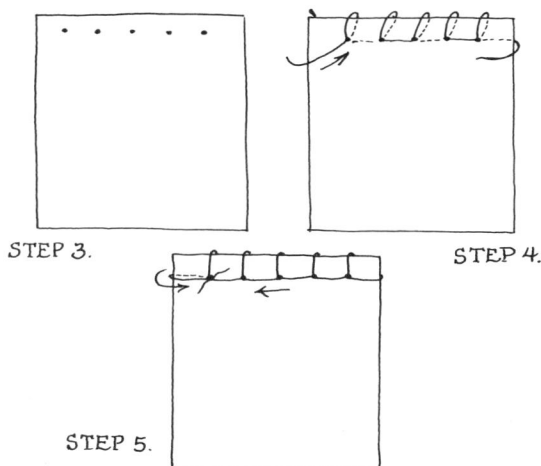

STEP 3.   STEP 4.

STEP 5.

A How-to-Make-Books Book

How to Make Your Own Books, by Harvey Weiss (Thomas Y. Crowell, $7.95), is an easy-to-read, well-illustrated guide to making personal, one-of-a-kind books—diaries, stamp albums, travel journals, flip books, comic books, and more. In addition to clear directions on how to make a variety of simple bindings, *How to Make Your Own Books* includes a good selection of ideas for the kinds of books you might want to make.

JIM BLAKE and BARBARA ERNST
The Great Perpetual Learning Machine

LEARNING TO READ

Skip the Bad Parts

One day soon after school had started, I said to [my new fifth-graders], "Now I'm going to say something about reading that you have probably never heard a teacher say before. I would like you to read a lot of books this year, but I want you to read them only for pleasure. I am not going to ask you questions to find out whether you understand the books or not. If you understand enough of a book to enjoy it and want to go on reading it, that's enough for me. Also I'm not going to ask you what words mean.

"Finally," I said, "I don't want you to feel that just because you start a book you have to finish it. Give an author thirty or forty pages or so to get his story going. Then if you don't like the characters and you don't care what happens to them, close the book, put it away, and get another. I don't care whether the books are easy or hard, short or long, as long as you enjoy them. Furthermore I'm putting all this in a letter to your parents, so they won't feel they have to quiz and heckle you about books at home."

The children sat stunned and silent. Was this a teacher talking? One girl, who had just come to us from a school where she had had a very hard time, and who proved to be one of the most interesting, lively, and intelligent children I have *ever* known, looked at me steadily for a long time after I had finished. Then, still looking at me, she said slowly and solemnly, "Mr. Holt, do you *really* mean that?" I said just as solemnly, "I mean *every* word of it."

Apparently she decided to believe me. The first book she read was Dr. Seuss's *How the Grinch Stole Christmas,* not a hard book even for most third-graders. For a while she read a number of books on this level. Perhaps she was clearing up some confusion about reading that her teachers, in their hurry to get her up to "grade level," had never given her enough time to clear up. After she had been in the class six weeks or so and we had become good friends, I very tentatively suggested that, since she was a skillful rider and loved horses, she might like to read *National Velvet.* I made my sell as soft as possible, saying only that it was about a girl who loved and rode horses, and that if she didn't like it she could put it back. She tried it, and, though she must have found it quite a bit harder than what she had been reading, finished it and liked it very much.

During the spring she really astounded me, however. One day, in one of our many free periods, she was reading at her desk. From a glimpse of the illustrations I thought I knew what the book was. I said to myself, "It can't be," and went to take a closer look. Sure enough, she was reading *Moby Dick,* in the edition with the woodcuts by Rockwell Kent. When I came closer to her desk she looked up. I said, "Are you really reading that?" She said she was. I said, "Do you like it?" She said, "Oh, yes, it's neat!" I said, "Don't you find parts of it rather heavy going?" She answered, "Oh, sure, but I just skip over those parts and go on to the next good part."

This is exactly what reading should be and in school so seldom is—an exciting, joyous adventure. Find something, dive into it, take the good parts, skip the bad parts, get what you can out of it; go on to something else. How different is our mean-spirited, picky insistence that *every* child get *every* last little scrap of "understanding" that can be dug out of a book.

JOHN HOLT
The Underachieving School

They Learned It By Doing It

A seven year old boy explained it this way: "I learned how to read by sounding out letters. You should learn how to read by real easy books. And you keep on going and going, and when you think it's time to have real hard books, you should have them."

If you distrust this simplicity, reflect on the fact that your students have already learned how to talk, and they did not do this by being told where to put their tongue and lips and how to vibrate the sound box in their throats. They learned it by doing it. They did it by exploring sounds, by feeling the way their tongues, mouths, and sound boxes felt when they made different noises. Educators agree that learning to speak is far more complex than learning how to read and write, and in most cases children will learn to read on their own if they are placed in an environment where books are accessible and where reading is highly valued.

HAL BENNETT
No More Public School

We Are All Teaching and Learning Reading at Different Moments in Our Lives

There are four people in our family in addition to me: my wife Judy, my daughters Antonia who is five and Erica who is three and a half, and my son Joshua who is a year and a half. Josh is learning how to talk and he has four teachers on different levels of competency with the language themselves. Because Judy and I have a greater mastery of spoken English than Erica or Antonia does not mean however that we are more effective teachers of Josh. The girls spend a lot more time playing with Josh than we do and he follows them around and talks to them all the time. They sometimes seem to understand him a lot better than we do.

I notice they correct him every once in a while or name objects for him and ask him to repeat the words. It is a game for the most part but they want to communicate with him and he wants to communicate with them so there is a natural reason for them to guide and assist him with language, and for him to accept their help.

The girls are also learning how to read in a natural manner. There are a lot of books around our house and the kids see the adults reading and want to do it too. Josh picks up a book and pretends to read. So do Antonia and Erica, only in different ways. Tonia knows which side is up or down, how the pages turn, and how the writing moves across the page. She's heard us read some books so often that she feels she can read them herself and does in a way—moving her finger across the page and reciting the story she knows by heart.

She also knows the alphabet and some words.

Erica knows which side of the book is supposed to be held up, but forgets which way the pages turn and the writing goes. Tonia helps her and sometimes reads the stories she has memorized to Erica who follows avidly.

Erica on the other hand helps Josh turn the book right side up, talks to him about pictures, imitates Judy or me reading a story.

Whenever there is a question about a picture or a word the kids bring the books to one of us and we tell them.

Judy and I in turn are still learning how to read—she has begun to read texts in ethology and has a new technical language to figure out. I am trying to make my way through Paolo Freire's *Pedagogy of the Oppressed* and have to learn his special use of some words as well as the meanings of some of his statements in the original Portuguese, a language I do not know. I have to deal with a translation and learn whether the translation distorts Freire's thoughts.

With the exception of Josh, we are all teaching and learning reading at different moments in our lives. There is no one of us who is always a teacher or always a learner. In fact the children often teach us to look at something differently— a story or picture, which they see more clearly than we do.

HERBERT KOHL
Reading, How To

———————◆———————

Motivation Is Part of Learning

There's no point to a child's reading—or at least he or she won't know there's a point—unless it's clear that you're a reader yourself. Read books and stories out loud, and point out what you learn by reading, in *every* sense of the word. By reading a clock, you learn what time it is; by reading music, you can play the piano; by reading a recipe, you can cook; by reading the numbers on a stove, you know how hot the oven is; by reading the radio or TV section of the newspaper you can find out what programs are scheduled; by reading the instrument panel of a car you can tell how fast you're going, how to turn the wipers on, whether the lights are on or off, what gear you're in. I never stopped pointing out to my kids how miraculous reading is, and I'm convinced that healthy, normal children who *want* to read *do* read.

PHYLLIS CERF WAGNER

The Code People Versus the Meaning People

If we consider the approaches [to reading] independently of historical patterns, we see them as falling roughly into two groups. Stated as simply as possible, the distinction between the two is this: One group (let us call it the "code-emphasis" group) believes that the initial stage in reading instruction should emphasize teaching children to master a code—the alphabet code. The other (the "meaning-emphasis" group) believes that children should, and do, learn to read best when meaning is emphasized from the start.

DR. JEANNE CHALL
Learning to Read

[The debate between the code-emphasis people and the meaning-emphasis people, with its many ramifications, is the subject of Jeanne Chall's *Learning to Read,* published by McGraw-Hill in 1967 and available in paperback for $3.95. Dr. Chall's conclusions, based on clinical research, favor the code approach. —Eds.]

Sylvia Ashton-Warner: Learning to Read "Organically"

In spite of studies that support the teaching of reading by some sort of code recognition (e.g., phonics), I find Sylvia Ashton-Warner to be the reading teacher a parent could most easily emulate without adding to the trauma that learning to read can become in our culture. Believing that children will most easily learn to read the words they want to learn, Ashton-Warner begins her teaching with words chosen by the children, words that best describe their inner world of loves, fears, and imaginings. "Daddy, Mummy, ghost, bomb, kiss, brothers, butcher knife, love, dance, cry, fight, hat, bulldog, touch . . ."; such words were among those chosen by the five-year-olds to whom Sylvia Ashton-Warner taught reading and writing during her tenure at a Maori school in New Zealand— a tenure she describes in her acclaimed book *Teacher* (Simon and Schuster, 1963, hardcover; Bantam Books, 1971, paperback).

"I call a child to me and ask her what [word] she wants," writes Ashton-Warner. "She may ask for 'socks' and I print it large on a card. . . . She watches me print the word and says it as I print, then I give it to her to take back to the mat and trace the characters with her finger. . . . These self-chosen words mount up and are kept in a box. . . . When they have collected their own [words] they choose a partner and sit together and hear each other, their own and the other's words. . . . The only words [they keep] are those that have come from deep within . . . and have to be told only once. . . . The longer [a child's] reading is organic, the stronger it becomes, until by the time he arrives at the books of the new culture, he receives them as a joy rather than a labour."

If you're thinking that this sounds a little too much like the open-classroom techniques that are supposed to have failed and been abandoned, you should read Sylvia Ashton-Warner's later book, *Spearpoint: "Teacher" in America* (Knopf, 1972), in which she describes her feelings of alienation in a Colorado school too insistent on freedom for its four- and five-and six-year-olds. The children (and consequently the teachers) were ruled by wanna-do-wannas, mostly dowannawork. Energy spent deciding whether or not to work was energy lost for the work itself.

As Ashton-Warner discovered what she calls the key vocabularies of each child, she found a replacement of the native imagery common to children she had worked with in other cultures. Children had always asked first for words of home—for Mommy and Daddy and sisters and brothers—and proceeded from there to the outside world. But here were Jonathan and Gelo and Durla and Peter asking for words outside the home—for friends at school, and bikes, and helicopters, and pets, especially dogs. "Dogs are affectionate," explained one parent. "They're always there when the children go home. It's the dogs they turn to for their love." Here were children who never asked for the words "love" and "hate" until finally they were suggested by the teacher (in a rare disregard of the principle not to impose words that are not already in the child's mind). They were children who didn't ask questions, having been socialized by TV to sit and absorb without response;

children whom the author observed to be on the spearpoint of civilization, their stimuli so different from past generations as to cause a mutation in the human personality. (You'll find an excerpt from *Spearpoint* in the SCHOOLS AND LEARNING section).

RS

The Cafeteria Approach

One problem with the field of reading instruction is that experts tend to be extraordinarily doctrinaire about their own points of view. The only method is phonics! Phonics are terrible! Sight reading is the answer! Sight reading doesn't work! Controlled vocabulary lists are everything! Controlled vocabulary lists are useless! And so on. The fact is that all these techniques can help. And they can all be misused. And a little bit of everything might be the best recipe of all.

What *Sesame Street* and, to an even greater degree, *The Electric Company* have done is to use what Joan Ganz Cooney calls "the cafeteria approach": they've tried to combine everything with the assumption that some things will help some kids, and other things will help other kids.

A case in point was an experiment we've heard about in which a school split classes in order to compare the effectiveness of teaching reading skills with the Initial Teaching Alphabet (an alphabet where there are symbols for each phonetic sound) with the results achieved using more traditional techniques. As part of the test, family members attending the school were split up: one sibling would be taught ITA while the other received instruction in straight phonetics. More than one instance was reported in which both siblings fared poorly in their respective ITA and traditional classes, but met with considerable success after switching to each other's former group.

SHARON LERNER and CBC

READING GAMES AND ACTIVITIES

If It's Words You Want, It's Words You'll Get

When my son was starting to want to know words, I gave him words. Applying Sylvia Ashton-Warner's notion of learning to read "organically," I tried labeling things that were important to the kid in his everday life. His lunch packed for school (and this was only when I

had time) would have a sign: "Nick's lunch. Peanut butter and honey, apple juice, and 1 granola bar." I would read it to him first, he'd read it back, and perhaps sometime during the day he'd look at it again and "read" it (which was partly remembering what it said, but only partly).

His bureau drawers had labels: shirts, pants, socks, and underwear. When there was something to remember for the next day, at night we'd put a note next to his bed: "Mail letter to Ian." Or "Fix bike." Sometimes promises we made to each other would get written down—and when they were mine to him he had a good incentive for learning to read.

ELS

The Same and Different Game

Learning to read is about as miraculous as a spy's breaking a code—once you've learned to see likenesses and differences and to recognize combinations of letters, it all becomes easier. You can help a young person with the code-breaking process by encouraging her or him to observe similarities and differences. There are many ways to do this: perhaps the most enjoyable one—both for you and the child—is games. There are many on the market—lotto, for example—but you really don't have to purchase anything if you use your imagination a bit.

Here's a sample game: draw a circle, then suggest to a child that she pick up or point out, in the room or in a magazine, things that are round like a circle—a ring, a clock, a bottle cap, the top of a glass, the tire of a car, the full moon, the letter "o," knobs on a drawer. Anything. Play the game of seeing circles as you walk on the street or drive in a car.

You can play the "same and different" game with vertical lines too (including the letter "l"). Try it with a horizontal line also; eventually, you'll be able to demonstrate how these lines get put together to make letters that spell out the child's name. Buy large crayons for her to write with—in the beginning, a child's small motor muscles are hard to control. Print big and let the child copy you.

Once children can recognize their own names, they're on the way toward breaking the reading code. But remember, it's a game. Don't push!

PHYLLIS CERF WAGNER

Sometimes the Words Turned Corners

When he was just beginning to feel ready to learn to read and write, Nick discovered the perfect forum for expressing words he knew. One of his "activity books" had a crossword puzzle page which, though simple, was too advanced for him. What he did with the crossword puzzle was to fill in the squares with words he knew—any words. Sometimes the words turned corners, sometimes they connected with or ran into letters of other words, sometimes there were empty spaces left over—it didn't much matter. What did matter was that the kid was teaching himself to read. On occasion, when Nick got stuck, he would say, "Can you think of a word that has four letters and the third letter is 'e'?" and I would say, "Tree, t-r-e-e," and he would write it in and later he would be able to read the word back to me when he was showing me the crossword puzzle he'd "done."

It worked well, and for once I did not get caught up in telling him how one is "supposed to do" crossword puzzles; I did not start teaching him. I let him do what he wanted to do and get what he wanted to get from it. (I was so proud of myself for not butting in.) And, as I've always felt that kids will find a way of learning to read when they are ready to read, this was a living example.

ELS

Correspondence Course

One event that became increasingly important to my son when he was first learning to read was the morning visit to the mailbox. Grandma and Aunt Shirley had figured out that Nick liked their correspondence and from time to time they'd send mail for him to read. The letters started out simple. "I love you," Aunt Shirley would write frequently, and that was the first sentence Nick learned to read. Or Grandma would send a postcard after a visit: "I had a good time with you on Sunday. See you soon." It's enough to give a kid a reason to read.

ELS

Flash Cards: Breaking the Barrier Between Play and Work

Reading flash cards were the best investment I ever made for my child. I brought home a box of large hold-up, red-lettered cards with thirty different words—from "Mommy" and "Daddy" to "Horse," "House," and "Belly-Button." The idea was to introduce five new cards each week for six weeks. My 2½-year-old daughter trotted out these cards every night for months—first to learn, then to display her skill. It was a priceless experience. She broke the barrier between play and work early, a process which flourished into a love of reading and learning as her greatest pleasures.

GAIL SHEEHY

The Words Began to Seem Like Objects

I opened the new word cards. José lay full length on the desk, and I sat beside him. He objected to the great number of cards—there were about a hundred—but I said, "These are new words. Don't try to read them. Let's just see what we have." I flipped the cards one by one. He recognized many—to his own surprise—and these we put on a separate pile. I made a second pile of words I thought he might like to learn in the near future. The third pile was for hard words. Now each card became the occasion of a little conference. I turned up the word "pretty." "Yeah," he said brightly, "put it there," meaning the second pile. And so with several others. And in the process of saying that he wanted to learn them soon, he learned them on the spot and was unaware of it. It was odd. The cards themselves were physical objects, and the words began to seem like objects, too,

as if we were sorting out possessions. Soon I asked him to make up sentences for each word, even the ones he couldn't read, and we kept turning cards and talking about words for a long time, a very peaceful, easygoing kind of game.

GEORGE DENNISON
The Lives of Children

◆

Robororo, Robororo

Nonsense syllable games help build up an ability to read longer words easily. For example, here is a list of nonsense words.

> inmar   willoway
> robororo   millpasser

Pronounce them, make up meanings for them, use them in sentences.

A variant would be to list some syllables:

> ir   ick   un
> ark   ir   ine

and some letters:

> l   v   m   n
> r   t   s   b

Combine the syllables and letters to make:

> nasty sounding words
> sweet sounding words
> silly sounding words
> angry sounding words
> filthy sounding words

HERBERT KOHL
Reading, How To

READING PROBLEMS

There Is No Reading Problem

In *Reading, How To* (Dutton, 1973), Herb Kohl dares to say that the teaching of reading is not a sacred profession. "There is no reading problem, " he tells us. "There are problem teachers and problem schools." Kohl encourages children and adults alike to recognize their own potential as teachers, provides an understanding of the process of learning to read, proposes that reading can be taught more informally than it is in the schools today, and suggests a way to replace specific testing (IQ tests) with general evaluation of skills and attitudes at four levels of reading (Beginning, Not Bad, With Ease, Complex). If you've been told your child has a reading problem, or if you're interested in the teaching of reading, you should work with this book and be reassured by it.

RS

It turned out that Lillian had a problem focusing her eyes on the written word. I didn't need a test of perceptual skills to see that, it was only necessary to look at her. I suggested she follow along the page with her finger, and it seemed to work during the lessons at home. It created serious problems at school, however. Her teacher refused to let her use her finger while she read. Somewhere he had picked up the notion that it was a bad thing to do. The remedial reading specialist agreed. I spoke to the teacher about it. He could not give me any reason why reading with one's finger on the page was wrong or harmful, so he referred me to his supervisor, who took the same position in the same irrational way. Finally, I had to get a doctor's note and threaten a lawsuit to enable Lillian to read in school in a way that was obviously helping her.

HERBERT KOHL
Reading, How To

Dyslexia

Parents and educators want more than anything for kids to learn to read. At the same time, some statistics claim that 10 percent of the children in this country have reading problems.

One of the main causes of reading problems is dyslexia. This term has become more popular in recent years, having a clinical ring without all the negative connotations usually associated with other causes of reading problems ("slow," "retarded," "disturbed," etc.). But in some instances, the label "dyslexia" is used to conceal the primary problem of the school's inability to teach. That's the problem with neat labels.

ALLAN SHEDLIN, JR.

Sometimes children hold back from reading for seemingly arbitrary reasons. It may help to consider that one of the reasons for this reluctance may be the child's fear that if she learns to read, her parents will stop reading to her or with her. Reassuring the child that after she can read on her own you will still read together may help a lot.

SALLY LANGENDOEN

WHAT IT'S LIKE TO HAVE DYSLEXIA

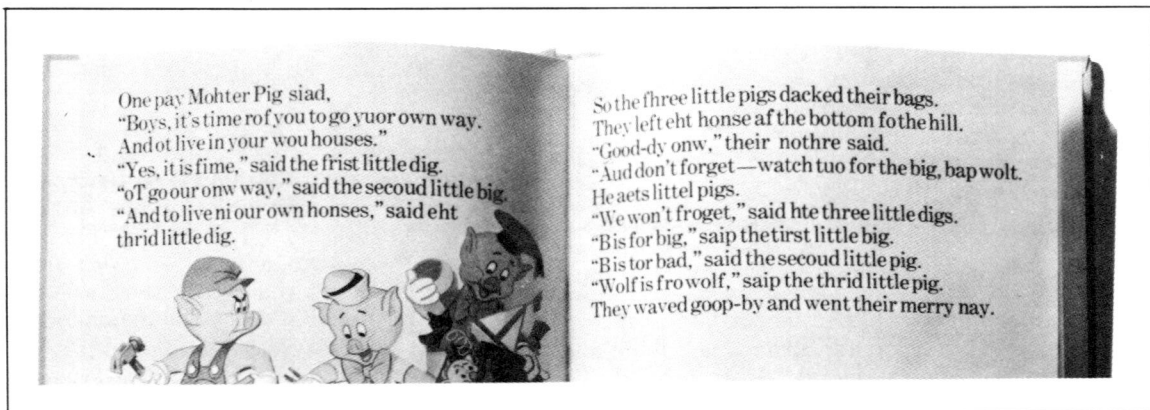

One pay Mohter Pig siad,
"Boys, it's time rof you to go yuor own way.
And ot live in your wou houses."
"Yes, it is fime," said the frist little dig.
"oT go our onw way," said the secoud little big.
"And to live ni our own honses," said eht thrid little dig.

So the fhree little pigs dacked their bags.
They left eht honse af the bottom fo the hill.
"Good-dy onw," their nothre said.
"Audd don't forget—watch tuo for the big, bap wolt.
He aets littel pigs.
"We won't froget," said hte three little digs.
"B is for big," saip the tirst little big.
"B is tor bad," said the secoud little pig.
"Wolf is fro wolf," saip the thrid little pig.
They waved goop-by and went their merry nay.

You're looking at what it's like to have dyslexia. Words are jumbled. Letters transposed. Upside down. Mirrored. Often speaking, even hearing, is affected. [From *Specific Learning Disabilities Gazette*]

Making Children Hate Reading

From the very beginning of school we make books and reading a constant source of possible failure and public humiliation. When children are little we make them read aloud, before the teacher and other children, so that we can be sure they "know" all the words they are reading. This means that when they don't know a word, they are going to make a mistake, right in front of everyone. Instantly they are made to realize that they have done something wrong. Perhaps some of the other children will begin to wave their hands and say "Ooooh O-o-o-oh!" Perhaps they will just giggle, or nudge each other, or make a face. Perhaps the teacher will say, "Are you sure?" or ask someone else what he thinks. Or perhaps, if the teacher is kindly, she will just smile a sweet, sad smile—often one of the most painful punishments a child can suffer in school. In any case, the child who has made the mistake knows he has made it, and feels foolish, stupid, and ashamed, just as any of us would in his shoes.

Before long many children associate books and reading with mistakes, real or feared, and penalties and humiliation. This may not seem sensible, but it is natural. Mark Twain once said that a cat that sat on a hot stove lid would never sit on one again, but it would never sit on a cold one either. As true of children as of cats. If they, so to speak, sit on a hot book a few times, if books cause them humiliation and pain, they are likely to decide that the safest thing to do is to leave all books alone.

JOHN HOLT
The Underachieving School

Books That Have Helped Me Help Others to Read

I have found a number of books useful in my work helping others to read. Naturally a dictionary (I recommend the *Shorter Oxford English Dictionary* or the *American Heritage Dictionary*) and a copy of *Roget's Thesaurus* are useful. In addition to these, however, are other less familiar but equally useful books:

a. Eric Partridge's *Origins,* which is one of my favorite books. It gives the origins of words as well as their original meanings. Partridge has also put together two other useful and fun books:
Slang Today and Yesterday, Bonanza Books.
A Dictionary of Slang and Unconventional English Macmillan, 1970.

b. Other interesting collections of words from our language are:
Major, Clarence, *Dictionary of Afro-American Slang,* International Publishers, 1970.
Wentworth, Harold, and Flexner, Stuart Berg, *Dictionary of American Slang,* Thomas Y. Crowell Co., 1970.

HERBERT KOHL
Reading, How to

[For information about a special comic-book series, starring Marvel Comics' Spider-Man, that's specifically designed to help kids learn to read, see page 291.]

P.S.: Reading Isn't Everything

The solution to [the reading] problem is, conceptually, not very difficult. To begin with, we are not suggesting that reading skill is unimportant. We probably ought to repeat the last sentence to avoid misunderstanding: we are not saying that reading skill is unimportant. What we are saying is as follows:

1. It is a mistake to *equate* reading skill with intelligence (which is now the case in many schools).

2. Schools must elevate the value they presently place on nonprint communication skills so as to give all students a fair chance to learn and to express what they know through the media they most favor.

3. Schools should undertake a realistic analysis of exactly what society's requirements are in relation to reading skill.

4. Schools should start questioning their obedience to the concept of reading grade levels. Without such a concept, it is quite possible that more students would learn to read competently than presently do, although they would do it in their own time at their own rate.

In other words, we are saying that the schools, to a large extent, have *created* the reading problem by making reading skill (almost) the only key to a successful experience in school.

NEIL POSTMAN and CHARLES WEINGARTNER
The School Book

BOOKS FOR BEGINNING READERS

The Cat in the Hat: The Space-Age Answer to Dick and Jane

The saga of *The Cat in the Hat* (Random House) began in the late fifties when, suddenly and without warning, there was an extremely foreign object sailing through the sky, a tiny new moon named *Sputnik* that beeped derisively as it whizzed overhead. Nobody quite knew what it portended, but everybody knew one thing: America had had its pants snatched by a bunch of Cossacks. How had it happened? The answers were many, but none was so gratifying to a nation of petulant ex-schoolchildren as this one: Blame the teachers!

"Why is it," trumpeted the headlines, "that Johnny Can't Read . . . and *Ivan Can!*" Hardly

"Remember the Maine!" but it did get some people thinking. John Hersey was one of them, and he did it out loud in *Life* magazine, opining that the problem was quite possibly Boring Books. If only someone with talent, he dreamed, like Dr. Seuss, would tackle the question of how to write interesting books for those kids struggling to break the code of the written word. Then maybe children might learn to *like* to read, and, conversely, like to *learn* to read. Then watch our smoke! (Just what beguiling books Ivan had been immersed in all along, I've never even *wanted* to know.)

Dr. Seuss, who is an extremely logical man (and a former *Life* subscriber), liked that. He got hold of a somewhat ridiculous list of three-hundred words guaranteed by its heavily

Ph.D.'d compilers to be familiar to most first-graders. He ran his practiced eye along it. Where in this pile of rubble so often quarried for endlessly running Spots seen and seen again by joylessly voyeuristic Janes might there be an undetected keystone? "Cat?" Kids liked cats. A rhyme? "Hat." BANG! The mother lode. Into the lives of children sauntered a six-foot-tall cat wearing a hat that looked like a limp barber pole. Books for beginning readers have never recovered.

Hard on the Cat's heels came a host of others. The Cat became the symbol for two series edited by Dr. Seuss, "Beginner Books" and "Bright and Early Books." Together these now number about a hundred volumes and include the work of such writers and illustrators as Roy McKie, P. D. Eastman (whose 75-word-vocabulary classic, *Go, Dog, Go,* is, for me, the quintessential example of how to combine words and pictures for beginning readers), Stan and Jan Berenstain (and their famous family of bumbling, but scientifically knowledgeable, bears) and, of course, the Doc himself.

(In closing, it should be noted that, exactly ten years after the publication of *The Cat in the Hat,* an American first set foot on the moon.)

MICHAEL FRITH
Former editor of Dr. Seuss's books

Do-It-Yourself Beginner Books

In the last few years, without fanfare, and even without a series label, a new "do-it-yourself" kind of Beginner Book has been created. The lead item in this mini-line from Random House is *My Book About Me, by Me, Myself, with Some Help from My Friends Dr. Seuss and Roy McKie.* Not only is it simple for young readers to handle, it encourages children to pursue revealing, if sometimes insane, examinations of themselves and their surroundings, as they attempt to fill in the numerous blanks in its pages. Examples:

"My longest hair is _____ inches."
"There are _____ forks in my house."
"I can make noises ☐ like a rooster ☐ like a dog ☐ like a goose ☐ like a train . . ."
"My family loves my noises. Yes☐ No☐"

Dr. Seuss's second entry in the "do-it-yourself" sweepstakes is *I Can Draw It Myself,* an oversize, spiral-bound creation that combines quintessential Seuss verse with partially completed drawings that the child is encouraged to finish. One page, for instance, offers an illustration of the front half of a strange antlered beast with the following bit of poetry:

I'm so good,
I drew half of a Yill-ya-yakk.
Dr. Seuss drew the front half, and
I drew the back.

Finally, Michael Frith's *My Amazing Book of Autographs* assumed the scope of a lifetime quest for at least one child whom we gave it to last summer. What it sets forth, in second-to-third-grade prose, is the task of collecting different kinds of autographs from a staggering assortment of people. Your child will need, among other things, an autograph from a friend who wrote his name blindfolded, seven autographs of friends with stores, an autograph from someone whose middle name begins with "V," a left-handed autograph by a right-handed person, and "the hardest one of all—a foot-autograph done by a foot." It may not be literature, but it's a book your kid won't put aside after one reading.

CBC

I Can Read Books: Little Bear Leads the Way

Among the finest series of books for beginning readers is Harper & Row's I Can Read Books. Perhaps the most famous of these—and deservedly so—are the Little Bear books, written by Else Holmelund Minarik and illustrated, magnificently as usual, by Maurice Sendak.

Where Dr. Seuss's *The Cat in the Hat* wins kids with a combination of mischievous nonsense, raucousness, and chutzpah, Little Bear and his family and friends project a simple warmth that charms children and parents alike. "Sendak's forte," writes Selma G. Lanes in *Down the Rabbit Hole,* "is making us feel, and come to cherish, the quality of warm relationships developed pictorially through an entire book, a sustained feat of magic."

CBC

A MESSAGE TO PUBLISHERS OF BOOKS FOR VERY SMALL CHILDREN, AS TOLD TO A PARENT BY A LIFE-LONG LOVER OF BOOKS, AGE TWO AND A HALF

Little readers like books they can handle all by themselves. The first requirement is that a book should lie open with very little help from the reader. This becomes so obvious when you watch a child alone with a book that it is remarkable how often it is ignored by manufacturers.

In our house we have (almost) gone so far as to refuse to buy books that require two firm adult hands to keep the pages open (where the binding is too tight at the spine). Not only does a child find it difficult to look at such a book by himself or herself, but he or she cannot even have the pleasure of turning the pages when being read to.

PAULA GLATZER

SELECTING BOOKS FOR KIDS

When I was in grammar school I faked illness and spent a long delicious day in bed reading *Huckleberry Finn.* Of course my mother was angry when she learned my aches were nonexistent, but I cherish the memory of that day. I remember that I loved the story, but I also remember the thrill I felt from the knowledge that a great book had the power to reach me without the intervention of parents, teachers, or friends. I can encourage my children to read and share my thoughts with them, but I believe they must ultimately discover for themselves the joy and value great literature can give them.

MARJORIE LIPSYTE

I should like to see children taught that they should not say they like things which they do not like, merely because certain other people say they like them.

SAMUEL BUTLER
The Way of All Flesh

If your child is interested in football, don't try to get him to read a book about how to grow plants. You really must think of your youngster's own interests if you want to encourage him to read.

PHYLLIS CERF WAGNER

There's More to a Book Than Just the Reading

[Maurice Sendak's] sister Natalie gave him his first book, *The Prince and the Pauper.* "A ritual began with that book," Sendak once told Virginia Haviland, "which I recall very clearly. The first thing was to set it up on the table and stare at it for a long time. Not because I was impressed with Mark Twain; it was just such a beautiful object. Then came the smelling of it . . . it was printed on particularly fine paper, unlike the Disney books I had gotten previous to that. *The Prince and the Paper—Pauper—*smelled good and it also had a shiny laminated cover. I flipped over that. I remember trying to bite into it, which I don't imagine is what my sister intended when she bought the book for me. But the last thing I did with the book was to read it. It was all right. But I think it started then, my passion of books and bookmaking. There's so much more to a book than just the reading. I've seen children touch books, fondle books, smell books, and it's all the reason in the world why books should be beautifully produced."

JONATHAN COTT
Rolling Stone

Why the Same Few Books Keep Getting Read

I've noticed that the majority of children's books that we have accumulated simply sit on our bookshelves. The same few books keep getting read and the same few are requested for bedtime stories read by my wife or me. My second son, Paul, keeps requesting *The Bible in Picture for Little Eyes,* and then returns over and over again to the same few stories. He loves the David and Goliath story and the story about Joseph and his brothers. Think about those stories for a moment. How many "kiddie stories" can you remember that contain action such as a small boy overcoming a giant of a man, or a favorite son being sold into bondage by his brothers? Both stories allowed him to vicariously work out his own aggression; both when discussed in the context in which they took place allowed me to clarify experiences with him.

FRANK McLAUGHLIN
School Library Journal

In the Great Tradition of Jacqueline Susann . . .

If your child brings home from the library—and loves—a book you think worthless, you should certainly not spoil his pleasure by supercilious comment. ("That's trash. Let me find you a *good* book, like *Tale of Two Cities.*")

FREDELLE MAYNARD
Guiding Your Child to a More Creative Life

Kids choose stuff which adults are put off by, the Hardy Boys and Nancy Drew books being classic examples. Adults have decided that that's bad. I don't find anything wrong in a kid's choosing the Hardy Boys and Nancy Drew, just as I don't find anything wrong in an adult's choosing Jackie Susann.

HENRY GREENWALD

Assuming you agree with Mr. Greenwald that there's nothing wrong in a kid's choosing Nancy Drew, you may wish to enroll your child in *Parents' Magazine's* Nancy Drew Twin-Thriller Book Club (52 Vanderbilt Avenue, New York, NY 10017). As was pointed out in the *New York Times Book Review,* Ms. Drew was "liberated long before Gloria Steinem"; membership in the club entitles you to two of her adventures in one $2.49 volume per month. (Postage and handling are extra, natch.)

CBC

"Lacking Genuine Nutrition, You Can Starve on a Full Stomach"

It's that great gray area between the good and the bad that is so stultifying. Generally speaking, the bad stuff in reading—the commercialized series, the sensational mysteries, the sickening romances—are at least not pretentious and a position on them can easily be explained or discussed with a child. What I principally object to are all our dreary, smug books about growing up and coming to terms with oneself, that purport to be "with it" and are merely another brand of conformity; all the books on race relations that are little more than a condescending, inverse form of racism; all our books of dull facts that take the excitement out of science, or history, or other countries. It's really hard to explain one's stand on this "ho-hum" stuff unless you take each book individually and put a better book up beside it. Tolkien rather than Frank Baum, Sendak rather than Nan Agle, O'Dell rather than Wojieckowska, Patricia Wrightson instead of Jean Little. . . .

It's the mediocre that drags us all down to a common denominator; common is fine but does it have to be the lowest? It's mediocrity that deprives us of judgement; it's mediocrity that closes our minds to new ideas; it's mediocrity that particularly deprives us of a sense of humor.

SHEILA EGOFF
School Library Journal

You Are What You Read

Nobody told us, in school or elsewhere, what a child between the ages of nine and twelve should be reading and what he should read from twelve to fourteen, etc. We read everything that took our fancy, whether we understood it or not, from Nick Carter to Kant and *Penrod and Sam* to Joyce. And when we became infatuated with some writer, we stopped barely short of total impersonation. When I read that Shelley had carried crumbs in his pocket, I started to do likewise and practically lived on breadcrumbs for days.

STUART BRENT

Librarians and children would rarely give first prize to the same book or group of books. Perhaps this is because librarians have read so much and children have read so little. Children's bodies need to grow, and so do they have to grow in their ability to appreciate and understand literature before they and librarians will agree on just what constitutes a good book.

PHYLLIS CERF WAGNER

For What Age Group Is a Book Intended? The Publisher Will Tell You (But He'll Do It in Code)

Have you ever noticed the odd series of numbers that often appear in one corner or another on the front jacket flap of a juvenile book? "07211," you'll be informed, or "90014," or some such. In most cases these numbers are there to tell you (or someone) the intended age range of the volume in question. (The first example, of course, means seven to eleven; the second, nine to fourteen).

But why the code? Perhaps it's to keep a child from reading the numbers and being offended at your estimate of his reading ability—or lack thereof. Maybe it's meant to make booksellers appear omniscient when they miraculously group their children's books according to difficulty. Or it could have been created so that those of us who are offended when chil-

dren's products are pigeonholed according to age level won't take notice.

Whatever the case, the suggested reading level is there if you want it—as long as the book is sold with a dust jacket, that is. (*Note:* If the number is preceded by "ISBN," it's not the one you're looking for. And there *are* some books whose jackets don't carry the code.)

CBC

◆

List of Lists

In her book *A Parent's Guide to Children's Reading* (Doubleday, 1975, $8.95 hardcover; Bantam, 1975, $1.95 paperback), Nancy Larrick, former president of the International Reading Association, offers a comprehensive list of children's booklists. You may find her inventory helpful, especially if you're searching for a book of a particular type or on a specific topic.

—Eds.

OF KIDS' BOOKS, RELEVANCE, AND REALISM

The New Realism

There are no longer any taboos in children's books, except that of good taste. (And depending upon your taste, you might say that even that has fallen by the wayside.) What was once not even whispered in the parlor, and only snickered at in the barroom, is now legitimate fare for young readers.

The old-fashioned view that certain things should be taboo for children simply because they are young is no longer in style. Librarians, who are often caricatured as conservative, accept this, too. (Though occasionally there are librarians whose overzealous guardianship of the "morals of minors" make their sister and brother librarians blanch. For example, in 1972, the American Library Association was in an uproar when some misguided librarians painted diapers on the little naked boy-child in Maurice Sendak's prize-winning picture book, *In the Night Kitchen*.)

The reasons for this opening-up of subject matter in children's books are many and varied. I think that three factors have been most instrumental in bringing about this new phase: the change in readership, the rise of mass media, and especially the advent of television.

Certainly the reading public has changed. Children who were once-upon-a-time chained to long days in a factory are being compulsorily and compulsively "educated." Reading is no longer the royal prerogative of the privileged upper classes. Children at all levels of society are opening books—and opening worlds.

The superabundance of brightly-colored magazines in every household also has a lot to do with the striking down of the taboos. Easily accessible to the youngest children, these periodicals talk about drugs, death, and divorce in the same attractive fashion with which they tout cigarettes, sleeping pills, and beer.

And finally television, perhaps the real reason that so much has changed in the last fifteen years in children's books. . . . Even a child who does not yet read has easy access to television.

So all the deadly sins, plus sex, death, drugs, drunkenness, divorce, poverty, hunger have all become the subjects of children's books. *Sounder* (William H. Armstrong) looks at white man's brutality to blacks; *My Darling, My Hamburger* (Paul Zindel), at premarital sex, pregnancy and abortion; *I'll Get There: It Better Be Worth the Trip* (John Donovan), at homosexuality; *The Pigman* (Paul Zindel), at senility. But at the same time, these books also look at hope, perseverance, determination, strength, belief, and all-encompassing love.

Such books are often lumped together under the heading "relevant books." They are stories that utilize the strong, realistic material already familiar in other forms to many children. The worst of the "relevant" books merely exploit this material. The best explore.

JANE YOLEN
Writing Books for Children

I Rewrite My Child's Books!

I've begun to rewrite my child's books. I darken faces, exchange traditional masculine/feminine jobs, block out inane or frightening sentences, and neatly print in more helpful facts or dialogue to go with the pictures. This does take a lot of time, so I only re-edit those books which appear promising to start with. It's surprising how very few of these there seem to be.

As my husband and I waded through books about little bunnies, puppies, and kitties, *ad nauseam,* we wondered who decided, and why, that children couldn't meet life directly. They are condemned instead (along with us parents who are the readers) to make all sorts of translations, extensions, and mental gymnastics to comprehend what little bunny is doing, and why... (And damn if it isn't always a little bunny *Momma,* always in the kitchen—or some other place reserved for mothers, bunnies or not. And does human life really seem better if Dad is a walrus?)

I have learned that authors and publishers (with some notable exceptions, of course) know little about what information growing children need, are concerned about, and are confronted with in their attempts to comprehend and function in the world around them; the world's wonders and beauty, as well as that which is frightening and confusing.

And so, a defender of civil liberties became a censor—or, at least, a super-editor—and many of Allie's books have been de-sexed, re-sexed, integrated, non-violenced, texts added to and deleted to present life and an approach to its problems in as non-sexist, non-capitalist, cooperative, friendly, factual, and scientific a manner as possible.

We have women truck drivers talking to black women doctors working out problems with daddies cooking supper and caring for baby, while discussing with baby the surface of the moon or how the body heals a cut.

Of course the editing (in, as well as out) gets harder as the child gets older, and as information in the books becomes more complex. Our next venture, aside from pressing publishers for more rational, meaningful books, will have to be to write our own.

BARBARA JOSEPH

So Much for Realism

Say what you will about children's desire for books where they can confront the realities of life directly. My favorite book as a child was *Pollyanna,* because she always looked at the bright side of things, and because everything always turned out all right in the end.

GENEVIEVE CERF

The Council on Interracial Books for Children publishes a bulletin eight times a year which recommends and reviews the latest children's literature dealing with the portrayal of minority groups in both fiction and non-fiction. The bulletin highlights books for all ages concerning black, Chicano, Native American, and feminist subjects, among others. The bulletin is $10 from the Council on Interracial Books for Children, 1841 Broadway, New York, N.Y. 10023.

RUSTY UNGER GUINZBURG

Nurturing Fathers

Just as children's books have denied that some 40 percent of women work outside the home, so they have denied the fuller roles that men play—or can play—in childrearing.

A few books are, however, starting to depict men in more intimate contact with children. *Martin's Father,* published by the feminist collective Lollipop Power, takes us through the routine that preschooler Martin shares with his dad (there's no mother present). After father cooks breakfast for them, they do the laundry, go for a walk, make sandwiches, and so forth, until bedtime: "And last of all, he played a tune on Martin's xylophone, *every evening the same one.*" As a work of literature, *Martin's Father* is not very engaging; but given the absence of books showing men in caring roles, it is an important beginning.

Zeek Silver Moon by Amy Ehrlich is a superb piece of literature, and one of the rare books to capture the spontaneous flow of feeling between father and child. When baby Zeek is born, his father makes him a cradle and, in a scene unique for children's books, makes up a lullaby for singing him to sleep. There is more to this father–son relationship than roughhousing or Little League; mother and father share equally and naturally in . . . their responsibilities as parents . . .

The only book (as of this writing) to show a homemaker-father, *Hello, Aurora,* was published in Norway in 1966 and brought to America in English translation eight years later. In the Tege family, father takes care of six-year-old Aurora and six-month-old Socrates, while mother practices law in Oslo. Even in Norway, it is an unusual life-style, and the book explores sensitively and humorously, from Aurora's viewpoint, what it feels like to be doing something that is natural, sensible, *and* at odds with the culture's norm about childrearing.

JAMES A. LEVINE
Who Will Raise the Children?

Non-Standard English: Indulging the Natives?

Respecting the language and culture of the learner implies taking a nonelitist attitude toward language.* It implies that one does not believe that one's own way of speaking is superior as well as that one is curious about understanding the structure of other dialects. These last remarks are specifically addressed to white middle-class people. It is fashionable to be interested in so-called non-Standard English, in Black or Chicano or Puerto Rican dialect in a condescending paternalistic way. I have seen many young teachers who say they believe that kids should be allowed to speak and write in their own dialects. The tone these teachers take implies that the natives should be indulged a bit before being raised to the level of "our language." One has to listen to how people speak, to think about language, to be aware of how one's own values slip into so-called objective statements about language, in order to undo the racist sense of the superiority of white middle-class language that is part of the legacy of American education.　　　HERBERT KOHL
Reading, How To

* *Black English* by J. L. Dillard (Random House, 1972) substantiates the points made [here] with respect to the speech of Black Americans. It should be read by anyone who thinks about language and culture.

I think the "black culture" books for children that have become fashionable these days are great—for parents. But a *kid's* concept of himself and his people comes from how you relate to him. Your heritage comes from your mother and your father—not from books.

From an interview with NIKKI GIOVANNI

Roots, Jr.

All Us Come Cross the Water, by Lucille Clifton (Holt, Rinehart & Winston, 1973), is a book for preschoolers and early-grade-school children that effectively and poignantly tells the story of a young black boy, Ujamaa, whose teacher stimulates his curiosity in his family's ancestry. Ujamaa and his friend Malik learn from an old man in the community about their heritage and the heritage of all African-Americans. With this information, Ujamaa returns to his class and presents his story with much pride and dignity.

This book, written in black dialect, is a warm and moving story with dynamic pictures by the noted children's illustrator John Steptoe. A white colleague who picked up the book in my office said, "I could never read this to my child." And I agreed that indeed he could not. As he was reading it out loud to me, I knew he was hearing Amos and Andy, or the people who worked in his kitchen as a child, because these were the only blacks he heard speak that way. But if I read it to my kid I'm freer about it.

There have been other attempts to use the black English idiom in fiction for young readers, attempts which have failed miserably. Sentences begin to sound alike, phrases are repetitious, and not at all as effectively rendered as Lucille Clifton's *All Us Come Cross the Water.* It's often a case of people trying to exploit what they think the market is but not having any relevant experience or sense of excellence in terms of the story.

MARIE BROWN

Some Depressing Books Are Written for Good Reasons

Some depressing books are written for good reasons. This is notably true of many books inspired by the Women's Movement (designed to promote a more active, achieving female image) and those intended to provide a wholesome self-image for blacks. Stories like *Mommies at Work* and *Martin's Father* may aid in the disintegration of sex-role stereotypes, but they are not likely to take the place of *Kathy and the Big Snow* (about a heroic tractor who just happens to be female) and *Pippi Longstocking,* with its liberated heroine who has never heard of Women's Lib. And some of the books most likely to promote a black child's self-esteem don't talk about blackness at all. They simply feature a black protagonist.

FREDELLE MAYNARD
Guiding Your Child to a More Creative Life

Letters and Phone Calls from Irate Readers and Contributors Notwithstanding . . .

To the question "What books should our children read?" there's no simple answer. Since there are hundreds of kids' books published every week—and tens of thousands already in print—it is impossible to present a comprehensive list, or even a list of just favorites. Our "must read" lists are changing from day to day; we have lost our definition of what a classic is. (Invariably, the books I like most are my son's least favorite, and vice versa.) Part of the problem lies in the fact that the classics we grew up with have been translated into other forms for our children's generation.

Kids who watch *Sesame Street* think that Goldilocks answered Baby Bear's "Who ate my porridge?" with a flip "Don't looka me!" And they don't bat an eye when the storybook characters—Cinderella, Snow White, et al.—are interviewed by a frog!

Good grief, these kids wouldn't be at all surprised if Huck Finn ran into Barbie and Ken getting stoned along the banks of the Mississippi or if around the next corner Curious George was visiting a lesbian community.

These are the kids we're choosing books for? When we asked some kids to help us with our list of books kids love, they were unable to be critical. They liked everything. They thought it was like school where they are supposed to find everything "interesting." So we asked adults what they remembered loving or what they think their children really do love. They mentioned Pooh and Black Beauty, the Madeline books, fairy tales (Andersen's and Grimm's), *The Wind in the Willows,* Heidi, Babar, Mary Poppins, *The Velveteen Rabbit.* The Howard Pyle books kept coming up. A few people who loved Lewis Carroll said they couldn't see how anyone under twenty-one could understand *Alice in Wonderland.* Another generation of "classics" includes *Millions of Cats, Make Way for Ducklings, Mike Mulligan and His Steam Shovel.* And *The Red Balloon* is treasured by many children and parents.

What we have included in the reviews that follow, finally, is only a small portion of those books that came to our attention that we liked. Only a few of them will survive to amuse your children's children, but if you and your child will be reading lots of books, these are some worth knowing about. You may find your favorites elsewhere in this book. Or, and heaven forgive us all, they may have been overlooked entirely. I have imagined the letters and phone calls from contributors and readers, admonishing: How can you have forgotten Manus Pinkwater? And Fernando Krahn? You left out Segal's *Tell Me a Mitzi* and Kotzwinkle's *Elephant Boy.* Didn't you mean to include Robert Welber's *Winter Picnic?* Or Robert Kraus's *Leo the Late Bloomer?* And speaking of Leo, dear me, how about Leo Leonni's *Swimmy?* Or Dennis Nolan's *Big Pig?* Or Susan Jeffers' *Three Jovial Huntsmen?* Didn't you love William Weisner's *Moon Stories,* or Benjamin's *365 Birthdays* by the Barretts? You mean you overlooked *Paddle-to-the-Sea* (and who could forget a name like Holling C. Holling?)—a book that in fact *will* be around for your children's children.

Help! There's no more time or space. There are too many books. (Anyway, we must hurry to get out our second-grade "Limited Vocabulary Edition" of *Oedipus,* starring Mickey Mouse and his Mom.) ELS

. . . Here's a List of Some of Our Favorite Books

(Listed Alphabetically)

ALEXANDER AND THE TERRIBLE, HORRIBLE, NO GOOD, VERY BAD DAY, *by Judith Viorst (Atheneum, 1972, $6.95 hardcover; $1.95 paperback).*

Judith Viorst's books work for my kids and me. My children identify with her boys and the problems they face—toilets not being flushed, zippers that get stuck. In *Alexander and the Terrible, Horrible, No Good, Very Bad Day,* Alexander is dreaming of how it might go better for him in Australia, and his Mom says, "Some days are like that. Even in Australia." Of course.

BOBBIE MALONE

ALICE'S ADVENTURES IN WONDERLAND, *by Lewis Carroll (various editions).*

The mysteries of big and little, innocence and perversity, stuff and nonsense, are best preserved in *Alice in Wonderland,* judging by the night-after-night return to its delights on demand from my daughter. We found a version just light enough to keep a three- or four-year-old from falling asleep on the exposition. (It was a sixty-six-page excerpt in a funny little pink book called *The Best in Children's Books,* published by Doubleday in 1958, and now, unfortunately, out of print [try your library]. The bonus was another beloved tale, Phyllis Krasilovsky's *The Man Who Didn't Wash His Dishes.*)

GAIL SHEEHY

[Is the unabridged *Alice* too difficult and obscure for contemporary American kids? Martin Gardner, who, as editor of *The Annotated Alice* (NAL, $3.95) and an expert on Lewis Carroll, should know, suspects that it is. See his article below.]

A CHILD'S GARDEN OF BEWILDERMENT

My own view is—though it arouses some Carrollians to a pitch of frenzy—that *Alice* is no longer a children's book. I do not deny that here and there a few unusual children, more in England than here, are still capable of enjoying it, but I believe their number is steadily diminishing. Like *Gulliver's Travels, Robinson Crusoe,* and *Huckleberry Finn, Alice* has joined that curious list of books that librarians call "children's classics" but which are read and relished mostly by grownups. I myself have never met a child who said that *Alice* was one of his or her favorite books, and I have met only two U.S. adults who said they had enjoyed it as a small child. (Please don't write me an angry letter saying you have just read *Alice* to your five-year-old and she *loved* it. Try reading to her *A Midsummer Night's Dream* or Norman Mailer's *American Dream;* you'll find she loves them, too.)

The truth is that, from a modern child's point of view, the Alice books are plotless, pointless, unfunny, and more frightening than a monster movie. . . .

For intelligent children over fifteen and adults who, unlike Mencken, are not bored by fantasy,

the Alice books are rich in subtle humor, social satire, and philosophical depth. Both books, especially the second, are crammed with paradoxical nonsense of exactly the sort that mathematicians and logicians revel in. It is no accident that you are likely to find more references to *Alice* in a book by a modern philosopher of science than in a book by a literary critic. . . .

Moreover, *Alice* swarms with jokes that no American child will catch (e.g., the Ugly Duchess's clever double pun on the proverb "Take care of the pence and the pounds will take of themselves"). And there are jokes not even an English child today can understand (e.g., the parodies on poems, now forgotten, that Victorian children memorized). . . .

It is all this, from the obscure word plays to the philosophical and mathematical paradoxes, that keeps the *Alice* books alive among adults long after they have ceased to delight the average child. . . . My advice is: Give *The Wizard* (in its handsome Dover paperback edition, with its bibliography of Baum's other books) to that ten-year-old; send *Alice* (*The Annotated Alice,* of course) to anyone over fifteen who is bored with reading novels about psychotics in a real world.

MARTIN GARDNER
Saturday Review

ALL THE WAY HOME, *by Lore Segal, illustrated by James Marshall (Farrar, Straus & Giroux, 1973, $4.95 hardcover).*

Juliet falls down in the park. She cries, at which her baby brother George grins maniacally. The mother announces they will have to go home. Juliet cries all the way home.

As they proceed, they meet a dog who wants to know what all the noise is about. He gets behind Juliet and barks all the way home. They meet a cat who meows all the way home. They meet a bird who squawks all the way home. It is a regular racket.

At home the doorman will not let them in because they are making too much noise. They are consigned, like a group of Ancient Mariners, to walking on and on. Finally Juliet whispers to her mother that she doesn't feel like crying anymore and that she wants to go home. That whisper is courageous and powerful. Juliet's

family can enter the apartment building. The animals keep walking.

The pictures in this book are very funny—check the expressions on the mother and the hateful little sibling in particular—and the story will appeal to any child who has ever gotten out of control in public and not quite known how to collect himself.

JENNIFER CARDEN

AMELIA BEDELIA *by Peggy Parish (Harper & Row, 1963, $3.95 hardcover; Scholastic, 1970, paperback 95 cents).*

A maid causes incredible havoc in the household by following the literal meaning of every instruction given to her. Imagine what happens when she is told to "dust the furniture" or "dress the chicken" . . .

JIM BLAKE and BARBARA ERNST
The Great Perpetual Learning Machine

AND THEN WHAT HAPPENED, PAUL REVERE?, *by Jean Fritz, illustrated by Margot Tomes (Coward, McCann & Geoghegan, 1973, $5.95 hardcover).*

It's a well-known fact that Paul Revere rode around the countryside warning everyone that the British were coming. Ms. Fritz tells us all about that. What she also tells us is that Paul left home in such a hurry he left the door open and his dog got out; that he forgot his spurs and retrieved them only by sending his dog back home with a note attached to his collar; that he was arrested by the English at one point and relieved of his horse; and that the opening shots of the Battle of Lexington found him helping John Hancock carry a trunkful of secret papers through a hail of enemy gunfire—a trunk that had accidentally been left in a tavern.

Harrowing and suspenseful? Definitely. And the ridiculousness of it all is not lost on Ms. Fritz, either. "Paul Revere felt bad, of course," she writes, after relating the story of his unfortunate capture by the English, "to be on his Big Ride without a horse."

CBC
With thanks to Joe Raposo

AND TO THINK THAT I SAW IT ON MULBERRY STREET, *by Dr. Seuss (Vanguard, 1937, $3.95 hardcover).*

[Dr. Seuss's] first book for children, in 1937, *And to Think That I Saw It on Mulberry Street,* was a prototype, low-key version of all Seuss plots and characters to follow. The hero, Marco, is—like his creator—a varnisher of truth. Despite his father's stern warnings to

Stop telling such outlandish tales.
Stop turning minnows into whales

(precisely the talents that have won the book's author a firm place beside Edward Lear and Lewis Carroll as one of the inspired creators of nonsense in the English language), he cannot. Left to his own devices on a walk down Mulberry Street, Marco finds it impossible to suppress his gift for brightening up reality. From a garden-variety horse and wagon he sees on his walk, Marco compulsively builds bigger and better variations until he ends up with "a Rajah, with rubies, perched high on a throne" atop an elephant who, with two giraffe assistants, is pulling an enormous brass band, with a trailer behind—the entire entourage escorted by motorcycle policemen past the mayor's reviewing stand while a small airplane drops confetti down on the frenetic scene . . . The reader is at a mild fever pitch by the time the final invention is heaped on Marco's rapidly expanding universe. It is a blessed relief when the hero, home at last, is confronted by his fact-loving father's query: "Did *nothing* excite you or make your heart beat?" and he replies:

Nothing, I said, growing red as a beet,
But a plain horse and wagon on Mulberry Street.

SELMA G. LANES
Down the Rabbit Hole

THE UNREAL WORLD OF DR. SEUSS

Adults are just obsolete children . . . and to hell with them.

DR. SEUSS

I love Dr. Seuss and I love his books. That doesn't mean, as some would have it, that I don't love P. L. Travers, A. A. Milne (and the wonderful Sheperds *père et fille*), William Pène du Bois, Howard Pyle, Rudyard Kipling, Edward Gorey, Crocket Johnson, Charles Kingsley, and Arnold Lobel. These and a host of others I do also love. But there are many who get positively exercised about Dr. Seuss, who somehow feel that if you're nuts about Beatrix Potter, you can't also be nuts about *him.* I'm willing to wager that B. Potter (a little nuts herself) would have understood Dr. Seuss rather better than the rest of us, would have understood his unwavering vision, his dedication to craftsmanship, the extraordinary amount of work that goes into his books. It's just that his come out looking a little different.

The problem is that people seem to want little children to read about tiny, furry things that live in burrows and wear bonnets and aprons of a sort worn only by tiny, furry things that live in burrows in children's books. As they grow older, children are then expected to suddenly switch their attention from furry animals to people (also frequently modishly furry) who wear earth shoes and cope endlessly with the problems of the Real World. Then, finally, fully prepared for life, the kids are at last allowed to return to fantasy by graduating to *Cosmopolitan, Penthouse,* and the *Harvard Business Review.*

Alas, while Dr. Seuss's creatures occasionally do live in burrows (usually rather noisy and, we suspect, smelly places), they tend to be a pretty raffish lot, frequently without manners and generally with their fur growing in absolutely the wrong places. And they almost never wear earth shoes—though I think I spotted them once on a camel. That particular camel had problems all right, but they were far from the usual, dreary earth-shod variety: he had come down with the wubbles and had started to bubble. And, in the Unreal World of Dr. Seuss, a world around which generations of children have gleefully followed him, that's a pretty serious condition.

The three-most-often-asked questions about Dr. Seuss are:

(1) What is his real name?
(2) Where does he live?
(3) Is he really a doctor?

And the true answers are:

(1) Theodor Seuss Geisel (he sometimes spells it backward).
(2) On a mountaintop (in La Jolla, California).
(3) Yes. But he wasn't always. At first he just called himself "Dr. Seuss." Then Dartmouth, his alma mater, gave him a doctorate. Now he calls himself "Doctor Dr. Seuss." (He calls his wife "Mrs. Dr. Seuss.")

MICHAEL FRITH
Former editor of Dr. Seuss's books

AN APPLE A DAY, by Judi Barrett, illustrated by Tim Lewis (Atheneum, 1973, $3.95 hardcover).

It happens that Jeremy hates apples, so every night after dinner when his mother gives him an apple he hides it away uneaten in his room. Soon his room is so overrun with apples that he can hardly walk around in there. He tries to eat his way out, and becomes sick. A doctor is summoned, and cannot get the door to Jeremy's room open because of the wall of apples. An apple a day has *almost* kept the doctor away, but he enters through the window, a delightful moment in the illustrations. Children love stories in which things get out of hand and then are restored to order. In this case Jeremy's mother makes a great deal of applesauce, which she and her husband eat. Jeremy has a pear.

JENNIFER CARDEN

THE BAD ISLAND, by William Steig, illustrated by the author (Simon and Schuster, 1969, $5.70 hardcover).

The Bad Island is my favorite book in the world, yet no one ever seems to know about it;

it's never in any of the bookstores. It's about an island that nurtures grotesque things—everything that lives on it is *bad.* The whole place reeks with monstrous characters and warts and things crawling out of trees. And the words that describe the island's badness, and the brilliant watercolors in the illustrations, get more and more grotesque with each passing page.

Then one day a flower grows, and everybody freaks out. A storm comes, all the awful things get killed, and all that's left are the flowers!

The Bad Island is more bizarre than Maurice Sendak's *Where the Wild Things Are,* and William Steig's art is extraordinarily beautiful.

SUSAN KANOR

THE BEARS' ALMANAC, written and illustrated by Stan and Jan Berenstain (Random House, 1973, $3.95 hardcover).

When I say "the best of the Berenstains," I'm *saying* something. No previous Stan-and-Jan jamboree has had the frolic, fun and facts that fill these page-after-pages. A wacky array (hooray) of happy bears take young readers through the months and seasons of the year, with a goofy character called Actual Factual Bear flipping facts that kids enjoy—how the wind blows, what snow is, how to tell it's summer. It rhymes, it entertains, it instructs, it's a bargain.

GENE SHALIT
Ladies Home Journal

BENJAMIN & TULIP, by Rosemary Wells (Dial Press, 1973, $4.95 hardcover; 1977, $1.50 paperback).

Tulip is a female bully raccoon who sits around in tree branches waiting to terrorize Benjamin when he passes underneath. Benjamin's Aunt Fern thinks Tulip is a sweet little girl, which shows how much she knows. This is an absolutely hilarious little book, with funny illustrations and funny text. You will be delighted to hear that at the end Benjamin smashes a watermelon in Tulip's face. This puts the relationship on a more equal footing, and the two of them sit down to spit seeds at each other and eat the remains of the melon.

JENNIFER CARDEN

THE BEST WORD BOOK EVER, by Richard Scarry (Golden Books, 1963, $4.95 hardcover).

Occasionally . . . genius will out and a product hard-headedly devised for the mass market proves so lastingly popular that the author-illustrator becomes more important than the product he has helped to produce. Such was the case with Richard Scarry, whose lively and individualized little animals had been appearing in Golden books of varied format for more than a dozen years before his first Golden giant encyclopedia—*The Best Word Book Ever*—became a best seller in 1963. Crammed full of small animals totally absorbed in the objects and activities of daily life, it continues to sell remarkably well. Though [former Golden Books editor Roberta] Miller has said that "the one thing merchandise books cannot do is provide just the right book for Suzy"—meaning that books which seek a common denominator for multitudes of children cannot hope to appeal to the individuality of any given one—Richard Scarry has managed to get around this problem by covering all contingencies in his books. When Scarry depicts houses, foods, trucks, boats, etc., he provides so many specific varieties within the general category that he usually manages to hit the very truck, house or boat that speaks volumes to any given small viewer. This probably explains why so many young children will pore over his busy, narrative illustrations, by them-

selves, for unnaturally long periods of time. Scarry's more recent volumes, *What Do People Do All Day?* and *Great Big Schoolhouse,* employ the same winning encyclopedic approach, but they are now done under the Random House imprint.

SELMA G. LANES
Down the Rabbit Hole

RICHARD SCARRY A SEXIST? RICHARD SCARRY?

Richard Scarry is big. He's an institution. I never questioned his books; rather I accepted them happily as hand-me-downs, gave brief thought to the slightly controversial question of the busyness of his pages, wasn't crazy about the style of art, but wasn't offended either. Then I finally *read* one of the books. I think the first one I read was *What Do People Do All Day?,* a very popular book, one that sets out to tell kids about the jobs people have.

On the first twenty pages of the book (a section that starts with "Everyone is a worker"), besides the Mommy, the only working characters that are clearly female are the dancer, the dressmaker, the beautician, and the laundress. In the course of this section, Daddy buys Mommy some earrings and, for taking such good care of the house, a new dress (which, to free her hands for giving Dad a big hug and kiss, she hangs on the handle of her vacuum cleaner—without which none of this would have been possible).

Following that is a section called "Mother's work is never done," in which it certainly isn't. At the start of the day mother and daughter cook and serve breakfast to father and son, who are sitting at the table with forks poised. Daddy gives Mommy money; Mommy gives Daddy a kiss. The problem is that the book suggests no options. The thing to be if you're a woman is a mommy (and women who are not mommies are nurses or stewardesses—they don't work on ships, farms, trucks, in factories).

It's a pity, too, because the books have so much in them that is good and information that is useful to a pre-schooler: how seeds grow; how wood is used, paper is made; how we get electricity, cotton; where bread comes from. We might forgive Scarry because in the sixties, when most of the books were published, not many consciousnesses were raised, but we should be aware of the one-sidedness when we read these books, mention it to our kids, and hope Scarry will come around (or that his publishers will let the old books go out of print).

ELS

THE BOY WHO PAINTED WALLPAPER, *by Mark Rubin (Watts, 1974, $4.90 hardcover).*

A fast-paced story with comical line drawings, Rubin's book is about a famous, rich, and clever little boy who paints hundreds of rolls of wallpaper to look like hundreds of little boys painting wallpaper.

RS

CAPS FOR SALE, *by Esphyr Slobodkina (Young Scott/Addison-Wesley, 1947, $4.25 hardcover; School Book Service, 1976, 95 cents paperback).*

Here is a ridiculous story that kids love to hear. A man wears a lot of different colored caps on his head. He falls asleep by the side of a tree, and the monkeys steal all the caps, one by one. When the man wakes up all the caps are gone and the monkeys are up in the tree imitating him with the caps on their heads. And the old man says, You give me back my caps . . . and the kids all go crazy. Finally the monkeys throw the caps out of the tree. It's a wonderful, repetitious story.

JUDY GRAHAM

CHARLIE AND THE CHOCOLATE FACTORY, *by Roald Dahl (Knopf, 1964, $5.95 hardcover; Bantam, 1977, $1.95 paperback).*

In *Charlie and the Chocolate Factory*, rotten adults are punished as well as rotten children, which makes it especially fun to read. I recommend it highly.

MARC ALONSO
Age ten

CHARLOTTE'S WEB, *by E. B. White (Harper & Row, 1952, $4.95 hardcover and $1.50 paperback.)*

Charlotte's Web is as moving a fantasy as there is.

VIRGINIA HAVILAND
Horn Book

My father came home one day from work to find my mother and me dissolved in tears. "My God," he shouted, fearing the worst had happened to my baby brother. "What is it, what has happened?" "Oh, Daddy," I cried, "Charlotte is dead." "Charlotte? Charlotte? I don't know any Charlotte," he said, puzzled. It took several minutes of misunderstanding before we could make it snufflingly clear that a spider in a book called *Charlotte's Web* had died. We had just been reading it together. My father, though, was quite right. He did not know any Charlotte, for he had never read the book. But my mother

and I knew Charlotte. We both knew her well. And we had been with her when she died.

JANE YOLEN
Writing Books for Children

DAWN, *by Uri Shulevitz, illustrated by the author (Farrar, Straus & Giroux, 1974, $5.95 hardcover).*

Dawn is a beautiful book, a small gem of a book that is fun to share with a child. Uri Shulevitz has adapted an eighth-century Chinese poem on the coming of dawn into the world of nature as experienced by an old man and his grandson. The watercolors are exquisite, and the text is properly terse. Shulevitz paints nature with craft and guile. He succeeds in illustrating "quiet" and "still," surely no small accomplishment. The color at the end of the book is both inevitable and thrilling. I found myself showing this book off and sitting back and waiting for the magic to take hold.

SHERMAN DREXLER

A DAY NO PIGS WOULD DIE, *by Robert Newton Peck (Knopf, 1972, $6.95 hardcover; Dell, 1974, $1.25 paperback).*

This is a strong, uncompromising story of Shaker farm life told through the eyes of a twelve-year-old boy on his way to becoming a man.

His father, Haven Peck, is a pig slaughterer and farmer, full of plain truth and abiding love for his family, his land, and the work of God.

The language shines in its simplicity, and my children are delighted with the novel use of certain words and phrases: "Papa burdened me upstairs to my room"; "a warm glass of milking"; "She [a cow] was looking clean as clergy."

There is sorrow and death in this little book, but it is presented as a natural part of life, as natural as dawn and rain and spring.

This is an excellent reading-out-loud book because conversation seems to result from sharing its pages with someone, and I think any moderately sensitive, well-informed child from about eight years on would enjoy it, even though it is not, strictly speaking, a children's book.

RUTH PELMAS

FAIRY TALES, *by E. E. Cummings, pictures by John Eaton (Harcourt Brace Jovanovich, 1950, $6.95 hardcover; 1975, $1.75 paperback).*

These four fairy tales have the informality and spontaneity and light sense of fancy of stories that a father makes up for his daughter when the father happens to be E. E. Cummings. A butterfly visits an elephant, a bird makes sweet mosquito pie for a lonely house, an ageless fairy eats plates of light and glasses of silence for lunch and tries to stop an old man from constantly saying *why*. John Eaton's illustrations are as airy and whimsical as E. E. Cummings' words.

RS

With thanks to Jim Silverman

FORTUNATELY, by Remy Charlip (Parents' Magazine Press, 1964, $5.95 hardcover).

Chris, who's seven, brought over a picture book his younger brother had been enjoying, and held the book up for me to see the pictures (he knew the text by heart). "When Ned's plane exploded . . . Fortunately he had a parachute . . . Unfortunately the parachute didn't open . . . Fortunately there was a haystack . . . Unfortunately there was a pitchfork in the haystack . . ."

I hadn't read Remy Charlip's *Fortunately* in a while, and it was wonderful to experience again what fun it is for people of all ages. (Fortunately, the book is available in a Scholastic paperback. Unfortunately, the paperback publisher didn't think kids would understand the words "fortunately" and "unfortunately," so they changed the title and text to read "What good luck . . . What bad luck." Fortunately, there are libraries, so if you don't buy the original version in hardcover, you can borrow it.)

FREAKY FRIDAY, by Mary Rodgers (Harper & Row, 1972, $5.95 hardcover; 1973, $1.50 paperback).

One Friday, Annabel Andrews awakens in her mother's body, having kept her own thirteen-year-old mind, sense of humor, and viewpoint. Coping with Ma's hectic schedule and trying not to slip out of Ma's character while still in Ma's body, Annabel finds out how family, teachers, friends see her. She's amazed that her brother, Ape Face, knows she hates him and that Boris (*sigh!*), the boy upstairs, thinks she is a drip. By the end of the day Annabel has vowed to be different, and even if the only change is in having gained increased sympathy for Ma—whose life, she has discovered, is no picnic with Annabel's adolescent ways—well, then it all was worth it.

Mary Rodgers' keynote is humor, and her saga, on which the Disney movie was based, will captivate readers from about the age of nine. Fast reading, zippy dialogue, lots of laughs.

ALICE BACH

FREDDY THE PIG BOOKS, by Walter R. Brooks (Knopf)

There are few, if any, books from my childhood days that I remember more fondly than Walter R. Brooks's Freddy the Pig series. Brooks created Freddy for eight- to twelve-year-olds, but I remember coming across him at a younger age: when I was in kindergarten or first grade, one of my teachers—who obviously had a good nose for satire—would read a Freddy novel to us, one chapter a day, during rest period. It wasn't long before the entire class was hopelessly addicted, and I made my parents go out and buy me the whole series.

So who is Freddy the Pig? Well, he's one of the inhabitants of the Bean farm near the town of Centerboro. Mr. Bean's farm is hardly typical: his animals are very much a part of the family, and, indeed, tend to live much more interesting, varied, and influential lives than their owners. At various times in his career, Freddy—"detective, pied piper, newspaper editor, poet"—has managed the political campaign of Mrs. Wiggins, the cow (she was running for president of a republic established to keep a dictator woodpecker from taking over the First Animal Bank, which Freddy had founded to prove to the Beans that the animals could manage the farm while the family went to Europe); traveled the world in a balloon, with two brave ducks as companions (this story is related in *Freddy and the Perilous Adventure*); set up a travel agency (the first excursion cow carried thirty mice "down the river road for a mile or two, crossed the canal and came back the other way, stopping at the cheese factory for lunch"); and tried to help Mr. Camphor, a local estate owner, rid his summer house of his two aunts ("There's two kinds of aunts," Mr. C. was fond of saying. "There's the regular kind, and then there's the other kind. Mine are the other kind").

And that's only the beginning. There are more than a dozen Freddy books in all, and most are still available from Alfred A. Knopf, Publishers. Leafing through the series I was reminded of reading Orwell's *Animal Farm* as a young adult and thinking, "Hmph, it's Freddy the Pig."

CBC

THE GIRL WHO LOVED THE WIND, by Jane Yolen, pictures by Ed Young (Crowell, 1972, 24 pages, $6.95 hardcover).

Danina's father, a widower and wealthy merchant, determines that his daughter's life should be always happy. He shuts her away in a carefully regulated, lovely, lonely place where Danina grows up "knowing everything that was in her father's heart but nothing of the world."

One day she hears something sad but beautiful. It is the wind, who explains who he is and affirms that he is "not always kind." Danina begins to ask questions of her father about a world in which things are sometimes sad, where there is challenge, and where "nothing is always."

Danina's father, assuming she has been talking to a flesh-and-blood person from the outside, takes steps to protect her further. Ultimately, however, Danina (on a billowing cape) and the wind manage to sail far to the west into the ever-changing world.

This is one of the best picture books I have ever seen. The watercolor and collage illustrations are lush; the text is beautiful. Its implications are many, and will provoke thoughtful discussions with youngsters about feelings, adults, freedom, risks, and all manner of things having to do with realistic living.

JENNIFER CARDEN

THE GIVING TREE, *by Shel Silverstein (Harper & Row, 1964, $4.95 hardcover).*

The Giving Tree is the most important book my children had—and to think that it took four years for the publisher's salesmen to agree that the book should be published. The ending, I understand, was thought by them to be too sad for children. How sad.

The Giving Tree is also available in French, as *L'Arbre au Grand Coeur.*

JEROME AGEL

HARLEQUIN AND THE GIFT OF MANY COLORS, *by Remy Charlip and Burton Supree, illustrated by Remy Charlip (Parents' Magazine Press, 1973, $5.95 hardcover).*

What a wonderful introduction this book is to a tale that has many variations—in dance and music as well as in literature. *Harlequin* is a story about not having enough and sharing, about children as a subculture, about carnivals as they used to be—a story told as much in the beautiful pastel illustrations as in the words.

RS

HARRIET THE SPY, *by Louise Fitzhugh (Harper & Row, 1964, $5.95 hardcover; Dell, 1975, $1.50 paperback).*

One of the best books in the world. About a tough and truly nasty little kid who does all the horrid things that kids do. *Harriet the Spy* is not an adult's romanticized view of childhood. It's

miserable and unhappy and horrible, and that's just fine because it's a marvelously good story.

BECKY CORWIN

HIGGLETY PIGGLETY POP! OR THERE MUST BE MORE TO LIFE, *by Maurice Sendak (Harper & Row, 1967, $4.95 hardcover).*

Higglety Pigglety Pop! or There Must Be More to Life perhaps comes closest to Sendak's ideal of the perfect mix of original conception, words and pictures. It is the waggish tale of Jennie, a Sealyham terrier. Jennie is the dog "who has everything," yet leaves home because, as she says, "there must be more to life." Carrying her Gladstone bag in her mouth, she sets off for new experiences, which include being a nursemaid for a baby who will not eat and losing her charge to a lion who will eat anything. Jennie finally lands on all four feet in the World Mother Goose Theater's staging of the nursery rhyme: "Higglety pigglety pop!/ The dog has eaten the mop!" The book is never cutesie or cloying. Like *Alice in Wonderland* it can transform a narrative non sequitur into art. At its best, it achieves levels of fond comedy that are more touching if you know—as Sendak's readers rarely do—that the author actually had a Sealyham named Jennie who died in 1967.

From *Time* magazine

HORTON HATCHES THE EGG, *by Dr. Seuss (Random House, 1940, $3.95 hardcover).*

Of all the Dr. Seuss books, *Horton Hatches the Egg* is our family's very favorite. Underlying the humor is a deeply moving story of a dear elephant whose stubborn, if misplaced, loyalty finally triumphs over greed and irresponsibility. After countless readings, we still love it.

RUTH PELMAS

I MET A PENGUIN, *by Frank Asch, illustrated by the author (McGraw-Hill, 1972, $4.95 hardcover).*

I am a new fan of Frank Asch. *I Met a Penguin* is a sweet, nutty book which delights me and the young children I've read it with. The female penguin—"as strong as an elephant . . . as gentle as a dove . . . as pretty as a peacock"—that the lion meets after he has been shipwrecked at the South Pole is a noble creation. The book is subtitled "A Love Story," and it really is.

Frank Asch is an original, someone in touch with his own fantasies. He draws with the same personal feeling he gets into his writing, and his

later book, *Gia and the One Hundred Dollars Worth of Bubblegum* (McGraw-Hill, 1974), lives up to its predecessor. Mr. Asch and his books are a find.
SHERMAN DREXLER

I'M NOBODY! WHO ARE YOU, *by Mary Anderson (Atheneum, 1974, $6.95 hardcover).*

This starts out as a story of a lonely girl with no friends. Sound familiar?

At the start of a new school term, lonely, fat, freckled, poetry-loving Ellie Grogan meets poetry-loving, pretty unusual—pretty *and* unusual—Stephanie. A strange force pulls the girls together, and they become fast friends.

Stephanie enjoys psychic power, and wants to share it with Ellie. She is able to describe Ellie's most secret thoughts. And she can transmit pictures to Ellie's mind; when the picture is "received," Ellie is convinced. She agrees to follow Stephanie wherever weird adventure and disaster lead.

In *I'm Nobody! Who Are You?*, two once-lonely people find friendship in each other and share lively experiences. (I'm still shivering.) There are many strange things in this novel—even the dust jacket is spooky—and I would recommend it for fifth- to seventh-graders. Adventures of the mind will always find explorers, and Stephanie and Ellie are on the right path.
JULIE AGEL
Age fourteen

IN THE NIGHT KITCHEN, *by Maurice Sendak (Harper & Row, 1970, $5.95 hardcover).*

When I was a child, there was an advertisement which I remember very clearly. It was for the Sunshine bakers, and it read: "We Bake While You Sleep!" It seemed to me the most sadistic thing in the world, because all I wanted to do was stay up and watch . . . it seemed so absurdly cruel and arbitrary for them to do it while I slept. And also for them to think I would think that that was terrific stuff on their part, and would eat their product on top of that. It bothered me a good deal, and I remember I used to save the coupons showing the three fat little Sunshine bakers going off to this magic place at night, wherever it was, to have their fun, while I had to go to bed. This book was a sort of vendetta book to get back at them and to say that I am now old enough to stay up at night and know what's happening in the Night Kitchen!
MAURICE SENDAK
As quoted by Virginia Haviland in an article by Jonathan Cott, in *Rolling Stone*

THE J.C. PENNEY CATALOGUE

My son, at three, went crazy over the colorful catalogue from J. C. Penney. After a year it was still one of his favorite books and could occupy him for half an hour.
BART POTENZA

[To get yourself on the Penney mailing list, go to the nearest catalogue store or telephone the catalogue department of your local Penney's. For $2, which is deductible from your first purchase, you can have their big catalogue (over 1,000 pages, and not exactly comfortable for lap reading). There are several smaller, free catalogues available at the beginning of each season, but they go quickly.—ELS]

THE JUNIPER TREE AND OTHER TALES FROM GRIMM, *selected by Lore Segal and Maurice Sendak, translated from the German by Lore Segal and Randall Jarrell, illustrated by Maurice Sendak (Farrar, Straus & Giroux, 1973, 2 volumes boxed, $12.95).*

Whatever cautionary words one might say about *The Juniper Tree*, it's destined to wind up on every middle-class child's bookshelf. In a way, it deserves to be there: the stories are high camp, for the most part gorgeously written (and translated) and Sendak's illustrations are, as ever, *wonderful.* One tale, "Mrs. Gertrude," a two-pager in which an "obstinate and willful" little girl who does not obey her parents winds up transformed into a log to brighten the hearth of a witch (don't listen to mommy and you'll burn—one way or the other) may alone be worth the book's price; it's an exceptionally fine short story. But the real question, it seems to us, is whether you really want your children to read these items. . . . The stories are wildly sexist—as well as racist and classist. Peasant women (do consider your forebears . . .) are ugly, greedy, incompetent, with "coarse arms and legs" ("The Three Feathers"). In "Hans My Hedgehog," black skin can be changed to white (the more desirable) by a "special salve." In the same story, daughters are given away by their fathers as payment for services rendered. Throughout, male children are prized more than female children, women give birth while their husbands (kings or princes) are off hunting. Witches abound and are burned. Husbands commit bigamy, one wife being returned to her family, out of favor, used goods. Disobedient women (those who exercise minds independent of men) are literally hacked to pieces. Interior decoration is proselytized as a way to catch a prince. Wives are driving, avaricious, greedy, heartless (the momma's the real bad guy in "Hansel and Gretel"). Violence—not just sexist/sexual violence—appears throughout. And, of course, only beauties "catch" princes. . . . One could conceivably argue that Grimm is closer to the way things really are than some of the beatific non-sexist non-violent children's books now being produced. But that's your decision. To us, *The Juniper Tree* seems to demand more polemical sophistication than most children can muster. But buy a copy for yourself, you'll love it.

From *New Times*

CHILDREN AND FAIRY STORIES: AN ACCIDENT OF HISTORY?

Fairy stories have in the modern lettered world been relegated to the "nursery" as shabby or old-fashioned furniture is relegated to the playroom, primarily because the adults do not want it, and do not mind if it is misused.* It is not the choice of the children which decides this. Children as a class—except in a common lack of experience they are not one—neither like fairy stories more, nor understand them better than adults do; and no more than they like many other things. They are young and growing, and normally have keen appetites, so the fairy stories as a rule go down well enough. But in fact only some children, and some adults, have any special taste for them; and when they have it, it is not exclusive, nor even necessarily dominant. It is a taste, too, that would not appear, I think, very early in childhood without artificial stimulus; it is certainly one that does not decrease but increases with age, if it is innate.

It is true that in recent times fairy stories have usually been written or "adapted" for children. But so may music be, or verse, or novels, or history, or scientific manuals. It is a dangerous process, even when it is necessary. It is indeed only saved from disaster by the fact that the arts and sciences are not as a whole relegated to the nursery; the nursery and schoolroom are merely given such tastes and glimpses of the adult thing as seem fit for them in adult opinion (often much mistaken). Any one of these things would, if left altogether in the nursery, become gravely impaired. So would a beautiful table, a good picture, or a useful machine (such as a microscope), be defaced or broken, if it were left long unregarded in a schoolroom. Fairy stories banished in this way, cut off from a full adult art, would in the end be ruined; indeed in so far as they have been so banished, they have been ruined.

J. R. R. TOLKIEN
Tree and Leaf

* In the case of stories and other nursery lore, there is also another factor. Wealthier families employed women to look after their children, and the stories were provided by these nurses, who were sometimes in touch with rustic and traditional lore forgotten by their "betters." It is long since this source dried up, at any rate in England; but it once had some importance. But again there is no proof of the special fitness of children as the recipients of this vanishing "folklore." The nurses might just as well (or better) have been left to choose the pictures and furniture.

JUST SO STORIES, by *Rudyard Kipling* (various editions).

The book from our childhood that has been most enjoyable to share with our children is Kipling's *Just So Stories*. The stories are a delight to read over and over again, and the words—marvelous-sounding words, with lots of repetition—fascinate the children as much as the plots do. Because we loved the book so much as children, we get a special pleasure out of our own children's enjoyment of it and they, in turn, get a kick out of knowing that their parents once had the same stories read to them when they were little.

BROOKE ADLER

Just So Stories by Rudyard Kipling is the one book I hadn't expected to hold up, but it does, it does.

JOEL OPPENHEIMER

THE LITTLE HOUSE BOOKS, by *Laura Ingalls Wilder (Harper & Row).*

The Wilder books are not so complicated that you have to ask what does this mean and not so easy that they're just dumb. They're very, very good.

JENNY WIRTSCHAFTER
Age nine

[For more on the Little House books, see Leslie Jones's review on page 276]

LITTLE TOOT, *pictures and story by Hardie Gramatky (G. P. Putnam's Sons, 1939, $6.95 hardcover).*

At the foot of an old, old wharf lives the cutest, silliest little tugboat you ever saw. A *very* handsome tugboat with a brand-new candy-stick smokestack. His name is Little Toot. And this name he came by through no fault of his own. Blow hard as he would, the only sound that came out of his whistle was a gay, small toot-toot-toot.

And therein hangs one anthropomorphic tale that many of us grew up on. *Little Toot* is a wonderful book for children, still. It's all about a childlike tugboat who plays instead of working. A real kid is Little Toot. Then he has a change of heart, roughly analogous to the end of adolescence.

He realizes he comes from a great family (Big Toot and Grandfather Toot). Now he too should be pulling his own weight, as it were. So he tries to help out. Naturally, none of the other tugs will take him seriously at first because he has a history as a cut-up. He has such a hard time trying to establish himself as a grown-up tugboat, in fact, that he becomes preoccupied with the problem and drifts out to sea.

Things get really exciting. A terrible storm comes up. Little Toot is frightened, because tugboats are not comfortable at all at sea. But look! An ocean liner is jammed between two rocks and in distress. What to do? Little Toot puffs SOS in smoke, and the entire fleet of tugs sees the signals from downstream. They mobilize to save the ship, Little Toot's father, Big Toot, deliciously in the lead. Little Toot pulls the liner free, and now he is a hero. *Quelle rite de passage,* all here in a book for four-year-olds!

JENNIFER CARDEN

MARTHA ANN AND THE MOTHER STORE, *by Nathaniel and Betty Jo Charnley (Harcourt Brace Jovanovich, 1973, $5.50 hardcover).*

© 1973 BY JEROME SNYDER

Mothers beware! There is a store where those of us who insist on straightened rooms, sensible bedtimes, and clean shoes can be exchanged for new mothers. You and your kids can read about it in *Martha Ann and the Mother Store.*

Martha Ann trades her mother in for Mrs. Harris, who doesn't care about tidiness. But unable to find anything in the mess, Martha Ann exchanges Mrs. Harris for Mrs. Dunne, who is not strict about bedtime. Exhausted from staying up late, Martha Ann exchanges her for Mrs.

Allen, who is not fussy about wiping feet or keeping things clean, but the house gets too dirty even for Martha Ann's taste.

Next comes Mrs. Clemington, who wears an attractive red pants suit which, it turns out, she doesn't like to get wrinkled, so she cannot cuddle Martha Ann. Mrs. Clemington is finally exchanged for Martha Ann's own mother, who has been patiently drinking root beer and waiting all this time down at the Mother Store where Martha Ann has parked her.

Unnervingly similar in mood to scripts for *The Twilight Zone,* this story makes the point that, though there may be things about her you don't like, when you put it all together she spells Mother, and she is uniquely irreplaceable. The black-and-white line drawings are humorous. We don't know where the fathers are.

JENNIFER CARDEN

© MUPPETS, INC

THE MONSTER AT THE END OF THIS BOOK, *by Jon Stone, illustrated by Mike Smollin (Golden Books, 1971, $1.50).*

Grover, the furry blue Muppet protagonist of this book by *Sesame Street*'s executive producer, Jon Stone, is desperately anxious to keep readers from reaching the book's final pages. Why? Because a terrifying monster is supposedly lurking there. As a result, Grover ties down pages, nails down pages, evens builds a masonry wall across a double-page spread, all the while begging his audience "Please don't turn the page!" Needless to say, children are more anxious than ever to turn the pages, and in the course of doing so, they're likely to notice something about beginnings, middles, and ends.

Perhaps it was only my infectious enthusiasm, but after I finished reading *The Monster at the End of This Book* to one four-year-old, he went running into a roomful of adults calling out, "Everyone has to read this to me. Oh, you're all going to be so scared!"

The monster at the end of the book, incidentally, turns out to be Grover himself, and boy, is he embarrassed.

RS

THE OZ BOOKS (various titles), by L. Frank Baum (Reilly and Lee).

I never read an Oz book when I was a child! Not for me were the earthly paradise of the Emerald City and the surrounding four Oz countries with their swarming little utopias and nightmares and the enclosing Deadly Desert, nor the fairylands beyond and the far, far country of the American middlewest, nor little Dorothy from Kansas and Betsy Bobbin from Oklahoma and the Shaggy Man from Colorado and the humbug Wizard from Omaha, nor the crowd of Oz names and Oz faces, Ozma and Glinda the Good and Ozga the Rose Queen and Polychrome the Rainbow's Daughter, the Scarecrow, the Tin Woodman, Ojo the Unlucky and the Patchwork Girl, Tik Tok and the Gump and the Private Citizen and the Incubator Baby; these and all the children and simpletons, animals and freaks and fairies that make up Oz eluded me. I must have felt the lack, because when my little boy was four I started reading him Oz books.

My little boy now has a large collection of Oz books which he reads, rereads, and ignores on his own. I found most of them in second-hand bookstores. The Oz books are still in print, but the new printings omit the lavish and fantastic colour plates that graced the early editions. There must be attics all over the country—thousands of attics in the middlewest alone—where set upon set of the resplendent original Oz books, painstakingly gathered by children of two or three generations ago, lie neglected and preserved like so many child's gardens.

Those who read the Oz books when they were children say that you can never recapture the magic of Oz on rereading them. A stranger to Oz, I was spared such disappointment.

JORDAN BROTMAN
Chicago Review

THE SECRET GARDEN, by Frances Burnett (Dell Yearling paperback, $1.50).

This is a book in its third or fourth generation. The girl in it is unpleasant and badly behaved, but she is presented with understanding and sympathy. The girl also overcomes her personality defects and changes her situation through her own efforts and independence—she is a child with her own mind. She works hard bringing the garden to life. I was very pleased that my daughter, a very pragmatic, modern, outdoors girl, would be touched by the romantic, imaginative quality of the story.

ELIZABETH EHRENFELD

The Secret Garden was and still is one of my favorite books, because of its great sensitivity and beautiful evocative prose. There is also a sense of adventure, of children creating something special without adult help or intervention, and the great optimism in the face of skepticism which the children maintain. My boys, aged seven and nine, both enjoyed having *The Secret Garden* read to them at bedtime two years ago, and the nine-year-old is now reading it himself.

JACQUELINE CRAVEN

SEND WENDELL, by Genevieve Gray, illustrated by Symeon Shimin (McGraw-Hill, 1974, $6.84 hardcover).

Wendell is just about the right age to be the errand person for *every* member of his family. It seems that everyone else is always busy and it is quite convenient to "send Wendell"—to the store, to pick up orders, and on and on. Every child and adult who has ever been the "go for" can relate to Wendell's experience.

A sensitive, loving story, beautifully, warmly illustrated.

MARIE BROWN

SOUNDER, by William H. Armstrong (Harper & Row, 1969, $5.95 hardcover; 1972, $1.25 paperback).

The most important thing to me in a children's book is that it not leave the child indifferent. It shouldn't just have used him and taken up his time; rather, it should have really made an impression on him. This is one of the reasons I have such tremendous respect for *Sounder*.

I know the prejudice that exists against *Sounder*: the militant blacks don't like it, because it shows a kid who doesn't strike back. But in the old days, you know, blacks couldn't strike back; they didn't have the weapons or the wealth or the organization. There's a marvelous scene in the book involving a redneck guard who viciously lashes a lead pipe against the boy's knuckles, and his knuckles start bleeding, and you find yourself shouting to yourself, "Kid, pick up a brick! Brain this guy or something!" But he can't. He has to take it.

Another controversial episode in *Sounder* involves stealing. The librarians are very uptight about it—you mustn't steal! Militant blacks, on the other hand, feel that the father didn't steal *enough* to feed his hungry family. This is the whole point. Sometimes you have to support something that on the surface looks immoral; the point is you have to *live*. You're entitled to life, and this is what *Sounder* proves so marvelously. There's a starkness there, a kind of simplicity that pervades every page. It's one of my favorite books.

From an interview with GEORGE WOODS

SPECTACLES, by Ellen Raskin (Atheneum, 1972, $1.95 paperback).

Kids who need glasses (and even kids who don't) will delight in the funny fuzzy world of a near-sighted Iris Fogel who sees fire-breathing dragons and other unlikely sights. The text is short and simple, fun to read aloud, and perfectly integrated with the wonderful illustrations of how the world looked to Iris before and after getting glasses. (That fire-breathing dragon, by the way, turns out to be Iris's great-aunt Fanny standing in front of a tree which is in front of a house with a smoking chimney.)

ELS

THE STONE-FACED BOY, by Paula Fox (Bradbury, 1968, $6.95 hardcover).

My first encounter with Paula Fox's fiction came when I was an editor of children's books, and merely curious to see what the competition was publishing. A few pages into the first chapter of *The Stone-Faced Boy* I discovered one key to Fox's genius: her ability to distill emotions and experiences, capturing their intensity in a totally controlled literate language. I savored the prose, lingering over the words, wanting to make the story last as long as possible.

I need not have worried. Gus's journey through the horrors of the night has stayed with me. There are still moments when the image flashes into my mind—Gus, a frightened, introspective little boy battling real and imagined shadows that darken his world, and the solace he is able to take from the light contained within the crystals of a geode. Not a Hollywood sunset. Gus does not change into a burbling, happy-go-lucky child. It's a softer, more subtle light that sheds promise on the lonely world through which Gus has been struggling.

Because Fox does not sprinkle fairy dust over the wounds of her characters, because she respects their pain, we trust her vision. She is offering no magic except the magic that was there undetected all along, the untapped resources buried within Gus's own soul.

Reviews of Fox's children's novels are often studded with comments from librarians and educators—"for the special child"; "sensitive character portrait." When was the last time a critic encapsulated an adult novel with the observation "for the special adult"? Not likely. Perhaps librarians are somewhat nervous

around the prose of Paula Fox because her novels for children carry the same seriousness, the same belief in her reader's ability to relate to her material, as her adult novels.

ALICE BACH

THE STORY OF BABAR, by Jean De Brunhoff (Random House, 1937, $3.95 hardcover).

I loved all Jean De Brunhoff's original Babar books, especially the very first one, *The Story of Babar,* in which Babar the elephant comes from the jungle to civilization (for "civilization" read "Paris"). The artwork in these books is light and airy, humorous and ingenious—one scene showing Babar in an open department-store elevator has stayed with me vividly down through the years. Also exquisite: *Babar and Zephir* (Random House, 1942), which relates, among other things, the adventurous encounter of Zephir the monkey with a group of mermaids and sea monsters.

Early editions of the Babar books were printed in magnificent script, and I wish they still were. But it appears that the champions of the "Century Schoolbook is the only typeface that children can handle" philosophy of reading instruction have won the day.

SARAH KLEE

THE STORY OF FERDINAND, by Munro Leaf, illustrated by Robert Lawson (Penguin, 1977, $1.50 paperback).

© 1964 BY MUNRO LEAF AND JOHN W. BOYD

I came across a copy of this book secondhand, in mint condition, just as it was when my parents read it to me in 1942. Simple, gracefully illustrated, it is the tale of Ferdinand, a young bull whose mother worried because he wasn't aggressive and who chose to lie under the cork trees smelling the flowers. Alas, an untimely reaction to a bee sting made the bull fanciers think he'd be a winner in the ring, and they brought him there amid great pageantry. But when he smelled the audience's flowers, he sat down and refused to fight. The matador wept with rage. They had to take Ferdinand home, where he remains to this day under his favorite tree smelling the flowers.

Although the real world is in general more brutal to pacifists than this story suggests, still I read it to my son with thankfulness, and wish there were a dozen like it.
MICHAEL ROSSMAN

SYLVESTER AND THE MAGIC PEBBLE,
by William Steig (Simon and Schuster, 1969, $6.95 hardcover; Windmill, 1973, $1.95 paperback)
AMOS AND BORIS, *by William Steig (Farrar, Straus & Giroux, 1971, $5.50 hardcover; Penguin, 1977, $1.95 paperback).*

A friend to whom I'd recommended William Steig's books complained that there were too many big words in them for his four-year-old. It may be that Steig far exceeds vocabulary limits designated for his reader level, but there is always enough substance to the tales and enough going on in his careful, beautiful, true-to-the-story watercolors to keep even an alert three-year-old interested and wide-eyed. (And, most important, Steig's books can hold the interest of a thirty-year-old who might have to read them aloud with some frequency.)

COPYRIGHT © 1969
BY WILLIAM STEIG

Steig's stories are not what you'd call child-like, though there is a playfulness to his fantasies. In one, *Sylvester and the Magic Pebble,* a donkey turns into a rock and stays that way for a long time, through seasons, and no one knows until, by a curious turn of fate, he turns back again and lives happily as ever with his mother donkey and father donkey.

COPYRIGHT © 1971 BY WILLIAM STEIG

No less fantastic a story, *Amos and Boris* tells of a mouse who builds a boat, sets sail, then falls into the middle of the ocean, where he floats resignedly, wondering what it's like to die ("Will I go to heaven? Will there be any other mice there?"), until he's rescued by a whale. The whale becomes the mouse's best friend—a friend who, in turn, is rescued by the mouse later on in the book. So moved are they by the depth of their friendship that they both cry in the end. "They knew they might never meet again. They knew they would never forget each other."

These are the books I recommend to babysitters who get to read to my child. I've even lent them to friends who have no children.
ELS

THE TALE OF PETER RABBIT *and other works by Beatrix Potter (various editions).*

Do the works of Beatrix Potter still appeal to kids? The opinions we sampled were divided. Jacqueline Craven, for example, recalling that she loved all the Beatrix Potter books as a child, thinks they're as relevant as ever. "They're pure fantasy, delightfully illustrated," she writes. "And they're published in 'child-size' books which don't immediately overawe a child with their great length and volume."

John Donovan, director of the Children's Book Council, disagrees. "I think Beatrix Potter is terrific," he says. "But a lot of young contemporary American kids, seven or eight years old, look at Potter's books and see that they're old-fashioned and look babyish. They bear absolutely no relationship to the other visual things that are being fed to them on television and which they see in ads. Beatrix Potter is an acquired taste for most people. And most children probably won't (and shouldn't have to) appreciate Beatrix Potter until adulthood.

An important thing to realize about Potter is that she was always willing to deal with the harsh, as well as the sweet, side of reality. "Don't go into Mr. McGregor's garden," Mrs. Rabbit warns her offspring in *The Tale of Peter Rabbit.* "Your father had an accident there; he was put in a pie by Mrs. McGregor." Some modern publishers have tried to temper this facet of Beatrix Potter by abridging or re-editing her original works: such editions are most definitely to be avoided. (The most flagrant bit of tampering, Jason Epstein has noted with disgust, was the addition of a sign over Peter Rabbit's bed which read "Good Bunnies Always Obey.")
CBC

THE 21 BALLOONS, *written and illustrated by William Pène du Bois (Viking, 1947, $6.95 hardcover; Dell, 1969, $1.25 paperback).*

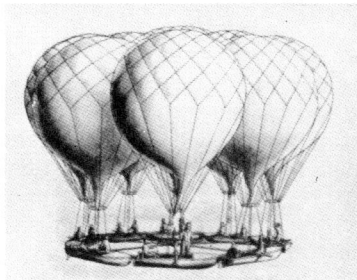

© RENEWED 1975 BY WILLIAM PÈNE DU BOIS

The 21 Balloons relates the story of one Professor William Waterman Sherman, who set out in a balloon from San Francisco with the intention of flying across the Pacific, and was discovered a few weeks later in the *Atlantic* Ocean hanging on for dear life to the wreckage of a platform attached to not one, but twenty, hydrogen balloons which when filled had "a combined lifting strength of 45,360 pounds." The only stop Professor Sherman made along the way was on the Pacific Island of Krakatoa, which blew up, moments after the Professor left it, in what is reputed to be the most violent explosion in the history of the planet Earth.

"Half of this story is true," the author tells us, "and the other half might very well have happened." Well, Krakatoa did blow up in 1883. Whether your kids choose to believe the remarkable tale of Professor Sherman's voyage and of his "unusual life on the Island of Krakatoa," is a matter for them to decide. Suffice it to say that *The 21 Balloons* was just about my favorite book as a ten-year-old, and upon rereading it as an adult I found it to be just as marvelous as I remembered.
CBC

WHERE THE WILD THINGS ARE, *by Maurice Sendak (Harper & Row, 1963, $5.95 hardcover).*

There's a specific reason that I particularly like *Where the Wild Things Are:* Maurice Sendak made monsters legitimate. After Sendak, we got all the monsters in the world, and I must say, most of them were inept monsters. You know, *There's a Monster in My Closet,* and all those other books that came out.

Sendak's book is all so terribly natural. Just look at the way the trees spring up from the bedroom floor. Notice the way the carpet just kind of goes up along the base of that tree!

And the monsters are composite monsters, winged and spined, taloned and beaked. None of them are menacing or threatening. The Child Study Association protested to me because *The New York Times* had called this the "best illustrated book of the year." They said it was going to give children nightmares. I said there's nothing I can do about it. You've got to use common sense. If a child has to go to bed with a light on in his room, you don't give him a book like this. Being afraid of the dark is part of growing up. And overcoming that fear is terribly important. In fact, there's nothing wrong with a *rational* fear of the dark: too many people go blundering down dark alleys and end up dead as a result.

From an interview with GEORGE WOODS,
Children's Book Editor, New York Times

TAMING THE WILD THINGS

[There are] games children must conjure up to combat an awful fact of childhood: the fact of their vulnerability to fear, anger, hate, frustration—all the emotions that are an ordinary part of their lives and that they can perceive only as ungovernable and dangerous forces. To master these forces, children turn to fantasy: that imagined world where disturbing emotional situations are solved to their satisfaction. Through fantasy, Max, the hero of my book, discharges his anger against his mother, and returns to the real world sleepy, hungry and at peace with himself.

Certainly we want to protect our children from new and painful experiences that are beyond their emotional comprehension and that intensify anxiety; and to a point we can prevent premature exposure to such experiences. That is obvious. But what is just as obvious—and what is too often overlooked—is the fact that from their earliest years children live on familiar terms with disrupting emotions, that fear and anxiety are an intrinsic part of their everyday lives, that they continually cope with frustration as best they can. And it is through fantasy that children achieve catharsis. It is the best means they have for taming Wild Things.

It is my involvement with this inescapable fact of childhood—the awful vulnerability of children and their struggle to make themselves King of All Wild Things—that gives my work whatever truth and passion it may have.

MAURICE SENDAK
upon receiving the 1964 Caldecott Medal,
as quoted by Jonathan Cott in Rolling Stone

THE WONDERFUL O, by James Thurber (Simon and Schuster, 1957, $4.95 hardcover; 1976, $1.95 paperback).

We read to our [six-year-olds] from James Thurber's splendid book, *The Wonderful O*, about the fellow who hated the letter "O" ever since his mother got stuck in a porthole and they couldn't pull her in so they had to push her out. He left that letter out of his kingdom later, your child will be happy to know, and Ophelia Oliver became Phelia Liver.

That's very ribald to a Six.

MARGUERITE KELLY and ELIA PARSONS
The Mother's Almanac

ZEELY, by Virginia Hamilton (Macmillan, 1967, $5.95 hardcover; Collier, 1971, $1.25 paperback).

Sometimes in the snowiest days of winter when you're walking head down to avoid your breath being stolen by the monster wind, you notice a patch of violets sitting there, as if some grave mistake had been made on their timetable. Always there is a problem of whether or not to pick them.

Sometimes when spring has just begun to settle in, you're in the park and spy a tiny mud puddle, calling to your toes.

Mostly you avoid the small pleasures of life, but sometimes when your heart is bursting for something to love you reach beyond the "proper" toward the fantasy and rediscover joy. *Zeely* is like cotton candy on a rainy day—a pleasant fanciful memory; the smell of bread baking; a little piece of warmth that makes us happy we still smile. I like *Zeely* because I think love is one of life's little pleasures. And we ought to share it.

NIKKI GIOVANNI

The Books I Liked Best:
A Cynical 15½-Year-Old Remembers

Having an avid appetite for reading, I frequently overstepped the limits of "children's literature" and read Thurber, Agatha Christie, and Tolkien, among others. But the main bulk of my reading between the ages of seven and fourteen came under the headings of nostalgia, humor, mystery, and, biggest of all, fantasy. These are some of my favorites:

The Wolves of Willoughby Chase, Black Hearts in Battersea, and *Nightbirds on Nantucket,* by Joan Aiken (Dell Yearling Books, about age 7 and up). These three books are connected by the character of Simon, who is a minor character in the first, the main character in the second, and constantly mentioned in the third. They are full of malevolent and scheming governesses and orphans-home mistresses, dippy but kindly aunts and doctors, lovely parents who are being schemed against (see governesses, above), one hot-tempered little girl and one shy and retiring one who are the best of friends due to the whole mess concocted by the schemers. The books are adventurous and the perfect thing to read on a cold rainy day with a cup of hot tea.

The Little House books, by Laura Ingalls Wilder (Harper & Row, ages 7 to 11). These nine books about growing up in the pioneer days are infinitely superior to the lukewarm TV series that they inspired. They are autobiographical but fantastic in the best sense of the word. There aren't many dangerous Indians and the like; the weather is the main enemy. Laura is of course the principal character and believe me, she is a character. How the family put up with everything that happened to them is a lesson in perseverance.

Little Women, Little Men, and *Jo's Boys,* by Louisa May Alcott (Grosset & Dunlap, ages 7 to 14). A classic group but often overlooked by thrill-crazed modern readers. They are nice and homey and full of motherly advice and prudence, balanced by wild young children. They are the kind of book that you read on a summer's afternoon on the front lawn, or in bed on a winter morning, or in the bathtub.

Greenwillow, by B. J. Chute (Dutton, ages 9 to 14). A very nice, enveloping story, definitely for girls. It takes place long ago and far away, maybe, but not now, not here. It's the country, and maiden aunts, and little towns.

Gone-Away Lake and *Return to Gone-Away,* by Elizabeth Enright (Harcourt Brace Jovanovich, ages 9 to 14). These two are really fun to read. It all starts when two cousins find an old, dried-up lake bed and all the houses that used to be summer homes when there was a lake. A brother and sister, now in their seventies, still live in the houses. The cousins come back and back, learn all about the people who lived there around the turn of the century, and eventually their families move there too. These books are full of old things.

The Three Musketeers, Twenty Years After and *The Vicomte de Bragelonne,* by Alexandre Dumas (Dodd, Mead, ages 12 to 14). All right, swash your buckles, everyone! Get ready for intrigue, swordplay, romances, and all that fun stuff. I absolutely adore this period, despite the author's thick, archaic style. Let's bring back the sword instead of the pistol. It's a lot harder to conceal, to begin with. (Ah, but what about poison?)

My Life and Hard Times, by James Thurber (Harper & Row, ages 10 to 14). Oh boy, is Thurber nuts! His autobiography is full of burglars and ghosts, his grandfather (who thinks the Civil War is still on), beds falling, men standing up in the middle of *King Lear* and announcing that the world is coming to an end, and similar hysteria. Absolutely hilarious. Anything else by Thurber is good, too.

The Pogo books, by Walt Kelly (Simon and Schuster, ages 12 to 14). This may seem a strange selection, but I find Pogo to be the most insane thing I ever read and I love it. *Ten Everlovin' Blue-eyed Years with Pogo* is best because it's got all the really good stuff from Walt Kelly's best years, and it's hard to get hold of the old comic books now.

The Nancy Drew mysteries, by Carolyn Keene (Grosset & Dunlap, ages 7 to 10). I still read these for kicks. They were my first mysteries, discovered in the first grade. Now they seem terribly funny in my cynical old age (15½), but I really love them. There are at least fifty in the series, with the list growing all the time. Nancy has a whole slew of friends, a "sporty blue roadster," and a faithful dog whose name I always forget.

Agatha Christie's mysteries are the next step up from Nancy Drew. I read them between the ages of about 9 and 14. Some of my favorites are *Halloween Party, The Moving Finger, Cat Among Pigeons, Crooked House,* and millions more.

Alice in Wonderland and *Through the Looking Glass,* by Lewis Carroll. My absolute favorites. They're classics, and I suppose everyone over the age of five has heard of them, but classics often go unread—too obvious, I suppose. Anyway, the poetry is great and the stories equally wonderful, always twisting and turning on you. Absolutely no one should go through life without having read these books. The ones with illustrations by Tenniel are best.

The Wind in the Willows, by Kenneth Grahame (Scribner's, ages 7 to 14). I grew very fond of this book after I took it to camp one summer and found myself with little else to read. It is remarkably well written, with no feeling of cutesy, Bambi-type anthropomorphism. The antics of the famous Mr. Toad are hilarious, and poor Mole and Water Rat and Badger are certainly equal to the occasions Toady puts on them. This book contains some of the warmest and most beautiful scenes I've ever read, such as the mice caroling at Mole's door, the feast at the end, finding Muskrat's son, and on and on.

The Gammage Cup, by Carol Kendall (Harcourt Brace Jovanovich, ages 9 to 14). A heroic tale of ostracism, getting back to the land, and caring. It also deals with narrow-mindedness and distrust of change and difference. The Minipins, or Little Ones, dwell in the Land Between the Mountains, where they fled long ago from the terrible Mushroom People, under the leadership of Gammage. Gammage brought with him the precious Cup of Wisdom, which resides in the main town of the Land Between the Mountains. The tale centers on the village of Slipper-on-the-Water and "Them," five Minipins who don't conform. When a contest between the villages for the Cup of Wisdom is announced, all the prejudices of the average Minipin break out, and heroism is rediscovered. A marvelous story.

Once on a Time, by A. A. Milne (Avon Books, ages 8 to 14). A fairy story for adults, supposedly, but I read it in third grade. It's a crazy little tale about two tiny countries, Euralia and Barodia, and what happens when they go to war because the King of Barodia's favorite whisker got bent. The story is mainly about Prince Udo of Araby, who is invited to stay at the palace of Euralia by Princess Hyacinth and is changed en route into a beast who is a mixture of a rabbit, a sheep, and a lion. Need I say more?

The Chronicles of Narnia series, by C. S. Lewis (Collier Books, ages 9 to 14). This is the first real fantasy I read, and with one book I was hooked. There are seven in the series, peopled with talking animals (*intelligent* talking animals)—fauns, dwarfs, centaurs, unicorns, flying horses, sea serpents, dragons—and, of course, a few people. But the main inhabitants of Narnia are nonhuman, and they are real. The enemy is personified by various witches, giants, and the Calormenes (who are Saracens in disguise). The central and stabilizing force of the series is Aslan the Lion, creator of the Narnian world and personification of all goodness and strength. Various children from our world (England) go to Narnia at times, to help it in its hours of need. The stuff is authentic adventure, no prissy little Disney types leaping around. This is reality.

The Oz books, by L. Frank Baum (Reilly and Lee, ages 7 to 10). The Oz stories are very unreal, but you know for sure that everything's going to work out all right, and Ozma will forgive the villains and they'll reform. Everyone knows *The Wizard of Oz,* but the other thirteen books are less well known. They have a regular cast of characters which increases as the books go along, so there's always someone to appear to save the day. The ones with illustrations by John R. Neill are nice and give quite a flavor of the time when they were written (1900–1920).

The Mary Poppins books, by P. L. Travers (Harcourt Brace Jovanovich, ages 8 to 12). Good ol' Mary Poppins. I've seen the movie seven times at last count and I'm good for at least seven more. Here, too, reality and unreality merge. Everyone knows Mary Poppins, but by reading the books you get to know her better and longer, and you can always flip back to the beginning.

Taash and the Jesters, by Ellen K. Mackenzie (Harcourt Brace Jovanovich). I was the only person to take this book out of our middle-school library for two years, and I had it out all the time. Then they split the schools into intermediate and junior high, and that was the last I saw of it. Anyway, it's a fantasy. Taash is first an apprentice, I think, then he lives with an old "witch" on the outskirts of town, and then strange things start happening. He gets mixed up with two jesters (twins) and with the Forces of Evil, who are trying to kill him because he's really the heir to the throne. I could read this book over and over and over (and I have!).

These are the best of the books I know. The publishers, by the way, are those of the copies I own; some of the classics are published by all and sundry. And now I am seized with a mighty yearning to read!

LESLIE JONES

SCIENCE FICTION

Until someone actually does invent a time machine, science fiction is the best way we have to examine tomorrow. That's why young people love it, and that's why they read it.

BEN BOVA
School Library Journal

S-F for Kids: A Brief Overview

A discussion of fantasy and science-fiction books for kids raises two questions: What are fantasy and science fiction? and What is a children's book? Is Homer's *Odyssey* any less a work of science fiction than Robert Heinlein's *Space Cadet?* Is J. R. R. Tolkien's "Hobbit" trilogy—*The Fellowship of the Ring, The Two Towers,* and *The Return of the King*—for children or for adults? I won't try to answer those questions here; what follows is a selective guide to authors who have written stories with a "sense of wonder," stories whose realities expand from our own, and which offer a world of the fantastic to children of all ages.

Those who've read the Nancy Drew mysteries, the Hardy Boys, or the Laura Ingalls Wilder books will not be surprised to find that the series approach is also popular in children's fantasy and science fiction. In addition to Tolkien's trilogy, the best of these is Ursula K. Le Guin's Earthsea trilogy (Bantam): *A Wizard of Earthsea, The Tombs of Atuan,* and *The Farthest Shore.* The last won the National Book Award for Children's Literature in 1973, and all demonstrate Ms. Le Guin's remarkable talent for creating unique worlds and characters. Earthsea, a realm of magic and sorcery, has its own legends and prophecies which its inhabitants must fulfill to maintain the kingdom's well-being. C. S. Lewis's Chronicles of Narnia—the core of which are *The Lion, the Witch, and the Wardrobe; Prince of Caspian;* and *The Voyage of the "Dawn Treader"*—are classics. Other Narnia titles are *The Silver Chair; The Horse and His Boy; The Magician's Nephew;* and *The Last Battle* (all Collier paperbacks).

For younger readers, the Finnish writer Tove Jansson has created Moominland, set in northern climes and populated by a Moomin family, animals, and creatures of Jansson's invention. *Finn Family Moomintroll; Moominland Midwinter; Comet in Moominland;* and *Tales from Moominvalley* (all from Walck) interrelate, but are less dependent on each other than Tolkien's or Le Guin's works. Another "family" group was created by Mary Norton. Her books *The Borrowers* and *The Borrowers Afield* (Harcourt Voyager paperbacks), are chronicles of the adventures of miniature people who co-exist (not peacefully) with a normal household.

There are many examples of writers known for their adult s-f who have produced books for

children as well. Le Guin is one, and Heinlein is another. Widely known for *Stranger in a Strange Land,* Heinlein wrote several children's books during the forties and fifties. They have dated somewhat, but like Jules Verne's tales (another good bet) they still have much appeal. Try *Rolling Stones* (Ace paperback), *Farmer in the Sky* (Dell paperback), *Space Cadet* (Scribners), and *Rocketship Galileo* (Ace paperback).

Andre Norton is perhaps the most prolific of all s-f writers for young people. She has produced literally dozens of titles and all are remarkably similar in their conventional morality and values. Her most recent book, *Here Abide Monsters* (Atheneum), comes closest to having a hero who loses out.

More interesting are the works of Lloyd Alexander. He has created a wonderful otherworldly cat named Gareth whose journeys are recounted in *Time Cat* (Holt). Alexander's other books include *The Book of Three; Castle of Llyr; Black Cauldron; Taran Wanderer* (all Dell paperbacks); and *The Foundling and Other Tales of Prydian* (Holt). Some of these bring the "sword and sorcery" side of science fiction to children's literature. Little sword, but much sorcery, comes from L. Frank Baum, whose *Wizard of Oz* and related titles open the door to a debate on what s-f is. Lewis Carroll's *Alice in Wonderland* might also, but it must be admitted that both books are fantasy at its best.

Madeleine L'Engle's *A Wrinkle in Time* (Dell paperback) was awarded the Newbery Medal in 1963. She says it is based on the principles of Einstein's theory of relativity and that her most recent children's book, *A Wind in the Door* (Farrar, Straus & Giroux), applies the current thinking of cellular biologists. Both books are superb. A British writer, Alan Garner, is deserving of attention for *The Owl Service* (Walck), *Red Shift* (Macmillan), and *Elidor* (Walck). Garner's strong plots and vivid language create haunting atmospheres such as Elidor, a "green isle in the shadow of the stars," a twilight world of fear and darkness.

If you aren't sure whether any of these individual works would be of interest, there are several recent anthologies which offer a good range from which to choose. *Tales Beyond Time,* edited by L. Sprague de Camp and Catherine Crook de Camp (Lothrop, Lee & Shepard), is a fine collection of contemporary s-f and retold legends. Jane Yolen's *Zoo 2000* (Seabury) offers twelve stories of fantastic animals by authors such as James Thurber, Arthur C. Clarke, and Philip José Farmer. *Deep Space* (Nelson), edited by Robert Silverberg, has eight fine stories, including one each by Damon Knight, Harlan Ellison, and Silverberg himself. Andre Norton and Ernestine Donaldy have combined to select the stories for *Gates to Tomorrow: An Introduction to Science Fiction* (Atheneum). Although the stories were not explicitly written for children, it's a good collection, incorporating a variety of themes which really do accomplish the purpose expressed in the subtitle.

If you can't find any of these titles locally, the Science Fiction Shop, 56 Eighth Avenue, New York, N.Y. 10014, will try to fill your mail orders. They also carry a variety of board games and educational materials with science-fiction themes—"Space Hop: A Game of the Planets" from Games by Teachers; the Waddington House of Games' "4000 A.D.: An Interstellar Conflict Game" (for ages 12 and up), and "Triplanetary: The Game of Interplanetary Warfare." The last was developed by restaging the events of s-f novels, and attempts to simulate the movement of a body in space. A grid composed of hexagons rather than squares and rules which adhere to the principles of Newtonian physics make this game more sophisticated (and more fun) than the others. It can be ordered from either the Science Fiction Shop or from Game Designers' Workshop (Box 582, Bloomington, Ill. 61701), for $7.95 plus postage.

BILL STRACHAN

On Selecting Books for One's Parents to Read

I had a voracious appetite for science fiction as a kid. Why? Well, for all the obvious reasons. But the most important factor of all was that science fiction was just about the only field of literature—at least the only field *I* cared about—in which my father wasn't an expert. What a thrill it was to find *him* a new story that he would read and love, rather than the other way around.

CBC

REFERENCE BOOKS AND MAPS

A Good Reference Book Is to Grow With

A good reference book is to grow with. It's not a book that you read from cover to cover and swallow whole. If it's around the house, every now and then you go back to it and get more out of it.

One thing to keep in mind is that, children have very poor skills for using reference material. For instance, most children cannot use an index. They think of the word that labels what they're looking for; they don't know a set of related follow-up words or ideas to pursue.

Another thing to consider is that dictionaries and almanacs, which come immediately to many people's minds when they think of reference books, are fact-checking books and won't teach you about a subject as a whole. And encyclopedias, I think, are impersonal and sort of dull. The information has all been put through a mill and comes out fairly standardized. Encyclopedias provide a very good way of doing the least possible work on an assignment for a teacher, but they don't encourage curiosity in the way that a single author's writing can.

But there are reference books that one would love to have around the house. I think the children's version of *The Way Things Work* (Simon and Schuster, $12.95), or even the grown-ups' version, which can be used by kids (though it's much more difficult), is a nifty book to own. So are those big *Life*-type picture magazines that you can buy in foreign cities. And I can't imagine a house without an atlas. They come in all prices, and it really doesn't matter which one you buy, as long as you look for excuses to use it. If you can afford the *Rand McNally International Atlas* [$45], it is wonderful. Its maps are topographical (with shading to indicate hills, etc.), and it includes a superb set of maps of the large cities of the world, all drawn to a common scale. *The New York Times Atlas* [$35] is the other great big one: it's more complete, and features a better index than the *Rand McNally Atlas,* but its maps don't give anywhere nearly as good a feeling of what the land is really like.

A good cookbook is a very important reference book. It gets used, it enlarges your world, and it makes for safe experimentation with cooking, which, when you think about it, is a large part of what a family does. And *The Oxford Book of Food Plants* (Oxford University Press, 1969, $16.00 hardcover), a nature guide to the vegetable shelves in the grocery store, is a reference book that children can and will use. Six-year-olds like to look at the color illustrations, and an eight-year-old might tackle one or more of the short paragraphs of botanical and geographical information that the book provides.

And finally, there's the Bible. It doesn't mean what it meant to our grandparents, and yet it is still a great book to own and read.

From an interview with PHYLIS MORRISON

How to Crack Nuts So You Don't Look Like an Idiot, Etc.

Okay, dummy. If you don't want to tear that piece of bread you're spreading with cold butter, put another piece of bread underneath. If you've spent your whole life relying on some sort of sixth sense to tell you which is your right hand when the teacher asks, place both of your hands in front of you with the thumbs extended at right angles. The index finger and the thumb of the left hand will make a nice big *L* for left. (On the right hand you'll have a big *J*. We don't know what that is for, so disregard it.)

These and other tips are to be found in *The Easy How-To Book,* by Seymour Reit, illustrated by William Dugan (a Golden Book, 1973, $5.95). It is a book especially beloved by eight- and nine-year-olds, who tend to read it straight through and then, at dinner time, apprise you of everything they've learned (how to tell if your pet is sick, for example, or how to step out of a boat properly—pieces of information you will then have at the ready whether or not you in fact own a cat or ever go near the water).

The Easy How-To Book is based on a single great idea: letting kids in on the true existential secrets of our culture early on. Much of the book is truly valuable, although some sections give the distinct feeling that they were included mainly for fleshing-out purposes. And would that they had not dodged some real problems! (Example: tying a shoelace securely. The author says to tie a regular knot and then do it again. Well, if we *knew* how to tie a regular knot, Ollie, we wouldn't be in this mess in the first place.)

Still and all, you pay your money and take your chances. While you're doing that, keep in mind that this book seems primarily intended for children in the intermediate grades, and that a nursery-school child, intrigued by the colorful pictures, may be frustrated by it. It's a nice book, one in which your youngster is bound to find something you didn't know before.

JENNIFER CARDEN

Kids' Dictionaries: From the Delightful to the Deadly Didactic

The best dictionary for a child who is just beginning to read has a warm lap, lots of patience and speaks most times only when spoken to. But parents can't be expected to do all the work. . . . So, I've looked over 15 [dictionaries] that would seem appropriate for a child between the ages of 4 and 8.

The list got narrowed down rather quickly; I was so paralyzed by the mediocrity of seven of them that I had nothing of substance to say. Three others were so deliciously terrible that I think it important to include them to strike a blow for freedom from a claque of educators and publishers who have found it economically rewarding to keep us from trusting our intuition. Their ploy is to promote the Deadly Didactic that learning to read and to use organized knowledge is terribly hard work and most definitely should not be fun, especially for children.

This Deadly Didactic virtually ignores that fact that most children have a spontaneous interest in and fascination for words, first in speech and, in all good time, for speech written down, which is, after all, what reading is all about. The remaining five have something to commend them, but in all, I don't think that we should take too seriously the dictionary aspect of children's dictionaries. As books that do well by words, some of them are quite good, but as books that have embarked on a serious mission of teaching a six-year-old dictionary skills, that is a mission that simply isn't very serious.

The Picture Dictionary for Children, by Garnette Watters and S. A. Courtis (Grosset & Dunlap, $3.95), contains 5,084 words, the most comprehensive selection of any of the dictionaries reviewed, and most of them are defined in a way that can be only described as insulting. Lack of clarity, dull sentences reminiscent of the old basal reader and absurd stabs at defining characterize this book. Just a couple of examples, and by no means the worst ones, should suffice. The word "rat" is defined with a drawing together with two sentences: "This is a rat. It is like a mouse but much larger." Tell that to a child who's met one on a stairway. The word "road" is explained with a 1941 De Soto parked in the middle of the highway. "The auto stood in the middle of the road," says the accompanying sentence. That seems like a foolish thing for a car to do. Foolishly patronizing is the tone of this book.

My First Dictionary, by Laura Oftedal and Nina Jacob (Grosset & Dunlap, $3.95), and *A Child's First Picture Dictionary,* by Lilian Moore (Grosset & Dunlap, $1.95), may appear to be attractive because of their modest prices, but don't be misled. Both dictionaries are written in that stilted style so favored by reading specialists. The latter one may be a good buy, however, if you want to teach your child some history. The word "up" is illustrated with a plane writing BUY BONDS in the sky. I haven't seen that since 1947, which is about when both of them should have been taken off the market.

In delightful contrast to these, there is *Richard Scarry's Storybook Dictionary,* by Richard Scarry (Golden Books, $5.95). Scarry has used a standard list of words—there appears to be a formula for doing children's dictionaries—but what he does with the list is remarkable. With a cast of characters that includes Pickles Pig, the happy glutton who opens the refrigerator door so often he catches cold, lovable Big Hilda the Hippo, and my favorite, Brambles the Warthog who is obsessed with grooming his impossible hair, Scarry makes language what children intuitively know it is, something alive and lively.

I've known educators to take a look at a Scarry book and go into a long rage that they are too jumbled, too confusing, too much on a page. But I've met few children who would agree, and I think it is Scarry's respect for children that makes the difference. He assumes that children have curiosity, resources and intelligence that can be appealed to rather than ignored.

Another good one is *Cat in the Hat Beginner Dictionary,* by P. D. Eastman (Random House, $4.95). Here, too, is respect for the intelligence and resourcefulness of children. Words are clearly defined, though not perhaps as richly as in Scarry's book. The author does a fine job with the so-called empty words like "across," "after," "here," words that some children seem to have difficulty with. And if you've never heard of Zyxuspf birds, well, there is a whole nest of them in this zesty book.

The New Golden Dictionary, by Bertha Morris Parker (Golden Books, $4.95), is comfortably in the middle ground and will likely appeal to those of us who feel uneasy with the idea that learning to read and to use words well can be mostly fun. It is unabashedly a dictionary dictionary, and by its format suggests that it will not hurt at all if children learn some skills. It does not offer any suggestions as to its use, however. The author seems to trust parents' intuition, which is commendable. The definitions are somewhat matter-of-fact and a bit dry (Boat: "A boat is for riding on the water"), but most relate well to a child's perception of things. The illustrations are none too humorous but clear and helpful.

There are also two excellent paperback dictionaries. *First Dictionary,* by John Trevaskis and Robin Hyman (Young Reader's Press, 95 cents), is notable for its handsome layout, its colorful illustrations (some are a bit too stylized), and its clarity of definition. Its size, too, is handy and its binding is sturdy enough to take lots of wear by young hands. With some 2,000 words presented, it is a good buy as an only dictionary, but I would suggest it as a good complement to the Scarry book.

Finally, the four volumes in *Pyramid Primary Dictionary Series,* by Amy Brown, John Downing and John Sceats (Pyramid Publications, 95 cents for Books 1 and 2; $1.25 for Books 3 and 4), offer an excellent selection of words, departing significantly from the standardized list used in most others. Definitions are precise and the illustrations are colorful and cheerful.

JACK McGARVEY
The New York Times Book Review

Dictionaries: Exploring for the Fun of It

I think a big, unabridged dictionary is a fine thing to have in any home or classroom. No book is more fun to browse around in—if you're not made to. Children, depending on their age, will find many pleasant and interesting things to do with a big dictionary. They can look up funny-sounding words, which they like, or words that nobody else in the class has ever heard of, which they like, or long words, which they like, or forbidden words, which they like best of all. At a certain age, and particularly with a little encouragement from parents or teachers, they may become very interested in where words came from and when they came into the language and how their meanings have changed over the years. But exploring for the fun of it is very different from looking up words out of your reading because you're going to get into trouble with your teacher if you don't.

JOHN HOLT
The Underachieving School

Encyclopedias: For Younger Kids, *World Book* Is the Best

Just about everybody we've asked tells us that the *World Book* encyclopedia, with its highly visual style of presenting information, is the best encyclopedia to buy for pre-teen-age kids.

It presents "good, simply written, well-illustrated general information," says David Shetzline, whose six- and seven-year-old daughters use it "to teach each other." "It's simple enough for kids starting at age eight or nine," reports Annette Fidler, "yet detailed enough for my fifteen-year-old."

Victor and Anne Navasky also give high marks to the *Childcraft Encyclopedia,* the junior edition of the *World Book.* "It's got enough pictures and is organized well enough," they tell us, "so that the child who reads, and wants to, can use it by himself."

If you do make the decision to invest in an encyclopedia, by the way, you'll find that the lowest-priced edition should be perfectly serviceable. "I've always been amused that encyclopedia companies command premium prices for such extras as washable bindings," remarks Robert Bernstein. "How many times have you washed your encyclopedia?"

CBC

◆

If You Think "G" Was Exciting, Wait Till You Get to "H"!

The *World Book* encyclopedia was to me as engrossing as a novel might be. Written in that homogenous, dispassionate third-person style, with very little opinion thrown in, the books allowed me to fill my brain with data, and then decide what should be kept and what should be discarded.

Between my eighth and tenth years I read every article in the *World Book,* from one end to the other. About midway through, I realized how things crossed over and interrelated, even in a body of knowledge that was organized arbitrarily from aardvarks and airplanes through zebras. As I was reading through, I'd realize that something in Volume G was relevant to something in Volume A which also related to an idea in Volume L. And it helped me to organize my mind in that way, making a lot of social science and hard science and arts and history relate to each other.

CHIP BLOCK

What to Do Until the Encyclopedia Salesman Gets There

The *Tell Me Why* series, published by Grosset & Dunlap, is a fantastic reference work for kids from the age of four or five right up through the later years of childhood. Like many parents of young children, we haven't been able to invest in an encyclopedia as yet, and these books have filled the gap beautifully, answering most of the questions a child will ask about "What makes . . . ?" or "Why does . . . ?" and so forth. The articles are simply enough written to be clear to the younger kids, but not so simplistic that they aren't interesting and informative for an older audience.

BROOKE ADLER

◆

Time-Life Books: Learning by Osmosis

Exactly the things that make Time-Life Books somewhat weak for adults make them strong for children. An adult can't sit down and read them and learn about a new subject; the books are too much in little pieces, too episodic and unconnected, too cut and pasted. But that's exactly what makes them a great resource for kids: it's clear you aren't supposed to read the whole book.

You can start by just looking at the pictures. Having done that, you can go back and read a few captions. Then you might come back later and read a page relating to some pictures that particularly interested you, and from that you might begin reading forward—or backward—in the book. The pictures, which are superb in all Time-Life Books, serve the same purpose for children that an index or provocative chapter heads might for adults.

Time-Life Books are wonderful to own if you have children: taking them out of the library and then having to return them is almost a wasted endeavor, since your kids won't really have a chance to follow up on the things that catch their attention.

The science and math series seem to be the ones that kids love most. But the assorted history series are appealing, too. For a catalogue, write: Little, Brown and Company, 200 West Street, Waltham, Mass. 02154.

From an interview with PHYLIS MORRISON

A Map with Your House on It?

Did you know that you can get a map of your area on which a half-mile is scaled to one inch? First write to the Superintendent of Documents, at the U.S. Geological Survey, and ask for an index map of your state, which they'll send you for free. Individual maps that are available are indicated on the index map: simply choose the one you want. Most of the maps are 23 by 27 inches, and cost $1.25 each. They're beautiful. Every street is marked, and if you live in a less congested city, every house.

For maps of areas east of the Mississippi River, write to Distribution Selection, U.S. Geological Survey, 1200 South Eads Street, Arlington, Va. 22202. For areas west of the Mississippi: Distribution Section, Box 52286, Denver Federal Center, Denver, Colo. 80225.

From an interview with PHYLIS MORRISON

Maps for Beginning Readers

What, really, is a map? Dorothy Rhodes's book *How to Read a City Map* (Children's Press, 1967, 46 pages) explores the basic concept that a map shows something larger made smaller. As one proceeds through Ms. Rhodes's pages, one comes across a progression of new symbols: a school, a city street, a broad avenue, a freeway, a bridge, a lake; and throughout the book, line maps and photographic maps are juxtaposed.

How to Read a City Map is a nice gift for beginning readers; I know one child of four who thoroughly enjoyed it.

RS
(recommended by Phylis Morrison)

Map Reading from Your Plane Window

Erwin Raisz Landform Maps (130 Charles Street, Boston, Mass. 02114) offers incredibly detailed maps, based on air photographs, of the United States (in various sizes), Canada, Japan, Italy, Europe, and some individual states. The maps reveal plains, hills, mountains, and if you use a hand magnifying glass, you'll locate even smaller features with little difficulty. Erwin Raisz maps are terrific to take along on a cross-country flight (I recommend the 17 by 11–inch map of the U.S.) because you can see the detail on the land just about the way the map shows it. Write the company for a complete list of maps and prices (which, incidentally, are most reasonable).

BURT SINGER

Maps of mass transit systems are often available for free—ask bus drivers and token sellers. Maybe one day there will be maps of bicycle paths.

RS

Books from NASA: "The Map Made Real"

The National Aeronautics and Space Administration has published many books featuring aerial photography of the earth, some of them very good indeed. One we particularly recommend is:

Exploring Space with a Camera, by E. M. Cortwright (NASA, 1968, 214 pages, $9.15), a pre-man-on-the-moon NASA photo album featuring color photos of our planet from orbit (some of the whole earth), many black-and-white shots of the moon, and dramatic shots of Mars, from close up and far away.

To order NASA publications, write the U.S. Government Printing Office, Public Documents Department, Washington, D.C. 20402.

PHYLIS and PHILIP MORRISON

POETRY

Poet Kenneth Koch has been acclaimed for his contributions to the art of helping kids learn to appreciate—and create—poetry. His techniques for introducing "great" poetry to children, outlined in the following article, are described in greater detail in his books *Rose, Where Did You Get That Red?* (Random House, 1973) and *Wishes, Lies, and Dreams* (Random House, 1970).

Teaching Poetry to Children

Last year at PS 61 in New York City I taught my third-through-sixth-grade students poems by Blake, Donne, Shakespeare, Herrick, Whitman, William Carlos Williams, Wallace Stevens, John Ashbery, and Federico García Lorca. For several years before, I had been teaching poetry writing to many of these children, and they liked it so much that I thought there must be a way to help them read and enjoy great poetry by adults.

I found a way to do it, in conjunction with my students' own writing, which enabled the children to get close to the adult poems and to understand and enjoy them. What I did, in fact, was to make these adult poems a part of their own writing. I taught reading poetry and writing poetry as one subject. I brought them together by means of "poetry ideas," which were suggestions I would give to the children for writing poems of their own in some way like the poems they were studying. We would read the adult poem in class, discuss it, and then they would write. Afterward, they or I would read aloud the poems they had written.

When we read Blake's "The Tyger" I asked my students to write a poem in which they were asking questions of a mysterious and beautiful creature. When we read Shakespeare's "Come Unto These Yellow Sands," I asked them to write a poem which was an invitation to a strange place full of colors and sounds. When we read Stevens's "Thirteen Ways of Looking at a Blackbird," I asked them to write a poem in which they talked about the same thing in many different ways. The problem in teaching adult poetry to children is that for them it often seems difficult and remote; the poetry ideas, by making the adult poetry to some degree part of an activity of their own, brought it closer and made it more accessible to them. The excitement of the poem they read inspired them in their writing.

I had used poetry ideas in teaching my students to write poetry before, to help them find perceptions, ideas, feelings, and new ways of saying things, and to acquaint them with some of the subjects and techniques they could bring into their poetry; I had proposed poems about

FRANK DERBAS

wishes, dreams, colors, differences between the present and the past, poems which included a number of Spanish words, poems in which everything was a lie. I would often suggest ways of organizing the poem as well: for the Wish Poem, starting every line with "I wish"; to help them think about the difference between the present and the past, I suggested alternating line-beginnings of "I used to" and "But now"; for the Comparison Poem I suggested they put one comparison in every line, for a Color Poem the name of a color in every line. These formal suggestions were most often for some kind of repetition, which is natural to children's speech

and much easier for them to use in expressing their feelings than meter and rhyme.

With the help of these poetry ideas, along with as free and inspiring a classroom atmosphere as I could create (I said they could make some noise, read each other's lines, walk around the room a little, and spell words as best they could, not to worry about it), and with a good deal of praise and encouragement from me and from each other, my students in grades one through six came to love writing poetry, as much as they liked drawing and painting, sometimes even more.

KENNETH KOCH
New York Review of Books

ACCESS TO KIDS' BOOKS

Bookstores Serious About Children's Books

Few bookstores are well stocked in children's titles. They tend to carry a few classics and a few current titles. George Plimpton once suggested that one ought to be able to dial B-O-O-K

or L-I-B-R-A-R-Y and order any book, to be shipped from a nearby distribution center. You would be billed on your library card or telephone bill. It's a great idea, but it hasn't happened yet. So, listed below, alphabetically by state, are stores that were recommended as "serious about children's books." The asterisks denote stores that carry children's books only.

- Borealis Book Store, 503 Second Avenue, Fairbanks, Alas. 99701, (907) 452-5549.
- Hunter's Books, 7213 East First Avenue, Scottsdale, Ariz. 85251, (602) 947-7271.
- Books Unlimited Cooperative, Inc., 1975 Shattuck Avenue, Berkeley, Calif. 94704, (415) 845-6288. Will make individual lists on request; specify interest or need.
- *The Magic Horse, 2118 Vine Street, Berkeley, Calif. 94709, (415) 845-3430.
- *The Magic Fishbone, Mission and 7th, P.O. Box 3473, Carmel-by-the-Sea, Calif. 93921, (408) 624-4444.
- *The Children's Bookshoppe, 3707 East Coast Highway, Corona del Mar, Calif. 92625, (714) 675-1424.
- John Cole's Book Shop, 780 Prospect, P.O. Box 1132, La Jolla, Calif. 92038, (714) 454-0814.
- *Of Books & Such, 132 South Beverly Drive, Beverly Hills, Calif. 90212, (213) 275-0169.
- *Once Upon a Time, 2309 Honolulu, Montrose, Calif. 91020, (213) 248-9668. Carries book-related toys as well.
- Vroman's, 695 East Colorado Boulevard, Pasadena, Calif. 91101, (213) 449-5320. Catalogue four times a year, free.
- University Bookstore, P.O. Box 5800, Riverside, Calif. 92507, (714) 787-4211.

- *The Red Pony, 284 Ladera Country Shopper, Alpine Road, Portola Valley, Calif. 94025, (415) 854-6891.
- *Bookplace, 50 Clement Street, San Francisco, Calif. 94118, (415) 752-4800.
- Tecolote Book Shop, Studio 51, Montecito Village, Santa Barbara, Calif. 93108, (805) 969-4977.
- The Chinook Bookshop, 210 North Tejon Street, Colorado Springs, Colo. 80903, (303) 635-1195. Mail order catalogue available at Christmas.
- The Denver, 16th & California, Denver, Colo. 80201, (303) 534-2111.
- Cobble Court Bookshop, Litchfield, Connecticut 06759, (203) 567-0084.
- New Canaan Book Shop, 59 Elm Street, New Canaan, Conn. 06840, (203) 966-1684.
- Francis Scott Key Book Shop, 1400 28th Street, N.W., Washington, D.C. 20007, (202) 337-4144.
- Smithsonian Bookstore, a McGraw-Hill Enterprise, 14th and Constitution Avenue, N.W., Washington, D.C. 20560, (202) 381-5248. Specializes in Americana.
- Rich's, Book Department, Broad Street, P.O. Box 4539, Atlanta, Ga. 30302, (404) 586-4636.
- Marshall Field & Co., 111 North State

Street, Chicago, Ill. 60690, (312) 781-1000. Book selection listed in Christmas catalogue.
- Stuart Brent Book Store, 670 North Michigan Avenue, Chicago, Ill. 60611, (312) De 7-6357.
- Cannon's Book Store, 150 North Oak Park Avenue, Oak Park, Ill. 60301, (312) 386-2288.
- Julia Marwick Books, 320 Happ Road, Northfield, Ill. 60093, (312) Hi 6-8244.
- Goldsmith's, Inc., 116-118 South Topeka Avenue, Wichita, Kan. 67202, (316) 263-0131.
- *The Owl and the Pussycat, 314 South Ashland Avenue, Lexington, Ky. 40502, (606) 266-7121. Catalogue available $2.
- *Maple Children's Shop, 7529 Maple Street, New Orleans, La. 70118, (504) 861-2105.
- *The Children's Book Shop, Riverside and 81st Street, #6401, Cabin John, Md. 10731, (301) 229-7972. Mail order only, specializing in American historic and regional fiction. Catalogue available once a year for 25 cents.
- The Book Shop, 40 West Street, Beverly Farms, Mass. 01915, (617) 927-2122. Mail-order catalogue available at Christmas.
- Lauriat's, Inc. (and suburban branch stores), 30 Franklin Street, Boston, Mass. 02110, (617) 482-2850.
- Harvard Cooperative Society, 1400 Massachusetts Avenue, Cambridge, Mass. 02138, (617) 492-1000, ext. 268. Christmas catalogue, free.
- Concord Bookshop, 65 Main Street, Concord, Mass. 01742, (617) 369-2405.
- Hathaway House Bookshop, 103 Central Street, Wellesley, Mass. 02181, (617) 235-2830.
- Dartmouth Bookstore, 33 South Main Street, Hanover, N.H. 03755, (603) 643-3616.
- Bamberger's Book Office, 6th Floor, 131 Market Street, Newark, N.J. 07101, (201) 565-1234.
- Princeton University Store, 36 University Place, Princeton, N.J. 08540, (609) 921-8500.
- Books 'n' Things, 1868 Pleasantville Road, Briarcliff Manor, N.Y. 10510, (914) Wi 1-5688. Mail-order catalogue six times a year.
- *Child's Play, 226 Atlantic Avenue, Brooklyn, N.Y. 11201, (212) 237-2656. Catalogue of non-sexist children's books available for 50 cents.
- Eeyore's Books for Children, 2252 Broadway, New York, N.Y. 10024, (212) 362-0634. Mail-order catalogue available.
- F. A. O. Schwarz, 745 Fifth Avenue, New York, N.Y. 10022, (212) 644-9444. Catalogue twice a year, free.
- Scribner Book Store, 597 Fifth Avenue, New York, N.Y. 10017, (212) 486-4013. Mail-order catalogue available at Christmas.
- The Higbee Company, 100 Public Square, Cleveland, Ohio 44113, (216) 579-2580.
- *Mother Goose Book Shop, 325 Seventh Street, Findlay, Ohio 45840, (419) 422-0422.
- Sanford Books, King of Prussia Plaza, King of Prussia, Pa. 19406, (215) 265-5075.
- *The Growing Tree, 202 South Allen Street, State College, Pa. 16801, (814) 237-3655.
- *Bo-Peep, 3830 North Lamar, Austin, Tex. 78756, (512) 452-2402.
- Rosengren's, 312 Bonham Street, San Antonio, Tex. 78205, (512) 226-3473.
- Rule Book Shop, Boonsboro Shopping Center, Lynchburg, Va. 24503, (804) 384-5982.
- Scribner Book Store, Merchant Square, Williamsburg, Va. 23185, (804) 229-9821.
- University Book Store, 4326 University Way, N.E., Seattle, Wash. 98105, (206) 634-3400.
- Jeanette Schaffer Books, 2521 East Belleview Place, Milwaukee, Wis. 53211, (414) 964-9181.

Paperbacks for Kids: By Mail and Otherwise

Scholastic Book Services (904 Sylvan Avenue, Englewood Cliffs, N.J. 07632) . . . is a superb source for children's paperbacks—possibly the largest selection in the country. They have an excellent selection of biographies, record–book combinations, Charlie Brown stories, activity books, discovery science books, and award-winning "classics." Send for their *Readers' Choice Paperback Catalog* (Kindergarten–12th Grade) for a complete, descriptive list of titles.

Scholastic also has two book clubs specially geared to elementary students. A monthly selection of books can be ordered at reduced rates through classroom teachers—write for bulk order forms of Lucky Book Club (K–3) or Arrow Book Club (4–6).

Dell's Yearling Books (Dell Publishing Company, 1 Dag Hammarskjold Plaza, 245 East 47th Street, New York, N.Y. 10017) are designed for children in grades two to eight. Although the selection is smaller than Scholastic's and includes fewer books for primary children,

these paperbacks are among the best around. *Charlotte's Web,* the *Paddington* series, *Island of the Blue Dolphins, J.T., Pooh* books, *The Secret Garden,* and Lloyd Alexander's *Book of Three* series are only a few of their award-winning titles. Send for their free catalog, *Dell Paperbacks for Elementary Schools,* for a complete listing.

JIM BLAKE and BARBARA ERNST
The Great Perpetual Learning Machine

Resources for Out-of-Print Books

1. The library.
2. Your own shelves or attic.
3. Family and friends; ask if they've stored any books away.
4. Secondhand bookstores. Ask if they advertise in *Bookman's Weekly* or if they're going to put your request in a file. Unless the store will actively search (many will, and some charge for the service), you're not likely to get the book.
5. *AB-Bookman's Weekly,* Box AB, Clifton, N.J. 07105, (201) 772-0020, is a trade journal that advertises books being sought and being sold. Search ads are available only to trade outlets (e.g., secondhand bookstores); private individuals may advertise to sell but not to buy. You pay per ad, through the secondhand bookstore. Single copies of the journal are available for $2.
6. Catalogues of rare and out-of-print children's books are available from Justin G. Schiller, Ltd., P.O. Box 1667, FDR Station, New York, N.Y. 10022, (212) 832-8231, one of the most active dealers. He won't search for you, but will put you on his mailing list. Prices are high but fair.
7. Victoria Book Shop, 16 West 36th Street, New York, N.Y. 10018, (212) 683-7849. Here you'll find high-cost collectors' items. In fact, their prices are considered "outrageous" by some secondhand bookstore people, but their catalogue is useful for information.
8. *The New York Times Book Review* has a book exchange page which includes classified ads for out-of-print search services.
9. Frances Klenett will search for any out-of-print book you name (she's got twenty-five years' experience). Ms. Klenett receives her commission from the seller, and does not charge for quotations. Call or write Frances Klenett, 13 Cranberry Street, Brooklyn, N.Y. 11202, (212) Ul 2-2424.

RS

Secondhand Books

When my son was a tot, we had that rarest of urban treasures, a secondhand magazine store, within blocks of our house. Old issues of *Arizona Highways,* special editions of *Life,* sixty years' worth of *National Geographic,* infinite resources for pennies. When he got interested in insects we walked to the store, found some glorious color spreads, took them home and cut them up to paste into a book of our own.

The store burned down this year and has not reopened, but our town (Berkeley, California) is still rich in secondhand book shops with large sections of children's books, and every so often we go to browse in them. Except for a few lines of paperback editions, kids' books cost so much these days that to buy them new is a special event, and our money goes thrice as far for used books. In the secondhand stores, the ratio of junk doesn't seem much worse than what holds for new kids' books, and it's more comfortable to browse there than in the more chic retail outlets.

There are some subtler benefits to buying used books. It offers my child a chance to pick and choose at his own whim rather than just mine, at a price that doesn't make me wince, and that will fit his budget too when he comes to shopping on his own. Periodically we go through his books with him, and take what he doesn't want and give them to someone or trade them in at the bookstore for credit on more books, in this way reinforcing in him a philosophy of recycling. Most of all, perhaps, it introduces him to the pleasures of old bookstores as friendly places.

MICHAEL ROSSMAN

Libraries

Don't forget your local library; the children's section is a pleasant place to pass some time.

Remember that these are *lending* libraries. So borrow books—on your own card, if your youngster is too young. In our house, we're big book people—have lots and read lots—and the pleasure of new ones weekly (at no cost!) is tremendous.

Many libraries have story hours. Some have film programs. My three-year-old loves the weekly story hour, and it has been a great preschool experience.

PAULA GLATZER

Dial-a-Story

Dial-a-Story? You can if you live in San Francisco, where two telephones, sponsored by the Public Library, answer 626-6516 with a three-minute story, twenty-four hours a day. (If you want to call long distance, the area code is 415). The stories are impeccably read, change weekly, and all end with a suggested activity combined with instructions to hang up the phone: "Now why don't you ask your mother for a carrot and tell her the story of *The Runaway Bunny*. Hang up the phone now. Goodbye." "Now hang up the phone and see if you can whistle like Peter did." "Now hang up the phone and draw a picture of a wild thing for your room. Goodbye."

What will we have when picture phones are introduced? Perhaps the librarian's answer to *Sesame Street*.

MARIANNE SMITH and RS

COMICS

Suppose Michelangelo were alive today and suppose Shakespeare wanted to collaborate with him on a comic strip. Would the product of their collaboration be any less important because it was a comic strip?

To me it isn't the form that's important. It's the content. You can have a comic that is a masterpiece just as you can have an epic novel that doesn't succeed at all.

STAN LEE
as quoted by Howard Kissel in the
Denver Rocky Mountain News

Comic Relief

Children hungry for reasons are seldom given convincing ones. They are bombarded with hard work, labelled education—not seen therefore as child labor. They rise for school at the same time or earlier than their fathers, start work without office chatter, go till noon without coffee breaks, have waxed milk for lunch instead of dry martinis, then back at the desk till three o'clock. Facing greater threats and riskier decisions than their fathers have had to meet since their days in school.

And always at someone else's convenience. Someone else dictates when to rise, what's to be good for breakfast, what's to be learned in school, what's to be good for lunch, what're to be play hours, what're to be homework hours, what's to be delicious for dinner, and what's to be, suddenly, bedtime. . . .

It should come as no surprise, then, that within the shifting hodgepodge of external pressures, a child, simply to save his sanity, must go underground. Have a place to hide where he cannot be got at by grownups. A place that implies, if only obliquely, that they're not so much; that they don't know everything; that they can't fly the way some people can, or let bullets bounce harmlessly off their chests, or beat up whoever picks on them, or—oh, joy of joys!—even become invisible! A no-man's land. A relief zone. And the basic sustenance for this relief was, in my day, comic books.

With them we were able to roam free, disguised in costume, committing the greatest of feats—and the worst of sins. And, in every instance, getting away with them. For a little while, at least, it was our show. For a little while, at least, we were the bosses. Psychically renewed, we could then return above ground and put up with another couple of days of victimization. Comic books were our booze.

JULES FEIFFER
The Great Comic Book Heroes

Comic Books: The State of the Art

For as long as there have been comics, there have been parents who restrict their children from reading them. And, despite the experts' concern over eyestrain, suspicion of story content, and rejection of the form as "illegitimate" literature, the fact remains: *kids love comics*.

Published and sold by the millions, comic books continue to find their way into American homes, where television and radio have rapidly replaced the bookcase as the center of entertainment. Individual editions of many comic books continually outsell hardcover best-sellers (the average monthly issue of *The Fantastic Four* sells 240,000 copies).

At present there exist no fewer than eight major comic book companies in the United States. Europe, Latin America, and the Far East produce their own comics. Superman appears in languages ranging from Arabic to Japanese. Popeye is printed in Israel. Each fall in Italy, over 40,000 adults gather in the town of Lucca to seriously discuss comics as an art form of equal status to television and the movies. Even in the United States, comics have been receiving increasing attention from an older market, especially college students. A new name has been coined for the tales spun with panels and balloons: graphic stories.

Are comic books today so much different from what they were in the 1940s and 1950s? Is the material for which your child plunks down his or her not-so-hard-earned money radically changed from the SOK! BAM! POW! funnies that you purchased as a grimy-handed eight-year-old?

Yes and no.

The cost of a 32-page comic book has risen from 10 cents to 25 cents since the early 1960's. The number of story pages has frequently dropped below 20 as the number of ad pages has climbed.

With rising paper and production costs, the major publishers have been making an effort to develop new formats for comic books. The classic 32-page book is being pushed off the stands by 68- and 100-page color comics and a variety of other new formats. Today you can find giant comics in a 10⅛ by 13¾-inch size, or mini-comics in a *Reader's Digest*–size book, or black-and-white comics in a standard magazine form. The prices for these variations range from 50 cents to $1.50.

If your kids haven't yet delved into the adventures of Spider-Man or the House of Secrets, it may be more than the higher costs that's been keeping them from doing so. A more likely cause might be the unavailability of the material which for so long could be found on the racks of candy stores and "Mom and Pop" shops. In the age of the supermarket, comics have become much harder to find. Subscriptions are available for most titles, but the opportunity of selecting a comic book from among hundreds of brightly colored covers remains a treat unto itself.

There are many types of comic books published in America. Some companies specialize in one particular type among these several variations:

• *Superhero comics.* Having their roots in the old "pulps" of the 1930s that featured such characters as Doc Savage and the Black Bat,

superhero comics tend to portray larger-than-life individuals who are in perpetual combat with larger-than-life forces of evil. Hero/heroine vs. villain/villainess is a predominant theme. The classic superheroes include Batman, Superman, Wonder Woman, Captain Marvel, Captain America, and the Human Torch. Beginning in the "golden age of comics" (circa World War II) with Bill Everett's *Sub-Mariner* and Will Eisner's *The Spirit,* another main type of superhero has emerged: the super-anti-hero. He or she is usually at odds with the local police, although down deep being on the side of good. Marvel Comics has been the main promulgator of the super-anti-hero, having introduced the Hulk, Spider-Man, and the revived Sub-Mariner during the 1960s.

> Not satisfied with being heroes . . . the characters of the group Marvel know how to laugh at themselves. Their adventures are offered publicly like a larger than life spectacle, each searching masochistically within themselves to find a sort of maturity. . . .
>
> We cannot die from obstacles and paradoxes, if we face them with laughter. Only of boredom might we perish. And from boredom, fortunately, the comics keep distance.
>
> FEDERICO FELLINI
> Introduction to *The Steranko History of Comics*

For the record, some of the top superheroic rivalries of the twentieth century include: (1) Batman vs. The Joker, (2) Captain America vs. The Red Skull, (3) Superman vs. Lex Luthor, (4) The Fantastic Four vs. Dr. Doom, and (5) Spider-Man vs. The Green Goblin (and son).

In addition to individual heroism, it is common for superheroes to band together. The Avengers, the Defenders, the Justice League of America, the Justice Society of America, and the Legion of Superheroes are all collections of superheroes united (however tenuously) in the cause of justice.

• *Horror comics.* A consistently lucrative, if not healthy, type of comic book has been the horror/terror/supernatural variety. The big comics crackdown of the early 1950s stemmed in part from the unwholesome nature of horror comics of the period. As a result, comic book companies have been more cautious about their horror books, and most submit their tales to the censorship board of the industry, the Comics Code Authority.

Many large black-and-white comics, however, feature violence and gore to match '50s standards. Most of the color stories are milder by comparison. A typical color comic book horror story features a weird occurrence stemming from some immoral act: Man kills wife by pushing her down the stairs. Man starts dreaming that his wife will return to get revenge. Man grows increasingly tense. Man thinks he sees wife coming toward him on street. Man runs and falls down subway stairs. Man dies. Bystanders wonder what upset him. Mistaken woman makes ironic comment. Many of the stories are much more embellished, often with beautiful illustrations of a particular historical period.

The classic mold for a horror comic was developed by EC Publications in the 1950s. It involves a narrator (witch, ghoul, horror aficionado) presenting each tale with a twisted and somewhat humorous introduction. Among present-day hosts are "Uncle Creepy," "Cousin Eerie," "Dr. Graves," and Boris Karloff.

• *Funny animal comics.* Mickey Mouse is a funny animal. Casper the Friendly Ghost is a funny animal. Nonhuman characters presented in light, humorous fantasies are funny animals. The movie cartoon stars of the Disney and Warner Brothers studios are perhaps the most famous, but a host of others such as Yogi Bear, Funky Phantom, and the Pink Panther appear regularly in comic books. Many of the tales, particularly those of Carl Barks (Donald Duck) and Sheldon Mayer, are warm, intelligent, and delightful.

• *Teen-age comics.* Short, funny stories are the meat of these books. Most deal with the antics of suburban high school students in a lighthearted manner. *Archie* is probably the best known of these comics; *Scoobie Doo Mystery* and *Millie the Model* are among the others.

• *Sword and sorcery comics.* A more recent trend in comic books has been "barbarian" stories, usually set in a mythical age. A heroic prototype for these characters is "Conan," a wanderer, soldier, and adventurer created by Robert E. Howard. Most sword-and-sorcery tales feature three main elements: wizardry (mysticism), violence, and a beautiful girl. These serve as a backdrop for the actions of the predominantly male s-and-s stars.

• *Monster comics.* A variation on the horror theme, monster comics usually feature a single character in a recurring milieu. Among the monsters with their own books are Dracula, Frankenstein, Swamp Thing, Man-Thing, Man-Wolf, and Werewolf. Many of these series are sympathetic to their monsters, taking the "poor, misunderstood creature" attitude epitomized in Karloff's *Frankenstein.*

• *Underground comics.* Legally, kids are not permitted to buy most of these books, which multiplied in the late 1960s and early '70s, but have been on the wane of late. The "undergrounds" are a predominantly black-and-white group of comics produced by independent publishers. Many of the books are heavily involved with the portrayal of explicitly violent, sexual, and drug-oriented material. Other themes commonly explored are women's liberation, horror, and political repression.

BYRON PREISS

"Should My Child Read Comic Books?"

Having looked at the comic book scene, we now face the classic question: Should my child read comic books?

The most compelling argument against comic books is the violence they depict.

Those who argue in favor of comic books cite literate scripts, healthy speculative fantasy, and beautiful artwork. Many people attribute their kids' progress in learning how to read to their interest in comic books. Some children get involved with drawing by tracing pictures of their favorite comic book characters.

If you don't wish your child to read comic books, it shouldn't be out of disdain for the graphic story form. *Kids like it.* If you have objections, discuss them. After all, Batman explained things to Robin.

BYRON PREISS

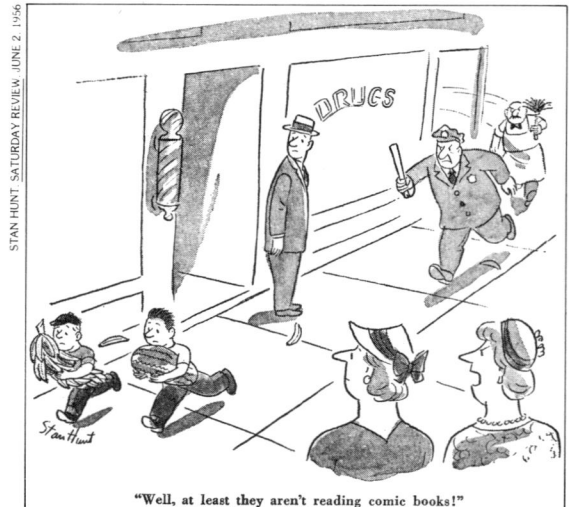

"Well, at least they aren't reading comic books!"

[If this cartoon, drawn in 1956, were done ten years later, it would have the caption: "Well, at least they're not watching television!"]

"I Don't Read Comics (But I Used To)"

Comics, many librarians would have you believe, are deplorable. I don't agree. Of course, I don't read comics; I really don't like them now. But I used to.

When you stop to think about it, reading comics requires a very sophisticated visual perception. A child has to figure out how to relate words to pictures; which characters are talking and what their emotional state is as they speak their lines; how to recognize the difference between spoken dialogue, thoughts, author's asides, and sound effects. At the same time, she or he will be exposed to every kind of punctuation under the sun, not to mention a surprisingly rich vocabulary of words and ideas.

I firmly believe this visual training is good for young readers—in fact, the kids know they're learning from comics, whether the librarians like it or not.

PHYLLIS CERF WAGNER

A Word About Ads

Ads are one of the really negative aspects of comic books. Ads for which TV networks would come under vehement attack—for BB guns, X-ray glasses, and toy armies—are frequently found in comic books. The overall quality of the ads has improved, but the situation is still far from acceptable. The Comics Code Authority (41 East 42nd Street, New York, N.Y. 10017), which approves comic book story content, is the body to contact if you have a problem with any comics-advertised product. One more thing: be prepared to wait a long time for any item ordered through a comic book ad.

BYRON PREISS

Fanzines

There are a number of limited-edition magazines published *about* comic books. Some are made up predominantly of ad material. Others feature "scholarly" articles. Some of the more popular fanzines are:

The Comic Reader: The "TV Guide" for comic books. Published monthly; 75 cents from Street Enterprises, P.O. Box 255, Menomonee Falls, Wisc. 53051.

The Buyer's Guide: Packed with ads for old comic books, this is a place where you can find the missing books for your kid's (or your) collection; $5 for 26 issues from The Buyer's Guide, 15800 Rt. 84 North, East Moline, Ill. 61244.

Mediascene: Coverage of comic books, paperbacks, and movies in a handsomely packaged tabloid; $1.75 per issue from Supergraphics, Box 445, Wyomissing, Pa.

BYRON PREISS

Spider-Man to the Rescue

To catch the eye of a slow-reading child and lure him into a story is not easy, not even with comic books. Not today, especially, when he can gaze at the television screen instead and watch pictures that talk to him out loud.

But there is a project going on now that nevertheless hopes to win the slow reader over to the written word through a well-researched use of the comic book format.

The project is run by the Children's Television Workshop. . . . Its comic book series is called Spidey Super Stories. It sells for 35 cents per monthly issue, 10 cents more than its competitors, but unlike them it carries no advertising. The Spidey series is aimed at 6- to 10-year-olds reading at a second-grade level. Or, for that matter, any child reading at a second-grade level.

The comic books are produced in conjunction with Marvel Comics. Spidey, who is based on Marvel's Spider-Man, looks just like him, armed with web-shooters in his hands, dressed in what appears to be a blue body stocking and wearing a red net over his head. But the big difference is that the Spidey stories are much gentler. . . .

Because there is less violence in this new comic than any other of the superhero genre, the Workshop tries to keep the action as lively as possible in the hopes that nobody will notice that this Spider-Man is a bit of a softy.

The most productive aspect of the Workshop's research is the work of Dr. Kenneth O'Bryan, a Canadian psychologist who traces the eye movements of children as they read. The reflections of beams of light striking the cornea are measured so precisely that Dr. O'Bryan can create a map showing how a poor reader's eyes move through a comic strip—he knows which elements are attractive and which are frustrating.

That knowledge led him to recommend several ways to guide poor readers, who tend to approach the reading matter, he says, with a "haphazard attack." For example, the word balloons should be close to the speaker and the action. And irregularly shaped balloons—jagged balloons such as the ones used to depict radio bulletins and the bubbly surfaced ones used to convey thoughts—should be kept in mind because they act as magnets to the eye.

Dr. O'Bryan advises artists not to tell too much of the story in the pictures so that the children will have to read to find out what's going on.

And he found that children tended to ignore information in the lower half of the frame, that they preferred to read balloons or boxes that were vertical rather than horizontal (so the lines would be shorter, only two or three words each) and that too much detail in a frame, the kind of detail comic-book creators are so proud of, can confuse the slow reader and stop his eye movement dead in its tracks.

When the child stops reading the game is lost. The object of these comics isn't to challenge a child but to give him a taste of success.

For that reason, too . . . the words used are constantly tested. A recent field trip to a local school revealed that the writers ought to avoid using "masks," "thefts," "ghosts," and "loony bin." On the other hand, "pickpockets," "crawling," "master," and "mystery" were just fine.

Controlling the vocabulary doesn't mean that the editions have deleted all the conventional comic expletives. They still allow ZAP, BAM and an occasional

RICHARD FLASTE
The New York Times

The Original Comic Strip Bad Boy

Created in 1904, published in Hearst's New York *Journal,* Richard F. Outcault's Buster Brown was the original comic strip "bad boy." And although each episode ends with Buster making resolutions to improve himself, we know not to expect miracles. He will invite eighty children for a surprise birthday party for himself without informing his mother; tie a visiting dog's tail to the pull of a windowshade; try his luck at "setting" on a dozen eggs on the best chair in the parlor, etc. Fifteen of these comic strips, collected in a $2 Dover paperback and reproduced in the original full color, are good fun for *everybody.*

MARIA POLUSHKIN ROBBINS

The French Way

The Adventures of Tin Tin, the French comic series, has now been translated into English (Atlantic–Little, Brown, $2.50 to $2.95 each, paperback). They are quality comics—good adventure stories with nice illustrations—for seven-to-ten-year-olds. (The biggest difference I've noticed between these and American comics is that the text of *Tin Tin* is not written all in capitals.)

My son isn't into big books, and when he's finished one of these—they're about sixty pages long—he feels as though he's really achieved something.   LIZA WERNER

[Next time you're in Port Chester, N.Y., look for the Museum of Cartoon Art. For a description of it, see page 355.]

MUSIC

293

INTRODUCING KIDS TO MUSIC

The Environmental Approach

There are two ways to introduce kids to any-thing: environment (accepted by the child as his "background") and instruction ("Eat it, it's good for you"—generally rejected by the child, although he may temporarily seem to accept it in order to please his parents). If the arts are part of a child's environment, the child will more likely be interested in wanting what his or her parents have in order to seem "grown up." Parents who enjoy good music should take their children to musical events that they as adults are interested in, rather than just taking them to children's events. Children should not be dragged to something that is of no interest to the parent.

Expose children to as much music as pos-sible, whether it be Prokofiev's *Peter and the Wolf* or Bach's *The Art of the Fugue*. Don't worry that a child may be too young to "under-stand" what he is hearing. One cannot truly un-derstand great art any more than one can truly understand an ocean or a mountain range. One of the basic premises of any great art is that it will mean different things to different people. There is a beautiful story of how Toscanini, near the end of his sixty-eight-year career, was discovered engrossed in the score of Bee-thoven's First (and simplest) Symphony. Asked why he was still studying a piece which he had been conducting from memory for over half a century, he replied that every time he looked at it he discovered new things in it. In my own personal experience I fell in love with Bach's *The Art of the Fugue* as a child, went about whistling tunes from it, and made it part of my deepest pleasure experience, though it was not till many years later that I learned what a fugue was.

Art must always be immediately accessible, never removed to lofty heights. From earliest childhood one should always think of the great-est creators and their art in the spirit of Pablo Casals, who, when asked why he played Bach so frequently, replied simply, "Because Bach is my friend."

GILMAN COLLIER

Mozart Had Secret Thoughts, Too

Music educators sometimes remind me of sex educators in the diffident way they approach their subject. . . . They're afraid that we're han-dling a great masterpiece, a fine piece of china. How much easier for those kids to accept Mo-zart if they read some of his letters. Those same thoughts that they lock up or laugh over in the bathrooms, Mozart wrote. Schubert—if they knew what this young boy was feeling at school. Beethoven—if they knew what Bee-thoven felt as he was losing his hearing. Satie—he was into mysticism and it came out in his music . . .

LORIN HOLLANDER
quoted in *Music Educator's Journal*

Real People Playing Real Music

If parents don't care about music very much themselves, it's hard for them to do much to encourage their kid's interest in music except to provide instruments if the kid wants them, or concerts if the kid wants to go. An introduction to people who make music would be much more meaningful to a child, especially real live people making music in a small room rather than in a concert hall. Chamber music—if you can find people to play string quartets in some-one's living room—would be immensely excit-ing for a child.

JOHN HOLT

A Young People's Concert— Right in Your Own School

There are subsidized bands of professional per-formers all over the country who will put on concerts and dance recitals at schools and other community centers for an unbelievably reason-able price.

Through a nonprofit organization known as Young Audiences, Inc., you can arrange for whatever kind of program best suits you: string, brass, percussion, or wind ensembles; jazz or electronic music; ballet, modern dance, opera, etc.—often with only a week or two's notice. And, at this writing, the cost to the school or other youth group for a New York appearance is a mere $180, all expenses paid (Bradford Lewis of Young Audiences tells us the rates are fairly consistent from one chapter to another). In addition to two full performances, children get to handle and play the instruments, converse with the musicians, offer opinions on the musical and dance selections—even lead the orchestra. All that for just a couple of dollars per student.

Young Audiences has over forty regional chapters in such major cities as New York, Boston, Chicago, Los Angeles, Philadelphia, Detroit, New Orleans, Minneapolis–St. Paul, San Francisco, and even Las Vegas, just to name a few. To find out the address or phone number of the one nearest you, call or write Young Audiences, Inc., 115 East 92nd Street, New York, NY 10028, (212) 831-8110.

CBC
(recommended by Danny Epstein)

◆

Rock: Support Your Kids' Interest

It took some time before rock music was accepted as legitimate, but by now even most classical musicians acknowledge it. Leonard Bernstein was influential in this effort, including pieces like Janis Ian's "Society's Child" in his Young People's Concerts.

In an address to music teachers, Lorin Hollander talked about the importance of supporting a kid's interest in whatever kind of music he or she is interested in. If it's rock, the child should be able to study rock. And if you want to turn that kid on to classical music, the way to do it is through good rock music. If you try to impose an "alien" music on kids, they'll rebel.

I went to talk to some teachers who were trying to force classical music on their students, black kids between six and twelve years old. I told the teachers, "Let the kids listen to Aretha Franklin and Ray Charles. Let them listen to Stevie Wonder, whose genius and talent is recognized by all musicians today; and the old Beatles albums, still some of the best rock music around. 'She Loves You' is loved by five-year-olds and eighty-year-olds." It's been said so much, but the Beatles are good clean music. I suggested that the teachers listen to rock and soul music, find artists and cuts that they like, and share their choices with the kids.

The important thing is for parents to give kids all types of music—rock and classical and jazz and folk—without making value judgments. There's good and bad in all genres; you learn to choose unless psychological barriers have been created.

WARREN SPAETH

◆

How Can a Child Who Has Not Yet Learned to Read and Write Dabble in Creative Music?

The answer lies in the inexpensive tape recorder. Have the child make any music he wants—on any instrument, be it the piano or the coffee table—and play it back to him. Does he like what he hears? If not, why? Let him, as they say in the profession, make another "take." Does he like this one better? The child will be encouraged to continue not only by his interest in the sounds he makes but also by his fascination with the tape recorder itself. In this way he can formulate his own ideas in music while at the same time realizing, long before it is ever presented to him scholastically, that there is form, structure, timbre, plasticity—in music and in all objects of beauty. All this can be done spontaneously, not as assigned work.

Another idea: suggest that the child make up a story or paint a picture inspired by a musical piece. (Don't impose your own interpretations on the child.)

GILMAN COLLIER

I remember going to a symphony orchestra performance and sitting next to a man I had seen at a number of concerts. He told me he had been trying for years to get his teen-aged children to go with him to a concert. "I offered them tickets and everything else," he said. "I just can't seem to get them to hear good music." "Is that what you call it?" I asked. He said, "Yes." "Could I possibly persuade you to call it something else?" He smiled and said, "Ah, I see what you mean." "Call it orchestral music, call it symphonic music, but don't draw a line between you and them and put them on the wrong side."

JOHN HOLT
Music Educator's Journal

Music is feeling, then, not sound
WALLACE STEVENS

The Mini-Moog Method

The Mini-Moog—a small electronic synthesizer available at many music shops—is the best instrument I've found for developing aural acuity in children. Within an hour most kids catch on to its operation—then they can use it to try to approximate different sounds from their environment. It's remarkable how quickly one can learn to listen. PAUL BEAVER

"Tell Me What You Hear"

One of the best ways to train a child's ear is by guessing games . . . Begin with the simplest sit-very-quiet-and-tell-me-what-you-hear variety. You'll be surprised to discover how many noises an alert child will detect in a "quiet" house: the refrigerator hum, the clock tick, the *whoosh* of a car going by, footsteps in a distant room, a pot boiling, his own heartbeat. . . . Now reverse the procedure. Have the child shut his eyes while you produce noises for him to identify: a drawer closing, a light switch snapped on, the winding of a watch, knuckles tapped on the table, a shoe dropped, paper being crumpled. Or ask the child to make noises imitating common sounds, while you guess. Children are often startlingly adept at reproducing siren howls, the clop of horses galloping, the screech of brakes and the cork POP when a bottle's opened. Of the many special-sound-effects records which can be used in conjunction with these games, two are notably good: *Muffin in the City, Muffin in the Country* (Young People's Records), about a little dog who learns to listen when he can't see, and *The Lonesome House,* which reproduces lovely spooky empty-house noises.

FREDELLE MAYNARD
Guiding Your Child to a More Creative Life

Songs for Any Occasion

My son is always asking me to sing to him and because of that I discovered that I have a perverse and unpredictable repertoire that dredges up, from unknown depths and resources, songs appropriate for any occasion. Consequently my son has learned a lot of songs. It all started when "Sweet and Low" and "Go Tell Aunt Abby" failed as lullabies and I resorted to "Michael from Mountains" (from Judy Collins' album *Wildflowers*), which became his favorite and which I was trying to memorize at the time. After a year and a half of singing it to him, I played the record so he could hear the real thing, and he was transfixed. Since then, we've ridden seven hours in the car alongside the Erie Canal, so we learned the song "The Erie Canal" (see below); he had a rotten chest cold and his Granny rubbed it with camphorated oil, so I sang "John Brown's Baby had a cold upon his chest . . . so he rubbed it with camphorated oil"; he was saying things like "Rzpfh spells racing car, "so I sang "B-I-N-G-O," a song that spells out the dog's name; "Jack-o'-Lantern" at Halloween; "Over the River and Through the Woods" at Thanksgiving and Christmas or any time we're going to Granny's house. Not the greatest songs? Maybe. But my kid loves to sing. FLAVIA POTENZA

MUSIC BOXES

Snoopy and Friends

A friend of mine decided that her daughter should have a music box collection—it would be a good idea for grandparents' gifts. So her daughter has Pied Pipers with little animals, ballerinas in glass houses, and ballerinas in velvet houses. She loves to listen to them, even though she can't touch.

At the other end of the scale are the Fisher-Price music boxes, which parents swear by because, like most Fisher-Price products, they're indestructible. If longevity is a criterion, be assured that neither stuffed-in pennies nor ice cream nor stomping feet nor winding in reverse can destroy the Fisher-Price offerings. (No one mentions much about the *music* they play. The Ferris wheel turns to "In the Good Old Summertime," and the merry-go-round lulls with "Skater's Waltz." Both sell for around $13 in discount stores, which makes them expensive for what they are.)

If you query a few parents, you'll find that one has a Mattel Jack-in-the-Music Box (purists would call Snoopy singing "Where, Oh Where Has My Little Dog Gone" a $7.00 toy rather than a music box), one has a Japanese import from the stationery store, and one has the wooden Creative Playthings box ($5.25), the one you can see through that plays "Swan Lake" for as long as you're willing to turn the handle. ("It's one of the few commercial boxes that's in pitch," says pre-school music specialist Cindy May).

But if you are willing to spend a little more money on a music box than you would on a toy, one standout is a five-inch-high wooden circus backdrop featuring a clown who clicks his heels to "La Machiche." One young friend has played with his for three years and it seems indestructible (he's thrown it twenty feet across the room and nothing's broken). It has a Swiss mechanism, winds like a clock, and can't be overwound. I haven't found it in any of the big stores, but it's available for $30 by mail from Rita Ford, 812 Madison Avenue, New York, N.Y. 10021, (212) 535-6717.

Although Ms. Ford carries mostly antique music boxes that you wish had been passed down in your family, she also has a number of enchanting new ones. My personal favorite is a shadow box whose doors open on Pierrot and Pierrette dancing to "Clair de Lune" ($45). Others are less extravagantly priced: a solid wooden box with a gremlin on top revolving to the tune of "Frère Jacques" ($12.50); an austere bust of your favorite composer and a selection of his music ($22.50); carved Anri figures revolving to your choice of "Danny Boy" or "My Wild Irish Rose" ($27.50). Ms. Ford will send a catalogue upon request ($3).   RS

[The Fisher-Price music-box record player is discussed in the Phonograph section, below.]

PHONOGRAPHS

A Child Needs His or Her Own Record Player

Even where a family owns a first-rate stereo system, a child needs his own record player. The quality of sound reproduction will be inferior, certainly. But there's no substitute for the child's being able to control his own music time—play the same record over and over if he chooses—and to listen in absolute privacy. Besides, there's a special delight in squatting on the floor, beside the player, watching the disc spin around and around. I recall, from my older daughter's first years, her passion for a record called *Train to the Zoo*. "The train is in the station, It's going to the zoo, It's full of little boys and girls, But there's still room for *you*. Choo-oo CHOO! Choo-oo CHOO!" The summer she was three, we spent several weeks with friends who owned a phonograph and a sizable collection of juvenile records. Rona listened with polite interest. But *every* afternoon, before nap time, she would sit on the floor by her bed and, crouched over an imaginary record player, would flip an imaginary switch. "Click! Wait until it warms up. . . ." A minute later, we'd hear singing, very soft. "The train is in the station, It's going to the zoo. . . ." Whatever it was that moved this three-year-old—images of animals, promise of friends, or simply a familiar melody—it had become an important part of her life rhythm.
                              FREDELLE MAYNARD
                    Guiding Your Child to a More Creative Life

A Real "Phoner"!

Records have been one of the greatest kids' pleasures in our house—and at a much earlier age than I had expected. (I guess you can begin anytime; I have friends who introduced classical music to their son the day he came home from the hospital.) The real fun came for our daughter (and for us) with the gift of a real "phoner" she could operate all by herself (which she did competently enough at around two and a half—before she could pronounce it). It's a small plastic portable/plug-in Panasonic that has withstood more than a year of not-so-gentle treatment (we did replace the needle).
                              PAULA GLATZER

◆

Buying a Kid's Record Player

A child of three (sometimes even younger, see above) can be taught to use a simple record player. Before buying one, listen to the tone of it. Although for storytelling records high fidelity is not as important as for music, it is unfair to your child to get a record player that sounds outrageously bad.

Battery-operated machines aren't a wise choice because of the quality of the sound (usually terrible) and the cost of changing the batteries (kids have a tendency to leave the player on); however, they are safer than electric machines and can easily be carried around. Record players with automatic changers break too easily and are best left for older children.

A decent child's record player can be had for about $15 to $25. They're mostly portables in a carrying case, which is an advantage if you aren't planning to keep it out all the time. A plastic case might crack, but it's more practical than the cardboard ones if you'll be scraping bubble gum off the bottom.   ELS

Children's Record Players: Some That Work

The Fisher-Price music-box record player (around $13 in discount stores, includes five records) is really better than a music box that you just watch because it teaches a very young child how to use a real record player. You turn if off and on, and you have to get the record on in the right place or it won't play, and you have to put the arm on the record. Matthew has thrown pennies down the slats and it still works. The kids stand on it and throw the records around and they haven't broken (they're about a quarter-inch thick). When Michael learned how to use this, we got him a cheap regular electric record player for $10 at a discount store (it's in its second year and it hasn't broken yet). Now that they have a real record player they put cowboys and Fisher-Price people on the old turntable and watch them go around. ANN FINK

Marsh was given a Teletone record player a year ago which has kept him occupied for hours and hours. He's given it tremendous abuse, and it's like new—it seems indestructible. It has three speeds, mono, one on-off-volume control. Often, instead of a story at nap time, Marsh will go in, put on a record, and go to sleep listening; later I'll turn it off. ANNE GARDINER

It is important to have an arm that is housed in sponge rubber, because one of the first things that breaks is the arm. I've been extremely lucky with the Newcomb Educational Model, (R124 Serial 250587), which may cost you $100 but in twelve years of classroom use I've never had to have it repaired. It's had peanut butter in it and all kinds of things—and I've only had it cleaned. It's got four speeds, the feet are on springs so when the children jump the record doesn't get scratched, and you can lock the needle if you want. It's expensive, but if you buy the $20 or $30 department store special and it ends up in the shop, it's going to cost you $14 every time.

Newcomb record players are available from Newcomb Audio Products Company, 12881 Bradley Avenue, P.O. Box 4476, Sylmar, Calif. 91342. CINDY MAY

Close and Pray

It stinks, say several parents whose kids have lived through more than one broken Close and Play phonograph (Kenner, $10 each time you or Grandmother buys it). It plays 45s only, and one problem is that as the batteries wear, the records slow down.

Another parent said she didn't even consider getting it for her child because "it would become a toy, not a functional thing."—Eds.

Facing Reality

Kids and diamond needles really don't mix, and why should they?

We have had a series of players that were bought on the cheap. Dreary affairs that are now stacked up in a closet on the theory that you can't throw them out, they must be fixed—but leaning against the sad reality that to fix them is more costly than to replace them. JENNIFER CARDEN

TAPE PLAYERS

Child's Play

We never bought a children's record player. David's been using our compact radio-stereo-cassette correctly since he was two. It's really a very simple operation, and he knows which button to push (though often the babysitter does not). He's been taught, he knows, but I wouldn't let any of his friends use it. SALLY LANGENDOEN

An Electronic Companion

The Panasonic tape recorder is a little plastic box with color-coded keys so that you know to press the red and black to record (the rewind mechanism is more difficult). Although they are marketing it for teen-agers, my three-year-old learned how to work it in a day. The day she got it—we didn't even know she had it on—she walked around with it, talking to it and telling stories. Then she played back a half hour of our lives. To hear the way we talk to her was sometimes a little scary for us. But she was thrilled to hear herself. What she talks about on the tape follows pretty closely what she does in her independent play: fantasy conversations with her real friends, conversations with a doll, and music. The reproduction is a little tinny, but it's clear enough. I think it's a better investment than a record player for that age. And although pre-recorded tapes are more expensive than records, you can record from the radio or a friend's records.

MARIE BROWN

[For some ideas on how to use a tape recorder to encourage a child to be creative musically, see Gilman Collier's article on page 295. Also, a few thoughts on using a cassette player for long-distance storytelling can be found in the BOOKS section, page 242.]

RECORDS AND TAPES

Records Are a Good Investment (Even Though Your Kid Will Destroy Them)

Parents have to steel themselves to the slow destruction of kids' records; but Gaby has been satisfied with such a small collection of favorites that I consider them a worthwhile investment. Favorites, by the way, are the *Sesame Street* albums, *Free to Be You and Me,* and assorted nursery songs. (*Note:* She never really liked any record on the first hearing, so have the patience to play it until it's familiar.)

PAULA GLATZER

Which Record Should I Buy? (Don't Take the Choice *Too* Seriously)

It seems to me that in dealing with records and children it's best not be be reverent. Of course, I am speaking from a non-musical family, so you have to take that into account.

For us the record collection is rather like the book collection. It has gotten added to over the years, and, as with books that are now dirty, torn, under beds, passed from child to child, ripped, drawn in, and read from upside down, the records are in the wrong slipcases, left on radiators to melt, and generally under beds too.

What records have we bought? Serious, sensitive John Philip Sousa marching band collections. Woody Guthrie with the great work songs. Peter, Paul and Mary in concert at an elementary school. Mr. Rogers telling us we are fine in ever so quiet a voice—we are so fine, it turns out, that we don't have to assert that fact. (I don't know how the kids feel about Mr. Rogers, but he makes *me* feel terrific.)

Besides, we have tons and tons of little records with little books. The narrator reads the story and "when-you-hear-the-bell-turn-the-page." There was a time when the children loved those, and huddled cross-legged on the floor grabbing at every line and turning the pages rapidly in order to keep up.

Now it's the Bee Gees. What can I say? These are played on the regular family player (the needle doesn't get damaged anymore). The children know *every* word. And dance. Adolescence may be approaching.

JENNIFER CARDEN

The Most Often Played Records

Records seem to provide company for our three-year-old when she is alone in her room drawing, building with blocks, playing with clay, etc. Children do not need a lot of records, they enjoy listening to the same record, even the same side, over and over again.

The most often played records in our house fall into three categories:

1. Records related to TV shows, plays, puppet shows, or movies the child has seen. These include any of the twenty or more records put out by CTW—featuring material from *Sesame Street* and *The Electric Company*—Mr. Rogers' records and Captain Kangaroo records, as well as records made in conjunction with children's plays and movies, like Mary Poppins or Winnie-the-Pooh. The children are familiar with the material from the movie or show, and they seem to delight in memorizing the words and performing what they have seen.

2. Records on a holiday theme, usually Christmas or Easter. The current favorite for our child, which she started to listen to months before Easter, is *Peter Cotton Tail.* The songs are charming, bouncy, and all about rabbits in simple fantasy stories.

3. The old standards. These songs which children love, and are able to learn easily, are scattered throughout the first two groups. Captain Kangaroo's *A Treasure House of Best Loved Children's Songs* has one of the finest selections of old favorites, including "In the Good Old Summer Time," "The Bear Went Over the Mountain," and "She'll Be Comin' Round the Mountain."

ELIE WARD

Amanda Guinzburg's Top 11— and Her Mother's Bottom 2

I asked my daughter, Amanda, five years old, to pick her favorite records. Here are her choices and my comments:

1. *Cock-A-Doodle-Doo & Mother Goose Too/118 Children's Classics* (Telecast Marketing, 12715 B State Highway 55, Minneapolis, Minn.)

   A four-record set containing *every* standard kids' song in varied renditions, so that each one has a unique sound. Never cloying or condescending, some of these songs are very funny. Especially good for kids between two and four.
2. All Sesame Street Records.
3. *The Wizard of Oz* (MGM Records).

   For any child who has seen the movie this is a must.
4. *Moving*, by Peter, Paul and Mary (Warner Bros.).

   Especially "Puff, the Magic Dragon" and "This Land Is Your Land."
5. All Mister Rogers Records (Pickwick International Records).

   She likes him. Maybe it's because she doesn't live with her father.
6. All Disney records that go with movies (Disneyland Records).

   If she has seen the movie, she loves the record. They all come with books.
7. *50 Happy Years of Disney Favorites* (Disneyland Records).

   Never too much of a good thing. Contains two records and an eleven-

page book; includes *every* classic Disney song in its original version.
8. *Christmas with the Chipmunks,* Vols. I and II (Monarch Music).

   Kids think these are hysterical and love to hear Christmas songs all year round. To me, they sound as if they're being played at the wrong speed.
9. *Bozo's Christmas Sing-Along* (Peter Pan Records).

   Not as hard to take as the above. If a kid wants to have Christmas in August, why not?
10. *Disney Christmas Favorites* (Disneyland Records).

    Okay, okay, so she's a little obsessive.
11. *Snow White and the Seven Dwarfs, Sleeping Beauty, Rumpelstiltskin* (Great Children's Classics—MGM Records).

    Great for days when parents don't feel like telling the stories themselves, have laryngitis, or hangovers, this record contains stories told with sound effects and music.

Once I went out and bought some records recommended by child-rearing books. Two of the *least* successful—and there were others— were:

1. *Action Songs and Rounds* (Honor Your Partner Records).

   "Push the Damper In," "Put Your Finger in the Air," "Little Tommy Tinker," ad nauseam—if anyone sang like this to you, you'd punch him.
2. *What's the Good Word,* by Jackie Roach and Mel Poretz (Peter Pan Records).

   "What's the Good Word," "With a Wink and a Nod," "The Dic-Dic-Dictionary," "A-E-I-O-U," "Sing a Song of Synonyms," etc. Amanda put her hands over her ears for this one.

RUSTY UNGER GUINZBURG

COURTESY OF SESAME STREET RECORDS

© 1969 WALT DISNEY PRODUCTIONS

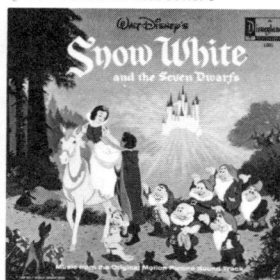

© 1977 WALT DISNEY PRODUCTIONS

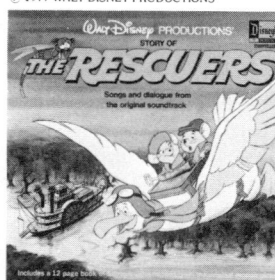

COURTESY OF POLYDOR RECORDS

Records: First Things First

As soon as a child is playing "Peek-a-boo," she is ready for "first things first" records—records designed to help a child learn to sing on pitch, or sing in different kinds of musical patterns, or develop motor skills. You don't really need very many of them. Most young children will love to listen to the same record over and over again, until they know what's coming next—that's what they really enjoy. And they'll love whatever adult records you love if you share your listening with them.

When ordering by mail (which you may have to do, children's records being poorly stocked in most stores), specify whether you prefer LPs or 45s (if you don't, they'll most likely send 45s).

Here are my favorites:

A CHILD'S FIRST RECORD, by Frank Luther (Vocalion, $2.49).

Frank Luther has done a lot of records, and this album is great fun. It features games ("Mulberry Bush," "Tiddledywinks"), animal songs ("Mary Had a Little Lamb," "Three Blind Mice"), and toy songs. A parent could spend a year enjoying this record with a child.

ALLEY CAT AND CHICKEN FAT (Golden Records, $2.98).

These songs were originally designed to get children up and moving, probably around a classroom with limited space. The record encourages gross motor movement, fine motor movement, singing . . . and children can grow up with it. The activities it includes range from the very simple, like "Clap Clap Clap Your Hands, Clap Your Hands Together," right up through pattern dances, like the "Hokey Pokey."

EARLY, EARLY CHILDHOOD SONGS and AND ONE AND TWO, both by Ella Mae Jenkins (Folkways, $7.98).

These are fun for children and parents, as are all of Ella's records. CINDY MAY

The New Schools Exchange Newsletter reports that a "good source of records for school programs, children, and folks in general is Folkways Records (43 West 61st Street, New York, N.Y. 10023, [212] 586-7260. Free catalogue, individual orders accepted). We have been receiving lovely review copies which, when played, brightened our days. Records like *Jambo—and Other Call-and-Response Songs and Chants* by Ella Jenkins, which is the most

involving children's record I've heard in a long time—a favorite around here, and *Small Voice, Big Voice* by Dick Lourie and Jed, a nice sing-along. Folkways has a fantastic ethnic series."

Where Music Paints a Story

I think the most useful records for children are those in which the music is tied directly to a story. There are some in which instruments—each with its own particular tonal color—are used to represent characters. *Peter and the Wolf* is, of course, the most famous example. There are lots of fine recordings of it, including a very good one narrated by Peter Ustinov.

Taking an even more direct approach are the records by George Kleinsinger and Paul Tripp. Together they created several albums in which orchestral instruments were used as the characters themselves; Kleinsinger wrote and conducted the music, and Tripp (you may remember him as "Mr. I. Magination") was responsible for the narration. Their first record—and still their best-known one—was *Tubby the Tuba,* which they followed up with *Peewee the Piccolo.* Later, they produced *The Story of Celeste,* which, in case you haven't guessed it, is about a celesta.

Even though the Kleinsinger-Tripp recordings date back to 1950 or so, they've never been equaled, and they're not likely to be. It's just too expensive to record a symphony orchestra these days.

A good transition record—when *Peter and the Wolf* and Tubby and his friends have been exhausted—is Saint-Saëns' *Danse Macabre,* an orchestral piece in which the instruments are used so graphically they almost speak the story—the oboe crowing as a rooster, the xylophone as the bones of a skeleton, and so on.

But the main thing in leading a child to an appreciation of music is appreciating it yourself. We were always playing records or tapes at our house. Besides, my daughter, Ivy, heard me practicing on the xylophone at some point every day. It's no wonder she got interested.

DANNY EPSTEIN

Children's Records:
The Best Defense
Is a Good Pair of Earphones

A woman who was driven batty by her son's playing the same song over and over and over again finally invested in a pair of earphones for him. Now everyone's happy—even the neighbors.

ELS

A Word About
Spoken Word Records

If we played word association and I said "record," you'd probably say "music." But why not present a record that talks a child's language—famous books and stories read on discs by famous casts? [Here are favorites:]

The excessively versatile Peter Ustinov reads THE LITTLE PRINCE by Antoine de Saint-Exupery. This classic, delving into child-and-adult visions of the world, is illuminated by Ustinov's voices. He brings a marvelous new dimension to the story (Argo ZSW 520–1). And if you'd like to give the book as well, Harcourt Brace has . . . a lush 30th anniversary edition. Both would make an imaginative gift.

No other poet wrote as rapturously for the ear as did Dylan Thomas. And except for Thomas himself, I haven't heard anyone read his poems with the reverberating richness of Emlyn Williams. A two-LP set called A BOY GROWING UP includes *A Child's Christmas in Wales, A Visit to America,* and *A Visit to Grandpa's.* For older children—and surely for you—this is a treasure (Argo TA 509–10).

Don't confuse LASSIE COME HOME with the stuff on television. This is the real thing—the Yorkshire story by Eric Knight, read for all it's worth (and it's worth plenty) by David McCallum, who should not be confused with his stuff on television. He gives a terrific reading that will spellbind children, and if *you* wander into the room, you won't get back to whatever it was you were doing until both sides have been played out (Caedmon TC 1389).

If records *do* mean music to you—or at least words and music—what can compare to

PETER AND THE WOLF by Prokofiev? There are two exceptional versions. The first has Boris Karloff narrating with The Vienna State Opera Orchestra (Vanguard S-174). The other is the version I was brought up on: Richard Hale reading with the Boston Symphony conducted by Serge Koussevitzky. This one may not be in print anymore, and I don't have the number, but it's worth looking for. In any case, the Karloff version with the virtuoso playing of the solo instruments is just fine.

GENE SHALIT
Ladies Home Journal

Storybook Records:
A Collection of Classics

PETER RABBIT, *with narration by Vivien Leigh and an English boys' choir taking the part of the rabbits (Golden, $2.98).*

This has got to be included in any list of "classic" recordings. When Wonderland first put it out, it came with a beautiful book containing all of the Beatrix Potter *Peter Rabbit* pictures. Then Golden Wonderland reissued it for $2.49 without the pictures. But it's still a great record, and you can always buy a Potter *Peter Rabbit* book to go with it.

PETER AND THE WOLF *(various recordings).*

You can pay $2.98 for the Golden version (mono), which is cheap and good. Or you can buy a $7 version (Children's Records of America) by the New York Philharmonic, narrated by Leonard Bernstein, with *The Nutcracker* on the other side.

WESTON WOODS.

Weston Woods (Weston, Conn. 06883, [203] 226-3355), one of the finest companies for children's filmstrips, also produces records, cassettes, and books (hardcover and paperback). Their list includes many classics in the art of combining music with narrative: *The Fox Went Out on a Chilly Night,* for example, and *London Bridge, Hush, Little Baby,* and *Mommy, Buy Me a China Doll,* all very good nursery rhymes for young children. Also excellent is the haiku book *In a Spring Garden.*

The Weston Woods list includes so many favorites, generally so well performed, that it's worth writing for their catalog. (The books are publishers' editions, the records and cassettes Weston Woods' own.) Some of their materials are available in other languages.

CINDY MAY

THE WIZARD OF OZ, *original recording with Judy Garland and Bert Lahr (MGM, $6.49).*

Four- and five-year-olds, who have all seen the movie version and read either the original or an abridged version, listen to the record over and over for weeks. They memorize every word, act it out, and eventually go on to a new record. But while their fascination lasts, they adore it.

LIZA WERNER

THE ERIE CANAL, *illustrated by Peter Spier (Doubleday Zephyr paperback, 1970, $1.95).*

Everybody (well, almost everybody) knows the song "The Erie Canal," and all the text consists of (well, almost all) is the lyrics to the song. So why this and not some songbook? Because of Peter Spier's illustrations, because the words and music are in the back of the book, because a brief history of the canal is in the back of the book, too. Spier makes life on the canal look as though anyone who ever worked on it never had a bad day in his life (except for a cross-looking mule getting harnessed up for work. But even she smiles later on). Still, Spier's talent for historical detail is fascinating and makes for a whole other story that the reader can glean from the pictures. And, at last, I know the second verse.

FLAVIA POTENZA

MUSICAL INSTRUMENTS

I love to blow on instruments I don't know how to play.
JOHN HOLT

Random Notes

When I was working with first-graders, I used to take an old bugle to school and take it outside at recess. Twenty kids would line up to have a turn. A lot of them would put the mouthpiece inside their mouths like a lollipop—and I would just take it away from them, put it up to my lips the right way, give it back and they would go blatt. (A French horn is a lot easier to blow, but it's also a lot more expensive and you'd be more worried about its getting dropped.)

JOHN HOLT

My seven-year-old has a trombone; it's bigger than he is, he can't even reach the last position. I thought he chose the trombone because he's very mechanical and it moves around and you can take it apart. But then I asked him why he picked it. "It was the only instrument I knew the name of," he said.

JIM TURNER

Greatest recommended value in pianos: a good secondhand Steinway grand. In future years, should the child quit lessons, you will always be able to recoup your investment on a resale.

GILMAN COLLIER

A piano should be in a kid's room instead of in a "family room." The child has access to it any time, and some privacy with it.

JOHN HOLT

To buy an instrument because you want your kid to develop an interest in it is probably not a great idea. It's very expensive and it puts a lot of heat on. There's always going to be a little bit of feeling: gee, we went out and bought that instrument for you; why don't you play it. You can always borrow or rent.

JOHN HOLT

Anything can be a horn to a two-year-old—even a candlestick and some good, strong toot-toots.

Making Your Own Simple Musical Instruments

She picked long blades of grass to play with. By stretching the grass between her two thumbs, she created a fine instrument. She blew her breath against her thumbs; the blades vibrated. After a few tries, she was able to make two pure notes of sound.

VIRGINIA HAMILTON
Zeely

Music in the Kitchen

- An empty coffee can with a few beans makes a great rhythm sound.
- Fill a few water glasses with different amounts of water, tap lightly with utensil, and you have lovely music.
- Two pot covers make fine cymbals.
- Bang a wooden spoon on an aluminum pie plate for your percussion section.
- Stretch various widths of elastic bands across the back of a chair or around an empty box, and strum for a good string sound.
- Look into your cupboard, even your egg beater makes a pretty sound.
- Don't forget the unused washboard— with a thimble on your finger, rubbing it up and down, you have a happy noise.

DOROTHY LOHMAN

And More Ideas

Interested in learning more about making your own musical instruments? If so, the following books should prove helpful:

MAKE YOUR OWN MUSICAL INSTRU-MENTS, *by Muriel Mandell and Robert Wood (Sterling, 1957).*

Don't be fooled by this book's old-fashioned format and amusingly out-of-date photographs. It's full of good ideas.   CINDY MAY

RHYTHMS, MUSIC AND INSTRUMENTS FOR CHILDREN TO MAKE, *by John Hawkinson and Martha Faulhabe (Albert Whitman, 1970).*

This is the second volume on the subject: it contains more information than the earlier *Music and Instruments for Children to Make.*

CINDY MAY

THE MUSICAL INSTRUMENT RECIPE BOOK *(Elementary Science Series, 1971).*

Simple and inspiring, *The Musical Instrument Recipe Book* features the most accessible format in its field. (Perhaps the excerpt below— the formula for making an ear harp—will whet your appetite.) You may have trouble locating a copy; if so, you can order one from its distributor: McGraw-Hill, Princeton Road, Hightstown, N.J.   RS

How to Make an Ear Harp

MATERIALS

15″ length of board (pine or other soft wood) about ¾″ × 12″ (sold as 1″ × 12″ at lumberyards). If possible, get "select" pine which has no knots in it.

nylon fishline (Squidding line is best.)

6 or 8 nails about 1½″ long with heads

either 6–8 screw eyes (size #112) and a large nail *or* 1½ ft of ¼″ dowel and masking tape for tuning pegs

TOOLS
    hammer
    ruler
    saw

drill (hand or electric)
¼″ bit   } for tuning pegs
sandpaper

Draw a line near and parallel to one edge of the board.

Then draw a slanting line from an opposite corner.

Hammer an evenly spaced row of nails partway into the board along one of the lines, one nail for each string.

TWO WAYS TO FINISH
YOUR EAR HARP

1. *Screw Eyes.* Using the large nail to start the hole, insert a screw eye partway into the board along the other line opposite the first nail.

Then attach a piece of fishline to the nail with a good firm knot. Pull the string fairly tight and tie it securely to the screw eye. You can make the strings tighter by turning the screw eyes.

Do the same for the other strings.

Screw eyes are easier to turn if you use a nail through the eye as a lever.

After the rest of the strings are connected, tune them as you like by tightening or loosening them.

2. *Tuning Pegs.* These can be used for other string instruments, as well. Instruments with tuning pegs seem to have a richer sound than those with screw eyes. Screw eyes are easier to insert, but pegs can be twisted farther for tuning, and they look nicer!

To make tuning pegs, you need:

¼″ diameter doweling (2″ piece for each peg)

drill (hand or electric)

¼″ bit for drill

sandpaper

saw

masking tape

Saw the doweling into 2-inch pegs. (Make one for each string.) Sand each peg on one end so that the last ½ inch is flat on one side. Then flatten the other side on the same end. (Wrapping the sandpaper around a ruler makes it easier to sand flat.) Drill a ¼-inch hole through your board for each peg. Attach one of the strings to a nail on the other end of the board with a good firm knot. Then put about 3 inches of masking tape along the free end of the string—sticky side toward the string. Wind the taped part of the string around the peg just below the flat end. Force the round end of the peg into its hole until it is firmly in place. You can tighten or loosen the string by turning the pegs. A wooden clothespin fitted over the flat end of a peg makes it easy to turn the peg for tuning.

HOW DOES IT SOUND?

If you hold the back of the harp against your ear while you play it, the sound will seem richer and warmer to you. Also some ear harps sound stronger if you prop them up on a table with a block of wood under one corner. If you want your harp to sound *much* louder, hook up a microphone to the loudspeaker system of a tape recorder or a phonograph and put the microphone on the board while you pluck the strings. Try this with other instruments, too.

from *The Musical Instrument Recipe Book*

The Seed Pod: A Multipurpose Instrument

A seed pod that you find on the street in October when it falls off the tree makes nice music— *chchchchchchchch.* Then, when you're finished playing music with it, you can take out the seeds and plant a tree—and use the pod for a moustache.

NICHOLAS SCHARLATT
Age five

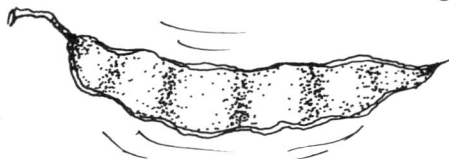

MUSIC LESSONS

The End Depends on the Beginning

When your child is old enough—four or five— you can enroll him in a class where he will sing, clap hands, and bang percussion instruments in rhythm. The class spares the child the feeling of isolation that so often comes with private music study. The rigors of studying a particular instrument should not begin until a child is physically and psychologically ready—rarely before he has had a year of academic work and can read and write.

First of all, provide the child with a good instrument. Here I recall my own school's motto, *Finis origine pendet* ("The end depends on the beginning"). As one cannot draw blood from a stone, so one cannot extract beauty from an instrument so cheap and bad that it cannot produce it. Too often as a piano teacher have I had the experience of trying to teach students tone color, knowing that they will go home and practice on miserable little spinets that can only make music in black-and-white.

Similarly, be very careful to choose a good teacher. Go to a specialist in the instrument. Just as .in this eighth decade of the twentieth century we do not expect the doctor who examines our children's eyes and the doctor who fills their dental cavities to be the same person, so avoid the "instrumental music teacher" (usually provided—often free—by the public school system) who gives lessons on any and every known musical instrument. Do not say, This teacher is all right for now—later if my child shows serious interest I will take him to a better teacher. "Later" may be too late. It is like saying you will feed your baby junk and if he grows up to be strong and healthy, then you will switch him to wholesome, nourishing food.

Just as a child is taught to spell correctly and do correct arithmetic even though he may not be destined to become a famous writer or scientist, so he should be taught to play correctly even if there is not the slightest intent to steer him toward music as a career.

GILMAN COLLIER

How to Keep a Kid from Learning to Play an Instrument

A perfect way to discourage kids from playing an instrument is by telling them they have to practice an hour every day. As long as a kid is small enough so that he's afraid not to do it, he will practice an hour a day (that is, when pushed hard), and then when he gets big enough so that you can't make him do it anymore, he'll quit. That's exactly what happens to 99½ percent of the kids who're made to take music lessons. There are millions of kids who acquire a fairly proficient skill on an instrument, play in high school bands or marching bands; then they graduate and the instrument is put away. "Oh, I used to play the clarinet when I was a kid," I used to play such-and-such when I was a kid—it's one of those things you do as a kid.

Jenny watched me play and she saw my cello around my office and she got the idea, when she was about six or seven, that she wanted to play the cello. There was a child's-sized cello in the family, and her mother got it fixed up for her. A few times we'd play together and explore together on the instrument, and after a while I could see that at that particular time in her life it wasn't what she'd thought it was going to be. I said to her mother, "I think it's terribly important for us to make it easy for Jenny to stop playing the cello—not to have any well-we-spent-the-money-to-have-it-fixed or that kind of thing—because the easier it is for her to stop, the easier it will be for her to start it again if she

wants to—and to stop and start as she chooses."

Now she has spells of hardly playing at all, spells of being discouraged, spells of enthusiasm, and she gains in great spurts. It's a very funny thing about learning—I learned a lot about the cello in the seven or eight years I wasn't playing (between ages forty-two and fifty). I don't know exactly what it is, but when I began again, I was much more of a musician than when I stopped—I'd heard other music, I'd seen a lot of cellists, I was learning even though I wasn't playing.

JOHN HOLT

Recordings with a Part for You

MMO—Music-Minus-One (43 West 61st Street, New York, N.Y. 10023) is a company which produces recordings of duets, trios, larger ensembles, piano accompaniments, and orchestral accompaniments to concertos. There is always something missing—a part to be filled in by the player at home. In their very large catalog one finds a wide variety of music. . . . The printed music is included for the missing part. In recent years, most of the recordings have had a wonderful feature: the complete music may be heard by using the volume controls set equally for each speaker, but by turning down the volume on one channel one can hear only the desired portion—either the student's part or the supplementary parts. The violin duets such as Bartok and Pleyel wrote are particularly effective this way.

ELIZABETH MILLS and PARENTS of SUZUKI STUDENTS
In the Suzuki Style

Parents say to me, "Johnny doesn't study his scales. He's always improvising the way he wants to." My God, let him! This is the free imagination. He's composing, he's letting his mind go, he's listening to the sounds. That is what being a human being is about. And when he says, "My mind is going this way, but I can't move my hands," he'll have to know about muscle relaxation and those little black dots.

LORIN HOLLANDER
quoted in *Music Educator's Journal*

TELEVISION

JAY GOOD

307

The Dream Hearth

Television is not a toaster. Yet we treat it as another household appliance, we are unconscious of it to that degree. It reaches us at such an indirect level of awareness that we think we ignore it—like the toaster, or the blender, or a lamp.

When the technology brought us television, however, we ended up with something far more pervasive than hot bread and homemade milkshakes. Television has taken us to new places in our minds, if not our spirits. Day in and day out, it is continually telling us disparate, divergent, and contradictory things. If somebody talked at us that much, telling us of cops and foreign countries in crisis and relationships falling apart and aspirin and oil and orange juice and the numbers one through ten and a long pass intercepted and auto insurance and Victorian English family life and class structure and the weather and life in Queens and working at a TV station in Minneapolis and rescuing people and killing people, we would collapse under the strain. We would not and could not tolerate all that.

So how is it that the average American home keeps the television fires going over six hours per day? In many homes it is the center of activity, or at least of sitting—sometimes built-in, literally included in house plans, or else portable, so as never to be too far away. If not a member of the American family, television is a part and perhaps the center of the American home, replacing the hearth around which our ancestors gathered for warmth and togetherness and food.

In view of the range and scope of material that television conveys, the question of its influence becomes not so much how much does it communicate, but how much does it connect? How much does it connect us to those with whom we watch and to the experiences and far-off places it portrays? When we sat around the fire, we experienced a sense of closeness with others in the room. It was a tacit bond, not requiring comment. It provided affirmation without words. What does television provide without words?

PETER ALMOND

AT THE BIRTH OF TV . . . OPTIMISM

Foremost in significance will be the strengthening of the home ties, especially for the younger set. If the program directors of television do well their part, it will no longer be difficult for parents to induce their children to spend evening hours in the family circle.

LEE DeFOREST
Television Today and Tomorrow (1942)

Television: The Broad View

It seems to me that three conditions have shaped the structure and determined the character of American television. The first of these is a technical condition, namely that the number of available channels has been very few and the possible variety of programs which could be offered simultaneously has, therefore, been very small. The second is an economic condition, namely that the financial basis of television has been advertising, and this has meant that a great system of public communication was financed by payments from producers who were not concerned primarily with public communication but with the sale of whatever it is that they happen to produce. The third is a social condition, namely that the audience for American television is what may be called a mass society. . . .

One asks is this primarily a medium of public entertainment which happens to be supported financially by advertising, or is it primarily an apparatus for the marketing of consumer goods which uses public communications as part of the marketing process? . . . The financial support which shapes the programs of the millions is . . . provided . . . by the makers of automobiles, detergents . . . depilatories, packaged foods, headache remedies, shampoos . . . [who] have no special competence for the role which history has whimsically assigned to them as arbiters of American entertainment and shapers of policy in the field of public communications. . . .

I do believe that television falls distressingly short of fulfilling its social potentialities and that it gives little of the nourishment to the human spirit which a great and vital medium of communication can give and ought to give. But I also believe it is unrealistic to be shocked when an advertising medium resorts to advertising practices. Men who live by advertising must sell, just as men who live by soldiering must fight and men who live by politics must make compromises. A person who wants to understand soldiering, or politics, or television will not do so by attributing the shortcomings of the system to the personal qualities of the men involved in it. Instead, he will examine the dynamics of the system itself.

DAVID POTTER
"The Historical Perspective"
The Meaning of Commercial Television

TUBE OR NOT TUBE?

At Home with Flipper

People fuss a lot about what kids watch on television. People fuss a lot about kids, which I guess is a good thing. They deeply want their kids to be "well educated," and so spend immense sums of money on new schools and go racketing around in the evenings to meetings where they discuss the hiring of teachers, the firing of teachers, the revision of the Alchemy Department in keeping with the New Alchemy—all very laudable—and in the meantime their own kids, who . . . will by the age of eighteen have devoted more of their lives to watching television than to any other single activity except sleep, are home watching "Flipper."

MICHAEL J. ARLEN
Living Room War

A Fan's Notes

I am and always will be an avid television fan. My viewing freely encompasses game shows (*Hollywood Squares*, *Match Game*, and the *Pyramid* shows), certain carefully selected "soaps," sit-coms (*M*A*S*H*, *Maude*, *Chico and the Man*, *Mary Tyler Moore*, *Good Times*, *All in the Family*, *Barney Miller*, and *One Day at a Time*), *Upstairs-Downstairs*, *Nova*, *Walsh's Animals*, plays, ballets, and concerts, seasonal specials, *Night Stalker*, *Rockford Files*, *Cannon*, *Mannix*, and *Police Story*, to say nothing of *Sesame Street* and *The Electric Company*, plus the myriad sporting events, nightly newscasts, and, last but not least, *Star Trek* reruns.

My reason for listing all these programs is that these are, school and bedtime permitting, what our daughters ages eleven and twelve watch with us; and most important is the conversation that these programs provoke. Our children have learned more from television and our answers to their questions arising from television than from any other factor in their lives.

In the last five years we have discussed politics (their solutions seem naive and probably workable), war, peace, race relations, poverty, surgery, humor (its nature and origin—a terrific subject), fidelity in marriage, infidelity in marriage, friendship (what it is and how it works), dating (still in the hypothetical stage), kissing, rape, abortion, and the law, from all angles. We have gone into the burning question of the news media's responsibility to present the events of the day and how far that responsibility goes.

We have laughed, cried, been scared, outraged, annoyed, and even bored, but we have done it together. And we have all come to one conclusion: that we have learned from our experiences, not only about the world around us, but more important, about each other and ourselves.

RUTH PELMAS

◆

Life Without Television

We have several times lived without television, and after the kids go through the initial withdrawal, after they get past shaking at 5:30 when *The Flintstones* are on, they begin to find other things to do. When kids live in a home that has a television, they become very passive; they expect everything to appear before their eyes as they sit there in a funk. They become very irritable and get bags under their eyes. If there isn't anything on that they want to watch, they sit there and watch something they don't want to watch. Or they say, "We have nothing to do," and wander aimlessly around the house and whine.

But when we're living without a television, a change comes over the kids: they play games, they play outside more, they build houses with blankets and furniture, they start putting on shows, cutting things out with scissors, making things, they do all kinds of things that simply don't occur to them if they have a TV in the house. (We do, too.)

We would rather give up even the good stuff that's on and not have a television around, than to try to screen shows or have "Two hours of television a day," which is extremely arbitrary.

CAROLYN and ORSON BEAN

◆

You Can't Insulate Your Child (and Maybe That's Good)

In the past we tried to ban this or that silly or violent or morally evil television program from our son, five and a half, but we have come to believe that there's no way to insulate a child. Even if you throw out your own television set, there are always playmates who watch everything. And the attraction of a forbidden program will increase for a child especially if his peers watch it. On the positive side, I think it is good for a child to know that there are facts and ideas transmitted on television (and later in movies, plays, and books) that his parents find untruthful and morally wrong. The values of the parents can prevail, provided they monitor and comment on what their child is viewing.

MARJORIE LIPSYTE

◆

The Waltons: It Gave Us a Chance to Talk

My nephew, Steven, had been watching an episode of *The Waltons* while I was busying myself with preparations for our drive to La Honda. Several times I drifted in and out of the room (he was curled up in an overstuffed chair, absent-mindedly sucking his thumb and staring intently at the TV), but I hadn't really focused on the program. I do remember an old man and a young boy talking earnestly.

Later, in the car, Steven began to shiver. Since it was a fairly warm California evening, I was surprised. He shuddered and grew very agitated. "What is it to die?" he asked. "What does it mean? Can't you ever talk to the person again?"

And a stream of questions on time and death

and why and why and why followed. Each question was repeated in one form or another, and he asked if I ever thought of death and does it mean that I might die someday too. The questions were interspersed with a recounting of the Waltons' story, or at least fragments, the important ones. Apparently the old man had told the boy about someone who had died whom the old man had loved very much. It was something like that, all serving as a metaphor for the likelihood of the old man's death and the effect it might have on the young boy.

Steven worries a lot anyway. He doesn't exactly cry all the time. But he stays awake and wonders about things and asks a lot of questions about very large and unanswerable matters like death and time and space.

That evening, had his brothers been there—either Mike, his twin, or David, their senior by two years—one or both of the boys might have tried to take care of Steven, comfort him somehow. I don't think they would have teased him, not about something like this. They knew when to back off; besides, Steven acted out concerns his brothers shared, maybe providing them some kind of outlet.

We were there alone that night. Somehow, we faced it together. This experience with the television death seemed like a good thing, despite all the shuddering and agitation it set off. Maybe it's risky. But it gave us a chance to talk, really talk and worry together about death and friendship and closeness and space beyond time where you still stayed in touch with the spirit of someone you love. And I wished I had bothered to sit down and watch that *Waltons* episode.

There was no conclusion, no neat explanation for either of us, I suppose. We both kind of drifted off, calmed down a bit, and took to looking off in the middle distance as we made our way toward La Honda.

PETER ALMOND

◆

Spectators vs. Doers

I seldom watch TV and never encourage my children to do so, since watching teaches them to be spectators rather than "doers." Because of *not* watching much, though, my four-and-a-half-year-old daughter often stops in the middle of a show to play with her puppets or do something inspired by the program.

ARLENE HEISS

TV Can Foster Curiosity

What about the effect of television on the development of the imagination? Parents who grew up in pretelevision days and who were great readers of classical literature have been suspicious of television. They feel that the stories and commercials are mostly trash and that having a story presented visually in full detail induces passivity in the viewers and relieves them of any necessity to use their own imaginations.

Educators do not generally agree with this judgment. They believe that the over-all effect of television has been to foster children's imagination, intelligence, and curiosity, especially children from families that provide only an average or less-than-average amount of intellectual and cultural stimulation. In particular, the experts point to the way in which children go to libraries to read about topics that have been featured on television.

It is probable that comic books, which similarly have been abhorred by sensitive parents, also have been valuable in fostering children's imagination and intelligence.

DR. BENJAMIN SPOCK
Raising Children in a Difficult Time

ANYTHING HEREINABOVE TO THE CONTRARY NOTWITHSTANDING . . .

Newsweek reported that Dr. Benjamin Spock once brought his stepdaughter and granddaughter to New York to expose them to the city's cultural fare. But when it came time to sally forth, the world's most famous childcare expert could not persuade the kids to leave their hotel room. "I couldn't get them away from the goddamned TV set," the magazine quoted Spock as saying. "It made me sick."

TV Is a Parent's Cop-Out

TV has been every parent's cop-out: "Go watch TV," we suggest, whenever we're getting a bit tired of having the kids underfoot. The temptation is irresistible—I'm not condemning it, because I've done it so often myself when we've had children visiting the house.

What's important to note is that, although kids do like to watch television, they'd prefer, by and large, to do other things. Fred Rogers, of *Mister Rogers,* and his staff did a survey of children in primary grades, asking them to rate their fifteen favorite activities. Believe it or not, TV came in fourteenth. The only item lower on the list was "petting my dog."

What I'm trying to say is that instead of blaming TV for tempting kids to remain passive, we should note that children really prefer active play. Thus, even though it's often easier for us to let TV babysit for them, our kids would welcome our encouragement and guidance toward more active pursuits.

JOAN GANZ COONEY

SCRAMBLED THINKING

Television scrambles time, and consequently scrambles thinking. Many kids today think that Liza Minnelli is Judy Garland's mother. They also see the letters "o" and "u" where the rest of us see a toilet seat.

ALAN LAKEIN
It's About Time and It's About Time

"Switch Awareness"

We've decided that what's most important is that a child be aware that the TV has an off switch. Kate comes home from school at 4:30, and from then until bath time at 7 p.m. is allowed to pick three shows on during that period. Her current choices are the *Mickey Mouse Club, Electric Company* and *Bewitched*—a rather strange mixture, but certainly no odder than the programs I watch.

DICK ADLER
Los Angeles Times

---◆---

Help Your Kids Be More Selective

Use *TV Guide* to help kids be more discriminating in their television viewing. Make "viewing profiles" of the programs you watch, then switch profiles and watch TV through someone else's eyes. Classify programs and talk about them. Establish some days on which you have to watch only programs you've never seen before. (As TV becomes a habit, few children seek out new shows to watch. There is often very little knowledge of the breadth of the programing that is available.) Child and adult, devote a whole Saturday morning to watching TV; no other activities allowed—no games, no conversations, no snacks.

KIT LAYBORNE

We Can't Watch TV? How 'Bout Letting Us Listen to It?

Video Voice, a television-listening radio from Hong Kong ($29.95), [will take you back to] the good old days of radio when only your imagination supplied the picture. It's good to find out your imagination still works.

HAMMACHER SCHLEMMER, 147 EAST 57TH STREET, NEW YORK CITY

Video Voice lets you listen to the sound part only of all VHF/TV channels (2 through 13) and the full band of FM radio broadcasts. The radio is completely solid state and operates on 4 penlight batteries (supplied), but unfortunately it is not convenient to carry around. An earphone is also supplied for private listening. The whole works, including telescoping antenna, is housed in a 5″ plastic cube.

Video Voice has been great for getting the kids away from the TV and involved in other activities—yet they can still listen to their favorite shows. When travelling, it will keep you and the kids unbored. Remember, it's also an FM radio. Or, use the earphone even if you still want to watch the picture on your TV set—no one will be disturbed. Get the kids in bed early and let them "listen" to TV—it will help put them to sleep. And for those who have been holding out on buying a television set, here's your chance to give in half-way.

STEVEN CANEY
Toy Review

Striking a Blow for the Pleasure Principle

The simplest benefit we can expect for our children from television is the one that it seems to have been supplying throughout its history and the one that many people attack as exactly what is wrong with television: It gives children an important source of pleasant enjoyment.
. . . It is no small achievement in itself.

GERALD S. LESSER
Children and Television

And shall we just carelessly allow children to hear any casual tales which may be devised by casual persons, and to receive in their minds for the most part the very opposite of those ideas which we would wish them to have when they are grown up?

PLATO
The Republic

Keep 'Em Alert

It's okay with me if Nick watches TV, I have told babysitters, as long as you talk to him during the program. Talk about what's going on on the screen, interrupt, ask if he wants an apple—anything that will keep him out of a trance and in reality. It may be foolish, but it makes me feel better.

ELS

Let's Teach "Media Literacy"

The best way to regain control over the television set is to learn its language. It's called media literacy, and should be available for kids to study in every school in a land where, according to Nicholas Johnson, "by the time the average child enters kindergarten he has already spent more hours learning about his world from television than the hours he would spend in a college classroom earning a B.A. degree."

RS

DRAWING BY ROBERT DAY ; 1970 THE NEW YORKER MAGAZINE, INC.

"Don't you understand? This is life, this is what is happening. We can't switch to another channel."

COMMERCIALS

Time Out for a Word from . . .

Jennifer was telling me about her nightmare: "I was running up the stairs and a man was chasing me and then the ad came on."

I was startled. "Then what came on?"

Jen repeated disgustedly, "The ad. You know, that one about the lady in the long dress and the car, and then the dream came back on again and the man . . . "

How do you deal with something so ingrained?

MARY ANN BUCKLEY

◆

"My Dog's Better Than Your Dog,"
or
A Look at the National Association of Broadcasters' Guidelines for TV Advertising to Children

NAB: "Broadcasters believe that advertising of products or services normally used by children can serve to inform children not only of the attributes of the products or services but also of many aspects of the society and world in which they live."

"My kids are totally cynical about TV advertising," a Washington, D.C., parent writes. "They have learned, through bitter experience, that merchandise is misrepresented, and that they are lied to."

NAB: "Appeals shall not be used which directly or by implication contend that if children have a product they are better than their peers or lacking it will not be accepted by their peers."

But it's okay to say, My dog's better than your dog because my dog eats Ken-L-Ration.

NAB: "Children shall not be directed to purchase or to ask a parent or other adult to buy a product or service for them."

"In September," a mother in Queens reports, "my seven-year-old already had a two-page Christmas list. All the requests came from things he had seen advertised on television." No doubt each commercial met the letter of the NAB code.

NAB: In order to help assure that advertising for children, designed primarily for children, "is non-exploitive in manner, style and tone, such advertising shall avoid using exhortative language. It shall also avoid employing irritating, obtrusive or strident audio techniques or video devices such as cuts of less than one second in length, a series of fast cuts, special effects of a psychedelic nature . . . "

Although advertisers meet code requirements, if you observe the cuts and angles and language you will begin to get some insights into the subtly persuasive methods of this strange and uniquely American art form—the filmed or taped commercial.

The code principles and interpretations go on for pages. The advertisers are required to submit storyboards to code editors, who review and usually make extensive and highly detailed criticisms, suggestions and, finally, deletions where the ad agency has failed to meet one code requirement or another.

It is strange to consider the lengths to which the NAB, in the form of the Code Authority, and advertisers go to protect the consumer from manipulation. Yet, read it and weep, because common sense tells us that the commercial works for the purpose it serves: not the viewer-consumer's protection, but to sell whatever it happens to be the advertisers are selling to pay for whatever time slot they've bought.

PETER ALMOND

◆

Teach Skepticism

My kids sing advertising jingles much as I sang nursery rhymes. When they demand to buy something, we go to the store, compare the product to others, reiterate what it is supposed to do, and see if it does. Teach skepticism.

REP. PATRICIA SCHROEDER

At first my children believed every word they heard between cartoons, but when they saw the toy or product for real, without TV props, sales spiel, most advantageous camera angle, etc., they wised up on their own to some extent. Their father and I were then able to explain the whole idea of using your own judgment and not expecting claims to be entirely true. At the moment they're both very skeptical of TV ads.

JOY KLOTZ

TV advertising has made my children very discerning. At an early age we bought them each one coveted TV toy, which of course did not perform as per TV ad. They are now super-skeptics. They like to go to a store that has touchable open box displays of expensive imported dollhouses, forts, miniatures of all sorts, and they make requests based on firsthand experience.

SHEILA SACHS

The Thumbs Down Method of Dealing with Commercials

At three and a half our son learned that there were programs on television he wanted to watch other than *Sesame Street* and *Mister Rogers.* And he learned that there were commercials.

From the beginning we put thumbs down on commercials. *Boo,* we'd yell at a particularly offensive commercial, and he'd boo and put his thumb down too. We told him that commercials often tell you things that are not true because they want you to buy what they are selling. Of course we buy things that are advertised, but just because the commercial says something doesn't mean it's true. Hershey's milk chocolate is good for you, the commercial implies. Any candy is bad for you, we explain, but sometimes we eat things that are bad for us because they taste good. In the supermarket I am firm (most of the time, *sigh*) and won't let him fill the basket with his choices. He has never had a sugar-coated cereal, though at one time he talked about Kellogg's Sugar Pops constantly. In the battle between us and Tony the Tiger we must assert our right to determine what is best for our children no matter how much easier it is to give in to the nagging.

MARJORIE LIPSYTE

A Cure for Television Toy-itis

We gave up, several Christmases ago, any toy that was advertised on television. Our children really balked the first year, and my husband and I found what proved to be a really lasting solution. We gave each of our daughters a certain amount of money and let them go to the store and buy—for themselves—one of the television toys that we had failed to give them. Both toys broke within a week, and the girls certainly got the point.

ILENE GOLDMAN

A Game That Talks Back to the Tube

It's Switch, available from ACT (46 Austin Street, Newtonville, Mass. 02160, $1.50). Pick a number. Move your "knob" the appropriate

number of spaces. If you land on a commercial spot you draw from the deck of "commercial" cards—Boredom Berry, Sugar Flops, No-C Juice, Muck Donald's, Good and Empty—they look like Wacky Packs. When you accumulate three commercials, you are set back. And so it goes as you try to reach the commercial-free "Sign Off Zone."

A dollar and a half buys you the game and helps support Action for Children's Television, which is selling Switch as part of their two-pronged fight to change television advertising and educate consumers to fight back in the meantime. Lots of kids can play (knobs enough for nine or ten kids), and it's a lesson in efficient packaging: no cardboard box, just a big piece of heavy paper with punch-out cards and a paper board.

—Eds.

◆

Two Good Films About Commercials

One of the most valuable things that Action for Children's Television has done was to put together a fifteen-minute, 16-mm. film of the commercials that appeared in one hour of children's programing, accompanied by comments from psychologists, toy makers, and children. It's a scary film—one which *every* parent ought to see. It's called "But First This Message," and you can rent a copy for $25 by writing ACT, 46 Austin Street, Newtonville, Mass. 02160.

From an interview with CHRISTOPHER SARSON

SEEING THROUGH COMMERCIALS, *a 16-mm. color film produced by Larry Stein and Ruth Arens (Vision Films, P.O. Box 48896, Los Angeles, Calif. 90048. Purchase, $220; three-day rental, $20).*

The film consists of a series of fictitious advertisements for equally fictitious products, each carefully dissected by the film's narrator. Nevertheless, the techniques used in these hypothetical commercials will be all too familiar . . .

The use of sound effects to add excitement to a product, the practice of distorting a product's appearance by unusual camera angles or close-ups, and the importance of advertising disclaimers are all clearly demonstrated.

One particularly vivid segment chronicles the magical treatment showered on a teenage fashion doll, undoubtedly a descendant of the Dawn, Barbie, and Skipper line. The toy is initially shown unadorned by the special glamor that TV advertising can bestow. In the next sequence the doll is placed against a velvet backdrop; music is added, followed by colored lights, and a camera filter adds the final touch of class. Commercials for a candy bar, a new "fun" cereal and a racing car are similarly demystified.

The film concludes with a commercial simulation featuring many of the techniques demonstrated in the film, but without the benefit of a narrator's interpretation. This final segment, which challenges viewers to unmask the commercial, could stimulate students to analyze ads for products which are currently promoted on television.

JEAN JOHNSON
Action for Children's Television *News*

VIOLENCE, OR, THE SATURDAY MORNING SPECIAL

A study estimated that by age 14, the ordinary child has been exposed to 11,000 murders on television.

WILLIAM V. SHANNON

When I see something unique and exciting on TV, like a high-speed auto chase or a burning and a dousing with gasoline, I say to myself, "I'll see this in court." And I do.

JUDGE PATRICK TAMILLIA
Pittsburgh Juvenile Court
Quoted in the New York *Daily News*

◆

Kung Fu: Caine Was Nonviolent, but Did Anyone Get the Message?

Kung Fu was the only Western I ever saw that acknowledged the fact that Chinese people lived in the old American West (and indeed that a Chinese person could be a hero). And though the hero was superhuman in the tradition of most TV heroes, he was wise, gentle, nonviolent but masculine; he fought only in self-defense, and used no weapons except his body in the martial art of kung fu.

But it is doubtful that the message of nonviolence is what had meaning for the viewer. The cowboys in the show were generally portrayed as the traditional gun-shooting, guts-splitting, bloodthirsty, prejudice-ridden villains. I've been told that it is currently popular among children to imitate kung fu. If a new way of fighting is what children perceived as the message of the show, then we must ask what interests and values children are bringing with them to TV.

LAURA EBY

For information on local PTA activities in the area of television violence, contact the National PTA, Project on TV Violence, 700 North Rush Street, Chicago, Ill. 60611.

"Relevant Idiocy"

There have been efforts "to clean up our act," says Squire Rushnell, ABC vice-president in charge of children's programming. Mostly, this has meant taking some of the violence out of a cartoon series and replacing it with a dose of do-goodism, leaving in the same old absurd characters. Rushnell notes that much of the reduction of violence was inspired by pressure from the FCC and parents' groups.

Saturday morning now finds violence replaced, as one network official puts it, by "relevant idiocy." Now children can watch "Super Friends"—Superman, Batman, Aquaman, and Wonder Woman—"assembled in the Hall of Justice, The World's Four Greatest Heroes, along with their super friends Wendy, Marvin, and Wonder Dog. Their mission," booms a Clark Kent–like voice, "to fight injustice, right what is wrong, and to serve all mankind." A child might wonder if they work for the Justice Department.

JOSEPHINE FRANKLIN CAPLAN
Tuesday magazine (*Chicago Tribune*)

To the extent that television does not reflect reality, it socializes children into a fictitious social system, where criminals are always caught, . . . guilty people always break down under a good lawyer's barrage of questions, problems are solved in an hour, and things usually work out for the best.

AIMEE DORR LEIFER, NEAL J. GORDON,
and SHERRYL BROWN GRAVES
"Children's Television: More than Mere
Entertainment," *Harvard Education Review*

STEREOTYPES

SPOTTING SEXISM AND RACISM ON TV

An Exciting New Game for the Entire Family

I think the most "dangerous" shows on television today are reruns of programs that were made at a time when values were different from those we have today. For example, *The Three Stooges,* some of the early *Lucy* shows, and *Life with Father* are incredibly racist, incredibly sexist, and incredibly widely watched by youngsters when they get home from school. These shows can be subversive, because everyone dismisses them as pablum, and they're really not. They're where children are getting their stereotypes.

Kids want to watch these shows—they just won't ignore them. Therefore at our house we've designed a little game: we all try to best each other at spotting instances of racism and sexism as the program goes along. This can actually be fun, and it has the added advantage that you talk so much you miss most of the program. But, of course, you have to be alert enough to catch the offensive bits—some of them are remarkably subtle.

CHRISTOPHER SARSON

Sex Role Stereotypes

Television commercials tell children what is important to the sexes. In a Yuban coffee ad the woman is defined by the quality coffee she makes. Horrors, her husband will take a second cup of another woman's coffee, but never takes a second cup of hers. The ad, of course, never questions the basic assumption that coffee making is a female job, or opens up the possibility that a person who drinks coffee of an inferior variety might say, straight out, to the coffee maker, "Gee, I don't like this coffee. What's wrong?" Secrecy about coffee making and heaven knows what else between the sexes is sustained by the commercials.

CARRIE CARMICHAEL
Non-Sexist Childraising

SOME SPECIFIC PROGRAM RECOMMENDATIONS

Assuredly, one's children get no nightmares from [some of the children's TV shows], but where do they get dreams from . . .?

MICHAEL J. ARLEN
Living Room War

Merlin, the Cowboys, Mr. Rogers (and Reality)

Merlin, a seven-year-old from an upstate farm, had come into town with his parents for a holiday visit. One afternoon, when his parents had gone out to do some shopping, Merlin asked if he could watch television; he wanted to see a cowboy movie.

When the shooting started Merlin got very scared (he doesn't have a TV on the farm where he lives), and asked several times if it was real. The woman he was visiting assured him that the shooting wasn't real, that all the cowboys were actors, and that really it was just like somebody making a film of Merlin playing on a toy horse. Merlin remained fearful and was again reassured that it was just a story.

Then Merlin watched *Mister Rogers.* Is he real, Merlin wanted to know right away. Yes, the woman said, Mr. Rogers is real. Merlin watched intently, though he wanted to be told again that the man was a real person. This time the woman went a little further in her assurance, saying yes, he is not only real but he really talks to children that way all the time; he really cares about children and wants to answer the questions they ask.

Merlin watched the show a bit longer. Then he looked up and said to the woman, He really loves me, doesn't he?

Even though Mr. Rogers' warmth embarrasses many adults, it's important not to make fun of him, at least in front of the kids. Fred Rogers' nice quality is that he explores many of the issues that deeply concern children—sharing, moving, getting ready for school, prejudice. Sometimes grown-ups don't like to stop and talk about things this way, so a friendly voice matters a great deal to the children, particularly the continuing patience.

PETER ALMOND

Sesame Street and The Electric Company

Sesame Street and, in other ways, The Electric Company are, with lapses, the most intelligent and important programs in television . . . When a seven-foot yellow-feathered bird who is subject to depression attempts to seat himself upon the letter "h" and fails, it is no longer simply an event in children's television, or even in the media. It is part of the intellectual history of a generation, who are already in important ways the children of Sesame Street.

. . . [In 1972] in Jackson, Mississippi, Big Bird led an integrated audience of more than ten thousand children and their parents in a passionate recitation of the alphabet. He counted to ten. The audience, including a few retarded adults and spastics, clapped and counted with him. A Jackson policeman drove white, black, and Chicano members of the cast to the Jackson airport. The mayor had welcomed them when they came to town. Nation time.

RENATA ADLER
The New Yorker

Sesame Street/Electric Company: it's training to be super-hypo. It's training to take in advertising. It doesn't give any chance for thought—there's no extended dialogue, there're no extended stories, there's no real emotional depth, it's all very shallow and slick. Those are my objections. On the positive side, it's a painless way to learn the alphabet and some rudiments of reading on that level. All the kids in my class know the "Silent E" song from Electric Company—none of them learned anything from it about how to read silent e's.

But it's better to watch that than cartoons.

From an interview with HERBERT KOHL

To my three-year-old, "1-2-3-4-5-6-7-8-9-10" is a one-word song, nothing more.

ELS

What is disturbing is that a medium which, through Sesame Street and The Electric Company, is teaching pre-schoolers about reading, leaves them relatively bereft of any contact with literature the rest of their viewing lives.

RICHARD R. LINGEMAN
The New York Times Book Review

Because Sesame Street and The Electric Company teach middle-class morality—defined as civilized values in dealing with one's fellow men—the shows have come under attack from that fraction of the intellectual community which prizes improvidence and viciousness, the demand for immediate gratification. But as a serious matter C.T.W. [Children's Television Workshop, producers of Sesame Street and The Electric Company] has no enemies. What is odd is that so many of its friends—and the world at large—seem not to take C.T.W. very seriously. Let a couple in jeans shepherd a dozen youngsters to a "school" in backwoods Vermont to live on wheat germ and fried cockroaches and love, and the media swarm with tribute to their imagination and their contributions to education. Electric Company is being seen in 20,000 schools, as part of the basic instructional program in the most basic of all educational skills. There is a chance—not an assignable probability yet, but a chance—that this television show will in fact improve the average level of reading ability in the United States. In 15 years of examining these matters, I have seen nothing in American education of comparable importance.

MARTIN MAYER
The New York Times Magazine

CTW

SESAME STREET

CHILDREN'S TELEVISION WORKSHOP

A lot of people who've criticized Sesame Street have objected to it because it uses procedures borrowed from TV commercials. But, you know, commercials are audio-visual messages, and no one has mastered audio-visual techniques to the degree Madison Avenue has. They're the finest short-film makers in the world.

If you look at a TV commercial as a thirty-second film and ask yourself what's really wrong with it, chances are your answer will be, "It's selling something." That's what people object to. If you're equally offended by a similar film on, say, the letter "J," I think you're crazy. Because what you're doing is saying, "We'll leave to the salesmen the most effective, advanced audio-visual techniques designed by man, and, meanwhile, teaching techniques will be left somewhere back in the Dark Ages."

JOAN GANZ COONEY
Creator of Sesame Street

Me got major complaint about Sesame Street. There is no excuse for my child's hearing "Me got what me want" (the Cookie Monster) on a public television station. Sesame Street, of all programs, should use correct English.

ELS

COMMERCIAL TELEVISION

Tarzan

Many of the remarks you hear on television are questionable, except on the Tarzan hour, which I never miss if I can help it. In the jungle world men have managed to create for themselves, with its gloomy wars, its smashed atom, its hair sprays that threaten the ozone layer, its balance of power, and its absence of any sensible and orderly way . . . to settle the myriad things that need to be settled, Tarzan in his loincloth is the one person who seems at home in the environment, as he utters his wild cry and swings along on those old moss-covered docking lines. His speech nowadays is immaculate, and his rapport with animals has always been good. There is a little five-year-old girl in our town who can't tell time by the clock but knows instinctively when the hour of Tarzan is at hand.

E. B. WHITE
The New Yorker

◆

The Jacques Cousteau Specials

I'm a great admirer of Jacques Yves Cousteau, on television and also in a series of books published by Doubleday.

Cousteau is a scientist using technology to explore areas previously inaccessible; a man intellectually and emotionally exploring his relationship to the earth; a child simply playing in his most natural playground. Cousteau gives everyone something, whether it be beautiful pictures of marine life, a story of an endangered species, a tale of people working together harmoniously, a glimpse of a now extinct life form, a concept of future life. But Cousteau is above all a humanitarian, seeking further evidence of the natural state linking past to present to future.

STEVEN BAUM

◆

Afterschool Specials, Adult Programs for Children, etc.

ABC's *Afterschool Specials* particularly appeal to me, because very often they show me an aspect of childhood that I remember fondly.

I also think that a lot of programs meant for adults have special appeal for children. The television movie *The Autobiography of Miss Jane Pittman* provided children with a marvelous feel for black history in America. And, of course, there are the National Geographic specials and

all the regularly scheduled nature shows like *World of Survival* and *The Wild, Wild World of Animals.* The fact is that good programs are hard to produce, but once you've got one, it can appeal to all kinds of people beyond its intended audience. For example, *Zoom* is meant for eight- to twelve-year-olds, but we get a hell of a lot of response from parents, grandparents, and a lot from teen-agers, too—all, incidentally, apologizing for watching.

CHRISTOPHER SARSON
Creator of *Zoom*

◆

Religious Programs: Better Than *The Flintstones*

While I am probably God-fearing, I am not a religious person. I don't go to church; I don't read the Bible; I don't watch *Faith for Today* or *Oral Roberts Presents* on Sunday mornings. What I like to do on Sunday mornings is sleep. But with an early-rising son who likes to be entertained, this is not easy. Since ours is not a TV-watching household, I have been put in the curious position of having to urge my 3½-year-old to please watch some TV on Sunday mornings. Because I have made clear my disapproval of *The Flintstones* (I think it is among the worst shows for kids—demeaning to women, children, husbands, pets, neighbors—it makes everyone out to be a fool, and the jokes are always someone's being clunked over the head or else made fun of for being tricked), my son skips over it (I could never explain how that happened) and scans the channels for something else. Often it's Bugs Bunny or some other cartoon I've rejected because of the violence and foolishness and further flattening of people and animals—this time with steam rollers. Meanwhile, I doze off, happy for the quiet.

Recently, I turned over one Sunday and learned that my son has discovered something new to watch: the sanctum sanctorum of the early morning funnies. Disguised as animated adventure stories, shows like *Davey and Goliath* preach faith and virtue as a valuable and attainable alternative to the rage and violence of the steam-roller set. Davey sets out to find his lost dog and, keeping the faith, finds him ("God loves you in much the same way as you love Goliath," the boy's father explains, "and will look after you as you do your dog"). Davey runs away from home to join the circus and, discovering that it's better at home, returns ("I love you even when you make mistakes," Father intones, "in much the same way as God forgives us all our mistakes"). Davey is an ordinary "good" kid trying out a few of his mischievous fantasies, returning always to discover that his parents, and God, have not abandoned him. Falling just short of *Divini Redemptoris,* the situations in the program probably bear no resemblance to the life of most of the kids who end up in front of the screen at that hour, but the message, I've decided, is innocuous, and the extra hour's sleep is, for me, well, divine.

ELS

◆

Short Takes

I think children deserve to have their own favorites (I was addicted to *Buck Rogers* as a child). I have been through stages with each of my three daughters where they would "die" if they missed an· episode of, respectively, *Batman, Lost in Space,* and *Bonanza.* They eventually outgrew their fondness for these shows. The only program I forbid (and that jokingly) is *The Flintstones,* which I detest. What I am trying to encourage them to watch, with only slight success, is *The Evening News with Walter Cronkite.*

ELIZABETH EHRENFELD

Animal World and *Wild Kingdom* are good documentaries of lives and habits of various animals, all filmed in the animals' natural habitats. Also, Jane Goodall's documentaries of animal behavior don't come along often, but when they do they're not to be missed.

REBECCA and H. LE BARON PRESTON

Amie (fifteen months) most enjoys Marlin Perkins' *Wild Kingdom.* She is learning to identify animals, and it's terribly exciting for her to see in action what she has seen in books as inanimate objects.

SUSAN HOUGEN

Polly and Katie love to watch *The Brady Bunch.* For one thing, it's about a big, happy, expanded family, and they find that very appealing. Besides, it's on at six o'clock when, as they well know, I'd rather be watching the news.

JON STONE

We find several cartoons and one evening show (*Wait Till Your Father Gets Home*) objectionable because they picture fathers as fools and use terms we discourage, i.e., "shut up," "dumbbell," etc.

MRS. DAVID ASHTON

I prefer my kids to watch shows like *The Flintstones.* I'd rather have them see animated cartoon figures doing stupid things than real people doing stupid things.

DENNIS EICHLER

I asked a couple of six-year-olds if they think *The Muppet Show* is for kids or for adults. "It's a family show," Gaby replied, though her mother admitted that most of the jokes had to be explained to Gaby. But, clearly, gags that are over the heads of little kids make sense enough coming out of the mouths of furry Vaudevillian Muppets. Witness:

"Kermit's the star of the show," said Nick. "Things are funny when Kermit says them." And, looking at his mother, he added, "Things that wouldn't be funny at all if *you* said them."

ELS

Big Brother Is Trekking You

For a show which was only on the networks for three seasons (1966–1968), and has been in rerun syndication ever since, *Star Trek* has spawned a fandom akin to a religious cult. True believers—or trekkies, as the media have labeled them (much to the fans' indignation) —watch episodes five, 10, 15 times, know the dialogue by heart, know all of Spock's facial nuances by heart, buy *Star Trek* paperbacks (which are just novelizations of episodes they've already seen), and either delight or drive their parents up the wall with their full-hearted near-fanatical devotion to, of all things, a defunct television show . . .

The [ten] years that *Star Trek* has been in reruns has generated a legion of followers who form a large, ever-growing constituency, a constituency cutting across sexual, racial, geographical, and class lines. . . . Though *Trek* fans look cute in their pajama uniforms, and though many of them are so glassy-eyed that one imagines that their brainwaves sound like "Metal Machine Music," my initial frivolousness faded when I realized that trekkies are not just out on a lark. These kids are *serious.* . . .

The emergence of fandom is breathlessly told in a paperback entitled *Star Trek Lives!* written by Jacqueline Lichtenberg, Sondra Marshak, and Joan Winston. . . . The style of their enthusiasm gives much insight into the *Trek* fan's mentality. What one comes to understand is that aside from the show's superb production values, respectable acting, and intelligent writing, the real basis of *Star Trek*'s popularity is sex, cool, and technology. . . .

Trek fans believe in the inherent benevolence of the machine, and in the ability of men to use machines benevolently—beliefs rooted in an almost childlike fascination with gadgets. *Trek* fans love gadgets, they're a generation raised on intimate acquaintance with tape players, TVs, and radios—my 10-year-old brother, for example, never goes to sleep without his Sony AM-FM cradled in his arms—and the phasers, tricorders, and communicators on *Trek* are fanciful, ingenious toys.

Understand that this fascination with technology goes beyond affection into a fervent faith in the ability of technological means to master the future. . . . Of course, in *Star Trek* this faith in technology is swashbucklingly romanticized. William Shatner, who played Captain Kirk, based his characterization of Kirk upon the life of Alexander the Great—so he says—and in reference to a particular episode, the *Trek* triad comment: ". . . Kirk, knowing the greatness it took to achieve this mastery of our environment represented by the *Enterprise* and himself, to create the technology, the mechanization, the electronics that hurled us from the caves to the stars, would answer [his accusers] firmly: 'We armed man with tools. The striving for greatness continues.' " That sounds pretty—I'm ashamed to use the word—macho. The technology on *Star Trek* represents not just power, but masculine will because all those who firmly wield those tools (what a thicket of innuendo) are, of course, men. . . .

Aside from the mastery of power, and the sexual attractiveness of the comically handsome William Shatner (Kirk) and the imperturbable Leonard Nimoy (Spock), what we have here, bless Leslie Fiedler, is the return of the runaway boys on the biggest damn raft you can imagine—the U.S.S. *Enterprise*. Male readers have always been drawn to the story of two men venturing out together, but *Star Trek* also hooks the women by the sexual tension beneath that buddy-buddiness—a sci-fi variation of Newman and Redford. . . .

Spock is at the center of *Star Trek*'s appeal not only because women identify with his intensely sublimated sexuality—such women are only a portion of fandom—but because he's a hero to kids. Spock is physically strong, which most kids aspire to (which is why *The Six Mil-*

lion Dollar Man is also a success); literally alienated because of his mixed birth; freakish, because of his pointed ears (most kids feel self-conscious about their looks); and, in his calm earnestness, quite fatherly. . . .

But most of all, Spock is supremely cool. Cool is very important to kids. My brother reveres a character on *Happy Days* called Fonzie. Fonzie is the master of every situation, always in command, a shaman of high school cool—when Fonzie kicks the Coke machine, two free bottles slide out. Essentially, however, cool is holding your own, not losing inner equilibrium no matter what outside forces (teachers, parents, other kids) are battering away at you. If you're 10 years old, and your teacher is screaming out her lungs at you, and you just smile back, totally unfazed, totally cool; well, kid, such nonchalance is heroic.

No one, however, is *totally* cool since cool is the mastery of tensions; Spock is the coolest TV hero because his tensions run so deep, rooted in his divided biological/cultural heritage (half-earthling, half-Vulcan); so his mastery over himself—his control—has been won at no small psychic cost. I've seen kids weep at the episode entitled "This Side of Paradise," in which Spock falls in love and then surrenders that love because his tragically schizoid nature prevents him from abandoning himself to bliss. . . .

Nimoy's Spock embodies the notion that beneath the facade of cool is a vast potential for violence—violence needed to protect that cool. Kids idolize these men because *they* are frustrated—when they're yelled at by an adult for being "stupid" or ridiculed by other kids for being "fat" or "ugly"—they can't fight back effectively. They can throw tantrums, or they can endure the humiliation. Their heroes, then, are those who have obviously endured humiliation—a freakish alien like Spock—and transcended it with the crowning pride that comes from holding your poise no matter what pain you're suffering. . . .

JAMES WOLCOTT
Village Voice

Looking for the Silk Purses

We cannot say that all or most television is so many sows' ears, nor can we say that careful viewing will produce silk purses. But that idea brings us closer to television's potential if we take it seriously, if we view its kaleidoscopic offerings thoughtfully. The more we think about TV, the more room we give it to grow.

There are plenty of signs of its potential around already. We have seen in recent years an account of the life of a black woman from slavery to the civil rights struggles a hundred years later (*The Autobiography of Miss Jane Pittman*); a teen-age boy confronting not only his parents' separation, but the recognition of his father's homosexuality as well (*That Certain Summer*); a developing relationship between a young white priest and the inhabitants of an Indian fishing village in British Columbia (*I Heard the Owl Call My Name*), shot on location with a large cast from the community, accurately portraying the villagers' rituals. And we have seen the uneven, yet laudable introduction of so-called docu-dramas (*Potsdam*, James Whitmore's *Truman*, *Tailgunner Joe*, *Eleanor and Franklin*, *Thirteen Days*). These shows may demonstrate the formula-bound nature of television planning (one good—read successful, i.e., high ratings—show begets not just another in the same format but a whole slew of offspring), but they tend to be well produced. As dramatizations of "real events," however, they often play fast and loose with the facts, and for that reason alone it becomes essential to talk about television with kids, particularly kids who might not even know who Eugene McCarthy is, much less Joe McCarthy.

At the same time, more and more prime-time characters are becoming mature and realistic. Women are being portrayed as complex characters who do more than weep and cook supper, who hold jobs of some consequence, who may or may not have male friends over for the night. Blacks are shown as they live their lives in an inner-city black community. Many of the mystery, private eye, doctor, cop, and lawyer shows treat serious social issues as the core of their story lines: drug addiction, divorce, the women's movement, politics, corrupt business, war casualties. While the quality of writing and production varies, these shows suggest many issues that we could and should discuss with kids.

Roots is another story. Does its unprecedented success suggest that we Americans are ready to reconcile ourselves to our bitter history? Will we see more daring, "relevant" pro-graming since it has proved commercially and, in its way, socially and ethically meaningful?

In time slots designated for children, the trend has been toward increasing the number of positive social values. Unfortunately, many of the Saturday and Sunday morning shows (and reruns) remain in roughly the same animation form as the old cartoon; it's just the message that has changed. Archie becomes *The U.S. of Archie,* imparting history and morality. The emphasis is on efficiency: animation of the kind kids see on Saturdays is not very expensive by TV standards, and it appeals to the broad two-to-twelve age range as something of a young people's lowest common denominator.

The Instructional approach—whether teaching letters and numbers and words, or social values—still amounts to grown-ups telling kids what to know or how to act. It says, "Come see our world," rather than "Let's see your world." TV ought to recognize the serious and interesting thoughts on *kids'* minds and provide greater understanding of children by adults.

Several shows in varying formats have undertaken these tasks. CBS's *In the News* reports on serious subjects such as political crimes and water pollution in three-minute segments during the children's viewing schedule. Other shows present documentaries about real kids doing interesting things. The young people portrayed are not stars, nor are they turned into an attractive song-and-dance troupe; they're real kids. On public television, *Rebop* catches the spirit of teenagers on their home turf (frequently ethnic and racial minority communities). *Studio See* sweeps about the country effectively portraying a variety of phenomena: venomous snakes and their handling, the wild horses of Chincoteague Island, windsurfing on the Pacific. Between segments the crew explains some aspect of technical production, and transitions include readings of poems written by children.

Kidsworld darts around from a frog jumping contest, to a story of UFOs, to a bilingual school, to a story on a young cancer victim, to an interview with *Jaws'* and *Close Encounters'* director Steven Spielberg, with kids as anchor people and narrators. Zoomguests on *Zoom* have often included kids who could be considered handicapped in one discernible way or another, portrayed not as heroes or victims, just as people. On all these shows, the stories are well constructed and production standards are high. (Production is handled by adults, fortunately. It's great to see kids on TV, as reporters or subjects of stories; it's also great to have good productions on behalf of the kids, and adults, who watch the shows.)

Most of the public affairs shows that speak to young audiences are on in the morning or afternoon, and *Rebop* competes with the evening news, of all things. We need to see more of the quality children's programs aired at times when families could watch together. And we still need more shows aimed at specific age groups, instead of every show reaching for the largest possible share of the audience.

The point of aspiring to silk purses is to talk about what we see. Whether we begin with Walter Cronkite or the *Happy Days* crowd, *Today, Tonight* or *Tomorrow,* or *As the World Turns,* the dialogue connects us to the medium. If it is evocative and pervasive, our TV dialogue becomes a natural complement to viewing itself. A clunker of a show, a bona-fide sow's ear, can turn to silk if we're willing to participate.

PETER ALMOND

IMPROVING TV: WHAT CAN YOU DO ABOUT IT?

If You Want to Improve Children's Television, Get Up and Watch It

One of the reasons children's television—and children's TV commercials—is so bad is that the number of parents who are willing to get up at seven o'clock on Saturday morning is very small indeed. If one could somehow make adults get up, at least a few times, to watch television with their kids until eleven, I don't think it would be long before they barraged the net-works with mail. And maybe something would be accomplished.

From an interview with CHRISTOPHER SARSON

The people own the television air. The networks are the trustees. If the trustees are not doing an adequate job, a responsible job . . . it is up to the people to say so and to say what they want to make their voices heard.

You Should See What You're Missing!
(Television documentary)

TV Resource Directory

One way to work for the improvement of television is to contact networks and local stations about any program or advertisement that moves you. Executives and program people are surprisingly alert to viewer reaction, especially when people have taken the time to put their thoughts in writing. And it helps if you let them know about the good shows as well as the bad shows.

The following resource list, adapted from *The Family Guide to Children's Television* (reviewed on page 324), should help you direct your correspondence to the proper organizations and agencies.   PETER ALMOND and EDS.

◆

GOVERNMENT AGENCIES

Director, Consumer Product Information Center, Public Documents Distribution Center, Pueblo, Colorado 81009

Chairman, Consumer Product Safety Commission, 1111 18th St. N.W., Washington, D.C.

Chairman, Federal Communications Commission, Washington, D.C. 20554.

Chairman, Federal Trade Commission, Bureau of Consumer Protection, Washington, D.C. 20580

Director, Food and Drug Administration, Department of Health, Education, and Welfare, 200 C St. S.W., Washington, D.C. 20204

National Telecommunications and Information Administration, Dept. of Commerce, 1800 G St. N.W., Washington, D.C. 20504

Both the Senate and the House of Representatives have subcommittees responsible for television and communications. . . . Write to them at either the Senate Office Building or the House Office Building, Washington, D.C.

NETWORKS

Address your letters to the presidents of these companies.

ABC, 1330 Avenue of the Americas, New York, N.Y. 10019 (212-LT1-7777)

CBS, 51 West 52 St., Avenue of the Americas, New York, N.Y. 10019 (212-975-4321)

NBC, 50 Rockefeller Plaza, New York, N.Y. 10020 (212-664-4444)

PBS, 485 L'Enfant Plaza S.W., Washington, D.C. (202-488-5000)

STATION GROUPS

Some major groups owning television stations are listed below. Address your letters to the president.

Avco Broadcasting Corp., 1600 Provident Tower, Cincinnati, Ohio 45202

Capital Cities Communications, 485 Madison Ave., New York, N.Y. 10022

Cox Broadcasting Stations, 1601 W. Peachtree St. N.E., Atlanta, Ga. 30309

John E. Fetzer Stations, 590 W. Maple St., Kalamazoo, Mich. 49008

Forward Communications Inc., Box 1088, 1114 Grand Ave., Wausau, Wis. 54401

Hearst Stations, 959 Eighth Ave., New York, N.Y. 10019

Kaiser Broadcasting Stations, 300 Lakeside Drive, Kaiser Bldg., Oakland, Calif. 94604

Metromedia Inc., 485 Lexington Ave., New York, N.Y. 10017

Post-Newsweek, Broadcast House, 4001 Brandywine St., Washington, D.C. 20016

RKO General Inc., 1440 Broadway, New York, N.Y. 10018

Scripps-Howard Group, 200 Park Ave., New York, N.Y. 10017

Storer Broadcasting Co., 1177 Kane Concourse, Miami Beach, Fla. 33154

Taft Broadcasting Co., 1906 Highland Ave., Cincinnati, Ohio 45219

Tribune Co. (*Chicago Tribune*) Stations, 2501 Bradley Place, Chicago, Ill, 60618

Westinghouse Broadcasting Stations, 90 Park Ave., New York, N.Y. 10016

(Complete information available from Broadcasting Yearbook, 1735 DeSales Street N.W., Washington, D.C. 20036.)

LOCAL STATIONS

Every local television station has a call-sign beginning with "W" east of the Mississippi and with "K" west of the Mississippi. To find the addresses and phone numbers of your local stations, look up the call-signs in the phone book under "W" or "K" (WNEW, KRON, etc.). Address your letters to the president of the station.

ORGANIZATIONS AND GROUPS

Action for Children's Television, 46 Austin Street, Newtonville, Mass. 02160 (617-527-7870). National organization of parents and professionals, working to upgrade television for children and to eliminate commercialism from children's TV. Membership, newsletter, campaigns, research information, film, and library facilities.

Center for the Study of Responsive Law, P.O. Box 19367, Washington, D.C. 20036. Nader founded this group of lawyers who investigate a variety of areas in response to consumer needs. Provides legal advice, publishes books on areas studied.

Citizens Communications Center, 1914 Sunderland Pl., Washington, D.C. 20036. Provides legal assistance and advice to citizens interested in taking action in broadcasting area. Publishes annual report.

Council on Children, Media, and Merchandising, 1346 Connecticut Avenue N.W., Washington, D.C. 20036. The Council, created by Robert Choate, is most active in areas relating to nutrition and food advertising to children.

National Academy of Television Arts and Sciences, 110 W. 57 St., New York, N.Y. 10009. Professional organization of broadcast producers and performers. Publishes some materials.

National Association for Better Broadcasting, 2315 Westwood Blvd., Los Angeles, Calif. 90064. Oldest broadcasting organization. Has membership, publishes newsletter and annual critique of programs on the air.

National Association for the Education of Young Children (Media Committee, 1834 Connecticut Avenue N.W., Washington, D.C. 20009. Leading organization for teachers of preschool children, publishes journal and has special committee preparing materials about the media.

National Citizens Committee for Broadcasting, 1914 Sunderland Place N.W., Washington, D.C. 20036. Was active in 1960s and then lapsed. Now revitalizing as a national organization planning to coordinate all citizen efforts in broadcasting.

Office of Communication, United Church of Christ, 289 Park Ave. S., New York, N.Y. 10010. Dr. Everett Parker has made the Office of Communication a spearhead of legal efforts to improve minority representation in broadcasting. Publishes some materials, gives advice.

Urban Communications Group, 1730 M Street N.W., Washington, D.C. 20036. A group involved in minority ownership in broadcasting, especially cable TV.

Video Games: "A New Way of Interacting with the Tube"

Some of the skills you use when you're playing video games are identical to ones that schools are intent on developing. Hand–eye coordination, reasoning, accuracy, etc., are all involved in one game or another. I've been told that children with reading problems (like dyslexia) are helped by playing the games. But I would say that the main reason for getting them is that they're fun, and that they offer your family a new way of interacting with the tube—and with one another. BERNIE DE KOVEN

[For more about electronic games, see page 422.]

BOOKS ABOUT TELEVISION

LIVING ROOM WAR, *by Michael J. Arlen, (Viking, 1967, 242 pages, $5.95 hardcover).*

THE VIEW FROM HIGHWAY 1, *by Michael J. Arlen (Farrar, Straus & Giroux, 1976, 293 pages, $8.95 hardcover; Ballantine, $1.95 paperback).*

New Yorker essayist Michael J. Arlen's *Living Room War,* a collection of TV commentaries from the middle and late sixties, still stands up marvelously, and his second collection, *The View from Highway 1,* continues his deft and incisive observations into the seventies.

You do not hear Arlen passing · judgments from some Olympian transmitting tower. Instead, he shares his musings about the country as it is reflected in television. We join him as he somewhat absent-mindedly flicks on the set, as he lives his own life, as television weaves itself into his consciousness as he does into ours.

These two volumes contain, quite simply, the best writing ever done about American television.

PETER ALMOND

TV: THE MOST POPULAR ART, *by Horace Newcomb (Doubleday/Anchor Books, 1974, $2.50 paperback).*

Horace Newcomb introduces a refreshing perspective to the study of television. Examining what he calls the aesthetics of the TV art (methods, techniques, stories, details), Newcomb brings the study of TV nearest to what American viewers actually see when watching television. He analyzes, in simple terms, situation comedies (contrasting *All in the Family* with *Father Knows Best*), shows about doctors and lawyers, mysteries, westerns, sports and news, documentaries, soaps, adventure shows, and what he calls "new shows" (*Laugh-In, An American Family, Maude* for example). It is an approach that could well be adopted in schools, from early grades through college.

Newcomb cites an essay by Abraham Kaplan which puts the question of "value" of the popular arts against the high purpose of Art:

Aesthetic judgment is one thing and personal taste is another. The values of art, like all else aesthetic, can only be analyzed contextually. There is a time and a place even for popular art. Champagne and Napoleon brandy are admittedly the best of beverages; but on a Sunday afternoon in the ballpark we want a coke, or maybe a glass of beer. "Even if we have all the virtues," Zarathustra reminds us, "there is still one thing needful: to send the virtues themselves to sleep at the right time." If popular art gives us pleasant dreams, we can only be grateful—when we have awakened. [From *The Popular Arts, A Critical Reader,* New York: 1967]

PETER ALMOND

THE FAMILY GUIDE TO CHILDREN'S TELEVISION, *by Evelyn Kaye (Pantheon, 1974, $2.95 paperback).*

Darting around from criticism of industry structure to a workbook for viewing children's TV (for both grown-up and child), *The Family Guide* has plenty of advice on what shows and types of programing to avoid. All the arguments are well documented, but perhaps Kaye has tried to do too much at once.

The Family Guide is sponsored by Action for Children's Television (ACT) and the American Academy of Pediatrics, both of which represent essentially a middle-class, albeit healthy, perspective. They are fighting the good fight, and have a good writer in Evelyn Kaye, but sometimes you wonder if ACT and Ms. Kaye aren't overloading the parent with duties and responsibilities. (The author once pronounced on a midday TV talk show that any parents who allowed their child to watch evening television indiscriminately "should have their heads examined." Well, a lot of decent parents do allow exactly that, and to impose guilt for that is of questionable value.)

To anyone setting out to organize a community media group, *The Family Guide* provides valuable assistance in this effort. For those who want to know about the byzantine workings of the Federal Communications Commission the description here is a good one.

The book is, finally, a compendium of different perspectives and approaches to children's TV. Thought of that way—as separate pamphlets, each serving a different useful purpose—it may help the concerned adult make better use of television for children and the family.

PETER ALMOND

Other ways to support ACT:

For $15, a one-year membership, including a subscription to the organization's quarterly newsletter.

For $25, a one-year contributing membership, including the quarterly newsletter and a copy of *The Family Guide.*

Contributions should be sent to Action for Children's Television, 46 Austin Street, Newtonville, Mass. 02160.

THE PLUG-IN DRUG, *by Marie Winn (Viking Press, 1977, 231 pages, $8.95 hardcover).*

Reading Marie Winn's recent book on television, *The Plug-In Drug,* an attractively intemperate attack on the medium as the chief destructive force of our age, I was reminded how quickly thoughts about popular culture and its effect on children lead to larger thoughts about the function of art and literature in general. When we think of our children we all become philosophers. Of course, Winn's book is hardly philosophical: it's a fluent, very biased, journalistic dump on TV. Winn amasses wads of evidence, all negative: Television occupies more than one-third of the waking hours of preschool children, she reports, more time than any other activity; it perpetuates dependency, inhibits verbal, cognitive, imaginative and social development, and diminishes family life. It makes reality less real. Its function is to pacify and control children, just as gin and laudanum once did.

Hence, parents are pushers. Television watching is a kind of stupor, a trance state, a druggy trip. Even worse, she writes, it may be damaging our children's neurological development: There has been a serious diminution of verbal abilities and of reading and writing skills in the TV generation; television seems to encourage visual-spatial modes of thought, not verbal and logical ones. Before TV, parents resorted for relief to a daily nap-time for children, a time when they played alone and developed their sense of self. Today's parents are hopeless slaves of the tube; family meals, talk, games and rituals are destroyed, and children have a reduced sense of the actuality of other people. In an experiment in which TV was turned off for a few weeks, there was more interaction with adults, a more peaceful atmosphere in the home, a greater feeling of closeness as a family, more help by children in the household, more outdoor and indoor play, more reading, better relations between parents. In short, TV rots our brains, destroys our social and family life, and sets every man's hand against his brother. Winn even implies that it may lead to totalitarian government, along the lines of *Brave New World* or *1984.*

I enjoyed this polemic a lot; its missionary zeal confirmed my prejudices and swept the rational arguments in favor of limited TV aside for a few hours. And of course Winn's chief alternative to television as a cultural medium for the young was books. I liked that too. At a crucial juncture she cites the psychoanalyst Bruno Bettelheim: "Television captures the imagination but does not liberate it. A good book at once stimulates and frees the mind."

RICHARD LOCKE
The New York Times Book Review

And Now, a Word About Other Media . . .

Turn on the Radio: *The General Mills Adventure Theater*

Turn off the TV, pull down the shades, close your eyes and "come . . . to a theater whose stage has no limits. . . . Where you can be anything you dream. Sail seas, scale mountains and explore galaxies—all in your own mind."

Every Saturday and Sunday evening stories of intrigue, mystery and adventure will enter your house. *The General Mills Adventure Theater* . . . is a new radio show based on an old, time-tested, successful idea. . . .

Himan Brown, a veteran producer of great old radio shows . . . carries listeners into dark jungles, tropical swamps, haunted houses, and whaling ships. Brown hires about four actors and actresses for each show. Each performer plays as many as three characters, using different voices for each. And during each show the sound engineer stands ready to . . . produce anything from the squawk of an exotic bird to the pounding of galloping horses.

Some of the stories are familiar—*Moby Dick* and *Pinocchio.* Some stories are new and written especially for *Adventure Theater.* But all the stories stretch the imagination . . . and transport us to worlds and times far away from our living rooms.

GRETCHEN DYKSTRA
Junior Scholastic

Movies for Kids

MOVIES FOR KIDS, by Edith Zornow and Ruth M. Goldstein (Avon Books, 224 pages, $1.65 paperback), like everything good meant for children, is really for everyone. It is a gem of a book that shares, rather than preaches about, the love of films which its two authors obviously have.

A guide for parents and teachers on films for children between nine and thirteen, the book lists 125 features and 75 short films. With each entry is information on distribution, directors, actors, and a wonderfully informative description of the content of each film that is much more than a plot summary. There is a lovely short essay on "How to Look at a Movie" which should enrich film watching for everyone who reads it. On the practical side there is an exhaustive list of companies and film societies, so the book is also a directory of how and where to rent the films discussed. And the bibliography of more than 100 books on the subject of film is worthy of the best film study courses in the country. There are some special little gems listed here (the films of Robert McLaren and Eli Noyes for example), which one doesn't encounter in usual theatrical distribution, but which can be rented for a party or library screening.

Movies for Kids is written with great love and enormous knowledge, and no one who uses it will remain untouched by the power and joy of film.

NAOMI FONER

MAKING THINGS

When I was a child, my mother said to me, "If you become a soldier you'll be a general. If you become a monk, you'll end up as the Pope." Instead I became a painter and wound up as Picasso.

PABLO PICASSO
Quoted in *Life With Picasso*
by Françoise Gilot and Carlton Lake

ARTS AND CRAFTS

Supplies: What You Need and Don't Need

If crafts are going to be more than a three-rainy-days-a-year pursuit in your house, you should be set up for it. The best way is to have an area (it could be just a shelf or a carton kept on the bottom of a closet) in which you keep the kind of junk you once would have thrown away— string, wrapping paper, egg cartons, wine corks, packing materials, cardboard tubes, bottle tops, scraps of fabric, ribbon, yarn, wood—as well as the supplies you need to buy, such as paints, paper, glue, markers, nails, and so on. Poke holes in an upside-down egg carton to hold scissors, brushes, pencils. Another egg carton, right side up, could hold paper fasteners, toothpicks, buttons.

Really, you need very little. You needn't accumulate a lot of specialized materials. It's better to build gradually and try to stretch the basic materials. (It's amazing, for example, what you can do with just drawing paper and crayons: you can make crayon rubbings, or you can melt the crayons onto the paper for a raised design, and if you color over the drippings, then peel them off, you have a batik-like pattern. With glue, you can make collages, or rice or macaroni friezes.)

If you can stand to leave your kid to her own devices, you will be surprised at how resourceful she will be—much more so than when you intervene and start "showing" her how to be "creative." Nevertheless, we do have some suggestions for you. Read on. —Eds.

Artista Watercolors

When I buy watercolors for a classroom, I get the powdered colors in as big a jar as I can, and mix and match and dilute and thicken according to my needs. You can buy incredibly sophisticated, expensive kits with eight hundred colors, but I don't think you come up with anything better than if you have red, blue, yellow, and white and mix them yourself.

The powdered paints are good for home use because you can mix as much as you need— for one kid, you put a little in a pimiento jar; if you have eighteen kids, you put a lot in a big mayonnaise jar. With a pre-mixed watercolor, you don't have that flexibility. Artista is one of the better brands of powdered colors.

NANCY HAUSMAN

COMB

ZIPPER

COIN

BUTTON

WOOD

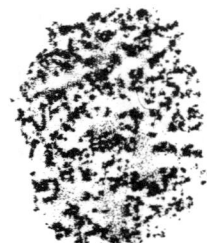

BRICK

Choosing and Using Materials in Child Care Settings, by Ann Dintenfass and Bernie De Koven, suggests the side of an old crayon as the best tool for rubbings. "Go on a texture hunt," the authors advise.

The Longest-Lasting Felt-Tip Pens

Not only do felt-tip markers provide more vivid colors than crayons, they serve well as body paint. If your family goes through a lot of them, you may want to hunt around for a brand that is recommended as "longest-lasting" by Sally Langendoen, whose son has a remarkable collection of them, and by Josh Robison and his class of nine- and ten-year-olds at the Bank Street School in New York. The markers are somewhat difficult to find and are packaged under at least two names that we know—Buffalo and Marvy, both made in Japan. The ink in these markers is water-based; it washes off hands and clothes. I paid $4 for a set of twelve Marvy pens (they come in larger sets, too) in an art supply store.

RS

◆

Cray-pas

Kids enjoy using Cray-pas—the colors are bright, the texture is interesting (it's a cross between a crayon and a pastel), and you can get different effects with them. I've seen kids go for the Cray-pas before the crayons, because they're less common.

NANCY HAUSMAN

◆

Containing the Mess

Messy Play and Hobby Tray, from Childcraft, $6.95, measures 23 inches square with a 1½-inch rim all around, and weighs half a pound. Kids can finger-paint right on it or play with clay, but it's also ideal for playing with those toys and puzzles that have a million tiny pieces. It's made of a bendable plastic that, while not sturdy enough to use on a lap or sickbed, is definitely suitable for table or floor. Order from Childcraft, 20 Kilmer Road, Edison, N.J. 08817.

FLAVIA POTENZA

◆

For Lefties Only

You can find left-handed scissors at a surgical supply house, and you can order an assortment of left-handed products from the Left Hand, 140 West 22nd Street, New York, N.Y. 10011. Their mail-order catalogue includes writing instruments, sports equipment, kitchen utensils, and more. The $1 charge for the catalogue is deducted from your first order. Gift certificates are available in multiples of five dollars (a free catalogue is sent with all gift certificates).

RS

Papers

Construction paper
  For drawing, painting, hats, masks, mobiles, collages. Comes in solid color packs or assorted colors. Buy some solid packs of red, green, blue, yellow, black. Basic size: 9″ × 12″ and 18″ × 24″.

Contact paper (clear)
  Use to coat game boards, lotto cards, etc. Very handy. Make nature samples by covering leaves, etc., with contact to preserve.

Corrugated paper (flameproof)
  Colorful as a bulletin board (use pins) or to cover the backs of furniture. 48″ × 25′ roll, 13 colors.

Crepe paper (flameproof)
  For costumes, decorations, puppets, hats.

Easel paper
  Newsprint is fine for tempera (easel paint), crayon, or chalk. BIG PAPER needs BIG BRUSHES for free, bold strokes. Flat ¾″ wide brushes or round 1″ long bristled brushes with long handles.

Finger-paint paper
  Heavily glazed white paper (you can use heavy glazed shelf paper or butcher paper or a formica tabletop as well).

Kraft paper (roll)
  Tan paper 36″ × 20 yards. Very useful for murals, displays, maps, stage or puppet sets, group pictures or collages.

Manila paper
  A basic all-purpose paper for crayon, paint, chalk. Cream colored, more expensive than newsprint.

Newsprint
  Newspaper without words. Good as easel paper (see above) or drawing paper (9″ × 12″, 12″ × 18″).

Railroad board (or oak tag)
  Cardboard with a color finish on both sides (lightweight), good for birthday charts, calendars, lotto games, etc. 22″ × 28″.

Tissue paper
  Many uses—cut snowflakes, unfold, lay on paper, paint with liquid starch to glue. Make wrapping paper—print with a fork, cork, etc., dipped in paint.

ANN DINTENFASS and BERNIE DE KOVEN
Choosing and Using Materials in Child Care Settings

Scrapbooks for Free

Wallpaper sample books make terrific scrapbooks—and you can get them free. They come in 8½- by 11-inch and 12- by 24-inch sizes, and are perfect for pasting things into and writing in. The books usually become available in the fall when the new designs come out.

BECKY CORWIN

A Classic Easel to Make Yourself

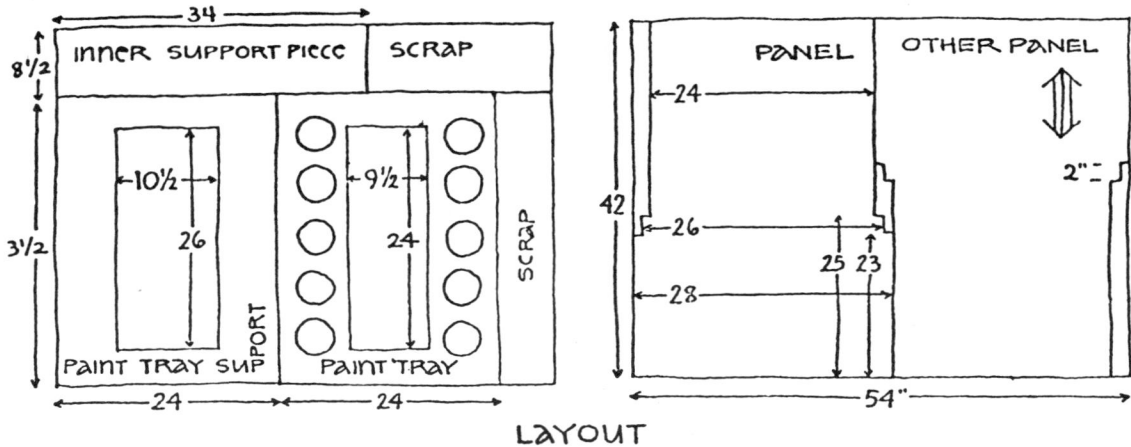

LAYOUT

This shows how to lay out a 42" high easel on 2 48" × 54" pieces of Tri-Wall. (The inner support piece will be a little loose in its position, so if you make this from other size pieces of Tri-Wall, cut the width of that piece to fit the slot.) Holes for paint containers: these should be cut to fit the containers you'll use. Many teachers use frozen orange juice cans: they are easy to come by, their height supports brushes well and their depth slows down evaporation from the paint. There is a small circle cutter that cuts 2¹⁄₁₆" circles, just the right size for these cans. If you plan to use something else, you'll need to measure its size before you cut the holes for it. You can punch a paring knife through and cut with it until you have a slot wide enough for your saw to slip into.

Assembly: tape the edges of the sides together with cloth or paper tape. Stand up in approximately correct position and lower paint tray support piece down over top until it rests on lower "step" at sides. Adjust position of sides so paint tray support piece fits. Lower paint tray to rest on upper "step." Slide inner support piece in from the side, resting it on paint tray support.

From *Cardboard Carpentry Workshop*

Jody Tiedemann's Favorite Art Supplies

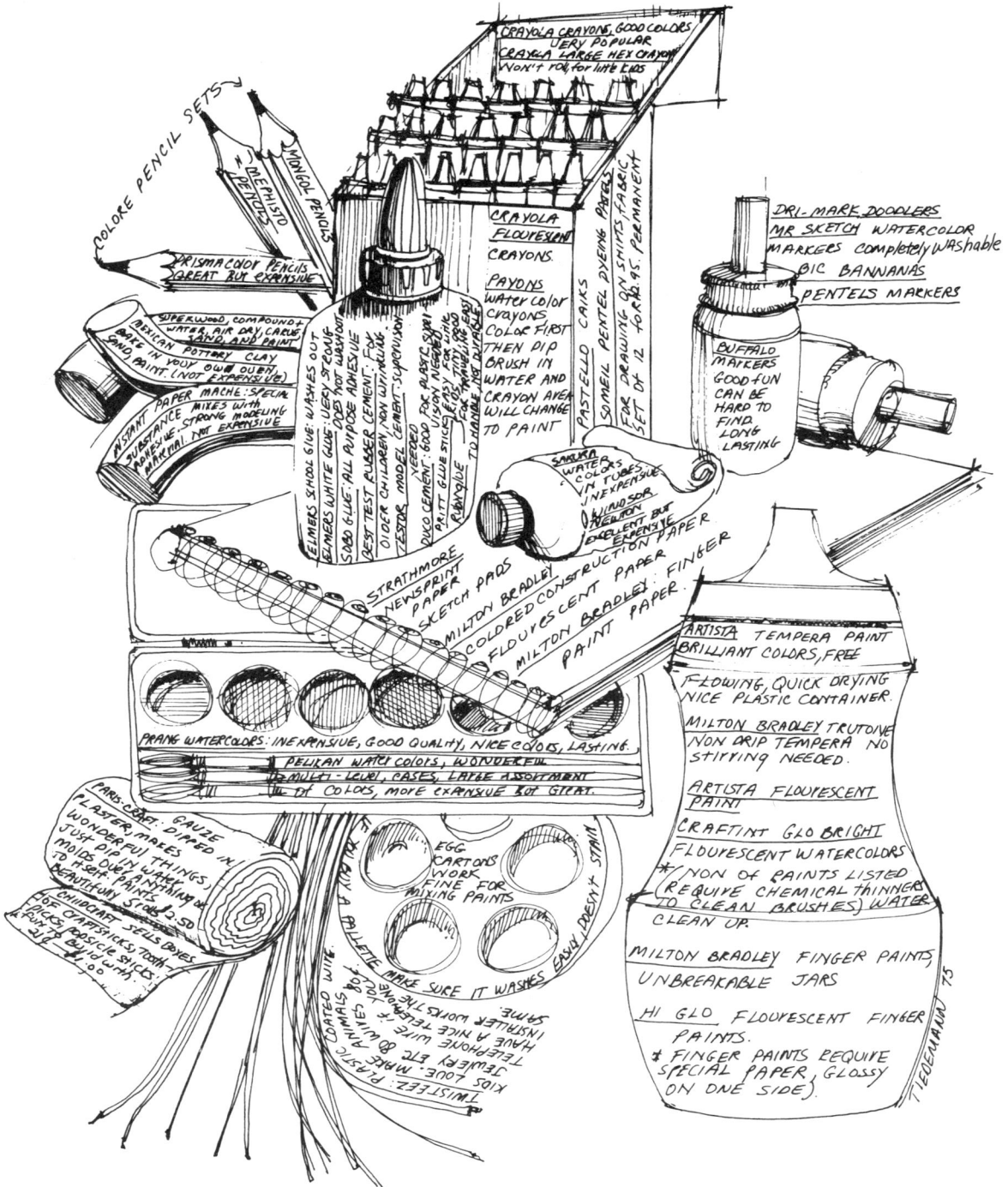

CRAYOLA CRAYONS, GOOD COLORS,
VERY POPULAR
CRAYOLA LARGE HEX CRAYONS
Won't roll for litle kids

COLORE PENCIL SETS

MONGOL PENCILS

MEPHISTO PENCILS

PRISMACOLOR PENCILS
GREAT BUT EXPENSIVE

SUPERWOOD, COMPOUND +
WATER, AIR DRY, CARVE
SAND, AND PAINT
MEXICAN POTTERY CLAY
BAKE IN YOUR OWN OVEN
SAND, PAINT (NOT EXPENSIVE)

INSTANT PAPER MACHE: SPECIAL
SUBSTANCE MIXES WITH
ADHESIVE, STRONG MODELING
MATERIAL, NOT EXPENSIVE

CRAYOLA
FLOURESCENT
CRAYONS

PAYONS
WATER COLOR
CRAYONS
COLOR FIRST
THEN DIP
BRUSH IN
WATER AND
CRAYON AREA
WILL CHANGE
TO PAINT

ELMERS SCHOOL GLUE: WASHES OUT
ELMERS WHITE GLUE: VERY STRONG
SO-BO GLUE: ALL PURPOSE ADHESIVE, DOES NOT WASH OUT
BEST TEST RUBBER CEMENT: FOR OLDER CHILDREN, NON WRINKLE
TESTOR, MODEL CEMENT, SUPRONIOXY
DUCO CEMENT: GOOD FOR PLASTIC, SUPER STRONG, VISION NEEDED
RUBBER CEMENT: EASY, FOR LINING
PRITT GLUE STICK: EASY, EASY FOR YOUNG CHILDREN (EXPENSIVE)
BANXQUE TO HANDLE NOT EXPENSIVE

PASTELLO CAIKS

SOMEILL PENTEL DYEING PASTELS
FOR DRAWING ON SHIRTS, FABRIC
SET OF 12 FOR 84S, PERMANENT

DRI-MARK DOODLERS
MR SKETCH WATERCOLOR
MARKERS completely WASHABLE
BIC BANNANAS
PENTELS MARKERS

BUFFALO
MARKERS
GOOD FUN
CAN BE
HARD TO
FIND,
LONG
LASTING

SAKURA
WATER
COLORS
IN TUBES,
INEXPENSIVE
WINDSOR
NEWTON
EXCELLENT BUT
EXPENSIVE

STRATHMORE
NEWSPRINT
PAPER

MILTON BRADLEY
SKETCH PADS

COLORED CONSTRUCTION PAPER
FLOURESCENT PAPER
MILTON BRADLEY FINGER
PAINT PAPER

PRANG WATERCOLORS: INEXPENSIVE, GOOD QUALITY, NICE COLORS, LASTING

PELIKAN WATER COLORS, WONDERFUL
MULTI-LEVEL CASES, LARGE ASSORTMENT
OF COLORS, MORE EXPENSIVE BUT GREAT.

PARIS CRAFT: GAUZE
PLASTER MAKES
WONDERFUL THINGS,
JUST DIP IN WATER
MOLDS OVER, MAINTAIN
TO HEAT, PAINTS
BEAUTIFULLY, $2.50
HOBBYCRAFT SELLS DOWELS
STICKS, POPSICLE STICKS
& PLYWOOD WITH $1.00

TWISTEEZ: PLASTIC
COATED WIRE
KIDS LOVE: MAKE
ANIMALS, ETC @ WIRES
TELEPHONE WIRE: IF YOU
HAVE A NICE TELEPHONE
INSTALLER WORKS THE
SAME

EGG
CARTONS
WORK
FINE
FOR
MIXING
PAINTS

MAKE SURE IT WASHES EASILY, DOESN'T STAIN

ARTISTA TEMPERA PAINT
BRILLIANT COLORS, FREE
FLOWING, QUICK DRYING
NICE PLASTIC CONTAINER.

MILTON BRADLEY TRUTOINE
NON DRIP TEMPERA NO
STIRRING NEEDED.

ARTISTA FLOURESCENT
PAINT

CRAFTINT GLO BRIGHT
FLOURESCENT WATERCOLORS
*(NON OF PAINTS LISTED
REQUIRE CHEMICAL THINNER
TO CLEAN BRUSHES) WATER
CLEAN UP.

MILTON BRADLEY FINGER PAINTS,
UNBREAKABLE JARS

HI GLO FLOURESCENT FINGER
PAINTS.
* FINGER PAINTS REQUIRE
SPECIAL PAPER, GLOSSY
ON ONE SIDE).

TIEDEMANN 75

WARNINGS

Art Supplies to Beware Of

1. Certain modeling clays are not meant for children. Plasticine (a clay mixed with oil and dough) is tempting because it comes in small packages, but it is very oily, does not come out of rugs, and has a disturbing odor which lingers on hands.

2. Be careful to check that any modeling clay you buy is nontoxic. Some of the clays are candy-colored and look very tasty. Ask to smell the clay before you buy; even Play-Doh has a strange odor. Read labels.

3. For older children working with model airplanes, cars, etc., make sure there is plenty of ventilation. No models should be worked on in a small enclosed space, especially when dangerous solvents (turpentine, benzene, thinner) or glues are used, which can ignite very easily.

4. Some paints (especially fluorescent paints) cannot be cleaned with water and need solvents; they are not for children. Examine containers carefully.

5. Certain glues (Duco Cement, rubber cement, Testor glues) have strong odors and should be used with proper ventilation.

6. All the new superglues (10-second drying) are extremely dangerous and certainly not for children. If these glues get on your hands they can bond to eyes, ears, etc., and must be cut apart. Nothing a child does requires this kind of glue.

7. Do not store crayons on radiators or in direct sunlight; they melt quicker than you think.

8. Check supplies before you buy them to make sure they aren't old, or dried up, or discolored. Many Magic Markers are dried up from shelf life. Test the ones you're buying before you leave the store.

JODY TIEDEMANN

Crafts Sets: Less Than Meets the Eye

Reviewing some arts and crafts material for the Federal Trade Commission, I found that much of it is deceptively packaged beyond belief. If you want to go out and buy an arts and crafts *set,* you're going to pay many times more than if you just got a wad of paper and crayons or paints. True, sets make nice gifts; but with a little ingenuity you can provide all of your child's arts and crafts supplies for next to nothing.

SHARON LERNER

Caution: Read Labels Fully

On the back of a package of Pactra Hi-Glo paints found on the toy shelf in a dime store and marked "Non-Toxic," I read the following:

Combustible.
Harmful or fatal if swallowed.
Contains petroleum distillates.
Do not induce vomiting. Call physician.
Avoid prolonged or repeated contact with skin, breathing of vapor.
KEEP OUT OF REACH OF SMALL CHILDREN.

I wonder, what do they consider toxic?

ELS

SOME PERSONAL FAVORITES

Color Stickers

Self-adhesive stickers in assorted shapes and colors—the kind that are pre-cut and come on sheets of waxed paper, so that even very young kids can peel them off—are perfect for collages and other decorative fantasies. My daughter loved them at eighteen months, though she decorated the kitchen cabinets as well as the construction paper; my nieces, ages four to eight, also found them irresistible.

An outfit named Avery makes some that are available in most stationery stores; they come on handy separate sheets of 35 and are even restickable—except that, at $2.85 a box, I'm making my daughter go through all 1,000 yellow dots before I splurge on red ones. Maybe we should organize an Avery cooperative, where different-colored dots are traded like baseball cards.

PAULA GLATZER

Yarn Drawings

Needlepoint canvas and blunt needles are a relatively safe way for children to be encouraged to create their own pictures with yarn, and learn to sew at the same time. Later the yarn can be taken out and the materials used again.

MRS. DAVID ASHTON

Soap Art

Drawing on windows with soap cleans windows, is harmless, and allows for larger drawing space than most paper. My fifteen-month-old loves it.

CAROLINE HARKLEROAD

I mix Ivory Flakes with a little bit of water to make a pasty substance. You can play with it on paper and let it dry in three-dimensional patterns. Occasionally I've been known to add food coloring. My three-year-old thinks it's terrific.

RONA ROBERTS

Body Murals

If you have big rolls of brown paper, or can tape together enough newspaper, it's fun to draw outlines of bodies. Younger kids can color them and older kids can draw the innards.

MATT HARRIS

Dough Sculptures à la Muppets

Jim Henson of *Muppets* fame and his family have been making sculptures out of bread dough for years now, particularly around Christmas time. "The kids find our dough mix-

ture easier to handle than modeling clay," says Jane, Jim's co-puppeteer wife. "And I certainly prefer making up a batch when we need it to the bother of keeping a supply of clay on hand!"

The Hensons' recipe is simple: combine four parts flour with one part salt, then add water and knead until the mixture reaches the consistency your child feels comfortable working with (usually the same percentage of water as salt).

After the masterpiece is complete, bake it in a 350° oven for a couple of hours, let it cool, then coat it with shellac to give it a rich glossy surface (and to preserve it for posterity).

CBC

Design-It-Yourself Iron-Ons

The idea behind iron-ons is so simple—and it really works. Any crayon drawing you make can be permanently transferred to cloth using a hot clothes iron. Or, you can crayon directly onto cloth and then iron the drawing into the fabric. For your design you might copy a picture, draw your own, write your name in fancy letters, think up a funny phrase, or just create colorful patterns. Your drawings can be ironed onto T-shirts, or on plain cloth to make banners, wall hangings, placemats, flags, or any sewing project you can do. Once the crayon has been ironed in, the cloth may be washed repeatedly in cold or warm water without running or fading.

Materials	Tools
crayons	clothes iron
cloth	

The details

Decide what your crayon project is going to be and organize your materials. Make your drawing either directly onto the cloth or onto a plain piece of paper. But remember, if you are going to transfer a drawing from paper to cloth the result will be in reverse. Either way, be sure to press hard on the crayons so that your colors go deep. Light crayon drawings just do not transfer well.

The ironing should be done, or at least supervised, by an adult. Set the iron temperature selector for the type of fabric you are applying the drawing to. Place the drawing on the cloth, crayon side down, or if you have crayoned directly onto the cloth, leave it crayon side up. Iron slowly over the drawing, giving the crayon enough heat to melt and impregnate the cloth. As the crayon melts, the colors will become a bit brighter and possibly spread a little. (You will also find that your drawing is still on the paper.) Remove the drawing, and your iron-on is complete. If any crayon remains on the iron, wipe it away with a wad of paper toweling while the iron is still warm.

From STEVEN CANEY'S *Play Book*
Workman Publishing

Busy Box

When the children were younger, if they were sick or if it was raining, I'd get out a "busy box" that I had put together: a shoe box filled with cotton balls, colored paper, toothpicks, glue, paper clips, scraps of wool, cloth, crayons, etc. Then the box was put away again until the next time. They loved it, and it was also a portable item for car trips or visits to other homes.

RUTH PELMAS

For Free

Go to the post office and ask them to save for you the ends of sheets of stamps. They're sticky and fun to tear apart and useful for collages. Some have the little zip-code man on them, but many are blank so that a child can design her own stamps.

ELS

Hardware Store Sculpture

A visit to our neighborhood hardware store with sculptor William Accorsi generated this list of materials for people exploring three-dimensional forms.

Brushes. If you don't limit your use of brushes to painting, then the whole gamut of paint and household brushes are possible components for pieces of sculpture. You can use them for faces, and then add arms and legs. The beautiful soft white fiber brushes you used to be able to get are becoming more scarce (and more expensive when you can find them); mostly what you find now is plastic, but they can still be fun to work with.

Cork. It's soft and will contain things well and is a nice base to begin building onto (try sticks, dried-out Bic pens, and pieces of wire just to see what you can do). You can paint it or draw on it with Magic Markers. Corks run around 15 cents each in the hardware store, so find someone to save wine corks for you. You can buy the big ones or tiny ones at hardware stores.

Eyelet refills. Little packages cost about 40 cents for 100, but sometimes you'll come across a whole lot more for almost nothing. Eyelets can be used to fasten cardboard arms and legs to a base material. They can give a cardboard cutout sculpture movable parts. (Paper fasteners can also be used for this, but they're more obtrusive.) To secure eyelets, you'll need a pair of gripper pliers (about $2.50).

Springs. Once you figure out how to do something with springs, they're a lot of fun to work with. For starters, drill or whittle a hole the size of your spring in a block of wood, put putty or plastic wood in the hole, and stick the end of the spring in the putty before it dries. You can then add papier-mâché, cardboard, or wire on the other end of the spring.

String. There's so much you can do with string that Dover Press has a whole book on it: *String Figures and How to Make Them,* by Caroline Furness Jayne ($3.50 paperback).

Upholstery tacks. They're expensive (roughly a penny apiece), but fun to work with. Call upholsterers listed in the yellow pages to see if you can get their rejects.

Wire. For creating marvelous sculpture, use relatively thin wire, around a no. 20 (about $2 for 300 feet), that is easy to bend. Coat-hanger wire isn't flexible enough to make much more than a basketball hoop, and you bust your hand trying to do anything with it. If you're working with wire, you'll need two different kinds of pliers: one with a cutting edge on the inside (they cost over $3), and a blunt-edged pair for shaping. Most useful: a pair of straight-nose pliers, which you can buy in hardware stores for a little over a dollar.

WILLIAM ACCORSI and RS

The Suitcase That Doesn't Go Anywhere

Tucked away in a closet of my house is a small suitcase full of treasures that would appeal only to a child's imagination. The stones my grandson and I collected on a walk in the country become mountains. The incomplete deck of cards we saved is a roadway for a little car. Bits and pieces of colored paper, a few twigs, a handful of buttons, some paste, a scrap of material or ribbons, some pine cones, a string of broken beads—that's all you need for a beautiful collage on a shirt cardboard. The plastic top from a coffee can is a magical flying saucer. The possibilities are endless for my grandson and me.

The little suitcase has given us hours of pleasure for no investment. It is reached for at *every* visit—always with a surprise: the treasures change from one time to the next.

DOROTHY LOHMAN

Papermaking

5-MINUTE RECYCLE RECIPE
Makes New Gray Sheets
(a little detergent added to the water helps
bleach newsprint ink)

◆

[The following is an excerpt from Making Things, *a "standout" among arts and crafts books according to Maurice Sagoff. For more on this book, see page 337.]*

Paper is one of the most important and useful materials man has ever created. Until a hundred years ago most sheets of paper in the world were made by hand, and mostly used for precious documents.

Wasps taught us how to make paper. (Have you studied a hive?) Wasps chew fibers and weeds into a kind of paste or mash, spit it out to form the walls and chambers of their hive, and when it dries it is a kind of paper sculpture.

The first people to make paper were the Chinese in 105 A.D. In the sixth century, when the Chinese lost to the Arabs at the Battle of Samarkand, captured papermakers were forced to share their craft with their new masters. A thousand years later the art of papermaking reached Europe.

Paper is made from fibers such as: weeds, bark, wood pulp, corn husks, rags, celery strings, sawdust and wood shavings.

Fibers must be mashed, melted, reduced to pulp by some method such as pounding, boiling, or beating. Try the easy ones such as: corn husks, dried leaves and weeds chopped fine.

The pulp mixed with water is called slurry. If you dip a piece of metal window screen into the slurry and raise it up slowly and drain it, blot out the extra water and press it dry you will have a crude sheet of handmade paper.

◆

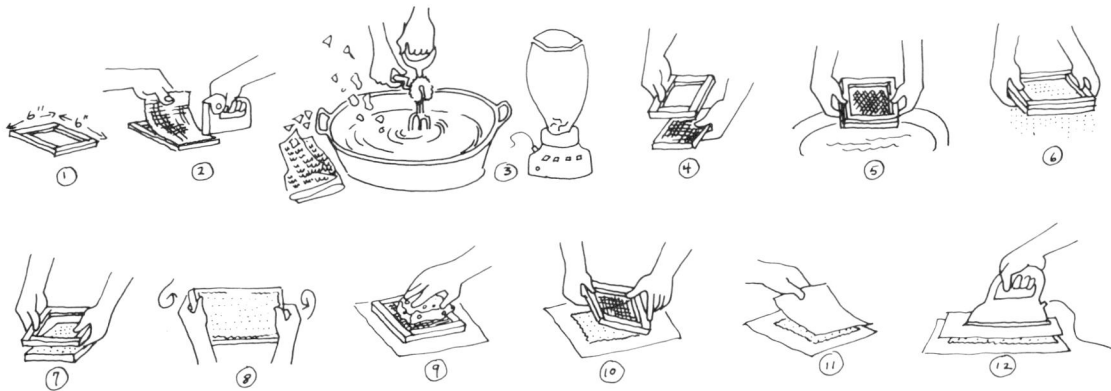

The Quick Recycle Papermaking Method is the best to start with (no chemicals, only use *water*):

1. Make two small frames (same size).
2. Staple wire screen to one frame called the mold.
3. Tear up old newspaper. Soak it, beat it or blend it. About one sheet of newspaper per dishpan of warm water.
4. Hold the mold, screen side up, place the empty frame on top. (The empty frame is called a deckle. It allows the water to drain slowly and forms the edges of the "wet-leaf.")
5. Dip both frames into dishpan of slurry.
6. Raise frames up slowly, and drain.
7. Remove top frame.
8–9. Turn screen over onto paper towel blotter and sponge screen dry.
10–12. Remove screen. Put another blotter on top of "wet-leaf" and iron dry. Remove blotters. See—you made new paper!

ANN WISEMAN
Making Things

CRAFTS BOOKS

Selecting a Crafts Book

Young kids should be free to develop their own styles, so they need ideas for crafts projects, not a whole set of instructions. It's when kids are older that they usually want to go into more detail. That's when plastic model kits become popular—the kind with detailed instructions requiring advanced manual dexterity. By that time kids are old enough to begin to organize and plan their own projects. That's the time to buy specialized books on macramé or candle-making or model rocketry.

In choosing a crafts book, look at several of the projects and consider the following: How accessible are the materials that are called for? (You may not want to go looking for #1032 machine screws with flat heads.) Do you have the tools required? What skills are needed? How structured are the projects?

Figure out beforehand what the purpose of the crafts project is. Is it to give the kid something to do, something you can get her started on? Or is it something you and your child will do together? (Most crafts projects in books require parents' help.) Is the craft something the child will play with? Many crafts projects end when you put on the last decoration; but there are some that become actual play products. That's the kind I prefer. Many crafts that have been written about over and over for many years sound exciting; on the assumption that they probably work, authors of kids' books copy them for their own books. But some of them don't work. One that I defy you to use successfully is the standard recipe for making rock candy. I've tried it many times and it won't work. Yet scores of crafts books contain the same recipe. The moral: Be prepared for trying projects that don't work out.

From an interview with STEVEN CANEY

I SAW A PURPLE COW, by Ann Cole, Carolyn Haas, Faith Bushnell, and Betty Weinberger, illustrated by True Kelley (Little, Brown, 1972, 96 pages, $3.95 paperback).

This book has basic recipes for the essential supplies—paste, finger paint, clay, "fun dough." The activities and crafts are presented very simply, and there is a great variety of things to do, some for a three-year-old child to do with an adult, and others for a seven-year-old to do alone.

SHARON LERNER

PASTE

YOU NEED:
    1 cup flour
    ½ cup water

YOU DO:
1) Combine the flour and water and mix until creamy.
2) Store in a covered container.
    (For a more durable paste, add ½ cup flour to 1 cup *boiling* water. Stir over low heat until thick and shiny.)

Paste is excellent when working with paper (for example, torn paper collages). Glue is useful when a more lasting effect is desired, such as with macaroni or dried bean decorations.

From *I Saw a Purple Cow*

THE AMERICAN BOYS HANDY BOOK, by D.C. Beard (Charles E. Tuttle Co., Rutland, Vt., 1966, 391 pages, $7.50 hardcover).

Subtitled "What to Do and How to Do It," this reprint of Beard's 1882 classic is full of innocent sexism (unchallenged by the first women's movement), and full of ingenuity. Its emphasis is on wholesome do-it-yourself adventure, and its philosophy, sexism aside, is delightful. In these pages you will learn how to make kites, water telescopes, hot-air balloons, soap bubbles, snow shoes and puppets; and blowguns, snares, knots, bends and hitches; how to blow birds' eggs and stock a freshwater aquarium and preserve insects and imitate birds and bind a prisoner without a cord. The book is sure to send your kid prying in your tool chest after pirate fantasies.

MICHAEL ROSSMAN

Yes, there is an *American Girls Handy Book*, by the Beard sisters, for the same price. There are some wonderful items, like how to make corn-husk dolls and flower dolls and fans; but too much of the book is devoted to holiday crafts and games for my taste.

RS

MAKING THINGS, *by Ann Wiseman (Little, Brown, 1973, 159 pages, $4.95 paperback).*

In the profusion of books about arts and crafts, one of the standouts is Ann Wiseman's *Making Things.* An artist and teacher, Wiseman is an experienced hand in the learning-by-doing art, and from her experience has put together this handbook of 150 "discoveries" using available materials, calculated to stimulate a child's creativity.

Step-by-step sketches and simple explanations show how to make paper from fibers such as weeds, bark, sawdust, etc.; how to make a salt pendulum; how to build disposable weaving looms that cost nothing; how to build mobiles and kites; how to turn odds and ends into toys, fish into fossil prints, leaves into lace, and scores of other "amazements."

MAURICE SAGOFF

ODD GLOVE FINGER PUPPETS

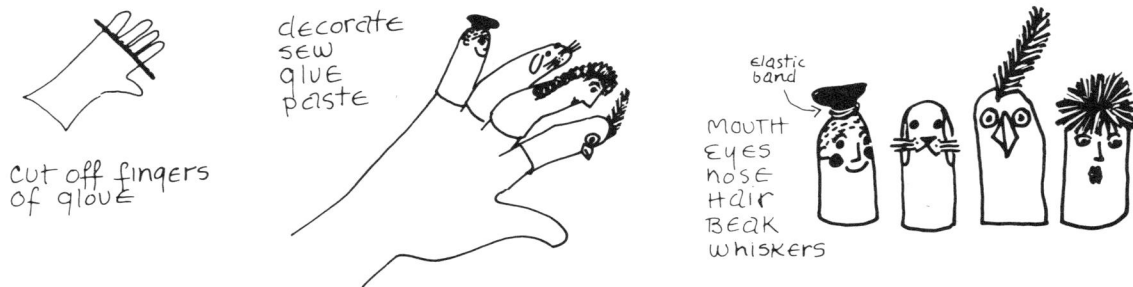

cut off fingers of glove

decorate
sew
glue
paste

elastic band

MOUTH
EYES
nose
Hair
BEAK
whiskers

BOX HORSE

USE: wooden box, hammer & nails, pine board, 4 furniture casters, Rope or string, 16 ¾" screws

use any ready made box! orange crate fish crate Liquor box

cut ears and slot

out of pine board and attach to box with nails.

ready-to-screw-on furniture casters, found at all hardware stores, make fine wheels.

cut slot same width as board so it fits tight.

a much easier, quicker way to serve the imagination

PiET

From *Making Things*

WHITTLING AND WOODCARVING, *by E. J. Tangerman (Dover Publications, 1936, 293 pages, $3 paperback).*

This book, for older children, is the classic on the subject.

WILLIAM ACCORSI

Some parents feel that dull blades are safer on a child's knife. Quite the opposite is true, providing the child is old enough to have a knife at all, because a dull blade forces excessive pressure behind it, thus causing slipping, splitting, snapping shut, and their attendant hurts. A good clean cut can be handled with a dose of iodine, a bit of a bandage, and forgetfulness. My four-year-old's favorite expression is "I didn't cut myself *berry* badly"—and it was mine too at his age. I remember once I did a very complete job of paring an index finger but didn't tell a soul about it for fear I'd have the knife taken away for a while. I had a boat to finish first.

From *Whittling and Woodcarving*

◆

CHILDREN MAKE SCULPTURE, *by Elizabeth Leyh (Van Nostrand Reinhold, 1972, 96 pages, $6.95 hardcover).*

An inspiring book, *Children Make Sculpture* shows what you can make out of common items you have around (and a few things you'll have to buy). Mostly the sculptures are made from cardboard, twigs, stones, wood scraps, matchboxes, plaster, and clay. The nicest thing about this book is that there's enough general guidance to get a child started, but there are no formal directions for how to make something. The charm comes from a kind of attitude, as if to say, "This sculpture made out of junk is pretty terrific, eh?" And it is—even when you see it here alongside a picture of sculptor David Smith's work, or a 3,000-year-old Egyptian carved granite baboon. The black-and-white photographs are great. A section called "Sculpture Is Everywhere" shows a partly eaten ice cream cone, a fried egg, a snowman, and an "arrangement" of silverware.

ELS

◆

WEAVING WITHOUT A LOOM, *by Sarita R. Rainey (Davis Publications, 50 Portland Street, Worcester, Mass. 01608, 1966, 132 pages, $10.95 hardcover).*

This is probably the best book that's ever been done on weaving, and one of my favorites in my crafts book collection. It covers every kind of weaving there is: weaving with paper, with straws (see below), on a pencil, on cardboard, into burlap. It suggests materials and supplies, and tells you where to get them. It's a book for the whole family, with very simple projects for young kids to do alone, as well as very complicated ones for adults.

STEVEN CANEY

WEAVING WITH DRINKING STRAWS

Basic Materials	Optional Materials
Straws (drinking or soda)	Thick and thin yarns
	Tinsel
Scissors	Fabric cut into strips
String	Ribbon
Yarn	Nylons cut into strips
	Cords

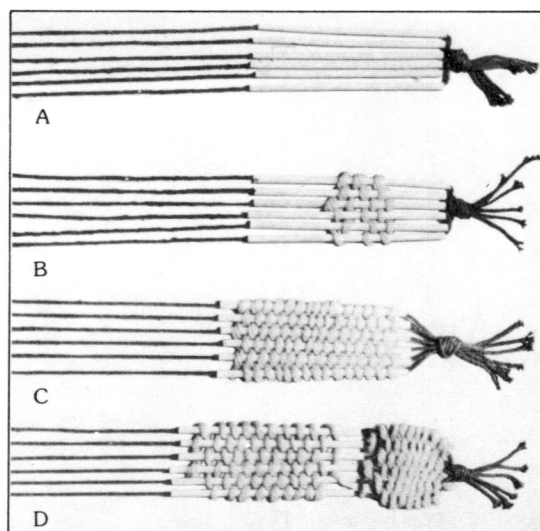

Procedure: For straw weaving, cut drinking straws in half and cut one warp string for each straw. Strings should be equal in length and as long as the finished product will be. Tie all the warp strings together in a knot. Place the knotted end of warp at the top of the straws, then thread each string though a separate straw. Suck on the straw to get the string through easily. Push the straws up to the knotted ends (Photo A). Weave over and under the straws, beginning a pattern (Photos B and C). Add new color by tying a knot to the previous color and continue the weaving. As the weaving progresses, push the woven section up and off the straws, freeing them for more weaving (Photo D). Slip the straws off the warp when the weaving is finished. Weave the end strings into one another so they will not ravel.

Variations: Use several strands of warp through each straw. Since this provides for additional warp threads, more intricate weaving is possible.

From *Weaving Without a Loom*

Those trying to explain pictures are as a rule completely mistaken.
PABLO PICASSO

CHILDREN AS ARTISTS

Process, Not Product

Kids' approach to art is quite different from the adult notion of art as aesthetics. Kids are trying to figure out the world around them, they're really wrestling with ideas of space and ideas of representing things. Often their drawings are not meant to be a final product. They *can* be finished products, but in most cases the drawings are attempts to figure things out, to explore various media, to examine geometric relationships.

When adults say "What a perfectly beautiful picture," that's usually not what the kid was waiting to hear. And if that product keeps being valued, then the kid starts setting out to make a beautiful picture for Mommy, instead of exploring her or his own world.

For kids it probably shouldn't even be called art. It should be called painting, or whatever the activity is. To the kid the activity is what's important: it *is* painting, it's not *a* painting.
BECKY CORWIN

But Sometimes It's the Product That Counts with the Kid

I don't like how-to-draw books either, but the ones by Ed Emberley (Little, Brown paperbacks, 95 cents) are better than most. He starts with a simple shape and shows many things that can be drawn from that one shape. His books have a sense of humor, are not rigidly prescriptive, and help give confidence and free the spirit. Drawings don't have to come out perfectly at all, and the material is usually what kids want to draw (especially his *Little Drawing Book of Weirdos,* which includes vampires, goblins, cats, monsters, witches, werewolves, devils). The step-by-step method also helps reinforce left-to-right movement for reading and writing, and gives kids an interesting opportunity to learn and use the basic geometric shapes.
ALLAN SHEDLIN, JR.

Hidden Messages

Through my child's artwork I have been able to discover many things about him. He is able to express his emotions while developing his drawing skills. Although at three years old, my boy's artwork does not look like much, when I ask him to tell me about it, it is amazing what all the different squiggles become. They really mean something to him. If he has gotten in trouble, he might say he has drawn a boy crying. If he misses his father, who is a fire fighter, he usually will draw a fire engine with his dad driving and the Dalmatian puppy beside him.
MRS. PAUL GRANT

Getting the Artwork Out of the House Without Hurt Feelings . . .

If your kid produces at least one painting, collage, or other masterwork every day, the accumulation may be more than any household can bear. Encourage sending it out to friends and relatives immediately. Save the cardboard tubes from paper towel rolls—they make fine mailers for rolled-up drawings and paintings.
ELS

. . . Or Soothing Hurt Feelings After the Artwork's Gone

My son told me he was unhappy because Mommy had thrown away some drawings he had made for her. I told him that it wasn't because Mommy didn't like them, that she'd thrown them away because she did not like to clutter her room with a lot of things. When I saw that this explanation wasn't really satisfactory, I hit upon the following:

"You know, David, Mommy is like a turtle. Turtles carry everything they need with them on their backs and don't have room for anything else. You are like a squirrel."

He thought for a minute, and then said, "Yeah, I'm like a squirrel because I like to save things. Mommy's like a turtle because she doesn't."

From then on, he wasn't unhappy about our not always saving the little things he'd given us.
TERRY LANGENDOEN

"They Always Need to Have Things Explained"

Once when I was six years old I saw a magnificent picture in a book, called *True Stories from Nature,* about the primeval forest. It was a picture of a boa constrictor in the act of swallowing an animal. Here is a copy of the drawing.

In the book it said: "Boa constrictors swallow their prey whole, without chewing it. After that they are not able to move, and they sleep through the six months that they need for digestion."

I pondered deeply, then, over the adventures of the jungle. And after some work with a colored pencil I succeeded in making my first drawing. My Drawing Number One. It looked like this:

I showed my masterpiece to the grown-ups, and asked them whether the drawing frightened them.

But they answered: "Frighten? Why should anyone be frightened by a hat?"

My drawing was not a picture of a hat. It was a picture of a boa constrictor digesting an elephant. But since the grown-ups were not able to understand it, I made another drawing: I drew the inside of the boa constrictor, so that the grown-ups could see it clearly. They always need to have things explained. My Drawing Number Two looked like this:

The grown-ups' response, this time, was to advise me to lay aside my drawings of boa constrictors, whether from the inside or the outside, and devote myself instead to geography, history, arithmetic and grammar. That is why, at the age of six, I gave up what might have been a magnificent career as a painter.

ANTOINE DE SAINT-EXUPÉRY
The Little Prince

Reproducing Children's Art

If you want to send reproductions of your children's artwork and writing to relatives or close friends, various methods are available:

Mimeographing and dittoing. These duplicating processes are probably available in your child's school, and are the least expensive way to reproduce medium quantities of simple artwork or writing. After one copies the drawing, writing, or tracing onto a stencil, the work is then printed on white or colored paper. Fifty copies should cost less than a dollar.

Photocopying. Photocopying machines are to be found in libraries, drugstores, office supply stores, and print shops. Prices vary from 2 cents to 25 cents, based on the number of copies desired.

For artwork, wet copy machines (Olivetti, Minolta) enable you to get adequate reproduction of color tones and shades of gray that would be lost on many dry copiers. Dry copy machines (IBM, Royalfax) retain black areas that would drop out or fade with other copiers.

For writing, dry copy machines are best, because wet copy machines will give a grayish tone to the reproduction.

Offset printing. If you want to use your child's artwork for the cover of a family Chanukah or Christmas card, offset printing will give you a high-quality reproduction for a reasonable price. Offset reproduction may be done in one to four colors. It is most economical in quantities of fifty and above. A printer makes an inexpensive copy of the drawing or work on a paper plate or a metal plate, and uses the plate to print copies. Metal is more expensive, but enables the printer to do more accurate reproductions of photographs, color artwork (with distinctive forms and contrasting tones), and pencil drawings. Simple line drawings, handwriting, and sharply contrasted pictures (even photographs) may be reproduced satisfactorily by paper-plate offset.

Card-stock paper, which is heavier than regular paper, can be used in both kinds of offset printing. To make greeting cards featuring your children's artwork, divide a sheet of paper in half, horizontally or vertically; the children can draw on the right half or the bottom half, and the work can be run off by a printer on a variety of colored stocks. All metal-plate and some paper-plate offset printers can enlarge or reduce the size of drawings to make them fit in a particular space.

Fifty card-stock pages should run about $6 for paper offset. One hundred regular-paper reproductions can average $3.50 to $5.50. Metal plate averages considerably more, and there are added costs when screens of photographs and complex drawings are required as an intermediate printing step.

BYRON PREISS

Pictures Can Be Reproduced on Plates, Too

Those plastic plates with your kid's very own drawing are a nice idea, but they can be expensive. Here's how it works:

You send $3.95 to Small Fry Originals, Plastics Manufacturing Company, 2700 South Westmoreland, Dallas, Texas 75224. They send you a Small Fry Originals Kit, which includes color markers and enough specially treated paper for up to 50 drawings. You send $1.25 along with each completed design (plus $2 postage and handling for one to ten drawings, a charge which they omit from the original brochure that describes the kit). Each drawing is molded to a plastic plate, which they send you in about a month (longer if it's around Christmas or Mother's Day). Buying from Small Fry Originals makes more sense if you do it with a group so you can share the kit and handling costs.

ALLAN SHEDLIN, JR.

Kiddie Kreations, 906 North Woodward Ave., Royal Oak, Mich. 48067, has a similar operation for 10-ounce thermal insulated drinking mugs (minimum order: 14 mugs). Seven ninety-five buys you the kit and the first four completed mugs (including postage). —Eds.

PRINTING

Demystifying Print

Children often think that anything in print is necessarily true. When they begin printing their own stories or books on a simple press, they come to see that the printed text is only a legible, easily reproduced version of something they themselves may have thought, said, or written. It is only as accurate as the words they themselves set in type—and perhaps invented. Thus the printing process becomes simply a useful tool, and any printed matter, no longer magic, can be read critically.

From *Children and Printing*
Published by Educational Development Corp.

Printing Supplies

You can print with just about anything; it's just a question of figuring out how. If you can make ink adhere to a surface, you can print with it. Thumbs, potatoes and other vegetables, erasers and sponges are what most people think of, but you can print with leaves, with bolts and screws, with an eggbeater or a potato masher. Dip the surface into paint or water-base ink (which you can buy in large cans in art supply stores—the little tubes are pretty expensive), and then print.

Other printing tools:

Alphabet stamps from the five-and-ten.

Styrofoam meat trays. Indentations can be carved on the convex side with a fingernail or a pencil. Mix tempera paint with Ivory Flakes (to make it adhere better) and spread it on the Styrofoam block. A paintbrush might fill in all the indentations, so it may be worth buying a proper tool to spread the paint or ink more easily and evenly.

Stamp pads are useful. The only problem is that the ink on the pre-inked pads isn't washable. You can buy blank pads and ink them yourself with washable ink.

An X-Acto knife for carving on erasers, etc. Any knife, of course, will do, but X-Actos are made for carving.

SUSAN KANOR

Stamps: Beyond A to Z

Geyer Instructional Aids (P.O. Box 7306, Fort Wayne, Ind. 46807) is a source for some amazing printing stamps: the ubiquitous circle, a multipurpose grid, a U.S. map. Others are more bizarre: a human skeleton six inches tall, or cross-sections of grasshoppers, eyeballs, plants, molars.

BECKY CORWIN

Charette (31 Olympia Avenue, Woburn, Mass. 01801) has plexiglass stamps of people, trucks, cars, and all kinds of trees (from the tops, from the sides, with leaves, without leaves). Architects use them to stamp plans, but kids could stamp miniature forests in their rooms or on their letters. Each stamp is around $3 (it can get expensive), but if you know a kid who is really interested in printing, this is a great gift. [Charette has another shop at 212 East 54th Street, New York, N.Y. 10022.]

BECKY CORWIN

The Workshop for Learning Things (5 Bridge Street, Watertown, Mass. 02172) has printing materials, from basic $8.25 sets to beautifully crafted $189 printing press kits. Their catalogue is 50 cents.

RS

Two Good Books About Printing

TAKE A HANDFUL OF LETTERS, *by Amy Orvell, illustrated by Kathleen Broderick (Education Development Center, 1974, $2.50 paperback).*

The introduction to this book about printing with homemade letters reveals its encouraging style and charm: "There is a tradition that when a Jewish child was introduced to study, he was given a slate covered with honey. As he licked the honey, the alphabet appeared. So the child learned to associate learning with sweetness. This book is intended to be in that tradition." And it is.—Eds.

FROM COVER TO COVER: PUBLISHING IN YOUR CLASSROOM *(an 11-page leaflet free from Encyclopaedia Britannica Educational Corp., Instructional Services Dept., 425 N. Michigan Avenue, Chicago, Ill. 60611).*

In case you're envisioning mammoth presses and a class register . . . think again. Publications can take the form of displays and charts as well as booklets and class newspapers. [*From Cover to Cover*] suggests briefly some of the mechanics of putting together publishing ventures.

From *Learning* magazine

PHOTOGRAPHY, VIDEO, AND FILM

Let us not delude ourselves by the seemingly scientific nature of the darkroom ritual; it has been and always will be a form of alchemy. Our overly precious attitude toward that ritual has tended to conceal from us an innermost world of mystery, enigma, and insight. Once in the darkroom the venturesome mind and spirit should be set free—free to search and hopefully discover.

JERRY HELSMANN
An Aperture Monography

Exploring the Camera

Before attempting to load film, take the time to thoroughly explore the camera. Take off the back. Turn any part that will turn; click anything that will click. Try to guess the function of each part before reading any instructions. When you begin to read, keep the camera handy and refer to it as you go along.

From *The Camera Cookbook*
Published by the Workshop for Learning Things

My Son, the (Flip) Movie Producer

Remember those little flip movie books? You'd run your finger along the edge of the pages, and a little animated "movie" would spring to life before your eyes.

When Brian was a child, not too many years back, he realized that he could make his own flip movies. He merely got some small white scratch pads and, starting at the back, drew little cartoons on each page, the action on each page being slightly advanced over that in the previous drawing. If your children like to draw, they can have hours of fun designing and making flip movies, starting simply—a rolling ball, a walking person or animal—and working up to more complicated actions or to something like one color gradually fading into another. Experiment.

JANET GARI

A Real Camera for Under $3

The Workshop for Learning Things has a little plastic camera styled after the ones given away at carnivals in Hong Kong. It's designed like a single-lens reflex camera: it has a lens cap, an adjustment for three light settings, and an adjustment for three distance settings, and it uses standard 120 black-and-white film (widely available in camera stores, but not in drugstores). If you drop it, one out of ten times it will break; and if you leave it on the radiator overnight it will melt. But the quality of the photographs produced by kids at the Workshop is high for the price.

When I gave this camera to a six-year-old, his initial enthusiasm (he was quite beside himself, really) faded only a little when he found the camera difficult to use (he couldn't load it himself, and his first roll resulted in blank negatives). A year later he still loves the camera, and about half his shots are printable. Perhaps it's a more appropriate gift for an older child, or for kids working with adult supervision.

Order from the Workshop for Learning Things, 5 Bridge Street, Watertown, Mass.

02172, $2.95 plus $1 postage and handling. Inexpensive, primitive darkroom materials, as well as a camera book by kids for kids, are available from the Workshop's catalogue.

RS

And a Real Camera for About $25

At three and a half, Muki loves the Kodak Pocket Instamatic. She doesn't have to do anything but look through the lens and press the button. The image is outlined, and the camera is light enough for her to carry. There is a big red button that you snap for the picture. And another little lever that you push to advance the film. All I have to say is "Keep the camera still and make sure you have Grandma in the box."

Three and a half isn't too young to have a camera. Some of the toys on the market are far more complicated than an Instamatic, and Muki understands that you can't throw a camera on the floor. The little Fisher-Price plastic camera, which they say is for ages three to six, operates on the same principle, but it's not real.

MARIE BROWN

Resources for People Doing Media with Kids

DOING THE MEDIA: A PORTFOLIO OF ACTIVITIES AND RESOURCES, *edited by Kit Laybourne and Pauline Ciancolo for the Center for Understanding Media (McGraw-Hill, 1978, $6.95 paperback).*

This is the best sourcebook for a wide range of media activities—from very simple ones requiring no sophisticated hardware, like "scratch and doodle film-making," to photography, super 8-mm. and 16-mm. film-making, and video—collected from a variety of teachers who have worked with kids on media projects.

VIDEO & KIDS, *an issue of the magazine* Radical Software *by the Center for Understanding Media (Gordon & Breach, 1 Park Avenue, New York, N.Y. 10016, 1974, 68 pages, $6.95).*

The same people who put together *Doing the Media* focus here on video exclusively.

TEACHING FILM ANIMATION TO CHILDREN, *by Yvonne Andersen (out of print; available in libraries),* and MAKE YOUR OWN ANIMATED MOVIES, *by Yvonne Andersen (Little, Brown, 1970, 101 pages, $6.95 hardcover).*

Film animation is one of the most popular and

satisfying media for kids. These books, one for teachers, the other for children, are the best aids in the field, written by the director of the Yellow Ball Workshop in Lexington, Mass.

BEING WITH CHILDREN, *by Philip Lopate (Bantam Books, 1976, 448 pages, $1.95 paperback).*

Read this one for its attitude toward working in media with kids, by a Teachers and Writers Collaborative poet who does it. It's accurately subtitled "A Highly Spirited Personal Account of Teaching Writing, Theater, & Videotape."

RS

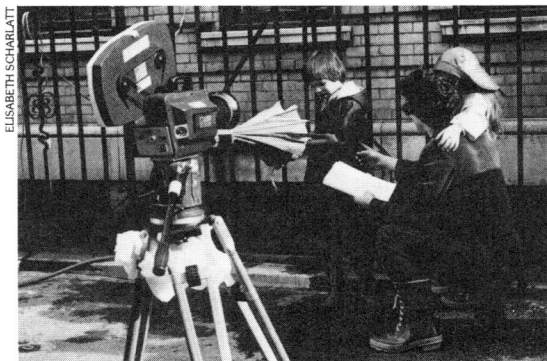

Audiences for Young Creators

PRINT AND GRAPHICS

Stone Soup. Elementary school children can submit poems, stories, plays, book reviews, and graphics to this fine magazine of children's literature, published five times each year. (A one-year subscription costs $8.50.) All work submitted should be labeled with the name, age, and address of the contributor, and should be accompanied by a self-addressed stamped envelope. Send submissions to *Stone Soup,* Box 83, Santa Cruz, Calif. 95063.

Shankar International Painting and Writing Competition. Over fifty children under sixteen years of age win medals, small prizes, and publication in an annual book of winning entries. For more information, write to the Shankar International Painting Competition, % *Shankar's Weekly,* Barakhambha Road, New Delhi, India.

VIDEO, FILM, AND AUDIO TAPES

Cable television companies, libraries, and *museums.* These are the places to contact about local audiences for videotapes and films produced by kids. *Note:* When you call a cable TV company, ask about time on public access and local origination channels.

Youth Film Distribution Center. The Center's catalogue of over 150 16-mm. films by young people is used by libraries, museums, community centers, and hospitals, among others. For a sample contract and other information, write to the Youth Film Distribution Center, 43 West 16th Street, New York, N.Y. 10011.

Young People's Radio Festival. Young people between the ages of six and eighteen who write, produce, and direct their own radio program can enter reel-to-reel tapes or cassettes in this contest, sponsored by National Public Radio and its member stations. Tapes should be under fifteen minutes in length, and should not be straight reproductions of music (even original music). News, documentaries, interviews, drama, sound portraits of your favorite places are the types of programming eligible for this contest. Prizes for local winners vary from community to community, but all local winners can hear their programs on a local radio broadcast. First-place local winners in three age categories (6–10, 11–14, and 15–18) are entered in the national festival. National winners in each age category are awarded cash prizes of $500, $300, and $200 for first, second, and third prizes, and their tapes are played on a nationwide Young People's Radio Festival Broadcast.

For more information, and guidelines on format, contact your local Public Radio Station or write to Young People's Radio Festival, National Public Radio, 2025 M Street, N.W., Washington, D.C. 20036. The annual deadline for entering tapes is usually sometime in January.

—RS

BUILDING MODELS

Model Rocketry: An Insider's Guide

I first started making model rockets when I was about nine years old (I'm now sixteen). My brother had sent away for a catalogue from Estes Industries and when it came we ordered rockets, engines, and a devilish device called the "electro-launch." (The Estes catalogue costs 35 cents. You can get it by writing to P.O. Box 227, Penrose, Colo. 81240.)

The theory behind model rockets always seemed reasonably straightforward. You took a long hollow cardboard tube for the body, traced and cut out some fins from a balsa wood sheet, sanded them, glued them to the body tube, attached something resembling a long rubber band cut open (called a "shock" cord) to the body tube, took a smooth lump of balsa, for a nose cone, and connected it to the other end of the shock cord by means of a screw eye. You then had but to cut a parachute out of very thin plastic film, rig it up with six cords of equal length, tie them together and tie it all to the screw eye. The rocket then, of course, needed to be finished, which involved brushing on countless coats of "sanding sealer," sanding between each coat, finishing finally with four coats of white paint and two coats of the color paint you had chosen. All that remained was to stuff some flameproof wadding down in the body tube, add the parachute and its cords and the shock cord, and fit in the nose cone.

Now the rocket was just about ready to be launched, missing only the thing to make it go—the engine. You selected your engine, taking into account rocket weight, wind, and a couple of other factors I'll mention later. You wrapped the engine with tape (to make it fit snugly), shoved it into the rear end of the body tube, and lastly, and with great precision, inserted an igniter into the business end of the engine. Then you took your fully "prepped" rocket, placed it over the launch rod onto the electro-launch pad, connected two micro-clips to the igniter leads, stepped back, inserted your "safety interlock" key into your controller, counted down from ten, and pressed the launch button.

STOP! I said back near the beginning that this *seemed* reasonably straightforward, didn't I? Well, let me tell you right now, this is not the way to go about model rocketry. I know, because for the first two years of my model rocketry career I did it the way I described above and I had a grand total of *one* successful launch. But I got wise, and I'm going to share my knowledge with you, the uninitiated.

Do not, I repeat, *do not*, get any device which, like the electro-launch, uses flashlight batteries to supply the power to the igniters. The batteries just don't have what it takes to get that igniter glowing. Get a launch system that has two big clamps designed to clip onto the terminals of an automobile battery. When I couldn't get my electro-launch to work, I went out and bought the other kind, and on the first subsequent launch attempt that rocket fairly *jumped* off the pad. One other note: tie the safety interlock key onto a good piece of string, and tie the string onto something you can't lose, like your neck. I'm serious. If you lose that tiny key, the whole system is useless until you get another key.

Next let's talk about the related topics of engine size and launch area. Estes Industries makes a particular rocket engine given the name "C6-5," which you should beware of. After using this engine on five successive launches and losing five successive rockets I began to think surely this engine was not meant to power *model* rockets! I finally got a rocket back using a C6-5, but it was a huge rocket and it still went 500 feet high. My final conclusion about C6-5's is that they are useful for one main purpose: if you have a rocket that you don't like (and *everyone* has at least one) put in a C6-5 and launch it. You'll never see it again.

Surprisingly enough, and quite contrary to what the model rocketry catalogues say, the size of the launch area doesn't matter at all. I have launched rockets in fields that were gigantic and I still lost them. They were usually the rockets I had built the most carefully, with the most coats of lovingly applied sealer and paint. A couple of years ago, near the end of my rocketry career, some friends and I got together and launched my remaining rockets in a backyard. The yard was literally ten feet square and we had to aim between the trees. After launching three rockets flawlessly and catching them as they neatly floated down between the branches, I started to get hysterical. For years I had been losing rockets in huge fields, and here they were coming back to me like homing pigeons. I had even used a C6-5 and the thing came back! In a last act of daring, I used an engine with twice as much power as the C6-5, the renowned D12-7, which delivers *nine pounds* of thrust, and I was sure that that rocket would be gone forever. Would you believe that the rocket, trailing a long orange streamer, dropped down not thirty feet from the launch pad!

I do have one secret which I didn't mention. The one thing all these rockets had in common was this: they were all poorly built, with terrible paint jobs. It may have become apparent what I'm leading up to. *Don't* spend a lot of time making your rockets if you want to get them back, and don't think you have to have acres and acres of field to launch them in. The best rockets to watch are the ones that look the cruddiest on the ground; remember this when you're building yours. (Nevertheless, a friend of mine launched a really ugly cluster rocket—one with three engines that fired at once—and because of some faulty workmanship it shot sideways for 100 feet and set fire to an acre of ground.) Use moderation, and if you want to, you might even occasionally work hard on a rocket and win with it at a hobby show. Just don't ever get the urge to launch it, because you're not likely to ever see it again.

ADAM GUSSOW

The Mattel Super Star Sky Show Plane (Damn It, I Love It!)

At first glance, the Mattel Super Star Sky Show Plane appears to be just about *everything* we consumers have learned we're supposed to avoid in a toy. It's expensive (over $20). It looks pretty flimsy (lots of thin plastic). It requires the use of a 6-volt battery, which, needless to say, is not included in the package. And it comes unassembled, which, for me, at least, automatically meant I'd never have it in one piece.

Seeing the sad look on my face as I stared at the components of my plane, my wife, Geneviève, took pity on me. (She's a Phi Beta Kappa, majored in physics and is halfway toward a Ph.D. in electrical engineering; thus, she's better qualified to put Mattel Super Star Sky Show Planes together than I am.) In less than an hour she had it assembled, and, to my surprise, she reported that (a) she'd had fun doing it, (b) it had been *truly* easy, and (c) the directions were remarkably clear and simple. Furthermore, she told me, the so-called "power plant" of the plane was intriguing: you charged the plane with a battery for a few seconds before you launched it; then, after you removed the wires, the engine would be ready to run for a certain specified fraction of the time you'd charged it.

The instructions said it was a big mistake to fly the Super Star Sky Show Plane on "very windy days." We checked outside. It was a very windy day. We shrugged, grabbed the plane, the 6-volt battery, and the "charging clip" and ventured out into the wind.

The Mattel Super Star Sky Show Plane comes with four flight plans: little circular plastic wheels whose irregular saw-tooth circumferences supposedly program its maneuvers in the air. We had selected one that would turn the plane in a tight squared-off circle around its launch point. Now we charged the plane for thirty seconds, removed the clip, faced into the gale and let fly.

To our amazement the plane leaped into the sky. Then, right according to plan, it banked for its first left turn. Suddenly a particularly strong gust caught it and flipped it over in midair. The plane went into a steep upside-down dive, narrowly missed the house next door, then, six feet off the ground, it abruptly righted itself and soared off for parts unknown. Across the road it flew, over the houses on the other side, pushed by its mighty tailwind toward the tidal swamp beyond.

Lack of space prevents me from recording here the details of the rescue of my Mattel Super Star Sky Show Plane from the mud flats of Shinnecock Bay by my friend Henry Beard. Suffice it to say that (a) the plane, flimsy though it looked, suffered no damage in its crash landing; that (b) overpriced though it may be, it still managed to provide me with many happy moments; and that (c) Mattel may be absolutely right to admonish us against windy-day flights, but the adventurous would do well to disregard their warning.

CBC

Two Books on the Paper Airplane

HOW TO MAKE AND FLY PAPER AIRPLANES, *by Captain Ralph Stanton Barnaby (Four Winds Press, 1969, $5.95 hardcover; Bantam, 1970, $1.25 paperback).*

Written by the man who won the *Scientific American* paper airplane contest, this is by far the best book on the subject. It's easy to read, and its organization—from very simple to complicated—gives you the history of the paper airplane. He starts off with dropping a piece of paper to see what happens, then builds up to instructions for making your first paper airplane. You start flying the paper as a wing, then you start adding things, bending the back of it; then you put a fold in the center so it has some stability and flies straight. Barnaby shows how the paper airplane relates to a real airplane. He discusses launching and actually flying a plane. You can read this book straight through; it's a crafts manual that is also interesting as a book. Though it shows you how to make a number of different planes, it does not offer the variety of the *Scientific American* book [see below].

STEVEN CANEY

THE GREAT INTERNATIONAL PAPER AIRPLANE BOOK, *by Jerry Mander, George*

Dippel, and Howard Gossage (Simon and Schuster, 1967, 128 pages, $2.95 paperback).

With good-humored fillers, this large-format paperback presents twenty of the 1,200 entries in the *Scientific American* first international paper airplane competition. It features photographs and scaled patterns on perforated pages. RS

[Can a kid who's fascinated by the joinings of the mast or the angle of a wing be equally fascinated with the parts of the human body? See page 47 for details on the Visible Man and Visible Woman.]

William Accorsi sells his model airplanes for $25 and up (Accorsi, 71 Irving Place, New York, N.Y. 10003). You could probably make something like this yourself (cigar boxes provide good wood for this purpose). Models needn't come in a kit.

Aurorasaurus

Ever since my son Jeremy visited the dinosaur hall at the Museum of Natural History in New York, he's had a passion for dinosaurs. We've tried several different kinds of models, and the best have been from Aurora, most of which are in the $2.50 to $6 range, although some go as high as $15. The pieces snap together, and although you can cement them, you don't have to. (The cheaper plastic models that require cement, the ones that sell for under $1.50, are really cheapo and I wouldn't recommend them.)

I have the usual parental complaints about Aurora: the pictures on the package are a lot more glamorous than the actual models, and the craftsmanship is mediocre. But for the most part Jeremy's been satisfied (except for Aurora's Cave Bear, which was made out of cheaper plastic and was tiny in comparison to some of the other models).

We also tried some of the motorized plastic models that sell for around $3 in the five-and-ten. They sounded terrific but they didn't work, and were dangerous—kids could get their fingers caught in the motor mechanism.

KAREN FREEDMAN

PARENT'S LAMENT

Here I am, a Ph.D. in thermonuclear dynamics, and I can't put together my child's model. How many more $3.99s will we spend on these before we realize they just don't fit together.

EMILY SHAW

TOOLS AND CARPENTRY

What Is a Tool?

While I was interviewing her father one day in the park, Tonia Kohl sat quietly with a piece of broken glass she'd picked up from the ground and whittled a piece of twig for at least an hour.

ELS

. . . And What Isn't a Tool

There's a thing out in the world called a child's hammer. To swing that tiny little hammer hard enough to be able to put a real nail into a real piece of wood would take a giant of a person. (In fact, I know several people who weigh well over 200 pounds and none of them has ever been able to drive a nail with a child's hammer.) So the child's hammer is a fraud, absolutely impossible, and over the years must have caused an enormous amount of frustration.

GEORGE COPE

Carpentry Tools: What You Need

When you buy tools for your kid it's best to do it in stages. Rather than buying a tool box with an entire set of tools, give a child one tool at a time, and a week or so to experience that tool, to learn how to use it. A hammer is a good one to start with. Get a bag of different kinds of nails and some scrap wood and show the child how to hold the hammer. Almost all kids will hold it too near the head, so show her or him where to hold it, and then to hammer with the wrist, not with the whole arm. After your child has worked with the hammer for a while, you might move on to a saw. And later you can get a screwdriver (younger children often can't manipulate a screwdriver) or a wrench and adjustable pliers.

Find someone in your area who is building and go pick up some scraps of wood to work with. In our house the Saturday project is to get a new supply of scrap wood and throw out the old used-up supply.

STEVEN CANEY

A Kid's Own Tools

Although our six-year-old shares most of our adult equipment with us (stereo, cooking utensils, etc.), I think it's important for him to have his own collection of hand tools—tools he can use safely and effectively and can learn to care for himself. Some I recommend for kids who are ready:

A good woodworking vise can add to the ease and safety of almost every tool operation—sawing, screwing, planing, drilling, sanding, filing, joining. Parents tempted to skip this investment should remember that the vise will help prevent needless medical bills. A number of fixed and portable woodworking vises are available in tool and hardware stores. A portable vise in the $5 to $12 range that opens up 2¾ inches to 3½ inches is adequate and easy to find. The jaws of the more expensive vises usually open up the widest and may be faced with pressed wood to protect the wood being worked. If you select a less expensive vise and are worried about marring the wood to be clamped in it, you can place or glue a piece of shirt cardboard alongside the inner jaw surfaces.

Clamps are good to have around even if you have a vise. They can hold together pieces that are to be glued and can serve as an extra vise when your kid has a friend over. C-clamps are commonly used for holding wood but require placing scrap wood under the jaws to protect good wood surfaces. A clamp that opens to 3 or 4 inches is a good starting size for general woodworking ($1.50 to $3 each depending on size and source), and smaller ones (under $1) are good for working on models and other small projects.

A *simple pocketknife* is another first tool of great use to a child. Often overlooked in the hardware store collection, its potential for direct and satisfying action is excellent, even for a four- or five-year-old. Some models, e.g., Swiss Army knives, have two knife blades and a saw blade (the saw works quite well for small pieces of wood secured in a vise). When choosing a pocketknife for a young child, make sure it opens and closes without snapping.

Compass or keyhole saws are excellent for straight rip and crosscutting by small persons who cannot safely and comfortably work alone with the familiar large rip and crosscut saws.

A *coping saw* ($4.50 and up) is most often used for curves, inside cuts, or intricate jigsaw cuts. Most models have a 5- to 7-inch-deep throat. The depth of the throat determines how far the blade can cut into the wood before the saw frame hits the wood edge—i.e., the deeper the throat, the farther you can cut before being stopped. Coping saws use pin-end blades, available by the package in several sizes (65 to 75 cents for a package of five).

The British fret saw does the same tasks as the coping saw but has some advantages for children. It sells for $6.25, has a 12-inch-deep throat, and 5-inch or 6-inch blades, which are easily replaceable and are available in two forms—the single edge and the spiral. The single-edge pinless blades are sold as jeweler's saw blades (package of ten costs $1.20 in a wide variety of sizes) or as jigsaw blades. Spiral blades, by virtue of their design—basically a "roughed up" wire—will not cut fingers. Fret saws and spiral blades, often not stocked in small hardware stores, are available by mail order from Constantine & Son, 2050 Eastchester Road, Bronx, N.Y. 10461. Write for a catalogue (50 cents).

Power tools, unlike hand tools, are adult tools and should be treated as such. If a parent feels a power tool is in order, I think the one that a child can use most safely—after thorough instruction and careful supervision—is a power scroll or jigsaw. These tabletop tools are quiet, have a super-safe blade guard, and permit straight cutting or intricate scroll work.

Before purchasing such an electric tool for a child, however, try to assess how much the child wants it. When I asked my six-year-old if he wanted an electric saw he said, "Well, maybe, sometime—but I really like working with my hands best." SALLY LANGENDOEN

For $20 you can get a pretty good two-speed, ¼-inch drill; something like a Millers Falls drill is reliable. A single-speed, ¼-inch drill is cheaper—you can get one for around $12—but it's very hard for a kid to handle because the fast start makes it difficult to get the hole started. (The size indicates the largest bit shank the drill will hold. There are ½- and ⅜-inch drills, but for kids get the ¼-inch.)

WILLIAM ACCORSI

THE TINY CARPENTER
A cardboard carton is great for hammering nails into for little kids who want to hammer and can't make it with wood. (Besides, wood is hard to have around all the time.) My three-year-old discovered this and used three-inch nails with large heads. Further, if your kid wants to saw and you don't mind giving her a turn, a cardboard box is the place to start. ELS

◆

The Jigsaw, Pro and Con

I find the jigsaw to be very fragile and hard to keep running. It's okay for a professional who knows what he can and can't do, but for someone with little experience with tools it's not much good. The minute it's pushed too far, the tiny thin blade snaps. GEORGE COPE

I've talked to a few people whose kids are as young as six and use a jigsaw. (They break blades, just as adults do, but they have such a good time working with the machine it's worth it.) It's a great experience for kids, because it can give them a sense of mastery, which is important in our culture. You can use many different blades, from very heavy to extremely fine, which enable you to cut just about anything, metal as well as wood. And you can cut just as you have drawn—very precisely.

WILLIAM ACCORSI

I think a jigsaw is safer and easier to use than a saber saw, which is portable—that is, you run it through a fixed piece of wood. With a jigsaw, you feed the wood into a stationary machine, and it's just easier to steer a piece of wood (and keep your fingers out of the way of the blade) than it is to steer a machine like a saw. You have more control since you can feed the wood as slowly as you like.

SALLY LANGENDOEN

The jigsaw to buy: You can spend a lot of money, but the best jigsaw for the lowest price, according to William Accorsi, is the Dremel #572, 60 cycles, 1.2 amp, 115 volts. It doesn't take a lot of electricity. The basic model (including rubber backing pad and adaptor, three sanding discs, four blades) costs around $50. A deluxe kit with additional attachments runs about $60.—Eds.

Using Tools Safely

Kids can learn a lot about the relative safety or danger of tools by experimenting a little. A good place to begin is down on the floor, with everybody sitting cross-legged. Let them "play" with the tools—and learn which instrument stabs, which scratches, which pinches—until it's not so scary.

You can build in some safety devices. For instance, get a castoff cardboard barrel with a metal lid at your local dump, then place cardboard or wood across the top of the barrel so you can saw with an electric saw; then, even if you saw straight toward you, when the blade hits the metal rim it will stop.

When children cut themselves with saws, it's usually not because they can't control the saws but because they can't control the wood they are trying to saw. There are several simple ways to hold a piece of wood firmly: clamps and vises, of courses, and also bench hooks (perpendicular structures that hold the wood; if the saw slips, it goes into the bench hook, not the other hand).

After getting kids used to tools, and employing whatever safety devices you can, you have to let the kids go. It's not the most relaxing thing in the world to stand around and watch a five- or six-year-old start to use a saw, but I know from experience that the best thing to do is turn around and walk away. Be near in case help is needed. But don't stand there and look over the kid's shoulder directing.

GEORGE COPE

HOW KIDS LEARN TO USE TOOLS

Learning by Imitating

Dad was . . . a city-boy intellectual who knew from nothing about houses. We bought an absolute leaky lemon of obsolete sub-code-standard construction. And over a decade of work and family hassle rebuilt it from top to bottom. As I went to bed, I saw him hunched over the midnight dining table, studying the government pamphlet on how to do electric wiring. And over slow afternoon years helping him, I learned how to shingle and sheetrock, plumb and stud, and care for the tools that gave us some power to change things. . . . The process of my learning was precisely this: I watched and questioned and imitated a person who was himself good at learning, and who was . . . not a specialist of skilled routine, but an amateur learning newly and rawly.

MICHAEL ROSSMAN
On Learning and Social Change

From Doghouse to Dream House

I can remember specific things that happened to me as a kid that, I think, made a big difference in my life. For example, when my dog needed a new doghouse my father and I sat down and drew up plans for what we wanted it to look like. And then we went and bought the lumber at the sawmill. I was just a little kid, barely able to hold a hammer, but Dad would have me hold a nail and then he'd pound it in and then he'd hold one and let me try to pound it in. And we'd cut the boards out and he'd saw a little bit, and then he'd say that he was tired and I had to finish it. We just built the damn thing together. He let me roof it by myself.

We built a really big doghouse. All of the neighborhood kids would come over and we'd sit around inside there with the dog and talk.

I know for sure that building with my father gave me enough confidence, years later, to go ahead and spend two years building my own house.

ELIOT WIGGINTON

Trial and Error

The way I teach is to try to have the students make as much as they can without too many skills. Let the skills come later. If you let people have the gratification of making something, in time they become fairly skillful.

WILLIAM ACCORSI

Hanging Out

If you live in a town that still has friendly artisans, find out if your child may hang out at the local carpenter's shop for a few hours just to watch. Preferably without you. If you can set up a midday meeting in advance, think about taking along a brown-bag lunch for your kid and for the carpenter.

ELS

◆

Useful Books on Building

WOODWORKING, by Roger Lewis (Knopf, 1952, $1.75 paperback).

Don't be put off by the old-fashioned format of this "father–son activity book." Though it includes a section on "what to make," its most useful (and very well done) feature is the easily understood one-page discussions on tools and equipment; each one is supplemented by a full page of clarifying illustrations—a handy reference format for the beginner. Safety is emphasized throughout, with diagrams showing how to hold a piece of wood correctly and securely in a vise or clamp. The sample below demonstrates the clarity of both text and illustrations.

SALLY LANGENDOEN

To saw a circular hole, first drill a small hole *inside* the circle. Loosen the blade [of the coping saw], and pass one end through the hole. Replace the blade, tighten the handle, and you are ready to saw. Afterwards, loosen the blade and remove it from the wood.

From *Woodworking*

YOU CAN BUILD A TABLE AND A CHAIR TOO!;
NOW YOU NEED A TOOLBOX;
SCOOTERS ARE GROOVY AND YOU CAN BUILD YOUR OWN;
IF YOU'RE READY, HERE'S THE CAR, by Ray Brock (Dell, 1974, paperbacks, $1.50 each).

Each title in this series addresses a single (and increasingly challenging) project. Each builds on the knowledge gained from the task covered in the preceding book. Though written simply

enough for a six-year-old to read, the suggested use of a large saw implies that the builder has to be somewhat older and larger. (You can use a smaller saw to do the projects.) The instructions on the use of a T-square, saw, and hammer, and later, brace and bit, pliers, and chisel and wrench are reasonably clear and relevant to the task at hand, with the general spirit of the books fun-loving and relaxed.

SALLY LANGENDOEN

◆

Cardboard Carpentry

Tri-Wall (³⁄₁₆ inch thick) corrugated cardboard, easy enough for children to work with, is sturdy enough to last in the form of tables, chairs, beds, and stages, not to mention easels, dollhouses, sandboxes, even wagons. To find it, look in the yellow pages under Corrugated, Boxes, Hardware, or Art Supplies. Or write to the Workshop for Learning Things, 5 Bridge Street, Watertown, Mass. 02172, for sources in your area.

The Workshop for Learning Things also has some tools just for cardboard—circle cutters (for wheels), slot cutters, and strip cutters (for repeated cutting of pieces of the same size). George Cope of the Workshop says: "These are indulgences for when you decide that cardboard has changed your life and you want to make a whole lot of things out of it. If you're just getting started in cardboard carpentry, don't buy any tools. Use whatever you have around the house—a paring knife or serrated knife from the kitchen, an old jacknife, an old saw no matter how dull it may be."

RS

Two Good Books on Cardboard Carpentry

BUILDING WITH CARDBOARD, *published by the Early Childhood Education Study (25 pages, $1 from Sales Section, Education Arts Association, 90 Sherman Street, Cambridge, Mass.).*

THE FURTHER ADVENTURES OF CARDBOARD CARPENTRY, *by George Cope and Phylis Morrison, illustrated with black-and-white photographs and line drawings (The Workshop for Learning Things, 5 Bridge Street, Watertown, Mass. 02172, 1973, 72 pages, $4.95).*

These books are recommended for their sound advice on construction with cardboard. The latter also gets high marks for its safety suggestions. For example:

[Cardboard] won't catch fire sitting on the radiator, but it will ignite with a match . . . as readily as a book or a tablet of lined paper. It spreads flame slowly and without excessive smoke. . . . Cardboard's resistance to fire can be further increased, if need be, by painting with a 10–20% solution of Borax and water (although you may not like the resultant milky look very much). Taping exposed edges of cardboard will retard its flame spreading rate, as the ability of the flutings to act like little chimneys is much restricted.

From The Further Adventures of Cardboard Carpentry

◆

To Inspire the Young Builder

ARCHITECTURE: A BOOK OF PROJECTS FOR YOUNG ADULTS, *by Forrest Wilson (Van Nostrand Reinhold, 1968, 96 pages, $8.95 hardcover).*

The first bridge I ever stood under was over a stream in the Catskills. I was trying to keep my new red shorts dry, but somehow the water had other ideas and there I was looking at the undersides of a stone bridge. To my nine-year-old mind, the stones should have been falling into the water. It was a long time before I found out why they didn't. Forrest Wilson's book would have provided the answers—with projects for building bridges and columns and beams out of sugar cubes, cardboard, and the like. The explanations and directions are clear and fascinating, and in those places my nine-year-old vocabulary would have stumbled over a word, the pictures would've had the answers. After careful consultation with my own child, I learned the book is still worth its weight in sugar cubes.

JO BUTLER

CITY, A STORY OF ROMAN PLANNING AND CONSTRUCTION, *by David Macauley (Houghton Mifflin, 1974, $7.95 hardcover).*

City would be a joy for any kid who's at all interested in how things work or how things were. Not only does Macauley transport you back two thousand years and show how a Roman city was built and how its people lived, but he provides endless parallels with our cities and our lives. I mean, who ever thought that ancient Roman cities had their own fast-food chains like McDonald's and Burger King?

City is full of such surprises; rich and endlessly fascinating in its details of life in a typical Roman town. It's a book parents and kids can really share. I found it stimulating, full of things to talk about, and eminently re-readable.

Also wonderful: *Cathedral*, Macauley's similar treatment of the construction of a fictitious Gothic cathedral (Houghton Mifflin, 1973, $9.95).

STEPHEN OLDERMAN

ARCHITECTURE WITHOUT ARCHITECTS, *by Bernard Rudofsky (Museum of Modern Art [distributed by Doubleday], 1964, 143 pages).*

This is an adult book capable of firing the imagination of a child. It is a study of architecture before the experts came along, and the photographs show the "anonymous" or "nonpedigreed" architecture of the world—communities carved in the walls and faces of cliffs, subterranean cultures, Mediterranean hill towns. The terraced mountaintops of Honan in China provide as vivid an example of the differences in culture East and West as any geography lesson could.

PETER ALMOND

THINGS TO BREAK

My child used to build fantastic towers out of blocks, panting with creativity; rest for an instant in triumph; and then, eyes gleaming with delight, step back and explode them all over the room; and then begin again. How many times I choked back my automatic protest—"Aw, don't spoil it!"—before I realized what a foreign sense of values I was forcing on him by wanting to freeze his accomplishments in admiration. He knew quite well that destruction is constructive, and integral to creation.

From the time we stop them from throwing their food on the floor to see the lovely splatter, we are constantly telling kids that their destruc-

tive urges are not just inconvenient, but nasty and creepy and shameful.

When my son and his playgroup were five and a half I let them tear down a plaster wall in the house we are rebuilding. They flailed away for fully ninety minutes with claw hammers and crowbars, exhausting themselves more thoroughly than I'd ever seen them do; then collapsed on the rubble, awed by their power. As was I: they had taken the wall out as high as they could reach, lath and plaster both, and wanted ladders. Now they tumble in the big open room and tell people, "There used to be a wall here; we helped take it out." And I know

they learned something that no creative plaything money can buy can teach.

Your four-year-old will get as much joy and learning from dismembering the clock you pick up for a buck at the junkstore as she will from your average $5 plastic impulse gift. Buy her her own adult-sized hammer and give her the dead toaster, remembering that grown-up people in engineering labs get fancy fees to study materials and stresses by destructive testing. Don't stop with a spectator tour of the city dump; get out with your kids and root around in the trash—they all love it, and for pocket change to the operators they can come away with a carload of busted bicycles to take apart,

maybe to put together into a whole one with a little help.

I like the weekly accumulation behind the electrical engineering lab up on campus. The discarded circuit boards are pure jewelry; kids like using wire clippers to snip the transistors and string them as necklaces, and maybe they won't be so reluctant to understand what goes on inside a television. When their bodies are big enough to use what they learn about leverage, $50 will get them a dead car, the tools to take it apart, and a book to understand it by. Once they get this far in genuine play, it is hard to resist learning how to keep a car running; even before this, the payoff is in growing up less alienated from machines and less helplessly at the mercy of the professional mechanic.

The opportunities for socially useful destruction are harder to arrange. Our playgroup likes to watch streets being torn up and restored, likes to go down to the end of the town to see stripped cars being broken up for scrap, the scrap passing on freight trains to the forge where old steel is hammered to new shapes in blinding sparks. My son helps me take the bottles to the volunteer recycling depot, awaits the day of his initiation into the mystery, when he too can shatter the crystal in the big cans, take his place in this ecology of industry. The full theme of destruction is endlessly creative. We burn our debris and take care to nourish the ground with the ashes, and eat of what it brings forth. And slowly we are learning to make parting and death not into tragedy only, but into the equal celebration of moving on.

MICHAEL ROSSMAN

GOING PLACES
WITH YOUR KIDS

The only true voyage of discovery would not be to visit strange lands, but to possess other eyes, to behold the universe through the eyes of another, of a hundred others —to behold a hundred universes that each of them beholds, that each of them is.

PROUST

IF YOU'RE IN THE NEIGHBORHOOD . . .

San Francisco's Exploratorium

Imagine yourself in darkness. You are making your way through a labyrinth. You crawl and climb up and down tunnels of plastic, sponge, metal, plush. Only your hands can guide you. The convoluted walls lead you to a chute, and you slide down into a chamberful of birdseed. If you can imagine it, you have just experienced a journey through the domed Tactile Gallery at the Exploratorium in San Francisco. The exhibits in this museum are designed to help you establish a relationship with the mechanics of perceptual phenomena. Step into the Shadow Box and with a flash of light your shadow appears on walls of phosphorescent vinyl; talk to a tree and it lights up at the sound of your voice.

The Exploratorium, with over three hundred exhibits, including the staples of every science museum (magnet, prism, battery, generator), invites visitors to investigate the possibilities of lasers, TV side bands, computer graphics. Exhibits are grouped under perceptual categories: light, color, patterns, electricity, sound, third dimension, and touch (the Tactile Gallery). Museum guides, known as "explainers," are available to answer questions, and are trained to elaborate on the more technical aspects of each exhibit's scientific derivation.

There are also concerts, a potpourri of musical genres, and special thematic exhibits.

A catalogue describing exhibits is available, as well as the "Exploratorium Cookbook," which details basic construction of exhibits, materials necessary to build them, and the scientific concepts behind them. To order these materials write to the Exploratorium, 3601 Lyon Street, San Francisco, Calif. 94123.

Admission to the Exploratorium is free. Note: Reservations are required for the Tactile Gallery—limit twenty persons.

MARIANNE SMITH

◆

The Children's Museum of Boston and Other Places

When anyone speaks of children's museums, it's the one in Boston that always seems to come up first. Designed to teach kids by allowing them to touch, probe, and experiment with objects and concepts, the Children's Museum of Boston (the Jamaicaway, Boston, Mass. 02130) provides access to real materials; kids are encouraged to use all their senses in explorations of the world, past and present. Examples: drawing a "movie" with crayons on a paper strip, spinning it in the zoetrope and seeing it become animated; grinding corn and scraping deerskin in an Algonquin wigwam; playing checkers or tic-tac-toe with a computer; taking part in a traditional tea ceremony in a real Japanese teahouse; trying on old-fashioned clothes in Grandmother's Attic; making a musical instrument out of junk materials; studying gerbils, turtles, rabbits, snakes—and lots more.

Parents, teachers, and community workers who come to visit from other cities—and from abroad—often ask, "What would it take to get a museum like this started in our city?" Mike Spock, director of the museum, tells us that plans are under way to put together a demonstration "package," a kind of starter set that will include basic information on methodology and costs, exhibit plans, training and workshop guides, perhaps a slide show—enough to get an interested community on the right track. But he cautions that the problems of organizing and financing a museum are formidable. "What looks like a cheerful, off-the-cuff, thrown-together experience is far from simple," he warns. The Children's Museum of Boston, now more than sixty years old, is the product of lots of hard planning and tough work. Nevertheless, enthusiastic groups in many cities—among them Portland, Maine; Tulsa, Oklahoma; and St. Paul, Minnesota—have tapped the experience of the Boston institution for their own prospective children's museums.

In Denver, the Children's Museum, which started in 1973 as a traveling exhibit visiting eight metropolitan localities, has grown so popular that it is now installed in a permanent home (931 Bannock Street, Denver, Colo. 80204). And the Smithsonian Institution in Washington, D.C., has opened a special area for hands-on, jump-into, swing-together, work-it-out activities that have caused the otherwise calm and staid Smithsonian to jive and vibrate as it never did before.

At Boston, the lively exhibit area of the Children's Museum is only one part of its program. Another large chunk is the resource center, a mine of educational materials for use in classrooms, neighborhood centers, and homes. The staff offers training and consultation services for anyone concerned with kids' education. Jim

Zien, director of the community services division, explains: "We see ourselves as an educational resource organization that grew up out of a museum." Originally set up to bring museum experiences to youngsters in outlying areas of the city using a traveling van (the "Earthmobile"), this division subsequently helped organize and staff a permanent center at the South Boston housing project on D Street, helping kids in the community in the visual arts, crafts, music, physical sciences, language, and mathematics.

MAURICE SAGOFF

There are other "museums of discovery" where you can touch and talk to and otherwise interact with the exhibits. The following have been recommended to us as memorable places to visit with children, if you're in the neighborhood.

The Ontario Science Centre, 770 Don Mills Road, Toronto, Ontario, has a television studio, a ship model shop, an ant colony, a talking typewriter . . . printers, weavers, weather forecasters, glass-blowers . . . a do-it-yourself computer center and a science game arcade . . . This one may be worth the price of the air fare.

The Brooklyn Children's Museum, 145 Brooklyn Avenue, Brooklyn, N.Y. 11213, is dominated by a multi-leveled transparent model of a diamond crystal that kids can climb around inside. The museum, housed in a sprawling, free-form building designed by Malcolm Holtzman, is dedicated to the proposition that artifacts should be handled, not locked away in display cases.

Another museum, so conceptually involving that you don't mind its lack of physical interaction, and particularly worth visiting with children: the Anthropological Museum in Mexico City.

RS and CBC

◆

The Museum of Cartoon Art and Hall of Fame

Anyone who enjoys cartoons and comic strips will enjoy the Museum of Cartoon Art on Comly Avenue, Port Chester, N.Y. 10573. The Museum has early American cartoons and some of the very first color Sunday comic pages. Little Nemo is there along with Buster Brown and old Dick Tracy and Beetle Bailey, as well as the modern heroes. I don't know how much comic art they have, but if you don't see something you are looking for, ask. The people who work there are nice and know what they're talking about. Cartoonists and their families are often

around the museum; for all you know, the man standing next to you might have drawn Spider-Man. The exhibits are changed every few months and feature foreign cartoons, comics by kids, in-depth studies of one cartoonist or a genre.

Hours are Tuesday to Friday, 10 A.M. till 4; Sunday, 1 P.M. till 5; closed Monday and Saturday. Suggested donation: adults, $1; kids, 50 cents. School bus loads of kids are welcome by appointment. Call (914) 939-0234.

JIM SILVERMAN

◆

The Best Zoo—Milwaukee County

Pressed to comment on the Victorians' enthusiasm for the newly created London Zoo, the historian Macaulay protested, "I have seen the Hippo both asleep and awake, and I can assure you that, asleep or awake, he is the ugliest of the Works of God."

Americans apparently don't agree. Once the poorest stepchildren of city government, rivaled only by libraries, zoos are so popular that beer companies and movie-studios-turned-conglomerates are rushing to build their own. The Walt Disney Corporation even has plans to add a flesh-and-blood Wild Kingdom to its Orlando extravaganza. The true zoo head will claim that the United States has at least a dozen fine zoos already. San Diego, the most famous, boasts a great collection of animals and a lush new 1,800-acre wild animal park in the suburbs, complete with monorail. Chicago's Brookfield is less elaborate, but houses a functioning wolf pack instead of the usual mangy individual specimens; Washington has two pandas, Nixon booty from his Opening to the Left. A private zoo, the Arizona–Sonora Desert Museum, provides air-conditioned underground views of its small collection that get you as close to desert life as you can ever hope to be. And what will someday be the best zoo in America, the well-heeled Bronx Zoo, contains a stunning World of Darkness in which usually shy night creatures come alive.

But none really compares with the Milwaukee County Zoo. Its main virtue is that it was started from scratch just twenty years ago—the 1950's site of the old zoo was victim to an Interstate highway. Every possible effort has been made to display animals in natural settings, a technique that is increasingly common, but nowhere else in so dedicated a fashion. Instead of cages, there are plains and rain forests—predators and prey are separated only by discreet moats.

Where the illusion of nature isn't possible, glass has replaced bars . . . It's even worth a visit in the winter—if only to see Siberian tigers taking dips in their half-frozen pool.

PETER PASSELL and LEONARD ROSS
The Best

"The Most Imaginative Playgrounds in the World"

When designer Eric McMillan opened his "Children's Village" at Ontario Place in Toronto in 1972, *Time* magazine hailed it as "one of the most imaginative playgrounds in the world." And indeed it is, for McMillan has broken away from traditional swings and see-saws to provide such wonders as a forest of punching bags, two giant air-mattress trampolines (one for big kids, one for small), a "foam swamp" for toddlers to crawl around in, a "cable slide" to take children on a breathtaking ride down a rope, pedal-powered water cannons for kids to shoot at one an-

other (complete with a "giant child dryer" designed, as McMillan puts it, "to make the parents feel safe"), and a remarkably beautiful system of nets, towers, and hanging bridges that take children—perfectly safely—high above the heads of their parents waiting below.

In recent years, three McMillan playgrounds have been built in the United States: at Sea World of Ohio, near Cleveland, and Sea World of California, in San Diego (both dubbed "Cap'n Kids World"), and at a San Francisco park with the unlikely name of Marine World/Africa U.S.A. Many of the same features are included in these newer play areas—some in "improved" second- and third-generation versions. And, for the U.S. parks, McMillan has developed what to me is his most delightful concept of all. Called the "Ball Crawl," it's an undulating ocean of colorful hollow plastic balls—tens of thousands of them!—for kids to swim through. If only they'd let grown-ups play in it.

CBC

Amusement Arcades

Amusement arcades as children's entertainment are relatively untapped in New York, Chicago, and some other large American cities. In New York (with the exception of one in Chinatown) they are concentrated in the Times Square area. That location is more than just a deterrent: it actually hides these places from middle-class consciousness, so that no one ever thinks of them as places to take kids.

But they are, and kids love them. They are either oblivious to the seediness or fascinated by it. Aaron is nine and Leah is six, and we're always looking for things all three of us enjoy equally. Arcades have a lot of things that are fun to do, some requiring skill, some offering rewards, and most of them are—ironically—wholesome. The Broadway Arcade in New York, which we patronize, is less unsavory in ambience than the other arcades in the area. The place is kept clean, and most of the machines are in working order.

Leah likes to have her fortune told, her personality traits called out on a lighted display board, and her snapshot taken by a machine.

Aaron gravitates toward target shooting and other games that are fast-moving. His favorite at this writing is a 25-cent coordination exercise that consists of maneuvering a car to keep it from being struck by other cars on a projected freeway. All three of us like skee-ball and having our feet massaged by a vibrator that was featured at the Brussels World's Fair. Amuse-

ment parks have always had these vibrators, but this one actually does seem to massage instead of just shaking.

None of this is cheap, or rather it is all cheap, but none of it is inexpensive. Skee-ball costs only a dime for nine balls, but each child is likely to want to play forever. There is an elaborate system of prize winning, based on coupons. In the end, even if your child is a skee-ball player of near professional caliber, you are still likely to find that you've paid three bucks for a plaster-of-paris statue of King Kong. But of course you haven't; you've paid for playing skee-ball. On Aaron's ninth birthday we took the whole party to an arcade. It beats hiring a magician.

Arcade employees, who are used to dealing almost exclusively with street people or tourists, are likely to be rude. Sometimes the rudeness is protective, as if they're asking, "What's a nice kid like you doing in a place like this?" Once Aaron wanted to browse at the souvenir stand, and complained that the woman kept chasing him away. I checked, and it turned out she had indeed been chasing him away. "He was trying to look at the dirty books," she told me.

RALPH CAPLAN
(with Aaron and Leah)

VACATIONS

Grossinger's in the Catskills

You don't have to be Jewish to love Grossinger's. That's the resort hotel in New York's Catskill mountains, and it's an ideal place for parents and children to vacation. The whole family can go—inexpensively. Or single parents can take their children and get in on a singles weekend.

Grossinger's, located near Ellenville, New York, and accessible by Short Lines bus from Manhattan's Port Authority, is open year round. For children from age four up there is a day camp every weekend, holiday, and all summer.

Counselors pick children up at their rooms at 8:30 in the morning and return them at dinner time. The camp is just like any good regular camp, except that children see their parents more. That situation is particularly reassuring for kids who find it difficult to be separated from their mothers and fathers, kids who need an extra measure of security. (Arrangements can also be made for children to spend only a half-day at the camp.) There are special features like hayrides and campfires, marbles tournaments and movies. Children can eat in the camp dining room or join their parents for meals.

Meanwhile, parents are able to vacation. Activities for adults and children alike include swimming, ice skating, snow-mobiling, skiing, and more.

There is no extra fee for the day camp. Grossinger's suggests only that a tip of $1 to $2 per day be given to the counselor in charge of your child's group. (Each group is generally comprised of eight to ten children.)

The hotel also has evening babysitters available, as well as something called the night patrol—a team of camp counselors who check each hour on children left in their rooms while the parents partake of the various entertainments offered by the resort.

JENNIFER CARDEN

Home Away from Home

House swapping is exactly what it sounds like—a vacation with all the comforts of home. I'm determined to try it someday. To find a house to swap yours for, you could advertise in newspapers and magazines in areas where you'd like to vacation. Or you could try one of the directory services listed below. The directories enable you to make contacts. Arranging the actual details—dates, use of automobiles, use of children's toys, who pays utility bills, caring for pets and plants—is up to you. (Note: There seem to be many more Americans looking to vacation elsewhere than there are people elsewhere looking to vacation in America.)

Vacation Home Exchange Bureau, P.O. Box 878, Belen, N. Mex. 87002. Begun in 1961. $20 entitles you to a year's subscription to their directory, which is updated monthly.

Vacation Exchange Club, 350 Broadway, New York, N.Y. 10013. Begun in 1960. A $13 membership fee entitles you to a listing in the directory (which appears in February), a copy of the directory, and a copy of the supplement (which appears in April).

RS

Camping: Some Advice for Beginners

Seven years ago I decided to purchase a tent and try camping as a means of cutting down on vacation expenses for my daughter Nancy, now thirteen, and me; the cost of lodging, I'd found, was becoming prohibitive. (We have always traveled with a cooler and a picnic basket, enjoying money-saving meals at roadside picnic areas.) I visited a local sporting goods store

(Morsan's, in Paramus, New Jersey) and looked over the variety of tents and camping equipment, obtained a store catalogue, and bought some small books on camping and a *Rand McNally Campground Guide* (now $7.95). Then I went home to study up on the subject.

Using the catalogue and camping booklets, I made a list of equipment I felt was necessary for our camping needs: a tent, sleeping bags, large ice chest for food, and a portable camp stove. I purchased a large Thermos Pop-Tent, at a cost of approximately $120. This tent, which looks somewhat like a green igloo under the pine trees, is large enough for two cots, with room to spare. It is easily handled and put up by one person. We are still using the Pop-Tent, its only sign of age being a few patches over the holes a mouse chewed in it one winter in storage. Using the *Rand McNally Guide,* I selected a campground not too far from home for our first camping venture. Our reasoning: if we didn't like it, we could easily go home. We liked it. We loved it! We became camping enthusiasts.

In the years since that first camping experience we have camped many times, many places. We often coordinate vacation schedules with other family members or friends who are campers, and we have learned much about family camping. We've learned that camping requires planning and preparation, and although experience is still the best teacher, perhaps the following information will help to make a camping adventure pleasant and encouraging for someone just starting out.

I keep an up-to-date camp file. Some of the items it includes are:

The Outdoor Cook's Bible, by Joseph D. Bates, Jr. (Doubleday, 1964, $2.50 paperback).
Equipment warranties and instructions.
Booklets of the "how-to" variety on camping. These booklets have chapters on equipment, safety, setting up camp, and cooking, and also provide checklists for camping needs and equipment. Two of the booklets are *Family Camping,* published (1965) by the National Safety Council, and *The Camping Blue Book,* published (1962) by Outdoors, Inc., Columbia, Missouri (this booklet was discovered in a shoe store).
The Camper's Bible, by Bill Riviere (Doubleday, rev. ed. 1970, $2.50 paperback). This book contains a massive amount of information, including an appendix listing sources of information on camping and campgrounds. Particularly useful are its photographs of various types of equipment, complete with brand names.
Brochures on campgrounds and places of interest. Chambers of commerce and state and federal agencies are good sources for free information.
Rand McNally Campground Guide. This guidebook contains road maps of all states, with campground locations indicated on the maps by numbers. Looking up the numbers on the campground listing enables one to select a campground best suited to his or her particular interests. The listing gives information such as the name of the campground and whether it is state, federal, or privately owned; access (how to get there from a main road or town); a description of the physical environment (trees, seashore, mountainous, etc.); the number of sites available; minimum fee; season (some campgrounds are open all year, some close for part of the year); whether reservations are accepted (many state parks operate on a first-come, first-served basis); time limit (some campgrounds have a two-week limit); facilities available, such as electricity, showers, flush toilets, air-conditioning, camp store, etc.; activities offered, such as swimming, fishing, playground, golf, horseback riding, etc.; the telephone number and mail address of the campground (especially helpful for obtaining more detailed information and making reservations).

I also maintain a camp notebook containing our camping diary and equipment checklist. As we camp, deletions and additions to this list are made according to our own particular needs. For example, we added cots to the list following one rainy weekend, as our sleeping bags got damp when we slept on the floor of the tent. The diary serves as a record of past camping trips, with cooking hints ("Start before dark"), campsite selection suggestions ("Don't pitch the tent next to the path to the washroom, because there will be constant traffic past the door"), and amusing experiences ("When it rained we discovered we had made camp in an 'instant lake' area!").

All our camp gear is stored in one place in the basement; the tent and sleeping bags are now stored in a mouse-proof barrel. (Everything is put away in good repair, and checked again prior to packing for a trip.) Some of our major items of equipment are:

Tent
Tarpaulin for dining area
Cots
Sleeping bags
First-aid kit
Propane lantern
Flashlights
Propane stove
Cookware
Water jug
Food chest (ice box)

A complete checklist should ensure that nothing will be forgotten, such as cameras, film, bird identification books, etc. Although such items are not essential, they can add greatly to the enjoyment of a vacation. Nancy makes a list of "Things to Bring" and packs a shopping bag with notepaper for writing to friends, games and puzzles, a book to read, etc. She also helps to check equipment, pack the car, choose a campsite, and set up camp on arrival.

A word about camping safety: Nancy and I take the same precautions about being alone as we do in our everyday living, i.e., we don't advertise the fact that we're alone, and we don't take chances that put us in dangerous situations. (However, I do prefer to camp with friends or relatives—especially since it adds to the fun.)

When Nancy was quite small, I didn't camp close to the water, and I accompanied her whenever we went over to the dock. Fire is always a hazard, and precautions must be taken, especially with small children around. Tents and other canvas items are not fireproof. There is also the danger of carbon monoxide poisoning

in the use of stoves and heaters, and campers should be aware of this.

JESSIE BAZZEGHIN TRABAND

◆

WHERE CAN I FIND A CHILD'S SIZE-8 HIKING BOOT?

A wide variety of sturdy, reasonably priced kid-sized camping equipment is available by mail through Recreational Equipment, Inc., 1525 11th Avenue, Seattle, Wash. 98122. R.E.I. is a co-op, offering rebates to members who join by paying a $2 membership fee.

A glance through their latest catalogue discloses such pint-sized items as polar cub sweaters, junior rainsuits, junior and tot-sized skiwear, small-sized sleeping bags, and two styles of hiking boots built with a child's growing foot structure in mind.

Their catalogue is available free of charge, and contains the information necessary for joining the co-op.

DEBBIE KOVACS
(with thanks to Amy Ephron)

A Vacation from "Activities"

It is good for children to spend some time in a place where a phrase such as "know the score" is never heard, where nobody is out to win first prize, where nobody is being urged continually to do something and do it better, and where the environment is not a constant assault upon quietness of the spirit. Children as well as adults need to spend periods in a non-communicative and non-competitive atmosphere. I am opposed to all those camps and summer resorts set up to keep the child engaged in a continuous round of play activities, give the body all it

wants, and pretend that an inner life doesn't exist.

At Bark Point [where we spend summers], our children can learn something firsthand about the earth, the sky, the water. They plant and watch things grow, build and watch things form. There is no schedule and no routine, but every day is a busy day, filled with natural activities that spring from inward urgings, and the play they engage in is something indigenous to themselves.

STUART BRENT
The Seven Stairs

Culture Shock: Williamsburg and Disney World, Back to Back

They blur in my memory, history and fantasy, now that the trip is done. Let me try to sort it out: The Governor's Palace, with its magnificent maze, is in Williamsburg, Va., but Cinderella's Castle, with its mosaic mural, is in Walt Disney World, Fla. The King's Arms Tavern is in the Colonial capital, but the Liberty Tree Tavern is in the Magic Kingdom. The Blue Bell is in Virginia, along with the Sign of the Rhinoceros, and Tinkerbell's in Florida, along with Dumbo, the Flying Elephant. . . .

If I am suffering from culture shock, I have no one to blame but myself. No one forced me to decide at the start of the summer that my 6-year-old son and 5-year-old daughter were mature enough for their, and my, first trip to Disney World. I elected to drive from New York because of a love-hate relationship: In a car, I would escape from telephones, which I love, and my wife would escape from airplanes, which she hates. I began to suspect that driving might be a mistake as soon as I emerged from the Lincoln Tunnel and, blinking into the hazy sunlight, realized that the twin towers looming in the distance were those of the World Trade Center, not Cinderella's Castle. "Are we there yet, Daddy?" asked my son.

I resisted the urge to quote Ring Lardner— " 'Shut up,' he explained"—and pressed on, heading for a quick stop in Washington to deposit a collie with a relative. His temperament had been adjudged too sensitive for a kennel; the collie's, that is, not the relative's. I realized that my children might not be eternally grateful for this terrific vacation I'd planned when my daughter, refusing to re-enter the car in Washington, cried out that she would rather spend a week with her cousin and her collie than with Mickey and Donald. Her cries fell on deaf ears, a natural result of the screaming and barking that took place between New York and Washington.

From Washington we cut over to Colonial Williamsburg, where we would spend the next three days—on the theory that we had to stop somewhere, that Williamsburg was only a few miles out of the way to Disney World and that it was, after all, the start of the Bicentennial year. We checked into the Williamsburg Lodge, got a good night's sleep and arrived early in the morning at the Information Center, just in time to queue up for a screening of "Williamsburg— The Story of a Patriot." The film, tracing the conversion of a fictional member of the Virginia House of Burgesses from royalist to revolutionary, acts as a perfect introduction to the Colonial city; such characters as George Washington, Thomas Jefferson and Patrick Henry wander among the restored and reconstructed buildings. As soon as the fictional "patriot" of the film's title appeared on the screen, my son snapped to attention. "It's McGarrett," he announced, his voice filled with the awe he reserves for all television law-enforcement officers above the rank of patrolman. And sure enough, it was: Jack Lord himself, at least 20 years younger, disguised in dark wig and fancy stockings, but still, unmistakably, Steve McGarrett, the head of "Hawaii Five-O," the scourge of the Honolulu underworld. Right away, my son's respect for Colonial Williamsburg doubled. He couldn't understand why there were no Orientals in the film.

Actually, my son recognized three people in "The Story of a Patriot"—McGarrett by face, and Washington and Jefferson by name. My son had never seen or heard of Patrick Henry before, but the most outspoken of the Williamsburg revolutionaries quickly became his hero. He was pleased to learn that Henry was elected the first governor of a free Virginia—he even seemed to grasp the difference between a free and a Colonial Virginia—and he was absolutely delighted by both the rhythm and sentiment of Henry's impassioned cry, "Give me liberty—or give me death."

Several times during the next few days my 6-year-old son ordered his 5-year-old sister to give him liberty or give him death, and although at times she obviously favored the latter, he always managed to wriggle free. When we dined one evening at the King's Arms Tavern, where my daughter pronounced the peanut soup a smashing success, I am fairly certain that my son, his newly purchased tricorner hat perched proudly on his head, told the waiter he would like either liberty or death. He got roast beef.

The foundry, the bootmaker, the Colonial Capitol building, the Bruton Parish Church, the Courthouse of 1770—none of these genuinely historical spots appealed to my son. But for some reason his complaints about too much walking and too much heat stopped when we visited the Governor's Palace. . . . "Which room did Patrick Henry sleep in?" he asked.

Aside from the Governor's Palace, and from the two swimming pools shared by the Williamsburg Lodge and the Williamsburg Inn, my son's favorite diversion in Colonial Virginia was the "Militia Muster," a parade each morning of fifes and drums, a firing of muskets and an explosion of cannon. My daughter resented the noise of the weapons, but she was compensated by a carriage ride through the heart of the 173-acre historic area. "Is this how you traveled when you were a little girl?" she asked my wife.

I could sense that it was time to move on to the Magic Kingdom.

The drive from Williamsburg to Orlando was uneventful, unless you consider attempted fratricide an event. My children insisted, repeatedly, that the ride was incredibly boring, yet both refused to sleep for even a minute. What? And miss something? Besides, sleep comes slowly in a growing mountain of empty soda bottles, discarded candy wrappers and the skeletal remains of Colonel Sanders. . . .

Quite by accident, we had arrived at Disney World at the best possible time—the weekend. Unlike most tourist attractions, Disney World is at its least crowded and most enjoyable on Saturdays and Sundays, when the armies of visitors are still advancing along the highways, and at its most crowded and least enjoyable on Mondays and Tuesdays. Crowded or comfortable, the place does defy belief. It is much easier for 5- and 6-year-olds to accept than it is for 40-year-olds. The children have grown up in an

unreal world of television and splashdowns, and to them the idea of riding a monorail over a lagoon, through the middle of a cavernous modern hotel and past a simulated Polynesian Village is not boring, but it's not exactly thrilling, either. "Oh, look, there's Space Mountain," said my son, pointing to an awesome futuristic structure with recognition and with no more excitement than I used to feel when I pointed from Brooklyn's Nostrand Avenue trolley and said, "Oh, look, there's Ebbets Field." In fact, I was probably more excited. They'll tear down Space Mountain some day, too.

We started our tour of the Magic Kingdom on Main Street, U.S.A., took a cruise in a Swan Boat, then strolled into Fantasyland for "The Mickey Mouse Revue," a musical kaleidoscope of the best Walt Disney films, and "It's a Small World," a boat ride twisting among magnificent dolls and a one-world philosophy, a hit, in its previous incarnation, at the New York World's Fair. Then we decided to try something a little more daring, a trip to the Haunted Mansion, which is in Liberty Square, right down the block from the Hall of Presidents, but bears no outward resemblance to the White House. The entrance to the Haunted Mansion is lined with tombstones, and once inside the gate, a portrait on the wall ages in the manner of Dorian Gray's, advancing from vibrant life to bony death. Doors creaked, walls moved, disembodied voices shrieked, and right before we stepped into small cars that would carry us deep into the terrors of the mansion, my son tearfully paraphrased his hero and demanded his liberty immediately. A guide, garbed as an undertaker, escorted us out through a side door, into bright sunlight that revived my son's shaky spirits. "*I* wasn't scared, I could tell my *sister* was getting scared," he explained, gallantly.

From the Haunted Mansion, we walked to Adventureland, to try out one of the most popular attractions at Disney World, the new "Pirates of the Caribbean." As soon as we settled

into the boats that would float us into pirate-infested waters, eerie voices began to chorus, "Dead men tell no tales . . . dead men tell no tales . . . dead men . . ." I got the feeling that any second my son was going to tell me that his sister was scared again. But the children survived the sad chorus—if I have one objection to Disney World, and to such Disney films as "Snow White" and even "Fantasia," it is that they tend to frighten more than seems necessary—and enjoyed the rest of the cruise, even the rather bizarre scenes of drunken pirates plundering and, evidently, raping. "What's that pirate going to do to that girl?" was one of the very few ticklish questions that my son failed to think of all week.

My children, my wife and I got equal pleasure out of driving the Grand Prix cars in Tomorrowland, my children and I got equal pleasure out of the submarine journey "20,000 Leagues Under the Sea" (my wife didn't like the attack by the giant squid any more than Captain Nemo did), and on the advice of earlier tourists we passed up the miniature space-shuttles within Space Mountain. The simulated space trip is apparently quite realistic—the impression persists of hurtling through the sky at supersonic speeds—and while the Apollo-Soyuz astronauts and cosmonauts had no trouble with the ride, other visitors might, especially those with less high-speed, high-altitude training. I was told that the Space Mountain ride is one hundred per cent enjoyable only for certain people—like National Football League linebackers in their prime.

For four days we sampled Disney World, and as the crowds swelled we took increasingly smaller doses. The long waits on Mondays and Tuesdays are very frustrating, yet the basic appeal of the place remains enormous. Disney World is like Muhammad Ali . . . sometimes annoying, sometimes repetitive, sometimes incomprehensible . . . but never dull. From the most complex rides to the simplest attractions, Disney World entertains. My children loved the multi-million-dollar parade, with its accompanying fireworks and electrical water pageants, but they got just as much pleasure out of sitting on the floor in the tiny Main Street Cinema and watching a rather frayed and fading print of the original Mickey Mouse cartoon, a non-talkie called "Steamboat Willie." The last thing my son and daughter wanted to do, in fact, before we fled from Disney World on the final day was to see the cartoon one more time. They were fascinated. Accustomed to the slickness of the Flintstones and a million other television cartoons, they had never seen anything so primitive as

"Steamboat Willie." That was the seed of *their* civilization.

A week or two later, after we had returned to New York, I wanted to see whether the historical lessons of Williamsburg had faded. I asked my son if he remembered who said "Give me liberty—or give me death." His eyes lit up—mischievously. "Steamboat Willie," he said,

knowing exactly what he was doing, deliberately making the mistake, deliberately distorting history.

He had, in his own way, made a strong point: George Washington may be the father of this country, Dad, but Walt Disney is its guardian.

DICK SCHAAP
The New York Times

BY CAR: TIPS TO MAKE IT EASIER, GAMES TO MAKE IT BEARABLE

Little Known Facts About Long Motor Trips with Small Children

1. Foods such as French fries and hot dogs, which are high in salt content, make everybody thirsty. Though almost impossible not to, it is wise to refrain from ordering them because once you are tripping on salt you will have to slow down for one pit stop after another. The thirst from the salt leads to gas-station soft drink machines, and the soft drinks lead to more gas-station restrooms. Now look at the time you've wasted.

2. As babies are lulled by motion (try driving a colicky infant around the block, by the way, if it's the middle of the night and nothing else will soothe him), so is everybody. Further, when you've decided to push on the eight hours to Detroit and are screaming down Interstate 75, it is nice to have the children asleep in the back seat. But suppose you have to stop for some reason? The children will wake up! Solution: don't stop the car.

3. Basically, children in the growing years are not interested in passing scenery. What they are interested in is license plates from other states and games involving the alphabet. Here are two of those: (*a*) Each child is assigned an opposite side of the road. It is a race to spot the letters of the alphabet in order on signs along the way. The prize can be anything from a firm handshake to a sno-cone. (*Note:* You'll probably have to pass an antique shop to find the letter "q.") (*b*) Make a list of license plates spied. Include the colors and the motto. Michigan's, for example, is "The Great Lakes State." Ohio's is "Seat belts fastened?" This activity can get about as instructive as you want it to. Why is the greatest variety of license plates seen on interstate highways, particularly near resort spots? How did each state decide on its motto? How did those plates saying Ontario and Quebec get here?

4. Children love to go to restaurants and eat food their mother didn't make. However, they do not particularly like waiting for it to be served, nor, for that matter, waiting for other diners in their party to finish. They have a habit of letting everyone know this by opening all the little packets of sugar, squirting out the contents of the squeezable ketchup bottle, bickering about the menu choice, and engaging in hand-to-hand combat. It is wise, therefore, to choose restaurants with attractive backyards and/or opulent bathrooms, so the kiddies can spend their time there during the waiting periods, showing up at the table only for the actual eating. A reasonable alternative is to take a supply of pencils and paper to the table with you.

5. Some children would like to know how to read maps. Also how to fold them. Make these children the pilots, arm them with an atlas, and toss out questions for them to research, like how far is it from Buffalo to Chicago. Also give them a felt-tip pen to trace where they've been, where they are now, and where they're going. Impress on them that the shortest route is not necessarily the one you want. Can they find the scenic way?

6. Long periods of driving are often tedious and frustrating for kids. Break the monotony every once in a while by doing something you wouldn't normally have chosen to do, but which will be nice for them. Most towns have some sort of playground with equipment fashioned after Disney characters, or a zoo, or caverns, or a ride on an antique railroad. Front desks at motels generally have lots of leaflets telling what the local attractions are. (There is no law saying you have to register and spend the night in order to help yourself to these.) Still, a stop at a neighborhood playground rather than family-oriented, souvenir-selling national attractions is a nice change.

7. On the subject of motels, it is worth a lot to stay at ones with swimming pools and to stop

early enough in the day to use them. That way everyone gets some exercise, cools off, relaxes, and doesn't have to take a bath. It's a whole new environment: there are "magic fingers," glasses wrapped in little wax-paper bags, toilets with strips of paper around the seats—lots of fun.

JENNIFER CARDEN

A Satchelful of Traveling Activities

I have a small satchel that is always packed for traveling activities. It contains pencils and paper, a paperback book, a car or truck, some sugarless gum, a couple of tiny toys, a bag of peanuts, one of those scrambled number puzzles, and a few other oddments which evolve and change from time to time, though the satchel is never really unpacked. Whenever we go anywhere that requires more than ten minutes in a vehicle of any kind, we take the satchel with us. It makes life bearable.

ELS

The Car Trip Snack: Wholesome Diversion

Candy never relieves the monotony of long family car trips half as well as an impromptu dispensation of sausages and cheese. Pepperoni, touristenwurst, landjaeger, cervelat, salami— name what you like—any of them, thrown whole into the back seat along with [a] pocketknife, will provide more wholesome diversion than chocolate ever could. If your children are contentious, of course, it will tend to bring out the worst in them. But then, with contentious children, so will anything else. At least it keeps them fighting with each other, and not with their parents.

ROBERT FARRAR CAPON
The Supper of the Lamb

But Hold the Cream Cheese

For little kids on big car trips, Emily Kingsley suggests putting a bagel on a string around the child's neck. "Your kid will chew on it for a while," she says, "and when he or she loses interest, it will fall—not onto the floor, but will hang there, right at hand when the kid is ready to chew again."

ELS

Tapes for Traveling

When we make long trips in the car, we take along a cassette tape recorder. It's simple to operate; Abigail, who is six, can do it easily. We have found that the cheap tapes stop working fairly soon, so now we buy the better ones. We also make our own tapes. In our best one, Abigail played Cinderella and I played the mean step-mother and both mean step-sisters.

CALVIN TRILLIN

Cow Poker

Cow Poker is a very pleasant riding-in-the-car game, as opposed to those not-so-pleasant ride-in-the-car games which build to a pitch of shouting and jumping up and down which drives the driver insane or into a bridge abutment.

Teams are determined by which side of the road riders are sitting nearest. Each team scans the landscape on its own side of the road for cows and white horses to count, and the other side of the road for graveyards.

Object: To have more cows than the other team by the end of the trip.
Rule: Cows must be counted one at a time (not in fives or tens or in estimated numbers), and only as long as they are in sight ("One, two , three, four cows!").
Rule: A white horse *doubles* the accrued number of cows. (Paul Hays holds the record for cow poker. He had 44 cows to his opponent's 178 until we came to a field of 10 white horses on his side of the road. His grand total, therefore, was 45,056.)
Rule: A graveyard on your side of the car means *wipeout!* But only if someone on the opposing team points it out ("Ha, ha! You lose all your cows!").
Rule: If the driver is playing, it is not fair to make a sharp left turn just before reaching a graveyard on the left side of the road. (I've been known to do that.)

ANNA JANE HAYS
(who learned the game from Janet Campbell)

A Car Game That Tells You Something About Your Kid

Grandma plays a game with Nick which she says never bores them and helps her learn his likes and dislikes. They call it "Choices." "If you had your choice, would you pick for a pet a puppy, a kitten, or a lizard?" "Would you travel by plane, by boat, or by bicycle?" And so on. "Once in a while we argue when he wants to choose more than one, or none at all, but we work it out," says Gram. With the older grandchildren, the nature of the choices changes: "Would you prefer a Rolls-Royce, a Porsche, or a Jeep?" "Would you rather play tackle, end, or quarterback?" The game even helps her decide what to serve when the kids come for dinner: "If you had your choice, would you pick broccoli, string beans, or peas?" It's so simple, but the kids love to play it—and it's even gotten Grandpa, who is most difficult to amuse, involved.

ELS

Help: the AAA

If you're going to be driving during your vacation, you might as well know as much as possible about the places you're driving through. That's where AAA comes in. Highly recommended, both for their routing services and for the information they provide, AAA will route you the fastest way possible (usually freeways) unless you specify otherwise (which you may want to do). The spiral-bound packet they prepare for your trip (it can be held in one hand while you drive) provides excellent map information as well as anything you'd ever want to know about the places you're driving through: local radio stations, population, history, economy of the area, names of hills, national parks, local crops, and on and on.

Thirty-five dollars covers one car for one year (and anyone driving that car); renewal in subsequent years costs $30.

RS

A FEW PRACTICAL SUGGESTIONS

Traveling with your child alone can be tough, but one imagines one is broadening her, building her character, shaping her intellect. It doesn't matter that you carry a Pamperful of doodoo through fourteen states, or have to sell your soul for a glass of apple juice, or crawl under a moving train to chase a rolling Oreo (your last); you can easily reconcile yourself to these hardships.

Below are a few practical suggestions.

◆

What to Do When You Leave a Best Pal Behind by Mistake

Once, when Nick went off to visit his cousins for the weekend, he forgot to bring his "Baby," an old Raggedy Andy who usually accompanied him on such trips. He felt pretty lonesome without Baby, but before he could get the notion in his head that sleep was out of the question, resourceful Aunt Carol supplied him with a *picture* of Baby, a Crayola technicolor special, which stayed with him beside his pillow through the night.

ELS

Alternatives to the Battery-Operated Rhinestone-Studded Plastic Glow-in-the-Dark Grand Canyon Stick-On Mickey Mouse Ashtrays

For children who insist they need a souvenir of a place they've visited: how about coming home with a pebble found at the site, or a flower? Or perhaps a paragraph written on-the-spot about the place. Something for remembering doesn't have to cost money. If worse comes to worst, you can always come away with a nickel postcard—it only costs a quarter.

ELS

Before You Load the Car . . .

The library is a good place to look for books on day trips in your own area. But check the copyright date—many libraries forget to weed out the old books and you might travel two hours to find a milking farm that's gone dry.

(*Note:* This advice itself may be out of date.)

ELS

THE CIRCUS AND OTHER OUTINGS

why i've never taken nathaniel to the circus

three years ago helen took nathaniel to the circus. nothing happened except that he spilled his coke all over and got bored. two years ago david wyland took nathaniel to the circus. nothing happened except that nathaniel had his head under the seat looking for his flashlight when the guy put his head in the lion's mouth. last year bob smith took nathaniel to the circus

and nothing happened except that nathaniel whopped himself and the old lady behind him both in the head with his flashlight when they told the kids to swing them around. i've never taken nathaniel to the circus partly because i know the above things are all guaranteed to happen and partly because i don't want to lay my paranoia, acrophobia, agoraphobia, and claustrophobia on him all at once.

joel oppenheimer
The Village Voice

How I Could Have Spent $48.30 in Four Hours and Twenty-five Minutes at the Circus

When we went to the 104th edition of the Ringling Brothers and Barnum & Bailey Circus, I could swear we had already been, in our eight years as a family with children, to 102 such editions, but that's another story. Supposedly, there were twenty-four brand-new acts in the 104th.

What you need to know about the circus is fourfold:

(1) *The circus is fun.* Whether it's the Red or Blue Team that visits your city, there is definitely a rush when the lights are turned out and you hear "Welcome, children of all ages . . ." That moment is also very pretty because everyone is sitting in the dark twirling around a $1.50 twirl-around flashlight, and it looks, oh, like a summer night with a zillion fireflies climbing to the top of Madison Square Garden, or the Coliseum, or the Civic Center, or wherever you happen to be.

There are lots of medallioned elephants and people dressed in costumes usually seen only in after-hours sections of the city. These are designed to sparkle and generally thrill you, and they will if you let them. The circus is ritualistic, predictable, and probably something you want to do for your child even more than he wants you to do it for him—but not that much more, when you get down to it.

Many parents want to know how young is

too young to go to the circus. We say take them whenever everyone feels like it. But be comforted if you think they're still too young, because you can have every confidence that the show will be back next year. And if animal trainer Günter Gabel-Williams is missing, at least there will be some good gymnasts.

(2) *The circus is expensive.* I actually can't complain, because our four-children-and-one-adult outing cost only $5.80, but that was because the tickets were given to us by a friend who knows a clown. They would have cost $8.50 apiece otherwise. Then there was $1.50 for the flashlight (which on first twirl ejected its batteries and had to be replaced in a Nader-esque maneuver with the concessionaire), 35 cents for a soft drink, $1.35 for three containers of ice cream (you can see we were sharing a lot), $2 for the souvenir program with a poster of the shortest man in the world, and 70 cents for subway fares. You may have other transportation costs and/or parking. We didn't. We bypassed (by parental dictum, I might point out, not popular consensus) cotton candy, peanuts, hats, pennants, and popcorn. (Be forewarned.)

(3) *The circus is long.* Consider it. You have animals, basketball players, clowns, high-wire artists, tumblers, dancers, tightrope walkers, and who-knows-what-all to get through.

Plus production numbers. This year one pro-

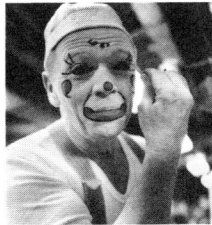

duction number involved some children from the audience, who got to wear hats emblazoned "I've been *in* the Greatest Show on Earth." They were led around from ring to ring by pirates and Little Bo Peeps and other fantastical creatures while the ringmaster sang a song about seeing the world through the eyes of children, the lyrics of which assured us that if we have any doubts, the kids will show us the way. I interviewed a few of these children later. One little boy remarked that as he was climbing out of the Happiness Duck in which he had been whirled in Ring Three, his shoe fell off. The kids, to a man, looked scared stiff, but reported they were happy they'd have something for Show and Tell in the morning.

And so it continued. Two hours and forty minutes into the circus, my children broke into fisticuffs, the exact reason for which no one seemed to know. They also began doing tricks at their seats, all featuring big, spread-arm finales as they popped up and down on the springs. They began asking when the circus was going to be over. Deciding to get a jump on the crowd, we left during the last number. One child gazed at the wind-up flourishes in the rings as we walked and pointed out, "The circus goes on forever. Even the ending never ends."

(4) *Learn some strategies.* Don't forget there is usually a menagerie before the actual circus. Get there ahead of time if you want to see it. It will be downstairs or backstage someplace. They close it down a half-hour before show time. Another thing, get up and walk around during intermission. They'll be bringing out the animal cages then and you can get up close. Neat.

JENNIFER CARDEN

Our Family's Annual "Nutcracker" Ritual

When December comes, we drive up the New Jersey Turnpike toward Manhattan past the green Statue of Liberty, solid and luminous against the darkening sky. We are on our way to Lincoln Center for the New York City Ballet's production of "The Nutcracker." . . . The day I purchased the tickets—weeks in advance—I grew warm with self-congratulation about my own graciousness and healthy generosity to my children: I felt myself on solid ground as a parent. I was seized with a sense of new potentiality. Self-approval informed my whole day. Since "The Nutcracker" visit with the kids is an annual ritual, these are feelings I had also experienced at the ticket window in previous years, but had forgotten.

At Lincoln Center, the air is clear, and the Metropolitan Opera House is a cage of light floating in blackness at the end of the square. This first moment is lovely. We run across the plaza, in the darkness and stinging cold, and burst into the State Theater lobby, which is thick with swarms of serene-looking little girls in velveteen ankle-length dresses. Three children enter behind us, wearing purple and green coats with mock chinchilla hoods. Their mother follows them through the door, eyes the crush, places her two spread hands on the children's hoods, and knocks their heads together. *"Stick together,"* she orders.

We rush upstairs to our seats, past a throng of cheery yet desperate people, little and big, mobbing the orange drink stand. A tall woman, stylish in boots, is speaking to four children who surround her knees. "Listen," she says: "I *know* where we're sitting. *I know* Jeffrey is sitting with Michelle. I heard you before, Jeffrey. I don't want to hear about it *one more time.*" Nora, who is 9, fixes her eyes on the curtain and takes a thousand infinitesimal steps backward until she is seated. She can't wait for the dazzling tree that grows up to the sky, can't wait for the war of the grey mice, can't wait for the dancers dreamily turning and turning with the imitation snow floating down all around. Zachary, who is 10, can't wait for the Cokes. Also, he is running a fever and has lost his glasses, and the fact that we are not sitting in the last four seats in the fifth ring, right next to the ceiling, is a source of bitter disappointment to him. The orchestra, stretching below us, is nearly filled. Massed with people sitting on their coats in dim light, it reminds Nora of the building in New York where you are supposed to be able to survive two weeks' worth of radioactive fallout. Zachary places his right shoulder against Nora's body and presses her with great force against the arm of her seat. "She keeps *bothering* me," he says, tears springing to his eyes.

The lights dim, to mild cheers. A man's voice speaks to us out of the walls, requesting that we not take photographs during the performance. At last, the curtain rises on a single glimmering star pendant over a sleeping town, deep blue, blanketed in snow. The star hangs in white light, the orchestra begins, the music swells around us in the darkness, and in hundreds of seats the grim and silent scuffles over the opera glasses begin to subside as easily as first flakes of snow settling to the ground.

The high moments of Act I come during the second half when Mary, the young heroine, leaves her genteel home—where an exceedingly refined Christmas celebration has been going on—and enters the magical, larger world of her own dreams. As Mary sleeps, we watch her dream come to life:

Grey mice begin to skitter across the drawing room. They are hideous and delightful, obese rodents on sticks of legs, swarming the stage and whirling in circles. The Christmas tree strung with candles begins to grow, swelling to a dazzling height; the mice grapple hand-to-hand with toy soldiers; the drawing room window becomes enormous, and Mary's doll's bed quadruples in size.

When at last the enormous, flashing Christmas tree slips out of view into the sky, the world of the drawing room is left utterly behind: Mary, lying in her white's doll's bed, glides away into snow, into a silent grove of fir trees draped in white. She sleeps on while snowflakes flutter down to dust her hair, the orchestra thunders, and the Nutcracker himself crowns her with gold sparkles after revealing himself to be a princely boy in kneebritches of pink satin. It is incredible. My husband is near tears. The stage is covered with drifting, swirling whiteness. "Is that real snow?" asks a child's small voice in the darkness behind me. "Yes," answers his father. "The hell it is," says the kid.

The second act is "The Land of Sweets," Mary's fantasy world full of confections. Here are dancing candy canes, and dancing marzipan and hot chocolate and Chinese tea, and even dancing petals of spun sugar. There is the huge and imperious Mother Ginger, in her enormous skirt which momentarily hides eight children and lists like a boat. And, of course, there is the Sugar Plum Fairy herself, coruscating and winsome and imperial, flushed with noblesse oblige, incomparably light on her pink satin feet. At last, she dances the grand pas de deux with her ardent cavalier, a climax of total glamour.

Mary and her Prince exit by sleigh, and it is over. The lights come up and we smile at the children, who are looking the other way. In the lobby, smiling people packed together are wrestling each other for a chance to purchase plaid angels, tiny furry stuffed mice, painted wooden nutcrackers, and plastic ballerinas in tutus who balance on one toe eternally. The woman behind the counter points out that for $21.50 the largest nutcracker actually works, and as she says this she gives it an indifferent tug so that its parts clack together and it cracks an invisible nut. "Don't spoil a nice evening, honey," says a father to his tiny daughter, sounding self-controlled but dangerously bored.

Nora is scandalized that the souvenir "Nutcracker" program sells for $2, but as she pulls on her mittens she looks at us with a wonderful look of real happiness. "It was great, Dad," Zachary says to Edward and me. And at last we swoop back across the plaza in the cold, past the slightly bubbling white fountain, to another solid year of Batman episodes.

JANE SHAPIRO
The New York Times

TAKE FOOD!

The secret of any successful excursion I have had with kids has always been, believe it or not, food. Whenever a kid is bored or restless, it seems, he becomes hungry. "I'm hungry, I'm starving, I need a Twinkie," he can exclaim, straight-faced, even if he's just finished a seven-course meal (or even if he's refused a roast beef sandwich). The reason for this is that after several hours of just sitting—in a car or train, or at a spectacle such as the circus or the Ice Capades—one needs some diversion, and, for kids, snacking is irresistible, especially when you're speeding past Golden Arch after Golden Arch or sitting at, say, a ball game where the ubiquitous soda and hotdog hawkers surround you on the aisles.

On long—and sometimes even short—train or car trips, or at the circus or a puppet show, I try always to have a bag of goodies. Fresh raw vegetables like string beans or peas or carrot sticks have worked wonderfully. Raisins are always good, or a little bag of peanut butter and crackers. With the homemade snack, you avoid the awful concession foods, cut down on sugar intake and cost, and, if the excursion turns out to be a flop, there is still the possibility that the picnic will have been a success. ELS

GOING PLACES WITH YOUR KIDS   367

The Magician Nonpareil

Doug Henning is the only magician I've seen. No doubt he'll be the best I'll ever see. The first ten minutes of Henning's *Magic Show* were so boring that I thought he was going to pull the magic trick of all time—making an audience of 1,000 people disappear. But soon he was up to his old tricks, and we were enthralled, bewitched, and bedazzled. Some of his tricks: transforming a lady into a mountain lion right before our very eyes (I think); sawing a woman into pieces; levitating a woman; tearing a newspaper and making it reappear as a single sheet. Believing isn't always seeing.

If Doug Henning appears in your town, you ought to take him in—before he takes you in.

JESSE AGEL
Age eleven

SPORTS

JOAN BINGHAM

CHOOSING SPORTS EQUIPMENT:
THERE'S NO NEED TO SPLURGE ON THE BEST
(EXCEPT SOMETIMES)

Baseball

• _Gloves._ The truth is that for a competent ball player, which glove he or she uses is largely irrelevant. Far more important than the original product is how the kid breaks in the mitt. Every glove when new requires a lot of attention. It must first be loosened up through the frequent application of leather conditioner in concert with all-purpose oil. The stuff should be kneaded into the glove with a vengeance, and it is hard to overdo this process (which has the added benefit of making the glove look better, used and worn, which for a kid is important).

Next, a "pocket" must be made in the glove. Actually, this point is largely misunderstood: what you don't want to do is make a small pocket in the palm of the glove with a baseball. A baseball is too small (remember, the glove will probably be used for softball), and the palm is not where you want to catch the ball. The glove is not especially well padded there, and properly so (padding limits flexibility), and if caught in the palm, a ball will sting pretty badly. More important, however, is that the fielder will have very little control over the ball if he or she makes initial contact in the palm area, and is just as likely to drop the thing. It is far better to form your principal catching area here:

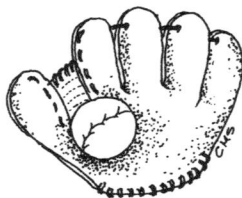

where you can utilize the webbing area as well as the fingers for maximum control.

To speed this crucial shaping process of a new glove, place a softball in the pocket area when the glove is not in use and tie it with string. Of course, the mitt should be played with and constantly flexed until it is worked into a comfortable shape.

You can probably buy a decent glove for $10 to $15 in most sporting goods stores. It would be easy to pay $30 without receiving a whole lot more for your money. Since baseball gloves really never wear out, and in fact usually get better with age, I wouldn't recommend spending under $10 unless the user is extremely young and incapable of controlling a relatively large glove. (This recommendation is based on the assumption that the glove will not be lost or stolen, an assumption that is risky.) I am still using, and quite happily so, the same glove I purchased some fifteen years ago. The glove is not an extraordinary piece of equipment—it cost me about $10 at the time. But I have over the years, through constant use and proper maintenance, created a work of art.

A word on specialty gloves. Unless a kid is sure—I mean really sure—about wanting to play first base and nothing but first base, or catcher and nothing but catcher, I would avoid buying a specialty glove. But for kids who are sure about their intentions, go along with it, and here a few extra dollars might be worth the investment. (Still, there is nothing more useless than a catcher's mitt not being used to play catcher, and a "firsty's" mitt isn't usually much more versatile.)

WILLIAM A. GOLDSTEIN

GLOVES ARE FOR BEING SMEARED WITH NEAT'S-FOOT OIL

My nine-year-old son, Tony, phoned me at the office at 4 P.M. It was at 8 A.M. that morning that we'd unwrapped his birthday present—a Wilson "Sparky Lyle" pitcher-fielder's mitt, which I carefully smeared with neat's-foot oil and, after having jammed an indoor ball into its pocket, wrapped tightly in a huge rubber band "to form a great pocket"—and I'd told him it would take about twenty-four hours to have the maximum effect.

"Hello, Dad?"—his small voice sounding as only a nine-year-old's voice could after having contemplated an oiled and wrapped-up mitt for eight hours—"would it be all right if I took the rubber band off my mitt now and played with it?"

ARTHUR SHIMKIN

• _Bats._ A bat pretty much is a bat. The only important variable here is size, and most youngsters feel compelled to use bats too big for them. Almost without exception, a kid under sixteen should never pick up a bat longer than thirty-three inches, and usually one or two inches smaller. Bats should be thought of as weapons, and as such, the player must be able to swing the thing fast. A bat which is not too heavy will reduce the number of embarrassing times when the batter is simply way behind the ball for lack of wrist speed. Of course, bats are altogether different for softball (most organized softball games exclude baseball bats, although I've never been able to figure out why). Softball bats are usually longer and thinner. We are seeing more and more aluminum bats in softball, which provide a certain "ping" that you don't get with a wooden bat. They also are about twice as expensive. I personally am a purist and usually stick to wood. Again, it's the size that remains paramount.

• *Balls.* For baseball, all balls are pretty much the same. In softball I would stay away from the rubber variety. They are too heavy (and may well hurt your arm from throwing), and they don't go as far. There is the advantage that they are not as subject to abuse from either weather or from the batter, but they are no fun to play with.

WILLIAM A. GOLDSTEIN

BASES: A GIFT TO PLEASE YOUR CHILD AND SAVE YOUR FURNITURE

One of the best presents my mother gave me as a child was a set of bases. They were the only "professional" set in the neighborhood, and they allowed for all kinds of play: well-organized baseball and softball games, sliding practice, games of "running bases," sharpening up control of my knuckle ball. Even more important (at least to my mother), the living-room cushions no longer had an essential place in my backyard activities. (Of course, if you have some *old* cushions you're about to throw out—well, these might serve your children very nicely. But I doubt they'll provide a thrill like the one I got when I received my "authentic" set of bases.)

CBC

Basketballs and Footballs

In choosing a basketball or football, you really can't go too wrong no matter what you buy. There just isn't that much difference between the worst piece of junk and the "professional" model, and what differences do exist don't matter much anyway. But a brief word on each won't hurt.

In basketballs, make sure the size is correct. If your child is playing basketball at school with full-size balls, a slightly smaller home version, although *easy* to succeed with, will make competition with the right size far more difficult.

Footballs are all pretty much the same size (although you can find some that are smaller than others). The key to a good football is in the lacings. Many balls come with a plastic-coated string lacing which will crack and peel and generally come apart in short order. You see, a good grip is essential in passing a football (especially for undersized hands), and balls of the same size can vary immensely in the grip across the stitching. Also, footballs are, to varying degrees, hard and soft. I used to have one made of hard rubber, and it stung pretty badly when caught improperly. Others are made of leather, and although not as durable, are a little more fun for those whose hands are not made of asphalt.

WILLIAM A. GOLDSTEIN

Golf Clubs: How to Buy Them

Golf clubs can be very expensive—you could easily spend $100 to buy a set of juvenile clubs. Certainly, no young child is in a position to appreciate the difference between a set of new and a set of used clubs. A good secondhand club—Spaulding or Titlist, for example—is a far better buy than a brand-new lousy discount-store club.

Golf clubs come in three sizes. A child won't really start swinging a club until he's six or seven, and there's a size for that age range. Then there's another size for eleven- or twelve-year-olds. Once a child gets up to fifteen or sixteen, he should be ready for an adult-sized club. Sports stores and, in particular, pro shops are continually turning over used clubs of all sizes: make sure you ask for clubs of the right length for your child.

What some parents attempt to do—I've done it myself—is to take a regular golf club and cut it down. This is *not* satisfactory. The club comes out balanced entirely wrong, and it also sits on the ground incorrectly. As for letting a kid "grow into" a set of clubs that's too big for him: it really doesn't work. If clubs are too long for a child to handle, he can't possibly learn to play correctly. It's like playing baseball with a lead bat.

BILL WHALEY

Tennis

• *Balls.* Tennis balls are pretty much all the same. You know, three balls in a can that goes *whoosh* when you open it. However, some manufacturers (Tretorn, for example) now make nonpressurized balls, which last about five times longer and don't seem to lack anything except the *whoosh*.

● *Rackets*. Here there are two variables, the frame and the string. As with baseball gloves, you can go crazy buying a tennis racket. If you want, it isn't hard to spend 60 bucks on one, but $25 will do very nicely. Get a decent frame, and initially at least, don't go to the aluminum or steel variety. These frames are harder to play with because the ball "pops" off faster and hence is more difficult to control. Additionally, many people who have used aluminum or steel frames complain of "tennis elbow," an aching ailment that has, among other characteristics, a tendency toward longevity. Certainly a beginner should not play with anything but a wood frame.

The stringing can either be nylon (cheaper) or gut (which is more professional, but subject to ruination in a hard rain). More important than the type of stringing is that the strings be as tight as possible, which you can test simply by pushing against them with your fingers. There should be very little give in the strings when you apply this pressure.

In size, tennis rackets are essentially all the same dimensions except in the grip. The grip is frequently labeled on the racket, e.g., 4¼, 4½, and this measurement refers to the circumference of the grip. The overall weight of the racket is usually also labeled on the racket, e.g., heavy, medium, or light. Hence, you can theoretically have a large grip and still have a light racket. I suggest that in purchasing a racket for a beginner you lean toward the lighter variety. Serving a tennis ball properly is a tiresome proposition, and that third set will seem a little less grueling if the racket doesn't feel like a sledgehammer. Finally, be sure to get a decent press, the frame in which the racket is stored when not in use. This will ensure against warping, which will almost certainly occur if you leave the racket out.

WILLIAM A. GOLDSTEIN

THE VIRTUES OF JAPANESE TENNIS RACKETS (MAINLY, THEY'RE *CHEAP*)

The Japanese tennis rackets we bought from Sears two years ago for $9.95 (made by Apollo) have a laminated construction, are lightweight, and extremely sturdy. Excellent for beginners.

RUTH PELMAS

◆

Ping-Pong: The Dick Miles Table Tennis Ball Test

To test a ball, spin it on a table with the seam up. If it wobbles, it will not play well. If it passes the roundness test, squeeze it in the middle by placing your thumb on one side of the seam and your forefinger on the other. It should give evenly.

DICK MILES
Table Tennis

◆

Rubber Balls: The *Ne Plus Ultra*

The best small rubber ball is still the Spaldeen (49 cents). The cheaper balls, when hit once with a stickball bat, become egg-shaped and thus are called "eggballs," our sources report.

However, in situations where it is likely that a ball will be lost down the sewer every day, surely a cheaper one will do.

ELS

How Necessary Is Certain Paraphernalia?

A child growing up in a relatively affluent neighborhood will see all around him new pieces of equipment which he will probably come to covet and, in turn, ask for. In most instances, the requests will be for things he can very well live without.

● *Bowling balls.* I would say that until a child can demonstrate an average in the 165 range using house balls, he surely doesn't require one of his very own. But the truth is that the fit of the house balls will never be quite right and a personalized ball will almost always, if properly drilled, improve someone's score at least 10 to 15 pins. But if a kid is slopping along rolling 130s and 140s, to give him his own ball is a little silly and he is likely to be laughed at by those who best him using the house specials.

● *Pool cues.* As long as the cue is not warped (and you can test it by rolling it along the top of the table), it will ordinarily do quite adequately. People who have their own cues—you know, those that come apart—had better be prepared to run 10 or 11 balls, because performance short of that does not necessitate personal equipment.

● *Fancy footwear.* When all is said and done,

the new $25 athletic sneakers are nice to have, quite nice in fact, and are usually more comfortable, and look better besides. Despite all that, an old pair of high-cut sneakers ugly with wear will serve just as well. If you have the money, fine, but as long as the size is correct and the kid wears a couple of pairs of socks to avoid blisters (one thin pair underneath a heavier pair), any damn sneakers will do.

Essentially, my message is that you must be careful not to put the horse before the cart. There is nothing more preposterous than a person (child or adult) equipped from head to foot with the finest stuff money can buy but who is unable to perform well enough to nearly justify the expenditures.
                                    WILLIAM A. GOLDSTEIN

[It may be true, as Mr. Goldstein states, that "any damn sneakers will do." But your child, and particularly your child's *peers*, may not agree. For a note on what can happen when you purchase an off brand of sports shoes, *see* Stephen Joseph's article on page 182.]

About Those Endorsements

Most famous athletes will endorse anything these days, and it seems that every sports product, no matter how shoddy, has some guy's signature and stamp of approval on it. When I was a boy I had a baseball glove which was supposed to be the "Lew Burdette" model. Well, I'm a righty and Mr. Burdette was a lefty, and my glove cost about 10 bucks and his was probably five times that. But still his name appeared on my glove, as if it were modeled after his very own. The truth is, of course, that all this endorsement business is nonsense, and should be completely ignored.
                                    WILLIAM A. GOLDSTEIN

Ten Ways to Save Money on Sports Equipment

1. When taking on a new sport, don't immediately splurge on the best equipment available. You may find that the "best" is not the best for *you*. Before making any purchase, read up on the sport and ask advice—not just from dealers, who may be out to load you up with everything they have in stock, but also from friends and acquaintances who have a practical knowledge of the sport and may be even better informed than a dealer. (Many sports equipment salesmen spend so much time in the store they have no time for sports!) Get several opinions before you make a buying decision.

2. If you're taking on a new sport, or plan to participate in a sport only rarely, try to borrow equipment rather than buy it. An avid golfer may not lend you his clubs, but a once-a-year duffer may be willing to do you a favor. (But make sure they're the *right* clubs for you.)

3. If you can't borrow, consider renting equipment you'll use only rarely, be it skis or scuba diving equipment. Some rental costs may seem high until you consider the cost-per-use. If you were to spend $300 for some sports equipment but use it only twice a year over a six-year period (and six years is about as long as you plan to keep it), your cost-per-use is $25 ($300 divided by 12).

4. Sell your old sports equipment in order to get money toward new equipment. Clean out the basement, attic or garage and clear out whatever you no longer use—old golf clubs, archery sets, camping gear, etc. Sell it to friends or neighbors, or run an ad in the classified section of the local newspaper. Or get rid of it at a garage sale. It's not doing you any good, and even if you only get 1/10th of what you paid for it, 1/10th is better than nothing.

5. If you don't want to sell your old gear, trade it in. A boat dealer won't accept an archery set toward a new boat, but a sporting goods dealer may accept it toward a table tennis outfit, or whatever else you're interested in—even if he ends up giving it to some charity. Certain lines of sporting goods must be sold at full list price, but a dealer can give you what amounts to a discount by offering an inflated value for your trade-in.

6. Planning to spend a sizeable amount of money on an outboard motor, a camping outfit or some other item you'll use only once or twice a year? Why not share the expense with a friend, relative or neighbor? Or with three or four others? To avoid ruining a beautiful relationship, put down in writing exactly how often each partner is entitled to use the equipment,

who stores it when not in use, who pays for repairs, etc. And work out a schedule so that vacation conflicts don't occur.

7. Where possible, buy *after* the season is over. In the late summer and early fall, you'll find bargains galore on boats, golf clubs, tennis rackets and other warm weather equipment. In the late winter and early spring, you'll save money on snowmobiles, skis, ice skates, etc. It means that you tie up your money for a few months, but the savings can be substantial. Preseason sales are also held, but the maximum savings is usually 20%.

8. Consider buying used equipment—from dealers or private parties. Dealers who take trade-ins always have used equipment to sell, and in some cases they fix it up so you can hardly tell it from new. And by checking the classified ads or attending garage sales, you can sometimes snatch up tremendous bargains. Sports equipment is often sold for very little just to get it out of the house, because a family is moving out of state, or because the youngster who used it has gone off to college, or because someone has died. Make sure to check it over carefully before buying, because you usually can't return it.

9. Shop at factory outlet stores if there are any near you. Manufacturers of sporting goods (like other manufacturers) often have merchandise that is slightly (or more than slightly) flawed—unsaleable through regular channels.

Or they somehow produce more items in a line than their wholesalers or dealers can handle. Or they are discontinuing a line. Whatever the reason, this merchandise is offered for sale at factory outlet stores, to anyone who wants it, dealer or non-dealer, in any quantity. For example, in Woodruff, Wis., a manufacturer sells first quality water skis at 20% off. In Fort Collins, Colo., a manufacturer sells first quality fishing lures at up to 50% off. In Forestville, Conn., a factory outlet store sells archery equipment, water skis and shuffleboard sets at 10% off (first quality) and 50% off (seconds and irregulars). And in Thompson, Ga., you can buy Keds tennis shoes at up to 60% off (irregulars).

10. Buy new, first quality equipment at a discount, from the dealers listed in [the *Consumers Digest*] Buying Guide. Generally speaking, you can save at least 33⅓% or 35% off list price on equipment for baseball, golf, squash, tennis and table tennis, and even more—40% to 43%—on fishing equipment. On boats, motors and trailers you can easily find discounts of 15% to 25%. Although certain brands—Johnson, Evinrude and Scott, for example—are supposed to be sold at full retail only, a dealer can still give you a discount of 15% to 20% by including these items in a package deal and pricing the other items extremely low. Or he can give you an inflated amount for a trade-in (see #5 above).

Consumer's Digest

HELPING KIDS WITH SPORTS

Okay, Coaches and Parents! Let's Get Out There and Accept Some Imperfection!

Coaches and parents have too often resorted to aversive or negative control when working with children (e.g., criticizing, ridiculing, blaming, humiliating, scolding, yelling, threatening, punishing, withdrawing approval, and so forth). This takes its toll on children, as can be attested to by dropout children and young participants alike.

To accept imperfection while a child is learning is important. An overconcern with perfection can make a child feel like a failure, causing him to subsequently lower his feelings of self-worth. You can make a child feel successful by rewarding any improvement or anything good and by making positive suggestions, or you can make the child feel like a failure by always criti-

cizing and yelling that he did this or that wrong, or that he wasn't as good as so-and-so was.

For example, a girl may come in last at a swim meet and feel happy and successful if you compare her to her past performance, but sad and unsuccessful if you compare her to the winner of the meet. In terms of over-all adjustment, as well as learning, to use the positive approach based on individual improvement is much more beneficial for the child.

TERRY ORLICK and CAL BOTTERILL
Every Kid Can Win

Don't Push

Right from Day One, I was interested in having my children involved in athletic programs, so I bought footballs and basketballs and golf clubs—the whole works—and literally forced them on Michael, my oldest son. The result: Michael is almost completely turned off sports.

The lesson I learned from this, of course, is that you shouldn't push too hard. I've *waited* for my other children to show interest in a particular sport, then helped them as much as I could without overdoing it. I play tennis or golf with them, throw the ball around, but we don't have any workouts or clinics as such. If I can give them a pointer or two, or teach them how to win and lose graciously, all well and good. But I've cut out the technical coaching.

It's one thing to set up equipment at home to help your child learn a sport, and quite another to *drill* him in it. Such forced instruction can build up tremendous pressures between parents and kids. When I put up a basketball net at our home, I immediately encouraged my son to invite his friends over to use it.

Get the kids doing it. Then, maybe, you can try it out with your children afterward.

BILL WHALEY

Good and Bad Models

When I was ten years old or so, just learning to play golf . . . I used to watch the club pro giving lessons, or hitting balls from the practice tee. Later, outside my house, I practiced my own swing in front of a window, trying to make it look like the pro's swing, and to remember what it felt like when it did. . . . Later, learning to play tennis, I did the same thing with forehand, backhand, and serve. Here my models—the best players where I played—were not quite good enough. They were fairly skilled, but, as I only learned later, they had some bad habits, which I copied, and then could not get rid of for years. Not until I saw Pancho Gonzales (who incidentally was almost entirely self-taught) at Forest Hills, the first year he won there, did I see how a tennis ball should be hit.

Today . . . we have learned a great deal about models and feedback. [One can] get and see quite easily films of champion athletes in many sports. The catalog of the Wolverine Sports Supply Co., [745 State Circle], Ann Arbor, Michigan, lists a large number of 8 mm. film loops of top athletes doing a great variety of movements and skills.

JOHN HOLT
Instead of Education

A Few Coaching Tips on Common Trouble Areas

• *Baseball.* Most youngsters don't know how to slide properly, and this ignorance causes many injuries, especially to the knee. Go to the beach to practice the basic hook slide; it will serve the potential star in extremely good stead. Essentially the hook slide is a three-part procedure: first, about 10 to 15 feet from the base, you throw your right leg out to the side sharply, simultaneously throwing both hands back over your head; and then, essentially, sit down. Your motion will carry you safely into the right side of the base, which you seek to hit with your left foot. Try it. It's not that hard, and actually a lot of fun. As the kid gets proficient, the same slide should be tried from the other side, that is, throwing the left leg out to the side and hitting the base on the left side with the right foot.

• *Basketball.* Ninety percent of the young basketball players in the country, and old ones too, never learn to dribble with both hands. Like most things, it requires practice and an awareness that you must vary your style when you play. As a means of instruction, set up some old tires in the backyard or corner lot and have the kid dribble around the tires alternating hands. In time, he or she should be able to do it without looking at the ball.

• *Football.* To catch a football with any degree of distinction requires a special kind of concentration. In most instances, even in easy, friendly "touch" games, the receiver will be forced to catch the ball under some form of pressure. So it is to the child's advantage if he or she is used to catching the ball in a crowd, so to speak. Get a group together, assign two kids to the defensive side, and let another be the end. This will ensure a little traffic and will require a lot of concentration to hold on to even a well-thrown ball.

• *Tennis.* An average tennis player can become a better than average one by simply learning what good position is on the court—generally nothing more than remembering to return toward the center of the backcourt after every shot (excluding net play, obviously). By doing the lion's share of the running before your opponent returns the ball, you are waiting for, not scrambling after, your opponent's shot, and so can be more aggressive. Additionally, always stop completely before you hit the ball; never hit the ball on the run if you can avoid it.

• *Track.* For kids who aren't terrifically gifted athletically, yet desire to succeed at a sport, track is the answer. Here, hard work is all there is to it. With the exception of the few short dashes, most events, especially the longer ones, require simple conditioning. Any youngster willing to go out and run a few miles a day can earn a letter in track.

WILLIAM A. GOLDSTEIN

Everything in Its Own Time

It's remarkable how few would-be basketball players ever learn to dribble with both hands. It's also amazing to note how many two-and-a-half-foot-tall kids you see futilely trying to sink a hook shot through a ten-foot-high basket.

There is a solution to all this. You might suggest to a child that there are certain things his body can't do yet, and others that it can. With this assurance, he'll feel less pressure to perform, and will find more enjoyment in sports. And, if you can encourage him to practice skills—like dribbling—that do fall within his ability, he'll be one up on a lot of his friends in years to come.

ANDY FERGUSON

Teaching Kids to Swim: Conflicting Theories

Water and the Limits of Courage

At one time or another I have watched a number of parents trying to teach their very little children to swim. On the whole, they don't get very far, because they are so insensitive to the rise and fall of courage in the child. . . . If we continually try to force a child to do what he is afraid to do, he will become more timid, and will use his brains and energy, not to explore the unknown, but to find ways to avoid the pressures we put on him. If, however, we are careful not to push a child beyond the limits of his courage, he is almost sure to get braver.

. . . When [Lisa] first went to a pool, she would not do anything more than sit on the top step and splash her feet, and her expression and manner showed that she thought that even this was a risky business. It was weeks before she was willing to get as much as waist deep, or to allow any of us to give her a ride. It was not until the following summer that she would let us tow her around without her holding on tightly with her arms. But we respected her natural timidity and caution. The result was that she wanted, and learned, to combat her fears and overcome them. Now, at the age of six, she is a fearless skier, going down difficult trails with children twice her age. In the summer she works hard at learning to swim, which she does as well as most of her friends.

JOHN HOLT
How Children Learn

Swim or Sink

I remember that morning exactly. I drove my six-year-old son, Matthew, to his special swimming class. I helped him change into his suit in the locker room.

Because we were early I went into the pool area and waited with him for the instructors to arrive, the ropes to be strung, the whistle to

blow. And for some reason I stayed even after the class began.

I sat in the bleachers while Matthew hesitatingly lowered himself into three and a half feet of warm blue water. He held on to the side and kicked a bit. He inched his way to the right, to the left, never letting go. His regular instructor tried to talk him into attempting a few simple basics with her: propelling himself with his feet while holding on to a Styrofoam kickboard; putting his face into the water; allowing the young girl herself to support him around the waist so he might go through the actual motions of swimming. But Matthew wanted no part of it. This warm, pretty pool terrified him. He had no idea what the water would do to him if he gave in to it. Swallow him up? Suck him under? Toss him, swirl him, engulf him until no one could hear his screams?

The young girl was patient enough. As an unpaid volunteer, she had no ax to grind, no deadline that had to be met. Like me, she was content with any tiny degree of bravado Matthew showed. Just his letting go of the side with one hand for a second could be this two-hour session's major victory.

But the man who ran the class was different. He was going to get these kids to swim, and nothing was going to stop him. He didn't want to hear any excuses, he wouldn't put up with any crying, he couldn't be satisfied with any performance less than 100 percent.

I knew this about him. I also knew that he only supervised and didn't usually spend his time working directly with the children. But that morning—maybe because I happened to be sitting there in the bleachers—he swam to Matthew and told him to take his hands. The supervisor merely meant to tow my son around the pool.

"What are you going to do?" Matthew began to cry.

"I'm just going to pull you along while you kick your feet. Like you do on the kickboard."

"I don't want that," Matthew's voice was becoming hysterical.

"Let's go, Matthew!" And the supervisor pulled my son from the security of the side wall.

"No!" Now Matthew was crying and clinging with all his strength to the supervisor, who began wrestling him off so to assume the position of the exercise he intended. But Matthew held on for dear life, screaming all the while.

The supervisor's face became red, his anger made his whole body thinner and more violent-looking. "Stop crying, Matthew. Let go of me!"

"I'm afraid! I'm afraid!"

What was I doing all this time? Believe me, I don't remember. It was one of those moments you experience from behind a sheet of glass—if you shout or bang no one will hear, events proceed ineluctably, in slow motion, your very own presence disappears.

"If you don't let go of me I'm going to dunk you in the goddamn water, Matthew!"

"*Noooo!* I'm afraid. Daddy!"

And damn if that son of a bitch didn't lift my son right up out of the water and then—*crash*—right back into it, under, in a little explosion of fury and fear, under and up and there was my son gasping and crying and still clinging, and the red-faced supervisor, sneering, nostrils flared, glasses spattered, torso visibly trembling, the water around them trying to settle, and I stood up and pressed against the glass and where were words, and where were actions, I couldn't, I dared not, I . . .

"Take a walk."

He was talking to me. The supervisor was chasing me out of there. I thought I detected him nod as if to say "Don't worry." To this day I wonder if he did.

Another man who swam with the children and sort of assisted, a man with a cerebral-palsied teen-ager and a well of kind sympathy, agreed that I should leave. The supervisor had assured me not to worry, I'm sure he had. In the locker room, behind the closed door, I could still hear Matthew screaming and the distorted admonitions of the incensed supervisor.

I walked through the locker room, out to the corridor, up the stairs, as far as to the outside door, and then went back down the steps, through the corridor, into the locker room, up to the door marked POOL. Matthew was still crying. I could hear the shouts of men and young girls. Some of the voices had an imploring tone. Again I walked to the outside door. I opened it, went to my car, started the engine, pulled out, stopped for a light, drove on toward the highway.

Suddenly the glass around me shattered.

What kind of father am I? Didn't I hear my boy crying out for "Daddy! Daddy!"? What the hell is so important about learning how to swim? What kind of a degenerate person would stand by and watch a maniac throw his own flesh and blood into water that was obviously terrifying? How could I have let him go on thrashing and screaming and pleading? Isn't that mentality obsolete—dunking a scared kid? Doesn't the philosophy of that madman go against everything I believe in? Where's the tenderness, the patience, the understanding, the wariness of trauma? Jesus Christ Almighty! I turned the car around. I don't know what I would have done if it hadn't been quiet when I got to the door marked POOL. I still don't know. But it was safe to go home.

My wife was as puzzled as I was. She guessed I had done the right thing and tried to see it from the supervisor's point of view. She also felt that I should reprimand the supervisor when I went back to pick up Matthew. Tell him I didn't approve of his wild style. Tell him how fearful Matthew was. But I knew that would do no good. The supervisor would simply counter with his primitive belief that the way to get rid of that fearfulness was to throw Matthew deep into the fear itself so that he could recognize its emptiness. I wasn't about to argue child psychology with a drill sergeant. So the decision was this: if Matthew was upset he wouldn't ever have to go

FRANK DERBAS

back and I would take the matter up with the administrators of the YWCA, which sponsored the special classes.

Anticlimactically, the first person I saw when I returned to the locker room was the supervisor. He was calm and eager to tell me how well everything had worked out. "Sometimes if a parent is present the child is distracted. That's why I wanted you to leave. But he was all right. I knew he could do what I wanted him to do because I've seen him do it. He was just being lazy. But he did it, it was all right."

The second person I saw was the kind assistant who, all smiles, congratulated me on the fact that Matthew was frolicking across the pool by the end of the class. Also, this incredibly decent man sort of apologized for the rough but results-getting manner of the supervisor.

Then Matthew came tripping into the locker room. "Daddy, Daddy, I was using the kickboard all across the pool. I was terrific!"

"Great," I said. "Did you have a good time?"

"Oh, I had a dy-no-mite time."

"You want to come again next week?"

"Yes, and I'm going to go across the pool on the kickboard all by myself!"

"But you were really upset when I left. Do you like John?"

"Yeah."

"But John dunked you, didn't he?"

"Yes, because I was crying."

A month later Matthew learned how to swim in our backyard pool. He submerged himself, did the dead man's float, swam, splashed, had a great time, and, in his own words: "My heart is thrilling and I'm so proud of myself in my brain."

Toward the middle of the summer I thought he might like to learn how to jump into the water off the deck. He said he was afraid and wanted only to lower himself in from the side. Gently I went over to him, put my arms around him, and said, "Matthew, it's going to be a lot of fun to jump into the pool." Then I tightened my grip, lifted him up, and threw him into the warm blue water.

ALAN SAPERSTEIN

There are two obstacles to get over when it comes time to get your child to consider swimming:

The first is face wetting. If a child can learn to feel comfortable getting her face wet—and you can try this in the bathtub—she has made the breakthrough.

The second obstacle is making the child be-

lieve that she will float. If she can come to understand this (and can get her face wet as well) she will be able to learn to swim very quickly.

ELS

Life Preservers: One Vote for the Egg-shaped Bubbles . . .

I had a summer camp for three- and four-year-olds, and I think the egg-shaped bubbles are worthwhile, the ones that strap across the waist. They're not for the two-year-old who doesn't realize that if he jumps in the pool with one, he stays up and without one he goes under; they're meant for slightly older children who're not afraid of the water. It lets them paddle out over their heads and begin to get the feeling of having their feet off the ground.

The good thing about the bubble is that the child uses the same muscles and practices the same movements as he would without the bubble (unlike training wheels on bicycles, which take over the job of maintaining balance). The bubble is out of the way, it leaves arms and legs free, and, I think, is better than the armbands.

LIZA WERNER

. . . and One for Inflatable Armbands

One parent recommends inflatable armbands for children from eighteen months to four years. "They help acclimate the child to water, but some effort is required to remain afloat. I like them because they do not inhibit the child's movement and aid in his learning to swim."

A Tip for Outgrowing the Bubble

John Holt suggests that one way to free kids of their dependence on the bubble is to carve little chunks off it so that it gradually gives less and less support. Very clever, John Holt.   RS

Floating Toys and Rafts

The only things I buy from F.A.O. Schwarz are their vinyl floating toys and rafts in summer. They're more imaginative than the ones you find elsewhere, and for some unknown reason, no more expensive (nearly everything else from Schwarz's is more expensive than elsewhere).

JUDY THORN

Helping Children With Sports:
Contraptions (to Make and to Buy)

THE TEE

In my Little League baseball days, there fell into my hands a book about hitting which featured a device called "the tee." (I can't remember the name of the book, but it seems to me it was written by a man named Dunne; perhaps one of our readers will recall it and will supply us with the title.) The minute I read about the tee I knew it could make me a star. After all, it was explained, Bobby "Doc" Brown, stalwart Yankee third baseman, couldn't hit worth a damn till—you guessed it!—his father made him a tee. And the rest is history.

So what's a tee? Simple. It's a plumber's friend (a plunger) with a few inches of rubber (or plastic) hose forced partway down the handle. It looks like this:

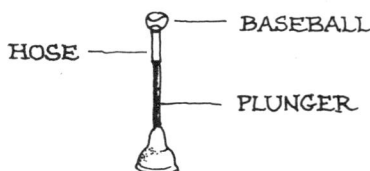

Just rest a baseball on top of the hose, get a bat, and swing away—you've eliminated the need for a batting-practice pitcher! Stand closer to the tee and you've simulated an inside pitch, stand farther away and you can practice hitting outside tosses to right field. And, if you *really* want to get into it, you can make a second tee for low pitches by getting another plumber's friend and sawing a few inches off the handle before you put the piece of hose in place. (Similarly, you can use a broom or mop handle, sawed to size, to make a tee for high pitches.)

Will the tee help your hitting? Well, my Little League average soared from .211 to .243 after I started using it. (No kidding, those are the actual numbers! The fact that I still remember them twenty-six years later should tell you something about how traumatic the pressure to achieve can become for young ballplayers.)

CBC

QUICK-PITCH MITCH AND FRIENDS

The Tomy Corporation and Remco Toys sell automatic battery-operated pitching machines that are lots of fun to play with. (Whether or not they'll help your kid improve his or her hitting skills is another question.) Both Tomy's (known as Quick-Pitch Mitch, retail price about $13) and Remco's (called Bat-Away, retail price about $20) use plastic balls that can be served high or low, inside or outside. Remco's machine hurls with more power and features a variable speed control and an automatic shut-off device, hence the extra cost. (It also uses four "D" cell batteries to Tomy's one.) Tomy attempts to turn its relatively namby-pamby delivery into a marketing advantage by claiming you can use its machine indoors. (Not at *my* house!)

For young pass-catchers, Coleco offers Mr. Quarterback, a contraption which can fling a "special light-weight football" up to fifty feet downfield. The device, which can be yours for about $25, is a real boon: for the first time, one kid can practice pass-receiving by him- or herself, or two kids can take turns defending each other. Instructions on the side of Mr. Quarterback advise you to "Pull release knob out and run"—a good idea, since the device's mechanical arm packs a mean wallop if you happen to get too close.

CBC

A TARGET FOR WOULD-BE PASSERS AND PITCHERS

An old tire hung from a branch makes an excellent target for young quarterbacks. A small child can try to throw a football through it from six to ten feet away; then, as he gets older and/or more proficient, he can move back.

The tire target is excellent for pitching practice too.

BILL WHALEY

A DEVICE TO HELP YOU PRACTICE YOUR TENNIS

Bancroft makes an item which features a tennis ball attached, by means of a long elastic rope, to a weight. You can put the weight on a tennis court—or in your driveway—and hit away at the ball: it'll keep coming back to you. The device has really worked for me and my kids, and I recommend it highly. The price: about $12.50.

BILL WHALEY

ORGANIZED SPORTS

The Little League: "What Strange Occurrences in the Play of Children"

What boys, left to their own devices, would ever invent such a thing [as the Little League]? How could they make such a boneheaded error as to equate competition with play? Think of the ordinary games of boys—in sandlots, fields, parks, even stickball in the street. They are expansive and diverse, alternately intense and gay, and are filled with events of all kinds. The boys make much of one another's personalities, one another's strengths and weaknesses, and their witticisms fly back and forth with unflagging vivacity. They do not stop their game to argue a fine point, but rather the arguments are great features of the game; they are vociferous and long-drawn and run the gamut from sheer emotionalism to the most legalistic pedantry. What may seem to be a shouting match is in fact filled with close distinctions. (I heard a boy win such a match by introducing the word "immaterial." "Whatta ya mean immaterial!!" "It's immaterial, that's all!" "Yeah?" "Yeah!" "Whatta ya mean it's immaterial!!" "It just doesn't matter, that's what!" "Oh . . ." If the other had lost his momentum before the mighty word, it was clear, too, that he was gaining the word.) Between innings the boys throw themselves on the grass. They wrestle, do handstands, turn somersaults. They hurl twigs and stones at nearby trees, and yell at the birds that sail by. A confident player will make up dance steps as he stops a slow grounder. If an outfielder is bored, he does not stand there pulling up his pants and thumping his glove, but plays with the bugs in the grass, looks at the clouds, makes up a droll saying to shout at the duffer at bat—who immediately answers in kind. There is almost always a dog on the field, and no part of the competition is gayer or more intense than that between the boys and the dog, who when he succeeds in snapping up their ball, leads them off in a serpentine line that is all laughter and shouts, the dog looking back over his shoulder and trotting with stiff legs, until finally he is captured and flattens his ears as they take back their ball. No one has forgotten the score or who was at bat. The game goes on. Often birds and squirrels share the field, and sometimes a noisy crew of younger kids, who must scamper out of the way from time to time, and

who shout childish versions of belligerent wit at their young elders. Everything is noticed, everything is used. The game goes on until darkness ends it, and the winners can hardly be distinguished from the losers, for by then everyone is fumbling the ball and giggling and flopping on the grass.

GEORGE DENNISON
The Lives of Children

Take the Decision Away from the Coach

When I was a little kid growing up in the Bronx, I lived next door to a playground. Kids used to gather at the park and play choose-up baseball games. We not only picked sides, but we also set the rules. The equipment was our personal property.

Adults had nothing to do with our games. We weren't an organized entity. The games were, in fact, disorganized fun. That's what sports for little kids should be—fun. My initial frustrations in sports began when I joined the local Little League as a 10-year-old candidate.

I have radical ideas on Little League, which has been a national preserve ranking alongside of mom and apple pie. I'll share some of my thoughts with you.

First, I think kids are pressured into being "stars" too early. Being good at anything takes a lot of time. Ask a watchmaker or an astronaut or, yes, a professional ballplayer. The star system should not be stressed in Little League, for it only leads to pressure.

Little League, with its short fences and 46-foot mound, is tailored for the big kid. If he is coordinated he will excel. This is wrong. The big kid has peaked too early. What happens to him when the other kids grow up and match him physically? Sometimes he can't cope with what he feels is a waning ability and quits the game. He's a has-been at the age of 13.

The real damage, however, is with the average-size 9-to-12-year-olds. They have to face the huge pitcher. The ball is often in the glove before the little kid has the bat off his shoulder. The kid doesn't hit, so he gets sparse playing time. Gone is his opportunity to play and improve himself. A coach has decided he isn't a player when the boy is still 9 or 10. Why stunt a boy and force him to quit when he has so much development time ahead of him?

These kids could become stars, even major

leaguers, if given a chance to play. It's not right that some coach, without professional ability, decides a kid shouldn't play. The boy himself should decide that. He knows better than anyone how much he really wants to play the game.

Take the decision away from the coach. An adult should not have the right to dictate a boy's recreational program, which really is what baseball is at the youthful level. Stop judging kids prematurely. Let's start giving them a chance to make their own decisions on a sport that really concerns only them.

I also disagree with the win, win, win philosophy of Little League. I don't say a boy should take the field and try to look bad. But I do say that after a kid does his best, losing isn't the end of the world.

I would do away with all the championships, from league crowns to the annual international competition at Williamsport, Pa. Look at some of the trophies kids are awarded. Where's the incentive to carry on after getting that kind of hardware?

Let's eliminate the all-star teams and cancel the pressure. Kids will develop without the frills. Let them enjoy themselves.

ED KRANEPOOL
With Ed Kirkman
Baseball

Organized Athletics: An Opportunity to Learn About Cooperation (But Can You Imagine Booing a Six-Year-Old?)

Organized athletics give many kids their first chance to function as part of a team. They provide a fine opportunity for a child to learn about

RICHARD HUTCHINGS

sharing and cooperation. Besides, it's their first shot at being in a competitive situation where they're asked to perform in front of other people.

I think all this is fine, but a parent absolutely must make sure that the proper weight is given to contests involving young children. Sometimes coaches get out of hand, and even more often, the audience does too.

When kids first team up in organized athletics, the idea is just to let them get in there and get involved. Now they have organized athletics in our town in the first grade. That's amazing, isn't it? For a parent to go out and boo a six-year-old is ludicrous.

BILL WHALEY

The Way It Is with Lower-Grade Football—An Insider's Report

First-, second- and third-grade football is interesting. First, it's about as fair as a fight between thirty teenage gang members with assorted knives and clubs against a one-legged middle-aged policeman with a night stick. And about as funny as that same one-legged policeman kicking down a door.

In the lower-grade football you have four good guys. These guys are really fantastic, and athletic, know about half the rules of the game, and really know how to cheat.

Then you have eleven rotten guys. They stink at the game and they are really naïve.

Now the four good guys take charge and put the eleven bad guys on one team and themselves on another. (I'm a bad guy.) Because we (the bad players) have more people, we kick off. It goes three yards. The good players pick it up and five bad guys touch the good guy with the ball, but all the good guys say they only touched him with one hand, when we should have touched him with two. Which is like believing in Nixon. Then the runner drops the ball and we (the bad guys) pounce on it. Instead of a fumble it's a dead ball and it's their ball. With other various ways of cheating, the good players win 48–0.

Sometimes the good players decide to split the teams up evenly, but again the bad players get the bad deal. It's bad guys who block and rush, and all they get for their effort is yelling from the captain. Then the two team captains get in a fight, they both quit, the game ends 0–0, and the two captains have a feud for the next two months.

Well, that's the way it is with lower-grade football.

SCOTT SEARS
Age twelve

What to Do If You Are a Hopelessly Inept, Totally Incompetent Little *Shlubber* Who Can't Run, Kick, Throw, Pass, Catch, Field, Block, Punt, Dribble, Shoot—Who Can't Do Anything at All in That Cruel and Merciless Big Bad World of Macho Sports

This article is dedicated to flops, to everyone who has ever chased a missed ball, dropped a fly, run after something which scooted between his legs, lost a dribble, lost a pass, lost a catch, lost a shot—in short, anyone who has been a total detriment to his team for his entire natural life and who has been razzed, blasted, totally humiliated because of it. It is a sport-by-sport account of how to avoid the horrors of most activities during the gym season and to escape with a minimum of psychic (and physical) injuries. (Parents: If by chance your school system still has the mentality of the 1950s, when it was considered "good mental health" to have your child participate in team competition—and when words like "sportsmanship," "good conduct," "winning" and "losing" still made the rounds of the rhetoric—it would do you good to read this article.)

LESSON ONE: HOW TO SURVIVE AT BASEBALL

(1) Play right field. Right field is where they invariably place the worst dingbats on the lot—the poor, hapless little donkeys who can't catch, run, throw, field, or anything; they just stick them out there in right field (preferably near the foul line), and—if luck comes their way—they'll never see a ball. Don't worry about left-handed hitters; they shift you over to left field for that one play (*Note*: On occasion, you might have to retrieve a foul ball.)

(2) Hit last. Get your obligatory out (they're counting on it anyway), and then just go and sit down. (I must admit it is a bit humiliating when you consistently go down swinging, so to speak, but this article promised to try to minimize psychic injuries, not eliminate them.) That's all for baseball.

LESSON TWO: HOW TO SURVIVE AT TOUCH FOOTBALL

Football, surprisingly, is even easier to get through than baseball (unless you are really skinny, in which case see Skinny People Note, below).

(1) Just block. Just place yourself there, in front of the other guy, and when your guy calls the signals you just charge ahead, hit some guy, he rolls over, you roll over, and soon, you sit up, look around, and the play will be gone, way off and down the field and carrying on without you. That's all you do: just block. (Don't worry about getting the ball, receiving the ball, passing the ball—they'll never give it to you, never, during the whole season. Just block, and you'll get by.)

(2) Punt, pass, and kick competition: This is a bit more difficult to get around. It can be (and was for me) downright shaming. (Especially when you miss the ball—trying to kick; or heave it a measly twenty yards—trying to throw; or dribble it a mere two feet—in a vain attempt at punting, and they all laugh.) My best advice here is to opt for being sick on this day—get a "gym excuse"—and then come back after school and just get it done in the relative tranquillity of after-school anonymity—with no one to be embarrassed in front of save the gym teacher, and where there are no cruel, meretricious "peers" to be castrated in front of.

[*Skinny People Note:* The author regrets to inform all skinny people that he has no solution. He does not know how you will get out of it, but suggests maybe getting a special pass saying you have delicate bones or something—they don't buy "delicate nerves" yet—but he admits that this is a far-fetched idea and cops to a personal failing here.]

LESSON THREE: PARALLEL BARS, THE HORSE, MATS, ETC.

Surprisingly, these are not all that bad. For this reason: they are basically "individual" sports—you just compete against yourself—so, logically, if you give up (which is the goal), there will be no one to really give a damn (except you—who doesn't anyway). So, you're out.

[*Special Warning to Fat People:* You are liable to run into some trouble here. Some of these ventures—especially the horse, the rope climb, and a few variations on the parallel bars—require a certain litheness and mobile agility which you may—forgive me—happen to lack. In any case, be advised: unless you are so outrageously obese that you can laugh at your own fatness, be prepared to be made fun of.]

THE WORST FOR LAST: BASKETBALL

This is real bad. Here's why: basketball is the only sport where you cannot engage in some form of disguised loafing around (which is what we have strived to do so far). Basketball is a sport where you must participate fully, all the time. This is why: there are only five or six or seven guys on a court—not enough to lose yourself, so to speak, in a sea of unfriendly faces. You must chase around, tear after some other guy, chase him all over, run back and forth, try to get the ball, try to block his shot, even try get the ball yourself. They pass it to you. And you must either dribble, shoot, or do something (and invariably you will foul it up. You will either lose it, or drop it, you will double dribble, have it stolen. If you shoot, chances are nine out of ten you will miss and they will laugh at you. You will get ridiculed, you will aggravate the other players. In short, it will be bad).

Also be aware of this: if you stand on the wrong side of some piece of masking tape under one of the baskets too long, some official will blow the whistle at you and point—and the rest of your team will give you dirty looks and hiss curses because you have screwed it up by breaking the three-second rule or whatever the damn thing is. Yes, basketball is the worst sport of all, and if you could break your leg or get some other injury that will last the entire season, you could do much worse, believe me. Better in a cast than at the receiving end of all that vehemence and hostility, yessir.

So, dear fellow *shlubbers,* follow the rules and perhaps you can avoid some of the crap which I was subjected to during my long and glorious reign as a complete flop and an inept little dork.

Boo on sports. Fie on machismo.

WILLIAM H. ELIN

◆

Noncompetitive Athletics

An excellent book for anyone interested in exploring some noncompetitive forms of athletics is *Everybody's a Winner,* by Tom Schneider (Little, Brown, 1976, 139 pages, $6.95 hardcover). The book includes everything from yoga to T'ai Chi Ch'uan. It provides rational, clear, easy-to-understand instructions on how to do it, how to start, how to get other people involved.

Running, weight training, swimming are all part of this overview of a form of recreation that is geared to self-fulfillment rather than public approval. There are photographs, drawings, charts, illustrations of how to make your own equipment, everything.

The book is subtitled "A Kid's Guide to New Sports and Fitness." But it's for people of all ages who appreciate their bodies and want to use them fully and lovingly. Yes, it's only an introduction—but what a way to begin!

BERNIE DE KOVEN

SPORTS AND PHYSICAL FITNESS

Probably one of the best things we can do for our youngsters is to interest them in regular exercise and to encourage them to keep it up as they get older. . . . We should encourage our children to establish proper habits in these areas, so that they do not have to change fixed patterns of living later.
BENNETT OLSHAKER, M.D.

Body Building

Far be it from me to offer particular advice on the subject of body building. But I would say that it is largely a worthless endeavor from the standpoint of improving athletic ability or coordination. To be sure, a stronger overall frame will usually do no harm, especially in heavy contact sports. But if kids want to improve their prowess in baseball/basketball/football/tennis, they probably would be better to strengthen their wrists rather than their biceps. A person's wrist strength is extraordinarily important and largely ignored.

If the kid insists, and he probably will, make certain he knows what he's doing. Lifting weights can be dangerous, and requires strict adherence to the rules of caution and balance. To be safe, a kid should lift weights with someone else around, and make increases in the poundage in a gradual progression. Any decent conditioning program will combine weight lifting with an equivalent running program, which for my money is worth far more.

At any rate, kids' interest in body building never seems to last very long, principally because it is brutally demanding and boringly repetitious.

WILLIAM A. GOLDSTEIN

Some Things to be Said for Jogging

1. Kids who are embarrassingly uncoordinated at organized sports can jog without shame.
2. Parents and children can jog together—

talking, or just enjoying each other's company. And let's face it, you could use the exercise.

3. Maybe all exercise is drudgery, but at least jogging lets you enjoy the outdoors. Country roads, beaches, city parks—even running around the block beats lifting weights in the basement.

4. Medical evidence is accumulating that "endurance fitness"—as opposed to mere muscle tone—is a key factor in longer life, and running is considered just about the best exercise to help your child—or you—achieve this.

CBC

The Sweet Smell of Failure: Sugar and Athletic Performance

A sweet tooth does not a sweet play make. So, in more scholarly language, says a report issued by the Department of Nutrition and Dietetics of the University of Montreal after a yearlong study of the effects of sugar on athletic performance.

An amateur hockey team was evaluated for performance, resistance to fatigue and playing ability. The control group was free to consume candy and chocolate bars, while the rest of the team was split into a sugar-free group and a test group given increasing sugar diets over an eight-month period. The sugar eaters, said the report, saw their ability to play drop to the level of incompetence as more and more gum and chocolate were added to their diets. Neither pep talks nor putdowns by teammates were sufficient to restore the original level of performance. Each youth on the sugar diet "had a severely weakened metabolism and was physically inferior to the rest of the team. Digestion of sugar and sugar substitutes in the candy robbed the body of its energy at the time when the game called for maximum ability. Concentration, resistance and physical strength dropped surprisingly, even for small amounts of sugar ingested."

Meanwhile, those on sugar-free diets improved their performances by 63%. In other words, where athletes are concerned, a sugar shortage would be a plus.

Sports Illustrated

[See pages 148–157 for more on sugar and some alternatives.]

OTHER SPORTS
(INCLUDING WORM-GRUNTING)

Some Thoughts on Fishing

A seven-year-old can fish; a ten-year-old can often cast better than her parents; and a three-year-old can sit in the boat and color and read and look around. And talk. One of the biggest thrills for my seven-year-old daughter came the afternoon she caught twenty tiny bluegill and we ate the biggest ones. (The only other equally thrilling experience was the first time she fed a bottle to a baby.)

Get the cheapest model of a good reel and rod—something like a Garcia, St. Croix, Pflueger, or Penn—it's superior to the five-and-ten variety or what you get at Sears. You can often get seconds at a sporting goods store, because the string is wound funnily around the lead line or it has some other minor quirk. The only upkeep is to clean and oil the rod and switch the line once a year.

Look in the sports section of the newspaper to find out which fish are running where.

For a kid who's really into it, think about a subscription to *Field and Stream* or *Fisherman's Digest* as a gift—there are nice pictures, good fish tales, and information about equipment.

GAY LORD and BARBARA HENRY

Worm Grunting, or, Fishing Worms Cost a Dollar a Dozen at the Bait Store, But You Can Make Them Come to You

What you do is, you cut yourself a length of hickory or sweet gum about four feet long and sharpen one end with an ax. Then you find yourself a length of flat iron—a leaf spring from a car or truck is ideal. Drive your stake into the ground. Rub the top of it *hard* with the flat of the iron. This will create a vibration you can feel in your feet, and an ugly sound. Every earthworm for about 20 feet around will find the vibration so disagreeable that it will crawl immediately to the surface. Stow your stake and your iron, fill your bait can and go fishing.

If you feel you need lessons, these are available free any morning outside Mr. M. B. Hodge's bait store in Sopchoppy, Fla. Mr. Hodge buys worms from dozens of people who make their living this way. In Sopchoppy, it is called "worm grunting." In neighboring counties of the Florida panhandle, it is also called "twiddling" or "fiddling" or "scrubbing" for worms, and it is thought that square stobs or triangular ones work best. People in Sopchoppy are contemptuous of these deviations from the common round stake and truck spring. More than 30 million earthworms a year are grunted around Sopchoppy, so Sopchoppy people know what they are talking about.

One word of caution, which sounds like a lie but is the truth: if you want to grunt worms for pay in a National Forest, you need a U.S. Worm Gathering License.

CHARLES KURALT
in *The Great Escape*

RONNIE SHUSHAN: THE PHOTO WORKS

The Proper Way to Go Inner-tubing

First, find some rapids in a stream. Get the inner tube from a tire and blow it up, but not all the way. If you blow it up all the way it will burst if you hit a submerged log. When that is finished, set the inner tube in the water and get on and sail down the stream. Remember to wear a life preserver; the best swimmer can drown. If you want to find a stream near you to go inner-tubing in, contact your local parks department.

JOE MICKIEL MEYER
Age twelve

Beachballs and Broomsticks

The Topanga Canyon *Messenger* reports the formation of local Broom Polo teams. Broom Polo, they say, is played on horseback "like the grownup stuff, but with brooms and a big beachball instead of lethal polo sticks and a wooden ball."

ELS

[According to Dr. Kenneth H. Cooper, inventor of aerobics, cycling—along with walking, jogging, and swimming—is one of the four truly useful forms of exercise. To learn more about cycling and about how to select the proper bike for your child, turn to pages 394–397, in the OUTDOOR PLAY section.]

A Mini-Olympics for Very Different Siblings

How do I find the time, energy, and ingenuity for three very different boys, one aged ten and twins aged eight and a half? Often my choice on-the-run is to try to do something with all three of them. This seems fairest, and most efficient. But for any one child this plan means his contact is diluted to one-third. Too often our four-man games break down into a squabble. The only exceptions to this seem to be outside-the-home activities that are defined by them as "treats" (such as miniature golf and bowling), and something I invented called "Rainbow Club," which is a mini-Olympics involving such youthful skills as breath-holding, tickle-withstanding, headstands, and other talents where they compete more against themselves than each other, and where I am not allied with any one of them.

RICHARD ALMOND

AND, FOR THE FANS . . .

The Book That "Begins Where Guinness Leaves Off"

If your child is going through the stage where he'll spout weird bits of sports trivia at just about any provocation (I'm still at this stage myself), then *Nestor Kraly's Amazing Sports Records and Other Oddities* (Fawcett, $1.25 paperback) is for him (or her). The book starts out touting Charles Zibbelman's world-record 168 consecutive hours of legless swimming and goes uphill (or downhill) from there. Thousands of entries later, with a passing reference to categories in which Russian women athletes never won an Olympic Gold Medal and a final burst of inspirational quotes, Mr. Kraly finally wears himself out. Perhaps he'll wear your child out too.

CBC

The Sporting News: A Statistical Gold Mine

Statistics are the stock-in-trade of the true sports addict. As a kid growing up in New York, it was essential for me to know the batting averages of not only *every* player on my beloved Yankees and Giants, but also of the leading prospects in their farm systems. And, naturally, an intimate knowledge of the up-to-the-minute performance levels of the major league leaders in *every* category—from outfield assists to being hit by pitched balls—was also an absolute requirement.

My main source for such information was a weekly tabloid known as *The Sporting News* (which is still going strong, and which has expanded its coverage to include all major spectator sports.) Not only did the newspaper provide me with one of my principal sources of recreational reading, but in studying the tables of winning, batting, and slugging percentages, I developed whatever aptitude I have for mathematics.

If your kid is an avid sports fan, a subscription to *The Sporting News* (about $20 per year) would be a marvelous present. You can find a subscription blank in each weekly copy (sold at most newsstands), or write to *The Sporting News,* P.O. Box 56, St. Louis, Mo. 63166.

CBC

The Baseball-Card-Flipping Guide

The competitive flipping of baseball cards is a great, honorable—and national—pastime that began simultaneously with the publication of the earliest baseball cards—as nearly as can be ascertained, about 1909—with "Talk of the Diamond" cards. It flourished through the 1915 Crackerjacks series, the nineteen-thirties' Goudey and Bowman bubble-gum sets, and reached glorious fruition with the bubble-gum cards of Fleers and Topps in the forties and fifties. Kids—both boys and girls—are still flipping today. Baseball cards are flipped not only in metropolitan New York—where flipping is high art—but in Boston, Chicago and Los Angeles and in the suburbs of America as well. This great American game is pervasive, but also largely unheralded—a situation that this Guide will attempt to remedy. Herewith a brief description of some of the rules, the techniques and the language of The Game.

THE COLLECTION

The ideal storage container for baseball cards has always been a cigar box. One remembers one's Garcia y Vega box with nostalgic fondness. Shoeboxes are acceptable, though inferior, substitutes. One's baseball heroes are carefully sorted into trading stacks, flipping stacks and collecting stacks. Sorted cards are, of course, held firmly by rubber bands. Generally, doubles or even unwanted singles are traded or flipped. Other precious cards are not flipped but are kept forever, or at least until mother cleans out the closet.

THE GRIP

The card—new and stiff—is held by all five fingers. They must rest on the long edges of the 3½-by-2½-inch card. The thumb is at the top edge, the other four fingers on the bottom; the card is positioned just back of the fingertips. There are those who pass sandpaper across the fingertip whorls to smooth off winter calluses before flipping. This is not regarded as cheating.

THE STANCE

The best flippers stand like Joselito, Hemingway's favorite *torero,* as he planted himself for La Faena: feet together; weight balanced on the balls of the feet and on the toes; spine arched backward, arms veed to the rear, pulling at the shoulder muscles. The store of cards to be flipped is held in the left hand and taken, one at a time, into the right hand—reverse this for southpaws—and then flipped into competition.

THE FLIP

Like the perfect golf swing or the tennis smash, a practiced flipping motion is the key to success in baseball-card competition. A player assumes The Grip and The Stance. Then, the arm is straightened and held downward, slightly to the rear of the player's own rear. The hand holding the card is palm forward. The flipper is required to look back, over his or her shoulder, down at the hand as it moves forward a trifle, pendulum-fashion, then into a modest backswing and then forward again. The card is released into the motion-manufactured breeze just as the hand passes the thigh. If released with precision, the card will flip slightly backward in its journey to the ground so that it comes to rest about a half foot behind the flipper—and will *always* be heads or tails, as demanded by the flipper. This is the most common baseball card flipping motion, and the technique for several games, including "Flips" and "Unmatch."

FLIPS

This game, sometimes known as "Singles," is your basic card-flipping contest. An opposing player gives a command—say, "Head, tail, tail, head"—and the flipper has to tumble his cards in precisely that order or lose either the four cards involved or an agreed-upon stake (today a Reggie Jackson or a Johnny Bench, in my day a Spud Chandler or Phil Rizzuto). "Singles" is the same game—it is believed to have originated in Richmond Hill—except that the demand for heads or tails is made one card at a time. The stake is the card being flipped. A variation is "Fives and Tens," where 5 or 10 cards are flipped to order.

UNMATCH

A perverse game, long a favorite in Park Slope, this is a variant of "Singles." The flipper is required to "unmatch" the specific order given. Authorities judge this a difficult game because a player not only has to flip his cards but must also *think* as well.

OFF THE STOOP

This contest is well worth mentioning because of its popularity. However, purists might say the game is analogous to church-bazaar wheels of chance, where success depends on luck. "Off the Stoop" is believed to have originated in Brooklyn Heights, where it still thrives; rarely if ever is it played in the suburbs, for obvious reasons. The players kneel on the top step of a stoop. With their thumbs and middle fingers, they shoot baseball cards outward to the sidewalk. The object of this game is not to *match* cards, but to cover one's opponent's card with one's own. If you cover the card, you own it. However, an important house rule, called "Tippies," could change the fate of a game. A "Tippy" occurs when a corner of one card barely touches the corner of another card. A "Tippy" is considered a miss unless the house invokes the rule that a "Tippy" wins. In a variant game, "Up Against the Wall," the card is slapped against a wall and permitted to flutter down.

PITCHING

This game, a product of Manhattan's Upper West Side, requires a unique grip and flipping motion. The baseball card is slid between the first two fingers of the hand and, guided by the thumb, tossed toward a wall. Follow-through is very important. Usually three or five cards are thrown in succession; the player owning the card nearest the wall gathers up all the cards thrown.

I would like to conclude this Guide to Baseball-Card Flipping with a reminiscence from my own playing days. During one competition—I think it was "Off the Stoop"—I had a "Tippy." My card, a Heinie Manush, was barely touching a Honus Wagner. Unfortunately the "Tippy" rule was not in force that day, so I lost.

ELISABETH SCHARLATT

Only recently has this ancient defeat returned to haunt me. I have learned, believe it or not, that the Honus Wagner card . . . is now worth about $1,500 to collectors. It seems that, originally, the card appeared in a pack of Sweet Caporal cigarettes, and was withdrawn when Honus decided the image he projected to American youth was not enhanced by appearing stuck into a pack of smokes. Only 96 Honus Wagners got into circulation and there are only about 10 or 12 around now, and thus the $1,500 value.

All of which goes to show you what happens when you don't call "Tippies."

FRED FERRETTI
The New York Times Magazine

GAMES FOR ARMCHAIR ATHLETES

Strat-O-Matic

Strat-O-Matic is played with dice and cards representing actual professional teams, basketball and baseball. The baseball teams range from the 1905 New York Giants (Christy Mathewson was 32–8 that year, the second year in which the World Series was played) to the great fence-busting New York Yankees and the current nines (or tens, in the case of the DH American League). The basketball teams are NBA.

The cards list the potential of the players. If Babe Ruth is at bat, your roll of the dice will be matched with his card and the chances are almost predictable that the Babe's roll of the dice will be identical to what he actually would have done on the diamond way back when. (In the Babe's case, it would probably have been a Ruppert Blast.) Strat-O-Matic baseball lets you manage, pull pitchers, give signals, pinch hit. Great World Series can be created—the 1927 Yankees against the 1955 Braves, even the 1927 Yankees against the 1949 Yankees, for example.

The basketball cards also let you razzle-dazzle. You can double team Jerry West—you can even keep the ball from him in the last three seconds when you're just one point up.

Strat-O-Matic is available by mail order; write to 46 Railroad Avenue, Glen Head, N.Y. 11545.

JESSIE AGEL

---

on his way

a couple of months back, in the midst of cold january, i picked up a sports illustrated baseball game, thinking there might be a piece in it for this space, something charming and witty and nostalgic about the hot stove league perhaps. but somehow i never looked at it much, maybe because this particular game, all-time all-star baseball, depended on computers for its origin and i'm still back in the spin-dial days, that glorious game we played as kids where the rosters were the previous year's all stars, each represented by a card that fit onto a spinner dial. each batter had his card divided pie-style to represent the number of homers, singles, strike-outs, etc., he might be expected to get under normal, i.e., average, circumstances. the new game had instead three weird dice, one black and two white, and you rolled them to get a number from 10 to 39, and then you looked that number up on the batter's or pitcher's card, and you got your answer, still dictated by the averages but, of course, somehow, to me, the old way was better.

in the new game the squads consisted of the 16 original major league clubs, each represented by a melange of old and new heroes,

based on a vote taken a couple of years back as to the all-time players in each city. so the dodgers had tommy davis as well as the duke and zack wheat, dazzy vance, and sandy koufax, and so on.

well, the game sat on my shelf, and i figured maybe nathaniel would get interested in it at some future date, maybe 12 or so. but spring came, and baseball started, and lo and behold, he found it now. he was playing ball all afternoon, and he asked if he could try it at night when it got too dark to play outside. soon we had a full league going in the house, him playing the dodgers, and all the other finky kids in this building taking the yankees. i don't need to tell you he kept getting clobbered. like i tried to explain to him, the yankees had 40 years of great players, and the dodgers had ten, so there was an essential imbalance, even when he had koufax pitching.

i tried to get him to make the other guys take somebody besides the yankees once in a while, but that seemed like copping out, so finally amidst many misgivings on his part, i talked him into trying the pirates. he knew nothing about them, had heard only of willie stargell, and was astonished to hear that ralph kiner on the card was the same one on television. of such things these days does history start.

he beat the yankees something like 7–5 in the first game, and the pirates became his club. the other night i was fiddling in the kitchen and i heard him and gabby starting a game. they were announcing their lineups complete with crowd echoes: "batting first-irst-irst, max carey-arey-arey, playing centerfield-ield-ield," etc., and then i heard him say: "batting third-ird-ird, playing shortstop-op-op, fast base stealer-ealer-ealer, good bunter-unter-unter (the game allows for such things), and my dad's favorite player-ayer-ayer, honus wagner-agner-agner!" "oh christ," said gabby, "not him again!"

well, i thought, dad, up there in heaven, the torch is passed on, you telling me in '37, '38, about the bowlegged dutchman, now the kid is playing him. he shifts him to third against right-handed pitchers so he can put arky vaughan at short. was i that smart that young? and that re-spectful of the old folks? later that night nathan-iel hauled out a book i'd picked up at a rum-mage sale a couple of years back about the original hall of famers and we read the section on wagner together. now he's got someone to counter gabby's ruth, dimaggio, and mantle, and he wins some games, too.

now i steal looks out the window at him play-ing ball, and the swing is good and straight, and he even begins to understand how to field. he's found a game to play that we all found, and the magic is beginning. he was in a cab last sunday with his mother and heard the cabbie's radio announce that harry parker had been hit in the knee by a line drive. the phone rang here at home and it was nathaniel: "how's harry? is he okay?" it took me five minutes of conversation to find out what he meant and then i told him the trainer had reported he was okay. he sighed his relief and went back to dinner with his aunt.

and yesterday he told me he had something wrong with his toes. they itched a lot and when he rubbed them they hurt. so today i went out and bought him his first can of desenex pow-der, his first tube of desenex ointment. the kid has athlete's foot. he's proud of it, and so am i in some warped way. he's on his way to man-hood in the american dream.

joel oppenheimer
Village Voice

Incidentally, that "glorious game" featuring pie-style batters' spinner cards that Joel Oppenhei-mer referred to above is still available. It's called All-Star Baseball, and it's produced and dis-tributed by Cadeco, Inc. ($4.99).

One of the charms of the game is that last year's cards fit on this year's game board. I still have my Danny Litwhiler, Ernie Lombardi, and Bill "Swish" Nicholson cards.

CBC

Table Hockey

I've been an addict of "table hockey" since my father gave my younger brother Jonathan and me our first model ice-hockey game back in the early 1950s. That primitive set boasted metal players that rotated in fixed positions when you spun the corresponding metal rods; with a little practice you could learn to slam a black marble with extraordinary speed toward your oppo-nent's goal. One of the highlights of the game was that a red light went on whenever you scored a goal—went on, that is, if your batteries weren't dead or if your shot went into the net at the correct angle to set off the temperamental trigger mechanism.

Table hockey has grown up a lot since then, and my brother and I grew—if not matured—with it. When the first set came out with players that could "skate" up and down the ice by slid-ing in grooves, we had to have it. When the first automatic puck dropper was introduced—by now a wooden disk had replaced the marble—we were among the first to own one. We even ended up purchasing the miniature replicas of National Hockey League trophies which the Colēco Company, which manufactured our set, so thoughtfully made available by mail.

Why all the excitement? Well, for one thing, table hockey seems to reproduce the sport after which it's modeled far more realistically than any of the simulated football and baseball games on the market. You really get the feeling, as you twist and pull those little knobs, that you're in the midst of a major-league hockey game. For frustrated athletes—and I was al-ready a frustrated athlete by the time I was eight—that feeling of realism is terribly impor-tant.

Secondly, table hockey is a game anyone—from age six or seven on up—can play and enjoy right away. But, silly as it seems, it's also a game of skill and cunning: the more you prac-tice—perfecting pass plays, learning how to fake, dreaming up your own strategy—the better you get.

The result of all this for Jonathan and me was that we acted out a great deal of our sibling competitiveness on our miniature hockey rink. Jon would work alone for hours to develop a new lift shot or a slap shot from the defense; then he'd beat me soundly for weeks until, after my own lonely hours of experimentation, I found a way to stop it. Once again my brother would retire to solitary practice until he had a new pass to center or whatever, and the cycle would continue.

So proficient did we become, in fact, that a few years ago, when a crazed editor-writer named Stanley Fischler announced he was organizing a World Table Hockey Tournament, we entered and won not only the T. J. Rugg Trophy symbolizing dominance of the international table-hockey doubles scene, but also the Pagello Award for goal-tending excellence. (Unfortunately, Stan Fischler's impressive publicity efforts on behalf of our victory attracted other fanatical adherents of table hockey from all over Canada and the U.S., and we lost our title the next year to a duo from Minneapolis.)

So, now that you've decided to invest in a table hockey set for your children (or yourself), which brand should you get?

Well, my *heart* belongs to the Colēco Stanley Cup model, since it's the set that Jonathan and I have played on the most. Its main features are a sliding plastic puck (as opposed to the ball-bearing-inside-a-disk used in the Munro Bobby Hull game), spring-activated players (as opposed to plastic gears in the Munro set), and relatively narrow goal mouths, which, as one's play improves, make for contests dominated by defense. There's a model that comes with its own legs, but putting them on is one of the

most complicated and frustrating tasks I've ever been confronted with, and you may prefer to use a table or the floor when you or your children play.

Munro's Bobby Hull Hockey Game is generally similar to the Colēco Stanley Cup model. The most apparent difference is that the Munro puck is a plastic ring with a metal ball bearing inside, which leads it to move straighter and more predictably—and with a good bit more force—than Colēco's. A second, more important difference is that a spin of a Munro knob is transmitted to a plastic player by means of miniature gears; this system seems to produce far fewer breakdowns than the Colēco spring action. Third, Munro's wider goals tend to produce a lot more scoring than Colēco's. This last, combined with a rather subtle flaw—that it's possible for an expert to manipulate the Munro puck from behind his own net to the front of the opponent's goal without the other player ever being able to touch it—leads many aficionados to favor the Colēco set. But, for general durability, and fun for the beginner, my unsentimental vote would have to go to the Munro Bobby Hull model.

CBC

CHILDREN'S SPORTS BOOKS

Thirteen Reviews, and Five Tough Questions

Sports books for children are the processed breakfast foods of publishing: overpriced, gaudy packages of leftover facts and empty truths and guaranteed pre-digested sentences. Now that "adult" sports books frequently contain Marxist exegesis and/or Nixonian expletive, children's books are heading on beyond sepsis into a world so free from those minor upsets due to words that a current biography of Vince Lombardi can rehash his final illness, operations,

death, and funeral without using the word "cancer."

Reviewing a batch of forty-one books was basically an exercise in consumer affairs. Herewith, five questions to ask yourself before buying, and thirteen acceptable purchases.

1. Is it readable?

Librarians and schoolteachers are always claiming that nonreaders have been "turned on" by a sports book. I believe them. But readers turned on to books filled with words like "unforgettable," "immortal," and "greatest" may have to lean on exclamation marks the rest of their lives.

Of the forty-one books, most were either ground out, or taken, like rubbings, from similar books now dead.

Breaking In, compiled and edited by Lawrence T. Lorimer [illustrated; Dell paperback, 198 pages, $1.25], was really stitched together, like a patchwork quilt, but it's the best buy. Lorimer's short, graceful introductions connect dramatic and meaningful excerpts from the autobiographies of Rube Marquard, Spencer Haywood, Mickey Mantle, Anthony Quinn, Dave Meggysey, Don Schollander, Althea Gibson, and Jackie Robinson.

For a very limited audience there is *Talking of Horses,* by Monica Dickens (illustrated; Little, Brown, 154 pages, $6.95), a charmingly personal, pastoral, anecdotal upper-class British ramble about the care, feeding, training and, mostly, loving of show and riding horses.

Henry Aaron: Quiet Superstar, by Al Hirshberg, updated by Mark Denton (Putnam's, 189 pages, $4.97), is a solid, no-nonsense career biography, long on game detail, short on boyhood stories or personal insight.

Satchel Paige, by Robert Rubin (Putnam's, 158 pages, $4.97), captures the black pitcher's voice by ripping off great chunks from his 1962 autobiography and enclosing them in quotes. This is "research." The original is *Maybe I'll Pitch Forever.* Get it if you can.

2. Can this book go the distance?

Younger readers tend to open their books on tables and floors and do push-ups on them. Check the durability of a prospect before you pay for it. Quite a number of the cheaper books with laminated covers—particularly the otherwise acceptable Random House Pro Basketball Library, Pro Hockey Library, etc.—are more vulnerable than Namath's knees.

These books are actually fan magazines between boards, offering inoffensive player biographies by competent working sportswriters. But the weaker among them will be loose-leaf in an hour, a consideration if this is a gift.

Dodd, Mead has a line of books with "reinforced durable bindings" which are sturdy and attractive. Two I particularly liked were by the prolific George Sullivan, *Baseball's Art of Hitting* and *Linebacker!* Illustrated, anecdotal books with some useful how-to.

Two other fairly durable books that might make nice presents are *Great Moments in American Sports,* by Jerry Brondfield (Random House, 152 pages, $5.99), and *Great Pro* *Quarterbacks,* edited by Lud Duroska (Grosset & Dunlap, 157 pages, $4.95). Both are large, well illustrated, and crisply written.

Great Women Athletes, by Martha Moffett (illustrated; Platt & Munk, 91 pages,) is a pedestrian effort in concept and execution. Presumably we can expect a flood of serious and funny and instructional books for the female fan and athlete. This will do until better appears.

3. Are the pictures clear?

Having watched the game on a 19-inch color set and seen the stunning photographs in *Sports Illustrated,* the young reader can hardly be expected to make do with poorly cropped black-and-white Associated Press wirephotos and diagrams that resemble electrical circuitry. Kids scrutinize art, especially if it is a stop-action of something they may have already seen. If the pictures don't have a clarifying value of their own, don't buy the book.

4. Can you understand it?

Many sports books contain instructional material that has been passed down for generations without a writer or editor ever having read it aloud. Read it aloud. If it doesn't make sense to you, it won't to a ten-year-old.

Even if it does make sense, be wary. Some directions—for football blocking and tackling, baseball pitching, and karate, for example—should be followed only with competent adult supervision. If you're not the coach, don't send in the play.

Some how-to books look better than they are; closer inspection will reveal ancient Safety Council photos, descriptions of out-of-date equipment, and dry treatises on the origin of the sport's name. If you're not sure of the material covered, don't buy the book just because you know the child is interested in the sport.

One reference book I saw seemed worthwhile, although its layout was crowded and its emphasis (11 pages for sailboating, 1 for table tennis) often seemed quirky. It's called *The Concise Encyclopedia of Sports,* edited by Keith Jennison (illustrated; Franklin Watts, 168 pages, $8.95).

5. Do you affirm the book's premise?

This is tricky and crucial, because giving a book to a child may be construed as a tacit affirmation of the book's implicit message.

Roberto Clemente, by Kenneth Rudeen, illustrated by Frank Mullins (Crowell, 33 pages, $4.50), is a short and simple biography of the baseball star's childhood, major-league career, and death, on New Year's Eve 1972, en route to help feed the survivors of the Managua earthquake. Economic, social, and racial problems are indicated, but not belabored. A fine springboard for further talk, especially if you're reading it aloud.

Inside Corner, Talks with Tom Seaver, edited by Joel H. Cohen (illustrated; Atheneum, 246 pages, $7.95), is a stupefying interview that allows Tom to offer advice ("Getting married and having kids right away is a no-no") and name the two people he most admires outside baseball (James Reston and Barbra Streisand). The Seaver presented here is cautious, decent, politic, dull; pretty close to the true Seaver.

Six Days to Saturday, by Jack Newcombe (illustrated; Farrar, Straus & Giroux, 93 pages, $6.95), is virtually a recruiting brochure for coach Joe Paterno and Penn State football. De-tail by detail, treating the players as nameless objects, Newcombe, who went to college with Paterno, shows a sample week of intensive preparations for a Saturday game. There is no critique of big-time college football, no perception of Paterno's exaggerated position as the progressive yet pragmatic Eastern Liberal Fantasy Coach.

In the quality of prose and art and production, this book is far superior to most of the others, yet it offers up the clearest example of the basic problem of these books. Unless you believe in its moral statement, giving such a book is a kind of abdication. It's like letting Tony the Tiger and Cap'n Crunch feed the children every morning.

ROBERT LIPSYTE
The New York Times Book Review

OUTDOOR PLAY

393

RIDE-ONS, SLIDE-ONS, AND WALK-ONS

"Big Wheels" and Other Low-slung Tricycles

The *Marx Big Wheel* has set off a fad for a new, low-slung type of tricycle that offers more play possibilities than a conventional tricycle. Except for the axle and pedal cranks, the *Big Wheel* is made basically of hollow plastic. It has a 16-inch front wheel, a low center of gravity, and plastic wheels that slide easily. The maker suggests it for 3-to-7-year-olds. Its success, due partly to the skidding games that can be played with it, has led to a slew of imitators and smaller variants.

The most popular maneuver performed with this type of tricycle is the "spinout," in which the youngster pedals briskly and then lifts his or her feet and performs an abrupt turn. About halfway through the turn, the rear wheels lose traction and the rear whips around about 180°. Some youngsters press it further and get a full-circle turn, winding up facing in the original direction. These maneuvers take lots of room but can be performed in reasonable safety (as long as they're not done in the street). The rear wheels slide easily and the seat is down between them, which minimizes the chance of accidental overturning.

Some youngsters, still not satisfied, will complete the skidding trick with a mock accident in which, with a considerable application of body English, they force a rollover at the final stage of the spinout. Although that can be scary to an onlooker, it usually comes off harmlessly, because the child, sitting only a few inches off the ground, just rolls over. Now add to that the game of deliberate collisions and you have a fair picture of the appeal of these toys.

Part of our evaluation of these tricycles was based on observing kids riding them. Our object was to assess how well the toys protect the children against their own antics and how well the machines stayed together. Fortunately, both the children and the tricycles survived without mishap. . . .

We think the *Big Wheel* deserves first consideration. Its all-plastic wheels and body could both give and take bumps harmlessly. More important, it was the most stable and most forgiving of the breed—not surprising since it has the widest rear-wheel spacing and one of the lowest seats. Its simple plug-in seatback made adjustment so easy that children could do it when exchanging turns. Finally, it had an important fea-

ture not found on the others: a small hand brake for one of the rear wheels. Youngsters used it both for braking and as help in initiating skidding maneuvers.

The slightly smaller *Sport Wheel,* by the same maker, lacks the brake but shares the other positive attributes of the *Big Wheel.* It came in second.

In third place by a narrow margin is the *Hot Cycle.* It was quieter than most and, like the two Marx models, all-plastic and non-hostile to flesh. With its narrower track and higher seat, though, it was apparently not quite as forgiving. When pressed, it would occasionally tip over accidentally. Also, tools were required to adjust the seat position.

The *AMF All Star* was also quieter than most and it, too, has a wide stance and low seat. But it was difficult to get moving or to control because its front wheel slipped excessively. In fact, about eight hours of hard use practically wore the front wheel out, whereas the others showed only minor wear. Its seat required tools to reposition, also.

The two machines that the children liked best ended up tied for last. The kids like their wild performance, which was just what concerned us. The *Hedstrom Super Cycle* and its little sibling, the *Sears Trail Cycle,* have a rubber tire on the pedal wheel that made spinouts particularly violent. Further, they lack the stable wide stance of the *Big Wheel* and the *AMF,* and their seats are higher than the rest. Spills occurred all too often. This pair was also the noisiest of the bunch, and they shared a seat-adjustment system that proved an annoyance. Their seats are held in place on their metal frame rails by bolted clamps. On our samples these clamps sometimes slipped, allowing the seat to slide to its rearmost position.

Since these low-slung tricycles encourage abuse by their very nature, we don't know if they'll survive to be passed from child to child, as you might expect with a conventional tricycle. We've seen them take incredible torture and come out undamaged. But after many skidding games, the plastic wheels do wear out. Replacement wheels and parts are available, however.

Because these machines invite children to be more daring with them, we think they call for extra prudence by parents, particularly in finding safe locations—off active streets or driveways—for their use.   *Consumer Reports*

Little Tikes' Ride-ons: Sturdy, Safe, Stylish—and Expensive

The Little Tikes Company (8705 Freeway Drive, Macedonia, Ohio) manufactures a variety of durable ride-on toys for pre-schoolers. They're more expensive than most, but well worth the price; they combine tasteful design, sturdy molded-plastic construction, lasting play value, and most important, soft-rounded corners as an added safety precaution against cuts and bruises.

CBC

ALLAN SHEDLIN, JR THE PHOTO WORKS

THE IRISH MAIL. You steer it with your feet, and you pump your arms and legs to make it go. It's great exercise, and was my favorite toy when I was a kid. I have a muscle in my arm that I'm quite sure I got from riding the Irish Mail. It comes from England and, unfortunately, isn't always easy to find in this country. F. A. O. Schwarz sometimes has them, for around $30. —ALLAN SHEDLIN, JR.

Don't Buy a Ride-on If Its Seams Are Showing

When purchasing a plastic ride-on, look for wheels that don't have a seam down the center. The ones with the seams split. (This tip came from an eight-year-old who prefers his 10-speed Peugeot to anything the toy industry can produce.)

RS

◆

Lowering (or Raising) the Decibel Level

If you live in an apartment building and want to keep peace with the neighbors (and can get away with it with your kid), you can remove the noisemaker from the Marx Big Wheel.

RS

If, on the other hand, you don't live in an apartment (or don't care about the neighbors), you can buy your kid R-R-R-Raw Power by Ideal, a device which fits over the handlebar of his trike or bike and instantly gives him the ability to produce the roar of a motorcycle with the mere twist of a handle. R-R-R-Raw Power requires no batteries and retails for about $5. It's not recommended for bikes with handbrakes, and with good reason: an inaccurate flick of the noise handle might produce a sudden stop that will send your little darling flying over the handlebars.

CBC

BICYCLES: BUYING, RIDING, AND TOTING

Buying a Bicycle: Some Slightly Contradictory Considerations

SIZE

Do not buy a bike for a child to grow into. People make the mistake of buying bikes the way they buy clothing. If the child needs a 16-inch bike, parents buy a 20-inch bike for the child to grow into, because bikes are expensive. But a five-year-old who needs a 16-inch bike is totally frustrated trying to ride the 20-inch bike. What parents either don't know, or don't take advantage of, is that most bikes have adjustable handlebars and seats so the bike can grow with the child. A 16-inch bike should serve a kid for four or five years. And if a small bike isn't adjustable, it should be rejected on the grounds that it has built-in obsolescence.

From an interview with STEVEN CANEY

SAFETY

Let's concede that there's an inherent danger in a two-wheeled vehicle that requires primarily rider skill in order to operate it. And if you lack sufficient skill, or you're just learning, you're certainly going to come up with a number of scrapes and bumps. But there's no question that manufacturers contribute tremendously to the dangers of bicycles.

Seventy-five percent of all the bikes that are sold to juveniles today (with the exception of 10-speeds or racing bikes, which are more or less functionally designed) are high-styled: they have high handlebars, which a child can't properly control; they have banana seats, which, if the rider leans back too far, cause the bike to tip backward; there are even bicycles with the gear-shift lever on the horizontal bar, so that if the kid bumps against a wall and slides he gets a crotch full of gear-shift lever. You can usually look at the styling and figure out the additional coordination needed to cope with the design.

I bought my five-year-old the plainest two-wheeler I could find: a Columbia for $44.95. A lot of the other 16-inch bikes I saw were in the $50 to $60 range, and were more expensive merely because of all that high-styled stuff on them.
                From an interview with STEVEN CANEY

BRAND

Many sources report excellent luck with Murray tricycles and Schwinn bicycles, and feel they are well worth the extra purchase price. —Eds.

PEER PRESSURE

If you want to buy a cheap bike, it's going to be a cheap bike. (You might be better off with a second-hand one, but test-drive it thoroughly before you buy.) If you want a good bike, it's going to cost more money than the cheap one. Chances are, though, that if your kid goes to school, it's peer-group pressure, not quality or safety, that will determine what kind of bicycle you are going to end up buying for your child. As with sneakers, notebooks, hairdos, and clothing, there is the "right" bike for each group and only that brand will do. (Isolation of parents being what it is, one couldn't possibly be trusted to choose a proper banana seat or chain guard.)
                                            ELS

The Best Ten-Speed Bicycle Under $300

Ten-speed bicycles aren't for everybody, though you would never know it from the sales. They are expensive—up to $600 for a production model—difficult to ride, and easy to damage. In city traffic you may find yourself, with a ten-pound anti-theft chain around your neck, shifting through seven or eight gears (one at a time) just to get up to cruising speed. Hit a pothole and you will bend a wheel ($15 plus). Even with the best of care you will need to service your ten-speed every few months. Figure $50 annually.

. . . With a ten-speed bicycle (and no other) a nonfanatic may look forward to easily pedaling forty miles of country road in five hours, all problems sublimated save the possibility of rain or truck traffic.

In essence, what you get for the money is a super-light bicycle frame—about fifteen pounds lighter than a sturdy Raleigh English Racer—and a set of gears that provide minutely graded choice over a rather narrow range. The virtues of light weight are self-evident, particularly if you plan to tour hilly country. And much of the

investment in a fine bike goes into the seamless manganese-molybdenum steel tubular frame, which has been braised rather than welded for maximum strength. (Welding increases the probability of undetectable structural faults at the joints.)

All those gears don't give you a wider range to work with than a three-speed. But the more gears you have, the more likely that you will be able to maintain a steady pedal rhythm over varied terrain. As in long-distance swimming or running, a paced effort just short of the level that winds the athlete is most efficient . . .

Our choice for the best, the Peugeot U10 ($250), is several hundred dollars cheaper than the most expensive. But what you get for the extra bucks—a few more pounds shaved off the frame, a classy one-piece aluminum crank—just isn't worth it.
                PETER PASSELL and LEONARD ROSS
                                        The Best

[*Consumer Reports* reported on ten-speed bicycles in February 1976. Their criteria and test findings generally provide useful guidelines for your own shopping. You can find back issues of *Consumer Reports* at many libraries.—Eds.]

Teaching a Kid How to Ride: Stay Invisible

I think the most important hint for teaching kids how to ride a bike is to remain as invisible as possible. A firm, straight arm which supports the kid's back, a tight grip on the seat of the bike, and keeping your whole body out of sight would be my recommendation. That way, as

soon as you feel your child gaining balance, it's possible to let go very unobtrusively, allowing those first few free pedals to happen on their own. Once your child has managed to stay up unaided, the rest comes quickly.

One final word of advice: if a big deal is made out of your releasing the bike, the kid is liable to be disarmed and will lose balance and, hence, confidence.
                                DEBBIE KOVACS

Learning to Ride a Bike: Down with Training Wheels (and Wood Blocks, Too)

Don't waste time and money on a set of training wheels for the youngster, unless he is not really ready to learn. Training wheels may help reduce the fear of falling, but no one learns to ride with them in place. Don't give a child, or a small adult either, a large-sized bike with wood blocks taped to the pedals. This is frightening and dangerous because it requires a balancing act to stay vertical.

MAX ALTH
Bikes and Bicycling

◆

Pretend It's a Scooter

My son Paul, six, learned to ride a bike on a virtually trafficless dirt road with a *very slight* incline. He would push his bike to the top of the hill, point it down the road, put his weight on the down pedal, and push off with his other foot. Off he'd coast, standing on the pedal, using his bike as if it were a scooter. The art of balance came quickly, and without pain: only when he felt totally comfortable with "scooting" did he try sitting down on the saddle.

ANNA JANE HAYS

◆

Mind Before Matter

. . . Friends of mine told me about one of their children, a girl of seven or eight. She had asked, begged, pleaded for a regular bicycle. They had given her one, and now, months later, she had not made the slightest attempt to ride it. What should they do, they asked. Try to teach her? Offer to help? Put on a little pressure—what's the point of having a bike if you never even take it out? I urged them not to do this. . . . I suggested that this child was perhaps learning to ride that bike in her mind, and that until she had ridden it there, there was no use trying to make her ride it anywhere else. Perhaps she was watching other children, and thinking, thinking about what it would feel like. Some time later they wrote me that after many more months of not touching the bike, one day the child had taken it out, ridden it on the grass a bit, fallen off once or twice without damage, and then gone riding off down the street with no trouble and had been riding ever since.

JOHN HOLT
Instead of Education

Bicycle Carriers for Children

I've been seeing a lot of a plastic bucket-type bicycle carrier for young children that looks far safer and more comfortable than the metal chair types that used to be common. The bucket seat fastens over the rear wheel. In addition to a seat belt, it has leg wells and a wraparound spoke guard to protect the child's feet from the wheel spokes.

There are several versions available, but a chorus of recommendations from *Consumer Reports Buying Guide for Babies,* my next-door neighbor, and a book I like called *Good Things for Babies* all point to the Sears Pak-A-Poose Baby Carrier as the one to buy. It's listed in the Sears catalogue for $15.99.

RS

Save Your Back

When it comes to gadgets, one that a parent should not be without on those interminable schlepps to the park is a tricycle (or bike) hook. It's about 20 inches long, made of one piece of heavy-duty wire which is bent so there's an oval hand grip, and a spot-welded 10-inch shaft which forks and bends around to form two blunt-end hooks that latch onto the handlebars.

No more the grumbling, lopsided simian gait as I push or pull my son and his trike by hand. No more discovering that it has taken us twenty minutes to go one block. And if he decides along the way that he doesn't want to ride his trike at all, something that provoked a major confrontation in the past, I just hook on and off we go. According to a friend of mine, a rope or a wire clothes hanger is just as efficient, but for my money (about $2), the tricycle hook belongs in the Hall of Fame alongside the safety pin and pop-up Kleenex. It's available (exclusively we're told) at Rappaport Toy Bazaar, 1381 Third Avenue, New York, N.Y. 10021.

FLAVIA POTENZA

SKATES, SKATEBOARDS, SLEDS, AND SUCH

Skate of the Union Message

My daughter's roller skates were manufactured by the Union Hardware Company, the same company that made *my* roller skates, which still work.

JESSICA TRABAND

Beginner skates (No.1) from Union Hardware, with non-ball-bearing metal wheels to control speed, fit shoe sizes 8 to 12, and cost around $3.50.

If for some reason your kid is learning to skate indoors, you might want to buy Union's plastic training skates (No. 9–03). They won't go very fast, but your kid will get used to standing on wheels without scratching your floors. They fit shoe sizes 8 to 1, and cost around $3.

JOAN BINGHAM

For size 3 shoes and up, Union's skates cost about $8 a pair. Before investing in these, however, be sure your kid is ready to handle the speed of roller bearings.

RS

Ice Skating: A Vote for Double Runners

I learned to ice skate on double-runner skates. (Are they still made?) [Yes!—Eds.] Instead of wobbling on a single runner, I stood reasonably erect thanks to the second runner, about ⅓ inch away from the first. My tumbles were fewer, and I'm convinced I gained confidence faster than your average single-runner learner does. I don't think double runners are analogous to training wheels (i.e., purposeless). They are useful and serve to encourage a young skater to move up to a single runner with very little fear.

DEBBIE KOVACS

Ice Skating: No Right Turn

On most city ice rinks, all skating takes place in a counter-clockwise direction. As a veteran of such rinks, I found to my horror, upon trying out for my school's hockey team, that although I was wonderful at turning left, I didn't have a clue how to turn right!

Thus, a hint to aspiring hockey players in urban areas: go find a pond somewhere and do some quiet clockwise skating.

JONATHAN CERF

Skateboarding Safety: "That's Not Snow or Water Beneath You"—Tell Your Kids

There's no question about it: if you ride a skateboard, you're going to fall from time to time. And, while skateboarding is less expensive and more accessible than surfing and skiing, that's not snow or water beneath you. . . .

The most basic safety consideration is making sure the area you plan to skate is safe. Since most skating is done on the road or sidewalk, the first thing to check out is traffic and pedestrian flow. Without going very far, just about anyone can find an area, that, if not totally free of cars and pedestrians, is relatively quiet. In skateboarding, enough is already demanded of

the rider physically, without bringing other factors into the picture. Inanimate obstacles are bad enough, but things that move, like people and cars, vastly increase the risk of collision.

A relatively unused part of a school yard is an ideal location. Without cars, animals, or package-laden pedestrians, it's just you and the skateboard. . . .

If you have to stick to the streets, pay careful attention to the slope of the terrain. Many hills are deceptive in this respect. If it's constant, even a relatively mild gradient can propel you at top speeds. Make sure the surface is sufficiently smooth and free of large cracks, bumps, and debris. Also, if the area you're skating is a slope, be certain you'll have enough room to stop at the bottom without drifting into traffic or crashing into walls or fences. . . .

As for safety equipment, ask yourself this question, "Would a 200-pound halfback stand up to a 270-pound defensive tackle without a helmet and pads?" The answer is obvious. Football pads were designed for a reason: the contact nature of the sport demanded it. Let me tell you, though, the concrete below you is infinitely harder than any football player's body. On top of that, you can run around a tackle, but you can't run from cement.

Safety equipment specifically designed for skateboarding is relatively scarce, even though more is becoming available. But there are plenty of adequate substitutes. You may not find a whole lot of skaters taking these precautions, but most of the best do. First of all, wear a shirt and long pants if you're going to be doing any kind of risky skating. For some skat-ers, that might mean a forty mile an hour down-hill run; for some it might mean an occasional tail or nose wheelie. Only you know how far you're extending yourself, and you should know how to protect yourself. If you have any doubt at all, use your head and don't be swayed by what you see others doing. Tennis shoes (preferably high-top for ankle support), knee and elbow pads, and gloves all offer good protection.

BEN DAVIDSON
The Skateboard Book

If your kids are serious about skateboarding, they'll want a copy of Ben Davidson's *The Skateboard Book* (Grosset & Dunlap, 1976). It's filled with information about different types of boards and wheel assemblies, tips on trick skating, advice on skateboarding clubs, and so forth, all presented with a wealth of detail. There's even a section on how to lobby for a skateboarding park in your community.

CBC

Sleds, Saucers, and Novelty Sliders

So you want to buy a sled? Well, just about everyone we've talked to recommends the Flexible Flyer, that old standby of "Gee Dad" fame. The company's 52-inch model sells for about $22, and five other lengths are available as well. Also highly rated: the Gladding American Flyer, whose various models sell from $2 to $6 cheaper than comparable Flexible Flyers.

Whatever brand you buy, it'll be easier to steer if the crosspiece that connects the runners (and by means of which the sled is maneu-vered) is *jointed* rather than rigid.

Saucers and other "novelty sliders" have no steering mechanism and, therefore, aren't as safe. But if you're sliding only a couple of times a year, a saucer ($4 to $9) or a sliding mat ($2 or $3) makes more sense than a sled.

Here are the criteria to consider when pur-chasing a novelty slider:

- Tug at the hand straps to make sure they are secure. Tug hard.
- Lift it to make sure it's as light as it looks. Some small sliders are heavier than sleds.
- If you want a *fast* ride, buy plastic.
- If you want a *smoother* ride, buy alumi-num. It dents easily, absorbing the shocks from bumps.

RS and CBC

Kangaroo Feet Belong on Kangaroos

Don't buy those shoes with Kangaroo springs on the bottom—they're terrifically good at causing fractures.

JOAN GUSSOW

[The Childcraft catalogue promotes Kangaroo shoes as being safe, but they're not. —RS]

Stilts: Making Them Is Child's Play

Stilts can probably be bought in toy stores, but you might check the lumberyard for scraps. Any child with the balance required to walk on stilts is old enough to hammer a few nails through the boards to attach the wedge foot-pieces. Straps are optional.

PRUDENCE MACKINTOSCH
Texas Monthly

THE BACKYARD AND BEYOND

Water and Sand and Dirt

People don't understand why kids will stand and wash their hands for a half-hour. And people think that kids dig in dirt just because they like to get dirty. Well, kids do like to get dirty and some kids get a kick out of getting clean. But a lot of what it's about is that water and sand and dirt are nondemanding and responsive materials with infinite potential for providing clues to the real world—math, physics, earth formations.

I think kids should be allowed to play with sand and water to their heart's content.

SUSAN KANOR

Get the Sand That Packs, or, Are There Mudpies on the Riviera?

Toy stores have duped mothers into filling the sandboxes with something called "Riviera Sand," a beautiful powdery white sand that shakes easily from hair and shoes and won't stain clothing but is utterly unfit for mudpie making. If you can stand it, get the sand that packs so kids can bury their feet and make substantial "frog houses" or elaborate terrains for trucks and bulldozers. Real sandpile work requires the use of the garden hose, so situate the sandbox accordingly.

PRUDENCE MACKINTOSCH
Texas Monthly

Black Sand: A Magnetic Attraction

Have you ever noticed the wavy patches of black sand that can often be found on an otherwise white beach? I always thought these were created by tar—pollution—until my wife, Geneviève, corrected me. "They're tiny grains of iron ore," she said. "You're supposed to be able to pick them up with a magnet."

On a recent summer weekend, when Geneviève's young cousin Cédric came to visit us at the shore, we decided to see if it was true. Cédric ventured out with a small magnet and came back a few minutes later, utterly delighted, clutching a bowlful of coal black sand. As visions of mining the beach with giant magnets filled my brain, Cédric proceeded to demonstrate that black sand is a wonderful toy: it acts much like iron filings and, in conjunction with a sheet of paper and one or more mag-nets, can be used to make a variety of interesting and attractive designs.

Incidentally, my colleague Elisabeth's son, Nicholas, was a bit more blasé about the joys of black sand than were Geneviève, Cédric, and I. Elisabeth sent Nick out with his magnet only to have him return without a single mention of his adventure.

"Did the magnet work on the black sand," she pressed him.

"Yes," Nick answered.

"Will you come and do it again so that I can see it?" asked Elisabeth.

"No," replied Nick.

"Why?" asked Elisabeth.

"Because," said Nick, "it's too much trouble to clean off my magnet."

CBC

Plaster Casting

Your children can use the beach, or a sandbox, for casting their own plaster sculptures. First, wet the sand; then draw or write in it—backwards, of course—to make a mold. Now mix the plaster. (You can pick up a supply at the hardware store.) Add enough water to the plaster to make it easy to work with (hurry, it sets fast); then pour the plaster into the sand mold. Smooth a board or a bit of driftwood across it to flatten it out, let the plaster set, and you have a plaster sculpture. Three hints:

(1) If you put tiny shells or other objects on the sand before pouring on the plaster, they'll stick to the mixture and become part of your sculpture. Try using a small mirror at the center of the mold, which can make an otherwise ordinary composition into something special.

(2) If you push a loop of wire into the drying plaster, you can hang it when you're through. But make sure you have it right at hand before you pour the plaster. If you go off to find it afterward, you'll be too late.

(3) Plaster-casters should clean up their spills (which harden into little rocks within minutes) so they don't litter the beach.

JANE HENSON

[A pond in your backyard can give your kids a chance to watch a cross-section of nature in action, day after day, without leaving home. For advice on how to build one yourself, see page 226.]

Sandboxes You Can Make

FROM TIRES

Some of the best sandboxes I've seen have been made from large truck or tractor or trailer tires. You just put one down on the ground and fill the inside with sand. And there's a place to sit around the outside of the tire. The hollow space inside the rim is what kids always seem to use the most.

It's fairly easy to come by a whole pile of big tire carcasses; when they can't be recapped they're discarded. In the country you can get them from a farm supply place, in the city from a trucking company.

STEVEN CANEY

FROM OLD ROWBOATS

If you can come by an old leaky rowboat, it can be a splendid sandbox. (All sandboxes should have covers, particularly in the country, to keep cats and other animals out of them.)

LIZA WERNER

FROM CARDBOARD

Tri-Wall corrugated cardboard, as shown in the following illustrations from *Building with Cardboard* (published by the Early Childhood Education Study—see the review on pages 350–351), makes a good sand or water box.

[To find out how to order Tri-Wall, see below and page 350.]

Triple-wall corrugated is not as readily available as we would like it to be. We hope in the near future it will be. In the meantime, Tri-Wall Containers, Inc. is one source where triple-wall corrugated can be obtained. . . . Their minimum order is rather steep for an individual. If you are embarking on triple-wall projects, it would be wise to involve a few other people to split the cost and the order. . . .

Orders for Tri-Wall can be placed with any of the following three branches.

Tri-Wall Containers, Inc.
100 Crossways Park West
Woodbury, New York 11797
Telephone: (516) 364-2800

Tri-Wall Containers, Inc.
Butler, Indiana 46721
Telephone: (219) 868-2151

Tri-Wall Containers, Inc.
7447 No. Blackstone Avenue
Pinedale, California 93659
Telephone: (209) 439-5222

BRUCE PALMER
Making Children's Furniture and Play Structures

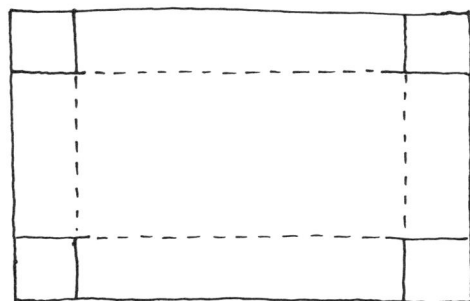

—CUT OUT CORNERS—

From *Building with Cardboard*

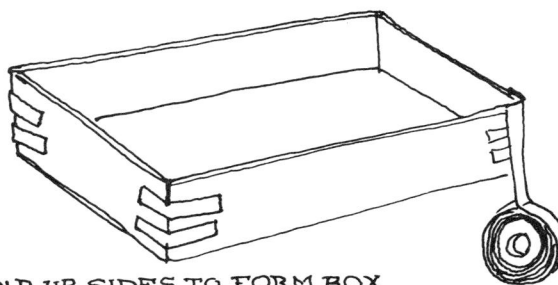

FOLD UP SIDES TO FORM BOX

FOR USE WITH WATER, LINE WITH POLYETHYLENE PLASTIC

TAPE ENDES

The Cheapest Place to Buy Sand

You need to keep extra sand to add as sand from the box gets scattered all over the yard. The cheapest place to get it is in a lumberyard—you can get a 75-pound bag for $1.50 or $2. I buy two or three bags at the beginning of the summer to keep in the garage so it's there when the box gets near empty.

BOBBIE ENTNER

The Art and Industry of Sandcastles, by Jan Adkins (Walker, 1971, $5.95), provides a wonderful look at sandcastles as they're supposed to be: stepping stones to fantasy, buildings on the beach, a bit of history, ephemeral things which disappear. It's a carefully handcrafted, lovely book.

BECKY CORWIN

A junk car that's been childproofed (strip the engine and smooth the rough edges) makes a fine piece of play equipment.

STEVEN CANEY

—————————◆—————————

Nesting Boxes

A friend writes: "A series of three (or more) large four-sided wooden boxes, designed to nest one inside another, makes for lots of cheap (and easily storable) fun. You can build a good set yourself, using ⅜-inch (or best-grade ¼-inch) plywood: glue the four sides together (you don't need a top or bottom) and use quarter-round stripping at the four corners.

"Children can paint the nesting boxes or decorate them with crayon or chalk. And they'll use them to make boats, huts, cars, etc., ad nauseam.

"If you're feeling adventurous, you can give the largest box (say three feet by four feet) a bottom for stability, or wheels for mobility. Or add a peaked roof piece that can double as a ship's prow. Just be sure you use a good glue (I think Titebond is the best) and many small finishing nails."

—————————◆—————————

Boffing

A Boffer is a three-foot duelling sword made of polyethylene foam, supplied with protective eye and ear guards. You can flail away at your opponent, unleash years of pent-up aggression, and still preserve your corporeal well-being.

You might get your ego dented a bit, though, if you drop your defense and let yourself be boffed in the belly by your opponent's rapier.

Actually, the classic rules of Boffing discourage wild swiping and pounding, provide that hits must be made between the shoulder and the waist, and award points only for a well-placed thwack with the tip of your sabre that produces a distinctive popping sound.

Commercially produced Boffers are made of triangular-shaped polyethylene foam wedges with plastic handles and come supplied with plastic goggles and doughnut-shaped polyethylene ear protectors. They cost about $14 for a pair. You can make your own set of "no-fault" duelling sabres by getting a four-inch by three-foot cylinder of polyethylene foam from a packaging supply company (check your Yellow Pages under "Plastics—Foam"). Slice the cylinder diagonally with a hacksaw or serrated knife to make two tapered, semi-circular forms. Punch holes in the ends of the forms, and insert one-inch-diameter wooden dowels, cut to ten inches in length, about five inches into each of the forms. (The best way to get the dowels to adhere to the polyethylene is to heat them almost until burning and plunge them into the forms so the foam melts.) Cover the dowels with bicycle grips or wrap with tape. Before you start Boffing, don't forget to get some eye protectors from a sports supply store.

SHOSHANA TEMBECK
and ANDREW FLUEGELMAN
The New Games Book

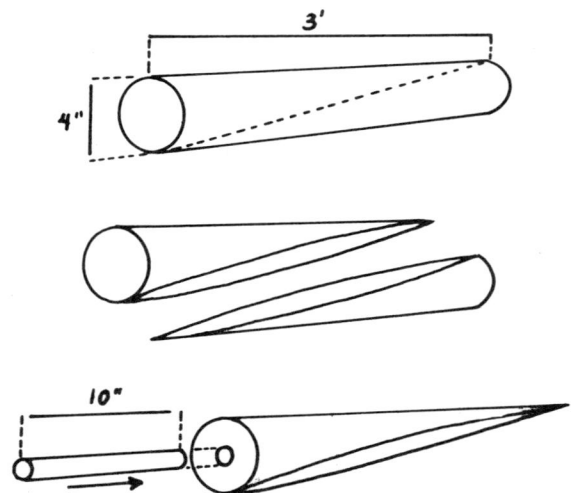

FROM THE NEW GAMES BOOK, PUBLISHED BY DOLPHIN BOOKS/DOUBLEDAY & CO., COPYRIGHT © 1976 BY THE HEADLANDS PRESS, INC. REPRINTED BY PERMISSION.

SWINGS AND SLIDES

Do You Believe in Swings?

When my son was nearly two, my cousin (whose son was also nearly two) telephoned to ask anxiously, "Do you believe in swings?" I'd never stopped to think whether I actually *believed* in swings—Nicholas didn't have one, I thought, because we simply hadn't got around to it. But now that the question had been put to me I had to give it some thought.

My cousin was averse to swings, because at the age of eight she was hit in the face by one, which broke off a front tooth and discouraged her from smiling into adulthood. But that wasn't all. She'd been advised by her sister-in-law that the dangers are greater than the benefits and that it was better to set up an environment in which the child does the moving and the equipment remains stationary. Sounds right, I thought, yet Nick gets a kick out of the swings in the park. So I began my personal, informal and subjective study in the playgrounds.

I found that the kids who were themselves causing the action on the slides and jungle gym definitely seemed more involved in their play than the kids who sat passively on the swings and merry-go-rounds being pushed. I later discovered that the currently popular notion is that the child must *do* something during play. But what is never considered in a discussion of play equipment is the interior life of the child—that is, the kid on the swing may have the space to think while the jungle-gym climber does not. As with everything else, I'm afraid, there is no right answer. You simply have to decide for yourself.

ELS

Rope Swings: Don't Make the Rope Too Long

I've seen people make gigantic swings on 25-foot-long ropes hung from a high tree branch. It's neat-looking and kids get excited by it, but they really can't build up any kind of momentum on so long a rope. It's better to limit yourself to ten or twelve feet. You can use sisal or nylon rope; polyethylene rope works fairly well too. Clothesline rope isn't strong enough.

From an interview with STEVEN CANEY

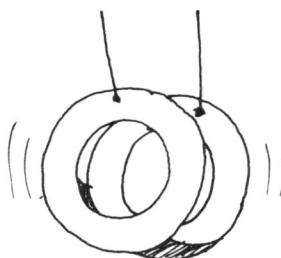

Tire Swings and Tire Cradles

Tire swings are very good and very cheap. Using a saber saw, cut the tread out three-quarters of the way around the tire. Then turn the tire inside out (the remainder of the tread makes the seat now) and hang it with ropes. A cushion is optional.

Hanging tires make great cradles too. Leave in about one-third of the tread for these.

SUSAN RUSSELL

"THE BEST SWING IN THE COUNTY"

Mr. Zuckerman had the best swing in the county. It was a single long piece of heavy rope tied to the beam over the north doorway. At the bottom end of the rope was a fat knot to sit on. It was arranged so you could swing without being pushed. You climbed a ladder to the hayloft. Then, holding the rope, you stood at the edge and looked down, and were scared and dizzy. Then you straddled the knot, so that it acted as a seat. Then you got up all your nerve, took a deep breath, and jumped. For a second you seemed to be falling to the barn floor far below, but then suddenly the rope would begin to catch you, and you would sail through the barn door going a mile a minute, with the wind whistling in your eyes and ears and hair. Then

you would zoom upward into the sky, and look up at the clouds, and the rope would twist and you would twist and turn with the rope. Then you would drop down, down, down out of the sky and come sailing back into the barn almost into the hayloft, then sail out again (not quite so far this time), then in again (not quite so high), then out again, then in again, then out, then in; and then you'd jump off and fall down and let somebody else try it.

Mothers for miles around worried about Zuckerman's swing. They feared some child would fall off. But no child ever did. Children almost always hang on to things tighter than their parents think they will.

E. B. WHITE
Charlotte's Web

Swing and Slide Sets

WHAT TO AVOID

The inexpensive metal-pipe swing and slide sets that you find at Sears and most toy stores are not worth buying. They tend to be flimsily constructed, rust-prone, and very tippy. The swing seats are usually made of a hard metal, which can be dangerous. And some of the cheaper equipment is falsely advertised. The ads feature illustrations in which the children are drawn half-scale to make the equipment look larger. (This is also often done with children's above-ground swimming pools.) Looking at one of these drawings for a lecture I was working on, I made the assumption that the child depicted was three feet tall. Scaling the equipment from that, I figured that the slides and swings would have to be nineteen feet in height!

If an inexpensive metal-pipe swing set is what you thought you'd buy (and it's what most people can afford), you're better off with simple home-made equipment [see page 405 for some useful do-it-yourself books].

WHAT TO BUY

The *other* kind of play equipment you can buy is expensive, but worth the money if you can afford it.

Child Life play equipment, for example, is made from beautiful woods that have been treated with a preservative so they won't rot. It's well made and adjustable and doesn't need to be staked into the ground. You can buy it assembled or as a kit with all the materials pre-cut and pre-drilled. And everybody in the family can get involved.

They say you don't have to paint Child Life equipment, that it will weather naturally. I would have preferred it that way, but there was a can of paint that came with the kit and the kids wanted to paint, so it's painted.

The only problem is that since Child Life equipment is very popular, you sometimes have to wait six to nine months for your order to arrive. If you want delivery in the spring you'd better order in the late summer or the fall.

(A note about Child Life's commitment to quality and service: while we were building our kit, one of the rungs broke. I called the people at Child Life and asked if they would please put another rung in the mail quickly. They had a truck coming my way that day, and I got the 14-cent rung at seven o'clock that night.)

From an interview with STEVEN CANEY

When we were investigating outdoor play equipment, one consideration was that our son disappears for long periods of time, as do the many other kids in the neighborhood. We thought that if we got something for our yard, maybe we could draw the kids to our place—and we'd know where they were.

Some friends of ours had a very simple wooden play structure from Child Life; they'd had it for twenty years. So we got the Child Life catalogue and went through it—they offer a rope ladder, a regular ladder, a jungle gym, four or five different swings, a rope to slide down, a house that fits on top of their basic play structure, an enormous sandbox. The basic frame alone costs over $150, but you can start with it and just a few other pieces, and add to it little by little over the years.

JIM TURNER

Ordering from Child Life

You save around 20 percent of the total cost by buying a kit rather than an assembled structure. And if you can get grandparents and aunts and uncles to forego individual gifts and make a donation toward the purchase of some play equipment, you can ease the dent in your own checkbook and avoid some superfluous toys at the same time.

The catalogue is free and enticing. Write to Child Life Play Specialties, 55 Whitney Street, Holliston, Mass. 01746, or call (617) 429-4639. Replacement parts are available.

RS

◆

THE WATER SLIDE

FROM THE NEW GAMES BOOK

Suppose someone were to spread a long plastic sheet on the ground and spray it with a hose. Would you be ready to take a running slide?

Shoshana Tembeck and Andrew Fluegelman
The New Games Book

COMMUNITY PLAYGROUNDS

In San Anselmo, California, a twelve-year-old girl campaigned for, and was appointed to, the city's Park and Recreation Commission. It sounds like a good idea. —ELS

Build Your Own

Playground building is an increasingly popular activity, warmly reminiscent of old-time barn raisings and other community endeavors. Empty lots, schoolyards, and already existing parks are fair game for volunteers with an abundance of free labor, energy, and inexpensive or scrounged materials. Some communities are just looking for a place for kids to congregate and play, some include vegetable gardens, some incorporate the needs of older people as well as youngsters into their plans.

Playgrounds can be built by the kids themselves, without a great deal of adult help. Some high school kids in Rabun Gap, Georgia (the same kids who put out *Foxfire* magazine), are working with elementary school children in the neighboring town of Clayton. Both groups get together, the younger ones talk about what they want, and together they build toothpick models and measure the site and size of the structure. The high school kids cut the logs from *Foxfire*-owned land (perhaps the parks department in your state could suggest a source of wood); they cut the notches and temporarily assemble the structure to make sure everything's in order, then number the pieces. When they return to Clayton with their "kit," both groups work on the final assembly. There's more than a playground in this process.

When I first heard about the *Foxfire* playground project, I sent several playground books to *Foxfire* adviser Eliot Wigginton for his opinion. I can't think of anyone whose recommendations I'd value more (see next article).

RS

A Playground Builder's Booklist

Of all the books we got, the one that grabbed us the most completely, got the kids' ideas flowing fastest, and presented the clearest, most concise diagrams and directions was *Handcrafted Playgrounds*, by M. Paul Friedberg (Vintage Books, 1975, 122 pages, $5.95 paperback).

Another book that proved quite helpful was *Play Structures*, by Gail Ellison (Pacific Oaks College Bookstore, 5 Westmoreland Place, Pasadena, Calif. 91103; 1974, 90 pages, $4 paperback, plus postage). It too is full of nice ideas, as well as lots of thought-provoking discussion that gets you thinking just what it is these structures are *besides* things for kids to play on.

We're just getting around to using *Building with Tires* (Advisory for Open Education, P.O. Box 158, Cambridge, Mass. 02140). It's got some fine ideas in it; we're going to use many of them in an obstacle course we're building for the fifth-, sixth-, and seventh-graders.

ELIOT WIGGINTON

TOP VIEW

LOOP CABLE AROUND POLES AND THROUGH TIRES ON THE BACK SIDE, AS WELL AS ON THE FRONT.

From *Building With Tires*

Designing with Purpose

The first question to consider in designing a play structure often goes unmentioned: *What is our educational and philosophical rationale for building a play environment? How does that affect the design of our structures?*

Play structures can have many qualities; they can be high or low, open or closed, simple or complex. The qualities you choose to emphasize or exclude will be determined by your phi-losophy. Most designers and educators agree, for example, that a good play structure *can offer*:

1. *Choices.* Different ways to get up and down. Routes which vary in difficulty so a child will not be forced to over-extend himself. Room for indecision at the top of a slide. A fireman's pole *and* a tire bridge *and* a ladder.

2. *Variation in topography.* Vertical levels and horizontal pathways. High platforms and low crannies. Stairs and ramps. Open spaces and tunnels.
3. *Privacy.* Hiding places for calm contemplation. Vantage points for quiet involvement in nearby activity.
4. *Group interaction.* Slides and swings for several people. Ropes for a dozen. Clubhouse enclosures or small platforms for group fantasies, stories, or free zones in group games.
5. *Opportunities for creativity.* Sufficient ambiguity that a child has to use his imagination. Stimulation of fantasy play.
6. *Exercise.* Opportunities for muscle building and energy release.
7. *Flexibility.* The capacity for the structure to be changed by the children and staff. The possibility of relocation or future additions.
8. *Risks. Safety and* challenge. A chance to develop judgment, and a test that makes a child feel proud when he masters the danger.
9. *Durability.* Relative immunity to vandalism and breakage. Easy maintenance.
10. *Varying surfaces and textures.* Sand and grass. Wood and concrete. Metal and rope. Sun and shade.

In the initial planning sessions it will be important to decide which of these qualities you want to include. You might want to try to incorporate all of them. On the other hand, it is quite possible that the aspect you think is obviously *the* most important has been omitted from the list. This decision can be made only by examining your philosophy—What do you think is most important for children? What kind of adults do you want them to be?

GAIL ELLISON
Play Structures

[Some of the most innovative playgrounds we've seen are Eric McMillan's. For details and locations, see page 356.]

GAMES, PUZZLES, AND MAGIC

407

Why does a child play a game with an adult? Usually to test himself against the adult world.

Why does an adult play a game with a child? For pleasure, to please, to be companionable, perhaps to win. Or, best of all, to help the child grow and become more comfortable with the adult world.

ROBERT WELBER

GAMES

LUCK, STRATEGY, CHEATING, AND THE MEANING OF IT ALL

The meaning and importance of games to children is often underestimated. Whether a mother or father or teacher or friend is involved, the adult can use a game to understand the child better. For within the game are the clues to unraveling the needs and fantasies of the child's inner life.

When I sit down to play a game with a child, I often ask her whether she wants to win, lose, or tie. The child is usually surprised to be asked this question in the first place. But I ask it and always find the answer interesting. Some kids feel that I should win so that they'll know that I did not "let them win." Others think I should win since I am the teacher. Still others *must* win. And, believe it or not, there are kids who feel much more at ease losing. In any case, it is educational to ask the question, and I usually know the child a little better for having it answered.

ROBERT WELBER

Games: Mysteries to be Explored

There are three stages through which children move in learning and playing tic-tac-toe (or any other game). These can be called: (1) making the contract; (2) playing the game; and (3) reviewing the contract.

I call the first stage "making the contract" because the primary concern is to establish and agree on the rules of the game. The nature of the contract depends as much upon the children as it does upon their understanding of the game. I have observed children playing the game without either of them understanding the nature of a win. They draw the grid, alternate turns, and when the grid is full they construct a new one and start again. They say they are playing tic-tac-toe, and even though another child may tell them they are not playing it right, they continue to play in the way they understand. Here the idea of winning the game is as foreign to the players as the idea of winning in a telephone conversation might be to you or me. In fact, what they are doing might be thought of less as playing a game than as conducting a conversation through the medium of pencil and paper.

Other children who have agreed that a win is possible and that it consists of a series of connected symbols of the same kind may play the game without stipulating that the symbols have to be in a straight line. In the following game, "X" used the same symbol each turn, as did "O." When "X" reached the position indicated in illustration A he announced that he had won. "O" then made his final mark, connected his symbols (illustration B), and announced that he had also won.

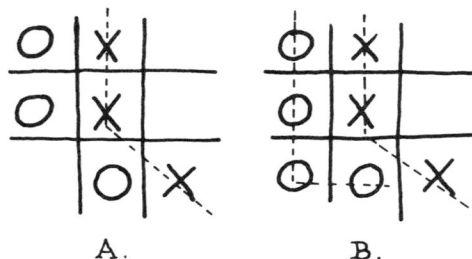

A.   B.

Even though "O" had won the technically correct game by having three of his marks in a straight line, he followed "X" 's convention by linking a fourth. And even though he had "won" after the other player had announced a victory, both agreed that he had, in fact, "won second."

The reason for playing a game may not be simply to master it, but to explore, with someone else, a mystery. As long as the form of the game encompasses a certain unknown area, one which is neither too easy nor too difficult to discover, the players recognize the game as being fun. That is, there is enough mystery within the game to allow them to explore it together without being overwhelmed. Once the mystery is fully understood the game is no longer fun.

BERNIE DE KOVEN

Winning and Losing and the Parental Fix

A lot of winning is helpful to a child's growth; so is a little losing, if the child's ego can accept it without damage.

ROBERT WELBER

◆

As a very young child our son liked our letting him win, but when he was five or so we had to be more skilled at purposely failing. He had to lose sometimes for reasons of reality and credibility. And by the time he was seven the games had to be played honestly, for he was beginning to measure himself against us and his friends—that is, he was defining his ability. Sometimes, in play, he would regress and insist on victory. His friends would not let him get away with that behavior, and neither would we—most of the time. Games, like gambling, are used to test not only ability, I think, but also one's relationship to "luck" or even "fate." I believe our son equated winning or losing with the random disposition of an Olympian god passing judgment. Emphasizing skill as a reason for winning or losing was important and helped combat his mystical thinking and to convey the idea that a bigger game was at stake—in the words of Satchel Paige, the baseball immortal: "Sometimes you win, sometimes you lose, sometimes you get rained out."

HARVEY JACOBS

◆

[Should parents, as Harvey Jacobs suggests, ever indulge in "reverse cheating"—intentionally "throwing" games to build the confidence of very young children? Alan Saperstein thinks so, a view which he expounds in his review (pages 417–18) of Winnie the Pooh, a board game which, he maintains, is singularly easy to lose on purpose.

Bernie De Koven, on the other hand, while recognizing a child's need to compete on an equal basis, is worried about the dishonesty inherent in the "parental fix." His solution: handicapping, outlined in his article on page 410.]

Beyond Chance

Most commercial games for children never go beyond chance. There are hundreds of games on the market that fall into the spin, penalty, reward, safe category—you spin the spinner or flip a die, you move x number of spaces, and, depending on where you land, you either receive a penalty (move back x spaces or miss a turn) or a reward (move ahead so many spaces or receive money), or you're safe. There's really little or no difference between these games and one of the simplest, Hi, Ho, Cherry-O, other than the title and theme of the game. These games are fine, but they serve only a limited purpose, are boring for an adult, and before long even your kid goes buggy. What happens is that at a certain point a child feels a need to use his special skills to feel that he's made himself win.

The first strategy that ever evolves out of a game of War, for example, is attempting to outwit one's opponent by organizing one's cards. Some kids put all their high cards up front; some in the middle, some in the back. But sometimes a kid thinks that he's employing a strategy and he's really not. He's sure he knows what will make him win. When he thinks he can win in Old Maid by picking the third card from the left, that's the clue that he needs to move on to strategy games.

The games that I prefer are ones that you can start out playing very simply, but that will allow you to build in more and more complex strategy as you get more experienced. Checkers, Go, Backgammon, and chess are good examples.

From an interview with STEVEN CANEY

Blind Luck: The Great Equalizer

Games that don't go beyond blind luck may, as Steve Caney suggests, grow a bit boring. But they do have the advantage of "equalizing" the abilities of kids and parents, or of younger and older siblings. Unless you're the kind of father or mother who exults at the prospect of winning fifty consecutive games of Scrabble from a seven-year-old, you'll probably be thankful that not all games depend on skill alone.

CBC

Handicapping

Nobody wants to play a game that is no contest. If you know you're going to win or lose even before you start playing, the game's no fun.

I want to play a game of checkers with my son, Chuck, who's six now. He knows the game, but he doesn't yet understand the strategies. He gets so intent on kinging one piece that he can't see that he's lost most of his other pieces in the process.

Now, my main reason for wanting to play checkers with Chuck is so that we can enjoy each other. The game itself isn't important. We've lots of games to choose from, and the only real question is which game we will both enjoy playing.

But I'm better than he is at checkers. I understand combinations, I can advance while blocking, etc. Should I play differently? Should I make mistakes on purpose? If I do that, if I move randomly or purposely set up big jumps for him, I wind up with a feeling of dishonesty. I feel I've fooled the kid for the sake of the game. I worry that he might detect my charity and feel cheated. Somewhere in the contract of the game is the assumption that we are both trying to do our best. If I help him, can I do it without violating that assumption?

In fact, what's happening to both of us is that we are handicapped by the rules of the game as we understand them. I am as much handicapped as he is by the difference in the level of our abilities. So why not handicap the game instead of the players? There are a number of ways to do this with checkers:

—The winner wins the game, but loses one checker for the next round. So the more I win, the more difficult it is for me to win the next game. Until it happens that Chuck wins. The score becomes a tool for equalizing the challenge.

—Make a rule that it is illegal for one player to ever be more than one piece ahead of the other. This little variation always results in a close game.

—At the end of three moves, the players change sides. Not only does this help to equalize the challenge, but it allows each player to see the game from the other's perspective.

—The checkers are numbered, 1 to 12. The player who is defending his championship has to throw one or a pair of dice. That player is not allowed to use the checker with the corresponding number.

One game with built-in handicapping is Nine Men's Morris (or Merels, or Mill), which was very big in the fourteenth century and is still played today. It has a unique rule which allows a player who has almost lost the game to regain his power. He is allowed to move his pieces anywhere on the board, while the other player must still move only to adjacent spaces. The result is that the player who initially had numerical superiority, unless he is particularly skillful, will lose most of his pieces, until he has only as many as his opponent. This same procedure can be adapted to checkers: when one player has lost most of his pieces, all the remaining pieces might be automatically kinged. (For more information on the game of Morris, see *The History of Board Games,* by Robert McConville, Creative Publications, 1974, $4.)

Try making up your own ways of handicapping a game. Remember, to young children "fair" means exactly equal, regardless of person or circumstances. If they—or you—find the rules of a particular game inappropriate, there are three options: change the rules, change games, or don't play.

BERNIE DE KOVEN

Cheating

Cheating is the first strategy many kids learn. They don't realize it's cheating. To the kid it's "I'll get away with this, it's something else I can do." It's testing, really.

STEVEN CANEY

What's a Poker Face, If Not Cheating?

Accidental cheating is built into some games: for example, misspelling a word in Scrabble and getting away with it. In other games it's more intentional. What's a poker face, if not cheating? Or is bluffing different from cheating?

We used to play a game called Famous People in which we tried to think of all the celebrities we could whose names started with "S" or "H" or whatever letter we had chosen. One way of cheating was looking at book spines (or more flagrant still, consulting the biography section of the dictionary). But the kind of cheating that was the most fun of all was making up fictitious names. We created more champion golfers and silent screen stars and famous novelists! Cheating well became a great challenge, and there was something special about the fact that we were conspiring with adults—my Aunt Shirley always made up the best names.

RS

Bored? Try Cheating.

Cheating is in most cases an attempt to alter the intensity of the challenge offered by the game. It is not an attempt to destroy the game, for the cheater always agrees, at least implicitly, to be bound by some of the rules. He is still enjoying the game with his partner.

Most often, cheating is an investigation of the implicit rules of the game; it serves to identify or transform those rules and can result in a better game. If both players are bored with a game, cheating can serve to enliven it.

BERNIE DE KOVEN
Adapted from *Outlook*

Rules and Rituals

[Seven to nine] is an age when rhymes and rituals seem to be a great help [to children] in their games. It is an age when they are prepared to pass harsh judgments on those who break the rules, even though they do not really observe them very well themselves. They do not realize this yet, however; although they lie without too much self-awareness, they con-

demn it as a major crime. In all of this they are helped by adults, who make rules very clear and are very fair in enforcing them.

Often their game rituals stray over into PRIVATE RITUALS, showing again a desire for ORDER in their personal feelings just as much as in their social world with other children. Thus, "You have to be on your bed before the door slams or else IT will come out from under the bed and get you" or "You have to get upstairs before the toilet stops flushing or else IT will get you." Sometimes the child's precarious relationship with God enters into these private dramas. "If I get to the utility pole before the bus does, God will be kind to me."

BRIAN and SHIRLEY SUTTON-SMITH
How to Play with Your Children (And When Not To)

God forbid I should intrude on my kid's secret rituals. It is doubtful I would ever be able to redeem myself. "Ma! Ma! Don't talk to me now! I have to beat the water." Beat the water? Dare I ask? All I wanted to do was brush the knots out before his hair dried, but I was interrupting a very important moment: with one foot in the bathtub and one foot out, he quickly released the stopper, then rushed to get dry and in his pajamas before the water drained out of the tub completely. I don't know what he's decided will happen if the water beats *him* out of the bathroom, but beating the water has become a regular ceremony for him and it is not for me to question. After all, it used to take him forty-five minutes to get out of the bathroom, and now he's out in five. (Starting with a full tub, that is.)

ELS

◆

Elimination Games: Cruel and Unusual Punishment?

There are some games, such as dodgeball, Monopoly, and musical chairs, in which players get put out of the game. Elimination games make sense to some groups of children, usually preadolescent, who are all too familiar with the tyranny of excluding or being excluded from their group. But for the majority of children, definitely children between the ages of four and nine, getting put out of a game is tantamount to cruel and unusual punishment. They simply don't understand why they can't continue to play. It makes as much sense to them as it would to you if you were to receive an anonymous phone call telling you that you shouldn't have answered the phone.

Take a game like musical chairs. It's really exciting knowing that there is one less chair than there are people. Every time you pass a chair, you get ready for the big sit. When the music stops, it's funny to see everybody try to sit down and claim their territory. If you miss, it's still funny. But if you're out, you can't be part of the fun anymore. So change the game. The challenge now is to see whether or not you'll make it the next time.

For a variation on musical chairs, try playing Upset. In this game, the chairs are placed in a circle. There is one less chair than there are players. Everyone, except "It," is seated; It stands in the middle of the circle. All the players are numbered. It calls any two numbers. Those players have to change seats. While they are about that, It tries to sit in one of the vacated chairs. The player left without a seat is the next It. If the players are too fast for him, It calls "Upset" and everybody has to change seats.

The same principle applies in other elimination games. If you get hit in dodgeball, you become one of the throwers. If you miss in jump rope, you become one of the turners. Instead of being punished, you exchange roles. If you're playing a game like Monopoly, you might have to define a new role. How about a realtor (who charges commission until he has enough to get back into the game) or a jailer (who demands bond or negotiates a trade) or a banker (who charges interest on loans and demands payment for services)? Since the fun is in the game, I find no real advantage to getting people out.

BERNIE DE KOVEN

PRE-SCHOOL GAMES

Hide and Seek: Variations

In this game, something, or somebody, is hidden and somebody else is trying to find it.

If "It" is hiding, everybody else is trying to find It (Sardines). If It is hiding something, everybody else is trying to find where It has hidden it (Hot Bread and Butter; Button, Button). If It is hiding an idea, everybody else is trying to find out what it is (20 Questions).

If the children are hiding, It is trying to find out where they are. If It has a base to protect, everybody else is trying to get to the base before It sees them (Hide and Seek). Sometimes It might be blindfolded (Blind Man's Bluff). Sometimes everybody is blindfolded (Proui). Sometimes the people It finds can get freed (Kick the Can).

Sometimes, if the children are hiding something, It has to guess who has the thing (Doggie, Doggie). Sometimes one person is hiding and It has to guess who that person is (Lost Child). Sometimes one person has a special role and It has to guess what it is (Indian Chief).

Or, It might have a code that everyone else has to figure out, and once they figure it out, they join It (Fannee Doolley, Hink Pink).

BERNIE DE KOVEN

A HIDE AND SEEK TIP FOR KIDS
BEGINNING TO LEARN MATH
Instead of counting from, say, 1 to 20, you can count to 100 by 5s, or to 60 by 3s. Experiment.

Follow the Leader

In order to be a good leader, you have to constantly provide just the right challenge for the followers. You must select obstacles that everyone else also wants to overcome, you must discover the appropriate speed, you must learn to be sensitive to the clues the followers give you. As a follower, you must not only keep up, but you must also find some way of communicating to the leader what you would like to do, where you would like to be led. It is a whole relationship of interdependent roles.

BERNIE DE KOVEN
New Ways

ELISABETH SCHARLATT

House Hockey

My 2½-year-old daughter's favorite indoor game is house hockey. Equipment: a long-handled wooden cooking spoon for each player (usually only two) and a lightweight hard-plastic ball (ours was left over from a kiddie croquet set). Best playing field: a long uncarpeted hallway, though the wilder the terrain (irregularly shaped room, with plenty of furniture obstacles), the more hysterical the fun. Gaby's a pro now, and invites everyone who enters our house to play—and everybody, from two years on up, seems to enjoy it almost as much as she does. Smack!

PAULA GLATZER

Horseplay

We've found that a length of almost anything—clothesline, a scarf, a jump rope—makes horse reins. Two people play: the horse holds the rope up against its waist, the driver holds both ends of the rope from behind. "Giddyap!"—and they're off. "Whoa," of course, stops 'em. There's "Right" and "Left" for those who know the difference, and "Haw" and "Gee" for the experienced cowpoke. After a couple of turns, horse and rider switch places. [Two years and up.]

PAULA GLATZER

Impressions

A favorite game of ours is Impressions. We've played it indoors or out, using a wad of clay or Silly Putty. The one who is "It" takes the clay, while the others hide their eyes, makes an impression of some object—the radiator grill, a design on the refrigerator door, the pattern on a drawer knob. The idea is to guess where the impression came from. Great fun!

ANNETTE B. FIDLER

The Kissy Monster

When my son's too full of energy, I turn into a Kissy Monster, chase him (or sometimes slowly stalk him, which makes the anticipation almost unbearable), and grab him and smother him with kisses and tickles. Those few moments of giggling frenzy seem to blow off that extra edge of energy—mine and his—that drives me crazy. Then he'll want to do quieter things.

FLAVIA POTENZA

"I CAN EAT ANYTHING FASTER THAN YOU CAN," ETC.

Kids treat so many things as games. They learn very early the pleasures of rules, repetition, and showing off. A couple of two-year-olds will go through the alphabet with each other until everyone else is driven from the room. Kids will see who can eat or drink something fastest. The more complex the rules, the more they seem to like the game.

BOB SHAPIRO

Broadcast

If you give [a four-year-old] a hairbrush and call it a microphone, he'll sing, broadcast, tell a story or just gab—a particularly good game of drama when you're on a car trip. Even the quietest child becomes garrulous in front of a mike.

MARGUERITE KELLY and ELIA PARSONS
The Mother's Almanac

How Do You Play Ha-Ha? A *Zoom* Viewer Will Tell You

When the television show *Zoom* asked its viewers to submit ideas for activities, jokes, riddles, and the like, it received a torrent of mail: some 200,000 letters and cards before the first season was even over.

A large-format paperback selection of the best material submitted to the show has been published under the title *The Zoom Catalog* (Random House, 1972, 128 pages, $3.50). In addition to some delightful original poems, stories, and illustrations (many of which will probably appeal as much to grown-ups as to kids), it offers a convenient and unusual treasury of traditional children's games, explained by the kids themselves. Among the selections: statues, haha, telephone, ghost, hopscotch, and Zzzz.

CBC

A Bookful of "Joyful Experiences"

Reading *Learning Through Play,* by Jean Marzollo and Janice Lloyd, illustrated by Irene Trivas (Harper & Row, 1972, 211 pages, $2.95 paperback), put me in touch with the most joyful experience of parenthood—the intense awareness of the wonder, freshness, and excitement with which children greet the most common object, the most natural occurrence. It is a reminder of how you, as parent or teacher, can enter into this exhilarating process of early growth and learning. Using materials easily found in and around your home, you can follow dozens of concrete suggestions for games to play with your pre-schoolers, and help them explore and understand concepts, their bodies and their relationships with others.

The book is filled with witty illustrations (see the excerpts below) that a child can "read" to get his or her own ideas. But beyond the specific ideas provided, *Learning Through Play* will spark your own creativity, and attune you to the many ways that children can learn from playful encounters with their world. SHELLEY KESSLER

SENSORY RIDDLES

Based on as Many Senses as Possible

This quiet guessing game is fun when riding in the car. You, or whoever is "it," think of something, and make a riddle about it, using as many of the five senses as possible. Whoever guesses the answer is "it" for the next riddle.

What is small, furry and says: MEOW?

What is yellow, gooey, moist, hot to taste, and eaten with hot dogs? (MUSTARD)

What feels like water, comes in small fancy bottles and smells beautiful?

What smells fresh and clean, makes suds, and tastes terrible?

What is brown, squishy, and fun to walk through?

What has numbers on a dial and goes "RING, RING"?

IRENE TRIVAS

WHAT'S WRONG HERE?

A Game for Identifying Problems

In this game the parent purposely makes obvious mistakes for the child to discover and correct. For each mistake the parent asks, "What's wrong here?" As you discuss the problem with your child, encourage complete answers as illustrated. Some "mistakes" to make:

Try to eat a banana without peeling the skin off.

Try to pour milk out of an unopened carton.

Try to put on your shoe when it is laced and tied.

Try to put on a shirt without unbuttoning it.

Try to pour soup out of an unopened can.

Try to eat with an upside-down spoon.

Try to sit on a chair that is turned on its side.

Try to brush your hair with the wrong end of the hairbrush

WHAT'S WRONG HERE! THE JACKET! WHAT'S WRONG WITH THE JACKET? IT'S UPSIDE DOWN!

JEAN MARZOLLO and JANICE LLOYD   *Learning Through Play*

CARD GAMES

Pre-school Card Games

There are innumerable games a young child can play with a deck of cards.

FOR A TWO-YEAR-OLD

Everyone thinks you can't play cards with a two-year-old. Of course you can: Put a hat, a bucket, or a big spaghetti pot on the floor. Each player takes an equal part of the deck and tries to throw the cards one at a time into the hat.

FOR A THREE-YEAR-OLD

A three is not ready for a proper card game, but can identify numbers, separate cards of color or suit, put them in order, backward and forward (the purist sorely misses number one). Don't try using playing cards for counting—the smaller symbols in the corners don't count and so are confusing.

FOR THE OVER THREES

Go Fish is low-key enough to appeal to Grandmother. Slapjack is best with another kid. But War is the big favorite. Deal out all the cards. All the players turn over their top card: the highest wins all the cards. If two cards match in number—not in suit—the two players take three cards of their hand, face down, and the fourth card face up. The highest wins all of those. The winner is the one with most cards when the deck has been used up.

ELS

FOR FIVES

Pig is just the kind of sober, intellectual game that five-year-olds love. To get ready to play, select from a standard deck four cards of the same denomination for each player in the game. Thus, if three kids are playing, you'll end up with a twelve-card deck containing, say, four threes, four sixes, and four sevens.

Now, deal out all the cards. Each player looks at his hand; then, on a given signal, everyone passes one card to the player on his left. The object of the game is to end up with four-of-a-kind in your hand: the moment you've achieved this feat, you must, as unobtrusively as possible, place your finger on your nose. It's up to the other players to notice this, and when they do, they must put *their* fingers on their noses too. The last player to do so is the pig. Oink.

CBC

And for Older Cardsharps . . .

KIDS OVER SIX can play various forms of solitaire.

OVER TENS can play gin or poker. Not only will they enjoy the game; they'll also feel terribly grown-up.

JUST ABOUT ANY KID can play Concentration. In fact, Concentration is one of the few games that children seem to play more skillfully than adults. So be prepared to lose. (Hint: the harder you take your defeat, the more your kids will love it.)

ELS

More About Card Games

To find out more about games that employ real strategy, send for *50 Card Games for Children, 150 Ways to Play Solitaire, Official Rules of Card Games, Poker, Fun with Games of Rummy,* and/or *How to Start Playing Bridge in Twenty-two Minutes.* They're all published by the United States Playing Card Company (Beech and Park Avenues, Norwood, Ohio 45212), and they sell for $1 each.

These little booklets have just about everything you need to know about card games. The *50 Card Games for Children* booklet runs 128 pages, and goes the gamut from simple games like Old Maid, solitaires like the Round the Clock, card tricks, and "grown-up" games like rummy and bridge. The *Official Rules* book (256 pages) is the most complete in the series, but has not as many elementary games. *150 Ways to Play Solitaire* includes solitaire so elaborate that you need four packs of cards to play. The poker book has interesting probability charts, and the family can find itself immersed in some pretty heavy mathematical inquiry (if it wants to).

BERNIE DE KOVEN

Pyramid

This is a fascinating form of solitaire. It requires a good deal of planning ahead; yet it is not at all difficult to play. And when you win you have a delightful sense of having been ever so clever to make those cards work out just right!

Deal out twenty-eight cards face-up, in the form of a pyramid, with seven horizontal rows, each overlapping the one above—as shown in the illustration. Hold the remainder of the pack in your hand, face-down.

The object is to remove all the cards in the Pyramid, by making combinations of *two* cards (only two) totaling 13—such as a 6 and 7, a 10 and 3. Jack counts 11, so it is removed with a 2. Queen counts 12, so it is combined with an Ace. The King, equaling 13, is removed alone.

The two cards that make 13 need not be in the same suit.

Only a card that is fully uncovered, with no card overlapping it, or partly overlapping it, may be used.

When the Pyramid is laid out, begin by removing any of the bottom-row cards that total 13, including any King. If two cards removed in this way uncover *completely* a card in the row above, it may then be used. (If a Nine partly covers a Four, and the Four will be free by removing the Nine, that combination may not be used, for both cards must be free to begin with.)

When no further cards can be removed, turn to the pack in your hand. Look at the top card. If you can use it to make 13 with any uncovered card in the Pyramid, do so, and remove them both to your discard pile of 13's.

If you cannot combine this top card of the pack with one in the Pyramid, lay it face-up on the table to begin a Boneyard pile. The top card of the Boneyard may be used at any time.

Look at the next top card in your hand, and use it to combine with and remove another card from the Pyramid, or if that cannot be done, place it face-up on top of the Boneyard.

And so on through the pack in your hand. If by that time you have not removed all cards in the Pyramid, you may turn the Boneyard over, and go through it, one card at time, as you did with the original pack. The Boneyard may be turned over in this way three times, but it must not be shuffled.

If by that time you have not removed all cards in the Pyramid, the game is lost. But you *may* be able to win without turning the Boneyard over even once.

From 50 Card Games for Children

The Most Sexist Card Game

The theme of a game can sometimes carry with it strong social implications. In the game of Old Maid, for example, the loser gets caught holding the Old Maid card at the end.
HERBERT KOHL
Math, Writing & Games

◆

The Oscar the Grouch Card Game (CTW/Milton Bradley) offers all the same thrills as old maid without the discrimination (unless, of course, you feel strongly about grouch stereotypes).
CBC

◆

In Growing Up with Toys, Irene Clepper describes the game of Old Bachelor, created by Mrs. Will Melbye: "A robot, who can't think, is the equivalent of the Old Maid, and he's the only 'put-down' in the deck. . . . Her card game has 19 pairs of matching vocations; each card is divided horizontally and there's a man and a woman each shown doing the job."
Eds.

For a Real Big Deal

When we first bought a deck of Giant Bicycle Playing Cards (U.S. Playing Card Co., $5.50), I played a trick on the kids. I showed them a regular deck of cards and asked them to select a card which they then had to give back to me. Then I turned my back to them and I pulled out a giant copy of the card they selected. When I turned around again and asked, "Is this your card?" they were very surprised. Then they all broke into a delightful giggle.

We first obtained these cards to see if they would be useful in working with kids that have visual problems. They are. But we also discovered that kids with little or no manual dexterity enjoy them as well—they are so big and clumsy that *every* one is at the same disadvantage. These are just like a regular pack of Bicycle playing cards in every way and detail except that they are 7 inches high and weigh about a pound. All the children in our neighborhood come to enjoy these cards. They play all sorts of games with the cards for hours. Frankly this is a lot of money to pay for a deck of playing cards, but then again you get a lot of card for your money!
LEWIS C. CLAPP
Toy Review

PACKAGED GAMES

Packaged Games: A Place to Start

Children's games come in every shape, form, price range, size. It is usually difficult to discern differences at the time of purchase without going through a retail trial-and-error approach. But some games, usually referred to as "classics," are better bets than others. Here are a few of the best-known games, arranged in order of difficulty.

LOTTO GAMES

The first games parents can usually introduce to children are lotto games, especially the ones that portray animals or household objects. Lotto, as just about everyone knows, consists of matching picture cards to pictures on a board. First try A-B-C or 1-2-3 lotto, played like bingo. "Go-together" lotto has more complicated pictures on the boards which need matching up with a related, rather than an identical, picture. There are many varieties of the game, some of which can get quite sophisticated and difficult.

JUDY THORN

CANDYLAND AND HI, HO, CHERRY-O

These classic children's games, very easy to play, are excellent for demonstrating to pre-schoolers the conventions of game play: i.e., taking turns, following rules, winning and losing. Candyland is the best game I've seen for very young children. It's the first board game two- and three-year-olds can handle. The only skill necessary is color recognition. The "spinner" points to a color, and the player moves his piece to the next space of the same color on the board. Then it's the next player's turn, and so forth—until one reaches the end of the multicolored path. Sound dull? Not at all! I've watched game after enthusiastic game between tots and much older siblings. There's enough action and competition to keep the older ones interested, and a great sense of accomplishment for the younger kids. And the winner is determined by sheer chance.

ANNA JANE HAYS

WINNIE THE POOH: A GOOD GAME FOR PARENTS TO LOSE ON PURPOSE

It is the "cheatability" of the pre-school board game Winnie the Pooh that makes it the best one, in my opinion, for parent–child participation.

When children play with each other they cheat by accident; they don't always recognize improprieties, and don't really need to in order to have fun. But parents need to impose structure in play. They also should want to let their children win, which sometimes flies in the face of fair play. But Winnie the Pooh makes it easy for parents to cheat. Instead of using a spinner on a multicolored wheel to determine which colored area a player may move to, Winnie the Pooh uses a bagful of colored disks that you reach into. Thus the color a parent winds up with doesn't have to be chosen in an above-board way. Without arousing the slightest suspicion, he or she can control the game so the child wins.

Some may be taken aback that I am endorsing a "fix." But my own instincts were reinforced by my son's kindergarten teacher, whom

WHITMAN/© WESTERN PUBLISHING. RACINE, WISCONSIN 53404

© MILTON BRADLEY

PARCHEESI®, ROYAL GAME OF INDIA, IS A REGISTERED TRADEMARK OF SELCHOW-RIGHTER, CO.

I watched tell her class the answers to questions before giving them the questions. Why? Because being right is very important to a child. It means approval, reward, satisfaction, and a host of other ego-building and confidence-restoring attributes. Good sportsmanship is surely a valuable lesson, but the fact remains that it is naturally discouraging, depressing, and even irritating to lose.

ALAN SAPERSTEIN

———————◆———————

CHUTES AND LADDERS

This game is for graduates of Candyland and has several of the same advantages, such as simplicity and wide age appeal. The spinner stops at a number which indicates how many spaces the player may move on a path that begins with number 1 at the bottom of the board and snakes in a path back and forth, numbers mounting, to the winning space—100—at the top of the board. But the excitement is in suddenly climbing from the second row of numbers all the way up to the eighth, simply by landing on a square at the bottom of a ladder. On the other hand, a great deal of ground can be lost by landing on a square at the top of a chute and having to slide down to a much lower number. This game gets very competitive, and can be as short as fifteen minutes or as long as an hour-plus. You see, there's this one gigantic, long chute in the 80s that can thwart a near-winner, sending him sliding back to the beginning.

ANNA JANE HAYS

———————◆———————

PARCHEESI

When a child has mastered Chutes and Ladders, a logical next step up is parcheesi. A simplified version of a backgammon-type game that originated in India, parcheesi confronts players with the task of moving *more than one* man around a board. Hence, planning and decision-making—albeit on the most basic level—begin to become important.

And after parcheesi, what? Monopoly can be mastered, after a fashion, by a game-playing child by the age of eight, and some who really enjoy games may start playing as early as six and a half. Of course, Monopoly played at its wheeling-dealing best can be one of the most delightfully vicious games there is—for more about it, see the following articles.

Eds.

Monopoly

To many players, Monopoly is almost a mystical, ritualistic thing.

PARKER BROTHERS EXECUTIVE
Quoted by Marvin Kaye in *A Toy Is Born*

Initially, of course, the timing for introducing Monopoly was perfect. People out of work loved playing tycoon, and men who were homeless needed to build dream castles.

But the game has far outlived its period, and it shows no signs of dwindling in appeal. Perhaps the reason for Monopoly's long-term success is simply that the game is just great fun. It provides opportunities for fantasized speculation, acceptable miserliness, and interpersonal conflict. Furthermore, Monopoly maintains an unusual balance between luck and freedom of judgment.

MARVIN KAYE
A Toy Is Born

I like it. You act cool, you think you're big. You act like you're Mr. Bad. GEORGE MAMLOUK
Age twelve

Computerized Monopoly: What Can You Learn From It?

Years ago, they computerized the game of checkers. Chess took a little longer, because it's a tougher game. And now, an eighteen-year-old high school senior has finally computerized Monopoly. His name is Lloyd Treinish. His advice: Don't buy Boardwalk! Well, I don't need a computer to tell me that. Boardwalk is too expensive, and nobody ever lands on it. Right?

But Lloyd's computer program for Monopoly has come up with several things I didn't know about the game. The very best properties are the red and the orange—the ones around Free Parking. According to Lloyd's computer, if you own those you're virtually unbeatable. Now Reading Railroad is the property everyone lands on the most, possibly because it's a few boxes from Go. And curiously, Short Line is landed on the least. Other than properties, more players land on Chance than on any other box. Now how many times have you said you wished you could *own* Chance!

Now, not only is what you buy important, but so is when you buy, according to the computer. Those railroads are fine to buy early in the game. But not later on, when other monopolies are being built up to bring far greater returns.

ROGER FIELD
WINS Radio

The Monopoly Book

If you don't have Monopoly strategies down, and you don't want to leave your playing to the computer or chance, you can make up for all the games you haven't played by reading *The Monopoly Book: Strategy and Tactics of the World's Most Popular Game,* by Maxine Brady (McKay, 1974).

If you already know the strategies, you may be interested to read how an unemployed Charles Darrow created the game from his memories of pre-Depression days in Atlantic City and made, by hand, two sets a day; and how Monopoly was at first rejected by Parker Brothers because it violated the "52 fundamental rules" for good family games.

RS

. . . and Anti-Monopoly

More than 8 million Monopoly sets have been sold since 1935, which means untold millions of citizens of all ages spending endless evenings trying to buy up all the available land, control the railroads, put the electric company and the waterworks under their private ownership, and take up to 225% profit on their capital investments.

Nevertheless, some people remain unconvinced that this is the American way. One of them, an economist named Ralph Anspach, has designed a game called Anti-Monopoly, with a few relevant lines from the Sherman Antitrust Law printed on the cover. In Anti-Monopoly, you get your financial glory from the satisfaction of managing a budget sensibly, while you go around selflessly busting trusts to win "social points."

JUDITH MARTIN
Vieux Carré Courier

Clue: A Logical Choice

Clue (Parker Brothers) is—and has been for many years—my favorite board game. Why? Because it encourages and rewards logical, orderly thinking. The object is to discover, by careful interrogation of the other players combined with sheer deduction, which of a suspicious array of Agatha Christie–type characters committed a murder, which weapon the felon used, and in what room the crime took place.

Because it is based almost entirely on skill (the only chance factor is that it's necessary to land in a "room" before one earns the right to ask a question), Clue is a marvelous instrument for helping a kid develop deductive strategies. In fact, it's a creative challenge for *adults* to

come up with a workable system of cataloguing information: everyone seems to have his or her own individual style of play.

One word of warning. Clue is one of those games that younger kids can't play too well with older ones: as in the case of other games of skill, the little kids will almost always lose and they *won't like it.* You might try waiving the rule that eliminates a player for making a wrong guess. Perhaps, if one or two misses per player were permitted, younger children wouldn't feel so overmatched.

SHARON LERNER

© 1972 PARKER BROTHERS

MOUSETRAP BY IDEAL TOY CORPORATION

"If a Man Makes a Better Board Game . . ."

Mouse Trap (Ideal Toy) is truly an incredible game, inspired by a Rube Goldberg invention. As you go around the board, every time you land on a white space you get to add one more piece to the structure. When it's all built you have little mice moving around the board; and when you land on the right square, you get to turn the crank that turns the gear that flaps the stop sign that kicks the boot that knocks over the bucket that gets the ball rolling down the steps through the rain gutter and hits the spring that sends another ball through the basket, hitting the diving board that knocks the man into the wash bucket. His weight dislodges the pole down which the basket falls to trap the mouse.

One thing that's really nice about Mouse Trap is that it's the only game I know where people cooperate. Everybody has to work together to get the mouse trap built; once you get it built, of course, you try to trap each other.

AMY SPAULDING

"Look, Mom, There's a Masterpiece!"

One Sunday afternoon in New York's Metropolitan Museum, my five-year-old son pointed to a painting: "Look, Mom. There's a masterpiece from the Chicago museum!"

I checked the plaque. Sure enough, the painting was on loan from the Chicago Institute of Art. "Right you are," I said, dumbfounded. "But how did you know?"

"It's in Masterpiece," replied Paul, "so it had to be from there."

Indeed. All the postcard-size reproductions in the game Masterpiece (Parker Bros.) are from the Chicago Institute of Art collection. The game (which belongs to my twelve-year-old daughter) offers opportunities to the players to auction off, bid on, purchase, or inherit paintings. The winner is the player with the most valuable collection when all the paintings have been acquired.

In our family, we add other goals by building our collections on different bases—such as style or period or artist preference. And when a player gets a painting, he shows it to the other players and announces the name of the painting and the "master" who painted it. Great fun.

ANNA JANE HAYS

Othello: The Excitement Is Justified

Othello (around $9 from Gabriel/CBS) is an excellent game. But ironically, Othello is virtually the same game as Reversi, with a few minor rule changes, and Reversi has been around for a long time—from Victorian times in England in fact. Moreover, Reversi has been introduced in various forms in the last few years by assorted publishers, including Mattel (as *Turning Point*), and by Four Generations and Products of the Behavioral Sciences as *Reversi*. In these previous incarnations, it never really took off. But now, with masterful packaging, a history of record sales in Japan, a lot of promotion, and a new name, Gabriel has made the game go. (Not *Go*.) The game Othello/Reversi is a very simple and elegant one, which permits much opportunity for strategy. The game is played on an 8 × 8 matrix, and each player has 32 playing discs, which are white on one side, black on the other. One player plays black; the other white. Four starter discs are placed in the center of the board to begin play. Then each player in turn places one disc on the board with his color up and must outflank the opposition by sur-

rounding one or more rows of his opponent's discs (there can be one disc in a row) with discs of his own color. After doing so, he flips each of the outflanked discs to his color. And that's all there is to the rules. The winner is the player with the most discs of his color on the board when all the discs have been played. The strategy comes in planning where to outflank to flip the most discs or to maneuver pieces to the strongest power positions on the board. . . . Even if it is a virtual copy of an old game, this is the best presentation of Reversi I've seen.

DR. GINI SCOTT
Games magazine

Master Mind: "An Excellent Strategy Game"

Master Mind (around $5 for the "original" version, around $3 for Mini Master Mind, and around $9 for Super Master Mind, all from Invicta Plastics Limited, 200 Fifth Avenue, New York, N.Y. 10010) is truly a phenomenon. After sweeping Europe, which generally has very different game tastes from America, it has captivated the U.S. as well. Since its introduction by an English company in 1975, this excellent strategy game in its several variants has sold in the millions.

In its original version, Master Mind goes like this: the codemaker (player 1) challenges the codebreaker (player 2) to duplicate a hidden code of four colored pegs, chosen from six possible colors. The codebreaker, starting from sheer guesswork, places four pegs at random in his first "guess row" (one row per guess, limit of 10 tries). The codemaker responds with clues. (A white peg for a right color, but wrong position. A black peg for a right color, right position.) The game ends with a cracked code or the 10th try, whichever comes first. And that's it—really quite simple.

DR. GINI SCOTT
Games magazine

Various electronic games have been created which secretly "choose" a mystery number for players to figure out—in effect, they're computer technology's answer to Master Mind. The most famous of these is probably Milton Bradley's Comp IV ($20 to $40, depending on where you buy it), which gives you the option of trying to guess three-, four- or five-digit numbers. Somewhat less flexible (*and* less expensive) are the more recent Digits (Coleco) and Think Tank (Interstate Industries).

Is it worth the extra money to buy an electronic version of Master Mind? Well, if you're anxious to play the game solitaire, it most certainly is. At the other end of the scale, Sharon Lerner points out that, for the two-player version of the game, you don't need to buy anything at all—two pencils and two pads are all the equipment that's required.

CBC

Spill and Spell and Scrabble

Spill and Spell (Parker Brothers) is a game for adults and kids with a built-in flexibility that makes it adaptable to children just beginning to build words.

Points are earned for the number of letters used, for words over six letters, and for speed. The letters are on cubes which are shaken up in a cup and spilled out. Playing against a sand clock, each player tries to make as many words as possible out of the letters which have turned up, in an allotted period of time. Parents can be handicapped by having only one minute, and children may be allowed to turn the sand clock and take more time, depending on their ages. When playing with five-year-olds just beginning to read, you don't have to use the rules. They can make words using any letter on the cube and forget about the timer. The game can be played alone, or in a foreign language, or using a certain theme.

A Scrabble set can be adapted to a word-making game for children of any age. If you have a sand-clock timer in the house, you can play a variation of Spill and Spell by shaking the letters up in a bag, dividing them among the players, and trying to form words. For this, you don't need the board, of course, and you can ignore the point values on each square.

RS and RUSTY UNGER GUINZBERG

Connect: A Game Without Words, Letters or Numbers

Connect is a game without words, letters or numbers. The challenge of play can be in simple visual matching or in the strategy of anticipating future moves and predicting the moves of others.

Connect involves a principle of play similar to that of dominoes—construction of paths by matching elements on the playing pieces. In Connect, the matching is of colored tracks rather than dots.

Each playing piece has a part of a track or tracks. The tracks are always red, blue or black, and a piece has one, two or three track lines on it. Some lines are straight, some are curved; some are beginning points, some are end

points. On some pieces the tracks divide, adding to the complexity and possibilities for strategy.

The rules folder suggests two to ten players. Connect also makes an interesting construction activity for one.

And if you shudder at the thought of 140 playing pieces floating around, you'll be glad to know that: (1) there is a 12-compartment tray inside the box for storage; (2) even if one or two pieces are mislaid, the game can still be played quite satisfactorily.

This is an English import and directions are provided in French, German and Spanish. English, too. *Order from:* Selective Educational Equipment, 3 Bridge St., Newton, MA 02195 ($5.25).

From *Learning* magazine

PACKING, STUFFING, AND EMPTY SPACE

Most games could be packaged with a board that folds four ways and could fit into a simple envelope.

HERBERT KOHL

We've developed a rule of thumb that the crappiness of a game is in direct proportion to the size of the box.

ZELDA WIRTSCHAFTER

The *ne plus ultra* in the packaging of space— empty as opposed to outer—was achieved by the Kenner Corporation in its promotion of *Star Wars* items during the fall and winter of 1977. Upon discovering that merchandise would not be ready in time for Christmas, they hit upon the idea of offering *Star Wars* IOU's in attractively designed boxes illustrated with scenes from the movie. The IOU's would be redeemable once the product started flowing off the assembly line, the company explained; cynics quickly noted that Kenner stood to garner a tidy extra profit from certificates sold but never redeemed.

CBC

What to Do When the Dog Eats the Spinner

I've always hesitated to buy any commercial games for my kids because usually within a week at least one, if not more, of the pieces disappears under the couch or behind the radiator and then gets sucked up by the vacuum cleaner or the dog, never to appear again on any game board.

Most manufacturers do supply replacement parts, however. Just write to them for what you need.

CAROL EICHLER

Bringing Yourself into the Game

What happens when you finally lose all the little "people" needed to move around the game board? One solution is for you and your kids to find objects which you think represent yourselves—something to suggest your individual traits or attitudes.

An alternative is to draw pictures of yourselves, tape them to pieces of cardboard or scraps of wood, and then play with the figures of you as you. (My colleague Christopher, who claims to represent those who can't draw, suggests using Polaroid snapshots instead of illustrations.)

ELS

Smart Electronic Games: At Last, an Opponent Who's Always Willing

You may be wondering, from the title of this article, if there is such a thing as a dumb electronic game. The answer is yes, and they've been around for years: their battery-operated spinners and whistles and bells and lights liven up the playing surface without contributing to the challenge of the game. But now we have games whose electronic components make it possible for you to find a willing and uncommonly skillful opponent whenever you want to play.

At the heart of these smart games are several hundred electronic parts packaged on a chip of silicon that measures 1/20 of a square inch in size. Technically, the chip is a microprocessor, not a computer: it performs some of the arithmetic and logical functions of a computer, but it has very little memory, and no generalized ability to generate or receive information. In short, it's a relatively simple integrated circuit programmed to play a specific game. The board or

DAVID AND ANNIE FOX

package for that game usually includes a few controls and a small read-out display.

Unlike mechanical games (and toys), which are forever breaking down, electronic games are as durable as small calculators (and more durable than transistor radios); the ingenuity of the program is usually more complex than the electronic circuitry. Inevitably, though, some units malfunction, and a ninety-day warranty is standard in the field; after that time there's usually a service charge for repairs. . . .

In a sense, these smart electronic opponents are tools for people who like to play games, perhaps not all that different from the tool kit that's been available to the amateur carpenter or photographer for years. Only instead of extending the hand or the eye, electronic games extend the mind.

DAVID H. AHL
Games magazine

A few popular electronic games are mentioned in connection with Gini Scott's review of Master Mind (page 420), and Bernie De Koven points out (page 323) the educational merits of video games. In general, though, we've shied away from reviewing specific electronic games, not because there aren't any we like, but simply because microprocessor technology is evolving so quickly that any games we describe are likely to be obsolete by the time you read this.

One suggestion: you might want to pick up a copy of *The Complete Book of Video Games,* by the editors of *Consumer Guide* (Warner Books, $1.75 paperback), which lists all the top manufacturers and describes their various models in exacting detail. Before you buy it, though, check the copyright page: if the edition's more than a year or two old, chances are it's out of date.

CBC

THE CLASSICS

Checkers

Checkers is a wonderful game to teach a child and one which kids learn surprisingly easily by the time they are four or five years old. The nice thing about checkers is that it enables the child to play with older siblings or friends a game of mutual interest.

JUDY THORN

[Bernie De Koven has developed several techniques for handicapping checkers so that an inexperienced player will have a 50–50 chance of beating someone skilled at the game. To learn about the De Koven system, turn to page 410.]

For the Sensually Aware Chinese Checkers Player

If your sensibilities can't tolerate a tin or cardboard Chinese checkers board, Berea Student Craft Industries, Berea, Ky. 40404, will sell you one in solid cherry, 14 inches square, for a mere $16.00 (plus postage and handling). An extra $1.50 will get you one in solid walnut. The price includes marbles.

RS

Backgammon for the Very Young

Using a backgammon board and four men, preschoolers can play an exciting chase game which, besides being fun in itself, is a first step toward learning how to play *real* backgammon. Here's how it works.

The players each get two men, which they position on the "point" farthest to the left on their respective sides of the board. Each player in his turn proceeds to roll the dice and moves one man (or, if your kid is old enough to understand, one or *both* men) counterclockwise the number of spaces indicated on the dice. The object of the game: to catch up with and pass your opponent's men.

In fact, my child and I spend most of our time counting the number of dots on the dice trying to figure out the moves; Sundance is not yet ready to chase me, or be chased, around the board.

REBECCA PRESTON

The Arrival Method of Chess Instruction

DAY ONE

My six-year-old son asks me to teach him how to play chess. He has seen other people play, and he can't figure out what they're so interested in. I am enraptured by the opportunity thus given me to impart the subtle harmonies and intricacies of abstract power configurations to the next generation of De Kovens. But first, I tell him, I must teach you the moves.

DAY TWO

My son asks me, once again, to teach him how to play chess. But, I say, we already are learning the game. But, he says, he doesn't want to learn the moves. He wants to play chess.

DAY THREE

I meditate on the varieties of chess instruction, which brings to mind the Chess Tutor game by E. S. Lowe and Co. of New York. Yes, the very thing I've been looking for. The moves are inscribed on each piece. All I have to do is show him how to interpret the drawings. And then I hesitate, seeing before us problems more complex than can be resolved by the Chess Tutor. I see the strategies, the concepts of check and checkmate. I see the two of us locked in confusion. And, knowing that my son's thirst for the wisdom of chess is not as great as his hunger for playful engagement, I abandon the Chess Tutor and consider other means.

DAY FOUR

I have evolved a plan. We will play with the chess pieces themselves. We will invent a variation of chess beginning with the piece which is most difficult to understand in terms of its moves and strategic capacity and arrive at a game which we find mutually intriguing.

The pawn is the most difficult piece to understand. Though it moves only in a straight line, it captures only diagonally. Its first move can be one or two squares, and its subsequent moves only one square. When two pawns confront each other on the same rank, neither can move.

When a pawn reaches the opposite side of the board, it metamorphoses into any piece except the king. No other piece on the board has so many different capacities.

We begin by setting up the pawns in their appropriate positions on the second and seventh ranks. The object of the game is to get a pawn over to the other side of the board. Since we have not as yet introduced any other pieces, the pawn has nothing into which it might metamorphose. Thus, we decide that when any pawn reaches the other side of the board, the player to whom that pawn belongs is the winner.

We play the game. It works beautifully. My son understands the moves and is really learning to appreciate the power of the pawns. I, too, am intrigued by playing pawns only. He learns the strategy quickly. So do I. We both enjoy the game. Though we're not playing chess, we're playing with chess pieces, and the game makes sense to both of us.

Eventually, we always tie the game. Since pawns have the bizarre feature of being able to immobilize each other, it is inevitable that a well-played game will result in a standoff. Thus, we are ready to explore the next complication, bringing the kings into play.

Now, the king is another peculiar piece. Though it can capture, it cannot itself be captured. But it can be attacked, and if it cannot move out of attack the game is lost (checkmate).

We now have a choice of goals—checkmate or getting a pawn to the opposite side of the board. We decide to pursue both. Again, we enjoy the game, and again we reach a standoff. My son and I both have clearer images of how the king moves, attacks, becomes threatened, of how the pawns support one another and can enter into protection pacts with the king.

Now we are ready for the knights. They are not as free-wheeling in their moves as the king or pawn, but they do have a strange way of getting around the board. They are the only pieces which are allowed to leap over others. Further, they move in a broken, L-shaped configuration instead of a line.

The knights, king, and pawns are a formidable combination. There are so many intricacies in their relationships that we have difficulty seeing the outcome of our strategies. Had we found this game clear, we would have continued exploring it. But we decided to eliminate the pawns.

Now we both have two knights and a king. Our objective? How about checkmate? We try. No, it is still too difficult. My son misses the feeling of the race. The game, without the element of trying to get the pawn to the other side of the board, loses its point for him. So we each get two pawns. We set the board up in the prescribed manner, the two pawns occupying the spaces in front of those for the king and queen.

This turns out to be our game. We dabble in other combinations: the queen, king, and pawns; the bishops and pawns. We've learned how all the pieces move, how they combine, attack, and defend, but we find the king-knights-two-pawns combination to be the most intriguing.

Maybe, when we want to use all the pieces, we'll decide to explore what would happen if the pieces started off the board and we introduced them one at a time. We'd have to enter the kings last or they might not be able to get the support they'd need. How safe a world could we construct for our kingdom?

DAY FORTY-ONE

I ask my son if he wants to play chess. He asks me which chess game I have in mind: the one with kings and pawns, the one with pawns only, with pawns and bishops, with bishops, knights, and kings . . .

BERNIE DE KOVEN

Go: ''A Good Game Together''

Go is the ultimate strategy game developed by human beings. In format and rules, it is about as simple as can be imagined. The board is a square grid with 19 × 19 intersections, including the edges and corners. (Square for all descriptive purposes—actually the traditional Japanese board is slightly longer in one dimension, for no apparent reason.) The pieces are 180 white and 181 black circular ''stones'' whose diameter should be about the same as the distance between two lines in the grid. The pieces are played one at a time, alternately, according to a very few simple rules. All the pieces are never used. The possible levels of strategy and complexity are endless.

The object is to surround and control as much territory as possible while avoiding having your own pieces surrounded and captured.

Scoring is done by counting the number of empty intersections controlled and subtracting the number of prisoners lost.

Even the simplest procedures of developing a game of Go are difficult for westerners, whose conceptions of strategy games are formed by chess. Chess provides two standing armies with a clearly defined front line, whereas Go begins with an empty board and no battle lines at all. Also, in chess, everything focuses on the one important piece, the king. In Go, there are no "important" pieces. *Position* is everything. Typically, among accomplished players, the game is developed in several different areas concurrently, always with an *eye* to their eventual interconnection, usually beginning in the corners, and extending along the sides of the board and ultimately into the middle. So there are many battles, all part of the same war, and no front line. . . . Go is the game of the guerilla war. . . .

The beginning western player, like his fellow novices in the Pentagon, tends to think of the game as a linear movement from one encounter to another, each completed by a "win" or "lose" before moving on to another part of the board. So even in the earliest stage of involvement, before there is the slightest grasp of the real game, you run into the need for a pretty drastic adjustment in your head. It gradually dawns on you that you have to see the thing as a whole from the time you play your first stone, because a linear game of Go quickly becomes trivial and therefore boring. If you can get into it, the struggle to alter the ways of perception you've grown up with can last the rest of your life. This is the first level at which Go can be an invaluable tool.

If you start getting serious about it you can refer to the many books around which describe the rules and some of the standard bases of strategy. You'll find graphic move-by-move descriptions of famous Go games of the past. Reconstructing one of these games can be mind-blowing—you can't figure out the remotest reasons for any of the moves, yet the game was played by acknowledged masters: most of us will never get there. But we can learn important things trying.

Go teaches balance; in fact, maybe Go *is* balance. An advantage taken somewhere will result in the need for a concession somewhere else. A gain here, a loss there. You cannot overcome this principle by clever playing—it's not a condition of strategy, but a law inherent in the nature of the game. Go is the pursuit, through the balancing of many "gives" and "takes," of the tiniest insuperable advantage. Every game is won by an advantage of one move, or by a count of one stone. If you win by twenty stones, you have merely duplicated your effort nineteen times. You begin to realize that the "score" (the *size* of the victory) is meaningless; and you begin to look for the nuance of an advantage, the simple announcement. Americans love to slaughter the other guy. In Go, the idea of a slaughter is imbecilic. The point is to win by one stone. This is very hard for us to accept, because our sensibilities are so gross. But Go bends over backwards, by an elaborate handicapping system, to equalize players of differing abilities so they will have a good game together. A good game *together*.

From *Big Rock Candy Mountain*

Convinced? *Big Rock Candy Mountain* suggests you'll do well to purchase your Go board and stones from J. Toguri Mercantile Co., 851 West Belmont Avenue, Chicago, Ill. 60657. Prices start at $13.50.

Marbles? What For?

In simpler times, with the annual onset of Spring, the fancies of most younger men used to turn to marbles. No more.

Oh, you'll find players—kneeling, squatting and knuckling down—in America's southern, western and border states and in isolated pockets in the east, and generally they'll be arrayed around a perfectly drawn large ring shooting tournament marbles, trying to eliminate each other so that they can be local, city, state, regional or national champions. But few youngsters—boys or girls—play for fun, or for keeps, just to kill time, simply for the hell of it.

Why not?

Once-empty lots are covered with apartments and whatever space is left over is blacktopped. Alleys are concrete ramps dipping into the darkness underneath buildings. Neighborhoods no longer exist, really. Dirt is something called soil and is packed in plastic for you to buy to put in window plant boxes. Curbs are rarely seen these days. They're for parking cars or for propping up garbage cans. There is so little space, and each year there is less.

And kids' heads have changed. Marbles? What for, when there are television and statically organized Little Leagues and GP and PG movies and elaborately packaged games that reduce cosmics to throws of the dice? What for, when there are cornet lessons and tennis instruction and planned after-school peer group interactivities?

What for?

Because marbles is fun, that's what for.

FRED FERRETTI
The Great American Marble Book

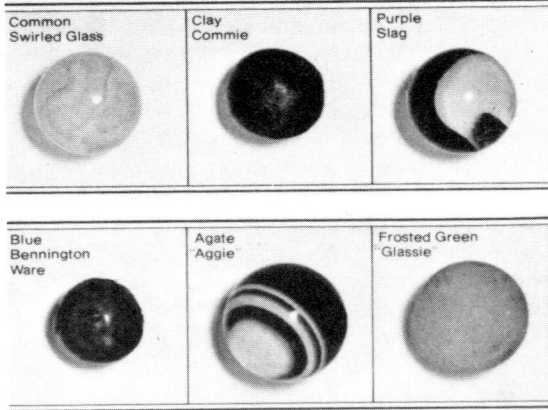

| Common Swirled Glass | Clay Commie | Purple Slag |
| Blue Bennington Ware | Agate 'Aggie' | Frosted Green 'Glassie' |

The preceding is reprinted from *The Great American Marble Book*, Fred Ferretti's delightful little paperback (Workman, 1973, 160 pages, $2.50). In addition to presenting a catalogue of legendary marbles (Who could forget the Cornelian "Blood" Alley, the Ginger Beer Glassie, or the incomparable Brown Bennington "Bonce"?), Mr. Ferretti outlines, in a fresh, breezy style, the rules of some fifty-six marble games. Two of our favorite examples are reproduced below.

CBC

BOSS-OUT

This appears to be the oldest marbles game as well as the oldest chase game, identical, it would appear, to that mentioned by Ovid and played by Augustus. It is described in Strutt as "a game at 'marbles" in which "one bowls a marble to any distance, which serves as a mark for his antagonist to bowl at, whose business it is to hit the marble first bowled, or lay his own near enough to it for him to span the space between them [i.e. a hand's span between them] and touch both the marbles" [Joseph Strutt, *The Sports and Pastimes of the People of England* (London, 1898)]. No specific distances are mentioned. If the antagonist can't hit the target marble or span to it, the roles change and he, the chaser, becomes the chased.

HOLY BANG

Place a marble in a dug out hole as a target. The first player able to get his marble into the hole and so hit the target marble three times is the winner and collects all of the missed marbles tossed in the game. . . .

An ideal hole slopes smoothly into the ground at an angle of about 45 degrees, and curves gently to the opposite slope. There should be no lip.

Pool and Bumper-Puck

Pool is a great game for all ages. It involves all kinds of skill development, such as hand–eye coordination, concentration, reasoning. The only problem is that a decent pool table (slate top, at least 4 by 8 feet), takes up a lot of room, is very expensive (at least $350), and frequently subjects its owner to varieties of paranoia (please don't put your drink on the table, please be sure you hold the stick right so you don't tear the cloth, please don't bounce the balls).

World Wide Games (Box 450, Delaware, Ohio 43015) makes a game they call Bumper-Puck. It's made of 3/4-inch solid chipboard with a hardwood playing surface and oak edges, and it sells for $70.00 (plus shipping). Instead of balls, you get little flat pucks with rubber rings around them. You sprinkle a little powdered wax (also included) on the surface, shoot the puck toward the cup on the opposite side of the table, and will be absolutely amazed at how easily it glides and bounces and misses the cup altogether. You can develop your skill at the game, but you'll probably find that your kids (any over seven) can beat you at it.

World Wide Games makes a quadpod, which is a metal game stand, invaluable if you want to keep the game accessible at all times. You'll need the tall one (34 inches), which will cost you another $23. Or use a card table.

BERNIE DE KOVEN

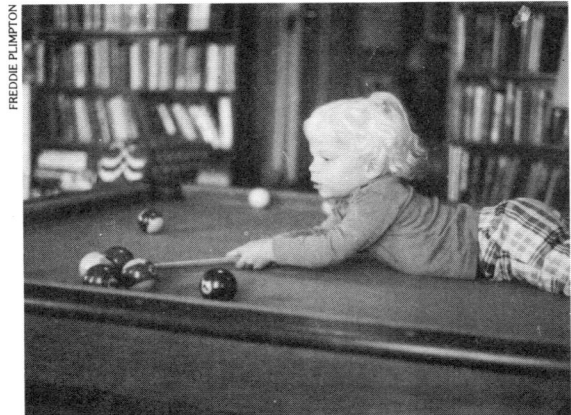

STREET GAMES

Telling It Like It Should Be . . .

Hangin' Out: City Kids, City Games, by James Wagenvoord (J. B. Lippincott Co., 1974, 128 pages, $5.95), is a book to be slowly savored on first reading, then dipped into again and again. Photos—there are over 120 of them— are the main part of the book; the well-written text serves mainly as a framework on which to hang them.

The book covers twenty of the games of the city, from skillzies and ringolevio to Chinese wall ball, with all the rules for each.

ADAM BLUMENTHAL
Age twelve

Backyard Games, by Eric Lincoln with Sam Fife (Stadia Sports Publishing, 1973, distributed by Dell). This unassuming paperback contains the rules for hundreds of yard games, street games, party games, table games, roller games, relay games, and lots more. There are games to improve one's skill at baseball (like "rundown," "flies up," and "pepper"), basketball ("h-o-r-s-e," "one-on-one," and "man-in-the-middle"), and football ("touch," "pass patterns," and "rolling-ball-pass"). There's a chapter on city games such as stickball, stoopball, and roller hockey, and another on self-challenges, like the standing jump, the "hill climber," and the "sixty-second count" (in which one tries to tell, without looking at his watch, when exactly one minute has passed).

You'll find a section on "combatives"— thumb wrestling and hand wrestling, for example—and another devoted to such team sports as volleyball, dodge ball, and box ball.

Traditional games such as potsy, jacks, and spud find their way into *Backyard Games* as well, listed under the sexist title "Games for Girls" (although the authors do their feeble best to absolve themselves by pointing out that girls' having their own chapter "does not preclude them from participating in all the sports" discussed in the book).

Finally, there's a handy section on pencil-and-paper games like "categories" and "dots-and-squares," and "automobile games" such as "license plates" and "station wagons."

An annoying feature of this otherwise extremely useful little book is that there is no alphabetical index of the games, so if you're looking up something specific you have to browse around in the appropriate section and hope for the best.

CBC

. . . And Like It Really Is

The authors didn't just talk to kids and ask them to teach them all their games. Nor did they merely reminisce with their friends and compile all the games they recalled from their childhood. They actually toured England, in the streets and lots and playgrounds, and they actually watched kids play.

The result of this effort, Iona and Peter Opie's *Children's Games in Street and Playground* (Oxford, 1969, $15 hardcover), is an amazing documentary of what goes on when kids play. This is no starry-eyed revisitation to the dreamland of childhood innocence, for the book includes such vicious games as Get the Coward, Chicken, Knifie, and Knuckles. These games hurt: causing pain is part of the fun.

You can use the book to learn a few hundred games that can be played informally with a small or large group. But I think its most fascinating aspect is as testimony to the intricacy and intimacy that exist within our children's culture [see the excerpt below].

BERNIE DE KOVEN

Often, when we have asked children what games they played in the playground, we have been told "We just go around aggravating people." Nine-year-old boys make-believe they are Black Riders and in a mob charge on the girls. They play "Coshes" with knotted handkerchiefs, they snatch the girls' ties or hair ribbons and call it "Strip Tease," they join hands in a line and rush around the playground shouting "Anyone who gets in our way will get knocked over."

. . . For a long time we had difficulty reconciling these accounts with the thoughtfulness and respect for the juvenile code that we had noticed in the quiet places. Then we recollected how, in our own day, children who had seemed unpleasant at school (whose term-time behaviour at boarding school had indeed been barbarous), turned out to be surprisingly civilized when we met them in the holidays. We remembered hearing how certain inmates of institutions, even people in concentration-camps during the war, far from having a feeling of camaraderie, were liable to seek their pleasure in making life still more intolerable for those who were confined with them. . . . It seems to us that something is lacking in our understanding of the child community, that we have forgotten Cowper's dictum that "Great schools suit best the sturdy and the rough," and that in our continual search for efficient uses of educational administration we have overlooked that the most precious gift we can give the young is social space: the necessary space—or privacy—in which to become human beings.

IONA AND PETER OPIE
Children's Games in Street and Playground

GAME ANTHOLOGIES

A Gentle Book About Playing with Your Kids

How to Play with Your Children (And When Not To), by Brian and Shirley Sutton-Smith (Hawthorne, 1974, $7.95 hardcover), suggests ways of playing with your children that you probably never thought were open to you. The book is arranged developmentally so you can understand the growing skills of your children and avoid under- or overestimating their abilities. It gives you a very gentle, responsive, playful approach to being with your children, and to leaving them alone.

BERNIE DE KOVEN

Handy Books: Short and to the Point

Ever need a game, fast, and find that you have to go through a couple hundred pages of your complete games anthology and then when you finally locate the game you're looking for, nobody wants to play anymore?

Handy Books (distributed by World Wide Games, Box 450, Delaware, Ohio 43015, approximately 24 pages each, $5.50 a set) are a series of booklets crammed with particular kinds of games. I use the following: *Outdoor Games,* *Active Games, Handy Stunts, All Time Games, Ancient Games, Games of Skill,* and *Puzzle Craft.* I take them with me whenever I visit a school, playground, or other gathering of kids. You can order either the Handy Games set or the Handy Folklore set.

Some of World Wide Games' booklets tend to get a little preachy, as though they're trying to convince people that it's all right to play.

BERNIE DE KOVEN

Pin a number in large printing on the backs of any two people who are opponents. Each is told to learn his opponent's number without revealing his own. Each player should hold his hands behind his back. Several two-man games can be started at once, although it's about as much fun to watch this one as it is to play.

From Active Games

For reviews of the latest games and game books, not to mention a bi-monthly potpourri of original puzzles, quizzes, and competitions, you may want to subscribe to *Games* magazine. One-year subscriptions cost $5.97—how they arrived at that particular price is a puzzle in itself—and you can get one by writing *Games,* P. O. Box 10145, Des Moines, Iowa 50340.

CBC

The Most Complete Book of Children's Games That Steven Caney Has Seen

The World Book of Children's Games, by Arnold Arnold (Crowell), is the most complete book of children's games that I've seen, with everything from how to play backgammon to street games to tricks and novelties. Though it's intended for parents, it's written simply and clearly enough to be used by an older child.

From an interview with STEVEN CANEY

The following diagrams show different Hopscotch diagrams used by children of the past and present, with and without numbers, played by hopping on a single foot, on both, or alternately on one and then on both. The rules are more or less similar [for all versions].

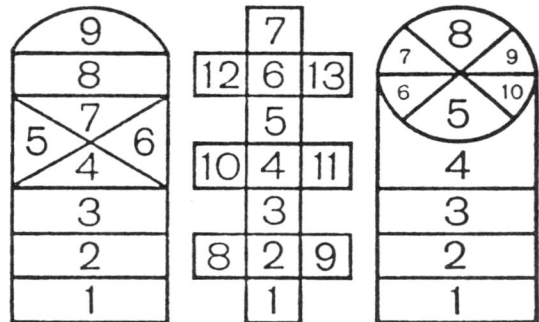

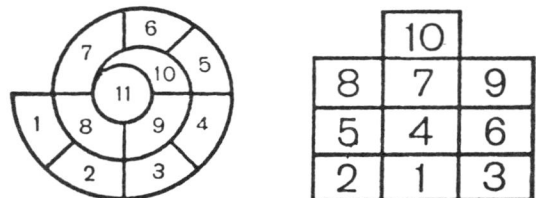

From *The World Book of Children's Games*

MAKING YOUR OWN GAMES

Watching children play, I decided if one presents young children with the components of games, they will generate games themselves. Children experiment with different ways of doing things whereas adults get accustomed to believing there is one right and one wrong way to do things. Creating a game is much like discovering how to write in one's own voice. Making games, writing, building are all ways young people can discover that they can put things into the world, that they can have some control over life.

HERBERT KOHL
Math, Writing & Games

Macaroni Monopoly? Bean Bingo?

It's certainly easy enough to make your own games, especially if you have a look at some commercial games first and see the stuff they're made of. Here are some items that might prove handy:

Cardboard (and paper for covering it) makes a fine playing board.

Pencils, rulers, compasses, and protractors for designing the board. (You can use magazine cut-outs, too, if you like.)

Playing pieces: buttons, pebbles, beans, macaroni. Or you might try bingo counters, which can be purchased in the dime store for about 29 cents per hundred (these used to be called teetotums, and one carried his or hers around always).

Play money. Buy some, or make it yourself.

Properties (if acquisitiveness is a theme of your game). Draw pictures of the items to be bought, sold, or owned. Or design deeds.

Dice can be made out of art gum erasers cut in half and decorated with the customary dots or with your own idiosyncratic symbols.

RS

The Road to Politics, et al.

Amy Spaulding worked with children making their own games at the Donnell Library in New York. The kids came up with a lot of gambling games, and a game based on *The Hobbit* and *Lord of the Rings,* with elaborate instructions sending players around the world of J. R. R. Tolkien. There wasn't a single antifeminist game invented; no contests to get Prince Charming, no dating games.

Richard Kronenberg invented something called "The Road to Politics" (he created it the month Nixon resigned). His board (with a college degree as the starting point) outlines three roads to becoming a political candidate: you can take the path of honesty, or the path of the crook working alone, or the path of the crook associated with the mob. As you move along your chosen path, you have to answer questions such as who was President during the Spanish-American War or at the time of the Alaska purchase. A wrong answer moves you back so many spaces. The object, Richard says, is to accumulate money as well as votes. He'll go far.

RS

Chess on Cape Breton Island: The Forest Men Versus the Ocean Men

Two under-twelves were on a hiking trip on Cape Breton Island. All they had was what they were carrying on their backs. One afternoon it was raining and they decided they wanted to play chess. So they looked at each other and one of them said to the other. "You go make a set of forest men and I'll go make a set of ocean men." So quick as a wink they did it, and they scratched out a chess board on the ground.

Since the most common things around were acorns, the forest guy made his pawns from acorn caps. His king and his queen were a round acorn and a tall acorn. His rooks were little pieces of bark with moss on them. His bishops were bracket fungus, that sort of tough mushroom stuff that grows on trees. And his knights were sticks.

It was a very pebbly beach, so the other guy used little black pebbles for his pawns. His king and his queen were two bigger pebbles, one with one white stripe and the other with two white stripes. His bishops were clam shells; his knights were snail shells; and I forget what his rooks were.

In no time at all, the two were happily at their chess game, having no trouble remembering which piece was which or which player it belonged to. Playing chess was a skill they had. But they also had the more important skill of knowing that they didn't have to stay within the confines of the game they had chosen.

From an interview with PHYLIS MORRISON

The Stretchy Loop

I recently invented a device, which I call the Stretchy Loop, which I have found to be just silly enough to open up the players to an exploration of what they want to do together. It's easy enough to make. . . .

Find an old inner-tube. Cut it in two-inch sections (or wider) so that you have rubber loops. Take equal lengths of rope and link them between the rubber loops, as if you were making a chain, alternating rubber and rope loops. Be sure to put two rubber loops on the first rope loop so that you can join the links in one complete circle. I've found it best to tape the rope knots with electrical tape—it makes them stronger and also less uncomfortable to lean against.

When you have the circle completed (it can be anywhere from ten feet in diameter up), put as many people as you can inside the stretchy chain. Have them lean back, and watch what happens. (I do recommend that everybody be of equal size.) Some of the games I've seen evolve are circular tug of war, some kind of absurd activity in which people on opposite sides of the circle try to change sides, and a kind of circular whirl-around. Try anything: have people hold on from the outside, have them alternate, or sit down, or whatever.

BERNIE DE KOVEN
New Ways

The Games Preserve Will Design a Game for You

As you'll note, this section is full of Bernie De Koven's ideas on games. We first encountered Bernie when we contacted a place called the Games Preserve. At its heart is a barnful of games, and people who are both serious and playful in their work. They schedule workshops throughout the year, and they also run a Games Library Information Bank, through which they offer to "locate, adapt, or design a game . . . that will explore virtually any area of rational process: scientific, musical, linguistic, social, psychological, sensual." They ask that you be concise and specific in outlining the elements and level of difficulty of the game you desire, and in describing the group that will play it. (For example: "a game which allows third grade children who have shown little confidence in their own abilities, who are withdrawn from the group, but who enjoy puzzles, to include other children in their play.")

So that's how we discovered Bernie De Koven. Corresponding with him is a game in itself; in fact, his stationery is designed as a gameboard (without any rules, of course).

For information, call or write the Games Preserve, R.D. 1355, Fleetwood, Pa. 19522; (215) 987-3456.

RS

[Specific kinds of games are dealt with in several other sections of this book. Sports gets an entire chapter of its own, for example; included there, in addition to such pastimes as golf, swimming, Ping-Pong, and worm grunting, are spectator-sports simulation games like Strat-O-Matic baseball and table hockey. The Outdoor Play chapter also offers some game-related ideas. Travelers will find suggestions for games to play in the car, plane, train, or restaurant—including Anna Jane Hays's incomparable Cow Poker—on page 363. And finally, for a game which pits a Hostess Sno-Ball (value −44) against a peach (+29), consult page 153.]

PUZZLES

JIGSAW PUZZLES

Selecting a Jigsaw for Your Pre-schooler

A puzzle teaches concentration, trains the eye to isolate shapes, and helps coordination—if it's easy enough. If not, put it away for weeks or even months, for nothing is more frustrating than a too difficult puzzle. We speak from experience, for to us, nothing's harder than those three-piece wooden puzzles cut on the color lines: no hints at all. Wooden puzzles are the most durable, the most expensive and the best, and cardboard puzzles in a frame are the worst, for the thin pieces are hard for a child to handle.

MARGUERITE KELLY and ELIA PARSONS
The Mother's Almanac

Knobs for Your Puzzle Pieces

You want to start introducing your baby to puzzles but his fingers are not quite coordinated enough to pick out the pieces. For some reason, the manufacturers of "first level" puzzles have not made any that are quite first level enough.

I bought a couple of Playskool inlaid woodboard puzzles—the kind with three or four pieces which do not butt up against one another; these are the easiest. Then I went to a hardware store and bought some unpainted wooden cabinet knobs. I glued one knob onto each piece of puzzle and now it is very easy for the baby to remove and handle the pieces.

In fairness, there is one company, Fisher-Price, that does put out a puzzle with knobs—but the pieces are tiny and the knobs are so small that you practically need tweezers to grip them. The knobs I recommend are good, round blobs that a kid can grab with ease. They glue on easily with Elmer's Glue. If you wish to be fancy, you can paint the knobs to match the puzzle pieces.

EMILY PERL KINGSLEY

Moving Up

Although wooden puzzles are better for little kids, five- and six-year-olds may label them babyish—even if the cardboard ones still prove too difficult. These kids are announcing that they want to move on to another, more grown-up stage.

ELS

Pre-school Jigsaws: The Shape's the Thing

Early in 1975, when the Milton Bradley Company and the Children's Television Workshop first decided to collaborate on a line of Sesame Street boxed jigsaw puzzles, the CTW research department began a study to determine the proper number of pieces to include: too few, we knew, and our intended audience of four- and five-year-olds would not be sufficiently challenged; too many and they'd walk away in hopeless frustration.

The researchers found that twenty-five pieces, the number tentatively proposed by Milton Bradley, seemed to be too many for the majority of the children tested. But when puzzle pieces with distinctly different shapes were introduced—interlocking squares, rectangles, circles, triangles, arrows, stars, and so forth—the kids were able to handle twenty-five pieces, and even more, with relatively little difficulty.

CBC

WHAT TO DO BEFORE YOUR KID MIXES UP ALL HIS PUZZLES

Whenever your child gets a new puzzle, scribble across the backs of all the pieces with a crayon, using a different color for each puzzle. When you have to separate a half-dozen puzzles, you'll find it a bit easier to sort them by the color of the scribbles on the back than by the color of the pictures on the front.

MARGUERITE KELLY and ELIA PARSONS
The Mother's Almanac

Jigsaw Puzzles: A Sampler

Playskool Match-Up Puzzles ($2.99 per box) are recommended for three- to six- year-olds, but I find they're good for lots of two-year-olds too. Each set—there are five in all—provides 24 two-piece match-up frame-tray puzzles; if your child is a puzzle-doer, he'll find a wealth of material for learning new vocabulary as well as puzzle skills. The best two sets by far, in my opinion, are Number Match-Ups and Animal Homes; they make good, inexpensive gifts for your kid, or someone else's.

Child Guidance offers a three-foot-tall Big Bird Floor Puzzle (about $6). Fashioned from heavy board, it's fairly easy and fun to do, especially if your child is not much for "tiny" puzzles.

JACKIE SHAPIRO

Otgari Pre-school Puzzles ($2.50 per box) are a great buy, if you can find them (try art, stationery, and novelty stores). Each box contains ten two-piece puzzles (See and Spell, Numbers, and others) or six six-piece puzzles (Travel Box or Safari Box). These colorful cardboard puzzles are small but simple; thus, they're a nice transition between large-piece wooden puzzles and regular jigsaws with hundreds of pieces.

RS

Fine Art Miniature Puzzles, by Springbok Editions, are 7 by 7–inch jigsaws, which are small enough so that they're manageable—you can finish one at one sitting. The pieces fit together really well, and when you're done you'll have a nice picture by a famous artist. All around, a really good buy.

CAROL PULITZER

Historically, jigsaw puzzles were maps. Gameophiles (16 Pine Street, Morristown, N.J. 07960, [201] 539-6884) makes city maps, subway maps, official Rand McNally maps, and navigation maps, all in jigsaw form. They're great if your child (or you) wants to learn her way around by piecing together a puzzle.

RS

Making Jigsaw Puzzles for Your Kids

The early childhood puzzles are often boring and ugly—or else $5—and fortunately it's easy enough to make your own.

For very small kids I take simple bold pictures from magazines and do two-and three-piece puzzles on cardboard. If you put clear contact paper over the picture, even cardboard puzzles will last a long time. Cut pieces with a matte knife or small saw. It's very inexpensive and a lot of fun to do.

JO BUTLER

◆

You can also mount posters or draw on ¼-inch plywood or Masonite, then cut with a saber saw or jigsaw if you have it. The possibilities are infinite. Four-dollar photo puzzles are advertised in the mail-order pages of magazines, but you can make your own easily enough. Even from a photograph that your kid takes—or from a picture she draws.

◆

If you don't want to cut your own puzzle, you can still design your own. Gameophiles (see address above) offers Design Your Own Puzzle, assembled or unassembled. Think about having to assemble a boxful of plain white pieces. Then, buy it assembled.—Eds.

THREE-DIMENSIONAL PUZZLES

Gradual Mastery: The Best Puzzles Allow for It

Once a puzzle is solved, it loses its value—it's worthless. On the other hand, it's not much fun to work hour after hour on a puzzle and make no progress at all.

My favorite puzzles, therefore, are those that present the possibility of intermediate levels of success—those you can't solve in an hour or two, but which give you the constant feeling you're making progress toward an ultimate goal.

Labyrinth (available from Brentano's, 586 Fifth Avenue, New York, N.Y. 10036, $17 plus $1 postage and handling), for example, requires that you tilt a playing surface by means of two control knobs in order to move a metal ball from one end of a maze to the other without its falling into any of a series of successively numbered holes. Obviously, this is a puzzle that calls for gradual mastery. The first time you try it, you'll be lucky to score a 6; later the first day, you may make it to 10, a week later to 21, and so forth. Every new high score produces its own moment of elation. And imagine how you'll feel when (and if) you finally maneuver your ball all the way to the finish line.

Another excellent puzzle is Pyschoteaze (distributed by the Chock Full of Everything Co., 307 Fifth Avenue, New York, N.Y.). Pyschoteaze is a flat wooden box containing interlocking rectangular pieces of varying size that can be slid around one another along the floor of the box. The object: to move the largest rectangle from the top of the box to the bottom. The farther you get before you can't make any more moves, the happier you'll be.

The puzzle I liked best as a child involved a cross made up of thirty-three holes; there was a peg in all but the center hole. One could remove a peg from the board by jumping it with another peg: the idea was to have only one peg left on the board at the end of the game. Here again, there was room for constant improvement; beating one's previous score was a cause for celebration. The puzzle is still available today in several incarnations. A hardwood one, made in the Philippines, is available from F. A. O. Schwarz (745 Fifth Avenue, New York, N.Y. 10022). You can order it by mail for $9.95 plus $1 handling charge; ask for item 54-23-704-0.

From an interview with JONATHAN CERF

◆

"A Real Brain Drain"

Penny Puzzlers, a series of twelve "movement puzzles" printed on Lucite, are appealing both to the eye and to the touch. They're rated according to difficulty from "easy as pie" to "a real brain drain," and you can order them ($1.99 each, plus 5 percent postage; minimum mail order $5) from Four Generations, 6005 Gravenstein Highway South, Sebastopol, Calif. 95472. It seems to me that Four Generations could have made these puzzles a bit more inexpensively, had they wanted to; still, they're well worth the price if you have a real puzzler in the family.

BERNIE DE KOVEN

◆

"Much Jollification"

Perplexing puzzles for adults and persistent children are made by [Pentangle (Blacksmith's Farm, Over Wallop, Hampshire, England; brochure free, 50 cents air mail)] . . . Puzzles include a glass marble to be removed from a cage, a silken cord to be removed from metal loops, and many wooden shapes to be constructed. Several of the puzzles have been chosen by the English Design Centre, and they are all coffee-table-worthy. On a lower level of humor, there is a tankard which only the owner will know how to drink out of, and a jug which can be made to suddenly start pouring from the center of the base "thus causing much jollification," claims the brochure.

MARIA ELENA DE LA IGLESIA
The New Catalogue of Catalogues

PUZZLE BOOKS

A Child's Gardner

I know several *Scientific American* subscribers—I'm one of them—who upon receiving their monthly copy of the magazine turn instinctively, with only the most cursory glance at the table of contents, to Martin Gardner's "Mathematical Games" column. Mr. Gardner is indeed a phenomenon: for more than twenty years he has playfully and inventively used mathematical principles as a framework to create (or report on) conundrums, "brain teasers," paradoxes, magic tricks, games, and sure-win bar bets that any confirmed puzzle fan—even one instinctively terrified of numbers—could not help finding fascinating.

Many of Mr. Gardner's more delightful columns have been collected in a series of books published by Simon & Schuster and Charles

Scribner's Sons. If you're a Gardner fan, you'll also be familiar with his witty annotated editions of the works of Lewis Carroll, himself a mathematician by trade: *The Annotated Alice* (Clarkson Potter, 1960) and *The Annotated Snark* (Simon & Schuster, 1962). What you may *not* know is that Mr. Gardner was for nine years a contributing editor of *Humpty Dumpty* magazine and has to his credit several books for kids, including at least three puzzle collections and a volume of cautionary verse.

A particular favorite, for eight- to twelve-year-olds, is *Perplexing Puzzles and Tantalizing Teasers* (Simon & Schuster, 1969, 96 pages, $5.95 hardcover, Archway Books, 60 cents, paperback). Attractively, if somewhat stiffly, illustrated by Laszlo Kubinyi (who, the book jacket tells us, "divides his time between illustrating children's books and playing the *dumbek,* a

Middle Eastern drum, in an Armenian orchestra''), the book contains a variety of diversions ranging from palindromes (words and sentences that read the same backward and forward, such as ''A man, a plan, a canal—Panama!''), through a collection of ridiculous riddles (Q. ''What has four stander-uppers, four pull-downers, two hookers, two lookers, and a swishy-wishy?'' A. ''A cow.''), to a paean, with examples, to Roger Price and his world-famous *Droodles.* The ''tantalizing teasers'' that tickled my imagination the most, perhaps because I grew up in a pun-loving family, were ''Thriftigrams.'' Mr. Gardner's chapter about them is reproduced below.

CBC

Read the Thriftigrams

The more words you use in a telegram, the more it costs, so you can save money if you can think of clever ways to cut down the number of words and still say everything you want to say. The thriftigram is a telegram that does this by using many single words that are puns for several words. For example, instead of saying, ''Thank you very much,'' you can say, ''Sanctuary much,'' and have only two words instead of four.

Now see if you can read correctly the three thriftigrams shown here.

MARTIN GARDNER
Perplexing Puzzles and Tantalizing Teasers

EASTERN UNION THRIFTIGRAM

MESSAGE:
OMNIVOROUS HAPPY SIAM
VENOM WITH YOU. LOVE
ENCASES.

EASTERN UNION THRIFTIGRAM

MESSAGE:
HAVE TOOTHACHE PLANE.
CANOE MIMI AT AIRPORT?

EASTERN UNION THRIFTIGRAM

MESSAGE:
VALUE BEMOAN VALENTINE?
OLIVE YOU.

LASZLO KUBINYI

Tangrams

A tangram is a puzzle consisting of a square cut into five triangles, a square, and a rhomboid, which can be combined so as to form a great variety of other figures. If the idea appeals to you, you'll be interested in a $1.50 paperback called, *Tangrams,* by Ronald C. Read (Dover, 1965, 152 pages). The following review by Steven Caney appeared in *Toy Review:*

[The Read book] shows 330 puzzles (and their solutions). Some are quite simple and can be done without too much brain straining, and others are quite perplexing and tricky. Included are puzzles for letter forms, numbers, animals, people, illusions, and double tangrams, as well as lovely bits of tangram history and instructions for making a special 15-piece puzzle.

Two Books for Would-be Cryptanalysts

I am planning to be a cryptanalyst (that's a code-breaker) when I grow up, so I especially like code books. My favorite is *Codes and Secret Writing,* by Herbert Zim (William Morrow, 1948, Scholastic abridged edition).

MICHAEL RINZLER
Age nine

For older kids, Philip and Phylis Morrison, writing in *Scientific American,* recommend *Secret Writing: The Craft of the Cryptographer,* by James Raymond Wolfe (McGraw-Hill, 1970, 192 pages, $5.50 hardcover). It's ''an exciting book,'' they report, ''a savory mixture of mathematics and the most raffish part of diplomatic history, a first-class introduction to the art. . . . [The author includes] an account of most of the main cipher systems, from a simple shift along the alphabet to a double-transposition cipher used in Italy by both German and American forces as a high-security field cipher.''

◆

A Puzzle Book That Can Make You a Game Expert

Your Move, by David L. Silverman (McGraw-Hill, 1971), presents, in turn, one chess problem, one checkers problem, one bridge problem, and so forth, along with the basic rules of each game and tips on strategy. The puzzles are great fun, and you'll sharpen your gaming skills too. In fact, I learned several new games as a direct result of Mr. Silverman's efforts.

From an interview with JONATHAN CERF

Mazes and Maze Books: The Labyrinthian Way

Why children and adults in the United States should develop a sudden hankering for mazes is a mystery. Increasing leisure naturally demands new time wasters, but that can't be the whole story. Is it because millions feel trapped in various kinds of labyrinths—religious, moral, economic, political—and finding a way out of a paper maze somehow helps relieve anxiety? That might apply to adults, but hardly to children. Perhaps it is just a case of publishers discovering an interest that children have had all along.

Of about 30 paperback books of mazes now on sale, Grosset & Dunlap has the lion's share. Thirteen of this publisher's books are by Vladimir Koziakin, a 31-year-old artist of Russian descent. His *Mazes for Fun,* volumes 1, 2, 3 and 4 ($1 each), in coloring-book format, and the smaller *ABC Mazes* (75 cents) feature pictorial designs for small children. For older children he has three pocket-size books: *Astro Mazes* (95 cents), *Mystery Mazes* (95 cents), and *Dinosaur Mazes* (75 cents). For those who prefer more challenging puzzles there are the abstract labyrinths in his middle-size books, *Mazes,* volumes 1 through 5 [$2.50 each]. Their striking patterns are arranged in order of increasing complexity, each bearing a rated time limit from a few minutes to an hour.

In addition to his maze books, the indefatigable Koziakin, surely the world's top maze artificer, draws a maze a week for the *National Enquirer.* From Gameophiles Unlimited (16 Pine Street, Morristown, N.J. 07960) you can obtain his 6-foot-long wall labyrinth, on vinyl, and his jigsaw puzzle maze. . . .

Greg Bright's *The Great Maze Book* (Pantheon, $2.50), first published in London and now available here, is the largest and handsomest of the maze books. Bright was a young rock musician in England until his passion for labyrinths got the upper hand. *Punch* has called his patterns "fiendishly difficult," and caricaturist Al Hirschfeld has paid tribute to their dazzling Op Art qualities. The book includes aerial photographs of Bright's Pilton Maze, a work of "earth art" that took him a year to dig in a field near Glastonbury. Bright is presently designing an outdoor maze, with bridges and underpasses, for Lord Weymouth's estate, at Longleat. . . .

The best of all the unorthodox maze books are by Rick and Glory Brightfield, two young graphic artists. In their *Amazing Mazes* and *More Amazing Mazes* (Harper/Colophon, $2.95) you will find labyrinths masquerading as

mushrooms, flowers, fish, birds, clouds, butterflies and abstract patterns as delightfully eye-twisting as they are ingenious. These are not just crooked roads inside a border that resembles something. The path itself is so artfully concealed that finding your way through a Brightfield maze is almost a new kind of cerebral experience.

MARTIN GARDNER
The New York Times Book Review

MAZES: "DON'T DRAW ON THE PAPER"

If you want to increase your pleasure in solving mazes, the first thing not to do is draw on the paper. Morons can be taught to solve a maze by shading blind alleys and detours until only a solution path is left. You should always work a maze with a toothpick or match, and not consider it mastered until you can touch the match to the starting spot and slide it unerringly to the goal.

Solving a maze that is spread before you is, of course, much easier than walking a hedge maze, like the famous English maze at Hampton Court. However, Greg Bright suggests a clever way to simulate such walking. Cut a small circular hole in the center of a sheet of cardboard. Place the hole over the starting spot. Now by sliding the cardboard, never seeing more than the spot along which you "walk," try to find a path to the goal.

MARTIN GARDNER
The New York Times Book Review

Superhero Stumpers

With characteristic modesty, Stan Lee, the guiding genius behind Marvel Comics, calls *The Mighty Marvel Superheroes Fun Book* "the world's most fascinating and unusual" puzzle book. The claim may or may not be extravagant, but there's no question that any kid (or adult) who enjoys "The Wonderful World of Marveldom" will find some pleasant hours between the covers of this 8½ by 11–inch paperback (Simon & Schuster, 1976, 128 pages). Reed (Mr. Fantastic) Richards, for example, has gotten his amazingly flexible arms hopelessly intertwined: in the puzzle "Farewell Two Arms?" the reader is asked to help him out. A few pages later, one is asked to have a heated (if somewhat scrambled) conversation with the Human Torch. Soon thereafter, one must straighten out Spiderman's webbing by filling in the appropriate words ("Oh, what a tangled web we weave . . ." mourns Spidey). And so it goes. It's all yours for $2.95.

CBC

MAGIC

A POTPOURRI OF TRICKS AND EFFECTS

Tricks to Get Started With

This article was going to be called "The Ten Best Magic Tricks with Props," but wasn't for the simple reason that I couldn't think of ten effects in that category. I could think of seven, however, and here they are. (They can all be ordered from Louis Tannen. See "Mail Order Magic," page 440, for details.)

• *Chinese sticks,* sold by all magic dealers, and at all prices. This is one of the classics of magic. You have two wands, each with a string going through one end. Pull on one string, the string in the other wand goes up. "Aha!" thinks the audience, "the string passes through one wand and into the other!"

"Not so," says the magician, as he or she puts one wand under his or her armpit and continues the trick.

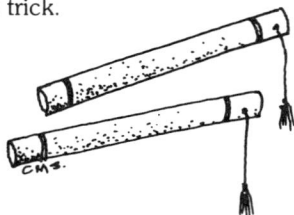

• *Spooky,* sold at most magic dealers for about $3.50. It is a beautiful effect, in which a silk handkerchief slowly forms a hump, conforming to the shape of Glorpy, your ghostly helper. (The silk is shown free of trickery before and after the effect.)

• *Anti-Gravico,* 50 cents at most magic dealers. Definitely uncanny. Borrow a bottle of soda, turn it upside down. Nothing falls out. Stick a few pencils up the neck of the bottle; still nothing comes out. Now, hand out the bottle for examination.

• *Chinese laundry ticket* or *paper tear,* sold everywhere, and explained in most books on basic magic. The performer tears up a piece of paper, realizes that it should've been in one piece, and restores it.

• *Sponge balls,* sold at most magic shops for about $2.50, or you can cut your own. Start with a ball of foam rubber. Put it in the spectator's hand—and she's holding two, or is that three? Or four? And that one just vanished, so God knows how many there are now. The foam rubber balls are just balls of foam rubber; the trick is knowing how to do it. *Sponge Balls,*

by Frank Garcia, is a very good book on the subject and costs $2.

• *Multiplying rabbits,* about $1. Basically a form of sponge balls, these are two foam rubber rabbits—a mother and a father. You put them in a spectator's hand and get four baby bunnies, also.

• *Chinese linking rings,* sold in all magic shops. Priced from $3 to $30, depending on the size. This is one trick that I hestitated on, because it *does* need some practice. Not a lot, but enough so that if you do it without practice, you may reveal the secret of one of the best tricks in magic. The effect is that of linking and unlinking eight solid steel rings which have been shown to be separate. The rings will come with instructions, but to have a really beautiful effect you need a book. Dai Vernon's *Symphony of the Rings* is probably the best book on the subject, if you can find it. Look in the library.

ADAM BLUMENTHAL
Age twelve

The Wizard

The Wizard is a marvelously effective clairvoyance trick. I particularly like it because it involves an ongoing conspiracy—often between a child and an adult. Moments after my mother first befuddled me with the Wizard, she let me in on the secret, and the two of us proceeded to pull it off, year after year, on a continuing parade of unsuspecting friends.

Here's the trick, as my mother worked it on me: One summer afternoon, in the middle of doing nothing in particular, she informed me that she had a friend, known as "The Wizard," who could guess any card I happened to think of. What's more, she said, he could exercise his power long-distance; all I had to do was tell her my card, then we'd call up the Wizard and he'd identify it. "Without your giving him any hints?" I asked. "Without my giving him any hints," she replied.

Skeptically I informed her of my choice—let's say it was the three of hearts. My mother dialed a number and asked for the Wizard. A moment later, after a cursory introduction, I found myself holding the receiver. "Hello, Wizard?" I said tentatively. "Hello," said a mysterious voice. "I believe your card is the three of hearts. And now, good-by." That was it: before I'd even had a chance to tell him he was right, he'd hung up.

How did my mother pull it off? Well, the Wizard was her accomplice, of course. He knew that as soon as he heard her question "Hello, is this the Wizard?" he should start slowly naming each of the suits: "Clubs . . . spades . . . diamonds . . . hearts." The moment he named the correct suit, my mother would interrupt him: "How're you feeling today?" she'd say, or something equally innocuous. Then he'd begin calling out card values: "Ace . . . two . . . three," and so forth. When he got to the correct number, she'd interrupt him again ("My son has a card for you to guess"). The Wizard would now have all the information needed to perform his miracle: it was as simple as that.

CBC

The Master Deck and the Demon Deck

When I was about ten, someone gave me a "stripper deck"—a deck in which one end of each card is imperceptibly narrower than the other. The purpose of the stripper deck is to enable a magician, after reversing a card in the deck, to remove that card simply by running his or her fingers along the edge of the pack, from the narrow end of the reversed card toward the wide end.

Obviously, by asking the victim of your magic to remove the card of his choice and then sneakily reversing the stripper deck before he replaces it, you can make the chosen card appear at will, even after shuffling. As a child, I succeeded in fooling my friends for weeks. (I may have *bored* them to death too, but they never guessed my secret.)

Browsing at Brentano's bookstore in New York, I recently came across a box labeled "2 Trick Decks—45 Terrific Tricks." Joyful memories stirred in my head. Could one of them be a stripper deck, I wondered.

Indeed, one of them was, relabeled the Master Deck by the manufacturer, Reiss Games, Inc. And the second pack of cards, called the Demon Deck, was even more remarkable: examining it, I noted that every other card was the same—the five of hearts. The fives, the instructions told me, were slightly shorter than the regular cards; as a result, when one riffled through the pack, only the regular cards would show. Consider the possibilities.

Of course, I bought the two decks, which together cost about $5, complete with two instruction books (including "patter"). I rushed home, and have been subjecting my bemused wife to my conjuring ever since. (Could it be she's begun to smell a rat every time she draws the five of hearts? If so, she hasn't said anything.)

CBC

Mom's Up to Her Old Tricks—And Here Are Two of Them

My mother is an inveterate collector of card and party tricks. Here, from a book she wrote many years ago with her friend Edith Young, are two that she thinks kids will find particularly enjoyable.

CBC

"THIGH, ATLAS, GOOSE, BIBLE"

This is an ancient card trick originally worked out in Latin and later translated into English. It is an excellent trick, impossible to detect, no matter how many times you do it for your audience. Yet it is simple to perform.

Take twenty cards from a regular deck. Any twenty will do. Now, lay them out face up, two at a time with *every* card showing, so that they look like this:

Ask your audience mentally to choose one of the ten pairs. In this case one might choose the Ace of Hearts and Jack of Spades. All the people who are watching may choose a pair. After this is done, gather up the cards, being sure to keep all of the pairs, such as the Ace of Hearts and the Jack of Spades, together, but otherwise picking them up haphazardly. Now, comes the trick. The key to it is the following four words:

T H I G H
A T L A S
G O O S E
B I B L E

After glancing at these words you will note that each word has a letter repeated in it (the H

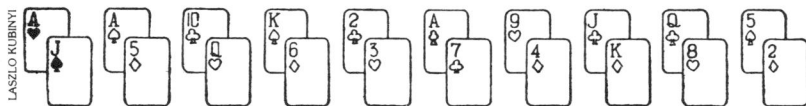

repeated in Thigh, the A in Atlas, etc.), as well as one letter that appears once in the other three words. (The I in Thigh is also in Bible, the G in Thigh is also in Goose, etc.) You must memorize these words in the order shown. These words set the pattern for your laying out of the cards for the second time for your audience. The first time you laid out the cards, you put them in twos. Now the second time, you use the letters in the four given words and lay out the cards face up, in the following manner:

You put five cards across the first and every row thereafter, as there are five letters in each of the words, and make four rows for the number of words used in the key. Now, as you start putting down the cards you must mentally spell out the key words. The first card will cover the T in Thigh; the second card must cover the T in Atlas, the third card will cover the H in Thigh and the fourth card will cover the other H in Thigh, the fifth card will cover the I in Thigh and the sixth card will cover the I in Bible. In other words, every time you cover a letter in the mentally spelled words, you must cover its corresponding letter in the same word or in one of the other words with a card. To illustrate, the moves are numbered:

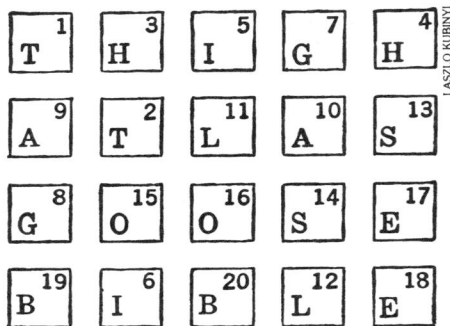

After you have laid out the twenty cards for the second time, you ask your audience, one by one, what row or two rows their chosen pair of cards appear in. If, for example, they say the first and second row, you know the only letter that appears in the first row and also in the second row is T. So you know the pair they have chosen covers the T's in your mental diagram. If they say both cards appear in the first row, then the cards they have chosen are covering the H's in Thigh and so on throughout the diagram. It is a really a baffling trick for an audience, and we hope you have fun fooling them.

COLLABORATION

Two people must collaborate on this trick, but no one else should be aware of the alliance.

One of the two leaves the room while the remaining guests choose one member of their group whom the absent man must name when he returns to the room. He looks around the room carefully and then points to the man who is picked by the group. Everyone gasps in wonder at this evidence of mental telepathy.

The trick is very simple. No two people sit in exactly the same position. The collaborator assumes the exact sitting position of the man or woman chosen. Naturally, he changes his position if the chosen person moves. If the unknown collaborator is chosen, he assumes a position unlike any other in the room.

PHYLLIS FRASER (CERF WAGNER)
and EDITH YOUNG
Puzzles, Quizzes and Games

———————◆———————

Pocket Calculator Magic

One of the more curious recreational uses for the pocket calculator is as a device for performing magic tricks, most of them of the ESP variety. Here is a stunt that children find particularly amusing. Ask a child to enter 98765432 and divide by 8. He will be mildly surprised by the result: 12345679. The digits are in sequence except for 8, the divisor, which has mysteriously vanished.

Ask the child to name his favorite digit. Suppose he says 4. You immediately say: "Very good. Multiply the number on display [12345679] by 36." Now he is really surprised, because the number he gets is 44444444 (or nine 4's if the readout can accommodate that many). The multiplier you give is always the product of 9 and the named digit. The working is easy to understand: $111111111/9 = 12345679$. Since 9 times 12345679 is 111111111, a multiplier of $9n$ (where n is a digit) is sure to give a row of n's.

Dividing a row of 1's by integers other than 9 until the quotient has no fractional remainder produces other "magic numbers." For example: $111111/7 = 15873$. Multiplying 15873 by $7n$, where n is a digit, produces a row of n's. Again: $111111/33 = 3367$. Multiply 3367 by $33n$ and you get a row of n's.

A trick I call the Arabian Nights Mystery, because it is based on the properties of 1,001, begins by asking someone to think of any three-digit number, *ABC*. Tell him to repeat the number to make *ABCABC* and enter the six-digit number in the calculator. While he is doing it, stand with your back turned so that you cannot see what is going on.

"I'm beginning to get some vibes," you say, "and they tell me that your number is exactly divisible by the unlucky number 13. Please divide by 13 and tell me if I'm right."

Your companion makes the division. Sure enough, there is no remainder.

"It's strange," you continue, "but my clairvoyant powers tell me that the number now on display is exactly divisible by the lucky number 11." He makes the division. You were right again.

"Now I have a strong impression," you continue, "that the number on display is exactly divisible by the still luckier number 7." This proves to be the case.

Tell your companion to take a good look at the readout. It is *ABC*, the number he first thought of.

The trick cannot fail. Multiplying any three-digit number *ABC* by 1,001 obviously produces *ABCABC*. Because the prime factors of 1,001 are 13, 11 and 7, dividing *ABCABC* by those three numbers must result in *ABC*.

MARTIN GARDNER
Scientific American

[Martin Gardner, author of *Scientific American*'s monthly "Mathematical Games" column, has compiled several marvelous puzzle books for children; see our review "A Child's Gardner" on pages 433–34.]

LEARNING MAGIC

Books to Conjure With

The Amateur Magician's Handbook, by Henry Hay (Thomas Y. Crowell Co., 3rd ed., 1972, 338 pages, $10.95 hardcover; New American Library, $1.95 paperback), covers close-up magic (using cards, coins, balls, cigarettes, and other small objects) very thoroughly, and has smaller sections on mind reading and stage magic. The book is clearly written and has photographs to show the moves, which I consider a decided advantage. So, if you're interested in learning how to do card tricks or magic with small objects, this book is a good buy.

If, on the other hand, you want to learn how to do stage magic or magic with larger objects, buy *How to Entertain Children with Magic You Can Do,* by the Great Merlini (Clayton Rawson) (Simon & Schuster, 1962, 175 pages, $2.95 paperback), or *Magic Digest: Fun Magic for Everyone,* by George B. Anderson (DBI Books, Northfield, Ill. 1972, 288 pages, $6.95 paperback).

The Illustrated History of Magic, by Milbourne Christopher (Thomas Y. Crowell Co., 1973, 425 pages, $14.95), is not a book of magic, but a book of magicians, from Dedi, who claimed to be 110 years old when he performed for Cheops, through Katterfelto, who performed in the late 1700s and who gave science lectures along with magic, up to today's Kreskin and Mark Wilson. Besides being well written it is beautifully and profusely illustrated, with some very good color plates of old magicians' posters. All of these combine to make it well worth $15. Because of the high price, though, it might be a good idea to see if they have it in your library, and find out if you like it enough to buy it.

ADAM BLUMENTHAL
Age twelve

[Walter B. Gibson's *Magic with Science* (Grosset & Dunlap, 1968, 120 pages, paperback) is a bookful of tricks based on sound scientific principles. For more about it, turn to page 217, in the SCIENCE section.]

◆

Magic Magazines

Each issue of *Genie* (Box 36068, Los Angeles, Calif. 90036; $8 per year, for 12 issues; sample copies $1) contains about forty pages, and it includes a column by the extremely eccentric Al Flosso, explaining five to ten tricks. There's a lot of advertising, by magic dealers from all over the world, so you know what magic materials are around. *Genie*'s motto is "Always late, always great." And it's true; I got last October's issue the following June.

I like *Genie* a lot more than *Tops,* a magazine published by Abbots ($11 per year, for 11 issues; a dollar a copy; see next article for address). *Tops* is thicker, and it also features articles and tricks, but I find its design off-putting, and, to my way of thinking, it gives too much patronizing advice.

ADAM BLUMENTHAL

Ordering Magic Tricks
and Books by Mail

Our sources tell us that you shouldn't order magic by mail unless you're familiar with the product or it has been called to your attention by a bona-fide source whose recommendations are without trickery! Being forewarned, the following are the most complete sources. You can probably get almost anything cheaper by shopping around, but maybe you don't have the time.

Abbots Magic Manufacturing Co., Colin, Mich. 49040, said to be the largest magic dealer in the world.

Louis Tannen, 1540 Broadway, New York, N.Y. 10036, (212) 541-9550, offers both tricks and books, all featured in a 700-page hardcover catalogue which they sell for $3.50. Tannen's minimum order is $3, postage prepaid. (Parcel post and handling charges are as follows: 75 cents for orders under $7.50; $1.25 for orders from $7.50 to $20; $2 for orders from $20 to $35; $3 for orders over $35.)

Magic, Inc., 5082 North Lincoln Avenue, Chicago, Ill. 60625, (312) 334-2855, publishes a 47-page catalogue (priced at $2).

ADAM BLUMENTHAL

A Word In Closing

If you decide to take up magic as a hobby, the one word you will read in every book you buy is *practice*. Most likely, you won't do it and you'll wonder why people don't enjoy your magic. You'll decide the fault was with the trick, and you'll learn a new one. And, when nobody likes that, you'll give up magic.

Moral: PRACTICE!

Also, *please* don't buy a trick just to find out how it's done. If you do, three things can happen:

1. The trick will turn out to be very simple, and you'll feel stupid for not having figured it out.

2. You'll have ruined your enjoyment every time you see the trick from then on.

3. You'll have wasted your money.

I know all this from personal experience.

ADAM BLUMENTHAL

TOYS AND DOLLS

441

TOYS

The Obsolete Child

Somewhere along the line the people who produce our toys began to take themselves seriously. They were no longer only interested in making money, but suddenly they were determined to re-create the world after their own vision. So toys took over and became the real world and children became the toys. Dolls that could be happy when their two- and three-year-old mommies or daddies were happy began to cry all the time. Trucks that would haul dirt across oceans if their little drivers asked began running their own blind routes into table legs and walls.

When I was growing up my favorite toys were clothespins. They were cowboys, football players, cops, robbers, anything I wanted them to be. And though I'd ask for more official (advertised) playthings from time to time and even get them when the getting was good, always I drifted back to my canvas bag full of sleek heroes and splintery villains, lantern-jawed quarterbacks and knotty linebackers.

Nevertheless, in those days, toys were toys. You could count on blocks to be nothing more than geometric hunks of wood that toppled as easily as the magic kingdoms built out of them, not specially grooved and numbered feats of engineering that when properly assembled improperly assemble a child's dreams. Those were the days when dolls were all Mona Lisas, mysterious, half-smiling, as unpredictable as their mother's imagination. Today a doll must dance or iron its way into a young heart. And if its hair miraculously grows before your eyes, then it will not speak, and if it miraculously speaks via that Frankensteinesque little pull string in its neck, then it will not wet its diaper, and if it wets, it won't do some other irresistible thing.

I'm as much a patsy for advertising and salesmanship as anyone else. I've bought my son toys he can only look at, can't even touch. Toys that only do a single preposterous thing like chug along a roller-coaster track right side up and then upside down. And then I can't understand why he prefers playing with spoons or his own socks or the food on his plate or toilet paper or my bed at seven in the morning. And then I remember my clothespins, how they never fought back or controlled me. I remember the child's boundless joy of manipulation and drama.

Other people have taken themselves too seriously and they have juggled our sense of reality. Machines have become more important than those who listen to them, operate them, and even create them. Politicians have made us believe that they elect us. Television would have us think that its camera eye sees truer than our own. Everywhere and every way we have allowed ourselves to become so finely developed that we no longer need ourselves.

ALAN SAPERSTEIN

CHOOSING TOYS

Coming to Terms with What Kids Like

So enlightened a parent am I that when my son was only three I let him use my heavy steel hammer to "build" to his heart's content. When he became more articulate, he told me that the hammer was too big and heavy for him. Indeed it was. "We'll get you a smaller one when we go to the hardware store," I told him. "Aw, can't I just have a *toy* one," he replied.

A lesson for me: many kids like junky plastic toys, even occasionally prefer them to the real or better thing, and no matter how much you feed them sleek wooden Brio trucks and handsome forest-artisan–made dolls, no matter how much of a purist you are or how high you think you've raised their toy-quality consciousness, they will still want the dime-store metal car facsimile, lust after the cereal-box plastic loop-de-loop with a life span of about forty minutes, grab for the 89-cent Fisher-Price look-alike—

and worst of all, not mind a bit that it lacks the longevity of a sturdier toy.

I am one who finds nearly all toys a nuisance, who prefers to see a kid play with real-world things—starting with the usual pots and pans and wooden spoons and grocery packages and cans right up to sand and rocks and pianos and chemical mixtures. (My friends think I overdo it—and perhaps I do—but in theory only, for my own child's room is full of molded plastic, name brand and otherwise.) I will concede that there are many toys that have given my child great pleasure and amusement and—even though I think the label "educational" is taken much too seriously by us all (there were a lot of smart people before there were "toys that teach")—have provided him with some understanding of the world.

Many of the toy companies that have a "bad name" for one reason or another among serious anti-consumers like me, the big companies are guilty of nothing more than performing in the American way: they are, they think, giving the public what it wants. (There will always be the question of whether they are trying to create the need rather than merely filling it. That is, would nine-year-old girls have conjured up Barbie if no one else had?) But it is also true that many of the arty handmade toys are not so great.

Most of us have come to terms with the fact that our children will have a shelf or box full of toys. The question is really how to fill that shelf or toy box so that both the parents and the kids can live with the choices.

ELS

Amortizing Toys

Our philosophy in terms of toys is to spend some time and effort shopping around, looking in catalogues and special stores, and once or twice a year buying something really good (and often expensive) that can grow with the child—like wooden blocks or the Skaneateles wooden train or Lego or an electric train or good outdoor play equipment—rather than spontaneously buying a lot of junky toys that fall apart. The one or two items that we decide to buy only seem more expensive: most of us have never worked out the concept of amortizing toys over time.

JIM TURNER

"May I go over to Jim's house and play with his toys? Mine are all educational." Wall Street Journal

What to Look for When You Go Into a Toy Store

We know that chemistry sets and electrical toys are for older children. We know that all toys should be nontoxic and nonflammable. We know, too, that toys with tiny parts shouldn't be given to kids who will swallow them. We think a toy should last, perhaps teach, certainly amuse, challenge, delight. We know a toy should be safe, we've read all the articles, heard the warnings, even listened to our own mothers' suggestions. But why is it that when we go into a toy store we are immobilized, we don't know where to begin, we end up buying what we think is right, and still it breaks down or loses its appeal? Here are some suggestions for what to look for when you go into a toy store.

Big blocks. The big wooden blocks are usually called kindergarten blocks and are worth buying

if you can't find someone to pass a set on to you. Decide whether you want hardwood or softwood. Hardwood has the advantage of not splintering and being long-lasting. But it has the disadvantage of denting softwood floors and furniture. Softwood probably won't dent most floors, but it may splinter sooner than the hard. I prefer hardwood (Creative Playthings or Childcraft or, for mail order only, Community Playthings, Rifton, N.Y. 12471; phone [914] 658-3141), though they tend to cost twice as much as most softwood blocks.

Good blocks will last nearly forever, and kids play with them for a long time. They provide a backdrop for play with smaller blocks, toy soldiers, little Fisher-Price people, Matchbox cars, or Hotwheels (be sure the set you buy includes at least one ramp-shaped block). They also make a lot of good noise when they are knocked down.

Wagons. Ask to see inside the box when you buy a wagon. Sometimes what's inside is not the same as the display sample. Check to see that the wheels are rubber, not plastic; squeeze them with all your might. If you can feel that they are hollow inside, then they're plastic and will not last through a week's worth of pulling. Some manufacturers have started putting on handles with plastic pull-ends. Don't buy these. A wagon without a handle is useful only as a coffee table.

AMF makes a perfectly fine, reasonably priced metal wagon. Creative Playthings has an expensive but beautiful wooden one with removable sides. Both need to be taken in when it rains.

Trucks. Kids conjure up incredible strength when it comes to pulling a toy apart. Try to pull off the wheels or other movable parts. If you can do it, don't buy the toy. (The store owner should send the pieces back to the manufacturer for credit.) Tonka trucks and cars as a rule hold up well and are certainly worth seeking out. A cheap truck from an unreputable or anonymous manufacturer is guaranteed to lose at least one wheel very quickly.

Dolls. Again, pull at the head, arms, and legs of the doll before you buy. Better to leave a limb on the toy-store counter than to find it under your refrigerator when you move. If the doll is a rag doll, make sure the stuffing contents are listed. I know of a couple who took their daughter to an allergist every week for months and months and spent hundreds of dollars before they discovered her sneezing was being caused by the stuffing of the favorite dolly she carted around constantly. Never buy a doll with anonymous innards (usually, if they list their polysyllabic synthetic contents at all, they're okay). If you have to poke your finger through the wrapping to read the label, do it—it should be where you can read it before you plunk down the money. (Many stores have re-wrap machines in the back.) Keep away from dolls that have wire skeletal frames inside (those with bendable though jointless limbs are suspect); they are likely to pierce the outside of the doll before too long and poke someone in the eye.

Battery-operated toys. Generally we feel that these are a waste of money because kids tire of them very quickly. But sometimes, we know, you find one that's irresistible. (Every Christmas I pass a guy on the street hawking made–in–Hong Kong trains that back up when they hit a wall, puff "real" smoke, and blow a believable

whoo-whoo over a realistic *ch-ch-ch-ch*. Two of them are on the top of my closet in disrepair, but still I can't promise that I won't give this mystery vendor one more chance come December.) Generally, battery-operated toys are so fragile that after just a few sessions of play the wires disengage and even new batteries can't bring them back to life. When the toy doesn't break, the battery replacements can be an expensive proposition.

Art materials. These are not toys and are best bought in places other than toy stores. (See MAKING THINGS, page 327.)

Games. Think about whether it is purely a game of chance or whether it allows the players to develop strategies. If it's a game of chance, is it different enough from games you already have? Can parts be replaced with common household or dime-store items? (See GAMES, page 408.)

Toys that pretend to be grown-up things. Don't buy a "toy" anything if the real thing will do better. Toy typewriters are consistently terrible: the keys on the Sears model are tight even to adult fingers; the Marx brand doesn't always type whole letters and the ribbon cannot be removed and changed. And that's $16. For probably $10, certainly $15, you can buy a second-hand typewriter in good working order. (My child's grandmother insists that if you give a kid a toy when the real thing is accessible, he will never learn respect for the real thing. How can you let him throw his toy watch into the bathtub, for example, and expect him to know that he can't do the same with your hundred-dollar Omega?)

Toy stores carry facsimiles with names like "Jr. Groom 'n' Shave" so a boy can emulate his father, and hair-fixing sets called "Betty's Beauty Shoppe" so a girl can discover Mom's beauty secrets. But a toy comb and brush? What's wrong with the real thing?

Those toy baking ovens that actually heat up are constantly being investigated for safety. If a child is old enough to operate a toy one, he is probably responsible enough to learn to use a real one—in your presence, of course—and before long he'll be making dinner for the family. And toy popcorn poppers don't work nearly as well as real ones (and are more likely to break down before next Christmas).

Musical toys. Though there are some exceptions, it is generally not a good idea to buy a toy musical instrument. The 98-cent plastic harmonica in the dime store doesn't make music. For a couple of dollars more you can buy a real harmonica that does, and as a bonus it won't crack or break as the plastic one will. A $2 plastic ukulele or guitar will not even last an hour. My son was so frustrated by one that was given to him when he'd gone visiting that he didn't even want to take it home—the instrument itself was unattractive, and the strings became loose and unplayable. He seemed to prefer playing the string that tied up the box.

Now you needn't go out and buy your five-year-old a Stradivarius, but you should consider the negative consequences of a crappy toy. A secondhand shop or flea market is again a good place to scout for this kind of item—you can often pick up a musical instrument that may not be great, but at least will let your child see what the real thing looks like and feels like. (For more on making music, see page 303.)

ELS

Toy Bargains at the Five-and-Ten

Elisabeth Scharlatt and I recently toured the toy counters of several local Woolworth's and Lamston's in search of "low ticket" play items that seemed to be good values. And, there amid the junk, we discovered all kinds of treasures that a child could enjoy—indeed, many which had the potential to provide more hours of play than items costing considerably more. Here's an annotated list (in alphabetical order):

Balloons. We found bags of balloons from several companies, most selling for under 40 cents. A particular bargain was Eagle's bag of "Twisty Animals," containing sixteen of those long, skinny balloons you can twist together to make wild beasts (which somehow always come out looking like dachshunds). Also worth considering: the "Eagle Party Pump Pack"—sixty balloons plus a little cardboard pump (which can save an awful lot of lung power), all for 98 cents.

Balls. Always fun. The whiffle ball, retailing for under 50 cents, is a classic. Air slits in its plastic surface allow one to curve it easily, and they also slow it down to the point where a direct hit from a distance of anything more than a few feet won't even smart. Small plastic whiffle bats are also available.

Foam balls, for under two dollars, are also a good buy. Parker Brothers' Nerf Balls are probably the most famous, followed closely by the Puff Basketball, which comes with a plastic-rimmed net that fastens, by means of rubber suction cups, to your mirror or window (well) or your wall (badly). (My wife gave me a Puff Basketball set and a huge carton full of Nerf Balls last Christmas; they're a permanent fixture now in my bathroom.) Foam balls are suitable for indoor play—the smaller ones, that is. The large ones are heavy enough, despite their low density, to cause extensive damage inside your house.

You shouldn't give foam balls to very young children, by the way—the foam tears quite easily, and once a piece is ripped away, it can become lodged in a youngster's throat.

Bingo markers. Elisabeth and I hadn't realized they were available separately, but they are. (My family used to use shell macaroni.) You can probably make up other games to play with these boxed markers as well. But we wouldn't recommend them for the under-five set, as they're easy to swallow. (Incidentally, there's a bingo game that uses a spinner, available for under $2. It's called Mini-Bingo.)

Bubbles. A bottle of bubble mix goes for about 35 cents these days. Keep an eye out, too, for the new bubble rings that allow your child to make monster-sized bubbles.

Card games. Edu-Cards and Whitman each produce many card games that sell for 59 cents. There are several Disney titles available, and also many of the old classics like Authors and Old Maid. Keep in mind, before you buy, that some of the games offered—Crazy Eights and Concentration, for example—can be played perfectly well with an ordinary deck of playing cards.

Digit Box. "Digit Box" is the trade name for those little plastic square puzzles in which interlocking numbered tiles can be slid around into different arrangements. As you'll perhaps recall, placing the tiles in order from 1 to 15 is relatively easy. But the reverse order—starting from 15 and working back to 1—is impossible. (I remember spending hours trying to prove the manufacturers of the Digit Box were wrong when they said it couldn't be done. But, sadly and predictably, I failed.) All in all, an excellent investment for 69 cents.

Dolls. An inexpensive cloth or rag doll can provide at least as much enjoyment as the large, TV-promoted ones like "Baby Alive" and "Luv-A-Bubble Tender Love." Knickerbocker's Raggedy Ann and Raggedy Andy ($1.59 at Lamston's) are still classics, and I've always found Knickerbocker to be particularly quality-conscious.

Dominoes. Fun, and educational too (a study by *Sesame Street*'s educational staff showed that numbers over three were much easier for pre-schoolers to learn when arranged in the traditional domino patterns). Elisabeth and I found a lovely set of genuine wood, "Dragon Double Six" dominoes, selling for $1.59.

Label makers. You may not have thought of label makers—the kind that emboss letters on colored tape—as toys. But children can have a tremendous amount of educational fun with them. The ⅜-inch tape seems to be the size most readily available these days. Avery makes a very satisfactory ⅜-inch label maker for the bargain price of $2.99.

Gummed letters, numbers and stars. Another can't-miss item from the stationery counter. Denison makes a fine letter and number assortment that retails for 69 cents.

Markers. These are fast replacing the crayons and colored pencils of our day. You can buy a set of twelve, in different colors, for under $2; make sure the ones you get are nontoxic!

Money changers. Here's an item that doubles as a bank and a role-playing device when your youngster feels like playing "bus driver" or "cabbie" or "conductor." It's not good for children under five, though, since it contains small metal parts that can be torn loose. The four-barrel money changers we saw retailed in the $2 range.

Paddle and ball. Like the whiffle ball, the paddle-with-elastic-band-and-rubber-ball-attached (how else can you describe it?) has become an old-time favorite. I'll never forget the scene from the 1950s 3-D movie *House of Wax* in which a museum barker blasted his "Bo-lo Bouncer" directly at the audience's head. The Bo-lo still seems to be the leader in its field; it retails for 39 cents.

Play money. Play $100,000 bills for 99 cents seem like a tremendous value! But we really don't understand why people would invest in the phony pennies, nickels, and dimes we saw at Woolworth's. It's nearly as cheap—and certainly more educational—for your child to play "store," or some such, with real coins.

Puzzles, frame tray. Whitman used to put out an extensive line of 39-cent cardboard "frame tray" puzzles (the kind of jigsaw puzzles that come with their own backed "frames" to hold the assenbled pieces together). Unfortunately, inflation has hit the Whitman puzzles from two sides: the prices have gone up—to 59 cents and 69 cents—and the size of the puzzles has gone down. The artwork was never anything to write home about. But, if your youngster is in the four- to six-year-old bracket, you'll still get pretty good value for your money.

In the $3 price range, Playskool has a broad range of hardwood frame-tray puzzles; these are much more durable, and satisfying to the touch. Playskool's puzzle illustrators aren't about to win any art awards either, though there's been a marked improvement over the past few years.

Puzzles, steel ball. These are those pocket-sized, sealed plastic cases with tiny steel balls inside; by manipulating the case you try to get the balls into the proper holes. The going price of steel-ball puzzles these days appears to be 19 cents—yet one or two of them can keep a child busy for hours. Again the warning, though: a pre-school child might crack these puzzles open and get at the metal pellets inside.

Rocket, air and water powered. This was just about my favorite toy as a ten-year-old, and I was thrilled to find it still on the market, courtesy of the Parks Company. It's a hollow plastic rocket, about 8 inches long. You fill it partway with water; then, with a lock-on plastic pump that comes with the toy, you compress the remaining air inside the projectile. Release the pump lock and *whoosh!* the rocket shoots up to altitudes approaching 100 feet, spraying everything below with water. Refuel it from the bottom and you're ready for another flight. It all costs less than $2, and I'm told that for a little more you can get a two-stage rocket that goes even higher!

Rubber stamps. Kids love rubber stamps, and there are some remarkable bargains around. One set of stamps we found retailed at 15 cents; it contained an assortment the logic of which could be comprehensible only to a Taiwanese toy manufacturer specializing in exports to the United States—the numbers 1 to 8, a zero, one dog, and one cow.

Silly Putty. Only $1.20. But remind your child that it leaves its mark when it gets too warm, so it really shouldn't be played with in the vicinity of your best furniture.

Slinkies. The traditional Slinky sells at Woolworth's and Lamston's for about $1.80. If that's too rich for your blood, 99 cents will buy you a Slinky, Jr. The smaller version has a narrower diameter than the Slinky, Sr. It works the same way, and probably just as well. But, to our way of thinking, it lacks the necessary oomph. Go ahead, be a big spender!

Susy Shopper's Supermarket Kit. Here's a super-schlock toy that caught my fancy—but most definitely not Elisabeth's. It presents supermarket miniatures in soft, flexible plastic: tiny cobs of corn, cheeses, cans of "Libby" vegetables and fruits—all for $1.19. I saw a great opportunity for role play; Elisabeth said, "*Real* cans and boxes from the pantry are better." But, she conceded, "A make-believe turkey is definitely preferable to a real one for playing 'store' or 'house' on your Aubusson rug.''

Water pistols. If you're opposed to children playing with any toy that symbolizes violence, or if you don't like being unexpectedly sprayed with water, you won't want to give your child a water pistol. But if you don't object to them, you can give him a great deal of pleasure for 39 cents. In addition to the marvelous array of more or less standard models, two designs particularly attracted me: a grotesque replica of Spiderman's head that spits water when you squeeze the trigger, and a small, hand-contoured model that can be totally concealed in your fist as you fire. The clerk informed me the latter was known in popular parlance as the "Green Destroyer."

CBC

Some Personal Favorites
(For Young Kids)

Creative Playthings and Childcraft both have a wooden sink with a make-believe faucet, and a wooden stove with burners painted on it and storage space underneath. They're hardwood, absolutely durable, but cost over $40 each.

For $14.99 Sears has a great three-in-one appliance—a fiberboard stove, sink, and oven (with plastic work surface). Even though it won't last forever, as the more expensive models seem to, it really looks a lot better to kids: the sink has a dispenser that holds a sack of water and so provides real running water. More for less on this item.

JUDY THORN

Blow-up clowns: most kids punch them; some have been known to sleep with them. After the first few times you tape up the holes, you have to throw them out, but you can find them again for a couple of dollars, and kids love them.

RONA ROBERTS

Fisher-Price is much better than Playskool-anything. I love the interchangeability of Fisher-Price's little people. We never seem to lose or break any of their stuff.

JILL SCHICKEL

Fisher-Price Happy Whistlers is a walker with three people who alternate popping up and down as it's pushed along. Hysterical.

JUDY GRAHAM

The Fisher-Price Tumble Tower ($4 at discount stores) is a good toy. You have to get all the marbles down through the holes on four levels before the sand in the timer runs out. One level has a pull-out knob, another turns, and so on. The toy is self-contained, there are no loose parts, and it doesn't break. It helps coordination for pre-schoolers, but adults get a kick out of it too.

Shake and Sort, by Child Guidance, is similar to the Fisher-Price Tumble Tower but is better for younger children. The tumbling and sorting happens when the toy is turned; the child doesn't control it. It's a good crib toy.

SUSAN LAWRENCE

I think that the little people that come with most Fisher-Price toys are priceless. They go anywhere, provide hours of imaginative play, whether at home, in the car, or put to use with other toys. From crabby-faced boys to sweet grandmother types, they work in very nicely with fantasy play as well as in conjunction with the Fisher-Price school, house, garage, city, etc.

JEANNE DUNN

Child Guidance makes all those old toys we've known about for years: Nuts and Bolts, Shake and Sort, Kitty in the Kegs, the Learning Clock, Play Counting Eggs, Sewing Cards, Color Cards, and, of course, Tinkertoys. There's nothing wrong with any of these toys. And, with the exception of Tinkertoys, they're all for very little kids, some of whom might learn something from them (though kids who do not have the Play Counting Eggs are likely to learn to count anyway).

ELS

"It's encouraging to know that we're teaching kids to laugh at themselves at a very early age," observed one parent when we talked about that classic crib toy, the mirror. Creative Playthings has a steel mirror with finger holes in a wooden rim for $6.25 (plus 15 percent for postage and handling). If you'd prefer a chewable plastic frame, Childcraft has a hexagonal double-sided non-glass mirror (also with finger holes) for $4.95. They're both, of course, unbreakable.

RS

Any parent whose kid has had one will tell you that Tonkas last. The parts still move after years in the sandbox, and although they'll rust in the rain, a little oil restores them. —RS

Trains

BRIO TRAINS

A train set isn't simply choo-choo locomotion. Like a dollhouse, it's an excuse for constructing a whole little universe. The froms and tos nestled in the topology of the track become real, become farms and factories and all the places people work; mountains and rivers come under your hand, along with the mastery of space.

Electric trains grow more costly and breakable, and more for older users. But even two-year-olds can enjoy an unpowered set, and the standout seems to be Brio. Ten bucks will buy an engine and three magnetically coupled cars (which are more fun than the hook-coupled ones.) But the tracks are expensive—about $1.50 per running foot, with switches and elaborate overpasses costing from $6 to $10. That's the price of buying a Swedish import, but you get value for the money. All Brio pieces are simply designed and of sturdy hardwood, and anything that breaks can easily be glued. A set will last six years and still be fit to hand down. And it may be used actively for at least this long, if your child begins adding her building blocks, cars, and figurine populations to the layouts she creates.

A tip to the thrifty: the straight Brio track and most of the accessories are simple in design and easy to duplicate in a basic woodshop.

MICHAEL ROSSMAN

MATTEL PUTT-PUTT TRAIN

My three-year-old is wild about a friend's Putt-Putt Train (around $14 in discount stores) and wants one of his own. It looks to be a good sturdy item: wind-up, no batteries, hardwood, an easy-to-fit-together track. He can work it without a fit of frustration—quite a relief after our experience with our older son and electric trains.

LINDA WEST ECKHARDT

ELECTRIC TRAINS: TIMING IS IMPORTANT

We bought a Tyco train when our older son was seven, and it drove us all mad. If all the wheels weren't on the track it didn't run at all, and he could never get it to work. It was a disaster. We put it away, and now, two years later, our son has taken it out again and is enjoying it. The main problem was that we bought it two years too early. The boy simply didn't have the coordination to put it together at seven.

Now he wants all the accessories from the hobby shop—bridges and country towns and stations. He wanted a second engine, but they're $22 so he's having to make do with one. Cars are $2.50 and up—it gets expensive.

LINDA WEST ECKHARDT

I know one man who has his electric trains at the office so his wife won't find out. And another who built a coffee table of a glass-encased train system. And I remember when I was a little kid my dad bought me an electric train and it was mine because it was just a circle—too simple for him to be interested in.

ROGER LOEB

[How do you make space for the damn things? See instructions for the Murphy Play Table, page 174.]

SKANEATELES

At about two years Marsh became obsessed with trains, anything and everything having to do with trains. The most successful have been Skaneateles wooden train and track sets which can be added to. They come with trestles and you can build huge bridges, and even incorporate wooden blocks in with them.

ANNE GARDINER

Skaneateles trains, the same ones that Playskool used to sell, can still be found in many toy stores. (They are no longer distributed by Playskool.) They can also be ordered directly from Skaneateles Handicrafters, the people who have been making them for thirty-seven years. All the Skaneateles pieces are made of hand-finished hard maple. They can be bought in sets, ranging from $11 to $30, or as individual components. In addition to trains and tracks, they make cars, trucks, and a tug and barge set.

Skaneateles guarantees every piece they make; if a wheel comes off or a piece splinters, send it back and they'll fix it or send you a new one free (even if it's a train your mother played with thirty years ago). For a Skaneateles brochure, write to Skaneateles Handicrafters, Skaneateles, N.Y. 13152.

RS

War Toys

SO MUCH FOR GOOD INTENTIONS

I was a big peace demonstrator and said my kids wouldn't have any war toys. My oldest son, who spent his infancy at peace demonstrations, got to where he had guns all over—he was stealing them from friends, he made them with his hands. My children believe in no more war, no more pollution. And so I really have to smile when I see a mother say her kid absolutely will not play with war toys.

JUDITH VIORST
Redbook Toy Conference

WAR IS INTERESTING

"Mostly I like to read books on war. I'm a real war nut," Richard Kronenberg told me. "I hate war itself, but hearing about it is so interesting— the courageous acts, the things people do under stress of war."

When I asked Richard (who's twelve) about grown-ups thinking kids shouldn't play with guns, he said, "I never play war now, and I didn't much when I was younger. Yes, my parents discouraged it, although every now and then I'd talk them into letting me have a water gun—it's not really any big deal. I hate any kind of war, and I know that when I grow up if there's a war I'll probably have to go. But I think kids should know about it at a very young age, because if they find out later, it's going to be quite something."

Richard told me that he's read so much about war that he's going to have to go on to another subject.

RS

NO GUNS ALLOWED

We just don't allow guns at school. There are some parents who feel strongly about not wanting their children to have guns. Eliminating guns from the environment might or might not make for a better world, but I think the school has to respect their beliefs and feelings about it.

LIZA WERNER

FOR WHAT IT'S WORTH . . .

My sister had always said, "*My* child will never play with toy guns," and she kept such things out of his sight. But then one day, barely three, he came in from playing and pointed his index finger at her: "Bam! Bam!" he said. "Pchoo! Bang! You're dead." Before he was five he was making guns out of wood, clay, clothespins, anything he could find. He went to nursery school and began trading his "harmless" toys with friends who were fortunate enough to have dangerous ones. He built up a cache of guns of all kinds.

The boy is now twelve and quite peace-loving and considerate of others.

ELS

Bath Toys

DUCKY'S RETIRED. NOW WHAT?

It's a good thing that plain old water is so much fun, because a good bath toy is hard to find. Rubber Ducky, alas, was finally outgrown, every boat seemed to sink (or at least capsize), and the battery-powered novelty I couldn't resist died a mucky, rusty death.

I even tried fancy (expensive, but sometimes worth it) Creative Playthings, only to get ripped off for $5 by their Splashtimers, a dozen plastic odds and ends that don't even fit together properly, and don't seem to do much anyway. (Unforgivably, there are no instructions or suggestions.)

Only one commercial bath toy has appealed to me—though to be honest, the cat has enjoyed it more than my three-year-old—a collection of foam-rubber blocks in different shapes and colors that (more or less) stick together when wet. (They're made in Japan by a company called Asahi, and F. A. O. Schwarz has them for $7.95.)

An old hand assures me that the only successful bath toys are assorted plastic containers. My daughter's personal favorites are Johnson Baby Shampoo clear plastic bottles in various sizes, which make great bubbles as they are filled, pour easily, and have good caps for screwing open and closed. For special occasions, have a tea party, with a kid's plastic tea set.

Speaking of water fun: if you don't mind a small (but controllable) flood, the same containers are as much fun at the sink—the kind of play my daughter never seems to tire of.

PAULA GLATZER

MAKING SURE IT LEAKS

When my son was in his twos I had a hard time keeping him from drinking his bath water—so I'd never choose a cup for a bath toy (he'd learned, finally, that a cup is for drinking). All household items used in the tub were selected on the basis of non-water-retention qualities: a slotted spoon, colander, garlic press, plastic flowerpots, funnel, bulb baster, tea ball, eggbeater, strainer, wire whisk, potato masher—and of course boats, sponges, rocks, seashells.

ELS

Building Toys

There is a category of playthings known as ''building toys.'' If any toys are educational, these are (though most don't have that magic word on the box). The most popular ones are wooden blocks (large and small), Lego, Tinkertoy (also Giant Tinkertoy), and Lincoln Logs. All are loved by children and loved by adults (except, perhaps, when it comes to picking up all the pieces at the end of the day). One parent is known to have spent several hundred dollars on Legos, building up an elaborate structure which, by that point, would have likely excluded the child.

The one thing that needs to be said about these building toys is that many of them that come in small sets are quite limited as to what one might build with them. I wish that, like registering a silver pattern at Tiffany's, I could make it known that my child could do with a few more hardwood blocks to add to his small set. Though several different building toys do give a child a crack at other kinds of putting-together skills, finally I think it's more rewarding to have one large collection of Legos or one double set of Tinkers instead of a little of each.

ELS

The American Toy Institute's Guide to Choosing Toys

Always keep in mind that from the time a child first uses a certain kind of toy, his interest will usually carry through more than one age period. For example, a youngster who enjoys riding a tricycle when very young will likely continue to be interested in wheel toys right into the teens.

The same is true of such playthings as construction toys and sets, board games, books, paint sets, handicrafts, musical instruments and sports equipment.

In the following tables, therefore, particular types of toys are initially listed within the age group in which interest in them is first apt to appear.

UNDER 18 MONTHS

rattles	nested boxes or cups
nursery mobiles	push-pull toys
soft animals	floating tub toys
squeak toys	musical and chime toys
crib-gym exercisers	pounding toys
strings of big beads	stacking toys
picture blocks	small light wagon
books with rhymes, pictures, jingles	simple take-apart-and-assemble toys

18 MONTHS TO 3 YEARS

first tricycle	stuffed animals
ridem to straddle or wagon to get into	dolls and doll furniture
small low gym and seesaw	simple puzzles
hobby horse	take-apart-and-put-together toys with large parts
wading pool and sandbox	clay, modeling dough
sand toys	large crayons
balls of all sizes and balloons	blackboard and chalk
child-size play furniture	simple musical instruments
simple dress-up clothes	blocks of different sizes and shapes

3 YEARS TO 6 YEARS

additional dress-up outfits	items for bathing, feeding dolls
puppets	larger tricycle and other wheel toys
storekeeping toys, cash register	easy construction sets
toy phone and toy clock	sled
more housekeeping toys	larger backyard gym
farm, village and other play sets	coloring books, puzzles
small trucks, cars, planes and boats	books and records
	trains and auto racing layouts

6 YEARS TO 9 YEARS

board games
tabletop sports games
fashion dolls
doll houses
paper dolls
typewriter
printing set
racing cars
electric trains
marbles, tops, kites

construction sets
science sets, under adult
    supervision
handicrafts
sports equipment
swim fins and masks
larger bicycle
skates
pogo stick
scooter
books

9 YEARS TO 12 YEARS

model kits
chemistry and other
    science sets

advanced contruction
    sets
marionettes

table tennis
billiard table
magic sets

jigsaw puzzles
team-play sports
    equipment
card games

OVER 12 YEARS

target games (with
    supervision)
shuffleboard
woodburning and
    woodcarving sets
more difficult handicrafts
party games

added equipment for
    train and auto race
    layouts
teen-size bicycle
movie projector
tennis racket
junior golf set
first skis

ⓒ American Toy Institute, Inc.

[For a word about age designations in toys, see page 477.]

It's No Longer True That "Made in Japan" Means the Toy Is Crummy

There was a time when toys not manufactured directly by Santa's Workshop all seemed to have been made in Occupied Japan. Toys from Occupied Japan usually fell apart quickly but generally cost very little. Things have changed on both scores.

Some American toy manufacturers still contract to Japan either for components or for whole products, though most now look to Hong Kong, Taiwan, Korea, and the Philippines for work once done in Japan. The reason to stick with Japan in the 1970s is precisely for the high-quality products the increasingly sophisticated Japanese technology can offer. The reason to leave Japan in the 1970s is that production there is no longer inexpensive.

"Practically all American manufacturers use the Far East for production," says a spokesman for the Toy Manufacturers of America. It is difficult to tell at first look which toys have been abroad and which have stayed home since the majority of toys made in Japan for the American market were conceived and designed here and have an "American" look.

You may not know the product was made overseas until you get inside the packaging to the item itself. By law, the place of manufacture must appear on the product. (Apparently, no one ever said anything about the package, though. Usually the package says "Printed in USA.")

But the heyday of cashing in on Japanese labor is just about over for American toy manufacturers. Toys made in Japan are no longer very cheap. Highly competitive, the Japanese do not feel compelled to present inexpensive design ideas to the American firms. Besides, according to Bill Crain, former president of Child Guidance toys, they are afraid that American manufacturers will take Japanese ideas elsewhere in the Far East where labor is cheaper. But even in Hong Kong, Taiwan, Korea, and the Philippines, the price advantage for contracted work is no longer enough to make a big difference in production costs. "Lots of companies are coming back home to the U.S. for total manufacture," says Crain.

JENNIFER CARDEN

There's No Such Thing as a Montessori Toy

There is no such thing as a Montessori toy. There are Montessori materials made (after extensive research) by authorized manufacturers. These materials are part of a complex system and are of little use outside a prepared environment that includes a well-trained teacher, a large group of children, and a full set of equipment (a lot of which is assembled and made by the teacher). "Do-it-yourself Montessori" books and kits are not recommended.

This is not, I promise, said for self-serving reasons, that is, we are not saying "send your child to a Montessori school because you can't possibly do it at home." What we are saying is that you can't produce a school at home—but you can produce a "Montessori home."

The best Montessori in the home comes from understanding the philosophical aspects of Montessori and from making use of the child's own environment. An annotated book list is available for $1 from Association Montessori Internationale-USA, 16 Forest Street, New Canaan, Conn. 06840.

KARIN SALZMANN
Coordinator, AMI-USA

My Kid's Never Had a Sorting Toy—Will He Never Learn to Sort?

My son dug out an old toy that I'd been hiding in the hopes of phasing it out secretly. "Hey, Mom," he called, "remember that old Mickey Mouse doll?" "Yes," I replied. "Well," he announced, "it still works." It was one of my least favorite toys, one of those dolls with a pull-string that makes Mickey say things like "I come from Disney World" (never hurts to get in a little plug) or "You are my best friend" (to which my kid replied: "You said that already!" after the seventeenth declaration of friendship). The doll is not soft and cuddly (though he says, "I'm soft and cuddly"), but it does no harm and my kid gets a kick out of it.

He has other toys he enjoys:
Matchbox cars
Tonka trucks
Tinkertoys
Fisher-Price school bus
Fisher-Price houseboat
Creative Playthings' Big Red Super Magnet
Mattel's Putt-Putt Train
Caran D'Ache Modela modeling clay
Mattel's Cat-in-the-Hat in the Music Box

And when he goes visiting, he discovers there is even more treasure out there than he'd ever dreamed. At his cousins' house he gets to play with some of the toys and games that are still left after four brothers have had their turn. Those intact:
G.I. Joe
Playskool garage with wooden cars
More Matchbox cars and Tonka trucks
Lincoln Logs
He has played with these at different times, and times have passed when he's played with none at all.

So what can we conclude? That all toys are terrible and all toys are wonderful. That whatever you feel like getting is going to be fine. That whatever you end up with in your house is probably all right. That none of the toys your kid plays with is likely to do her or him any harm. That what is *not* played with won't matter (My God, my kid's never had a sorting toy—will he never be able to sort?). That some toys are better than others. That quality will probably not affect your decisions about which toys are bought and which are left behind as much as what's on TV and what the other kids on the block are getting for Christmas. (I once dragged around to no fewer than six stores with a friend whose seven-year-old would give her no peace until Gargantua, the toy of that season, was in their house—nothing else would do.) And finally, that your child will grow and learn with or without any toys.

ELS

TOYS: GETTING THEM

Don't-Jump-to-Conclusions Department

My nearly-three-year-old, looking through a toy catalogue, noted about eight items he wanted. Now hold it, I warned him, that's rather a lot; perhaps you can choose one that you like more than the others. No, no, he assured me that he had to have all of them: the fire engine, the truck, the car, the camper, etc.—he couldn't understand my limitations. It was a while before I realized that what he wanted was the *picture* from the catalogue; he hadn't made the connection that what he saw in the catalogue represented something he could buy in the flesh. I gladly cut out for him all the pictures he wanted, and even let him, the next day, paste them on a piece of construction paper and hang them on his wall. (Oh, what a good mother am I.)

ELS

Ordering Toys By Mail

HANDCRAFTED TOYS

People who seem to have sworn off toys retain their enthusiasm for the handmade wooden playthings that turn up at local crafts fairs and small shops. If you can't find any of these in your area, here are some available by mail that our sources have recommended:

R. Voake of Thetford Center, Vermont (tel.: [802] 785-2837), is a craftsman par excellence. As an adult I am still fascinated by a well-constructed wooden train, airplane, or truck. I first came across Voake at a craft show, where his woodwork stood out because of its fine, detailed construction and workmanship and its extremely reasonable prices, especially when compared to the commercially made stuff. (You should have seen his expression when I told him I thought he should raise his prices.)

ALLAN SHEDLIN JR.

Anne Gardiner recommended the Different Drummer Workshop in Solon, Maine 04979, for their wooden toys; her son loves the four-foot Iron Horse train pictured here ($40). They have a smaller train, 40 inches, for $29.

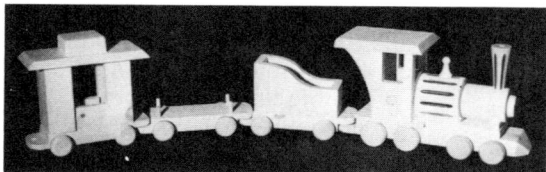

Timber-line Toys, 7015 Julian, Denver, Colo. 80030 (phone [303] 426-1624), has well-made vehicles with no sharp edges. Many of them come with little people. They are mostly made of unfinished sugar pine, but can be custom-made out of cherry. You can write for a free catalogue.

ROGER LOEB

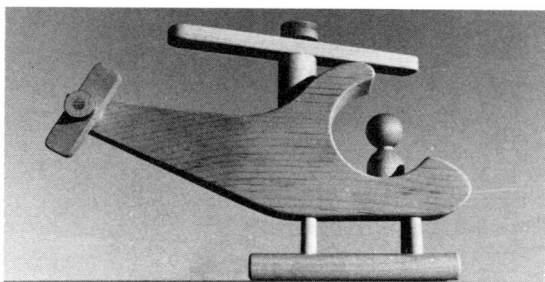

FINISH YOUR WOODEN TOYS

Handcrafted wooden toys are generally unfinished, which means they are neither waterproof nor stain-resistant. You may want to paint them yourself with a nontoxic paint (we used polyurethane). This is especially important if you want to use boats in water.

JUDY THORN

GALT TOYS

If you shop the Creative Playthings and Childcraft catalogues—and can afford their prices, which are high—you might want to look at the offerings from Galt Toys as well, the quality English supplier that now has several U.S. and Canadian outlets. People have spoken highly of their friendly and prompt service, as well as the quality of their toys. For a free mail-order catalogue (which includes a list of Galt toyshops around the world), write Galt Toys, 63 Whitfield Street, Guilford, Conn. 06437. Tel. (203) 453-3366.

RS

SEARS TOYS

I buy a lot of mail-order toys from Sears. Their Christmas catalogue has a better selection of toys than any other store, and their prices are consistently cheaper. Sometimes Sears has an item packaged specially for their catalogue, at even larger savings than other Sears toys. Although the toy may not be advertised as Fisher-Price or Mattel or whatever, the manufacturer's name is often on the photograph of the toy, and if it's not and you're not sure, your children can usually tell you.

Delivery is good, two to three weeks or less. Order at least a month before Christmas. Also at Christmas, Sears gives a 10 percent discount on orders of $75 or more if you order by a certain date in October (the date changes from year to year, so you have to check).

The main problem is that it's difficult to get a Sears catalogue (especially the Christmas edition). You have to write to Sears Roebuck and Co., 4640 Roosevelt Boulevard, Dept. 139, Philadelphia, Pa. 19132, and if catalogues are available they'll send you a card instructing you to pick up a copy within ten days at the nearest Sears store, or mail the card in and they'll send the catalogue.

JUDY THORN

Close-out Artists

If you have occasion to buy toys in carton lots—say for a school or day-care center, or for any kind of fund raising—you can hit the close-out artists of the toy industry. (Consider joining forces with one or two people from other organizations in your area.) Be forewarned that close-out shopping in no way resembles retail shopping; you go for bargains, not service. But astute shoppers can find crayons, pencils, and erasers for 10 to 15 cents on the dollar; $16

Lego sets for $3 to $4; $20 electric train sets for $4.50; $35 Gilbert chemistry sets for $4 to $5. Many of the items are overruns from Federated Department Stores, Sears, and other mail-order chains, and often they come in plain unmarked boxes (although a label may be inside), and you have to recognize the contents to know what it is you're buying.

For outlets in your area, look in the Yellow Pages under Salvage, Railroad Salvage, Close Outs, Toys, School Supplies. —Eds.

Borrowing Toys and Even Animals

Many of the toy (or pet) lending libraries currently springing up are either affiliated with the public library system or funded in some way. But the best example of this idea being translated into a successful community effort without either of these supports is the Pittsburgh Toy Lending Library.

The idea began with a federally funded pilot project in Washington, D.C. That was dramatically curtailed when the grant ran out and about half the toys were donated to Pittsburgh. A branch of the Pittsburgh Community Health Center sponsored the new library, providing it with two rooms, and when it opened in 1974 one hundred families registered within a month. It's open four half-days a week to children up to five years, who must be accompanied by an adult. Parents volunteer their time as supervisors.

The program was begun by new parents who, feeling isolated, had a need to connect with other parents. Because children are allowed to play there, it's a good place to take the child who has no other children to play with. Out of that concept, a parent-toddler co-op has formed, using the space one day a week when the library is closed.

Little by little, and with minimal advertising, they've become a resource and information center. They find babysitters, offer workshops in toy repair and first aid, and, incredibly, help teen-age parents learn about parenting. The possibilities are endless. For more information, contact Harriet Baum, Pittsburgh Toy Lending Library, 5410 Baum Boulevard, Pittsburgh, Pa. 15232.

FLAVIA POTENZA

Tips for Starting Your Own Toy or Pet Lending Library

WHAT TOYS ARE BEST

Try to collect things that parents tend not to have; crib and pull toys for infants; as well as building toys such as blocks, Legos; trucks, cars, airports, etc.; play kitchens, clothes to dress up in; puppets, dolls, and dollhouses; puzzles, lotto, magnetic wooden puzzles.

The Pittsburgh Toy Lending Library found the best commercial brands to be Creative Playthings, Fisher-Price, Playskool, Childcraft, and Tonka. Have a look at nursery school catalogues as well. The toys are expensive but they last (the Childcraft fire engine, for one). Look for heavy plastic (not brittle) and wood toys. Keep in mind how portable and how easy the toys are to keep clean, and, of course, make sure they're safe. For example, exclude teethers, plush animals, unwieldy or sharp toys, and those with tiny pieces easily lost or swallowed.

GETTING STARTED

Ask for donations from the community. And not just for toys. Find someone to contribute printing services or an artist to design a letterhead or a sign. There may be parents who are amateur toy-makers. Stores have after-Christmas surplus toys—three cannibalized Fisher-Price airports from which two complete sets can be made; dolls with smudges that can easily be wiped off; perfect merchandise in a broken box. Contact the Junior League for funds and/or volunteer services. "We even found local prison inmates who want to make toys," says Elizabeth Goldstein, co-founder of the Pittsburgh library. "The important thing is to talk to as many people in as many places as possible."

FINDING SPACE

Contact church councils, local shopping centers (merchants may be willing to support such an effort because it brings customers to them), the public library system, your department of parks and recreation, school boards, nursery schools, community mental health programs, university departments of child development, social work, or psychology, and the local "Y." Community coalitions might rent space in order to get the library in their neighborhood.

THE LEGALITIES

"Find a good-hearted lawyer who will help you incorporate," Elizabeth Goldstein advises. "It costs about $60 for the forms and processing. Then, when you are incorporated, apply for tax exempt status, without which you are not eligible to receive foundation support. Even without space or toys, being incorporated will help your credibility."

Insurance may not be as much of a problem

now as it was for the Pittsburgh library, whose insurance company was reluctant to cover them inasmuch as there was no precedent. You can check with nursery schools and day-care centers regarding their insurance and ask their company about coverage.

GETTING HELP

Contact your local library for advice on cataloguing. For information on consultation and training for a toy lending library, contact Ms. Ann Sarmento, Director, User Services, Far West Laboratory for Educational Research Development, 1855 Folsom Street, San Francisco, Calif. 94103, (415) 565-3100, or for $1.55 you can obtain the "Guide to Securing and Installing the Parent/Child Toy Lending Library" from the Superintendent of Documents, Government Printing Office, Washington, D.C. 20402.

FLAVIA POTENZA

MAKING TOYS

From *Consumer Action Now Newsletter*

Books on Making Toys

TOYS, A Step-by-Step Guide to Creative Toymaking, *by Charlene Davis Roth and Jerome Roth (Lancer, 1972).*
Hobby horses, sock puppets, jigsaw puzzles, etc.—175 toys children can make with the help of adults, all for $1.95. Although some of the instructions are rather elaborate and call for extensive sewing or tools such as a drill or a coping saw, they are always clear and easy to follow, and include many photographs, illustrations, and patterns.

ANDRA SAMELSON

AMERICAN FOLK TOYS, *by Dick Schnacke (Penguin, 1974, $3.50 paperback).*

This is a unique book which includes eighty-five folk toys for children and adults to make to-gether, ranging from easy-to-make toys and crafts like rope dolls and finger puppets to more challenging ones like miniature honeysuckle baskets and peach-seed carving. The complicated ones require much patience. The selection of toys is less conventional than that of most toy-making books. There are also instructions for skill toys, puzzles, tops, noisemakers, and some exotic amusements like the original 1891 Flipperdinger. There are concise directions for each toy.

ANDRA SAMELSON

THE TOY BOOK, *by Steven Caney (Workman, 1972, 176 pages, $3.95 paperback).*

When it came up in conversation, people I talked to were glad we were including Steve

Caney's *Toy Book.* It's that kind of book—people who have used it feel good about it. It's selective and simple in its presentation of toys, games and crafts that require a minimum of materials and tools, and best of all, a minimum of instructions. Bird feeders and cardboard looms are the stuff of this book. I've seen a five-year-old who could just barely read describe a project from the one picture. Appropriately, the book is dedicated to the refrigerator carton.   RS

The best recommendation for *The Toy Book:* at the age of seven Marc Eichler made every toy in the book by himself. This is one of the few books of its kind that a child can use without parental intervention, and Caney does not talk down to kids.   ELS

TOYS: LOOKING AFTER THEM

What Do You Do with Them at the End of the Day?

I have tried every possible means of storing my child's toys—every one: boxes, toy chests with tops, toy chests without tops, baskets, bags, barrels, everything. It seems to me that the point is simply to avoid slipping on roller skates or tripping on blocks or sitting on little plastic objects of all shapes and at the same time to make it easy for your kid to get those things out of sight—and then find them again. Truly the best receptacle for storing toys is the good old-fashioned bookcase. Open shelves offer a full view of what's there, allow for easy putting away, and, most important, serve well for the infant as well as the teen-ager (they easily adapt when rows of rattles and teddy bears change to books, records, and collected treasures).

If you don't believe me, try other ways and you will see what doesn't work. Toy chests with tops are a nuisance and can be dangerous (*The New York Times* last year reported the death of a child on whose head a toy-chest top came crashing down). Chests without tops, barrels, wastepaper baskets can work, but the problem is that you can't see what's in the heap. If you try any of these, keep in mind that a horizontal receptacle is much better than one that is so deep you cannot see what is at the bottom of the barrel. The same problem arises with those drawstring bags that have the word "Toys" appliquéd on the front. It's a great idea for putting toys away forever to hang inside a closet; but for everyday use, a kid simply will not play with a toy she cannot see.   ELS

You may possibly be aware that there is a certain amount of reluctance on the part of some children to pick up. One way to make it easier is to have general rather than specific organization for the room. If the trucks go in this bin and the dolls in that, it's a lot easier than if this red truck here goes next to that yellow car there two inches behind the blue bus. Generally, the larger the receptacle, the easier it is for a child to put things away—just think how easy it would be if you just told him to toss it all in the closet.

Vegetable bins that stack make much better holders for toys of many parts than the boxes they come in. Plastic refrigerator containers are much easier for a pre-schooler to put crayons into than a crayon box (try it). A record rack makes a better bookshelf than a bookshelf.

CAROL EISEN RINZLER

Sharing Your Space

To occupy your child while you're busy with your own work or play, if you can spare the space, make a special play drawer or cabinet in the room you spend your time in—kitchen or study—and fill it with the child's toys and other interesting things to discover and play with. Try to rotate the contents so that there will be a discovery when he opens the drawer. For pre-toddlers, if you make this drawer the second one up, you will encourage pulling-up-to-standing, stretching, reaching, and standing-up-while-rummaging activities.

EMILY PERL KINGSLEY and JERRY STALLER

Getting Rid of the Clutter

Don't forget about cup hooks or coat hooks for hanging toys. You can put up a strip of wood or molding at kids' eye level, then attach the hooks. On this can go pails full of tiny toys like marbles, beads, jacks, or pieces from games with a thousand pieces.   ELS

Ways of Coping with the Toy Explosion

1. Never buy, and encourage relatives never to buy, any toy consisting of more than three

parts if there are any children under five years old in the house.

2. Two or three times a year, weed out. Get two big cartons; in one put the toys that never seem to get played with, and stick it on top of a closet. In the other carton put all the toys with missing parts and toss the parts in as you find them. If you really truly think you might do it, you can make a third carton of toys that need to be fixed. But better to grit your teeth and throw them out. Bring back the good toys after three or four months. Some children (I heard of one once) can be conned into believing they're getting a whole lot of new toys.

3. Try the "Anything I have to pick up goes into the top of my closet and you won't get it back for a week" routine. This has worked for some people but must be said in a firm but friendly voice. Also, you have to stick to it (it doesn't have to be a week, a day will do).

4. Work along with the kid. For some reason, sharing a pick-up of Loony Links means more to a kid than if you pick up the Loony Links and he picks up the Silly Sponge.

5. Say, "If you can't take care of your toys, then I will take them all away and give them to the poor children, who would be happy to have them and would take good care of them. When I was a child I didn't have half the toys you have." Oh, go ahead and say it. How do you know it won't work?

CAROL EISEN RINZLER

Winterizing Your Toys

HOW TO WINTERIZE

Every Fall our children gather together all their toys that have been outside and in use for the summer months. The shovels and pails, the trucks and cars, the wagons are all brought to one spot for their winter check-up. We designate a maintenance area—the garage floor or patio will do—and use as supplies a bucket of water, rags, a can of oil, some steel wool and a few cans of spray paint of the anti-rust variety. (We never paint very young children's toys without checking the paint for toxic contents.) Each toy receives a check-up, is given maintenance if needed, and is assigned storage facilities if it will not be used for the winter months. Here are some specific methods we have used for upkeep of toys.

Metal trucks and cars. Wipe each vehicle clean with a damp rag. Don't forget the underside where most cobwebs and dirt will collect. If you then "road test" the truck by rolling it back and forth to check for dragging wheels, you'll find in nine out of ten cases the axles have rusted. A drop of oil at each point where the axle passes through the truck body will do wonders and certainly impress the child; the vehicle will usually run better than when new. If the outside of the body is dented and rusting, lightly steel wool the area and give it a coat of paint. (The parent should do this operation for younger children.) Protect plastic windows on cars and trucks from paint with masking tape. If any part of the metal is torn and has sharp edges exposed, discard the vehicle; it is potentially dangerous. Wagons require the same type of maintenance as cars and trucks and, if done at the outset of the project, become a great storage area on wheels. When we complete the maintenance operation, we end up with a wagon piled with repaired toys, covered with an old sheet and ready to be rolled into the garage or basement for the winter. In place of a wagon you can turn any cardboard box into a personalized storage garage with a magic marker. . . .

Wooden toys. After wooden cars and trucks have been wiped off with a damp rag, we "road test" them in the same manner as the metal vehicles. If the wheels are binding, apply some vaseline with a tooth pick to that part of the axles between the body and the wheels. The results are usually excellent. If the toy is painted and the paint is peeling, sand lightly and repaint. If the toy is unfinished, some common household furniture wax will do wonders in bringing the toy back to life. Do not wax toys that very small children will chew on.

LAST SPRING'S FORGOTTEN CHORES

By checking and preparing winter toys in advance, you avoid the headaches and the hectic scramble when the pond finally freezes and you find that the children's ice skate laces have rotted.

The following are some hints on preparing winter toys for play. In the spring use the same methods we discuss to prepare them properly for summer storage.

Sleds. The wood should be checked for dryness and splintering. Pull splinters off; sand and wax the wooden surface with furniture wax. The wood should be waxed at least a couple of times a season to create a seal against moisture. Clean off all metal parts and the runners, then wipe with an oiled cloth. *After* you have oiled the metal, clean the sliding surface of the runners with steel wool and rub them down with either soap or a bar of wax. Check the steering bar and oil if necessary. The sled should now run like new.

Skates. First remove the laces; check for wear; and replace if necessary. Now wax the skates and clean and oil the runners. After this is completed, have the older children's skates sharp-

ened. This is a good time to find the children's skating socks and place them inside the skates.

These projects present a great potential for learning through play. The child experiences fun in the care and upkeep of his toys and learns the joys of responsibility for his personal possessions. Often the hardest part of the whole process is persuading our children to put away a toy they have just restored.

PAUL J. GRUEN
Toy Review

THE CAREFUL CONSUMER

Small Enough to Swallow? The Truncated Cylinder

How can you tell if a toy is too small to be trusted in the hands of a child under three years of age? According to the Toy Manufacturers of America, a plaything presents an unacceptable risk of being swallowed if it fits, "in an uncompressed state," inside a "truncated right cylinder" with these dimensions:

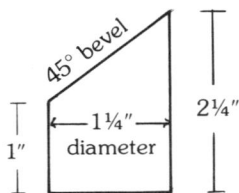

Remember that "too small" applies not only to the whole toy, but also to pieces or fragments that can easily be removed or broken off.

How did the TMA arrive at the truncated-cylinder shape? "Well," said a spokesman, "we started with the idea of a sphere 1¼ inches in diameter. But we quickly discovered that very long, thin objects could still present a swallow-

ing hazard. The truncated right cylinder took care of this problem nicely." CBC

cylinder alone

Bird in cylinder   *yo-yo in cylinder*

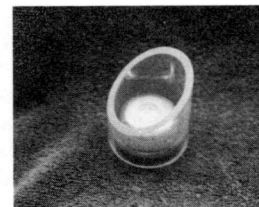

The truncated right cylinder. A Big Bird finger puppet passes with flying colors, but a sterling silver Tiffany yo-yo fails to make the grade. (No need to fret: if you've passed your third birthday, you're entitled to use the yo-yo.)

A Problem . . .

Sometimes I get the feeling that our house is one vast conveyor belt onto which the toys enter through the front door, ride up to the playroom, get stomped on and mutilated and dismantled and ignored—then down the stairs, out the back and into the trash can. And this really troubles me because—it's not just the gross extravagance and waste—my kids are picking up the notion of a disposable society in which shoddy materials are used carelessly and discarded, immediately to be replaced by more

of the same. . . . At a birthday party for my five-year-old . . . I was struck by a very, very unusual fact. He received as gifts three records, a set of posters, a knapsack, a baseball mitt and one toy—just one. I don't even know what the toy was, because by the end of the party it had been completely destroyed and I just found some pieces of mutilated red plastic on the stairs.

JUDITH VIORST
at the *Redbook* Toy Conference

. . . And Where to Complain

When you write to any of these organizations to complain about toys, it helps to put cc: Ralph Nader; cc: your congressperson; cc: their congressperson. You don't actually have to send copies to these people, but it doesn't hurt to do it.

If you want to register a complaint with the government:
>   Commissioner Susan B. King
>   Consumer Product Safety Commission
>   Washington, D.C. 20207

If you want to register a complaint with the toy industry:
>   Mr. Walter Armatys
>   Toy Manufacturers of America
>   200 Fifth Avenue
>   New York, N.Y. 10010

If you want to register a complaint about children's commercials:
>   Federal Trade Commission
>   Bureau of Consumer Protection
>   Washington, D.C. 20580

and
>   Action for Children's Television
>   46 Austin Street
>   Newtonville, Mass. 02160

and
>   Council on Children, Media and Merchandising
>   1346 Connecticut Avenue, N.W.
>   Washington, D.C.

If you want to support a toy consumer-action group, financially or with a letter stating your concerns:
>   Public Action Coalition on Toys
>   38 West 9th Street
>   New York, N.Y. 10011

CPSC Hotline: Don't Expect Too Much

The Consumer Product Safety Commission touts a "hotline" that supposedly answers questions on what products are unsafe. You can call 800-638-2666, toll-free from anywhere in the United States, except Maryland, where the number is 800-492-9237. The only problem is that they rarely (if ever, in my experience) give any concrete information. On separate phone calls I asked them about the stuffing in dolls and toys, about Halloween makeup, bicycles, and balls we'd heard were flammable. Each query got the same response: "You can buy anything on the market; our job is to make sure what's there is safe." And we know that isn't true. So the hotline sounds good, and only works if you need the information they have.

I was able to get some information (both on crib safety standards and on the hotline itself) from the commission's New York area office. I was told that the hotline's specialty is giving current recall information—that is, if you hear on the evening news that certain camping tents have been found flammable, you can call the hotline the next day for brand and model numbers. If your question is not answered to your satisfaction, ask to speak to the bureau director handling your area. If you leave your number and are not called back, you just have to persevere. "These things can't be solved one-two-three in a snap," I was told. That we all know. A list of CPSC's area offices is printed below.

RS

U.S. CONSUMER PRODUCT SAFETY COMMISSION AREA OFFICES

Atlanta Area Office
Consumer Product Safety Commission
1330 West Peachtree Street, N.W.
Atlanta, Georgia 30309
404-881-2231

Boston Area Office
Consumer Product Safety Commission
100 Summer Street, Room 160
Boston, Massachusetts 02110
617-223-5576

Chicago Area Office
Consumer Product Safety Commission
230 South Dearborn, Room 2945
Chicago, Illinois 60604
312-353-8260

Cleveland Area Office
Consumer Product Safety Commission
Plaza 9 Building,
55 Erie View Plaza
Cleveland, Ohio 44114
216-522-3886

Dallas Area Office
Consumer Product Safety Commission
Rm 410C, 500 South Ervay, P.O. Box 15035
Dallas, Texas 75201
214-749-3871

Denver Area Office
Consumer Product Safety Commission
Suite 938, Guaranty Bank Building
817 17th Street
Denver, Colorado 80202
303-837-2904

Kansas City Area Office
Consumer Product Safety Commission
Traders National Bank Building
1125 Grand Avenue
Suite 1500
Kansas City, Missouri 64106
816-374-2034

Los Angeles Area Office
Consumer Product Safety Commission
3660 Wilshire Boulevard, Suite 1100
Los Angeles, California 90010
213-688-7272

Minneapolis Area Office
Consumer Product Safety Commission
Federal Building, Fort Snelling, Room 650

Twin Cities, Minnesota 55111
612-725-3424

New York Area Office
Consumer Product Safety Commission
6 World Trade Center, 6th floor
Vesey Street
New York, New York 10048
212-264-1125

Philadelphia Area Office
Consumer Product Safety Commission
400 Market Street
Continental Building, 10th Floor
Philadelphia, Pennsylvania 19106
215-597-9105

San Francisco Area Office
Consumer Product Safety Commission
100 Pine Street
San Francisco, California 94111
415-556-1819

Seattle Area Office
Consumer Product Safety Commission
3240 Federal Building
915 Second Avenue
Seattle, Washington 98174
206-442-5276

Toy Recall

The manufacturer, the distributor, and the retail dealer of a product that has been banned by the Consumer Product Safety Commission are "required . . . to give notice of the fact that they have sold a banned article or substance and to repurchase it from the person to whom they have sold it, reimbursing that person the reasonable and necessary expenses incurred in returning it."

If you are returning a toy it helps, of course, to have a receipt. But if you don't have any proof of purchase and the retailer gives you a hard time, you can apply to the manufacturer for a refund. The manufacturer is not required to refund the consumer directly, but often it will.

If both the retailer and the manufacturer refuse to "repurchase" the product from you, contact your area office of the Consumer Product Safety Commission.

RS

I have returned every toy that fell apart soon after being played with—and the stores will take them back (if not, they lose my business—though not many of them care). Perhaps if enough parents return shoddy toys the stores will stop carrying them and the manufacturers will stop making them.

CAROL EICHLER

How You Pay Extra for the Package

For $4.98 you can buy a crafts kit that contains approximately $1.08 worth of materials. One kit I saw on the shelves at Christmastime featured the "makings" of doll clothes for a Barbie-size doll: one needle, thread (not even a spool—just some thread wrapped around a piece of cardboard), a few remnants of material, and, most notable, a big box to put them in.

Whenever you are tempted to buy a kit, see what's in the box and consider what you can put together yourself for probably a fraction of the price. A woodcarving kit, for example, contained a good woodcarving implement, but inside the box with it was nothing more than a few scraps of wood which you could probably pick up at the lumberyard for free, some colors which your child is likely to have in his crayon and marker box, and some "suggested designs." The thing cost $7.95. If you bought the carving implement alone, you could get a better tool and spend less money.

So many kits are a packaging "idea"—some marketing executive comes up with the notion that if he puts together in one box all the things you need to make a rag doll, you will buy it— even though you already have all those things in your bottom drawer for free. If you took the materials out of your drawer and put them in a pretty box or basket, what a thoughtful surprise you'd have for any nine-year-old.

To give you another example, you can buy glow-in-the-dark models. But it might be more fun for your kid to build an ordinary model and then paint it with glow-in-the-dark paint.

Even Bargello and needlepoint kits, which may contain a design you love, overcharge terribly for the yarn. If you buy the canvas alone, the child could draw an original design or even trace one from a magazine or coloring book—and you'd pay about half the price for the wool.

ELS

DOLLS

Live from F. A. O. Schwarz

I am standing near one of the doll displays at F. A. O. Schwarz and a couple comes in looking for a doll for their daughter. *"Fifty-nine ninety-five?"* I hear the husband exclaim. "For a *doll?"* Sure, there are any number of dolls you can get for $59.95—this particular one, wearing a $50 dress, stands about twenty-one inches tall in her stocking feet. The couple stroll through the doll department, probably the largest selection in the world here at the Fifth Avenue store, picking up dolls that coo, cry, eat, wet, talk, sing, play tennis. There is, at $26.95, a doll that sings "Twinkle, Twinkle, Little Star" until I would think one would have to pick her up and smash her against the wall. And another, at the same price, that says, "Good morning, dear Mommy" in five languages so that any child who owns her will be right at home abroad.

I look for a wonderful doll that is worth its price, but I don't find it here. How do you go about picking a doll for your child, I ask the couple. Oh, it would be a problem, they explain, if she had not told us that she must have a doll that talks—so that narrows it down a bit. But how many times will the child listen to that little record, hearing the same thing over and over? Is a doll like that good company?

I must have picked up seventy-five dolls, turned them over, listened to them, talked to them. And I can conclude only one thing: You cannot get really close to a doll that says, "Hi, Mary. Hi, Jack. Wanna go to the cinema?" (an English import).

I picked a rag doll for my kid, a doll that has little personality of its own, a doll that will make my child use his imagination somewhat, that will make my child talk, and will listen to him, instead of singing "Twinkle, Twinkle, Little Star" at him over and over and over, a doll, alas, that costs only $6.95, and one that won't be broken before its clothes need changing.

ELS

Cloth Sculptures

Jody Tiedemann (417 Courtland Avenue, Glenbrook, Conn. [203] 359-1946) makes some of the most fanciful creatures. Their personalities—and each has its own—come from fabric (corduroy, linen, felt, old jeans) and expressions and the weirdest physiques. The creatures—Ooglebyrd, Rosenkrans, Rufus McTavish, the Great Snazeelo—are stuffed with nonallergic polyfil and, with the exception of ones made of felt, can all be washed by hand. They are really cloth sculpture, made one at a time, no two exactly alike. You might want to correspond with Jody and together create a very special something for your child—or yourself.

RS

The Enchanted Dollhouse

Dolls to look at and dolls to play with and books about making and collecting, some imported dolls, many handmade in Vermont, and all to be seen in "The Enchanted Dollhouse" catalogue ($2). Write to them at Manchester Center, Vt. 05255, (802) 362-3030. There are storybook dolls (Heidi, all the Little Women, Alice), Beatrix Potter folk ($6 to $40), Joan Walsh Anglund pocket dolls if you're so inclined, and bears and gray felt mice. And wooden marionettes from England ($6.50 to $20). Handmade dollhouses (kits, unpainted, $60 and up; assembled, $160 and up). In general, prices are a little lower than at F. A. O. Schwarz, and considerably higher than discount stores.

RS

Barbie and Friends

You buy a six-dollar doll and you acquire a six-hundred-dollar habit.

JOHN NOBLE
Curator, Museum of the City of New York

My two boys have Big Jim (his limbs move, his hip socket broke off), Big Josh, G.I. Joe, and the superhero dolls Spider-Man and Batman. I don't even want them to see that now there are dolls from *Star Wars,* and dolls from all the TV shows. I think five dolls, which is what they have, for the two of them is enough.

ANN FINK

Talking Big Jim is not as well constructed as the non-talking Big Jim. His voice box breaks and his head comes off more easily. A friend had warned me of this. I bought it anyway, and found she was right.

JUDY THORN

My sons have a Barbie doll, and it's like this terrible secret that she's in the house. She spends most of her time nude, always being roughed up by G.I. Joe. She's unrapeable, though, because her legs will break if they're pulled apart. But she gets it other ways.

JEAN GREEN

Liberating Barbie

I do not like Barbie dolls or what they represent. The dolls themselves are not so expensive. But they are surrounded by possessions that are meant to mobilize the greediest sentiments of young children. In the Barbie section of a toy store one can find Barbie clothes, Barbie wigs, Barbie cosmetics, a Barbie house, and even a Barbie camper complete with sleeping bag and camp stools. Still, my daughters love Barbie dolls. I broke down last Christmas and got Erica a Barbie camper. The camper is central to many of my daughter's most elaborate fantasies and games. It has been everything from an actual camper to an ice cream truck to a mystery car carrying superheroes and heroines to a boat, a plane, a raft. Barbie is Barbie one day, Wonder Woman the next. My wife and I don't buy Barbie's elaborate costumes, so the children create their own. The other night the Barbies in our house even had a political meeting on the top of the camper to decide how to create kid power.

It is probably true that there are children in this country who believe there is only one way to play with Barbie dolls. However, most children know how to discard the rules and create their own.

HERBERT KOHL
Math, Writing & Games

WHAT DOES BABY ALIVE EAT?

What does Kenner's superdoll, Baby Alive, eat? A nutritionist at General Mills (which owns Kenner) informs me that the ingredients listed on Baby Alive's food packets include U.S. certified color, imitation flavor (can Baby Alive taste?), sorbital, algin potassium sorbate, and fumed silica (for thickening). These ingredients are defined as nontoxic, but the salesperson in the Kenner showroom admitted, "I don't imagine you'd want your child to actually *eat* it."

RS

◆

Baby Wet & Care, a more recent arrival in the Kenner family of dolls, gets diaper rash, which can only be cured with the company's own special baby lotion. Alas, poor dolly is not likely to outgrow her condition. What's next? A doll that gets sick in the night?

ELS

TENDING THE DOLLS

Dressing Dolls on a Shoestring

For the price of a sewing pattern—which in the Simplicity catalogue is $1.15 to $1.75—one can make wardrobes to suit 11½-inch dolls. (As it happens, Julia, Maddie Mod, Dusty, and, yes, even Barbie, are all 11½ inches tall.) Then there are also the 15½-inch and 17½-inch dolls: Crissy, Talky Crissy, Look Around Crissy, Brady, Velvet, and Dina. There are patterns for their clothes, too.

Most children who enjoy having these dolls also enjoy having many costume changes for them. Unfortunately, the cost of each little outfit supplied by the manufacturers is so great that to many it is prohibitive, not to mention a national scandal. The answer is to make them yourself.

There are benefits besides the money-saving ones to making doll clothes (just as there are additional benefits to making real clothes). The seamstress can exercise her own imagination and self-expression. She can use remnants of finer fabrics than the manufacturer can for the same price. She can create lush, personalized costumes. In most cases the seamstress will have to be an adult, because the clothes are so small that fine coordination is required, but in some instances, making doll clothes can be a learning experience for children.

The McCall's catalogue also features fashions—including trousseaus—for those teen dolls (and for teen-aged boy dolls as well). Of course, the company promotes its own Betsy McCall, which is a size 4 lifesize doll. In addition, there are McCall's patterns for a baby doll wardrobe, complete with a sling carrier.

Simplicity caters to the babies too, with all sorts of ways to dress the vinyl-body dolls like Tearie, Betsy Wetsy, Ginny, Tiny Tears, Baby Tender Love, and Powder Puff.

JENNIFER CARDEN

Spruce-up Department

If you collect porcelain dolls or portrait dolls, you may want to know about the New York Doll Hospital (787 Lexington Avenue, New York, N.Y. 10021). But they're not the place to replace the rooted hair on your kid's favorite dolly. My daughter could tell that it was a glued-on wig, and it made such a difference to her, she was really uspet. The repair cost $5.

RONA ROBERTS

We have found that lint from the clothes drier is excellent material for restuffing our little friends when they occasionally come apart. And for do-it-yourselfers, it is good material for stuffing homemade animals and dolls.

RUTH PELMAS

You can give an old doll new life if you add a boutonniere, a new hat, or a fresh ribbon round its neck.

ELS

If [an old "lovey"] begins to fall apart and cannot be mended or refilled, find another, more durable toy. Tie or sew the old lovey to the new one until all the old smells and feelings have been transferred. Then, and only then, can the old one be discarded.

BERRY BRAZLETON
Toddlers and Parents

MAKING DOLLS

Here's How to Make a Sock Doll

You can use a new or discarded sock; any color or size will do. For stuffing use washable filler or old nylon stockings.

Cut off about one-third of the size of the foot at the toe. Cut that piece in half lengthwise. Sew up along the open seams, stuff, and set aside for arms.

Open the sock and cut up to the heel for the doll's legs. Turn inside out, sew up the seams, turn back, and stuff. You should have what looks like two little legs, the heel of the sock forming the doll's backside.

Stuff about two-thirds full and tie yarn, ribbon, or string for the neck. Stuff the head and tie tightly, leaving a border to turn down for a hat. Sew the arms on at the "shoulders" below the neck.

Use your imagination to decorate and add details. Make a face with yarn, permanent magic marker, or embroidery thread. Add hair, buttons, clothes, maybe even socks.

DOROTHY LOHMAN

Isabelle

Isabelle is a life-sized rag doll that I made as a Christmas present for my ten-year-old daughter. The main reason I made it life size was to have a doll my daughter could dress with her own clothes.

Since the doll was to be a surprise, I used a pair of jeans and a shirt for a pattern guide instead of the live model.

The skin of the doll is made of pink denim. The stuffing started out to be cotton but was discarded because it produced lumpy limbs. The final stuffing was a spun-plastic fiber material that is sold for pillow making.

Since this was practically my first sewing experience, I proceeded with caution. I first made a very rough model. My main concern was finding out whether or not I could make the complete doll by sewing two figure images (front and back) together and then turn this inside out to hide the seams. I was afraid I would lose an arm or leg in the process. I didn't.

I did discover that the head had to be separate from the body and sewn on later by hand. I was lucky, I think, that Isabelle's head held fast. If you need to reinforce the head, use a stick or

a dowel to connect the head to the body; be sure to wrap the stick well with fabric so that it won't go poking out through the doll.

Each seam was sewn twice for strength. The hair is heavy yarn. The facial features are felt, glued on.

Manufacture time, about three and a half days.

JIM ADAIR

Doll Making: Two Books

If your children are Beatrix Potter enthusiasts, and if you have a lot of patience, *Toys From the Tales of Beatrix Potter,* by Margaret Hutchings (F.W. Warne & Co., 1973, 315 pages, $17.95 hardcover; Hawthorne, $7.95 paperback) will help you to duplicate all the little creatures.

The Complete Book of Doll Making and Collecting, by Catherine Christopher (Dover, 1971, 290 pages, $3 paperback), is a thorough and sophisticated survey of dolls and doll making, including many intricate instructions for constructing novelty, soft rag, ceramic, and other varieties of dolls, their clothing and habitats. This is definitely a book which will be of more interest to adults than to children: the instructions stress precision and convention, and there are several chapters on the history of dolls and doll collecting.

ANDRA SAMELSON

Before You Dump the Old Teddy Bear . . .

"Real isn't how you are made," said the Skin Horse. "It's a thing that happens to you. When a child loves you for a long, long time, not just to play with, but REALLY loves you, then you become Real."

"Does it hurt?" asked the rabbit.

"Sometimes," said the Skin Horse, for he was always truthful. "When you are Real you don't mind being hurt."

"Does it happen all at once, like being wound up," he asked, "or bit by bit?"

"It doesn't happen all at once," said the Skin Horse. "You become. It takes a long time. That's why it doesn't often happen to people who break easily, or have sharp edges, or who have to be carefully kept. Generally by the time you are Real, most of your hair has been loved off, and your eyes drop out and you get loose in the joints and very shabby. But these things don't matter at all, because once you are Real you can't be ugly, except to people who don't understand."

MARGERY WILLIAMS
The Velveteen Rabbit

DOLLHOUSES

The Joy of Dollhouse-keeping

There's a dough you can make with flour, water and salt, which I used to mix up and form into food to put in my dollhouse when I was little. (And even, I admit, when not so little.) Tiny birthday cakes with corny sayings in the icing; large, messy submarine sandwiches (large for a doll, that is—they were less than two inches long); sheets of cookies; pizzas; slices of watermelon with minute seeds in them; and once a roast pig with an apple in his mouth. But the things that pleased me the most, and do even now when I think of them, were the eggs. Shaped just like real eggs, though uncrackable, each one had a dot of yellow flour-and-water dough in the center to represent the yolk. No one would ever see it, but I knew when I laid the eggs out on the dollhouse kitchen table or packed them (hard boiled) in the dolls' picnic basket that those yolks were there. Also that there were linens on all the doll beds and clothes in all the drawers and messy piles of shoes in the closets and real presents—not just empty matchboxes—tied with bows under the dollhouse Christmas tree.

How do I describe the kind of thinking, the yolk-making mentality, that seems to me essential in any dollhouse? Some of the most lavish ones I've seen in museums don't have it. The drawers aren't meant to open, the soap has been glued to the soap dish, the bedspread is painted onto the bed. To me those houses are assemblages of furniture. They may be beautiful, but rarely are they lovable as I like to think mine was.

My own dollhouse wasn't a house at all; it sprawled along rows and rows of bookshelves in my room, extended in the last years to shoe boxes and packing crates. The scale was jumbled; most of the furniture was homemade. It certainly wasn't that my dollhouse was more *realistic* than those museum pieces. I don't think realism is all that important in a dollhouse. (Often, incidentally, neither are the dolls.) The reason I put yolks in my dolls' eggs and letters in their envelopes was that those things gave the house a sense of depth, gave me a feeling of layers and layers existing to be uncovered. Photographs in the family album—Annabelle at age six, age ten, age twelve and age ten months, bare on a bear rug. A sense of life going on, time passing. Secrets, mysteries. Dust under the rug, mice in the attic. I once put a nearly microscopic chip of Ivory soap, carved

vaguely like a tooth, under the pillow of a doll of tooth-losing age, never imagining anyone would see. A friend, examining the bed (made from round-headed clothespins and odd bits of balsa wood) noticed it fall out. She knew at once what that chip of soap was meant to be. Years later she mentioned the joy of discovering it, and I think perhaps she remembers the tooth occasionally even now, as I remember and think fondly of those egg yolks.

JOYCE MAYNARD
Seventeen

Dollhouse Catalogues

Joyce Maynard recommends the following catalogues to fellow dollhouse enthusiasts:

Federal Smallwares Corp., 85 Fifth Avenue, New York, N.Y. 10003. The catalogue is free; send 25 cents for postage.

The Miniature Mart, 883 39th Ave., San Francisco, Calif. 94121. Their book is $2 "but really worth it."

Chestnut Hill Studio Ltd., Box 38, Churchville, N.Y. 14428, has "beautiful, fine-quality furniture." Its catalog is $1.50 (add 35 cents for first-class mail).

Creative Playthings Dollhouse

The Creative Playthings Dollhouse is well constructed and functionally designed. Each of the eight rooms in the two-story house is completely open, so the child can play alone or with other children without fighting. Even though Muki was a little young (not yet three) to play house with the dollhouse, she used it for her own play purposes.

I've had to give in to lack of space and collapse it temporarily. It's easy to put up and take down and store (it's flat when collapsed).

MARIE BROWN

[*Editor's note:* The Creative Playthings dollhouse is $39.95; kitchen furniture, $6.50; living room furniture, $9.50; dining room $7.50; bedroom $7.50; bathroom $7.50.]

Build a box to serve as a platform on which the dollhouse can sit. Much easier to get at than from the ground up.

Dorothy Muson's Dollhouse

Dorothy Muson—a professional portrait painter and occasional carpenter—began designing and building dollhouses several years ago after despairing of finding an attractive, well-constructed house at reasonable cost for her own children. One design led to others, and she now offers six models, all hand-made of ¼-inch and ½-inch plywood, fully decorated on the outside in bright colors with shutters, door, and white trim, and on the inside with patterned wall coverings, rugs and vinyl flooring, and window curtains. They are mounted on rollers for easy mobility and storage.

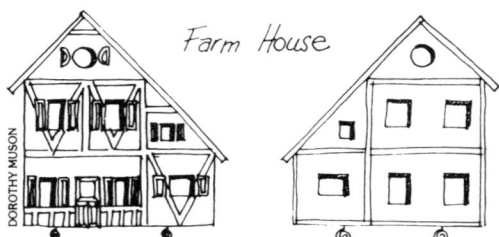

Farm House

Ms. Muson's dollhouses have stood up to the most devastating treatment; they've been climbed on, sat on, stood on, stomped, hammered, and ridden like skateboards. They simply won't fall apart (although the above treatment is not advised).

All six models are 12 inches deep. The large Victorian house ($150) is 44 inches high and 24 inches wide; the large Colonial ($90) is 30 inches high and 35 inches wide; the farmhouse ($60) is 32 inches high and 24 inches wide; and the small Colonial ($50) is 30 inches high and 24 inches wide. Both Colonials have side porches with lattice fencing. Any model may be purchased with plain interior at a 25 percent discount. In that case, instructions for interior decoration are provided. There is a choice of exterior colors.

The dollhouses are made to order; orders are filled within two weeks, except before Christmas, when one month's notice is requested. For more information contact Dorothy Muson, Bedford Artisans, Indian Hill Road, Bedford, N.Y. 10506, phone (914) 234-3275.

LOUISE JONES

The Doddhouse

The Doddhouse is the niftiest dollhouse around. It's huge, around three feet tall, and opens up to become twelve rooms. The reason it's relatively cheap is that it's made of corrugated fiberboard, not wood. I've tested it and it's strong, it holds up. People who don't take paper products seriously are missing out on this superwonderful house. (A wooden house this size would cost ten times more.) You have to add your own decorations, like windowboxes and door-knobs—which is as it should be.

STEVEN CANEY

My Doddhouse is 36 inches high and 24 inches square when closed. Each room is about 12 by 12 inches. The walls, all attached with fiberglass tape, do not need to be assembled; floors and roof segments have to be folded according to instructions, which I've been told are clear and easy. You can order the house from me, unfurnished, for $22 (including postage and insurance within the continental U.S.), at 745 Santa Barbara Road, Berkeley, Calif. 94707.

BRUCE DODD

Cape Cod and Georgian Dollhouses

A man in Kennebunk, Maine, makes fine, simple, well-designed dollhouses out of plywood. He has three or four models—Colonial, Cape Cod, etc. He includes a sheet of decorating ideas he has collected from his customers. If you're in Kennebunk, you can buy a house already assembled or in a knocked-down version that is cheaper and comes with instructions that he claims anyone can follow (I didn't take any chances; I got a refrigerator box from an appliance store and lugged home the assembled dollhouse on the plane). If you phone or write he'll send you his catalogue ($1). The name of his business is The House with the Blue Door, 23 Portland Road, Kennebunk, Me. 04043, telephone (207) 985-3461.

A store in England called Tridias has similar dollhouses, except in Georgian, etc., instead of Cape Cod, etc. Write for their catalogue (44 Monmouth Street, London WC2).

CALVIN TRILLIN

Toy Mouse House

Completely furnished, electrified, two-and-a-half-foot-high Cape Cod. Spacious livingroom. Woodburning fieldstone fireplace. Exposed chimney throughout. All modern kitchen (1940) including complete set of ceramic dishes, hand-painted. Full refrigerator and many other necessities. Light airy bedroom upstairs, floral wallpaper, fourposter, Franklin stove. Second-floor bath. Claw-foot tub. Chain toilet (can be replaced). Full attic wants "weeding out."

All furnishings are handmade and detailed. Some are made of found materials, so you will feel free to make your own additions over the years. You can get one made to order, all furnishings included, for $80. For more information write Elizabeth Radens at 6133 Tyndall Avenue, Bronx, N.Y. 10471   ANDRA SAMELSON

Making a Dollhouse—and Coming to Terms with Whose It Is

One summer vacation, Susan and I made a dollhouse for our kids. It was essentially a plywood box, completely ad-libbed, but it looked as much like a dollhouse as any "real" one looks. The key was an old book of wallpaper samples which we got from a wallpaper store for free. Once the rooms were papered (using Elmer's Glue) it began to look like a house.

The house was approximately one-half inch to the foot in scale as it turned out, although it wasn't planned that way. With a triangular scale rule (from an art supply store) you can measure anything according to one of six scales. We got balsa wood and matte knives and whenever I had a few free moments I made something for the house: a refrigerator, stove and sink, a double bed for the little parents, a crib for the baby, a bunk bed for the older child. And with little scraps of fabric on a bed or chair, the place began to take shape. When I stopped working on it, or lost interest after a while, we subsequently bought furniture, though the store-

bought stuff is really expensive.

The kids were not involved in the making of it at all—we did it after they went to sleep. And after it was turned over to them, the beautifully designed kitchen got painted kid-purple and there were drawings on the walls and the house began to deteriorate, but they loved it and I finally came to terms (intellectually if not emotionally) with its being their toy and not mine.

STEPHEN OLDERMAN

The Doll House Book

The Doll House Book, available from Kristin Helberg, Rainy Day Press, Box 471, Sausalito, Calif. 94965, (415) 454-7719 ($6.75 including postage and handling, allow three to four weeks for delivery) is one of the best alternatives to big, costly dollhouses (and expensive furniture) I've seen: a spiral-bound heavy cardboard book (6¾ by 8 inches) that opens up to make a four-room Victorian dollhouse. The rooms and twelve sheets of cut-out furniture are printed in black and white so you can color them. I first saw it at Design Research, and was delighted to find that it is available by mail order as well. (Also available, but not seen by me, are a Victo-

rian paper-doll family, and eventually a whole series of Doll House Books from different eras—including an Art Deco house.) It's probably a good idea to think about some sort of container, like a box top or a tray with sides, so that when the book is open and filled with furniture, it has something to hold it. That way, you can add trees and landscaping outside the house, too.   RS

SPECIFICALLY FURNITURE

A Short-term Solution

Architectural-model furniture that comes from Charette (31 Olympia Avenue, Woburn, Mass. 01801) is great for furnishing dollhouses. For example, they have plexiglass model furniture, very plain (modern) and not terribly sturdy (snaps easily with your fingers), that costs about

a quarter of the price of fancy traditional dollhouse furniture. You can get architectural models to scale, so conceivably you can build a dollhouse any size you want and then get some kind of furniture to fit.   BECKY CORWIN

[Charette also has a shop at 212 East 54th Street, New York, N.Y. 10022.]

Improvised Dollhouse Furniture

Most kids are not satisfied with unrealistic or imperfect homemade furniture unless they've "invented" it themselves. If you say: Hey, doesn't this yarn wrapped around this egg carton look something like a reclining chair, chances are the child will be dreaming about the tiny $17.95 version he or she saw in the F. A. O. Schwarz catalogue. On the other hand, if you keep a good-sized box around into which you toss household odds and ends, you might excite your child's creativity.

Some stuff to save for dollhouses:
Tiny paper cups (from pills in the hospital or your dentist)
Corks
Thread spools
Pictures of a TV, radio, refrigerator
Little brother's blocks

Pictures from magazines to paste on walls (you can always draw a window over a view you'd like to have)
Postage stamps for pictures on the walls (postcards if it's a big house)
Fisher-Price people
Clothespins
Shells
Fabric to cover anything, including raisin boxes
Paper clips
Shirt cardboard, cut with a matte knife and painted
Popsicle sticks or tongue depressors
Telephone wire, woven
Matchboxes, of course, and more, which the kids'll think up.

ELS

A Small Discovery About Making Dollhouse Furniture

Store-bought dollhouse furniture can be a very expensive proposition. But I've discovered that one simple trick (used even on the most expensive dollhouse furniture) can be employed by even an unskilled craftsman to make homemade dollhouse furniture that will delight any child.

My discovery is simply this: anyone can make a working door for stoves, refrigerators, cupboards, anything at all, with two straight pins, a pair of scissors, a matte knife, and a piece of balsa wood. Here's how to do it on, say, a refrigerator.

(1) You've already cut out the front panel of your refrigerator.

(2) Draw the outline of the door on the front panel.

(3) Cut out the door with a matte knife. Press the door out from the panel so you're sure it's been totally cut out. Then replace it in the panel.

(4) Stick straight pins in on the side you want hinged (see diagram). Push pins in as far as you can or until you're sure they're secure in the door.

(5) Swing door to test hinges.

(6) Snip off exposed pin ends with scissors or a wire cutter.

(7) Glue a handle on the door.

(8) Put the rest of the refrigerator together and attach the front panel with your working door.

STEPHEN OLDERMAN

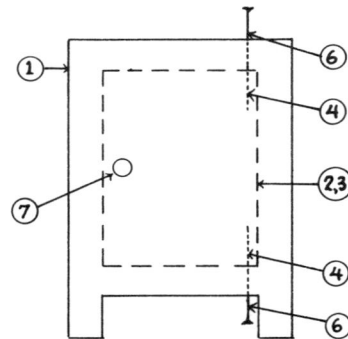

PUPPETS

Children as Impresarios

Children really love to put on shows—plays, puppet shows, magic exhibitions—for one another and for their parents. When Joan Cooney was a child, she and her friends used to do it on a paid basis: they'd write out tickets and charge everyone a penny to come. "Somehow," she says, "the idea we were running our own business made it even more fun. And it made our whole production seem more official and much more important."

CBC

Hand and Finger Puppets

The Possum Trot sock puppets require a child-size hand to bring them to life. There are twelve characters—a horse, a crocodile and a friendly lion are three we saw and loved. At Christmas I used one to decorate my hosts' gift, making it something of a found treat for their kid.

The puppets are $2.50 each. Write Possum Trot Corp., Box 249, McKee, Ky. 40447, for stores in your area that carry them. Worth chasing after.

RS

Grover, Cookie Monster, Bert, Ernie, Oscar, and other Sesame Street Muppet Puppets come from Child Guidance, $5 to $6 (more or less depending on where you buy them). And Sesame Street finger puppets (also from Child Guidance) are one of the great $1.25 buys. —Eds.

The Anything Muppet—a soft, blank face gives the imagination free rein; use accompanying accessories or scraps around the house to create the puppet of your dreams ($6, Child Guidance). The Sesame Street puppet collection reflects the nonracist intent of the program's producers. However, *every* puppet, white or black, is male: Oscar, Bert, Roosevelt Franklin, Grover, Ernie, and Big Bird. To protest this male bias, buy only the Anything Muppet.

LETTY COTTIN POGREBIN
Ms. magazine

Making Light Puppets

My light puppets are based on puppets I saw long ago from Pakistan. These were made from thin pieces of leather, oiled so that they were translucent and pricked with holes so that light from candles or lamps passed through.

I developed a similar one made from brown paper bags. For my young children I used the subject of insects, and as we made a butterfly or a ladybug or a grasshopper, we talked about where they had seen it and what it looked like and why the wings were so bright (camouflage) and what were those two knobby things that stuck out from the head and could they think of a machine in their house that had an antenna, etc. The conversations were silly, funny, and wonderful.

Here's the procedure:

(1) Using Magic Markers or crayons, make a drawing on a brown paper bag after talking about the butterfly or whatever.

(2) Color it "beautiful."

(3) Take a double piece of newspaper and line it with wax paper, then fold it in half.

(4) Enclose the drawing in the wax paper.

(5) Iron the drawing through the newspaper. (The wax will make the drawing translucent, while the newspaper keeps your iron wax-free.)

(6) Now cut out the butterfly.

(7) Prick holes with a toothpick or pin. Attach a string, find a beam of sunlight or a lamp, and let the magic begin.

JO BUTLER

◆

A Marionette from Wood and Screw-eyes

SCREW EYES:
pry open with
a screw driver,
close with a pliers.

USE SCRAP WOOD,
SAND THE EDGES.
(Its fun for kids to
work out the dimen-
sions for their
puppets)

from *Choosing and Using Materials*

◆

Shadow Puppets

Give a shadow puppet show using your hands, a wall, and a source of light (sun, lamp, or best of all a movie or slide projector). There are books on the subject (Bernie De Koven recommends Bursill's *Hand Shadows,* Dover, $1.25), but you can experiment easily enough.

RS

The Ol' Curtain Across the Doorway

One of the simplest puppet-theater setups is the ol' curtain-across-the-doorway device. Using one of those expandable curtain rods with a spring, you can hang a curtain or even a towel, behind which the players wait for their cues. If you can't get the curtain rod, and you don't mind a couple of nail holes in your doorframe, try a piece of string stretched across the doorway with a sheet hung from it.

ELS

Bringing a Story to Life

Always a favorite of mine and also loved by our sons, *The Pooh Story Book* was especially helpful one summer when we moved into a new community. Using Simplicity patterns, we made the characters, and the boys, who were a little insecure about a new home, had new cuddly toys. We spent hours with them retelling the stories and making up our own "Pooh Predicaments" and using the stuffed toys as puppets.

Pooh became such an important outlet for the older boys that they began to share him with the baby. He enjoyed the stories and plays as told by his brothers and soon had his own "Pooh-Bear." One day we decided to make Pooh a home, so we utilized the rather useless space at the bottom of a closet by putting in a shelf about three and a half feet high (it now holds shoes), which became a roof sheltering a perfect space for a small child to create a miniature world. The older boys built furniture, applied wallpaper, made bedspreads, rugs, etc., and created a perfectly charming home. The three-year-old has spent many hours mimicking Mommy and Daddy in the only room in the house where he is the *biggest* person (an idea that really fascinates a child with three brothers, who are so much older and bigger than he is).

JEANNE DUNN

Two Puppet Books

CREATING WITH PUPPETS, *by Lothar Kampmann (Van Nostrand Reinhold, 1972, 74 pages, $6.95).*

This book is for anyone who wants to make imaginative and unusual puppets—finger puppets, yam puppets, hand puppets, wooden marionettes—even for someone too young to read. The text is minimal (simple and helpful descriptions), and the photographs (most in color) will inspire you to turn spoons and slippers and other accessible and inexpensive materials into characters of your imagining. The book confirms what any three-year-old knows: that anything is everything.

LET'S START A PUPPET THEATER, *by Benny E. Andersen (Van Nostrand Reinhold, 1973, 91 pages, $4.95).*

Starting with simple puppet shows using just shoes, this book takes you through full-scale productions with lighting, music, and elaborate scenery and scripts. Materials range from household objects (mops, gloves, a mug with eyeglasses over the handle) to cut-out wood for marionettes and gauze-covered polystyrene for a boa constrictor. This is a delightful and instructive book, for someone who really wants to create a puppet theater and not just play with puppets.

ANDRA SAMELSON

GIFTS

471

WHERE, BESIDES A TOY STORE, YOU CAN GET A KID A GIFT

We've come to understand that the gifts we give to children and the playtime that fills their growing years carry an unspoken message about the kind of people we wish, hope, and believe they can become.

LETTY COTTIN POGREBIN

Some of the Best Gifts My Child Has Received or Given

- A small suitcase for overnights at friends' or cousins' houses: fill with soap, toothbrush, smallest-size toothpaste, a new face towel (wrap each item individually before putting them all inside the suitcase).
- An addition to a collection or hobby: some stamps, coins, seashells, special rocks or minerals (pack in an egg carton).
- A bowl of goldfish, food, gravel—all for probably under two dollars.
- Hardware store delights: a large-size nut and bolt make a good puzzle for a two- or three-year-old; some hinges (for older kids, add two pieces of wood and some screws); a retractable tape measure. Put together a toolbox (much better than buying an already-put-together one).

WRAP PRESENTS IN BROWN PAPER, COMICS, NEWSPAPER. INCLUDE A LITTLE TOY WITH THE RIBBON OR SOMETHING FROM A GUM MACHINE

- A clearly written recipe on an index card (whole cookbooks are sometimes intimidating for a kid) and all the ingredients: oatmeal cookies, puddings, baked apples. For non-reading kids, draw the recipe on a wall chart using symbols instead of words.
- A whistle.
- A magnet.
- A flashlight.
- A padlock and key—a great "toy" for a three-year-old.

- A metal lockbox with key—a treat for any child who has secrets to keep.
- A small seedling plant made from a grapefruit or orange seed; for the more ambitious, an avocado seed; or a sweet potato that has started growing.
- Directions for an at-home science experiment and all the materials needed. (You can go to the library and copy an appropriate experiment from any of the number of books on them, then put the whole thing in a shoebox).
- Some wood, a small hammer, and nails; or screws and a screwdriver.
- A simple-to-make pattern and some fabric. Put into a nice box with a spool of thread, a needle, hooks and eyes, and anything else that may be needed.
- Stationer's serendipity: a hole puncher, magnifying glass, label maker (the most inexpensive plastic one is as good as any other).
- A supply of stars, stencils, stick-on letters and labels, and a package of construction paper.
- A rubber stamp of the kid's name or a silly word.
- Our favorite Christmas present from Ian Gold: a beautiful seashell coloring book and crayons—and a collection of shells to go with it.
- A needlework design on canvas or a piece of linen with the yarn to make it. Draw the design to the child's interest—or the child's name alone would be enough.
- A pedometer, for children who want to know how far they walk to school.
- A bicycle pump, for an older, bicycle-obsessed kid.
- A cheap transistor radio (a terrific gift for a very young child—better than any $3 toy).
- From art supply stores and catalogues: intriguing devices such as plastic multi-shaped stencils and measuring and drawing aids to tempt the imagination.
- Jumprope, bag of marbles or jacks are still appreciated by older kid.
- Gift certificates: to a movie, an ice cream shop, toy store.

ELS

OBJETS TROUVÉS

Don't ever throw away a small container that could be filled with treasures for a small child. Fill it and give it to the child. Save:
- Cigar boxes
- Plastic medicine vials
- Film containers
- Typewriter ribbon boxes
- Tin cans (if you're sure there are no sharp edges left on)

Some treasures to fill the containers with (all for children three or over):
- Beans
- Macaroni (include a shoelace for stringing)
- Pebbles or a single big stone or seashell

- A button collection
- An old rhinestone button or broken piece of costume jewelry (these can be a great treasure for a child)
- Half of a cork, a toothpick, and a paper "mast"—these make a good boat "kit" for a four- or five-year-old
- Keys (and perhaps a chain or ring to keep them on)
- A found feather or leaf to look at closely
- A zipper (a good gift for a small child because it makes noise, moves, and is "real"; roll up one or two in a tiny box).

ELS

Christmas Books

Before we had kids, we used to make a Christmas book every year for the children of one or another of our friends. A month or so before Christmas, we would ask the parents to start collecting (secretly) the kid's drawings. I think if you take a dozen drawings by the same kid and rearrange them and look squinty-eyed at them, a story emerges. I was in charge of the text, and Alice was in charge of design. We always bought one of those hardcover sketchbooks that look like a real book. Alice used different-color construction paper to put the title on the front cover and the spine. We made up the name of a publishing company, although I can't remember what it was. She also used construc-

tion paper for the text—pasting in paragraphs in various shapes, which faced the illustrations (we always thought that her skill in this came from the fact that she has a four-year-old's imagination and is a neat gluer).

The part of the book the kids always liked best was the beginning. For Mary Kaye Schilling's book, for instance, one page said, in small letters, "Text by Bud Trillin." The next page said, in equally small letters, "Design by Alice Trillin." The next page was a double-page spread that said, in huge letters, "ILLUS-TRATED BY MARY KAYE SCHILLING."

CALVIN TRILLIN

One Thing That's As Good to Receive As to Give

When I was a child, the present I gave my parents that they liked the most was a book of coupons that I made up and designed myself. One coupon read, "Good for a half-hour of dishwashing"; another said, "Good to stop one fight with my brother," and so forth. The idea was, of course, that I was donating future time and services to my parents—time and services which they could make use of merely by presenting me with the appropriate coupon.

It wasn't long before I regretted giving my parents that booklet: they kept using the coupons! But now, as a parent, it occurs to me that one of the finest presents we can give our children is a gift of *our* time. Why shouldn't we make up coupon books for our kids, with certifi-

cates reading, "Good for one story-reading session," or "Good for one trip to school to pick up something you left there by mistake."

Such a book makes tangible your willingness to be close to and enjoy your child. At the same time, it may help give him a sense of budgeting, of handling money, of the true value of services and of time.

ILENE GOLDMAN

Gifts for Large Families

Ice cream maker
Popcorn popper
A rubber mattress for jumping
Ping-Pong table
Camping tent
Slide projector
Sports equipment everyone can use,
        such as a croquet or badminton set
A hammock   EDS.

◆

A Musical Christmas

My family, every year at Christmas, used to make a record. We'd all go to a recording studio, buy a disk, then we'd talk and maybe sing one song. Now we have these records from the time I was a year old until I was about twelve. They're hysterical.

LESLIE HARRIS

Surprise String Balls

Bob made all the kids (ages two to ten) surprise string balls for Christmas and Hanukkah. You need yards and yards and yards of brightly colored, strongish yarn or string, and at least half a dozen tiny treasures—mini-cars, balloons, doll toys, jewelry, candy. Begin with the biggest item (perhaps one of those large rubber self-sealing balloon balls with string attached, deflated of course), knot some yarn around it and start winding. Keep winding, adding another knotted-on treasure every several yards, until you have a ball four or five inches in diameter. Be sure to keep changing yarn colors (more knots) even more frequently than you add gifts, in order to make the unwinding a colorful adventure. You can top it all off with one larger gift hanging outside the completed ball, or something long and thin (special pencil or mini-flashlight) stuck through it.

PAULA GLATZER

More Good Gift Ideas

Box full of old costume jewelry
Complete dress-up costume
Knapsack
Magazine subscription
Disguise kit
Membership in a zoological society or a
        museum
Socks or mittens filled with magic markers or
        crayons
Things for looking: magnifying glass, colored
        lenses, microscope
                                            RS

And More . . .

One of my favorite gifts to give: a huge bottle filled with buttons and pieces of cloth and bits of paper and yarn and rocks . . . beautiful trash.

JEANINE WAGNER

A toy suitcase packed with embroidery floss, needles, transfers, and a hoop makes a wonderful gift. My daughter got such a homemade kit four years ago and has hauled it around, replenished it, and even learned to embroider with it.

LINDA WEST ECKHARDT

Mary Rodgers enjoys giving children "Important toys," her term for microscopes, adding machines, calculators, typewriters, tape recorders. Toys which will expand a child's mind, increase his or her experiences.

I give children plants. Any child can grow a coleus, a piggyback plant, a small jade plant, a philodendron, a spider plant, Swedish ivy. They are delighted to have a growing thing, and as long as they remember to water it, they will enjoy it for a long time.

ALICE BACH

I like to give kids big containers of glue and beautiful colors of tissue paper, the kind that mothers don't buy. They love it.

SUSAN KANOR

My favorite gift to give newborn babies is a big prism to hang in a window so that there is a moving rainbow in the room. (You can order one from the Edmund Scientific catalogue.)

From an interview with PHYLIS MORRISON

[For 75 cents you can give a kid an incredible map. See page 283 for information on U.S. Geological Survey maps, and order it about a month ahead of time.]

"Something They Can Actually Read"

I think personalized stationery is a marvelous present for kids, even when they're quite young. They don't even have to be old enough to write letters: they can draw a picture on it and still send off something with their name on it. Besides, the first thing children generally learn to spell is their name, so even if they're only four or five, you've given them something they can actually read.

And, for older kids, their own stationery might give them some incentive to send thank-you letters.

PHYLLIS CERF WAGNER

Instead of Stationery

Instead of the traditional box of engraved stationery, why not try a box of fine art postcards or notes. They're beautiful, different, and can be matted for framing. Museum shops are a good source. Or order by mail from a wonderful postcard shop called Untitled, 159 Prince Street, New York, N.Y. 10012. They have a list (with black-and-white reproductions) of 196 of their cards, which, to give you an idea, begins Albers, African, American Indian, Beardsley, Blake, Bosch. . . . Minimum order: 10 cards, $2 plus 50 cents postage and handling. (The people at Untitled inform me that there's also a good postcard shop, called Sublime, in Atlanta.)

For children who fancy fairy tale illustrations, there are posters, postcards, and note cards available from the Green Tiger Press, 7458 La Jolla Boulevard, La Jolla, Calif. 92037 (catalogue available; send 75 cents in postage).

RS

◆

For the Industrious or Tardy Gift-Giver

My friend Frannie makes beautiful gifts for children. If you can't take the time to make a splendid baby quilt like one of hers (my daughter Gabriela received the quilt originally intended for Fran's godson, born four years earlier), try her slightly-less-industrious project of embroidering the child's name in easy-to-read letters on a store-bought guest towel. Gaby's towel is bright yellow with an appliqué (by Springmaid) of a green crocodile in an orange bathtub, the name sewn (by Frannie) in orange embroidery thread, six strands strong. This is an especially good gift if you're habitually a year or more late with your baby presents.

PAULA GLATZER

An Old-fashioned Christmas

One of the best gifts my family ever received was from my mother. She filled a large carton with food. In addition to the staples—fresh-ground coffee, honey, brown rice, herbs and spices, breads for the freezer, whole wheat flour—there was a special treat for everyone: my favorite teas, fresh-ground peanut butter for the kids, nuts and raisins and dried fruits for all of us, and some delicacies we probably wouldn't have treated ourselves to. And we all felt virtuous rebelling against the modern Christmas.

ELS

Having Found a Use for Our Old Cigar Boxes and Oatmeal Boxes

Over the past few years we have really tried to cut down on the amount of crap that we give each other and the kids. This year at Christmas we got down to making everything by hand. It became an event that we built up to for two months. We all made the tree ornaments, and Orson helped three-year-old Max make a jewelry box out of a cigar box for me. The fourteen-year-old taught the five-year-old how to crochet on her fingers with big fat yarn, so she made me a belt. Orson made stilts for the two oldest kids, and all the kids helped Orson make three-dimensional pictures of the family, like shadow boxes, for me. One of the boys made a bank for his brother out of an oatmeal box with felt around it.

We wondered if at the last moment the kids weren't going to be disappointed, and if it was going to be an anticlimactic Christmas when they weren't up to their knees in broken plastic by noon. But they really were happy with it. If we had just suddenly announced on Christmas morning, "We're giving you stuff that we made," it would not have worked. But this was a family event. Everyone was involved. Two months before Christmas we had started planning what we would make, and there was much hiding in rooms. Everyone loved it.

CAROLYN BEAN

We All Do It, But . . .

Learn to avoid the following well-intentioned mistakes.

1. *The overboard gift.* The one where your kid asked one tiny simple quasi-scientific question and you rushed out and bought him a $35 chemistry set. Such behavior really has more to do with the parent's anxieties than the kid's curiosities, and the problem is that when the child can't handle the chemistry set, everyone feels resentful. No fun. When he asks about ink, tell him about ink. Don't lock into his future career plans.

2. *The peer-pressure gift.* This is the toy that every kid on the block has. Usually it is overpriced. Usually it breaks easily. Often it is boring. Practically always it has been advertised heavily on television during the Saturday morning cartoons when you were asleep.

Some parents are anxious about their children being different from others. Some parents think that it is cruel to deny their child what everybody else has. Some parents catch a whiff of their child's obsession and figure it won't work itself through until he has the actual object of his mania in hand. If your thinking is along those lines, go ahead and buy the dratted thing.

If on the other hand you refuse to be made a victim of advertising and give in to the unreasonable demands of a five-year-old child, you can use your wits. Present the child with something more interesting. Perhaps two inexpensive, constructive toys in place of the one worthless one. Better still, offer to build a tree house with him, or to put on a puppet show. Children are generally more interested in people than things. It's not really the objects they crave, but the doing.

3. *The peace-offering gift.* This is the one frequently purchased at the airport by the parent who feels guilty about being away from home so long. The irony is that it's not the toy the child wants, it's the parent. Better to forget the toy altogether, and bring yourself home. Go for a walk together. Build a card tower. Make a batch of cookies. It is important not to give toys as a substitute for yourself.

4. *The I-wish-I-had-it-when-I-was-a-kid toy.* The prototype here is the electric train set. If you really want electric trains, that's okay, but recognize your yearning for what it is. And prepare yourself for the possibility that your child won't be as excited by them as you are. Try to tune in to what he wants. (Maybe it is trains after all, terrific kid that he is.)

5. *The educational toy.* Any toy is educational if it intrigues your child and enlarges his experience. Toys which are designed to help your child read at a startlingly early age are probably not as educational as they are nerve-wracking. Frequently, toys classified as "educational" upset your child and cost you a lot of money. Abraham Lincoln did not have a lot of things hanging in his face as he lay in his cradle, and he came along just fine.

JENNIFER CARDEN
With thanks to STEVEN CANEY

Longing for the Trade-in

One relative, over the years, must have bought Nicholas no less than twenty $2, $3, or $4 plastic cars, trucks, motorcycles, boats, not one of which is still intact. How I wish I could trade in all those wheels, fenders, and plastic assortmentia for one well-constructed non-vehicle (no wonder we are a nation owning 1.8 automobiles per family)—a musical instrument, perhaps, that he'll have for a long, long time; or a stethoscope, a real one through which he can hear his own heart or mine. Surely it can't be the money: a wooden recorder, for example, could last his whole lifetime and could be had for about $5. A $3.98 transistor radio can be the child's very own. And he could have had his own Polaroid camera for less than what all those trucks cost.

Since, generally, worse comes to worst in these matters, I announced to Aunt Agnes one day that if she planned to give a gift, there were things Nick could use more than another car or truck. I'll be damned if he didn't decide right then that those crummy vehicles were his favorite kind of toy. And the stethoscope, which I finally got for him myself, is sometimes used as a towing device for those trucks with two wheels.

ELS

Give a child a present and he is ecstatic beyond description; give a child two presents and he is only interested in a third one.

ALAN SAPERSTEIN

About Age Designations on Toys (Also Games and Books)

We are all, no doubt, thrilled to see our clever two-year-olds putting together the puzzle intended for "three years and up," and our six-year-olds really reading and understanding a book labeled "for seven- to nine-year-olds." But what happens when your daughter who's eleven is reading a book she thinks is terrific and then discovers it's intended for the seven to nines (or how about if *you* discover it's for the seven to nines)?

One parent told me she finds that most things marked 3-to-6 are designed for the sixes more than for the threes, while another won't buy a 3-to-6 toy for her six-year-old because she thinks it will have too short an interest period for him and he'll probably tire of it before he's seven. My friend Jennifer observed: "Some children are quick with their hands and could manage a Davis weaving loom early on. Others are blithering dolts when it comes to such things, and might be happier with Play-Doh well into pubescence."

But how do you decide what would suit another person's child? Designations are useful for absentee grandparents or friends who haven't seen your kid since last summer. Still, it's unrealistic to establish a rule about age appropriateness. Generally, a child who has older siblings will pick up something belonging to an older brother or sister and figure it out simply to be like a big kid. Similarly, an older child might pick up his little sister's sewing cards or magnetic letters and find an afternoon's pleasure.

Thus, the only reasonable note a manufacturer could put on a package would have to go something like this: "While some 2- or 3-year-olds might be able to do this puzzle, it was essentially designed with 4s and 5s in mind, but we have discovered that a large number of 6- to 9-year-olds can work it with a sustained interest, and even the 12-year-old grandson of the president of the Marx Toy Company has shown a curiosity about it."

ELS

Hoping for the Best

For an adult who doesn't have children or know any child well, giving a gift can be a dreary chore or a challenge. Most adults in this situation ask one of the parents what might be suitable, a more careful giver asks someone else who has children what to give, or asks someone else to choose it, and the person who likes the child does the job alone. The choice of a gift can be difficult, but essentially it is like all gift-giving—you try to match up the gift with the person. It's a lot easier to try to buy off the child with something lavish, but children who care about their world will almost certainly like something small and unobtrusive that is right for them more than the big gift that *has* to be appreciated. You can never be sure what will work. All you can do is try to figure out who that child—that person—is, and hope for the best. (Most of the time you'll lose, but you will learn from it.)

A. OLSON

The Useful Presents and the Useless Presents

There were the Useful Presents: engulfing mufflers of the old coach days, and mittens made for giant sloths; zebra scarfs of a substance like silky gum that could be tug-o'-warred down to the galoshes; blinding tam-o'-shanters like patchwork tea cozies and bunny-suited busbies and balaclavas for victims of head-shrinking tribes; from aunts who always wore wool next to the skin there were mustached and rasping vests that made you wonder why the aunts had any skin left at all; and once I had a little crocheted nose bag from an aunt now, alas, no longer whinnying with us. And pictureless books in which small boys, though warned with quotations not to, *would* skate on Farmer Giles' pond and did and drowned; and books that told me everything about the wasp, except why.

Go on to the Useless Presents.

Bags of moist and many-colored jelly babies and a folded flag and a false nose and a tram-conductor's cap and a machine that punched tickets and rang a bell; never a catapult; once, by mistake that no one could explain, a little hatchet; and a celluloid duck that made, when you pressed it, a most unducklike sound, a mewing moo that an ambitious cat might make who wished to be a cow; and a painting book in which I could make the grass, the trees, the sea and the animals any color I pleased, and still the dazzling sky-blue sheep are grazing in the red field under the rainbow-billed and pea-green birds. Hardboileds, toffee, fudge and allsorts, crunches, cracknels, humbugs, glaciers, marzipan, and butterwelsh for the Welsh. And troops of bright tin soldiers who, if they could not fight, could always run. And Snakes-and-Families and Happy Ladders. And Easy Hobbi-Games for Little Engineers, complete with instructions. Oh, easy for Leonardo! And a whistle to make the dogs bark to wake up the old man next door to make him beat on the wall with his stick to shake our picture off the wall. And a packet of cigarettes: you put one in your mouth and you stood at the corner of the street and you waited for hours, in vain, for an old lady to scold you for smoking a cigarette, and then with a smirk you ate it. And then it was breakfast under the balloons.

DYLAN THOMAS
A Child's Christmas in Wales

PARTIES AND SPECIAL OCCASIONS

GREETINGS

Beware of Cuteness

A word to aunts and grandparents about birthday cards and picture postcards sent to little kids: It's a great idea—even two-year-olds like to get mail—but beware of cuteness. Kids are more interested in a card that shows something unusual or something real—in a picture even of a hotel or a mountain range. If you're sending a missive from the airport, don't pick out the most childlike card; find a picture of some planes or a city skyline or a scene that's slightly bizarre. Enough pussycats and little doggies and clowns and bunnies and duckies.

ELS

Cards That Tell a Story

For young kids the greatest birthday card (apart from the homemade kind) is a picture postcard. We've sent and received beauties of animals (pick up a few when you visit the zoo), boats (from fishing towns), Amish families on their horse-drawn carriages, cityscapes. Many of them tell a story.

ELS

Starting a Postcard Chain Letter

I received the following chain letter from Mike Frith—one of my few friends who has tried as hard as I have to remain a child (well, almost as hard):

Dear_____.

   This is a chain letter. Please send a PICTURE POSTCARD to the first person on this list. Then leave off the top name on the list, add your name to the bottom, copy this letter eight times, and mail it to eight of your friends. In eighteen days, with a bit of luck, you should receive 200 (count 'em!) postcards. Your letter should be in the mail within three days or the chain will be broken. *Please* don't break this chain!
   [List six names and addresses below]

   I'm afraid I broke the chain, but Mike (and some of the kids who sent him the letter) claims to have reaped quite a harvest (though hardly the promised 200 postcards).
   If your kid's a dreamer, show him the postcard chain letter and see if he's interested. At best, he'll get a few weeks' worth of fascinating mail from all over. At worst, he'll learn what you knew all the time: most chain letters are a hopeless waste of time.

CBC

Merry Christmas from the Giroux's Bathroom

A few years ago my friend Claude Giroux and his five daughters sent me an abstract painting as a Christmas card. It looked rather ordinary until I noticed an accompanying snapshot showing the card as a work-in-progress. The photo revealed the five girls making a hopeless mess in the bathroom, spattering paint this way and that and obviously having the time of their lives. I've remembered that card with pleasure: it certainly beats the stilted family portraits one often receives at holiday time.

From an interview with JOAN GANZ COONEY

Throwing in the Sponge (and the Potato)

Last year for Christmas cards Scott (then four) did potato prints of a piece of holly and berries. I wrote the message. This year he did temperas (or poster paints) on poster board using a sponge. He made about thirty or forty cards. It kept him busy, and got our cards done at the same time.

LAURIE GARDNER

[For other materials useful in making Christmas cards, turn to the PRINTING section on pages 341–42]

Bah, Humbug

Want to save money and energy on greeting cards? Consider these two alternatives. First, do away with envelopes—send postcards. A package of a hundred 4 by 6–inch index cards, blank on both sides, costs under 75 cents. Use one side for a personal drawing and message, and the other for the address. If you send 100 postcards, instead of 100 cards in envelopes, you save $5 in postage (enough to fill one or two stockings nicely), upwards of at least $10 by not buying commercially printed postcards; and think of the paper you conserve by not sending envelopes.

   The second alternative was suggested to me a few years ago when I received a recycled Christmas card from friends who had received that same card from their dentist. Now every Christmas card goes out again (except the ones that are just too ugly), and you and your kids will have a good time matching cards with people. If the back page of the card is blank, you can write the address there and staple it to the front so you won't have to track down assorted-size envelopes. Merry Christmas!

RS

The Picture Drawer

There's a drawer in the chest in Paul's room that we call the picture drawer. Every time he produces one of his 8½ by 11–inch master-pieces—crayon or pencil or watercolor or whatever—into the picture drawer it goes. Then, when it's time to send a birthday greeting or a get-well message or Valentine or Christmas cards, he rummages through his collection and picks out just the right picture for the occasion. He has a wonderful time doing it, and a Paul Hays original is, of course, far more personal than a store-bought card, especially after the artist has added his own hand-lettered greeting.

ANNA JANE HAYS

HALLOWEEN: COSTUMES AND CUTUPS

What Good Is a Halloween Witch Without Creepy Skin?

Real witches needn't have grotesque faces and black robes, but Halloween witches must. Since it's most important that people be frightened by you, and since no one, after all, is afraid of a little person in a black leotard carrying an orange balloon, try the following.

To create scars and warts and other distortions on hands and face, you need wax. Professional makeup artists use something labeled modeling wax or derma wax, which is hard to work with because it warms up and gets sticky from the oils in your hands. It comes in clear, light flesh, or dark flesh shades ($1.50 for a two-ounce container from Mehron, see below); if you use it, add some bits of cotton for warts (from cotton balls or rolls) and mold it with a small spatula or stick rather than your fingers.

Easier and cheaper and convincing enough to be used by some professional make-up artists is a dime-store product called Creepy Skin (made by Imagineering Inc., 49 cents for a small container). It's like modeling wax but contains a cotton fiber that makes it stronger and easier to mold; it also stays on better than modeling wax and is reusable. To make bloody wounds, for example, slap a layer on your skin, cut into it, and insert some vampire blood in the center (see recipe on the next page or spend about 40 cents for one fluid ounce, by Imagineering Inc., at Woolworth's et al.).

Another dime-store product you can use is Moleskin (39 cents for two ¾ by 6-inch sheets), which is self-adhesive and makes great warts and scars when painted. For other facial distortions, make a papier-mâché on your face with layers of Kleenex and Karo syrup (50 to 60 cents in the supermarket).

For fangs and other canine protrusions, den-tists make tooth caps out of hard plastic. But if that sounds like a bit of trouble and expense, for 29 cents or less the dime store sells evil teeth that glow in the dark, and penny-candy stores have 10-cent fangs covering the entire mouth or individual teeth for 3 cents. (Also 3 cents each are witches' nails and claws; they look deadly while they last, but break easily.) Mehron makes a stick of black tooth wax that makes a few hundred teeth disappear ($1), and the dime-store variety is reliable. To apply tooth wax: dry the tooth, take a few breaths with mouth open to remove moisture from your mouth, and, using a small spatula, apply as thin a coat as possible. (*Note:* We don't recommend covering braces with tooth wax.)

Then don a cloak, fetch your familiar brindled cat, gather friends (witches don't travel alone), and, most important of all, imagine a victim who believes in your power.

●

The professional makeup mentioned above was priced at Mehron Theatrical Makeup (250 West 40th Street, New York, N.Y. 10018, [212] 997-1011). Their products are available at retail outlets, but it's cheaper to buy from them directly. The problem is that there's a $15 mail-order minimum. When you stop to think about

PATRICK O'NEAL

it, though, colored pencils and rouges (good for clowns) begin to add up, and a $10 order would provide the materials for two terrific Christmas gifts. (A list of Mehron products and prices is available from the manufacturer on request.)

As for the dime-store products we referred to, they're most widely available around Halloween. You might want to buy some extra then for use at other times of the year. By the way, we *don't* recommend the 39- and 49-cent costume makeup sets you'll find in the dime store. In general, they seem to contain color sticks that don't work as well as crayons, nose putty that's cracked and hard, and tooth wax that, while perfectly usable, can be purchased separately. Instead of buying the sets, you're better off pur-

chasing the cheapest street makeup in whatever colors you wish, or using water-based Magic Markers.

Another product we found less than satisfactory was Scar Stuff, which seems to be harder to mold than Creepy Skin or Moleskin.

RITA OGDEN and RS

RITA OGDEN'S RECIPE FOR VAMPIRE BLOOD

Mix 1 cup Karo syrup, 3 tablespoons red tempera paint (preferably dry, but you can use wet if necessary), 4 drops red food coloring, and 1 drop yellow food coloring. It may stain your kids' clothes, but it *does* wash off skin . . . eventually.

Cardboard Masks

Special things must be considered when designing a mask. It must be comfortable to wear (not too hot and not too heavy), a mouth hole should be provided so that speech is easily heard, and vision should not be drastically blocked. If a kid can't see well through a mask, he is likely to trip or stumble on everything. And don't forget the mirror. You must look at yourself wearing a mask to understand the character you are going to be.

MATERIALS
cardboard boxes
yarn

TOOLS
pencil
scissors
crayons, markers, poster paint, etc.

CONSTRUCTION

Cut a long, rectangular-shaped piece from a corrugated box. If the box is large, one of the flaps will do. The long edge of the piece should go across the corrugations. Fold the piece in half back onto itself. If you open the piece to a "V" shape and place it over your face you will have the beginnings of a mask. With the piece held up against your face, try to "feel" where

the eyeholes should be. Mark the spot on one side only with your finger, and then mark the spot with a pencil. Do the same to find where openings should be cut for the mouth and ears. You only have to mark the position on one side of the cardboard. With the mask folded so that its shape will be symmetrical, cut out holes and spaces for the eyes, mouth, and ears.

Fig. 1 shows a simple cutting pattern for a first mask. The design of the face can be completed using crayons, felt markers, poster paint or collage. If you want a few ideas, just look in the mirror and twist up your own face. The theme of the mask is up to you—a sea creature, monster, clown, king, queen, or just any funny face. Punch a hole on either side of the mask at the rear, and tie a piece of yarn in one of the holes. Double-loop the yarn through the other hole so that it acts as an adjustable drawstring when fitting the mask. Put the cardboard mask over your face. The corrugated cardboard can be bent around your face for a better fit. Pull the drawstring tight so the mask won't slip down.

After making your first cardboard mask, you should experiment with cutting other shaped masks. A few suggestions are illustrated, but your imagination will work best for you.

STEVEN CANEY
Steven Caney's Play Book

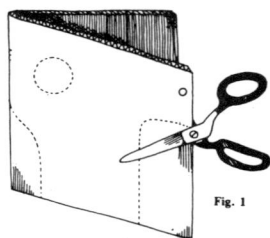

Fig. 1

Making Costumes for Your Kids: Simplicity Itself

Usually one of the nice things about sewing costumes for children is that if things do not turn out, the creation that was supposed to be a frog can suddenly be seen as a cucumber. For the American history play at school, however, if your daughter is to appear in a Puritan or a

Centennial costume of the eighteenth or nineteenth century, some exactitude is necessary. It is probably easier to go to the Simplicity pattern than to figure out on your own just how those little caps everyone wore at Plymouth Rock were constructed. Similarly for the Nativity pageant at Sunday school in which your child is curiously cast as an angel. Wings and halos can be tricky to make; Simplicity will show you how for around a dollar. Costume patterns can be a very good investment.

As for Halloween, it has been our experience that most young children like to dress up in the dime-store costume being pushed on television that fall. (However, if you envision your child as a tiger, dog, rabbit, cat, clown, angel, fairy, witch, princess, devil, skeleton, or astronaut, but do not know how to effect the transformation, check the back section of the Simplicity catalogue. There are patterns for each one.)

Remember the pattern catalogue too when the children are invited to costume parties (a type of fête distressingly popular in some areas). Maybe this is the time for an extravaganza in tulle and sequins, as your child may feel funny rigged out in your old nightgown, knowing that *no one* would believe she was a fairy godmother in that outfit.

Note: The clown costume offered by the Simplicity catalogue includes an adult size. A father we know dresses up in one of these and drops in at children's birthday parties in the neighborhood. He does magic tricks, wears a lot of lipstick on his nose, and is always well received. (He likes a piece of birthday cake for his trouble.)

JENNIFER CARDEN

For good patterns for costumes, send for a catalogue to Clothkits, 24 High Street, Lewes, Sussex, England.

How To Survive the Halloween Candy Frenzy

If you indulge in the Halloween tradition, it's hard to keep your own kids away from the bowl of candy kept at your door for other trick-or-treaters. Here are some candy substitutes: little boxes of raisins, sugarless gum, balloons, little toys. Check the dime store—there are still a few party favors or toys that can be had for about a dollar a dozen. Best of all, these leftovers will keep till next Halloween, which is more than you can say for Milk Duds.

ELS

Halloween Cutouts

Everybody makes pumpkin jack-o'-lanterns for Halloween. Why not try something different and see how many other kinds of vegetable and fruit cutouts you can make? Six-year-olds and up can do most of the hollowing and cutting by themselves. Here are some of the ones we've used:

Squash—all kinds, shapes, and colors
Gourds—ditto
Apples
Potatoes
Onions
Turnips
Carrots (fat ones)

At our Halloween party we put all our funny-face vegetables in a row and lighted them with tiny blinking Christmas tree lights.

We also bobbed for apples in a giant, hollowed-out pumpkin.

ROZ AULT and LIZ URANECK
Kids Are Natural Cooks

CHRISTMAS

Santa and His Helpers

You can give the Santa Claus legend as much or as little emphasis as you want—one of us thinks it should be a lot, to stimulate the imagination; the other, very little, to keep it in perspective. We do know, however, that if you deny the fancy of the elves completely, your child will not.

We remember a Six, reared with unbending realism, whose parents told the sitter to forget about reading "The Night Before Christmas" on Christmas Eve. "David," they announced, "has never believed in Santa Claus," and yet, the minute they left, David chortled and said his parents pretended every year that they bought all the presents but, of course, he knew better.

A child will believe in elves (and bunny rabbits and the tooth fairy) if he needs to believe and as long as it makes him happy to believe. No matter when a child accepts the truth, he always is wise enough to recognize the Santa story for what it is—another guise of your love.

The only bad effects seem to be caused by some department store ringers who misinterpret their job. Although your child will rationalize—without any help from you—that this man isn't the *real* Santa Claus, it's better to tell him beforehand that all the Santas he'll see in the stores and on the sidewalks will be only "helpers."

We've found the best helpers work in the swankiest stores, where they don't dare push or promise certain toys. The richer the customers, apparently, the softer the sell. To have this visit run even smoother, call the store first to check Santa's schedule and avoid a wait.

We almost guarantee that your child will be stricken with a chill of conscience late in the day on Christmas Eve, even though you've never mentioned charcoal and switches. Suddenly he wonders if he and Santa Claus really have the same standards for goodness after all. We find it helps to tell a child he's wonderful—about fourteen times—and then let him prepare the cookies and sugar cubes for Santa Claus and the reindeer. A little giving can assuage a lot of last-minute doubts.

MARGUERITE KELLY and ELIA PARSONS
The Mother's Almanac

In-Jokes at Christmastime: The Ritual of the Rubber Snake

Since we were tiny children, my brother Jonathan and I have shared an elaborate Christmas gift ritual involving a rubber snake. The basic idea is for the donor to wrap the snake in such a way that the recipient opens it without suspicion. Over the years this has been accomplished in a bewildering variety of ways: disguising it in a package shaped like a hockey stick; passing it off (with a carefully forged greeting card) as a gift from a seldom-seen distant relative; presenting it as a wrapped table favor at somebody else's dinner party.

Once the package has been opened and the snake discovered, the second part of the rite begins: the donor tries to recapture the snake so he can again be the prankster, rather than the chump, the following Christmas. (Once there was even an attempt to steal the snake, rewrap it, and present it again on the same Christmas—an inspired effort, which, unfortunately, proved unsuccessful.)

The Ritual of the Rubber Snake and other in-joke "traditions" have brought a lot of extra humor—and suspense—into our family's annual holiday celebrations. If your kids develop some of their own, you'll see what I mean. CBC

Christmas and the Single Parent: "To Hell with Tradition!"

As far as Christmas is concerned, I'm sorry I gave my son a sense of tradition because we are locked into it now. Our life has changed a lot since our earlier Christmases, but my son, longing for the old days, pushes us into trying for what we really can't recapture. I say to hell with tradition. Let him grow up and say to his wife and kids that he wants to have the kind of Christmas he never had as a kid.

JANE O'REILLY

A Christmas Notebook: Better Than Photographs

The protagonist in Richard Stern's novel *Other Men's Daughters* kept a notebook of his children's sayings. Every Christmas, for twenty years, he'd read from the notebook. "For this, the children sat around his leather chair. He and Sarah drank coffee, the others orange juice. The children knew the stories, but loved this annual reminder of their old innocence and wit . . . 'Like snapshots. They just remind you of different times.' "

ELS

Today's a Holiday
(And These Books Will Tell You
Which One It Is)

You say it's June 26 and you and your family feel like celebrating something? But what to celebrate?

Never fear. Just pick up a copy of *Every Day's a Holiday,* by Ruth Hutchison and Ruth Adams (Harper & Row, 1951, 304 pages), flip through the daily entries to June 26, and you'll see that that's the date of the yearly Feast of the Shepherds in Aragon, Spain. "Hurray!" you'll shout, and you'll rush out to buy mutton for dinner while the kids practice up singing *jota coblas* and prancing through the traditional stick dance.

Or could it be you're not ready to join in this particular Aragonian revel? "The description is interesting," you say, "but a bit dry"—a criticism, incidentally, which might apply to the entire Hutchison and Adams book. Well, then, perhaps *Chases' Calendar of Annual Events,*

published each year by William and Helen Chases' Apple Tree Press (Box 1012, Flint, Mich. 48501), will provide information more to your liking. Indeed, a glimpse at the June 26 entry reveals that it's National Fink Day, when people with the name of Fink from all over the nation converge on the tiny hamlet of Fink, Texas, for a day of merry-making. *Chases' Calendar* is filled with such vital information (including the dates for International Pickle Week, Foodservice Distributor Salesmen's Day, and the Annual Mermaid Reunion at Weeki Wachee Spring, Florida). No one, in my opinion, should be without a copy.

(Incidentally, if your name is Fink and you're interested in the Fink Day festival mentioned above, you should contact John Clift of the Denison *Herald,* Denison, Texas 75020.)

CBC

BIRTHDAY PARTIES AND OTHER DIVERSIONS

Dear Uncle Herbert,
Im sorry I didnt thank you for My Christmas present and it would serve me right if you forgot about my Birthday next Thursday.
Love
Jonathan

JONATHAN CERF
Age seven
Letter to his Uncle Herbert, 1953

Rather than trying to squeeze a dozen kids around a too-high table, my friend set up for her daughter's party on the floor. With a large paper tablecloth and place settings all around it, the party was contained in a small space with nothing—and no one—falling on the floor. ELS

How to Give a Birthday Party
When You Don't Want Fifteen
Kids in Your House or Even Five
in Your Backyard

1. Plan a ballgame (of the child's choice) at the park with a picnic lunch or dinner.
2. Throw a beach party—any season—with castle building, shell and rock hunting, and cake.
3. Set up a scavenger hunt.
4. Hike to a lake, or wherever your kid wants.
5. Take a trip to an orchard or factory.
6. Rent a truck and go someplace a little out of the way for a picnic.
7. Old favorites: a day at a bowling alley, movie, skating rink, or local theater.

CAROL EICHLER

◆

Cousin Leslie's friend reports that she has one rule: only as many guests as the year for a birthday party—three children for the third birthday, four for the fourth, etc.

ELS

Two Party Ideas for the Very Young

An Artistic Party. Provide various collage materials, play doughs made from flour (or oatmeal or sawdust), easels with paint, various mediums for finger painting. All activity should take place outside, or in a basement with supervision.

SUSAN HOUGEN

A Musical Party. Let the kids form a rhythm band to entertain the grown-ups. For small gatherings, invite a friend who plays an instrument (guitar, harmonica, cello—it doesn't matter what) to entertain. Most kids will appreciate the special intimacy of this.

ANNETTE B. FIDLER

◆

Parties For the Six-and-over Set: Some Ideas That Worked

THE MINI-CIRCUS AND THE QUIETEST PARTY POSSIBLE

Here's a party my kids really loved. Dad was made up like a clown, and the kids tried to hit his face (poked through a sheet) with a stuffed sock. We also had "Shoot Out the Candles with a Water Pistol," pitching pennies, and fishing with paper clips and magnetic clips.

ANNETTE B. FIDLER

Or: Make up all the kids as clowns—all you need is white pancake makeup, rouge, and an eyebrow pencil. And some hats. Remind the kids that clowns don't talk, they pantomime everything—this may make for the quietest party possible. Take a photograph of each kid made up and give it as a party favor.

◆

JUNE IN JANUARY, THE COUNTY FAIR, AND THE TRADING POST

I had a winter child and a summer child and gave a lot of seasonal parties, but two favorites were those in contrast to the time of the year.

For example, hot dogs and hamburgers, eaten on blankets on the floor, with open umbrellas for "shade" and crepe-paper-decorated pails and shovels, brought squeals of delight from the kids who attended my son Brian's fifth birthday party on a freezing February day. Ice cream was served in cones, and the cake was decorated with a sailboat.

Similarly, on a scorching day in September, the party guests, having received paper-snowman invitations, arrived at a "Frosty Frolic" for my daughter Amanda's sixth birthday party. We'd dragged out our sled and decorated it. The cake was a whipped cream snowman with chocolate bits for eyes, nose, and mouth and gumdrops skewered by straws for arms.

◆

Probably the most popular party my kids ever had was the "County Fair." Invitations were printed on balloons, which said, "Skip lunch and come to a county fair for Amanda Gari's birthday."

The night before the party, we turned everything around (bookshelves, desk, vanity, etc.) in my daughter's room to make counter space, adding two card tables and the ironing board! We covered everything with old sheets and attached signs reading HOT DOGS AND HAMBURGERS—25¢; CANDY—5¢ a scoop; RING TOSS—10¢ a throw; PHOTOS—25¢; SODA—10¢; POTATO CHIPS—5¢ a bag; ICE CREAM CONES—15¢; BIRTHDAY CAKE—free with any order.

As each child entered, he or she was given a packet of play money and set loose at the fair. I cooked the hot dogs and hamburgers at the "booth" on my electric griddle; my husband took Polaroids at the photo stand. The kids took it very seriously, and a couple of them nearly panicked when they ran out of play money. Of course, we promptly refilled their packets and sent them joyously on their way again.

It was hectic, but fun. If you have friends or relatives who would like to help out running the stands, grab them. There is no time or need for games, but have plenty of little prizes for the ring toss (or "Knock Down the Bottles with the Rubber Ball," etc.).

> Each birthday we try to teach the children something about themselves—their birthplace, their parents' and grandparents' birthplaces, what our name means. Sometimes we go through the baby book.
>
> MRS. DAVID ASHTON

We gave our kids a "Trading Post" party when Amanda reached her twelfth birthday; I borrowed the idea from my sister, who used to give a party like it—for adults—every summer. Guests are invited to lunch or dinner and instructed to bring along as many items as they want—in excellent condition only—to trade with the other guests. What might be a pain-in-the-neck pair of ice skates for one kid may delight one who has an unwanted tennis racket.

Or if the ice-skates kid wants the tennis racket but the tennis-racket kid doesn't want the ice skates, perhaps the ice skates can be traded for a third person's transistor radio, which the tennis-racket kid *does* want, etc.

Anyway, all you provide is the food and the space. It works terrifically in the backyard, but it's just as possible in an apartment. Guests come prepared to set up little booths (you provide old sheets and thumbtacks), and food is served either before or after trading. Everyone must be warned that anything left behind becomes your property (or that of your favorite charity). No games are necessary; the bargaining takes up the entire party.

JANET GARI

THE SPONTANEOUS PARTY

Mary McGrory once lamented in her syndicated column that Christmas belongs to the competent, "to those who can remember zip codes and shirt sizes, buy everything by Labor Day, mail it in October, deck the halls, trim the tree, make gingerbread houses, assemble 10-speed bikes, invite the entire clan over for Christmas dinner and go out caroling when they are not off to the Kennedy Center for Christmas concerts or 'The Nutcracker Suite,' for which they have booked well in advance." If it is true, as Ms. McGrory writes, that often "mechanics get in the way of sentiment" at Christmastime (and I think it is true), then it is also true that this happens with many other holidays—including one's own child's birthday.

Being one of the incompetent, to whom holidays do not belong—I can never seem to get the Christmas presents together by New Year's (I now try to get out of town so's not to have to face the embarrassment of friends dropping off gifts for us while I'm not sure I've even mailed the thank-you-for-the-baby-gift note)—I have figured out a few shortcuts to getting celebrations taken care of in a last-minute fashion. Here's one.

The Spontaneous Birthday Party (or Christmas Party or Halloween or Any Other Occasion Party) is based on two premises. The first is that kids will believe nearly anything; that is, if you tell them that this is a birthday party, then it is a birthday party—never mind that other kids' mothers have the temperament to blow up

thirty-five balloons. The second premise is that it does not matter if your kid does not have the best party on the block. If you can accept all that, you can have a spontaneous party for your kid with no trouble at all. We did it as follows:

We started by calling eight kids and telling them it was Nick's birthday (which it was) and could they come right over to celebrate with us. No presents, please, we said, unless it's something of your own that you want to give away and that still works (it wasn't easy to get Nick to agree to that, I must admit, but he finally gave in and I told him I'd give him a good present). Really, you cannot give people twenty minutes' notice of a party and expect them to run out and buy a gift on the way over. (And I generally don't welcome more of an accumulation of worldly possessions.)

So far so good: only five kids could make it. What I wanted to do for our first activity, and didn't—but I'll pass the idea on to you anyway, in case you can pull it off—was go with the whole gang to the supermarket. I thought I'd give the kids a chance to choose their own party food, with an allotment of something like fifty cents for anything sweet or junky, a dollar for anything with some food value (they could pool their money if they wanted to and, say, two kids pick out a half-gallon of ice cream). What I actually did was run out to the store myself and buy up a lot of junk and a cake and candles and race home with it all before the guests arrived. I also ended up buying a few small favors—bubbles (which accounted for another activity) and a little toy for each.

Next, on a huge piece of brown paper I drew a barely recognizable outline of an animal I called a donkey-moose. I put it on the table with a box of crayons and markers and asked the kids to cheer up the poor ol' animal, then gave them each smaller pieces of paper on which they were to design a suitable tail for the beast. They loved it (for some reason), and when they were through, a piece of tape on the end of each tail set them up for a game of pin-the-tail-on-the-donkey-moose. And a splendid beast it was—all polka dots and stripes and flowered ears.

We went on this way: an improvised game of waste-basketball, the bubble-blowing, a storytelling, cousin Marc's magic show, a round of lotto. Nobody "won" any games—there were no prizes—but there was lots of cheering and yelling going on and it was a very nice party that filled, I am proud to say, nearly three hours.

ELS

A TREASURE HUNT, CITY STYLE

It's a challenge to entertain children who have passed the pin-the-tail-on-the-donkey stage but haven't quite reached the I'd-rather-do-it-*my-self*-Mother stage. (And that's about the thirteenth birthday.)

For my daughter's party on that occasion, I decided to tap all that pre-adolescent energy and send it on a wild goose chase. I called the party a treasure hunt, but there was no pot of gold at the end of the rainbow, only reunion and refreshments and prizes for the winning team (favors for all, of course). The hunt itself was simply for one clue after another, and the team object was to find all the clues and complete the course first. If you decide to try such a party, your invitations should mention the hunt and suggest clothing appropriate to the activity and *weather*. Your preparations must be thorough if the hunt is to go smoothly once the party begins.

And here's the fun part: be diabolical in the diversity of your clues and the ways in which they are found—within limits, of course. (Our limit was about a fifteen-block radius of our home.) The greater the obstacles, the more excited the participants get about overcoming them. A warning though: make the clues challenging, but not impossible.

Muster your ingenuity and think of unique ways for clues to be found. My groups enjoyed scampering about Central Park from one statue to another, but they were enchanted at finding an envelope with a claim check in it for the hat-check counter in the Metropolitan Museum, and dazzled by an envelope containing a notice from the post office that a clue was waiting there—registered!

For my New York City treasure hunt, I decided to make the clues "puzzling."

For the clue to the Mother Goose statue in Central Park:

> "Old Mother Goose, when she wanted to wander,
> Would ride through the air on a very fine gander."
> . . . in Central Park!

To the neighborhood dry cleaners called "Miss Penny":

> A PENNY for your thoughts!
> Find a CLEANER clue at 88th and Lex.
> Ask Sam.

And to the post office:

> "Neither snow, nor rain, nor heat, nor gloom of night stays these couriers from the swift completion of their appointed rounds."
> Or keeps you from your clue at the *Gracie Station* Post Office, Registered Mail window, in the name of your *team captain*. . .

Leading to Alexander Hamilton's statue in Central Park:

> Visit my statue, if you will!
> My picture's on a ten-dollar bill.
> I was Secretary of the Treasury,
> So hurry up! Find a clue on me!

And so forth.

Before the party, plot the course of each team (I had three teams of four girls) so that the "reds," the "blues," and the "purples" all cover about the same distance and have the same stops to make, but *not in the same order*. I actually drew a map of the neighborhood, and with red, blue, and purple crayons traced the routes and numbered the stops.

When you distribute the clues shortly before the party (take lots of masking tape!), you'll leave three envelopes (marked "red," "blue," and "purple") at each stop. (The players should be warned that it is *cheating* to cop another team's envelope.)

Now twelve barely-teen-agers are gathered around you (having been divided into teams by drawing colored slips of paper from a basket) and are breathlessly awaiting instructions. Tell them the boundaries of the area covered, and read the guidelines:

1. Here is your first clue. When you read it and solve the riddle, it will lead you to a spot where you will find your next clue—and so on until you find the last clue, which tells you to race back here!

2. Here are three dimes for each team captain, and our phone number. Use them if you want to. The idea of this game is to have fun, and if you get lost, or stumped, or you find a spot and the clue is gone, call and we'll tell you where to go next. (*Note:* This is where the map comes in.)

3. It is *not* cheating to use your ingenuity in trying to finish first. Call anyone, ask anyone. But use common sense. You're old enough not to do anything stupid—like getting into a car with a stranger.

4. Even though you're in a race, follow all normal safety rules.

5. Be back by five o'clock, whether or not you've found all the clues.

6. Team captains, be sure you take your identification. (*Note:* See post office clue. If you use this idea, team captains must be predetermined and asked to bring identification in order to claim the registered letter.)

7. GO!

Fix yourself a drink, heat the spaghetti sauce, and make the cocoa. You've provided for all possible hitches—except acts of God or intervention of man. On the day of our daughter's party, we had to cope with both.

Five hours before the party that February day, the snow began to fall. By the time the girls arrived from school, there was a half-foot of snow on the ground and it was still coming down heavily. The snow hid and soddened most of the clues—but, fortunately, not the enthusiasm of the players.

As my husband was walking to the office, having taped all the statue clues in the park, he saw three workmen coming toward him carrying the dismantled bronze bodies of Mother Goose and her mount! Hanging from the goose by a strip of masking tape were two little envelopes. New Yorkers stared at the man running after three Central Park attendants carrying a statue, and shouting, "Come back with my clues!"

So you may well ask, was it worth it? Did the thirteen-year-olds appreciate all that effort? Did they ever come back? All I can tell you is that the four girls who burst into the apartment at 4:30 shouted "Are we first? Did we win?" And when I said yes, they jumped up and down screaming, hugged each other, and then hugged me and covered me with snowy kisses.

Even the losers admitted it had been a wor-

thy adventure, and they all compared trials and tribulations and funny incidents of the hunt over cocoa and, later, a spaghetti dinner.

ANNA JANE HAYS

The Half Birthday Party

Everyone gets half an invitation and receives half a cupcake and half a glass of soda, they have to sit on half a chair, wear half a hat, sing half of the Happy Birthday song, give half of a present. Best of all, parents: IT LASTS FOR HALF AN HOUR.

MAURICE SAGOFF

PARTY FAVORS

Most Supermoms have done away with party favors. "Unless you spend a dollar on each child, you're sending him home with more broken plastic junk to clutter the house," one mother said. It's better to spend the money on the party itself. With the extra cash you might take the kids to a children's theater performance or to a fancy ice cream parlor that specializes in birthday parties, and let the pleasant memory be their favor.

PRUDENCE MACKINTOSCH
Texas Monthly

Party games never seemed like real games (which were games without adults). They were obligations like going to church.

GRAHAM GREENE

PARTY GAMES

Two Party Games for People Who Hate Party Games

Like Graham Greene, I had (and have) an inherent aversion to organized party games. But I do recall that as a child there were two games that I found, if not wildly enjoyable, at least passably good fun. Here, in my mother's very own words, are the rules:

CBC

WHO AM I?

(For 6 or more people)

This is a particularly good game for a party at which the guests do not know each other very well. It will make them mix and begin to con-

verse with all the guests. Before the guests arrive the hostess must prepare slips of paper with famous names written on them—a different name for each guest. When the game begins, the hostess pins one of these famous names on the back of each of her guests. It is then each one's job to discover who he is by asking questions which may be answered only by "yes" or "no." As each guest may read everyone's famous name except his own, it is up to each one to ask one question about himself and then answer one for his informant. Thus it continues, with each guest roaming from person to person, asking a question and answering one until he has established his identity. There is always one person who has difficulty finding out who he is—and it usually ends with the whole group answering his questions to finish the game.

CAMOUFLAGE THE OBJECT

(For 4 or more people)

Five or more objects are chosen to be hidden, and shown to all players. Objects might be:

Wedding Ring	Rubber Band
Postage Stamp	Match
Thimble	Penny
Lump of Sugar	Key
Hairpin	Earring
Paper Clip	Button

After the rest of the players have left the room, one person hides the objects. No object may be covered. It must be placed so that it is in plain view and yet deceives the searcher. The paper clip, for instance, may be concealed in a glass of water, but must not be hidden in a closed cigarette box. Each player receives a list of the hidden objects, and starts his search. The players may look wherever they like, but nothing in the room may be moved or touched. When a player finds an object, he should move away from it (so he will not give the other players any clues) and then jot down on his list where he has seen the hidden object. The winner is the player who finds all of the objects first.

The trick in hiding the objects is simple. Place each object on a spot that more or less matches its own color. The penny on copper or brass, the thimble on top of a lamp covering the finial, and a postage stamp glued onto a liquor bottle over the revenue stamp.

Fifty-three Ways to Show Off at Parties

"We might as well admit it," write Tom Ferrell and Lee Eisenberg in the introduction to their book *Sneaky Feats: A Connoisseur's Guide to Casual One-Upmanship* (Pocket Books, 1976, 192 pages, $1.50); "it's a lot easier to roll a coin across your knuckles than to actually *think* of something terrific to *say*." Having stated this premise, the authors proceed to dazzle us with the instructions to fifty-three (count 'em) show-offy parlor tricks, including "Slicing a Banana Without Peeling It," "Making the World's Greatest Cat's Cradle," how to "Decapitate Yourself (and Live to Tell About It)" and the two useful stunts below.

Not only will *Sneaky Feats* provide your kid with the ammunition to "astound his friends and show up his rivals"; more important, it will enable *you* to amaze your children and their cynical (but naïve) acquaintances.　　　CBC

HOW TO LASSO AN ICE CUBE

This little number combines the show-off properties of ice cubes with the show-off properties of string—both articles easy to find, but not usually found in the same place at the same time, except in old-fashioned general stores with soda fountains. In order to score prestige points by lassoing an ice cube, it's usually necessary to carry the string with you. . . . The string should be the cotton kind, fibrous and easy to soak with water—positively not the newfangled nylon or synthetic sort that hardly gets wet at all.

So, here's what you do. You tie a one-or-two-inch loop in the end of the piece of string . . . and ask for a glass of ice water. The ice has to be in cubes, of course. Then you ask your nearest neighbor if he thinks he can remove the ice cube from the water by using the loop of string. He is not allowed to touch the glass with his fingers, or indeed to move the glass in any way. If you've picked a sensible victim, his most probable response will be: "No, I can't, and you can't either." Your only way out of this dilemma is to insist in a firm voice that you can so. Try to sound positive. Make him believe it. Then let him try.

After he's tried and failed long enough, then you step in. Your secret, of course, is that you cheat. You simply lower the loop onto the exposed top surface of the floating ice cube, so it just lies there on top of the cube. Try to get it to lie as flat as you can. Then, take a pinch of salt and sprinkle it on top of the ice cube, string and all. Wait a few seconds. The action of the salt on the ice cube will freeze the string solid to the cube. Then all you have to do is pick it up. Astounding! Of course, you probably won't want to drink the water after this. If your victim objects that you didn't say you were going to use salt in this trick, the best answer is that you didn't say you weren't.

HOW TO PUSH A PENCIL WITH YOUR MIND

A strong mind can do just about anything, though it can't move a mountain. It can, however, move a pencil across a table, and that's a fact. With the help of our brilliant assistant shown here, we will teach you how to move a pencil across a surface, without ever touching it.

In figure 1, our assistant holds up an ordinary pencil. For purposes that will remain a secret, make sure you use a round pencil, not one with edges.

In figure 2, our assistant begins summoning his strong mind to action. This is achieved by shaking the hands and arms. This action activates the very complicated "force-fields" that will ultimately move the pencil.

In figure 3, our assistant begins to circle the pencil with his finger. This action defines the "force-field" further and serves to focus all mental attention on the object. Make slow circles at first; then make a number of frenzied circles while increasing your mental concentration.

In figure 4, our assistant is shown making the pencil roll away from him. He is not, as you can see, touching the pencil with his hands. No, the pencil is miraculously following the man's finger, no strings attached. Well, one sort of string: our assistant is gently blowing air on the table's surface behind the pencil. He does this quietly and without notice.

The wild hand movements, you see, have distracted the audience's attention. So it looks as though nothing whatsoever is making the pencil move—nothing except the summoning of mental powers and a lot of ridiculous arm waving and finger circles. Practice by yourself— then go find someone to astound.

TOM FERRELL and LEE EISENBERG
Sneaky Feats

◆

[Tom Ferrell and Lee Eisenberg have dedicated their book to their mothers. "It's not their fault," they explain. —CBC]

CONTRIBUTORS

Accorsi, William
Adair, Jim
Adler, Brooke
Adler, Dick
Adler, Renata
Agel, Jerome
Agel, Jesse
Agel, Julie
Ahl, David H.
Albaum, Judy
Almond, David
Almond, Peter
Almond, Richard
Alonso, Marc
Alth, Max
Arlen, Michael J.
Ashton, Mrs. David
Ashton-Warner, Sylvia
Ault, Roz

Bach, Alice
Bain, Karren
Bakal, Steve
Baldwin, James
Baliotti, Dan
Barkman, Donna
Bauer, Caroline Feller
Baum, Steven
Bean, Carolyn
Bean, Orson
Beard, James
Beaver, Paul
Becker, Jonathan
Bennett, Hal
Berenson, Andy
Bernstein, Joanne
Bing, Elisabeth
Bingham, Joan
Blake, Jim
Block, Chip
Blumenthal, Adam
Boe, Eugene
Bookstein, Lynne
Borchardt, Anne
Boston Women's Health
    Book Collective
Botterill, Cal
Bova, Ben
Brazleton, Berry
Brent, Stuart
Brétécher, Claire
Brody, Warren
Brotman, Jordan
Brown, Marie
Buckley, Mary Ann
Buskin, Martin
Butler, Jo
Butler, Samuel

Cahill, Kathryn
Caine, Lynne
Caney, Steven
Caplan, Aaron
Caplan, Josephine Franklin
Caplan, Leah
Caplan, Ralph
Capon, Robert Farrar
Carden, Jennifer

Cardozo, Peter
Carmichael, Carrie
Carmichael, Luci Ann
Carroll, Lewis
Casriel, Daniel
Cavett, Dick
Cerf, Christopher
Cerf, Geneviève
Cerf, Jonathan
Chall, Jeanne
Clapp, Lewis C.
Cleaver, Diane
Cleaver, Lynne
Coles, Robert
Collier, Gilman
Cooke, Tom
Cooney, Joan Ganz
Cope, George
Corwin, Becky
Cott, Allan
Cott, Jonathan
Craven, Jacqueline
Curtin, Sharon

Davidson, Ben
Day, Robert
DeForest, Lee
DeKoven, Bernie
DeLuise, Dom
DeMott, Benjamin
Dennison, George
Derbas, Frank
Dewey, John
Dienstag, Eleanor
D'Incamps, Béatrice La
    Motte
Dintenfass, Ann
Dodd, Bruce
Dodson, Fitzhugh
Drexler, Sherman
Drymalski, Paul
Duhrssen, Alfred
Dunn, Jeanne
Dykstra, Gretchen

Eby, Laura
Eckhardt, Linda West
Egoff, Sheila
Ehrenfeld, Elizabeth
Eichler, Carol
Eichler, Dennis
Eichler, Todd
Eisenberg, Lee
Elin, William H.
Ellison, Gail
Entner, Bobbie
Epstein, Danny
Erikson, George
Ernst, Barbara
Ewald, Elin

Fellini, Federico
Feiffer, Jules
Feldgus, Karen
Ferguson, Andy
Ferrell, Tom
Ferretti, Fred

Fidler, Annette B.
Field, Roger
Fink, Ann
Flaste, Richard
Fisher, M.F.K.
Fluegelman, Andrew
Foner, Naomi
Ford, Ford Madox
Fox, Annie and David
Fraiberg, Selma
Francke, Linda Bird
Fraser, Phyllis
Freedman, Karen
Friedberg, Mark
Frith, Michael
Fuller, R. Buckminster

Gardiner, Anne
Gardner, Laurie
Gardner, Martin
Gari, Amanda
Gari, Janet
Gerson, Mark
Giovanni, Nikki
Gjersvik, Maryanne
Glatzer, Paula
Gold, Ivan
Goldberg, Lazer
Goldman, Ilene
Goldstein, William A.
Good, Jay
Gordon, Neal J.
Graham, Judy
Grant, Mrs. Paul
Graves, Sherryl Brown
Gray, Francine du Plessix
Green, Jean
Greene, Graham
Greenwald, Henry
Griffin, John Howard
Gruen, Paul J.
Gross, David
Gross, Leonard
Guinzburg, Rusty Unger
Gussow, Adam
Gussow, Joan

Hamilton, Virginia
Hansen, Janet
Harkleroad, Carolyn
Harris, Arthur S., Jr.
Harris, Leslie
Harris, Matt
Harris, Richard
Harrison, Lanny
Hart, Moss
Hausman, Nancy
Haviland, Virginia
Hayes, Jane
Hays, Anna Jane
Heiss, Arlene
Heller, Joseph
Helsman, Jerry
Henson, Jane
Hentoff, Margot
Hentoff, Nat
Herndon, James
Heylman, Katherine M.

Heyman, Abigail
Hoffman, Anne
Hoffman, Dustin
Hollander, Lorin
Holt, John
Hopkins, Douglas
Hougen, Susan
Howard, Jane
Huckaby, Gloria
Hutchings, Richard
Hutman, Sheila

Iglesia, Maria Elena de la

Jacobs, Adam
Jacobs, Estelle
Jacobs, Harvey
Jacobson, Linda
Jacobson, Michael
Jerrold, Walter
Johnson, Jean
Jones, Leslie
Jones, Louise
Jong, Erica
Joseph, Barbara
Joseph, Stephen M.
Jung, Carl

Kafka, Franz
Kanor, Susan
Karlen, Betty Madison
Kaye, Marvin
Kaye, Shirley
Kelly, Marguerite
Kennedy, Rose
Kessler, Shelley
Kierr-Bain, Susan
Kingsley, Emily Perl
Kirkman, Ed
Kirsch, Carol Goldberg
Kirsch, Howard
Klee, Sarah
Kliman, Gilbert
Klotz, Joy
Koch, Kenneth
Kohl, Herbert
Koren, Edward
Korr, David
Kovacs, Debbie
Kranepool, Ed
Krassner, Paul
Kubrick, Stanley
Kuralt, Charles

Lacombe, Brigitte
Lakein, Alan
Lanes, Selma G.
Langendoen, Sally
Langendoen, Terry
Lansing, Sydney
Lansky, Vicki
Lappé, Frances Moore
Laterman, Frances
Lawrence, Susan
Layborne, Kit

Lear, Edward
LeBaron, H.
Lee, Stan
Leifer, Aimee Dorr
Leitman, Allan
Lenzner, Allan
Lerner, Sharon
LeShan, Eda J.
Lesser, Gerald S.
Levine, James A.
Lewis, C.S.
Liebling, A.J.
Lilien, Leslie
Lingeman, Richard
Lipsyte, Marjorie
Lipsyte, Robert
Lloyd, Janice
Lobel, Arnold
Locke, Richard
Loeb, Roger
Lohman, Dorothy
Lord, Gay
Lord, Timmie and Charles
Lorenz, Konrad

Mackintosh, Prudence
Malone, Bobbie
Martin, Judith
Marzollo, Claudio
Marzollo, Jean
May, Cindy
Mayer, Martin
Maynard, Fredelle
Maynard, Joyce
McGarvey, Jack
McGuire, Thomas
McLaughlin, Frank
McLuhan, Marshall
Mead, Margaret
Merling, Nancy
Messenger, Kathy
Meyer, Joe Mickiel
Meyers, Stephen
Miles, Dick
Miller, Keith
Mills, Elizabeth
Mitnick, Karen
Moffat, Samuel
Montagu, Ashley
Morath, Inge
Morrison, Philip
Morrison, Phylis
Mortimer, Penelope

Navasky, Anne
Neill, A.S.
Nies, Anna May
Noble, John

O'Dwyer, Geraldine
Ogden, Rita
Olderman, Stephen
Olshaker, Bennett
Olson, A.
O'Neal, Cynthia
O'Neal, Patrick
Opie, Iona and Peter
Oppenheimer, Joel
O'Reilly, Jane
Orlick, Terry
Orwell, George

Padgett, Ron
Palmer, Bruce
Parents of Suzuki students
Parsons, Elia
Passell, Peter
Peck, Ellen
Pelmas, Ruth
Pène du Bois, William
Picasso, Pablo
Plato
Plimpton, Freddy
Pogrebin, Letty Cottin
Popper, Barbara
Postman, Neil
Postol, Flip
Potenza, Bart
Potenza, Flavia
Potter, David
Preiss, Byron
Preston, H. LeBaron
Preston, Rebecca
Proust, Marcel
Pulitzer, Carol

Radens, Betty
Rentschler, William H.
Reuben, David
Rey, H.A.
Rinzler, Carol Eisen
Rinzler, Michael
Robbins, Ken
Robbins, Maria
Roberts, Rona
Rogers, Gary
Rogers, Jennifer
Roiphe, Ann
Ross, Leonard
Rossman, Michael
Russell, Franklin
Russell, Susan

Sachs, Sheila
Sagan, Carl
Sagoff, Charlotte

Sagoff, Maurice
Saint-Exupéry, Antoine de
Salk, Lee
Salzmann, Karin
Samelson, Andra
Samelson, Judy
Sanborn, William B.
Saperstein, Alan
Sarson, Christopher
Saxon, Charles
Schaap, Dick
Scharlatt, Elisabeth
Scharlatt, Nicholas
Schickel, Jill
Schroeder, Patricia
Scott, Gini
Sears, Scott
Sendak, Maurice
Seuss, Dr. (Theodor Seuss
    Geisel)
Shalit, Gene
Shamberg, Michael
Shannon, William V.
Shapiro, Bob
Shapiro, Jackie
Shapiro, Jane
Sharkey, Tony
Shaw, Emily
Shedlin, Allan, Jr.
Sheehy, Gail
Sheraton, Mimi
Shimkin, Arthur
Shore, Mary Ann
Shushan, Ronnie
Silverman, Beverly
Silverman, Jim
Singer, Burt
Skelsey, Alice
Slater, Philip
Smart-Grosvenor,
    Vertamae
Smith, Marianne
Smith, Marjorie
Sontheimer, Stephen
Spaeth, Warren
Spaulding, Amy
Spock, Benjamin
Staller, Jerry
Stein, Cynthia
Steinberg, Dr. Burton
Steinbrenner, George
Stevens, Wallace
Stewart, Jayme
Stone, Jon
Strachan, Bill
Strachan, Pat Harding
Sugarman, Linda
Sutton-Smith, Brian and
    Shirley
Szasz, Thomas

Tamillia, Patrick
Tembeck, Shoshana
Thomas, Dylan
Thorn, Judy
Tiedemann, Jody
Tolkien, J.R.R.
Tolstoy, Leo
Traband, Jessie Bazeghin
Trillin, Alice
Trillin, Calvin
Trivas, Irene
Turner, Jim
Turner, Mary Dustan
Twain, Mark (Samuel
    Clemens)

Unger, Rusty
Uraneck, Liz

Van Buren, Abigail (Dear
    Abby)
Vander Wal, Mary-Claire
Vincent, Jo
Viorst, Judith
Vivian, Virginia M.
Von Hoffman, Nicholas

Wagner, Jeanine
Wagner, Phyllis Cerf
Ward, Elie
Warner, Naomi
Warren, Earl
Weber, Alan J.
Wechsler, Susan
Weingartner, Charles
Werner, Liza
Whaley, Bill
White, E.B.
Wiedrich, Bob
Wigginton, Eliot
Wilbur, Robert
Wilder, Laura Ingalls
Williams, Margery
Wirtschafter, Jenny
Wirtschafter, Zelda
Wiseman, Ann
Wolcott, James
Woods, George
Wray, Victor

Yolen, Jane
York, Jo Ann
Young, Edith

Zubrowski, Bernard

INDEX

Anderson, Yvonne, 343
And Then What Happened, Paul Revere? (Fritz and Tomes), 263
And to Think That I Saw It on Mulberry Street (Seuss), 263
Anger, related to fear, 66–67
    see also Fears and worries
Anglund, Joan Walsh, 462
Animal comics, 290
Animal Farm (Orwell), 267
Animal Park, San Diego, 355
Animals
    books about, 220, 221, 223, 227, 231–32
    emotions about, 228–30
    renting, 224
    World Pet Expo (animal road show), 224–25
    see also Animal Watching; Pets
Animal watching
    birds, 226
    butterflies, 227–28
    pond for, 226–27
Animal World (TV show), 319
Annotated Alice, The (Gardner), 262, 433
Annotated Snark, The (Gardner), 433
Annual Directory of Facilities for the Learning Disabled, 92
Anspach, Ralph, 419
Anthony, E. James, 19
Anthropological Museum, Mexico City, 355
Anti-Gravico (magic trick), 436
Anti-Monopoly (game), 419
Anything Muppet puppets, 469
Aperture Monography (Helsmann), quoted, 342
Appendectomy, children's books about, 40, 41
Apple a Day, An (Barrett and Lewis), 264
Appledorf, Howard, 151
Apron, unisex, 186
Aquarium, divided, 222
Archie (TV show), 321
Architecture, books about, 351
Architecture: A Book of Projects for Young Adults (Wilson), 351
Architecture Without Architects (Rudofsky), 351
Arens, Ruth, 315
Arizona Highways, 287
Arizona Sonora Desert Museum, 355
Arlen, Michael J., 324
    on television, 309
Arms, Suzanne and John, 60
Armstrong, William H., 258, 272–73
Army-Navy stores, 182
Arnold, Arnold, 428
Arrow Book Club, 287
Art, children's, 340, 341
    adult attitudes toward, 339–40
    audiences for, 344
    of blind children, 89
    reproducing, 340–41
    see also Art supplies; Crafts
Art and Industry of Sandcastles, The (Adkins), 401
Artificial coloring, flavoring, 150
    see also Additives

Artista watercolors, 328
"Art of the Essay, The" (White), 240
Art of the Fugue, The (Bach), 294
Art postcards, 475
Arts and crafts, *see* Art, Children's; Crafts
Art specialists, in schools, 106
Art supplies, 444
    craft sets, 332
    color stickers, 332
    Cray-Pas, 328
    easel, 330
    felt-tip pens, 328
    for "lefties," 329
    hardware store for, 334
    papers, 329
    scrapbooks, 330
    storage for, 328, 329, 334
    warnings on safety, 332
    watercolors, 328
Aruego, Jose, 231
Asahi Co., bath toys of, 449
Asche, Frank, 268–69
Ashbery, John, 284
Ashton, Mrs. David
    on birthday parties, 486
    on open classroom, 106
    on television, 319
    on yarn drawings, 332
Ashton-Warner, Sylvia, 19, 96
    on education, schools, 101, 116
    "organic" reading methods of, 249–250
    on touching children, 27
Aspirin, 35
Association for Children with Learning Disabilities, 84
As the World Turns (TV show), 322
Astounding Science Fiction, 204
Astronomy, 214–15
    books, book lists, 214–15
    telescopes for, 216
Astronomy Magazine, guide to telescopes in, 216
Athletics
    body building, 383
    noncompetitive, 383
    see also Outdoor play; Sports
Audiotapes by children, audiences for, 344
Ault, Roz, on Halloween cutouts, 483
Aurora Co., 347
Autism, mild, 82–83
Autistic children, 82–83
    camp programs for (directory), 92
    resources for help with, 91
Autobiography of Miss Jane Pittman, The (TV program), 318, 321
Automobile trips, *see* Car trips
Avery Co., 332
Avocado, how to grow, 234

Babar books (Brunhoff), 273
Babbitt, Natalie, 78, 244
Babies
    birth, books on, 59–60
    first-year difficulties with, 30, 31
    and older children, 22–23
Baby Alive (doll), 462

Baby and Child Care (Spock), 19, 189, 190
Baby food, commercial, 147
Baby food, homemade
    books on, recipes, 147–48
Baby food jars, uses for, 148
Babysitters, 127–33
    agency as source for, 129
    babysitting pool, 130–31
    child's opinion considered, 130
    friends, relatives as, 129
    glamorizing, for child, 131
    grandparents as, 130
    how to fire, 131
    instructions for, 131, 132
    interviewing, 128, 129
    males as, 133
    needs of, 131
    older persons as, 128
    to siphon off hostility, 132–33
    as stabilizing influence, 133
    teenagers as, 128
Babysitting
    in babysitter's own home, 128
    pool, 130–31
    see also Babysitters; Day-care centers
Baby talk, 58
Baby Wet & Care (doll), 462
Bach, Alice
    book review by, 273
    on learning how to spend, 200
    on plants as gifts, 474
Bach, Johann Sebastian, 294
Backgammon, 423
Backyard Games (Lincoln and Fife), 427
Backyard play, 400–02
    see also Outdoor play
Backyard pond, how to make, 226–227
Bacon, bacon substitutes, 150
"Bad children," 67
Bad Island, The (Steig), 264
Bagels, as car trip food, 363
Baggies, aid to putting on galoshes, 190
Bain, Karren
    book review by, 69
    on pillows as beds, 170
Bakal, Steve, on his can-recycling job, 199
Baldwin, James, on keeping promises, 14
Ballet, trip to, 366–67
Balloons, bargains in, 445
Ball-playing, indoor, foam balls for, 176–77
Balls
    bargains in, 445, 446
    baseballs, 370–71
    basketballs, 371
    beach, 385
    bowling, 372
    foam, for indoor ballplaying, 176–177
    rubber, 372
    surprise string, 474
Bancroft Co., 379
Band-Aid "kisses" and other helpful ornamentation, 35

facing schoolmates, neighbors after
bereavement, 75
of father, 73–74
funeral, child's attendance at, 74–
75
of grandmother, 75
mourning, delayed, for deceased
parent, 75
mourning, for pets, 228, 229–30
of young adult, family's feelings
discussed, 71–73
De Brunhoff, Jean, 78
De Camp, Catherine C., 279
De Camp, L. Sprague, 279
Decorating child's rooms
aesthetic and practical
considerations, 168
with flags and blow-up toys, 177
with window display items,
177–78
see also Furniture, children's;
Posters and wall decorations
Dee Dee's Heart Test (Children's
Hospital of Philadelphia), 40
Deep Space (Silverberg, Ed.), 279
De Forest, Lee, on television, 308
De Koven, Bernie, 137, 469
on art materials, 328–29
book reviews by, 89, 383
on children's games, 408–09, 410,
411, 412, 415, 423–24, 426–27,
430
on "de-school primers," 110
on puzzles, 433
on video games, 323
De Koven, Chuck, 410
Delights and Prejudices (Beard),
quoted, 160
*Dell Paperbacks for Elementary
Schools*, 287
De Luise, Dom
as disciplinarian, 10
on right to be destructive, 26
De Mott, Benjamin, 5
on "tired mother syndrome," 31
Dennison, George, 19, 96
on collaboration vs. compulsion, 9
on competitive sports, 380
on meaningful learning, 122
on teaching methods, 120
on reading games, 252
Dental floss, 43
Denton, Mark, 391
Denver, John, 182
Denver Children's Museum, 355
De Paola, Tomie, 77
Deprivation of Maternal Care
(Ainsworth *et al.*), 19
De-Schooling Society (Illich), 98
Designing a Day Care Center . . .
(Evans, Saia, and Evans), 141
Destructiveness
child's right to, 26
creative, 351–52
Developmental Learning Materials
catalogue, 93
Dewey, John, on education, 95
Diabetes, resources for, 91
Dial-a-Story San Francisco Public
Library service, 288
Dickens, Monica, 391

Dictionaries for children, 254
good and bad, 280–281
Dictionary of Afro-American Slang
(Major), 254
Dictionary of American Slang
(Wentworth and Flexner), 254
*Dictionary of Slang and
Unconventional English*
(Partridge), 254
Dienstag, Eleanor, on Montessori
nursery schools, 106
Diet, for good teeth, 44
see also Food and nutrition
Diet for a Small Planet (Lappé), 152
Different Drummer Workshop, 453
Different Woman, A (Howard),
quoted, 25
Digit Box (puzzle), 445
Digits (electronic game), 420
Dillard, G.L., 260
D'Incamps, Beatrice La Motte, on
mutual failure to listen, 13
Dinosaur models, 347
Dintenfass, Ann, 137, 328, 329
Dippel, George, 346
Directories
of camps, recreational facilities for
disabled, 92–93
of educational facilities, 92
see also Catalogues, directories,
pamphlets
Directory for Exceptional Children, 92
Directory of the National Association
of Private Schools for Exceptional
Children, 92
Directory of Summer Camps for
Children with Learning
Disabilities, 92
Directory of U.S. Facilities and
Programs for Children with
Severe Mental Illnesses, 92
"Dirty words," 52, 57
in school, 113
Disabled, see Handicapped Children
Disagreement with parents, child's
right to, 27
Discipline, methods of, 412
avoiding concepts "good" and
"bad," 10
"being yourself," 6
books on, 6
"bribery" as habit-breaking method,
6
of child who hits, 10
collaboration vs. compulsion, 9
compromise method, 7
"Klobber Method," Moss Hart's, 11
"logical consequences" approach, 6
money and, 201
punishment, 10–12; see also
Punishment
and self-demand schedules, 9
setting limits for child, 6, 7, 8–9
spanking, 12
tantrums, handling, 5
Diseases, immunization against, 38
Disney, Walt, 267, 355
Disneyland Records, 300
Disney World, trip with children to,
360–62
Dittrich, Lisa, 108

Divorce
books (for children) on, 68–69
children's feelings on, 68
Doctor's office, amusement for
examining room, 37
Dr. Seuss's Sleep Book (Seuss), 244
Dodd, Bruce, on Doddhouse
(dollhouse), 466
Doddhouse (dollhouse), 466
Dodgeball, 411, 412
Dodson, Fitzhugh, on spanking, 12
Doghouse, building, 349
Dogs, 220–21, 225
hints on buying, 221
mourning for, 228
Dog-walking, as children's business
venture, 198
*Doing the Media: A Portfolio of
Activities and Resources*
(Laybourne and Ciancolo), 343
Do-it-yourself Beginner Books, 255
see also Homemade books
Do-it-yourself iron-ons, 333
Doll hospital, 463
Doll House Book, The (Helberg), 467
Dollhouses
books about, 467
catalogues, 465, 466
furniture for, 467–68
housekeeping in, 465
kits for, 462
making, 467
sources for buying, 465–67
see also Dolls
Dolls, 461–64
baby, 462, 463
Barbie, 443, 462
books on, 464
buying tips, 444, 445
catalogues, 462
making, 463, 464
making clothes for, 463
repairing, 463
storybook, 462
superhero, 462
see also Dollhouses; Puppets
Dominoes, bargains in, 445–46
Donald Duck, 290
Donaldy, Ernestine, 279
Donnell Library, New York, 429
Donovan, John, 69
Donne, John, 284
Dough Sculpture, 333
Dowden, Anne Ophelia, 238
Down the Rabbit Hole (Lanes),
quoted, 245, 256, 263, 265
Down's syndrome children, 83
Dracula, fear of, 67
Dreams (E. J. Keats), 244
Dreikurs, Rudolf, 6
Dremel jigsaws, 349
Drexler, Sherman
book reviews by, 243, 266, 268–69
on Feiffer cartoon, 66
Drills, 348
Droodles (Price), 434
Drugs, for family medicine cabinet, 35
Drymalski, Paul, on building a bed
platform, 170
Duco cement, 332
Dugan, William, 280

Passell, Peter
    on bicycles, 396
    on zoos, 355–56
Paste, recipe for, 336
    see also Glues
Paterno, Joe, 392
Patterns
    for costumes, 483
    for doll clothes, 463
    and sewing supplies, as gift, 472
Peanut Butter Manufacturers and Nut
    Salters Association, 42
"Peanut butter pop," 156
Peck, Ellen, on child-free lifestyles, 56
Peck, Robert Newton, 266
Pedagogy of the Oppressed (Freire),
    249
Pediatric nurse practitioner service, 37
Pelmas, Ruth
    on art supplies, 334
    book reviews by, 266, 268
    on doll repair, 463
    on durable clothing, 184
    on menstruation, 57
    "Pelmas concoction" (baby food
        recipe), 148
    on television and family feeling, 309
    on tennis rackets, 372
Pene du Bois, William, 263, 275
Penney, J.C., catalogue, 269
Penny arcades, 356
Penny Puzzlers ("movement
    puzzles"), 433
Penrod and Sam (Tarkington), 257
Pentangle puzzles, 433
Penthouse magazine, 263
Perkins, Marlin, 319
Perls, Fritz, 19
Permissiveness, 10
    see also Discipline; Setting limits
*Perplexing Puzzles and Tantalizing
    Teasers* (Gardner), 433; *quoted,*
    434
Pet care
    pamphlets on, 224–25
    see also Pets
Peter, Paul, and Mary, 299, 300
Peter Rabbit, Tale of (Potter), 274–75
    Storybook Record, 302
Peter's Pockets (Barrett and Noonan),
    191
Peter and the Wolf (Prokofiev), 301,
    302
    "Spoken Word" record, 288
Pets, 220–25
    aquarium, divided, for fish, 222
    birds, 222, 224
    books and pamphlets about, 220,
        221, 223, 224–25, 231
    care of, 224–25
    cats, 221–22
    chickens as, 229
    death of, 228, 229–30
    dogs, 220–21, 225, 228
    exotic, 220, 223, 224
    feelings about, 228–30
    frogs, catching flies for, 223
    fruit fly colony, 224
    gerbils, hamsters, housing for, 223
    importing, 224
    rabbits, 223, 230

snake, care and feeding, 224
    turtle, funeral of, 230
    see also Animals; Animal watching
Peugeot U10 Bicycle, 396
Picture Dictionary for Children, The
    (Watters and Courtis), 281
Ping-Pong balls, 372
Phonographs, see Record players
Photocopying, for reproducing
    children's art, 340
Photography, 342–43
Piaget, Jean, theories of, 98
Picasso, Pablo, 328
    on explaining a picture, 339
Pickle dogs (recipe), 161
Pickles, 155
Pictures (of statues) for learning
    anatomy, 55
Pig (card game), 415
Pigman, The (Zindel), 258
Piggy banks, case against, 200
Pinkwater, Manus, 159–60
Pippi Longstocking, 260
Pittsburgh Community Health Center,
    454
Pittsburgh Toy Lending Library, 454
Pizza for a small planet (recipe), 158
Pitching machines, automatic, 379
Planets, see Astronomy
Planned Parenthood, 143
Plants and gardens, 233–38
    community gardens, 236
    food plants, 238
    gift plants for child, 472, 474
    identification, 238
    "instant" flowers (colchicum), 235
    in kitchen window, 234, 235, 236
    living Christmas tree, 234–35
    one-of-a-kind garden, 234
    toys and tricks from plants, 236–37
    vegetable dyes, 237
    weeds, 238
Plastic bottles, as bath toys, 450
Plastic plates, for reproducing
    children's art, 341
Plastic toys, children's fondness for,
    442–43
Platform for bed, how to build, 170
Plato, on stories for children, 312
Playboy magazine, children's
    enjoyment of, 52
Play-Doh, 332
Play equipment, see Equipment,
    indoor play
Playgrounds
    books on, 405
    community, 405–06
    McMillan's 356, 406
Playing cards, 445
    Giant Bicycle, 416
Play money, 446
Playskool
    puzzles, 431, 432, 446
    toys, 447, 448
Play Structures (Ellison), *quoted,* 405–
    406
Pleasant Valley School, Camarillo,
    Calif., 165
Plug-In Drug, The (Winn), 324
Pocket calculator magic, 437–39
Pocket knife, 348

Pockets, portable pin-on, 191
Poetry, by and for children, 284–85
Pogo books (Kelly), 277
Pogrebin, Letty Cottin
    conversation with daughters on sex,
        56
    on deeper message of gifts, 472
    on puppets, 469
Pollyanna (Porter), 259
Polly Designs (for children's clothing),
    185
Polushkin, Maria, 179
Pomeroy, Wardell B., 58
Pond life, ponds, 226–27
Pond Life (Golden Guide), 227
Pond on My Windowsill, The
    (Reynolds), 227
Pooh Story Book, puppet shows
    based on, 470
Pool, 426
Pool cues, 373
Poor, Paula, 148
Popper, Barbara
    on home vs. school values, 106
    on parents in hospital with sick
        child, 39
Popsicles, homemade, 157
Popular Arts, The, quoted, 324
Populations: Experiments in Ecology
    (Stone and Collins), 212
Pop-up books, 245
Possum Trot Corp., 469
Possum Trot sock puppets, 469
Postcard chain letter, 480
Postcards
    art, 475
    as greetings, 480, 481
Posters and wall decorations, 178–79
    ordering, 179
Postman, Neil, 96–98
    on reading problems, 254
Postol, Flip, on moving to new house,
    70
Postol, Steffi, 70
Posture, techniques for improving
    Alexander Technique, 42
    Rolfing, 42–43
Potato prints, as Christmas cards, 480
Potenza, Bart, on J.C. Penney
    catalogue, 269
Potenza, Flavia, 30, 329
    on allowing child to cook, 160
    on bicycle and tricycle hooks, 397
    on building a play table, 174
    on countering night fears, 65
    on games, 413
    on pet care, 224
    on posters for child's room, 178–79
    on school photographs, 113
    on singing together, 296
    on Storybook records, 303
    on toy-lending program, 454–55
    on waiting out early years, 31
Potenza, Vaj, 65
Potsdam (TV program), 321
Potter, Beatrix, 263, 274–75, 302
    dolls, 462, 464
Potter, David, on character of
    American television, 308–09
Powers of Ten (Eames) (film), 217
Power tools, cautions about, 348

Reference books for children, 265, 280–83
dictionaries, good and bad, 281–82
encyclopedias, 282–83
how-to books, 280–81
Time-Life Books, 283
see also Maps; Nature guides; specific subjects
Reiss games, 437
Reit, Seymour, 280
Relevance, in children's books, 258–260
"Relevant idiocy" vs. violence, on TV, 315
Remco toys, 379
Rentschler, Hope, 2–3
Rentschler, William H., 2–3
Reproduction
books on, 59–60
see also Sex
Resources
for blind, 88, 89
for handicapped children, 84
for improvement of children's TV, 322–23
for learning disabilities diagnosis, 84
for media work with children, 343
nursery school course for home, 141
for out-of-print books, 287
for retarded, 91–93
for sex education and information, 60–61
tutoring, 112
see also Books, book lists; Catalogues, directories, pamphlets; specific subjects
Retarded children
resources, 91–93
see also Handicapped children
Return to Gone-Away (Enright), 276–277
Reuben, David, 50
Revell company, 47, 54
Reversi (board game), 420
Reward
as habit-breaking method, 6
undesirability as discipline, 8
Rey, H.A., 39, 41, 214–15
Rey, Margaret, 41
Reynolds, Christopher, 227
Rhodes, Dorothy, 283
Rhythms, Music and Instruments for Children to Make (Hawkinson and Faulhabe), 304
Richard Scarry's Storybook Dictionary (Scarry), 281–82
Richmond, George, 201
Rich's Department Store, Atlanta, child care center in, 144
Riddles, sensory, 414
Rights (of children), see Children's rights
Rights Handbook for Ohio's Physically Handicapped, 87
Ringling Bros. Circus, 365
Rinzler, Carol Eisen
on candy, 157
on children's illness, injuries, 34, 35
on "tooth fairy," 45
on toy storage, 456–57

Rinzler, Michael (age 9)
book review by, 434
on parents' divorce, 68
Rituals, in children's games, 411
"Riviera Sand," 400
Riviere, Bill, 358
Robbins, C.H., 218
Robbins, Ken, on too-large clothing, 192
Robbins, Maria, 5
book reviews by, 162–63
Robbins, Maria Polushkin, on old comics, 292
Roberto Clemente (Rudeen), 392
Roberts, Rona
on doll repair, 463
on soap art, 333
on toys, 447
Robeson, Josh, 328
Robinson Crusoe (Defoe), 262
Rock collecting, 213
Rocketry, models, 344—45
Rockets, air and water powered, 446
Rocketship Galileo (Heinlein), 279
Rock music, favorable view of, 295
Rock sale, as business venture, 199
Rodgers, Mary, 267, 474
Rogers, Fred ("Mr. Rogers"), 71, 311, 316
Roget's Thesaurus, 254
Roiphe, Anne, on fads, 182–83
Rolf, Ida P., 42
Rolfing, for children, 42–43
Rolf Institute, 42
Roller skates, 398
Rolling Stones (Heinlein), 279
Rooms, see Children's rooms
Roots (TV program), 321
Rope swing, 403
Rose, Where Did You Get That Red? (Koch), 284
Ross, Leonard
on bicycles, 396
on zoos, 355–56
Rossant, Colette, 162–63
Rossman, Lorca, "setting limits," as taught to, 8–9
Rossman, Michael, 237
on backyard pond, 226–27
book reviews by, 273–74, 336
on "educational" destructiveness, 351–52
on Gray's Anatomy, 47
on ideal school, 114
on learning to use tools, 349
on science catalogues, kits, 205, 206
on secondhand books, magazines, 287
on setting limits, 8–9
on toy trains, 448
Roth, Charlene Davis, 455
Roth, Jerome, 455
Rouse Corporation, 144
Rowboat, converting to sandbox, 401
Rowell, converting to sandbox, 401
R-R-R Raw Power (bike accessory), 395
Rubber balls, 372
Rubenstein, David, 46
Rubin, Mark, 266
Rubin, Robert, 391

Rudeen, Kenneth, 392
Rudofsky, Bernard, 351
Rushnell, Squire, 315
Russell, Franklin, on life in a pond, 227
Russell, Susan
on taking child to work, 26
on tire swings and cradles, 403
Ryan, Cheli Durán, 243

Sachs, Marilyn, 69
Sachs, Sheila, on television advertising, 313
Safety
bicycles, 395–96
crafts materials, 332
fire, learning about, 214
fire-retardant clothing, controversy on, 189
skateboarding, 398–99
tools, 349
toys, agencies to contact, 459–60
see also First aid
Sagan, Carl
on science, 204
on space, 214
Sagoff, Charlotte, on toilet training, 21
Sagoff, Maurice
book review by, 335
on cooperative nursery-kindergarten, 108
on half-birthday party, 489
on making subjects come alive (MATCH Boxes), 110
on museum outing, 355
Saia, George E., 141
Saint-Exupéry, Antoine de, viii 288, 302
adult response to children's art, 340
Saint-Saëns, Camille, 301
Salk, Lee, 18, 19, 54
on helping child face pain, 37
on sex education, 60
Salzmann, Karin, on Montessori play materials, 451–52
Samelson, Andra
book reviews by, 455, 464, 470
on dollhouses, 467
Samelson, Judy, on Band-Aid decorating, 35
Samuels, Polly, 157
Sanborn, William B., on mineral collecting, 213
Sand
black (magnetic), 400
where to buy, 400–01
Sandboxes, 400–01
San Diego Sea World, 356
San Diego Zoo and Animal Park, 355
Sand sculpture, 400
San Francisco Exploratorium, 354
San Francisco Sex Information, 61
Santa Claus, belief in, 14
see also Christmas
Saperstein, Alan, 409
on children's emotions in hospital, 40
on company of peers for child, 134

on mildly autistic child, 82–83
on games, 417
on gifts, 477
on momentary pleasures of
    parenthood, 2
on non-books, 244–45
on overspecialized toys, 442
on public vs. private schools, 105
on second child, advantages of, 24
on teaching swimming, 376–78
Saperstein, Matthew, 24, 376–78
Saperstein, Stephen, 24
Sarmento, Ann, 455
Sarson, Christopher
    on teaching mathematics, 124,
        125
    on television, 316, 318, 322
    on television commercials, 314
    on "wrong" answers, 123
Satchel Paige (Rubin), 391
Satie, Erik, 294
Saucer (sliding toy), 399
*Save the Earth! An Ecological
    Handbook for Kids* (Miles and
    Nivola), 212–23
Save Your Child's Life! (Hendin), 36
Saving money, negative view of, 200
Saws, 348–49
Scandinavian Designs, Inc., 169
Scarry, Richard, 39, 178, 281, 282
    as "sexist," 265
Scarves, old, as playthings, 189
Schaap, Dick
    on taking children to the office, 26
    Williamsburg-to-Disney World trip,
        359–62
Scharlatt, Elisabeth, 54, 71, 269
    on "adopted," use of word, 78
    on age designation for books,
        games, toys, 477
    on art, art supplies, 332–34, 339
    on baby-food jars, 148
    on babysitters, babysitting, 129,
        130, 131, 133
    on bed as plaything, 170
    on bedtime stories, 70–71, 243
    book reviews by, 37, 70, 77, 78–
        79, 200, 231, 234, 273, 274, 338
    on books, reading, 17, 18, 76, 241,
        242, 246, 247, 250–51, 261, 265
    on breast-feeding, 146
    on child-care manuals, 17, 18
    on child-rearing (various aspects), 5,
        6, 7, 12, 21, 22, 23, 26, 27, 30,
        31, 51, 124, 179, 191
    on children's clothing, 185, 188,
        189, 190, 191
    on Christmas notebook, 484
    on consumer education for children,
        201
    on dolls, dollhouse furniture, 461,
        462, 463, 468
    on earphones, 302
    on ecology, 211
    on fears, death, dealing with, 64,
        65, 70–71, 73–75, 76
    on flammable clothing controversy,
        189
    on food, nutrition, snacks, 149,
        155–56, 157, 164, 165, 166,
        367, 483

on games, 411, 415, 422; traveling
    games and diversions, 363–64
on gifts (excluding toys), 472–73,
    475, 476
on greeting cards, 480
on handicapped, attitudes toward,
    82, 94
on hospitals, illness, 35, 36, 37, 39
on infinity, 217
on kitchen science course, 165
on nursery schools, day care
    centers, 64, 134
on parents, 14, 15, 30
on parties, 485, 487
on play equipment, 177, 372, 385,
    396, 403
on premiums in cereal boxes, 164
on puppet shows, 469
on record player for child, 297
on rituals, 411
on Scarry's books, 265
on schools, 107, 113, 118, 121
on teaching swimming, 378
on television, 312, 317, 318–19
on tools, carpentry, 347, 348, 350
on toys, 442–45, 447, 449, 450,
    452, 456, 461
on waste in packaging, 166
Scharlatt, Nicholas, 165, 246, 251,
    312, 318, 319, 364, 400, 403
    banana milk recipe of, 155
    birthday parties for, 487
    favorite toys of, 451
    gift preferences of, 472–73, 476
    on seed pod as musical instrument,
        305
Schickel, Jill
    on ice cubes as pain remedy, 34
    on "Supermom," 16
    on toys, 447
Schiller, Justin G., for out-of-print
    books, 287
Schilling, Mary Kaye, Christmas book
    of, 473
Schnake, Dick, 455
Schneider, Tom, 383
Scholastic Book Services, 286–87
School Book, The (Postman and
    Weingartner), *quoted*, 96–98
School cooperatives, food and
    transportation, 111
    see also Day care center collective
School food, 164–65
School Library Journal, 257, 278
School photographs, 113
Schools, 95–126
    alternative schools, alternative ways
        to learn, 96–101
    architectural plans, parents'
        involvement in, 113
    arts and music specialists, 106, 294–
        295
    authority, informed and fair, 101
    bad language, 113
    basic questions and givens, 96
    books on, 96, 105
    breakfasts and lunches, 164–65
    children as teachers, 112–13
    cooperatives (for food,
        transportation), 111
    criteria for choosing school, 101–06

days off (unofficial), 106, 120
dictionary of terms, 96–98
dissatisfaction with, 106, 107
hallways, ideas for using, 113
for handicapped, *see* Handicapped
    children
vs. home education, 98–100
ideals for, 114–17
innovations that work, 108–10
mathematics, 124–25
for mildly autistic child, 82–83
parents' visits to classroom, 118
and PTA, 119
public school vs. private, 105
recycling centers in school, 211–12
roles and purposes, 100–01, 117–
    118
"school within a school," 98, 109–
    110
sex education in, 61–62
special children, school directories
    list, 92; *see also* Handicapped
    children
staying in school with child, 64
teaching, 120–21; *see also*
    Teaching
theater games, 125–26
transportation, cooperative, 111
varying situations, children's
    reactions to, 106–07
ways of learning, 121–26
    see also Learning; Reading;
        Teaching
School Within a School (SWAS),
    defined, 98
Schroeder, Patricia
    on expectations from school, 118
    on television advertising, 313
Schubert, Franz, 294
Schwartzberg, Laura, 113
Schwinn bicycles, 396
Science(s), 203–18
    astronomy, 214–15
    blowing bubbles as, 210
    books, book lists, 212–15, 217–18
    catalogues for equipment, kits, 205,
        207, 209
    chemistry, 213–14
    ecology, environment, 211–13
    fire, learning about, 214
    infinity concepts, for young children,
        217
    to initiate observation process, 204–
        205
    kits, 207–09
    microscopes, what and where to
        buy, 206–07
    mineral collecting, 213
    museum exhibits, 354–55
    nature guides, 218
    and science fiction, 204
    scientific method as practiced by
        baby, 204
    telescopes, 216
    see also Animal watching; Pets;
        Plants and gardens
Science Fair kits, 209
Science fiction, as children's reading,
    278–79
    see also Fantasy
Science Fiction Shop, New York, 279

Science kits, what and what not to buy, 207–09
Scientific American, 2, 12, 433, 434; *quoted*, 438–39
　paper airplane competition, 346
　science book reviews, 218
Scissors, left-handed, 329
Scooters Are Groovy and You Can Build Your Own (Brock), 350
Scott, Gini, on children's games, 420
Scout Programs for the Handicapped, 93
Scrabble, 421
　cheating in, 411
Scrapbooks, 330
Sculpture
　cloth (fanciful creatures), 461
　dough, 333
　hardware store equipment for, 334
　sand, 400
Sears, Scott, on elementary school football, 381
Sears, Roebuck, 372, 404
　children's clothing from, 184
　Pak-A-Poose Baby Carrier, 397
　toy appliances, 447
　toys, 453
　toy typewriters, 444
　Trail Cycle, 394
Season to Be Born, A (Arms), 60
Sea World, San Diego, 356
Sea World of Ohio, 356
Second child, advantages of, 24
　see also Siblings
Secondhand books and magazines, 287
Secret Garden, The (Burnett), 240, 272
Secret Writing: The Craft of the Cryptographer (Wolfe), 434
Seed pod, as musical instrument, 305
Seeds, nuts, 152
　selling, as children's business venture, 198
Seeing Through Commercials (Stein and Aslens) (film), 315
Segal, Lore, 262, 269–70
Selective Educational Equipment, 421
Self-demand schedules, rigid conforming to, 10
Selfishness, child's right to, 26–27
Sendak, Maurice, 178, 221, 257, 258, 264, 268, 269, 270
　on beautiful books, 256
　on dream sources for illustrations, 241
　on fantasy as catharsis, 275
Send Wendell (Gray and Shimin), 272
Sesame Street (TV program), 242, 245, 250, 261, 271, 309, 314
　experimental program for retarded children, 87
　pros and cons, 317
Sesame Street jigsaw puzzles, 431
Sesame Street Muppet Puppets, 469
Sesame Street records, 299, 300
Setting limits
　collaboration vs. compulsion, 9
　as comfort for child, 7
　deeper lessons of, 8–9

Seuss, Dr., 244, 247, 254–55, 256, 268
　appeal of, 263–64
　on bad teacher, 121
Seven Stairs, The (Brent), *quoted*, 359
Seventeen magazine, 465
Sex, children and, 49–62
　anatomy, learning about, 54–55
　child-free lifestyles explained, 56
　"dirty talk," 52, 57
　discussing and instructing, pros and cons, 51–52
　"doing nothing" about, 52
　homosexuality, 52
　intercourse, discussing with child, 55–56
　masturbation, 52
　menstruation, 57
　myths, misconceptions, 56
　observing parental nudity, sex act, 52
　sexual development, 52
　sexuality of child, acknowledging, 50, 52
　single parents' sex life, 52–53
　touching, pleasures of, 61
　see also Sex education
Sex education
　books on, 58–60
　resources for, 60–61
　in school, pros and cons, 61–62
Sex roles, clothing and, 182–83
Sexual Adolescent, The: Communicating with Teenagers About Sex (Gordon), 58, 61
Sex and Your Teenager (Le Shan), 58
Sexist bias
　in *Sesame Street* puppets, 469
　on television, 316
　in Richard Scarry's books, 265
　see also in section Children's books
Shadow puppet show, 469
Shakespeare, William, 284
Shaler, Nathaniel, 99
Shalit, Gene
　book review, 264–65
　on "Spoken Word" records, 288, 302
Shamberg, Michael, on school hallways, 113
Shankar International Painting and Writing Competition, 344
Shannon, William V., on television violence, 315
Shapiro, Bob, on children's games, 413
Shapiro, Holly, 120
Shapiro, Jackie
　on child's private life at school, 120
　on jigsaw puzzles, 432
Shapiro, Jane, on trip to the ballet, 366–67
Sharing, child's right to refuse, 26–27
Sharing the Children (Harlowe), 141
Sharkey, Tony, on science, 204
Shatner, William, 320
Shaw, Emily, on model building, 347
Shay, Arthur, 41
Shedlin, Allan, Jr.
　book review by, 339

on legal rights, resources for handicapped, 84
on outdoor play equipment, 395
on reading problems, 253
on reproducing children's art, 341
on resources for special children, 91–93
on "special" education for all, 116–117
on strictness, 6
on talking books for blind, 88
on toys, 452–53
Sheehy, Gail
　book review by, 261–62
　on flash cards, 251
Sheep Book, The (Goodyear), 231–232
Sheffield, Margaret, 59
Shelley, Percy Bysshe, 257
Sheraton, Mimi, on fast-food hamburgers, 151
Shetzline, David, 282
Shimin, Symeon, 272
Shimkin, Arthur, on baseball mitt, 370
Shimkin, Tony, 370
Shoelaces, buying by the box, 191
Shoes, hard or soft, 185
Shore, Mary Ann
　on adoption, discussing with child, 78
　on guest artists in schools, 106
　on making child's clothes, 254
Shorter Oxford English Dictionary, 254
Showers, Paul, 46
Shrub Identification Book, The (Symonds), 238
Shub, Beth, 141
Shulevitz, Uri, 266
Shushan, Ronnie, 283
　on AAA, 364
　on art materials, 328, 329, 334
　on audiences for children's creative efforts, 344
　on babysitters, 131
　on beanbag chairs, 171
　on birds, 222, 226
　book reviews by, 42–43, 78, 90, 137, 141, 158, 159, 162–63, 191, 217, 227, 238, 244, 266–267, 268, 271, 304, 336, 343, 346
　on cameras, 343
　on cardboard carpentry, 350
　on children's gripes, 13
　on cleaning child's room, 179
　on community garden projects, 236
　on Dial-a-Story, 288
　on dirty words, 57
　on dolls, dollhouses, 461–62, 427
　on food and nutrition, 147, 149, 150, 152, 157, 158, 165
　on games, 411, 419, 423, 429, 430
　on gifts, 474, 475
　on greeting cards, homemade, recycled, 480–81
　on Halloween costumes, makeup, 481–82
　on "instant" blackboards, 171
　on life preservers, 378